Harrap's
English-Brazilian Portuguese
Business
Dictionary

edited by

Terence Lewis

with

Lígia Xavier
Cláudio Solano

HARRAP   LONDON

First published in Great Britain 1982
by Harrap Limited
19–23 Ludgate Hill EC4M 7PD

© Harrap Limited, 1982

ISBN 0 245-53820-8

Printed and bound in Great Britain
by A. Wheaton and Company Limited, Exeter

Preface

This *English–Brazilian Portuguese Business Dictionary* includes terms and expressions used in a wide range of commercial contexts such as Shipping, Air Transport, Banking, Stock Exchange, Accountancy, Insurance, Commerce and Law.

The editor has drawn upon a vast storehouse of primary materials including commercial correspondence, company reports, articles of association, contracts for services and similar documents, many of which have passed through his hands during the course of his work as a translator. He has also consulted business newspapers and magazines put out by commercial companies, banks and other institutions in the United Kingdom, the United States and Brazil.

Every effort has been made to ensure that the Portuguese used in the dictionary is authentic and up to date. This task could not have been accomplished without the patient and unflagging assistance of the editor's two Brazilian assistants, Lígia Xavier and Cláudio Solano. Our authority on matters of spelling and usage has been the *Novo Dicionário Aurélio*.

The aim of the dictionary is to provide a basic translating tool for everyday business language. As in all Harrap dictionaries, emphasis has been laid on giving practical examples to show terms and phrases used in context—rendering the dictionary of great value to the translator, the businessman, the secretary, the export manager and the business-school student.

In addition to the main text, the dictionary provides useful supplementary material concerning international currencies and international organizations and their abbreviations.

The user will find that many common English commercial terms have three or four Portuguese equivalents. In such cases, the order of the translations may be taken as a fair indication of their frequency. As language evolves continuously and is conditioned by the physical and social environment and the history, tradition and needs of those who use it, it is not possible to give a Portuguese equivalent for every single English term or expression. When equivalents do not exist, explanations or definitions of the English terms are provided.

Allowing for differences of spelling, some of the Portuguese terms included in this work are also used in commercial contexts in Portugal and Portuguese-speaking Africa. While the variants of Portuguese written and spoken in Brazil and in Portugal and its former colonies and overseas provinces differ significantly in certain respects, they are nonetheless mutually intelligible and, to that extent, it is hoped that this dictionary will also prove useful in Portugal, Mozambique, Angola, Guinea-Bissau and Macao.

Apart from his two Brazilian assistant editors, the editor would also like to thank Peter Collin for his constant support and encouragement and Eric Smith for his invaluable contribution to the final shape of the dictionary.

T.L. 1982

Prefácio

O *Dicionário do Empresário (inglês–português)* inclui termos e expressões utilizados numa vasta área de contextos comerciais tais como Navegação, Transporte Aéreo, Operações Bancárias, Bolsa de Valores, Contabilidade, Seguros, Comércio, Direito, etc.

Inicialmente, o organizador acumulou vasto material incluindo correspondência comercial, relatórios de companhias, estatutos sociais, contratos de prestação de serviços e documentos semelhantes, muitos dos quais passaram por suas mãos durante suas atividades como tradutor. Também foram consultados jornais e revistas especializados em assuntos comerciais publicados por companhias, bancos e outras instituições no Reino Unido, nos Estados Unidos e no Brasil.

Cabe também dizer que nenhum esforço foi poupado a fim de garantir que o português utilizado no dicionário seja autêntico e atualizado. Esta tarefa não poderia ter sido realizada sem a paciente e incansável colaboração dos dois assistentes brasileiros do organizador, Lígia Xavier e Cláudio Solano. Nossa fonte de consulta, no que diz respeito à ortografia e estilo, foi o *Novo Dicionário Aurélio*.

O objetivo do dicionário é fornecer um instrumento básico de tradução para a linguagem comercial do dia a dia. Como em todos os dicionários da editora Harrap, deu-se ênfase aos exemplos práticos que mostram termos e frases utilizados em determinados contextos, tornando o dicionário de grande valor para tradutores, homens de negócios, secretárias bilíngües, gerentes de exportação e estudantes de administração de empresas.

Além do texto principal, o dicionário fornece material complementar de grande utilidade no que se refere a moedas internacionais e organizações internacionais e suas abreviaturas e siglas.

O usuário notará que muitos termos comerciais ingleses possuem três ou quatro equivalentes em português. Nestes casos, a ordem das traduções pode ser tomada como indicação da sua freqüência. Como a língua está em constante desenvolvimento e é condicionada pelo meio físico e social e pela história, tradição e necessidades daqueles que a utilizam, torna-se impossível fornecer um equivalente em português para cada termo ou expressão em inglês. Quando os equivalentes não existem, explicações ou definições são fornecidas.

Com exceção das diferenças ortográficas e de construção, alguns dos termos e expressões em português incluídos neste dicionário são tembém utilizados em contextos comerciais em Portugal e nos países africanos de língua portuguesa. Embora as variações do português escrito e falado no Brasil e em Portugal e suas antigas colônias difiram significativamente em certos aspectos, permanecem mutuamente inteligível e, neste sentido, espera-se que o dicionário também seja útil em Portugal, Moçambique, Angola, Guiné-Bissau e Macau.

Além dos seus dois assistentes, o organizador deste dicionário gostaria de agradecer a Peter Collin o seu constante apoio e estímulo e a Eric Smith, cujos olhos de lince e colaboração metódica ajudaram a melhorar imensuravelmente o texto final do dicionário.

T.L. 1982

Abbreviations used in this dictionary
Abreviaturas usadas neste dicionário

a.	adjective	adjetivo
abbr.	abbreviation	abreviatura
Adm:	administration	administração
adv.	adverb	advérbio
Advert:	advertising	propaganda
adv.phr.	adverbial phrase	locução adverbial
Agr:	agriculture	agricultura
Am:	United States	Estados Unidos
a.phr.	adjectival phrase	locução adjetiva
approx.	approximate; approximately	aproximadamente
Aut.Ins:	automobile insurance	seguro de automóveis
Av:	aviation; aircraft	aviação; avião
Bank:	banking	operações bancárias
Book-k:	book-keeping	contabilidade
Braz:	Brazil	Brasil
Brit:	Britain; British	Grã-Bretanha; britânico
Cmptr:	computers; data processing	computadores; processamento de dados
coll.	collective	coletivo
conj.	conjunction	conjunção
Const:	construction industry	indústria da construção
Corr:	correspondence	correspondência
Cust:	customs	alfândega
Dom.Ec:	domestic economy	economia doméstica
Ec:	economics	economia
Eng:	England; English	Inglaterra; inglês
esp.	especially	especialmente
etc.	et cetera	et cetera
f	feminine	feminino
F:	colloquialism	expressão coloquial
Fin:	finance	finanças
fpl	feminine plural	plural de substantivo feminino
Fr:	France; French	França; francês
Geog:	geography	geografia
Hist:	history	história
i.	intransitive	intransitivo
ind.	indicative	indicativo
Ind:	industry	indústria
Ins:	insurance	seguro
inv.	invariable	invariável
Journ:	journalism	jornalismo
Jur:	legal term	termo jurídico
Lt.phr.	Latin phrase	locução latina
m	masculine	masculino
Meas:	weights and measures	pesos e medidas
mf	masculine or feminine	masculino ou feminino
mfpl	masculine plural or feminine plural	plural de substantivo masculino ou feminino

M.Ins:	marine insurance	seguro marítimo
Mkt:	marketing	mercadologia
mpl	masculine plural	plural de substantivo masculino
n.	noun	substantivo
N.Am:	United States and Canada	Estados Unidos e Canadá
Nau:	nautical term	termo náutico
n.pl.	plural noun	substantivo no plural
Num:	numismatics	numismática
num.a.	numeral adjective	adjetivo numeral
occ.	occasionally	ocasionalmente
Pej:	pejorative	pejorativo
pl.	plural	plural
PN:	public notice	aviso público
Pol.Ec:	political economy	economia política
Port:	Portugal	Portugal
Post:	postal services	serviços postais
pref.	prefix	prefixo
prep.	preposition	preposição
prep.phr.	prepositional phrase	locução prepositiva
Pr.n.	proper name	nome próprio
pron.	pronoun	pronome
Publ:	publishing	edição
Rail:	railways/railroads	ferrovia
Ret:	retailing	comércio a varejo
R.t.m:	registered trademark	marca registrada
Scot:	Scotland; Scottish	Escócia; escocês
sg.	singular	singular
sg. const.	singular construction	construção no singular
s.o.	someone	alguém
Stat:	statistics	estatística
St.Exch:	Stock Exchange	bolsa de valores
sth.	something	alguma coisa
subj.	subjunctive	subjuntivo
Tail:	tailoring	ofício de alfaiate
Tchn:	technical	técnico
Tel:	telecommunications	telecomunicações
Tex:	textiles; textile industry	produtos têxteis; indústria têxtil
Tg:	telegraphy	telegrafia
Th:	theatre; theatrical	teatro; teatral
tr.	transitive	transitivo
Trans:	transport	transporte
TV:	television	televisão
Typ:	typography	tipografia
UK:	United Kingdom	Reino Unido
usu.	usually	usualmente
v.i.	intransitive verb	verbo intransitivo
v.pr.	pronominal verb	verbo pronominal
v.tr.	transitive verb	verbo transitivo
=	nearest equivalent (of an institution, an office, etc., when systems vary in the different countries)	equivalente mais aproximado (de instituição, cargo, etc., quando se trata de diferenças entre os sistemas dos respectivos países)

A

A-1, *a.* de primeira classe, de primeira categoria.

abandon, *v.tr.* abandonar; *M.Ins:* abandonar, ceder ao segurador; **to abandon a ship,** abandonar um navio; *Fin:* **to abandon an option,** abandonar, renunciar a, uma opção.

abandoned, *a.* *Am:* **abandoned merchandise,** mercadoria não reclamada (em depósito, etc.).

abandonment, *n.* abandono *m* de um bem (de ativo fixo); *Ins:* **abandonment to insurers,** cessão *f* de todos os direitos aos seguradores; *Jur:* **abandonment of action,** suspensão *f* de uma ação judicial.

abate, *v.tr.* **1.** abater, deduzir, descontar; **to abate 10% on the selling price,** abater, deduzir, 10% do preço de venda. **2.** *Jur:* **to abate an action,** suspender, anular, uma ação.

abatement, *n.* **1.** abatimento *m*, redução *f*, desconto *m*; *Adm:* **tax abatement,** desconto tributário, desconto de imposto. **2.** *Jur:* **abatement of an action,** suspensão *f*, anulação *f*, de uma ação.

abbreviated, *a.* **abbreviated address,** endereço abreviado.

abeyance, *n.* **in abeyance,** em suspenso, pendente.

aboard, *adv.* a bordo; **to go aboard,** embarcar, ir a bordo; **to take goods aboard,** embarcar mercadorias.

above, *prep. Fin:* **above par,** acima do par.

above-line, above-the-line, *a. Book-k:* **above-line, above-the-line, expenditure,** despesas *fpl* acima da linha.

absenteeism, *n.* absenteísmo *m*, absentismo *m*.

absorb, *v.tr.* (*a*) absorver; **measures taken to absorb the surplus,** medidas tomadas para absorver o excedente; (*b*) absorver, incorporar; **the business was absorbed by a competitor,** a empresa foi incorporada, absorvida, por um concorrente.

absorption, *n.* absorção *f*, incorporação *f*, (de uma empresa por outra, etc.); **cost absorption,** absorção de custos.

abstract¹, *n.* resumo *m*, extrato *m*; **to make an abstract of an account,** fazer o extrato de uma conta, extratar uma conta; **to make an abstract of a document,** extratar, resumir, um documento; *Jur:* **abstract of title,** ementa *f* de título.

abstract², *v.tr.* extratar (uma conta).

accept, *v.tr.* **to accept the terms of a contract,** aceitar as condições, os termos, de um contrato; **to accept in payment,** aceitar em pagamento; *Fin:* **to accept a bill,** aceitar uma letra.

acceptable, *a.* aceitável.

acceptance, *n.* **1.** (i) aceitação *f*, (ii) recebimento *m* (de artigo encomendado, etc.); **qualified acceptance,** aceitação condicional; **unconditional acceptance,** aceitação sem reserva, incondicional; *Stat:* **acceptance sampling,** amostragem *f* para aceitação; *Ind:* **acceptance test,** teste *m* de aceitação, prova *f* de homologação. **2.** *Fin:* **acceptance against documents,** aceite *m* documentário; **acceptance supra protest,** aceite sob protesto; **bank acceptance,** aceite bancário; **trade acceptance,** aceite comercial, duplicata *f*; **acceptance credit,** crédito *m* de aceitação; **to present a bill for acceptance,** apresentar uma letra para aceite; **to refuse acceptance,** recusar o aceite (de uma letra).

acceptor, *n.* aceitante *mf* (de letra).

access, *n.* acesso *m*; *Cmptr:* acesso (a armazenador, etc.); **to have access to the board,** ter acesso ao conselho de administração; *Am:* **access (clerk),** encarregado *m* da caixa-forte.

1

accessory, *a.* acessório, adicional, complementar; **accessory expenses,** despesas *fpl* adicionais; *Jur:* **accessory clause,** cláusula acessória.

accident, *n.* acidente *m*; *Ins:* sinistro *m*; **industrial accident,** acidente de trabalho; **accident insurance,** seguro *m* contra acidentes; **motor accident insurance,** seguro contra desastres de automóvel; **accident policy,** apólice *f* de seguro contra acidentes.

accommodation, *n.* **1.** acomodação *f,* alojamento *m*; **accommodation allowance,** ajuda *f* de alojamento. **2. accommodation bill,** letra *f* de favor, *F:* papagaio *m*.

accord, *n.* **accord and satisfaction,** liberação *f* (de uma obrigação) a título oneroso.

accordance, *n.* **in accordance with your instructions,** de acordo com, em conformidade com, as suas instruções.

according to, *prep.phr.* **according to instructions,** segundo, conforme, as instruções; de acordo com, em conformidade com, instruções.

account¹, *n.* (*a*) conta *f*; **accounts payable,** contas a pagar; **accounts receivable,** contas a receber; **account rendered,** conta entregue; **account stated,** conta confirmada pelo devedor; **detailed, itemized, account,** conta com discriminação de verbas; **outstanding, unsettled, account,** conta não liquidada; **settled account,** conta saldada, conta liquidada; **to account rendered, as per account rendered,** conforme conta entregue; **to have an account,** *Am:* **a charge account, with a shop,** ter uma conta de crédito em uma loja; **to charge an article to an account,** debitar o preço de um artigo a uma conta, levar o preço de um artigo a débito de uma conta; **to settle an account,** liquidar, apurar, saldar, uma conta; **to pay $10 on account,** pagar $10 por conta; **to pay a sum on account of fees,** pagar uma importância por conta de honorários; (*b*) **the accounts (of a firm, etc.),** os livros (contábeis), a escrituração, a contabilidade (de uma empresa); **capital account,** conta de capital; **income and expenditure account,** conta de receitas e despesas; **payroll account,** conta de pagamento, de salários; **profit and loss account,** conta de lucros e perdas; **sales account,** conta de vendas; **stock account,** conta de mercadorias; **account book,** livro *m* contábil, livro de escrituração; **the account books,** os livros comerciais; **accounts department,** (departamento *m*, seção *f,* de) contabilidade *f*, contadoria *f*; **to keep the accounts (of a firm),** fazer a escrituração, a contabilidade (de uma empresa); (*c*) *Bank:* **bank account,** conta bancária; **credit account,** conta credora; **current account,** conta corrente; **debit account,** conta devedora; **deposit account,** conta de depósito; **external account,** conta externa; **joint account,** conta conjunta; **loan account,** conta de empréstimo; **overdrawn account,** conta a descoberto; **to open an account,** abrir uma conta; **to close an account,** encerrar uma conta; **to overdraw an account,** pôr uma conta a descoberto; **to pay money into s.o.'s account,** depositar, creditar, dinheiro na conta de alguém; **your account is in credit,** sua conta tem fundos; **statement of account,** extrato *m* de conta; (*d*) *St. Exch:* **the Account,** a liquidação (mensal); **account day,** dia *m* de liquidação; **dealings for the account,** operações *fpl,* negócios *mpl,* a termo; (*e*) *Advert:* conta *f,* cliente *m* de agência de propaganda; (*f*) **to set up business on one's own account,** montar um negócio por conta própria.

account², *v.tr. Book-k:* contabilizar, escriturar (despesas, etc.).

accountable, *a.* contabilizável.

accountancy, *n.* contabilidade *f*.

accountant, *n.* (*a*) contador *m,* contabilista *mf,* técnico *m* em contabilidade; **chief accountant,** contador chefe, chefe *mf* de contabilidade; (*b*) **chartered accountant,** *Am:* **certified public accountant** = (i) perito-contador *m,* (ii) conselheiro *m,* fiscal.

accounting, *n.* contabilidade *f*; **cost accounting,** contabilidade de custos, contabilidade industrial; **the accounting department,** a (seção de) contabilidade, o serviço de contabilidade; **accounting**

clerk, escriturário *m*, auxiliar *mf* de contabilidade; **accounting machine,** máquina *f* de contabilidade; **accounting system,** sistema *m* contábil; **accounting period,** exercício *m*; *Book-k:* **accounting equation,** igualdade *f* contábil, equação *f* contábil.

accredited, *a.* acreditado, autorizado.

accrual, *n. Book-k:* acumulação *f*; **accrual(s) basis,** base *f* de acumulação.

accrue, *v.i. (of interest)* acumular-se; **interest accrues (as) from . . .,** os juros se acumulam a partir de . . ..

accrued, *a.* **accrued interest,** juros acumulados; **accrued asset,** ativo acumulado.

accruing, *a.* (juros *mpl*) a vencer.

accumulated, *a.* **accumulated dividends,** dividendos não distribuídos.

accumulation, *n. (a)* acumulação *f*; **accumulation of capital,** acumulação de capitais; **rate of capital accumulation,** taxa *f* de acumulação de capitais; *(b) Ins:* retenção *f* de dividendos para distribuição posterior; *(c) Fin:* valorização *f* de título comprado com desconto.

acknowledge, *v.tr. (a)* **to acknowledge (receipt of) a letter,** acusar o recebimento, a recepção, de uma carta; *(b)* **to acknowledge a debt,** reconhecer uma dívida.

acknowledgement, *n.* recibo *m*, quitação *f*, (de pagamento, etc.); **acknowledgement of debt,** reconhecimento *m*, confissão *f*, de dívida.

acquittance, *n.* quitação *f*, liberação *f*, (de dívida, etc.).

acre, *n.* acre *m*.

act¹, *n.* **1. Companies Act,** lei *f* das sociedades; **Health and Safety at Work,** etc., **Act** = lei sobre acidentes de trabalho. **2.** *Ins:* **act of God,** ato *m* de Deus, caso fortuito; **act of war,** ato de guerra, ato bélico. **3. act of consumption,** ato *m* de consumo; *Jur:* **act of bankruptcy,** ato falencial.

act², *v.i. (a)* agir, atuar, obrar, (na qualidade de agente, gerente, etc.); **to act as manager,** exercer as funções de gerente; *(b)* **to act on instructions,** agir de acordo com as instruções; *(c)* **to act for,**

on behalf of, s.o., agir em nome de alguém, representar alguém.

acting, *a.* **the acting chairman, manager,** o presidente, gerente, interino.

action, *n.* **1. to take industrial action,** fazer uma greve. **2.** *Jur:* **action at law,** ação *f* judicial; **action for damages,** ação de perdas e danos; **to bring an action, take legal action, against** s.o., acionar, processar, alguém; intentar, levantar, mover, propor, uma ação contra alguém.

actionable, *a. Jur:* acionável, litigável.

active, *a.* **active money,** moeda ativa; **active population,** população ativa; *Book-k:* **active balance,** saldo *m* credor; *St.Exch:* **the most active shares,** as ações mais negociadas; **there is an active demand for cotton,** o algodão está muito procurado, existe uma grande demanda para o algodão.

actual, *a.* real, efetivo; **to give the actual figures,** dar os números reais; **on the basis of the actual value,** baseado no valor real, efetivo; **actual cost,** custo *m* real; *Ins:* **actual total loss,** perda total efetiva, perda total real.

actuarial, *a.* atuário.

actuary, *n.* atuário *m*.

ad, *n. F:* anúncio *m*; **to put an ad in the papers,** colocar um anúncio nos jornais; **small ads,** (anúncios) classificados.

add, *v.* **1.** *v.tr. (a)* **to add the interest to the capital,** somar os juros ao capital, acrescer o capital do valor dos juros; **to add five tons to the quantity ordered,** acrescentar cinco toneladas à quantidade encomendada; *(b)* **to add up the expenses,** somar, adicionar, as despesas. **2.** *v.i. (a)* **the assets add up to two million,** o ativo soma, importa em, se eleva a, dois milhões; *(b)* **this adds to our expenses,** isto aumenta nossas despesas.

adder, *n.* = adding machine.

adding, *n.* adição *f*; **adding machine,** máquina *f* de somar, somadora *f*.

addition, *n.* adição *f*, soma *f*, acréscimo *m*; **additions to the staff,** ampliação *f* do quadro de pessoal; *Fin:* **addition to the stock,** aumento *m* do capital (mediante transferência de reservas à conta de capital).

additional, *a.* additional expenses, despesas *fpl* adicionais, despesas suplementares; *Adm:* additional taxes, impostos *mpl* adicionais.

address¹, *n.* endereço *m*; *Adm:* name, address and age, nome, residência e idade; to change address, mudar de endereço; business address and home address, endereço profissional e residência; address book, caderneta *f* de endereços; *Jur:* legal address, domicílio *m.*

address², *v.tr.* (*a*) to address a letter to s.o., endereçar uma carta a alguém; to address an envelope, endereçar, sobrescritar, um envelope; (*b*) to address a meeting, fazer uso da palavra numa reunião.

addressed, *a. Corr:* please send a stamped addressed envelope (SAE), favor anexar um envelope selado e sobrescritado.

addressee, *n.* destinatário *m.*

addresser, *n.* remetente *mf* (de carta, etc.).

addressing, *n.* endereçamento *m*; addressing machine, máquina *f* de endereçar, adressógrafo *m.*

Addressograph, *n. R.t.m:* Adressógrafo *m.*

adjourn, *v.* 1. *v.tr.* to adjourn a meeting, adiar, suspender, uma reunião. 2. *v.i.* the meeting adjourned at 3.30, a sessão foi encerrada às três e meia.

adjournment, *n.* adiamento *m*, suspensão *f*, (de reunião, etc.).

adjudicate, *v.tr. Jur:* to adjudicate s.o. (to be) bankrupt, decretar a falência de alguém.

adjudication, *n.* adjudication of bankruptcy, decreto *m* de falência; adjudication of a bankrupt's debts, repartição *f* das dívidas do falido.

adjudicator, *n.* árbitro *m.*

adjust, *v.tr.* to adjust prices, reajustar os preços; to adjust wages to the rise in inflation, reajustar os salários de acordo com o aumento inflacionário.

adjuster, *n. Ins:* (loss) adjuster, árbitro regulador de avarias.

adjusting, *n.* adjusting of prices, reajustamento *m* de preços.

adjustment, *n.* reajustamento *m*, reajuste *m*; downward, upward, adjustment, reajustamento para baixo, reajustamento ascendente; *M.Ins:* adjustment of average, regulação *f*, repartição *f*, de avarias.

adman, *pl.* -men, *n. F:* publicitário *m.*

admin, *n. F:* = administration.

administered, *a.* administered price, preço determinado pelo vendedor, *Pol.Ec:* preço administrado.

administration, *n.* administração *f.*

administrative, *a.* administrativo; administrative expenses, despesas de, com, administração; administrative procedures, trâmites administrativos, burocráticos; administrative economics, economia *f* de administração; administrative law, direito administrativo.

adopt, *v.tr.* to adopt the advice of a consultant, adotar os conselhos de um consultor; to adopt the resolution put forward by the board, aprovar a proposta submetida pelo conselho de administração.

adoption, *n.* aprovação *f* (das atas de uma reunião, etc.).

ad valorem, *Lt.phr.* ad valorem duties, direitos *mpl* ad valorem; to pay a duty ad valorem, pagar um direito conforme o valor da mercadoria.

advance¹, 1. *n.* (*a*) to pay in advance, pagar antecipadamente; to pay a sum in advance, adiantar, fazer um pagamento adiantado; duty payable in advance, taxa *f* pagável antecipadamente, adiantadamente; prices fixed in advance, preços fixados de antemão, com antecipação; *Corr:* thanking you in advance, agradecendo-lhe desde já, afirmando desde já a minha gratidão, agradecendo antecipadamente; (*b*) adiantamento *m*, abono *m*, abonação *f*; an advance on a contract, um adiantamento por conta do preço contratual; an advance on wages, on income, um adiantamento, abono, por conta de salário, de rendimentos; to make an advance of $100, adiantar cem dólares; to make an advance on security, adiantar, emprestar, dinheiro sobre penhor; **advance account,** conta *f* de empréstimos, de adiantamentos; (*c*) aumento *m* (de salários, etc.); subida *f* (de preços); **the sharp advance in the platinum price,** a subida acentuada do preço de platina; **the advance on wheat,** a alta do trigo; (*d*) **advances in the mining industry,** avanços *mpl* na indústria de mineração; **economic advance,** progresso econômico. **2.** *a.* adiantado, antecipado; **advance bill,** letra aceita antes de embarque; **advance freight,** frete pago antecipadamente; **advance notice,** aviso prévio; **advance payment,** adiantamento *m*; pagamento adiantado, pagamento antecipado.

advance², *v.* **1.** *v.tr.* (*a*) aumentar, elevar, (o preço de algo); (*b*) **to advance money to s.o.,** adiantar dinheiro a alguém; **sums advanced,** adiantamentos *mpl;* (*c*) **to advance goods,** entregar mercadorias adiantadamente. **2.** *v.i.* (*of shares, etc.*) subir; **the shares advanced two points during trading,** as ações subiram dois pontos no pregão; **coffee advanced two cents,** o preço do café subiu (em) dois cêntimos, o café encareceu dois cêntimos.

advanced, *a.* **advanced economy,** economia adiantada, desenvolvida; **advanced country,** país desenvolvido; **advanced technology,** tecnologia avançada.

advancement, *n.* **economic advancement,** avanço, progresso, econômico.

advancer, *n.* **advancer of funds,** emprestador *m* de fundos.

advancing, *a.* **advancing economy,** economia progressiva.

adverse, *a.* **adverse budget,** orçamento deficitário; **adverse balance of trade,** balanço *m* de comércio desfavorável; **adverse economic situation,** desfavorável conjuntura econômica.

advert, *n. F:* anúncio *m*.

advertise, *v.tr. & i.* (*a*) **to advertise in a paper,** anunciar num jornal; **he advertised the car and sold it in two days,** ele anunciou o automóvel e vendeu-o em dois dias; (*b*) fazer a publicidade, a propaganda, (de um produto); **to advertise widely,** anunciar massivamente.

advertisement, *n.* anúncio (publicitário), reclamo *m*, reclame *m*; **classified advertisement,** (anúncio) classificado; **newspaper advertisement,** anúncio de jornal; **radio advertisement,** anúncio de rádio; **television advertisement,** anúncio de televisão, televisado, televisionado.

advertiser, *n.* anunciante *mf*, anunciador *m*.

advertising, *n.* publicidade *f*, propaganda *f*; **advertising account,** conta publicitária; **advertising agency,** agência *f* de propaganda, de publicidade; **advertising appropriation,** verba *f* de propaganda, dotação publicitária; **advertising budget,** orçamento *m* publicitário; **advertising campaign,** campanha publicitária, de propaganda; **advertising copy,** texto publicitário; **advertising executive,** executivo publicitário; **advertising expenses,** despesas publicitárias, despesas com publicidade; **the advertising industry,** a indústria publicitária; **advertising manager,** gerente *mf* de propaganda; **advertising medium,** veículo (publicitário), veículo de propaganda; **point-of-sale advertising,** publicidade no ponto de venda; **poster advertising,** publicidade de cartaz; **prime-time advertising,** propaganda de horário nobre; **radio advertising,** publicidade, propaganda, de rádio; **shop-window advertising,** publicidade de vitrina; **television advertising,** publicidade, propaganda, de televisão, televisada, televisionada; **to sell advertising space,** vender espaço para publicidade.

advice, *n.* **1.** conselho *m*; **to take legal advice,** consultar um advogado. **2. advice note,** aviso *m*; **letter of advice,** carta *f* de aviso; **as per advice,** conforme aviso; **advice of delivery,** aviso de entrega; **credit advice,** aviso de crédito; **payable without preliminary advice,** pagável sem aviso prévio.

advise, *v.tr.* **1. to advise s.o. on financial matters,** aconselhar, assessorar, dar conselhos a, alguém sobre assuntos financeiros. **2. to advise payment,** avisar pagamento; **to advise a draft,** mandar um aviso de saque.

adviser, *n.* conselheiro *m,* assessor *m,* consultor *m;* **an adviser to the manager,** um assessor do gerente; **financial adviser,** consultor financeiro.

affidavit, *n. Jur:* declaração escrita e juramentada.

affiliated, *a.* **affiliated to a trade union,** afiliado a um sindicato; **affiliated company,** (companhia) filiada, filial *f,* sociedade coligada.

affreightment, *n.* afretamento *m.*

afloat, *a. & adv.* **goods afloat,** mercadorias *fpl* a bordo; **to keep bills afloat,** fazer circular cambiais, manter letras de câmbio em circulação; **to keep s.o. afloat (financially),** ajudar alguém financeiramente.

after, *prep.* **bill after date,** letra *f* à vista pagável num determinado prazo; **bill payable 20 days after sight,** letra à vista pagável em 20 dias; **after January 15th,** a partir de quinze de janeiro, após quinze de janeiro.

agency, *n.* (*a*) agência *f;* **sole agency for a firm,** representação exclusiva de uma firma; **agency contract,** contrato *m* de representação, *Jur:* contrato de preposição; **news, press, agency,** agência de notícias; **employment agency,** agência de emprego, de colocação; **estate agency,** agência imobiliária; **shipping agency,** agência marítima, agência de navegação; **travel agency,** agência de viagens, agência de turismo; **literary agency,** agência literária; (*b*) *Bank:* agência (bancária), sucursal *f* (de banco).

agenda, *n.* **1.** ordem *f* do dia, temário *m;* **to draw up the agenda,** elaborar a ordem do dia; **to place a question on the agenda,** colocar um assunto na ordem do dia, incluir um assunto no temário. **2. the agenda is on the desk,** a agenda, a caderneta, está na escrivaninha; **the manager has a full agenda today,** a agenda do gerente está muito tomada hoje.

agent, *n.* agente *mf,* representante *mf;* **agent for the above firm,** agente, representante, da empresa acima; **agent on the spot,** agente de praça; **accredited agent,** agente acreditado; **appointed**

agent, agente autorizado; **commission agent,** comissário *m;* **(real-)estate agent,** agente imobiliário; **forwarding agent, transit agent,** despachante *m;* expedidor *m;* **insurance agent,** agente de seguros; **sales agent,** agente de vendas, agente comercial, representante comercial; **sole agent (for a brand),** agente exclusivo (de uma marca); **to appoint an agent,** nomear um agente.

aggregate, *a. Pol.Ec:* total, global; **aggregate demand,** procura *f* global; **aggregate expenditure,** despesa *f* total; **aggregate supply,** oferta *f* global; **aggregate output,** produção *f* global; **aggregate net increment,** aumento líquido global.

aggrieved, *a. Jur:* **aggrieved party,** parte lesada.

agio, *n.* ágio *m.*

agiotage, *n.* agiotagem *f.*

agree, *v.* **1.** *v.tr.* **to agree the accounts, the books,** aprovar os livros contábeis; **the figures were agreed between the accountants,** os contadores concordaram, chegaram a um acordo, sobre os números; **to agree the terms of a contract,** estabelecer, convencionar, as condições de um contrato; **to agree a price,** combinar, ajustar, estabelecer, um preço; **contract at an agreed price,** contrato *m* de preço global. **2.** *v.i.* (*of accounts*) conferir, concordar, bater; **the accounts do not agree,** as contas não concordam, não batem.

agreement, *n.* acordo *m,* convênio *m,* combinação *f,* contrato *m,* ajuste *m;* **agreement for sale,** contrato de compra e venda; **clearing agreement,** acordo de compensação, de clearing; **collective agreement,** convênio coletivo; **commodity agreement,** acordo sobre produtos básicos; **gentleman's agreement,** acordo de cavalheiros; **interim agreement,** acordo provisório; **written agreement,** contrato, convênio, acordo, por escrito; **by mutual agreement,** de comum acordo; **to abide by the agreement,** respeitar, cumprir com, os termos do contrato; **to break an agreement,** romper, quebrar, um acordo; **to enter into, sign, an agreement with,**

assinar, firmar, celebrar, um acordo, um contrato, com alguém; **to reach an agreement,** chegar a um acordo.

agricultural, *a.* **agricultural produce,** produtos *mpl* agrícolas; **agricultural economy,** economia agrícola; **agricultural profitability,** rentabilidade *f* agrícola.

agriculture, *n.* agricultura *f*; **agriculture and livestock sector,** setor agropecuário.

air, *n.* **by air,** por avião, (*of mail, goods, etc.*) via aérea; **air cargo, air freight,** frete aéreo; **air transport,** transportes aéreos; **air hostess,** aeromoça *f*; **air steward,** comissário *m* de bordo; **air letter,** aerograma *m*; **air ticket,** passagem aérea; **air waybill,** conhecimento aéreo.

aircraft, *n.* aeronave *f*, avião *m*; **charter aircraft,** (i) avião afretado, (ii) avião de aluguel, (*light aircraft*) táxi aéreo; **commercial aircraft,** avião comercial; **aircraft factory,** fábrica *f* de aeronaves; **the aircraft industry,** a indústria aeronáutica; **aircraft engineering,** engenharia aeronáutica.

airfreight, *v.tr.* aerotransportar, transportar por via aérea.

airfreighter, *n.* aerotransporte *m*, avião *m* para transporte de grande porte.

airline, *n.* linha aérea, empresa *f* de transportes aéreos.

airliner, *n.* avião *m* de passageiros.

airmail¹, *n.* correio aéreo; **by airmail,** via aérea; **airmail letter,** carta aérea; **airmail service,** serviço *m* aeropostal.

airmail², *v.tr.* remeter, enviar, (uma carta) via aérea.

airport, *n.* aeroporto *m*.

airproof, *a.* hermético, à prova de ar.

air-transported, *a.* transportado por avião.

all-in, *a.* **all-in price,** preço *m* global; *Ins:* **all-in policy,** apólice *f* de seguro contra todos os riscos.

allocate, *v.tr.* (*a*) **to allocate funds for research,** alocar, destinar, dotar, fundos para pesquisa; (*b*) *Ind: Book-k:* apropriar; **direct costs are allocated to a single product,** os custos diretos são apropriados a um só produto.

allocation, *n.* dotação *f*, (*amount*) verba *f*; **an allocation to the reserves,** uma dotação

às reservas; *Pol.Ec:* **allocations of special drawing rights,** alocações *fpl* de direitos especiais de saque; *Ind: Book-k:* apropriação *f* (de custos).

allot, *v.tr.* **to allot shares to an applicant,** atribuir ações a um subscritor.

allotment, *n.* (*a*) dotação *f* (de uma quantia para um fim específico); (*b*) atribuição *f* (de ações); **letter of allotment,** aviso *m* de atribuição (de ações); **allotment money,** entrada *f*, depósito *m* de entrada.

allow, *v.tr.* (*a*) **to allow a discount on cash sales,** conceder um desconto sobre vendas à vista; **to allow 5%,** deduzir 5%; **to allow a claim,** admitir uma reclamação, uma reivindicação; (*b*) **to allow for sums paid in advance,** deduzir as quantias pagas antecipadamente; **packing is not allowed for,** o custo de embalagem não está incluído; **breakages are not allowed for,** o custo de mercadorias quebradas não pode ser deduzido; **after allowing for commissions,** deduzidas as comissões; **to allow for the tare,** descontar, levar em conta, a tara; fazer desconto da tara; (*c*) *Cust: etc:* **goods allowed duty-free,** mercadorias isentas de direitos alfandegários; **the amount allowed per person,** a quantidade permitida por pessoa.

allowable, *a.* (*a*) permissível, admissível; **allowable discount, deduction,** desconto *m*, dedução *f*, permissível; (*b*) *Adm:* dedutível, abatível; **allowable expenses,** (i) despesas *fpl* dedutíveis, abatíveis, (ii) (*refundable*) despesas reembolsáveis.

allowance, *n.* **1.** (*as payment*) **accommodation allowance,** ajuda *f* de alojamento; **expense allowance,** ajuda de custo; **per diem allowance,** diária *f*; **entertainment allowance,** verba *f* de representação; **travel allowance,** ajuda de viagem; (*for importers, etc.*) **foreign currency allowance,** atribuição *f* de divisas. **2.** (*a*) abatimento *m*, desconto *m*, bonificação *f*; **to make an allowance on an article,** conceder um desconto, um abatimento, sobre um artigo; **allowance to the cashier for errors,** margem *f* de erro concedida ao caixa; **risk allowance,**

margem de risco; **allowance for exchange fluctuations,** provisão *f* para flutuações cambiais; **depreciation allowance, wear-and-tear allowance,** provisão para depreciação; (*b*) *Adm:* **income allowance,** abatimento da renda; **personal allowance,** abatimento da renda de pessoa física; **earned income allowance,** (limite de) isenção *f* de imposto sobre rendimento do trabalho individual; **capital allowance,** desconto *m* para depreciação.

alongside, *prep. Nau:* **free alongside,** livre ao lado; posto no cais, posto em barcaças encostadas ao navio.

amalgamate, *v.* **1.** *v.tr.* fundir, unir mediante fusão. **2.** *v.i.* unir-se mediante fusão.

amalgamation, *n.* fusão *f*; **amalgamation agreement,** contrato *m* de fusão.

amazing, *a.* **amazing offer,** oferta *f* excepcional.

amend, *v.tr.* retificar (uma conta); modificar, alterar, (as condições de um contrato, etc.).

amendment, *n.* retificação *f* (de conta); modificação *f* (de condições contratuais); **amendment of the articles of association,** reforma *f* do estatuto.

amicable, *a. Jur:* **amicable settlement,** acordo *m* amigável.

amortizable, *a.* **amortizable debt,** dívida *f* amortizável.

amortization, *n.* amortização *f*; **amortization quota,** taxa *f* de amortização.

amortize, *v.tr.* amortizar (uma dívida).

amount[1], *n.* quantia *f*, soma *f*, importe *m*, importância *f*, montante *m*, monta *f*, valor *m*, total *m*; **amount of expenses,** total de despesas; **amount of an invoice,** valor, montante, de uma fatura; **amount due,** importância a pagar; **amounts of stock negotiable,** quantidades *fpl* de títulos negociáveis; *Book-k:* **amount brought in,** saldo anterior, transferido do exercício anterior; **amount carried forward,** transporte *m*.

amount[2], *v.i.* (*of money, etc.*) somar, montar, importar; **the expenses amount to $300,** as despesas somam, montam a, importam em, trezentos dólares; **the total**

price **amounts to $26,** o preço total atinge, monta a, vinte e seis dólares.

analyse, *v.tr.* analizar (uma conta, o mercado, etc.).

analysis, *n.* análise *f*; **economic analysis,** análise econômica; **market analysis,** análise de mercado; **job analysis,** análise de cargos, de trabalho; **cost analysis,** análise de custos; **cost–benefit analysis,** análise de custos e benefícios; **cost-effectiveness analysis,** análise de custos e rendimento; **supply and demand analysis,** análise de oferta e procura; *Cmptr:* **systems analysis,** análise de sistemas.

analyst, *n.* **systems analyst,** analista *mf* de sistemas.

anchorage, *n. Nau:* ancoragem *f*.

annual, *a.* anual; **annual leave,** férias *fpl* anuais; **annual instalment,** prestação *f* anual, anuidade *f*, anualidade *f*; **debt repayable by annual instalments,** dívida anuitária; **annual general meeting,** assembléia geral ordinária; **annual report (of a company),** relatório *m* anual (de uma companhia); **annual accounts,** balanço *m* patrimonial e demonstrativo *m* de resultados; **he has an annual salary of $12 000,** ele ganha doze mil dólares anuais, recebe um salário anual de doze mil dólares.

annually, *adv.* anualmente, todos os anos.

annuitant, *n.* beneficiário *m* de uma anuidade; **life annuitant,** beneficiário de uma renda vitalícia.

annuity, *n.* **1.** *Fin:* **annuity in redemption of debt,** anuidade *f*. **2.** renda *f* anual, anuidade; **life annuity,** renda vitalícia.

annul, *v.tr.* anular, nulificar, invalidar, (contrato, escritura, etc.).

annullable, *a.* **annullable contract,** contrato *m* anulável, nulificável.

annulling, *a.* que anula; **annulling clause,** cláusula abrogatória.

annulment, *n.* anulação *f*, nulificação *f*, invalidação *f*.

answer[1], *n.* reposta *f*.

answer[2], *v.tr.* **to answer a letter,** responder a uma carta; **to answer the phone,** atender o telefone.

antedate, *v.tr.* antedatar (um documento, etc.).

anti-inflationary, *a.* anti-inflationary measures, medidas anti-inflacionárias.
anti-trust, *a.* anti-trust law, lei *f* antitruste.
apology, *n.* please accept our apologies for the delay, pedimos desculpas pela demora.
apparent, *a.* apparent consumption, consumo manifesto, consumo visível.
appeal, *n.* 1. the sales appeal of a product, o apelo de um produto. 2. *Jur:* to lodge an appeal against a decision, interpor um recurso contra uma decisão.
applicable, *a.* applicable penalties, penalidades *fpl* aplicáveis.
applicant, *n.* applicant for a job, candidato *m* a um emprego; applicant for a patent, requerente *mf* de uma patente de invenção; applicant for shares, subscritor *m* de ações.
application, *n.* (*a*) application for a job, pedido *m*, solicitação *f*, de um emprego; application for an import licence, requerimento *m* de uma licença de importação; application for payment, requisição *f* de pagamento; application form, formulário *m* de requerimento; to fill in an application form, preencher um requerimento; (*b*) *Fin:* application for shares, subscrição *f* de ações; to make an application for shares, subscrever ações; payable on application, pagável no ato de subscrição; application form, boletim *m* de subscrição; application money, entrada *f* (de subscrição); application is covered, todas as ações estão subscritas.
apply, *v.* 1. *v.tr.* to apply a payment to a particular debt, aplicar, imputar, um pagamento a uma dívida determinada; to apply penalties, aplicar penalidades; to apply profits, destinar os lucros (para determinado fim). 2. *v.i.* (*a*) to apply for a job, candidatar-se a um emprego; pedir, requerer, um emprego; to apply in writing, apresentar um pedido por escrito; to apply for a pay rise, requisitar, requerer, um aumento de salário; (*b*) *Fin:* to apply for shares, subscrever ações.
appoint, *v.tr.* to appoint s.o. to a post, nomear, designar, alguém para um cargo; to appoint s.o. as the new manager,

nomear alguém como o novo gerente; to appoint a commission, nomear, instituir, designar, uma comissão.
appointment, *n.* 1. (*for business, etc.*) entrevista *f*, encontro marcado, compromisso *m*; to make, fix, an appointment with s.o., marcar uma entrevista, um encontro, com alguém; to break an appointment, faltar a uma entrevista, etc.; to cancel an appointment, cancelar uma entrevista, um encontro, etc.; appointments book, caderneta *f*, agenda *f*; do you have an appointment, sir? o senhor tem hora marcada? 2. (*a*) nomeação *f*, designação *f*, (de alguém para um cargo); (*of shop, supplier, etc.*) by appointment to His, Her, Majesty, aprovisionador *m* oficial da sua Majestade; appointments board, junta *f* de nomeações; (*b*) posto *m*, cargo *m*, emprego *m*; to hold an appointment, ocupar um cargo; to advertise a secretarial appointment, anunciar uma vaga de secretária; *Journ:* appointments vacant, ofertas *fpl* de emprego, 'empregados procurados'.
apportion, *v.tr.* ratear, partilhar, (despesas).
apportionment, *n.* rateio *m*, rateamento *m*, partilha *f*, distribuição *f* proporcional, (de despesas, etc.); *Ins:* apportionment clause, cláusula *f* de atribuição de responsabilidade.
appraisal, *n.* market appraisal, avaliação *f* do mercado.
appreciate, *v.i.* (*of goods, assets, etc.*) valorizar-se; aumentar de valor, (*in terms of price*) encarecer; coffee appreciated by twenty-five per cent, o café encareceu em vinte e cinco por cento; appreciated surplus, valorização *f*; the pound appreciated in terms of other currencies, a libra se valorizou em relação a outras moedas.
appreciation, *n.* 1. estimativa *f* (do valor de um bem, etc.), avaliação *f*. 2. valorização *f* (de moeda, ativo, etc.), alta *f*, encarecimento *m* (do café, etc.); an appreciation of the company's assets, uma valorização do patrimônio social; these shares show an appreciation, estas

ações acusam, apresentam, registram, um aumento de valor; **appreciation in prices,** melhoramento *m* dos preços.

apprentice¹, *n.* aprendiz *m.*

apprentice², *v.tr.* empregar como aprendiz.

apprenticeship, *n.* aprendizado *m,* aprendizagem *f;* **to serve one's apprenticeship with s.o.,** fazer o seu aprendizado com alguém.

appro, *n. F: (of sale)* **on appro,** a contento.

appropriate, *v.tr.* **1. to appropriate the funds,** apropriar os fundos; apropriar-se, apossar-se, dos fundos. **2.** destinar, consignar, reservar, alocar, (**sth. to, for, a purpose,** algo a, para, um fim determinado); **to appropriate the net profit to the reserve,** dotar, atribuir, o lucro líquido à reserva; **to appropriate funds to the redemption of a bond,** destinar fundos ao resgate de uma obrigação.

appropriation, *n.* **1.** apropriação *f* (de fundos de outra pessoa, etc.). **2.** dotação *f,* consignação *f,* (para um fim determinado); **appropriation to the reserve,** dotação à reserva; **appropriation of the net profit,** distribuição *f* do lucro líquido; **proprietors' appropriations,** reembolsos *mpl* aos proprietários; **prior appropriation,** dotação prioritária; **appropriation account,** conta *f* de distribuição dos lucros; *Jur:* **appropriation of payments,** imputação *f* de pagamentos; **appropriation to a debt,** imputação a uma dívida.

approval, *n.* **1.** aprovação *f,* autorização *f;* **subject to board approval,** mediante aprovação do conselho de administração. **2.** *(of government, etc.)* ratificação *f,* homologação *f,* (de um acordo, tratado, etc.). **3.** *(a)* **on approval,** a contento; **sale on approval,** venda *f* a contento; **goods on approval,** mercadorias vendidas a contento; *(b) N.Am:* *pl.* **approvals,** mercadorias vendidas a contento.

approve, *v.tr.* aprovar, autorizar, sancionar; *(of government, etc.)* ratificar, homologar; *(of legal document)* **read and approved,** lido e achado conforme; **the**

proposal was approved (of), a proposta foi aprovada.

arbitrage, *n.* arbitragem *f* (de câmbio), arbítrio *m* (de câmbio); **arbitrage syndicate,** sindicato *m* de arbitragem.

arbitrate, *v.* **1.** *v.tr.* arbitrar, decidir por arbítrio. **2.** *v.i.* decidir como árbitro.

arbitration, *n.* **1.** arbítrio *m,* arbitramento *m,* arbitragem *f;* **arbitration award,** (decisão *f* por) arbitragem, arbítrio, julgamento *m* do(s) árbitro(s); **arbitration board, court,** juízo *m* arbitral, tribunal *m* de arbitragem; **arbitration procedure,** processo *m* de arbitragem. **2.** *Fin:* **arbitration of exchange,** arbitragem, arbítrio, de câmbio.

arbitrator, *n.* árbitro *m.*

architect, *n.* arquiteto *m.*

archives, *n.pl.* arquivos *mpl.*

area, *n.* **geographic area,** área geográfica; **free-trade area,** (i) zona franca, (ii) zona, área, de comércio livre; **currency area,** zona monetária; **sterling area,** zona esterlina; **development area,** zona de desenvolvimento; **shopping area,** zona comercial; **growth area,** setor *m* de crescimento.

arrangement, *n.* arranjo *m;* **arrangements for a new issue,** preparativos *mpl* de uma nova emissão; **to make an arrangement, to come to an arrangement, with s.o.,** combinar, ajustar, com alguém; **to make all the necessary arrangements,** tomar todas as providências necessárias; **price by arrangement,** preço *m* a combinar; *Jur:* **arrangement with creditors,** concordata *f.*

arrears, *n.pl.* atrasos *mpl,* contas atrasadas, pagamentos atrasados, prestações atrasadas; **arrears of pay,** salário atrasado; **arrears of interest,** juros *mpl* de mora vencidos e não pagos; **he is three months in arrears,** ele está com um atraso de três meses; **to fall into arrears with instalments,** atrasar-se no pagamento de prestações; **to make up arrears,** liquidar, saldar, apurar, os atrasos; **taxpayer in arrears,** contribuinte atrasado, em atraso; **salary with arrears as from 1st March,** salário com efeito retroativo a contar de primeiro de março.

arrival, *n.* chegada *f* (de navio, mercadorias, etc.); **advice of arrival,** aviso *m* de chegada (de mercadorias, encomenda, etc.); **arrival draft,** cambial *f* pagável a partir da chegada das mercadorias.
arrive, *v.i.* **to arrive at a price,** chegar a um preço; combinar um preço.
article, *n.* **1.** artigo *m*, produto *m*, mercadoria *f*; **to put an article on the market,** lançar um novo produto; *Ret:* **leading article,** artigo de ponta. **2.** (*a*) artigo *m*, cláusula *f*, item *m*, (de contrato); **articles of association,** estatutos *mpl* sociais, contrato *m* social; **as provided in the articles of the contract,** conforme as estipulações contratuais, conforme estipulado nas cláusulas do contrato; (*b*) **to be under articles,** estar sob contrato (de aprendizagem, etc.).
assess, *v.tr.* avaliar, estimar, calcular; **to assess the losses at $100,** estimar, calcular, os prejuízos em $100; **to assess a property,** avaliar uma propriedade; *Adm:* **to assess s.o.,** calcular a renda tributável de alguém.
assessment, *n.* (*a*) avaliação *f* (de danos, sinistros, etc.); (*b*) *Adm:* (*for taxation*) lançamento *m* (de imposto).
asset, *n.* bem *m*, haver *m*, componente *m* do ativo; **the assets of a company,** o patrimônio social, (*on balance sheet*) o ativo (de uma empresa); **available assets,** disponibilidades *fpl*, ativo disponível; **capital assets,** bens de capital, capital fixo, bens imóveis, ativo imobilizado; **circulating assets,** ativo circulante, capital circulante; **current assets,** ativo corrente, capital corrente, capital de giro, capital flutuante; (*of bank*) **earning assets,** títulos *mpl* de rendimento; **fixed assets,** ativo fixo, ativo permanente, (ativo) imobilizado; **intangible assets,** bens imateriais, bens incorpóreos, bens intangíveis; **liquid assets,** ativo líquido, capital líquido; **long-term assets,** ativo realizável a longo prazo; **net assets,** patrimônio líquido, patrimônio próprio, situação líquida; **net assets employed,** patrimônio líquido empregado (na empresa); **pending assets,** ativo pendente;

personal assets, bens pessoais; **real assets,** bens imóveis, bens de raiz; **realizable assets,** ativo realizável, bens realizáveis, ativo real; **short-term assets,** ativo realizável a curto prazo; **transferable assets,** bens móveis; **wasting assets,** bens esgotáveis; **assets brought in,** bens contribuídos para a formação do capital (de uma companhia); **excess of assets over liabilities,** excedente *m* do ativo sobre o passivo; **asset turnover,** giro *m* de capitais; **asset value,** valor *m* do ativo, do patrimônio; **asset valuation reserve,** reserva *f* para avaliação do ativo.
assign, *v.tr.* **1. to assign a bond by endorsement,** ceder um título mediante endosso; **to assign a lease,** transferir um contrato de aluguel; **to assign a contract, shares, to s.o.,** transferir um contrato, ações, a alguém; **to assign a patent to the receiver,** consignar uma patente ao síndico de massa falida. **2. to assign s.o. to a new post,** designar alguém para um novo cargo.
assignation, *n.* transferência *f*, traspasse *m*, (de contrato de aluguel), cessão *f* (de direitos, etc.); **assignation of shares,** transferência *f* de ações.
assignee, *n.* cessionário *m.*
assignment, *n.* **1.** transferência *f*, traspasse *m*, (de contrato de aluguel, de negócio, etc.), cessão *f* (de direitos); **assignment of shares,** transferência *f* de ações; **assignment of a patent,** (i) transferência de uma patente, (ii) concessão de licença para a exploração de uma patente; **deed of assignment,** escritura *f* de cessão; **assignment of debts,** cessão de dívidas. **2.** nomeação *f*; **his assignment as vice-consul,** sua nomeação como vice-cônsul, para o cargo de vice-cônsul.
assignor, *n.* cedente *mf.*
assistance, *n.* assistência *f*, ajuda *f*; **financial assistance,** assistência financeira.
assistant, **1.** *a.* assistente, auxiliar, ajudante; **assistant manager,** subgerente *mf.* **2.** *n.* adjunto *m*, auxiliar *mf*, assistente *mf*; **shop assistant,** caixeiro *m*,

vendedora *f*, balconista *mf*; **personal assistant (PA)**, secretária *f* particular.

associate, 1. *a.* **associate company**, companhia coligada, filiada (*f*); **associate director**, diretor associado. **2.** *n.* associado *m*, parceiro *m*.

association, *n.* associação *f*, agremiação *f*, organização *f*; **trade association**, entidade *f* de classe, associação profissional; **(restrictive) trade association**, sindicato *m* empresarial.

assume, *v.tr.* **to assume all risks**, assumir todos os riscos; **to assume liability**, assumir a responsabilidade.

assurance, *n.* **life assurance**, seguro *m* de vida; **term life assurance**, seguro de vida a prazo fixo; **assurance company**, seguradora *f*, companhia *f* de seguros; **assurance policy**, apólice *f* de seguro.

assure, *v.tr.* **to assure s.o.'s life**, segurar a vida de alguém; **to have one's life assured**, segurar-se, fazer um seguro de vida.

assured, *n.* segurado *m*.

assurer, assuror, *n.* segurador *m*.

attach, *v.tr.* **1. to attach a price list to a letter**, anexar, juntar, uma tabela de preços a uma carta. **2.** *Jur:* **to attach the goods of a debtor**, arrestar, embargar, os bens de um devedor; **attached account**, conta *f* em juízo.

attachment, *n.* **1.** (documento) anexo. **2.** *Jur:* arresto *m*, embargo *m*.

attend, *v.* **1.** *v.tr.* **to attend (to) a customer**, atender, despachar, um freguês; **to attend a meeting**, assistir (a) uma reunião. **2.** *v.i.* **to attend to an order**, despachar, atender, expedir, um pedido, uma encomenda.

attention, *n.* *Corr:* **your orders shall have our best attention at all times**, as suas estimadas ordens encontrarão sempre os nossos melhores cuidados; **for the attention of Mr. X**, aos cuidados do Sr. X.

attorney, *n.* (*a*) *N.Am:* advogado *m*; (*b*) procurador *m*; **power, letter, of attorney**, procuração *f*; **to grant s.o. power of attorney**, passar procuração para alguém; **attorney-in-fact**, mandatário *m*; (*c*) *Am:* **district attorney**, promotor público (de distrito).

attractive, *a.* **attractive prices**, preços atraentes, preços convidativos.

auction¹, *n.* leilão *m*, leiloamento *m*, licitação *f*, almoeda *f*, arrematação *f*, hasta *f*, praça *f*; **to put up for auction**, pôr em leilão, etc.; **to sell by auction**, vender em leilão, etc.; **auction room**, local *m* de leilão.

auction², *v.tr.* leiloar, arrematar, vender em leilão, etc.

auctioneer, *n.* (*a*) (*auctioneer and valuer*) leiloeiro *m*; (*b*) (*at a sale*) leiloeiro *m*, pregoeiro *m*.

audit¹, *n.* auditoria *f*, verificação *f* de contas, exame *m* de contas.

audit², *v.tr.* auditar, verificar, examinar, (as demonstrações contábeis).

auditing, *n.* auditoria *f*, verificação *f* de contas; **auditing procedures**, procedimentos *mpl* de auditoria.

auditor, *n.* auditor *m* (contábil), verificador *m* de contas; **auditor's report**, parecer *m* de auditoria, parecer do auditor; **a firm of auditors**, uma empresa de auditoria.

automatic, *a.* automático; **automatic vending machine**, vendedora automática, autômato *m*.

availability, *n.* **availability of stocks**, disponibilidade *f* de estoque; **subject to availability**, conforme disponibilidade.

available, *a.* disponível; (*of person*) livre; **items available in stock**, artigos estocados, disponíveis em estoque; **available at all branches**, à venda em todas as filiais; (*of product*) **no longer available**, esgotado; **available assets**, disponibilidades *fpl*; ativo *m*, capital *m*, disponível; **capital that can be made available**, capitais *mpl* mobilizáveis; **sum available for dividend**, lucro *m* atribuível para pagamento de dividendos.

average¹, 1. *n.* (*a*) média *f*; **daily average**, média diária; **weighted average**, média ponderada; **to take an average**, tirar a média; **on average**, em média; (*b*) *M.Ins:* avaria *f*; **particular average**, avaria particular, avaria simples; **general average**, avaria grossa, avaria comum; **usual average**, avaria ordinária; **petty average**, avaria pequena; **free from**

average, livre de avaria; **average adjustment, statement,** regulação *f* de avaria, repartição *f* de avaria; **average bond,** caução *f* para avarias; **to make good an average,** indenizar por uma avaria. **2.** *a.* médio; **average cost per unit,** custo unitário médio; **average price,** preço médio; **the average figures for the last five years,** a média dos números dos últimos cinco anos.
average², *v.tr.* **1. to average $5000 a year,** importar em uma média de cinco mil dólares anuais. **2.** *M.Ins:* **to average a loss,** repartir, ratear, um sinistro.
avoid, *v.tr.* **1. to avoid problems,** evitar problemas. **2.** *Jur:* resolver, anular, invalidar, rescindir, encampar, (um contrato, etc.).
avoidance, *n. Jur:* **avoidance of an agreement (owing to breach, etc.),** anulação *f,* resolução *f,* rescisão *f,* invalidação *f,* encampação *f,* (por inadimplemento, etc.); (*in a contract*) **condition of avoidance,** condição *f* resolutória, rescisória; cláusula resolutória, rescisória; **action for avoidance of a contract,** ação resolutória.
avoirdupois, *n. Meas:* **the avoirdupois pound is the pound of 453.592 grams,** a libra avoirdupois é a libra de 453,592 gramas.

award¹, *n.* (*a*) **arbitration award,** arbitragem *f,* arbítrio *m,* decisão *f* arbitral; (*in arbitration*) **pay award,** arbítrio de aumento salarial; **to make an award,** pronunciar, emitir, um arbítrio; (*b*) **award of a contract,** adjudicação *f* de um contrato; *Am:* **award clerk,** encarregado *m* de compras.
award², *v.tr.* (*in arbitration*) **to award a pay increase,** arbitrar um aumento salarial; **to award a supply contract to the successful bidder,** adjudicar um contrato de fornecimento ao proponente vencedor; *Jur:* **to award damages,** decretar o pagamento de indenização (para alguém).
awarder, *n.* adjudicador *m* (de um contrato).
awarding, *n.* adjudicação *f* (de um contrato).
axe¹, *n. F:* **the axe,** o corte das previsões orçamentárias; redução *f* do quadro do pessoal; **to give s.o. the axe,** demitir, despachar, alguém; mandar alguém embora.
axe², *v.tr. F:* **to axe public expenditure,** cortar as despesas públicas; **to axe officials,** licenciar, despedir, funcionários (por razões de ordem econômica).
axis, *n.* **axis of supply,** eixo *m* de abastecimento.

B

back¹, *n.* verso *m* (de cheque, letra de câmbio, etc.).

back², *a.* **back dividends**, dividendos atrasados; **back pay**, salário atrasado; *Ind: etc:* **back order**, pedido pendente; *Nau:* **back freight**, taxas cobradas pela devolução de carga não desembarcada por motivos alheios à vontade do transportador.

back³, *v.tr.* **to back a venture**, financiar, custear, um empreendimento; **to back a currency**, apoiar uma moeda; **to back a loan application**, apoiar um pedido de empréstimo; **to back a bill**, avalizar uma letra de câmbio.

backdate, *v.tr.* antedatar; **backdated pay increase**, aumento *m* salarial com efeito retroativo.

backed, *a.* **backed bills**, letras avalizadas.

backer, *n.* avalista *mf*, endossador *m*, endossante *mf*, (de uma letra); (*in partnership arrangement*) comanditário *m*; **backers for a film**, financiadores *mpl* de um filme.

backing, *n.* **financial backing**, financiamento *m*, custeamento *m*; **the backing of a currency**, o apoio a uma moeda.

backlog, *n.* acumulação *f* (de pedidos não despachados).

backshift, *n. Am: Ind:* (*a*) turno *m* da tarde; (*b*) turno *m* da noite.

backwardation, *n. Fin: St.Exch:* deporte *m*; taxa devida pela demora na entrega de títulos.

bad, *a.* **bad debt**, dívida *f* incobrável; **bad cheque**, cheque *m* sem fundos; **bad coin**, moeda falsa; **bad paper**, títulos *mpl* sem valor.

baggage, *n.* bagagem *f*; **baggage allowance**, franquia *f* de bagagem;

baggage room, déposito *m* de bagagem; **baggage check**, talão *m* de bagagem.

bagman, *n. Am: F:* caixeiro viajante *m*.

bail¹, *n.* (*a*) fiança *f*, caução *f*; (*b*) (*person*) fiador *m*; **to stand bail for s.o.**, afiançar alguém (para que este seja posto em liberdade condicional).

bail², *v.tr.* (*a*) entregar (mercadorias) sob contrato; (*b*) pôr em liberdade sob fiança.

bailable, *a.* afiançável.

bailee, *n. Jur:* depositário *m*.

bailiff, *n.* oficial *m* de diligências, oficial de justiça.

bailment, *n.* (*a*) prestação *f* de fiança; (*b*) entrega *f* (de bens ou mercadorias) sob contrato ou garantia.

bailor, *n. Jur:* depositante *mf*.

bailsman, *n. Jur:* fiador *m*.

balance¹, *n.* **1.** saldo *m*; **credit balance**, **balance in hand**, saldo credor, saldo positivo, saldo a favor; **debit balance**, saldo devedor, saldo negativo, saldo contra; **balance due**, saldo a pagar; **opening balance**, saldo de abertura, saldo anterior; **closing balance**, saldo de encerramento; **dormant balance**, saldo pendente; **balance brought forward**, transportado, transporte *m*; **stock balance**, saldo de estoque; **available balance**, saldo disponível. **2.** **balance of trade**, balança *f* comercial; **balance of trade deficit**, déficit *m* na balança comercial; **balance of trade surplus**, superávit *m* na balança comercial; **balance of payments**, balanço *m* de pagamentos; **invisible balance**, balanço invisível. **3.** **balance sheet**, balanço *m* (geral), folha *f* de balanço; **balance-sheet audit**, exame *m*, auditoria *f*, de balanço; **trial balance**, balancete *m*, balanço parcial; **periodic trial balance**, balancete

14

parcial; **trial-balance book,** livro *m* de balancetes.
balance², *v.* 1. *v.tr.* equilibrar (contas comerciais); **to balance an account,** saldar, liquidar, uma conta; **to balance a debt,** compensar uma dívida. 2. *v.i.* **the accounts balance,** as contas se equilibram, batem.
bale¹, *n.* bala *f*, fardo *m*; **bale of paper,** bala de papel; **bale of cotton,** balote *m*, fardo de algodão; **bale goods,** mercadorias enfardadas.
bale², *v.tr.* enfardar (algodão, etc.).
baler, *n.* enfardador *m*.
baling, *n.* enfardamento *m*; **baling press,** enfardadeira *f*.
ballast, *n.* lastro *m*; **vessel in ballast,** embarcação *f* em lastro; **cargo in ballast,** carga *f* em fundo de porão; **water ballast,** lastro de água.
balloon, *v.i.* (*of prices, etc.*) subir rapidamente.
ballot¹, *n.* (*a*) cédula *f*, chapa *f* eleitoral; (*b*) escrutínio *m*; **ballot box,** escrutínio *m*, urna *f* (eleitoral); **ballot paper,** cédula, chapa (eleitoral); **to hold a ballot,** organizar um escrutínio, proceder a um escrutínio; **to decide by ballot,** decidir, resolver, (uma questão) mediante escrutínio.
ballot², *v.* 1. *v.tr.* **to ballot the membership (of a union) on an issue,** conhecer as opiniões dos membros (de um sindicato) sobre uma questão mediante escrutínio.
bang, *v.tr.* *St.Exch:* **to bang the market,** fazer baixar as cotações.
bank¹, *n.* banco *m*, casa bancária; **agricultural bank,** banco agrícola; **central bank,** banco central; **clearing bank,** banco de compensação; **deposit bank,** banco de depósitos; **development bank,** banco de desenvolvimento; **investment bank,** banco de investimento; **land bank,** banco de crédito real, banco de crédito imobiliário; **merchant bank,** banco mercantil; **mortgage bank,** banco hipotecário; **private bank,** banco particular; **rediscount bank,** banco de redescontos; **reserve bank,** banco de reservas; **savings bank,** caixa *f* econômica, caderneta *f* de poupança; **the World Bank,** o Banco Mundial; **bank**

acceptance, aceite bancário; **bank account,** conta bancária; **bank balance,** saldo *m* em conta bancária; **bank book,** caderneta *f* de depósito; **bank clerk,** bancário *m*, funcionário *m* de banco; **bank credit,** crédito *m* em conta bancária; **bank debit,** débito *m* em conta bancária; **bank discount,** desconto bancário; **bank draft,** saque bancário; **bank examiner,** auditor *m* de bancos; **bank guarantee,** garantia bancária; **bank holiday,** feriado público; **bank manager,** gerente *mf* de banco; **bank rate,** taxa bancária; **bank statement,** extrato bancário.
bank², *v.* 1. *v.tr.* **to bank the takings,** depositar a féria no banco. 2. *v.i.* **to bank with,** ter conta (bancária) em (determinado banco); **I bank with the X Bank,** eu tenho conta no banco X; **where do you bank?** qual é seu banco?
bankable, *a.* **bankable bill,** efeito bancário, título *m* negociável em banco; **bankable currency,** moeda *f* aceitável em banco.
banker, *n.* banqueiro *m*; **banker's bill,** cambial bancária; **banker's cheque,** cheque bancário; **banker's draft,** saque bancário; **to pay by banker's order,** pagar por ordem bancária.
banking, *n.* 1. atividade bancária, operações bancárias; **banking house,** casa bancária, estabelecimento bancário; **banking services,** serviços bancários; **banking hours,** horário *m* de banco, expediente *m* de banco; **commercial banking,** atividade bancária comercial; **commercial banking system,** sistema bancário comercial; *N.Am:* **banking account,** conta bancária. 2. profissão *f* de banqueiro; **to be in banking,** ser banqueiro.
banknote, *n.* nota *f* (bancária), cédula *f*, bilhete *m* de banco.
bankrupt¹, *a. & n.* (*trader or firm*) falido (*m*); **fraudulent bankrupt,** bancarroteiro *m*; **to go bankrupt,** (i) falir, quebrar, (ii) (*fraudulently*) bancarrotear; **discharged bankrupt,** falido reabilitado; **undischarged bankrupt,** falido não reabilitado; **to adjudicate, declare, s.o. bankrupt,** decretar a falência de alguém.
bankrupt², *v.tr.* **high fuel costs bankrupted**

the company, os altos custos de combustível causaram a falência da empresa.
bankruptcy, *n.* (i) falência *f*, quebra *f*, insolvência *f*, (ii) (*fraudulent*) bancarrota *f*; to file a petition in bankruptcy, abrir falência, confessar falência; declaration of bankruptcy, declaração *f* de falência, decreto *m* judicial de falência; bankruptcy laws, direito *m* falimentar, direito falencial, leis falimentares, leis falenciais; bankruptcy proceedings, procedimento *m* falimentar; bankruptcy court, tribunal *m* de falências, tribunal falimentar.
bar, *n. Stat;* bar chart, gráfico *m* de barras.
bargain¹, *n.* 1. to strike a bargain, fechar um negócio, chegar a um acordo comercial; *St.Exch:* bargains done, negócios realizados, operações realizadas; *St.Exch:* time bargain, negócio a termo, operação a termo; *Jur:* deed of bargain and sale, escritura *f* de compra e venda. 2. (*advantageous purchase*) pechincha *f*, *F:* galinha-morta *f*; bargain hunter, pechincheiro *m*; bargain hunting, procura *f* de pechinchas; bargain counter, balcão *m* de pechinchas; bargain sale, liquidação *f*, saldo *m*, feira *f*; bargain price, preço *m* de ocasião, preço de liquidação; bargain basement, subsolo *m* de uma casa comercial onde se vendem pechinchas; to get a bargain, conseguir uma pechincha, comprar muito barato.
bargain², *v.i.* to bargain over the goods, pechinchar, regatear, as mercadorias.
bargainee, *n. Jur:* comprador *m*.
bargainer, *n.* regateador *m*, pechincheiro *m*.
bargaining, *n.* regateio *m*; *Ind:* barganha *f*, negociação *f*; bargaining power, poder *m* de barganha, poder de negociação; bargaining unit, unidade *f* de negociação, unidade de barganha; collective bargaining, negociação coletiva.
bargainor, *n. Jur:* vendedor *m*.
barge, *n.* batelão *m*, chata *f*, (*wooden*) barcaça *f*; barge crane, guindaste *m* flutuante; canal barge, batelão de canal; coal barge, batelão para carvão; motor barge, batelão a motor.

baron, *n.* oil baron, magnata *m* da indústria petroleira.
barrel, *n.* barril *m.*
barrier, *n.* barreira *f*; trade barrier, barreira comercial; customs barrier, barreira alfandegária, barreira aduaneira.
barrister, *n. Brit:* causídico *m*, advogado *m.*
barter¹, *n.* troca *f*, permuta *f*, permutação *f.*
barter², *v.tr & i.* trocar, permutar; to barter grain for heavy machinery, trocar, permutar, cereais por maquinaria pesada.
barterer, *n.* trocador *m*, permutador *m.*
base, *n.* base *f*; base period, período *m* base; base price, preço *m* de base; base rate (of taxation) alíquota *f* de base; *Book-k:* base stock valuation, avaliação *f* de estoques pelo método de estoque básico.
basic, *a.* básico; basic cost, custo básico; basic price, preço básico; basic commodities, produtos básicos; *Am: Ind:* basic crew, equipe *f* de base.
basing, *n.* basing point, ponto-base *m* (para estabelecimento de preços de venda).
basis, *n.* base *f*; on the basis of ..., à base de ..., com base em ..., baseado em ....
basket, *n.* basket purchase, compra *f* de diversos bens (geralmente por um preço global).
batch, *n.* batelada *f*, lote *m*; in batches, em bateladas; *Ind:* batch costing, custeio *m* por bateladas; batch processing, processamento *m* em batelada(s); batch system, sistema *m* de processamento em bateladas.
batch(ed), *a.* batch(ed) consignment, remessa *f* em bateladas, em lotes.
batchwise, *adv.* em bateladas.
bear¹, *v.tr.* to bear a date, estar datado; to bear the expenses, arcar com as despesas; all operating costs will be borne by the client, todos os custos operacionais correrão por conta do cliente; *Fin:* to bear interest, render juros.
bear², *n. St.Exch:* baixista *mf*; especulador *m* que espera uma baixa no mercado; bear position, posição *f* a descoberto.

bear³, *v. St.Exch:* **1.** *v.tr.* **to bear the market,** provocar uma baixa no mercado. **2.** *v.i.* jogar na baixa, especular na baixa. **bearer,** *n.* portador *m* (de título, etc.); **bearer share,** ação *f* ao portador; **bearer security,** título *m* de crédito ao portador. **bearish,** *a.* **a bearish stock-market operator,** um operador baixista; **a bearish market,** um mercado tendente à baixa. **behalf,** *n.* **payment on behalf of s.o.,** pagamento *m* a favor de alguém; **to act on behalf of s.o.,** agir em nome de alguém. **below,** *prep.* **below average,** abaixo da média; *Fin:* **below par,** abaixo do par; **below cost,** abaixo do custo, aquém do custo; *Book-k:* **below the line,** abaixo da linha (de demarcação de uma demonstração de lucros e perdas). **beneficiary,** *n.* beneficiário *m.* **benefit¹,** *n.* benefício *m,* proveito *m,* vantagem *f;* **for the benefit of,** em proveito de, em benefício de; **fringe benefits,** vantagens *fpl* adicionais, benefícios extras; **social security benefits,** benefícios da previdência social, benefícios sócio-securitários; **industrial injuries benefit,** indenização *f* por acidentes industriais; **sickness benefit,** auxílio-doença *m;* **unemployment benefit,** auxílio-desemprego *m;* **old-age benefit,** pecúlio-velhice *m; Jur:* **benefit of discussion,** benefício de excussão; *Jur:* **benefit of division,** benefício de divisão; *Jur:* **benefit of inventory,** benefício de inventário; *Ins: etc:* **benefit society,** sociedade *f* mutuante, mútua *f.* **benefit²,** *v.* **1.** *v.tr.* beneficiar, favorecer; **the new measures benefit taxpayers,** as novas medidas beneficiam, favorecem, os contribuintes; **a steady exchange rate benefits trade,** uma taxa de câmbio constante favorece o comércio. **2.** *v.i.* **to benefit from a rise in prices,** beneficiar-se de uma subida de preços. **berth,** *n.* atracadouro *m.* **bespoke,** *a.* **bespoke garment,** vestido feito sob medida; **bespoke tailor,** alfaiate *m* que trabalha sob medida. **best seller,** *n.* (i) (*of book*) best-seller *m,* sucesso *m* de livraria, (ii) (*of other*

merchandise) artigo *m* de grande êxito (comercial). **best-selling,** *a.* de grande êxito (comercial). **bid¹,** *n.* (*a*) (*at auction*) lance *m,* lanço *m,* monta *f;* **higher bid,** sobrelanço *m;* **to make a higher bid,** cobrir o lance; **closing bid,** lance final; (*b*) proposta *f,* oferta *f;* **bid price,** preço *m* de oferta, preço oferecido para compra; **to put in a bid for a contract,** apresentar uma proposta para um contrato; **bid bond,** fiança *f* de licitação, garantia *f* para licitar; (*c*) **takeover bid,** oferta pública de aquisição de controle. **bid²,** *v.tr. & i.* (*a*) **to bid a fair price,** oferecer um preço justo; (*at auction*) **to bid a hundred dollars for a table,** lançar cem dólares numa mesa, oferecer um lance de cem dólares sobre uma mesa; (*at auction*) **the buyers are bidding up well,** os lances estão subindo rapidamente; (*b*) *Ind:* licitar; **to bid for a contract,** apresentar uma proposta para um contrato. **bidder,** *n.* (*at auction*) lançador *m;* (*at judicial sale*) licitante *mf,* licitador *m;* (*for a contract*) proponente *mf,* licitante, licitador; **the lowest bidder,** o lançador da menor oferta; **the highest bidder,** o lançador da maior oferta; **the successful bidder (for a contract),** o proponente vencedor; **to knock down to the highest bidder,** arrematar a quem oferecer o maior lance. **bidding,** *n.* licitação *f,* leiloamento *m;* **bidding was very brisk,** houve um grande número de lances. **big,** *a.* **a big increase,** um aumento grande; **big profits,** altos lucros, grandes lucros. **bill¹,** *n.* **1.** nota *f,* conta *f,* (*as invoice*) fatura *f;* **itemized bill,** conta discriminada, fatura discriminada; **to make out a bill (for goods sold),** tirar, fazer, uma fatura (de mercadorias vendidas); **bill of sale,** nota de venda; **bill collector,** cobrador *m* de dívidas; *Book-k:* **bills payable,** contas a pagar, efeitos *mpl* a pagar; *Book-k:* **bills receivable,** contas a receber, efeitos a receber; *Jur:* **bill of**

costs, relação f, nota, de custas; *Ind: etc:*
the wages bill (of a firm), a folha de
pagamento (de uma empresa). **2.** letra f
(de câmbio), cambial f, efeito *m*
(comercial), efeito de comércio, papel *m*
(comercial); **bill payable to order,** título
m à ordem; **bill of credit,** carta f de
crédito; **bill of debt,** confissão f de dívida,
reconhecimento *m* de dívida; **short-dated
bills,** letras a curto prazo; **long-dated bills,**
letras a longo prazo; **clean bill,** letra (de
câmbio) sem documentos anexos;
documentary bill, letra (de câmbio)
acompanhada de documentos; **advance
bill,** letra (de câmbio) aceita antes do
embarque; **bill broker,** corretor *m* de
letras; **bill book,** (livro) registro *m* de
efeitos, de títulos; *Fin:* **Treasury bill,** letra
f do Tesouro. **3.** *N.Am:* cédula f, nota f;
five-dollar bill, cédula, nota, de cinco
dólares. **4.** (*poster*) cartaz *m*, (*handbill*)
volante *m*. **5.** *Jur:* **the Finance Bill,** o
projeto de lei das finanças. **6. bill of
lading,** conhecimento *m* de carga, de
frete, de transporte; **clean bill of lading,**
conhecimento marítimo limpo.

bill², *v.tr.* **to bill the purchases,** faturar as
compras; **to bill the company for the
goods,** cobrar o preço das mercadorias à
companhia.

biller, *n. Am:* (*a*) (*person*) faturista *mf*; (*b*)
máquina f de faturar.

billing, *n.* faturamento *m*; **billing machine,**
máquina f de faturar.

billion, *n. UK: Port: Fr:* bilhão *m* ($= 10^{12}$)
(*N.Am. word:* **trillion**), *Braz: N.Am:*
bilhão ($= 10^9$).

binder, *n.* **1.** *Am: Ins:* (*a*) documento
escrito que compromete a seguradora até
a emissão da apólice; (*b*) recibo
compromissório. **2.** *Am:* (*in real estate*)
(*a*) sinal *m*; **the real-estate agent accepted
our binder on the house,** o corretor de
imóveis aceitou o nosso sinal pela casa;
(*b*) recibo compromissório.

binding, *a.* obrigatório; **binding agreement,**
acordo obrigatório para todas as partes;
**the court's decision is binding on all
parties,** a resolução do tribunal é
obrigatória para todas as partes; **to make**
it binding for s.o. to do sth., obrigar
alguém a fazer alguma coisa.

black¹, *n. Book-k: F:* **in the black,** com
saldo credor, sem dívidas.

black², *a.* **black market,** mercado negro,
mercado paralelo, mercado ilícito; **black
goods,** mercadorias vendidas a preços
ilegais (ou no mercado negro); *Ind:* **a
black factory,** uma fábrica boicotada
pelos sindicatos; *Book-k: etc:* **black cash,**
caixa preta.

black³, *v.tr.* (*of unions*) **to black a factory,**
boicotar, boicotear, uma fábrica.

blackleg, *n. Ind:* fura-greve *mf*.

blacklist¹, *n.* lista negra; **to be on a
blacklist,** estar numa lista negra.

blacklist², *v.tr.* colocar (alguém) na lista
negra.

blame, *n. Jur: Ins:* culpabilidade f.

blank, **1.** *a.* **blank cheque,** cheque *m* em
branco; **blank endorsement,** endosso *m* em
branco; **blank credit,** crédito *m* sem valor
limite; **blank form,** formulário *m* em
branco. **2.** *n.* (*a*) espaço *m* em branco; (*b*)
formulário *m* com espaços em branco
para preencher; **cheque in blank,** cheque
m em branco; **to draw (a bill of exchange)
in blank,** sacar uma letra de câmbio em
branco.

blanket, *a.* global, geral; **blanket increase,**
aumento *m* global; **blanket price,** preço *m*
global; **blanket mortgage,** hipoteca f
geral; *Ind:* **blanket insurance,** seguro *m*
geral (isto é, sem especificação detalhada
dos itens segurados); *Adm:* **blanket tax,**
imposto único.

blind, *a.* **blind purchase,** compra f de um
artigo sem tê-lo visto; *Book-k:* **blind
entry,** lançamento *m* sem explicações
adequadas.

block¹, *n.* **1.** (*on form, etc.*) **block letters,**
letra f de forma. **2. a block of shares,** um
lote de ações; **a block booking,** uma
reserva em bloco; *Book-k:* **block method,**
método *m* de blocos.

block², *v.tr. Fin:* congelar, bloquear, (uma
conta, etc.); **blocked exchange,** divisas
congeladas.

blotter, *n. Book-k:* borrador *m*.

blue chip, *n. St.Exch:* blue chip f; título *m*
de alta rentabilidade.

blue-collar, *a.* blue-collar worker, operário *m* (de fábrica, etc.).
blurb, *n.* (*a*) *Publ:* publicidade *f* de capa; (*b*) anúncio *m* de ponto de venda.
board, *n.* conselho *m*, junta *f*; advisory board, junta consultiva; marketing board, junta de comercialização, junta comercial; (*in company*) board of directors, conselho de administração, conselho administrativo, diretoria *f*; board meeting, reunião *f* do conselho de administração; board of trade, (i) *UK:* departamento *m* do Ministério do Comércio, (ii) junta do comércio; the Chicago Board of Trade, a bolsa de mercadorias de Chicago; price control board, comissão *f* de controle de preços.
boardroom, *n.* 1. sala *f* da diretoria, sala do conselho de administração; boardroom battle, conflito *m* entre os diretores de uma companhia. 2. *Am: St.Exch:* sala na bolsa de valores onde as cotações estão afixadas em quadro.
body, *n.* body of technicians, corpo *m* de técnicos; international body, organismo *m* internacional; government body, órgão *m* do governo; *Jur:* body corporate, pessoa jurídica.
bogus, *a.* bogus currency, moeda falsa; bogus company, companhia fictícia.
bond¹, *n.* 1. (*a*) acordo *m*, convênio *m*; (*b*) fiança *f*, caução *f*; to give (a) bond, prestar caução, fiança; under bond, sob caução; performance bond, caução, garantia *f*, de execução (de contrato, etc.); bid bond, fiança de licitação, garantia para licitar; fidelity bond, seguro *m* contra infidelidade (de empregado); *Jur:* mortgage bond, caução hipotecária; *Cust:* goods in bond, mercadorias retidas sob caução na alfândega (até o pagamento de direitos); goods out of bond, mercadorias liberadas do depósito da alfândega; to take out of bond, tirar da alfândega. 2. *Fin:* obrigação *f*, título *m*, apólice *f*; bearer bond, obrigação, título, ao portador; registered bond, obrigação nominativa, título nominativo; debenture bond, debênture *f*; government bond, título da dívida pública; Treasury bond, letra *f* do Tesouro, bônus *m*; local

authority negotiable bond, título negociável emitido por municipalidade; instalment bond, obrigação resgatável em parcelas; income bond, título de renda, obrigação de renda; bond dividend, dividendo distribuído sob a forma de obrigações ou debêntures (da propria companhia); bond register, registro *m* de obrigações ou debêntures.
bond², *v.tr.* 1. *Cust:* depositar sob caução na alfândega. 2. to bond a loan, afiançar, caucionar, um empréstimo; (*of government*) to bond a debt, consolidar uma dívida; *Am:* to bond a property, hipotecar um imóvel para garantir títulos; *Ind:* etc: to bond an employee, contratar um seguro contra a infidelidade de um empregado.
bonded, *a.* bonded goods, mercadorias retidas sob caução na alfândega; bonded warehouse, depósito *m* da alfândega (onde as mercadorias são depositadas sob caução), entreposto aduaneiro; *Fin:* bonded debt (of government), dívida consolidada, dívida fundada.
bondholder, *n.* possuidor *m* de um título; *Am:* debenturista *mf*, obrigacionista *mf*, (de uma empresa).
bonding, *n.* 1. depósito *m* de mercadorias sob caução na alfândega. 2. bonding company, empresa fiadora (que presta caução contra pagamento de uma taxa).
bondsman, *n. Jur:* fiador *m*.
bonus, *n.* gratificação *f*, bonificação *f*, prêmio *m*, salário-prêmio *m*, abono *m*; incentive bonus, prêmio de produção; *Fin:* bonus share, ação bonificada; bonus issue, bonus stock, bonificação de, em, ações; bonus stock, bonificação em ações.
book¹, *n.* 1. livro *m*; the book trade, o comércio livreiro; book publishing, edição *f* de livros. 2. (*a*) registro *m*, livro-registro *m*; *Book-k:* book value, valor *m* contábil, valor segundo os livros; to put sth. on the books, contabilizar, registrar, escriturar, algo nos livros (contábeis); account book, livro comercial, livro contábil, livro de contabilidade; cash book, diário-caixa *m*; invoice book, registro de faturas; order book, livro de encomendas, carteira *f* de encomendas; purchase book, bought book,

registro de compras; **sales book,** registro de vendas; **stock book,** livro de estoque, livro de inventário; (*b*) **cheque book,** talão *m* de cheques; **receipt book,** talão de recibos; *Bank:* **savings book,** caderneta *f* de poupança, caderneta de depósitos. **3.** *St.Exch:* **to protect a book,** cobrir uma posição.

book², *v.tr.* 1. (*a*) **to book a conference room,** reservar uma sala de conferências; **to book a delivery request,** registrar um pedido de entrega; (*b*) **a consignment of eggs was booked for Chicago,** uma partida de ovos foi expedida para Chicago; (*c*) *Ind:* **the factory is heavily booked,** a fábrica tem muitas encomendas. **2.** *Book-k: etc:* **to book a transaction,** contabilizar, registrar, escriturar, lançar, uma transação nos livros apropriados.

booking, *n.* reserva *f*; **booking office,** guichê *m*, escritório *m*, de reservas.

book-keeper, *n.* guarda-livros *mf*, contabilista *mf*.

book-keeping, *n.* escrituração *f* (contábil, mercantil); **single-entry book-keeping,** escrituração por partidas simples; **double-entry book-keeping,** escrituração por partidas dobradas.

booklet, *n.* folheto *m*, brochura *f*, livrete *m*.

bookseller, *n.* livreiro *m*; **second-hand bookseller,** sebista *mf*, alfarrabista *mf*.

bookselling, *n.* comércio livreiro, comércio biblíaco.

bookwork, *n.* escrituração *f*.

boom, *n.* boom *m*, surto *m*; rápido crescimento econômico.

boost¹, *n.* **a boost in prices,** um aumento de preços; **a boost in production,** um aumento na produção.

boost², *v.tr.* aumentar (preços, produção, etc.).

borrow, *v.tr.* tomar (dinheiro) emprestado (**from s.o.,** a alguém).

borrower, *n.* tomador *m* de empréstimo.

bottom, *n.* **bottom prices,** (os) preços mais baixos; **the bottom fell out of the market,** o mercado sofreu um colapso.

bought ledger, *n.* registro *m* de compras.

bounce, *v.i.* (*of cheque*) *F:* ser devolvido por insuficiência de fundos.

bounty, *n.* subvenção *f*, subsídio *m*; **export bounty,** subsídio para exportação.

bracket, *n.* faixa *f*; **age bracket,** faixa etária; **wage bracket,** faixa salarial.

branch, *n.* (*a*) **the branches of industry,** os ramos da indústria; (*b*) sucursal *f*, filial *f*, (de uma empresa, etc.), agência *f* (de um banco); **branch office,** sucursal, filial, agência; **branch manager,** gerente *mf* de filial, de sucursal.

brand, *n.* marca *f*; **a new brand of coffee,** uma nova marca de café; **own brand,** marca privativa, marca exclusiva, (de uma cadeia de lojas).

branded, *a.* **branded goods,** mercadorias marcadas.

breach, *n.* **breach of contract,** violação *f*, infração *f*, de disposições contratuais; **a breach of protocol,** uma quebra de protocolo.

break, *v.tr.* **to break a contract,** romper, quebrar, anular, um contrato.

breakage, *n.* (*a*) quebra *f* (de artigos frágeis, etc.); (*b*) indenização (paga) por quebras.

break down, *v.* **1.** *v.tr.* desdobrar, discriminar, individualizar, (uma conta); analisar, classificar, (cargos, etc.). **2.** *v.i.* (*of talks, etc.*) ser paralisado(s), ser interrompido(s).

breakdown, *n.* **1.** desdobramento *m*, discriminação *f*, (de uma conta, etc.); **a statistical breakdown of data,** uma análise estatística de dados. **2. a breakdown in negotiations,** uma paralisação de negociações.

break even, *v.i.* (*of business*) funcionar sem lucros nem prejuízos.

breakeven, *a.* **breakeven point,** ponto *m* de equilíbrio, ponto morto (de custos); **breakeven chart,** gráfico *m* do ponto de equilíbrio.

breakthrough, *n.* **a breakthrough in steel prices,** uma subida importante nos preços de aço.

break-up, *n.* **break-up value,** valor *m* de liquidação.

bridging, *a.* **bridging loan,** empréstimo *m* a

curto prazo (até o tomador receber determinados fundos).
bring down, *v.tr.* baixar, rebaixar, reduzir, (preços, etc.); *Book-k:* transportar (uma importância, um saldo); **balance brought down,** transporte *m.*
bring forward, *v.tr. Book-k:* transportar (um valor, uma importância).
bring in, *v.tr.* **to bring in interest,** render juros.
bringing forward, *n. Book-k:* transporte *m.*
bring out, *v.tr.* **to bring out a new model,** lançar um novo modelo (no mercado); (*of shares*) **to bring out a new issue,** lançar uma nova emissão (de ações).
brisk, *a.* **brisk trade,** comércio ativo; **brisk market,** mercado ativo, animado; **brisk demand,** procura ativa.
brochure, *n.* **advertising brochure,** brochura publicitária, folheto publicitário.
broker, *n.* corretor *m*; **bill broker,** corretor de letras, corretor de títulos; **customs broker,** despachante aduaneiro; **exchange broker,** corretor de câmbio; **insurance broker,** corretor de seguros; *Am:* **real estate broker,** corretor de imóveis, corretor imobiliário; *Bank:* **broker's loan,** empréstimo bancário garantido por títulos negociáveis.
brokerage, *n.* (*a*) (*profession*) corretagem *f*; (*b*) (*commission*) corretagem *f*; **brokerage charge,** taxa *f* de corretagem.
broking, *n.* corretagem *f.*
budget¹, *n.* (*a*) orçamento *m*; **budget period,** período orçamentário; **budget planning,** planejamento orçamentário; (*of government*) **to present the budget,** apresentar o orçamento-programa; (*b*) **budget prices,** preços reduzidos; (*in shops, etc.*) **budget account,** conta *f* (que facilita ao consumidor a compra de mercadorias até determinado valor).
budget², *v.tr. & i.* orçar, fazer orçamento.
budgetary, *a.* **budgetary control,** controle orçamentário; **budgetary policy,** política orçamentária.
budgeter, *n.* orçador *m*, orçamentista *mf.*
build, *v.tr.* construir (uma casa, uma

fábrica, etc.); **to build a characteristic into a product,** incorporar uma caraterística a um produto.
builder, *n.* (*small-scale*) pedreiro *m*; empreiteiro *m*, construtor *m*, mestre *m* de obras; **ship builder,** construtor de navios, engenheiro *m* naval.
building, *n.* construção *f*; **building contractor,** empreiteiro *m* de obras; **building lot,** terreno *m* de construção; *UK:* **building society,** sociedade cooperativa de hipotecas e empréstimos, sociedade de crédito imobiliário.
build up, *v.tr.* (*a*) **to build up a business,** desenvolver um negócio; (*b*) **to build up a product,** fazer a publicidade de um produto.
build-up, *n.* (*a*) publicidade *f*, propaganda *f*; (*b*) campanha publicitária.
bulk, *n.* **in bulk,** a granel, em grande quantidade; **bulk shipment,** (i) embarque *m* a granel, (ii) partida *f* a granel; **to buy in bulk,** comprar a granel.
bull¹, *n. St.Exch:* altista *mf*; especulador *m* que espera uma alta no mercado; **bull transaction,** operação *f* altista; **bull market,** mercado *m* altista.
bull², *v.* **1.** *v.tr. St.Exch:* **to bull the market,** (i) usar manobras altistas, (ii) jogar na alta, especular na alta. **2.** *v.i.* acusar, apresentar, um aumento de preço.
bulletin, *n.* boletim *m.*
bullion, *n.* ouro *m* (ou prata *f*) em lingote, em barra; **bullion market,** mercado *m* de ouro; **bullion reserve,** reserva *f* de ouro; **gold bullion standard,** padrão-ouro *m.*
bullish, *a. St.Exch:* **bullish tendency,** tendência *f* altista.
bumper, *a.* **bumber crop,** safra *f* abundante.
buoyancy, *n.* animação *f* (do mercado).
buoyant, *a.* **buoyant market,** mercado animado.
bureau, *n.* **employment bureau,** agência *f* de empregos.
business, *n.* (*a*) comércio *m*, negócios *mpl*; **to be in business,** negociar, fazer negócios, comerciar; **it's a good piece of business,** é um bom negócio; **to be in business for oneself,** trabalhar por conta própria; **to set up in business,** abrir um

negócio; **what's your line of business?**
qual é seu ramo de negócios? **to travel on
business,** viajar a negócios; **to talk
business,** falar sobre negócios; **to lose
business,** perder freguesia, perder
clientes; **business agent,** agente *mf*
comercial; **business card,** cartão *m*
de visita; **business correspondence,**
correspondência *f* comercial; **business
deal,** transação *f* comercial; **business
hours,** horário *m* comercial; **business
lunch,** almoço *m* de negócios; **business
reply card,** cartão *m* resposta comercial,
carta *f* resposta comercial; **business trip,**
viagem *f* de negócios; *Ins:* **business
interruption insurance,** seguro *m* de lucros
cessantes; *Book-k:* **business income,**
receita *f* normal de uma empresa; (*b*)
empresa *f*, casa *f* comercial, negócio *m*;
he's the owner of a small business, ele é
dono de uma pequena empresa; **to sell the
business,** vender o fundo de comércio; **his
business is in the city centre,** o seu
negócio, o seu estabelecimento, situa-se
no centro da cidade.

businessman, *n.* empresário *m*, homem
m de negócios, comerciante *m*.

businesswoman, *n.* mulher *f* de
negócios.

buy¹, *v.tr. & i.* comprar; **to buy sth. from a
friend,** comprar alguma coisa de um
amigo; **to buy for cash,** comprar à vista;
to buy on credit, comprar a crédito,
comprar fiado; **to buy on hire purchase,**
comprar pelo crediário; **to buy wholesale,**
comprar por atacado, atravessar
(gêneros); **to buy in bulk,** comprar a
granel.

buy², *n.* compra *f*; **a good buy,** uma boa
compra, uma pechincha.

buyable, *a.* comprável.

buy back, *v.tr.* recomprar (especialmente
por retrovenda).

buyer, *n.* comprador *m*; **buyer's market,**
mercado *m* de comprador.

buy in, *v.* 1. *v.tr. (at auction)* comprar
aquilo que o próprio comprador colocou
em leilão. 2. *v.i.* comprar as ações de uma
companhia.

buying, *n.* compra *f*; **buying power,** poder
aquisitivo, poder de compra; **buying back,**
recompra *f*; **buying out,** compra *f* da parte
de um sócio; **impulse buying,** compra
impulsiva, compra emocional; *Fin:*
forward buying, compra futura, compra a
termo para entrega futura.

buy out, *v.tr.* **to buy out a partner,** comprar
a parte de um sócio; **to buy out a business,**
comprar o fundo de comércio; **to buy out
the minority shareholders,** comprar as
ações dos acionistas minoritários.

buy up, *v.tr.* (*a*) comprar em grande
quantidade; (*b*) açambarcar (cereais,
gêneros, etc.).

by-product, *n. Ind:* produto derivado.

C

cabinet, *n.* **filing cabinet**, fichário *m*, arquivo *m*.

cable[1], *n.* cabograma *m*; **cable address**, endereço telegráfico; **cable code**, código telegráfico; **cable confirmation**, confirmação telegráfica.

cable[2], *v.tr.* **to cable a message to s.o.**, enviar uma mensagem a alguém por cabograma; **to cable money to s.o.**, remeter dinheiro a alguém por ordem (de transferência) telegráfica.

cablegram, *n.* cabograma *m*.

café, *n.* café *m*, botequim *m*; **transport café**, restaurante *m* para motorista de caminhão.

cafeteria, *n.* restaurante *m* com auto-serviço.

calculate, *v.tr.* calcular, computar, (juros, etc.); **calculated risk**, risco calculado.

calculating, *n.* **calculating machine**, máquina *f* de calcular, somadora *f*, calculadora *f*; **calculating methods**, métodos *mpl* de cálculo.

calculation, *n.* cálculo *m*, computo *m*; **to make a calculation of the number of customers**, calcular o número de fregueses; **rough calculation**, cálculo aproximado.

calculator, *n.* máquina *f* de calcular, calculadora *f*, somadora *f*; **pocket calculator**, calculadora de bolso; **electronic calculator**, calculadora eletrônica, somadora eletrônica; **print-out calculator**, máquina de calcular com impressora.

calendar, *n.* calendário *m*; **calendar clock**, relógio-calendário *m*; **calendar year**, ano *m* civil.

call[1], *n.* 1. **a call on coal supplies**, uma procura de carvão, uma demanda para o carvão. 2. *Fin:* chamada *f* (de capital); **to meet calls**, atender às chamadas; **payable**

at call, pagável sob chamada, por chamadas; **withdrawal at call**, retirada *f* sem aviso prévio; **call letter**, (i) aviso *m* de chamada, (ii) aviso de resgate (de título, dívida, etc.); **call loan**, empréstimo *m* sob chamada, empréstimo à vista; empréstimo resgatável mediante solicitação por qualquer das partes; **call money**, dinheiro *m* reembolsável sem aviso prévio; **call note**, promissória *f* sem prazo fixo; **call premium**, prêmio pago pelo resgate de uma obrigação antes do vencimento. 3. *St.Exch:* **call option**, opção *f* de compra; **call price**, preço *m* segundo a cotação do dia (na bolsa de valores); **call system**, pregão *m* por chamada. 4. **(telephone) call**, telefonema *m*, chamada (telefônica); **call box**, cabina *f*, cabine *f*, telefônica, de telefone; **trunk, long distance, call** (telefonema) interurbano *m*; **international call**, telefonema internacional; **local call**, telefonema urbano; *U K:* **transferred charge call**, *N.Am:* **collect call**, telefonema a cobrar, chamada a cobrar; **to take, receive, a call**, receber um telefonema. 5. visita *f* (de técnico, vendedor, etc.).

call[2], *v.tr. & i.* 1. **to call s.o. on the phone**, telefonar, ligar, tocar, para alguém. 2. (*a*) **to call on s.o.**, visitar alguém; (*b*) **call on a bank, etc.**, recorrer a um banco, etc. 3. **to call a meeting of the shareholders**, convocar uma assembléia dos acionistas; *Fin:* **to call a bond**, dar aviso de resgate de um título; **to call a loan**, exigir o reembolso de um empréstimo. 4. **to call a strike**, decretar (uma) greve. 5. (*of ship*) **to call at a port**, fazer escala em um porto.

callable, *a.* exigível; resgatável à opção; **callable bond**, título *m* resgatável a

23

critério do emitente; **callable issues,** emissões *fpl* de títulos resgatáveis.
called-up, *a.* **called-up capital,** capital chamado.
call for, *v.tr.* exigir, reivindicar; **to call for a wage increase,** reivindicar um aumento de salário.
call in, *v.tr.* (*a*) retirar (moeda) de circulação; (*b*) **to call in a loan,** exigir o reembolso de um empréstimo.
call-in, *n. Am:* **call-in pay,** pagamento *m* de horas extraordinárias.
calling in, *n.* retirada *f* (de moeda) de circulação.
call off, *v.tr.* **to call off a deal,** cancelar, desistir de, uma transação; **to call off a strike,** encerrar uma greve.
campaign, *n.* campanha *f*; **sales campaign,** campanha de vendas; **advertising campaign,** campanha publicitária, campanha de propaganda; **press campaign,** campanha de imprensa.
can¹, *n.* lata *f*.
can², *v.tr.* enlatar (gêneros alimentícios, etc.).
cancel, *v.tr.* to cancel a cheque, cancelar um cheque; **to cancel an order,** cancelar uma encomenda; **to cancel a debt,** anular uma dívida; **to cancel a contract,** anular, rescindir, invalidar, um contrato; *Post:* **to cancel a stamp,** contra-selar um selo; *Book-k:* **the two entries cancel each other,** os dois lançamentos se anulam.
cancellation, *n.* cancelamento *m* (de encomenda, viagem, etc.); anulação *f*, invalidação *f*, rescisão *f*, (de um contrato); *Post:* (*mark*) contra-selo *m*, (*process*) inutilização *f* (de selos).
cancelled, *a.* cancelado; (*of contract, etc.*) anulado, invalidado; *Post:* contra-selado; *Bank:* **cancelled cheque,** cheque pago pelo banco sacado.
canned, *a.* **canned goods,** (produtos) enlatados; **canned foods,** lataria *f*, conservas *fpl*; gêneros alimentícios enlatados, alimentos enlatados.
canner, *n.* (*a*) enlatador *m*; (*b*) (*manufacturer*) fabricante *m* de conservas (enlatadas).
cannery, *n.* fábrica *f* de conservas (enlatadas).

canning, *n.* enlatamento *m*; **canning industry,** indústria *f* de enlatados, indústria de conservas; **canning factory,** fábrica *f* de conservas (enlatadas).
canvass¹, *n.* angariação *f*, solicitação *f*; **door-to-door canvass,** solicitação, angariação, de porta em porta.
canvass², *v.tr.* solicitar, angariar, (encomendas, fregueses).
canvasser, *n.* (*a*) (*general*) angariador *m*; (*b*) caixeiro-viajante *m*.
canvassing, *n.* angariação *f*, solicitação *f*; **door-to-door canvassing,** angariação, solicitação, de porta em porta.
capacity, *n.* **1.** capacidade *f*; **manufacturing, production, producing, capacity,** capacidade produtiva; **yield capacity,** produtividade *f*; **capacity cost,** custo *m* em razão da capacidade produtiva total; **capacity limit,** limite *m* de capacidade; **to work at full capacity,** trabalhar com máximo rendimento; **idle capacity,** capacidade ociosa, capacidade não utilizada; *Fin:* **profit-earning capacity,** capacidade rentável, rentabilidade *f*; *Cmptr:* **storage capacity,** capacidade *f* de armazenamento, capacidade de memória; *Ind: etc:* **capacity load,** carga máxima; *Jur:* capacidade. **2.** (*talent, ability*) **a capacity for business, business capacity,** uma aptidão para os negócios, uma habilidade nos negócios. **3. to act in the capacity of,** agir na qualidade de, na condição de, (representante, delegado, etc.); **to act in one's official capacity,** agir no exercício das suas funções.
capital, *n.* capital *m*, capitais *mpl*, patrimônio *m*, fundos *mpl*; **authorized capital,** capital autorizado; **circulating capital,** capital circulante; **fixed capital,** capital fixo; **floating capital,** capital flutuante; **invested capital,** capital investido, capital aplicado; **(net) capital employed,** patrimônio (líquido) empregado; **nominal capital,** capital nominal; **outside capital,** capital de terceiros; **own capital,** capital próprio; **paid-up, paid-in, contributed, capital,** capital integralizado, capital realizado; **risk capital,** capital de risco; **share capital**

capital-ações *m*, capital social; **subscribed capital,** capital subscrito; **working capital** capital de giro, capital de exploração, capital circulante; **capital allocation,** alocação *f* de capital; **capital allowance,** desconto *m* para depreciação; **capital appreciation,** valorização *f* de capital; **capital assets,** bens imobilizados, bens permanentes, ativo fixo; **capital bonus,** dividendo pago em ações; **capital budget,** orçamento *m* de capital, orçamento de bens imobilizados; **capital cost,** custo *m* de capital; **capital equipment,** imobilizado técnico, bens de capital; **capital expenditure,** despesas *fpl* de capital, dispêndio *m* de capital; **capital-exporting country,** país exportador de capital; **capital flight,** fuga *f* de capital; **capital flow,** fluxo *m*, movimento *m*, de capital; **capital formation,** formação *f* de capital; **capital gains (tax),** (imposto *m* sobre) ganhos *mpl* de capital, incrementos *mpl* de capital; **capital goods,** bens de capital; **capital imports,** entradas *fpl* de capital; **capital increase,** aumento *m* de capital; **capital intensity,** intensidade *f* de capital; **capital-intensive industries,** indústrias *fpl* em que o custo de capital predomina no custo total; **capital investment,** imobilização *f*, imobilizado *m*; investimento *m*, aplicação *f*, em bens de capital; **capital issue,** emissão *f* de ações; **capital-labour ratio,** relação *f* capital/trabalho; **capital liability,** passivo *m* exigível a longo prazo, passivo inexigível; **capital market,** mercado *m* de capitais, mercado financeiro; **capital mix,** densidade *f* de capital; **capital movements,** movimentos *mpl* de capital; **capital need,** necessidade *f* de capital; **capital outlay,** despesas *fpl* de capital, dispêndio *m* capitalizável, inversões *fpl* em bens de capital; **capital-output ratio,** relação *f* capital/produção; **capital project,** projeto *m* de investimento; **capital receipt,** receita *f* de capital; **capital reserves,** reservas *fpl* patrimoniais, reservas não exigíveis, reservas inexigíveis; **capital spending,** despesas *fpl* de capital, dispêndio *m* de capital; **capital stock,** capital-ações *m*,

capital social; **capital structure,** estrutura *f* financeira, estrutura patrimonial; **capital sum,** capital (original de um espólio, etc.); **capital surplus,** superávit contribuído pelos acionistas; **capital transactions,** transações *fpl* de capital; **capital transfer (tax),** (imposto *m* sobre) transferências *f* de capital; **capital turnover,** movimento *m* de capital; **capital value,** valor *m* do capital.

capitalism, *n.* capitalismo *m*.

capitalist, *n. & a.* capitalista (*mf*).

capitalizable, *a.* capitalizável.

capitalization, *n.* capitalização *f*; **capitalization issue,** bonificação *f* em ações; **capitalization unit,** unidade *f* capitalizável.

capitalize, *v.tr.* capitalizar; **to capitalize the interest on deposits,** capitalizar os juros de depósitos; **capitalized expense,** despesa levada a uma conta de ativo imobilizado; **capitalized surplus,** lucros não distribuídos, que estão incorporados ao capital; **capitalized value,** valor capitalizado.

capitation, *n.* **capitation tax,** imposto *m* de capitação, imposto per capita.

capture, *v.tr.* (*a*) **to capture the market,** conquistar o mercado; (*b*) **to capture investment,** captar investimentos.

car, *n.* carro *m*, automóvel *m*; **car factory,** fábrica *f* de automóveis; **car industry,** indústria automobilística; **car manufacturer,** fabricante *m* de automóveis; **car worker,** operário *m* da indústria automobilística; **car rental,** aluguel *m* de automóveis, locação *f* de automóveis; **car rental firm,** locadora *f* de automóveis; **rental car,** carro *m* de aluguel; **company car,** automóvel *m* de companhia; *Book-k: etc:* **car allowance,** ajuda *f* para despesas com o automóvel (paga a executivos, gerentes, representantes, etc.).

carbon, *n.* **carbon paper,** papel *m* carbono.

card, *n.* (*a*) cartão *m*; **business card,** cartão de visita; **business reply card,** cartão resposta comercial; **(bank) cheque card,** cartão de garantia de cheques; **sample, show, card,** mostruário *m*; **index card,** ficha *f*; **card index,** fichário *m*; (*b*) **punch**

card, cartão perfurado; **card punch,** perfuradora *f* de cartões; **card reader,** leitora *f* de cartões; **card counter,** máquina contadora de cartões perfurados; **card system,** sistema *m* de cartão; (*c*) *F:* **to get one's cards,** ser demitido, ser despedido, *F:* ser botado na rua.

cardboard, *n.* papelão *m*; **fine cardboard,** cartolina *f*; **corrugated cardboard,** papelão ondulado; **cardboard box,** caixa *f* de papelão.

card-index, *v.tr.* fichar (informações, etc.), registrar (informações, etc.) em fichas; catalogar.

card-indexing, *n.* fichamento *m*, catalogação *f*.

care, *n. Corr:* **care of (c/o) Mr X,** aos cuidados de Sr. X; (*on packing case, etc.*) **'handle with care',** 'tratar com cuidado'.

careless, *a.* negligente.

cargo, *n.* carga *f*; **air cargo,** frete aéreo; **deck cargo,** carga de convés; **full cargo,** carga plena; **mixed cargo,** carga mista; **cargo boat, ship,** (navio) cargueiro *m*; **cargo book,** livro *m* de registro de carga; **cargo handling,** manuseio *m* de carga, movimentação *f* de carga; **cargo homeward,** carga de volta; **cargo insurance,** seguro *m* de cargas; **cargo outward,** carga de saída; **cargo plane,** avião *m* de carga; **cargo waiver,** liberação *f* de carga; (*of ship*) **to take in cargo,** receber carga.

carriage, *n.* transporte *m*; **carriage free,** franco de porte; **carriage paid,** frete pago, porte pago; **carriage forward,** frete a pagar, porte a pagar; **carriage expenses,** despesas *fpl* de transporte; **terms, conditions, of carriage,** condições *fpl* de transporte; **contract of carriage,** contrato *m* de transporte.

carrier, *n.* transportador *m*, empresa *f* de transportes, transportadora *f*; **common carrier,** transportador comum, transportador público; **carrier's liability,** responsabilidade *f* do transportador; **carrier's waybill,** guia *f* de carga.

carry, *v.tr.* **1.** transportar, carregar, levar (mercadorias). **2.** (*in meeting etc.*) (fazer) aprovar (uma proposta); **the bill** **was carried by an absolute majority,** o projeto de lei foi aprovado por uma maioria absoluta. **3.** *Fin:* **to carry interest,** render, vencer, juros. **4.** (*of shop*) negociar com, vender, (mercadorias). **5.** (*of newspaper*) publicar (anúncio, etc.). **6.** *St.Exch:* (*of broker*) **to carry a client,** conceder crédito a um cliente.

carry back, *v.tr.* compensar um prejuízo com lucros de exercícios passados.

carry-back, *n.* sistema retroativo de crédito em favor de contribuinte de imposto de renda (pelo qual um prejuízo é passível de compensação com lucros de exercícios passados).

carry forward, *v.tr. Book-k:* transportar; (**amount) carried forward,** transporte *m*; **to be carried forward,** a transportar; **amount carried forward,** soma transportada.

carry out, *v.tr.* **to carry out the terms of a contract,** cumprir com as condições de um contrato; **to carry out plans,** executar planos.

carry over, *v.tr.* **to carry over a balance,** apresentar um saldo, *Book-k:* transportar um saldo.

carry-over, *n. Book-k:* transporte *m*.

cartel, *n.* cartel *m*.

carton, *n.* caixa *f* de papelão.

case, *n.* **1.** (*packing*) caixote *m*, caixa *f*. **2.** *Jur:* causa *f*.

cash¹, *n.* dinheiro (vivo), dinheiro em espécie, numerário *m*, moeda *f* sonante, caixa *f*, dinheiro em caixa, (*specific amount*) encaixe *m*; *Book-k:* ativo *m* disponível; (*on balance sheet*) **cash and banks,** caixa e bancos; **cash account,** conta *f* de caixa; **cash advance,** adiantamento *m* em dinheiro; **cash against documents,** pagamento *m* contra apresentação de documentos; **cash assets,** disponibilidades *fpl*, bens *mpl* de liquidez imediata; **cash audit,** exame *m* das operações de caixa; **cash balance,** saldo *m* em caixa, saldo de caixa; (**on a) cash basis,** à vista, em dinheiro; **cash basis accounting,** contabilidade *f* de caixa; **cash before delivery,** entrega *f* com pagamento antecipado; **cash benefits,** vantagens *fpl* em dinheiro, vantagens monetárias;

cash bonus, bonificação monetária, gratificação *f* em dinheiro; cash book, livro-caixa *m*, livro *m* de caixa; cash box, cofre *m*, caixa *f* para transporte de dinheiro; cash budget, orçamento financeiro; cash crop, cultivo *m* comercial; cash customer, freguês *m* que compra à vista; cash deal, transação *f* à vista, negócio *m* a dinheiro; cash deficit, déficit *m* de caixa; cash discount, desconto *m* à vista, desconto por pagamento à vista; cash dispenser, caixa automática; cash dividend, dividendo *m* em dinheiro; cash down, pagamento *m* à vista; cash flow, fluxo *m* de caixa, fluxo de liquidez; cash fund, fundo *m* de caixa; cash holdings, haveres *mpl* em dinheiro, efetivo *m* em caixa, saldo *m* de tesouraria; cash in register, dinheiro *m* na caixa registradora; cash in vault, dinheiro *m* na caixa-forte; cash items, comprovantes *mpl* a reembolsar; cash journal, diário *m* de caixa, livro *m* de caixa, livro-caixa *m*; cash loan, empréstimo *m* em dinheiro; *UK:* cash on delivery (COD), pagamento *m* contra entrega; cash on hand, dinheiro *m* em caixa, encaixe *m*; *F:* cash on the nail, pagamento *m* no ato; cash order, pedido acompanhado de pagamento; cash payment, (i) pagamento *m* em dinheiro (vivo), pagamento em moeda corrente, (ii) pagamento à vista (e não em prestações); cash position, situação *f* de caixa, disponibilidade monetária; cash price, preço *m* à vista; cash purchase, compra *f* à vista; cash ratio of a bank, relação *f* entre operações e reserva de um banco; cash receipts, receita *f* em dinheiro; cash records, livros *mpl* e registros de caixa; cash reserve, encaixe *m*; cash resources, recursos monetários; cash sale, venda *f* à vista; cash shares, ações subscritas em dinheiro; cash shorts and over, diferenças *fpl* de caixa, déficits ou excedentes *mpl* de caixa; cash statement, relatório *m* de caixa, relatório de disponibilidades (de caixa); cash store, loja *f* que não vende a crédito; cash voucher, comprovante *m* de caixa; cash yield, dividendo por ação, dividido pelo

preço da ação; *St.Exch:* cash contract, operação *f* à vista; *Ins:* cash (surrender) value, valor *m* de resgate (de uma apólice); to sell for cash, vender à vista; ready cash, dinheiro vivo; spot cash, dinheiro de contado; petty cash, caixa pequena; cash desk, caixa *f*; please pay at the cash desk, favor pagar na caixa; cash register, caixa registradora.
cash², *v.tr.* to cash a cheque, descontar um cheque; to cash a postal order, descontar um vale postal.
cashable, *a.* (*of cheque*) descontável; (*of bond, bill, etc.*) pagável à vista.
cash-and-carry, *n. & a.* (de) sistema *m* de compra (geralmente por atacado) com pagamento à vista e sem entrega a domicílio.
cashier, *n.* caixa *mf*, encarregado *m* de caixa; cashier's desk, office, caixa *f*.
cash in, *v.tr.* entregar (títulos, apólice, etc.) para resgate; to cash in a cheque, descontar um cheque.
cash up, *v.i.* fazer a caixa.
casting, *a.* casting vote, voto *m* de qualidade, voto de Minerva; to give the casting vote, dar o voto de qualidade.
casual, *a.* ocasional, eventual, casual; casual labour, mão-de-obra *f* ocasional; casual worker, trabalhador temporário; casual work, trabalho *m* eventual, *F:* bico *m*, biscate *m*; to live from casual work, *F:* viver de bicos, de biscates.
catalogue¹, *Am:* catalog, *n.* catálogo *m*; trade catalogue, catálogo comercial, catálogo para revendedores; mail order catalogue, catálogo para vendas pelo correio.
catalogue², *Am:* catalog, *v.tr.* catalogar.
cater, *v.i.* to cater for, fornecer serviço de alimentação (para escolas, fábricas, etc.); to cater for the consumer's needs, atender às necessidades do consumidor.
catering, *n.* (*a*) catering industry, setor *m* de restaurantes e estabelecimentos afins; (*b*) (*in factories, schools, etc.*) alimentação *f*; catering department, departamento *m* de alimentação; catering manager, chefe *mf* de alimentação; catering staff, equipe *f*, pessoal *m*, de alimentação.

cattle, n. gado m; cattle breeding, criação f de gado; cattle breeder, criador m de gado; cattle dealer, marchante m, negociante m de gado; cattle farm, fazenda f de gado; cattle hides, couros bovinos; cattle industry, (indústria) pecuária f; cattle market, feira f de gado; cattle show, exposição f de gado.

caveat, n. Jur: 1. advertência f; caveat against unfair (trading) practices, advertência contra práticas (comerciais) desleais. 2. embargo m de terceiro.

cede, v.tr. to cede rights, ceder direitos (to, a).

ceiling, n. teto m, limite m; output has reached its ceiling, a produção atingiu seu nível máximo; ceiling price, (preço-)teto m, preço máximo; ceiling value, (valor-) teto m; to fix a ceiling to a budget, fixar um teto para um orçamento.

census, n. censo m, recenseamento m; census data, dados mpl de recenseamento; census enumeration, coleta censitária; census enumerator, agente recenseador; census of housing, censo m de habitação; to take a census, fazer um recenseamento.

cent, n. N.Am: cêntimo m.

centavo, n. Braz: Port: centavo m.

central, a. central bank, banco m central; central planning agency, órgão m de planificação central.

centre, Am: center, n. centro m; business centre, centro comercial; industrial centre, centro industrial, eixo m industrial; tourist centre, centro de turismo; conference centre, centro de convenções; shopping centre, shopping center m, centro comercial; Book-k: cost centre, centro de custo, centro de cargas.

cereal, a. & n. cereal (m); cereal crops, cerais mpl.

certificate, n. certificado m, certidão f, atestado m; birth certificate, certidão de nascimento; medical certificate, atestado médico; share certificate, certificado de ação, cautela f; certificate of origin, certificado de origem; certificate of indebtedness, certificado de endividamento. Post: certificate of posting, recibo m de postagem; Fin:

Bank: certificate of deposit, certificado de depósito; Jur: certificate of incorporation, certificado m de constituição de uma companhia; Ins: certificate of damage, certificado de avaria; to issue a certificate, emitir, passar, um certificado, uma certidão; the holder of a certificate, o titular de um certificado, uma certidão.

certificated, a. (a) diplomado; (b) Jur: certificated bankrupt, falido reabilitado.

certify, v.tr. certificar, atestar; to certify a signature, reconhecer uma assinatura; certified (as a) true copy, cópia autenticada, Jur: pública-forma f; to certify a statement, autenticar uma declaração; Bank: to certify a cheque, visar um cheque; certified cheque, cheque visado; N.Am: Post: to certify a letter, registrar uma carta; certified letter, carta registrada; certified officer, funcionário m que emite parecer, atestado, etc.

cession, n. Jur: cessão f.

cessionary, n. Jur: cessionário m.

chain, n. cadeia f (de lojas, supermercados, etc.); chain-store, loja f que faz parte de uma cadeia; chain discount, desconto m em cadeia; Am: chain banking, cadeia bancária.

chair¹, n. presidência f (a assembléia, etc.); to take the chair at a meeting, presidir a uma reunião; to be voted into the chair, ser eleito presidente (para uma reunião, etc.); to speak from the chair, falar na qualidade de presidente (de uma reunião); to vacate the chair, vagar a presidência; to address the chair, dirigir-se ao presidente (de uma assembléia, etc.).

chair², v.tr. to chair a meeting, presidir a uma reunião.

chairman, n. presidente m(f); to act, serve, as chairman, exercer as funções de presidente; a committee with Mr X as chairman, um comitê sob a presidência do Sr. X; chairman of the board of directors, presidente do conselho de administração; chairman's report, relatório m do presidente (do conselho de administração).

chairmanship, *n.* under the chairmanship of Mr X, sob a presidência do Sr. X.
chairperson, *n.* presidente *mf.*
chairwoman, *n.* presidente *f*, presidenta *f.*
chamber, *n.* chamber of commerce, câmara *f* de comércio.
chance, *n.* oportunidade *f*; chance of making a profit, oportunidade de lucro.
chancellor, *n. U.K:* the Chancellor of the Exchequer = o Ministro da Fazenda.
chancery, *n.* chancelaria *f.*
change¹, *n.* 1. troco *m*; I've only got small change, só tenho dinheiro miúdo, trocado; to give change for $5, trocar uma nota de $5; to keep the change, ficar com o troco. 2. modificação *f*, mundança *f*, alteração *f*; change in demand, modificação da procura; change in price level, modificação no nível de preços; changes in stocks, variações *fpl* de estoques.
change², *v.* 1. *v.tr.* trocar; to change a faulty article, trocar um artigo defeituoso; to change a $5 bill, trocar uma nota de $5. 2. *v.i.* mudar; changing consumer tastes, mudanças *fpl* nas preferências dos consumidores; changing value of money, valor *m* variável da moeda.
changer, *n.* money-changer, cambista *mf.*
channel, *n.* canal *m*; channels of distribution, canais de distribuição; channel of trade, canal de comercialização; to go through the official channels, seguir os trâmites oficiais.
characteristic, 1. *a.* característico. 2. *n.* característica *f*; characteristics desired by purchasers, características desejadas pelos compradores.
charge¹, *n.* 1. taxa *f*, preço *m*, despesa *f*, encargo *m*; admission charge, entry charge, (preço de) entrada *f*; there is no charge (for admission), a entrada é gratuita; no charge is made for delivery, entrega grátis, entrega gratuita, não cobramos pela entrega; free of charge, gratuito; charges forward, despesas a pagar; advertising charges, despesas *fpl* com publicidade, despesas publicitárias; bank charge, taxa cobrada por banco; capital charge, serviço *m*, despesas

financeiras; customs charges, taxas alfandegárias; freight charge, frete *m*; interest charges, juros *mpl*, despesas com o pagamento de juros; postal charges, tarifas *fpl* postais; telephone charges, tarifa telefônica; *Book-k:* deferred charge, despesa diferida; *Book-k:* depreciation charge, taxa de depreciação; list, scale, of charges, tarifa *f* (de preços, etc.); *N.Am:* charge account, (i) conta *f* de crédito (com loja), (ii) *Book-k:* conta a receber. 2. *Jur:* gravame *m*, ônus *m*; to put a charge on a property, gravar um bem, impor um gravame a um bem; mortgage charge, hipoteca *f*; to register a mortgage charge on a house, inscrever uma hipoteca sobre uma casa. 3. to be in charge of the advertising, estar encarregado da propaganda, ser responsável pela propaganda.
charge², *v.tr.* 1. (*a*) cobrar; how much do you charge? quanto você cobra? we're charging two dollars a metre, cobramos dois dólares o metro; this shop charges too much for repairs, esta loja está cobrando caro demais pelos consertos; the plumber's charging twenty dollars an hour for overtime, o encanador está cobrando vinte dólares por cada hora extra; the bank charges a commission on all exchange transactions, o banco cobra uma comissão sobre todas as operações de câmbio; (*b*) debitar, imputar, lançar na conta (de alguém); to charge an expense to the customer's account, debitar uma despesa à conta do cliente; lançar uma depesa na conta do cliente; charge the meal to my bill, debite o preço da refeição na minha conta; this sum should be charged to the reserve, esta importância deve ser imputada à reserva. 2. *Jur:* gravar (um bem); to charge a property with a mortgage, hipotecar um imóvel, sujeitar um imóvel a uma hipoteca; property charged as security for debt, bem imóvel gravado em garantia de uma dívida. 3. to charge s.o. with a responsibility, incumbir alguém de uma responsabilidade.
chargeable, *a.* cobrável, a cargo (de alguém), debitável; **transactions**

chargeable to, against, a client, operações *fpl* por conta do cliente, operações a ser(em) debitadas na conta do cliente; **sums chargeable to the reserve,** importâncias *fpl* imputáveis à reserva.
chargee, *n. Jur:* credor privilegiado.
chargehand, *n. Am: Ind:* chefe *m* de turma, de equipe.
chart, *n.* gráfico *m*, quadro *m*; **bar chart,** gráfico de barras; **organization chart,** organograma *m*; **flow chart,** fluxograma *m*, diagrama *m* de fluxo; **chart of accounts,** plano *m* de contas, quadro das contas (de uma empresa).
charter¹, *n.* **1.** estatutos *mpl* (de uma sociedade); **charter member,** sócio-fundador *m*. **2.** (*a*) *Nau: Av:* afretamento *m*, fretamento *m*, fretagem *f*; **charter plane,** avião fretado; **charter flight,** vôo fretado, vôo charter; **charter company,** companhia *f* de fretamento; (*b*) *Nau:* **charter-party,** carta-partida *f*; (*c*) carta *f* patente.
charter², *v.tr.* **1.** fretar, afretar, (navio); **to charter a coach for an excursion,** fretar um ônibus para uma excursão. **2.** licenciar (alguém), conceder licença ou carta patente (a alguém).
chartered, *a.* **1.** **chartered accountant,** perito-contador *m*. **2.** **chartered ship,** navio afretado; **chartered aircraft, plane,** avião fretado.
charterer, *n. Nau:* afretador *m*.
chartering, *n.* afretamento *m* (de navios), fretamento (de aviões, ônibus); **chartering agent,** agente *m* de afretamento.
chattel, *n. pl.* **chattels,** bens *mpl* móveis; *Am:* **chattel mortgage,** penhor *m* de bens móveis.
cheap, *a.* (*a*) barato; **an exceptionally cheap article,** um artigo muito barato, baratíssimo; **cheap rate,** tarifa reduzida; **they are 50% cheaper,** custam 50% mais barato; **it works out cheaper to buy wholesale,** sai mais barato comprar por atacado; *F:* **these books are dead, dirt, cheap,** estes livros custam muito barato, *F:* são vendidos a preço de banana; **to buy sth. on the cheap,** comprar algo muito barato, por um preço muito baixo; **cheap**

labour, mão-de-obra de baixo custo, mão-de-obra barata; (*b*) *Fin:* **cheap money,** dinheiro barato.
cheapen, *v.tr.* baratear; **cheapened currency,** moeda desvalorizada.
cheaply, *adv.* barato, por um preço baixo, por um custo baixo.
cheapness, *n.* barateza *f*.
check¹, *n.* **1.** (*restraint*) restrição *f*; **to put a check on production,** restringir a produção. **2.** controle *m*, verificação *f*, conferência *f*; **check list,** lista *f* de conferência; **check figure,** número *m* de controle, de conferência; **check till,** caixa registradora. **3.** *N.Am:* **luggage, baggage, check,** talão *m* de bagagem. **4.** *Am:* = **cheque.**
check², *v.tr.* **1.** restringir (a produção, a subida dos preços). **2.** verificar, controlar, conferir, checar; **to check the sales records,** verificar, controlar, os registros das vendas; **the auditors check all the books,** os auditores examinam todos os livros; **the goods are checked on delivery,** as mercadorias são checadas, verificadas, na entrega. **3.** *N.Am:* registrar (bagagem).
check in¹, *v.* **1.** *v.i.* (*in hotel, airport, etc.*) registrar-se. **2.** *v.tr.* **to check in one's baggage,** (i) registrar a bagagem, (ii) entregar a bagagem no depósito de bagagens.
check-in², *n.* check-in *m*, registro *m*, (de passageiros, bagagem); **check-in counter,** balcão *m* de registro, balcão de check-in.
checking, *n.* **1.** controle *m*, verificação *f*, conferência *f*. **2.** *N.Am:* **checking account,** conta *f* corrente; **checking deposit,** depósito *m* à vista.
check-off, *n. Am:* dedução *f* do salario.
check out, *v.i.* **1.** sair; pagar a conta e deixar (um hotel). **2.** *Ind:* marcar o ponto de saída.
checkout, *n.* (*a*) (*in supermarket*) caixa *f* (à saída de supermercado); (*b*) (*in hotel*) saída *f*; **checkout time,** hora *f* de vencimento da diária de hotel.
checkroom, *n. N.Am:* depósito *m* de bagagens.
cheque, *n.* cheque *m*; **a cheque for twenty dollars,** um cheque no valor de vinte

dólares, um cheque de vinte dólares; **bank cheque,** cheque bancário; **bearer cheque,** cheque ao portador; **blank cheque,** cheque em branco; **counter cheque,** cheque avulso; **crossed cheque,** cheque cruzado; **marked cheque, limited cheque,** cheque marcado, cheque certificado; **open, uncrossed, cheque,** cheque aberto, cheque não cruzado; **pay cheque,** cheque salário; **personalized cheque,** cheque personalizado; **post-dated cheque,** cheque pré-datado; **traveller's cheque,** traveller's cheque *m,* cheque de viajem; *Am:* **certified cheque,** cheque visado; **cheque to order,** cheque nominal; **cheque without cover, worthless cheque,** *F:* **dud cheque,** cheque sem fundos, cheque sem cobertura; *F:* cheque frio; **cheque book,** talão *m* de cheques; **cheque card,** cartão *m* (de garantia) de cheques; **cheque paper,** papel *m* para a impressão de cheques e outros títulos; **cheque stub, counterfoil,** canhoto *m,* talão *m*; **to cash a cheque,** descontar um cheque; **to draw a cheque on the Bank of Brazil,** emitir um cheque contra, sacar um cheque sobre, o Banco do Brasil; **to make out a cheque to s.o.,** emitir um cheque em favor de alguém; **to pay by cheque,** pagar com cheque, pagar em cheque; **to pay in a cheque,** depositar um cheque (na própria conta ou na conta de outrem); **to refer a cheque to drawer,** recusar o pagamento de um cheque sem fundos; **to stop a cheque,** suspender o pagamento de um cheque; **to write a cheque,** escrever, fazer, passar, emitir, um cheque; **bearer, holder, of a cheque,** portador *m,* tomador *m,* de um cheque; **drawer of a cheque,** emitente *mf,* sacador *m,* de um cheque; **payee of a cheque,** beneficiário *m* de um cheque.

chief, *n.* chefe *mf*; **chief accountant,** contador *m* geral, contador chefe; **chief executive,** diretor *m* geral; **chief clerk,** chefe de escritório.

chilled, *a.* **chilled meat,** carne frigorificada.

chip, *n. Cmptr: F:* condutor *m* em circuito impresso.

chit, *n.* nota *f,* guia *f,* (de entrega, etc.).

circular, 1. *a.* **circular letter,** carta *f* circular; **circular note, circular letter of credit,** carta *f* de crédito circular; **circular economic flow,** circuito econômico. 2. *n.* circular *f.*

circularize, *v.tr.* **to circularize retailers,** enviar uma circular aos varejistas; **to circularize consumers on brand preference,** pesquisar as preferências de marca de consumidores mediante questionário; **to circularize a new product,** anunciar um novo produto mediante circular.

circulate, *v.tr. & i.* circular; **to circulate freely,** circular livremente.

circulating, *a.* circulante; **circulating assets,** ativo *m* circulante; **circulating capital,** capital *m* circulante; **circulating capital goods,** bens *mpl* de capital circulantes; *Fin:* **circulating medium,** meio *m* circulante.

circulation, *n.* (*a*) circulação *f*; **circulation of capital,** circulação de capital, de capitais; **to withdraw from circulation,** retirar de circulação; (*of money*) **to be in circulation,** circular, estar em circulação, ter curso; **to be out of circulation,** estar fora de circulação; **notes in circulation,** circulação monetária; **credit circulation,** circulação fiduciária; (*b*) (*of a newspaper*) tiragem *f.*

City (the), *n.* centro financeiro da Inglaterra (em Londres); **City man,** financista *m,* financeiro *m*; alguém que trabalha na *City*; *Journ:* **City article,** boletim financeiro; **the City immediately reacted to the news,** a Bolsa e as outras instituições financeiras reagiram imediatamente à notícia.

claim[1], *n.* 1. *Ind:* reivindicação *f*; **wage claims, pay claims,** reivindicações salariais; **to put in a large wage claim,** reivindicar um grande aumento de salário. 2. *Ins:* reclamação (submetida pelo segurado); **settlement of claims,** liquidação *f* de sinistros; **claims experience,** estatística *f* dos riscos; **claims expenses,** despesas *fpl* com a liquidação de sinistros; **claims department (in insurance company),** departamento *m* de sinistros (em companhia de seguros); **claims manager,** chefe *mf* do departamento de sinistros; **to put in a claim with an insurance company,** reclamar indenização a uma seguradora; **to fill in a claim form,** preencher um formulário para reclamações. **3.** (*of creditor*) direito creditório, crédito *m*; **to have a claim against a debtor,** ter (direito de) crédito contra um devedor; **to have a claim on the assets of a company,** ter privilégio sobre o ativo de uma companhia; **preferential claim,** crédito preferencial, crédito privilegiado, direito creditório preferencial. **4.** *Jur:* pretensão *f*, alegação *f*; **to bring a claim for damages against s.o.,** intentar uma ação de perdas e danos contra alguém; **claim for compensation,** reclamação de indenização; **to file a claim for compensation,** apresentar, entregar, um pedido de indenização (no tribunal).

claim², *v.tr.* **1.** *Ind:* reivindicar (aumento de salário, etc.). **2.** *Ins:* reclamar.

claimable, *a.* **1.** *Ind:* reivindicável. **2.** *Ins:* reclamável.

claimant,claimer, *n.* **1.** *Ind:* reivindicante *mf*. **2.** *Ins:* reclamante *mf*. **3.** *Jur:* requerente *mf*, pretendente *mf*.

claim back, *v.tr.* **to claim back an expense, a tax,** pedir a devolução de uma despesa, um imposto.

clampdown, *n.* **clampdown on credit,** arrocho *m* ao crédito.

clarify, *v.tr.* esclarecer.

class, *n.* **1.** classe *f*; *Av:* **economy class,** classe econômica, classe turística; **first class,** primeira classe; **he only travels first class,** ele só viaja na primeira classe, de primeira classe. **2. class of insurance,** ramo *m* de seguro; **class of risk,** classe do risco. **3.** *Trans:* **class rates,** tarifa cobrada por classe de produtos, na base do peso.

classification, *n.* **job classification,** classificação *f* de tarefas.

classified, *n. & a.* (anúncio) classificado (*m*).

clause, *n.* cláusula *f*, artigo *m*; **the clauses of a law,** as disposições, os dispositivos, de uma lei; **penalty clause,** cláusula penal; **saving clause,** ressalva *f*, cláusula restritiva; **no-strike clause,** cláusula contra-greve.

clean, *a.* *Fin:* **clean bill of exchange,** letra *f* de câmbio sem documentos anexos; **clean bond,** título *m* sem endossos; **clean bill of lading,** conhecimento marítimo limpo; **clean credit,** crédito *m* realizável sem apresentação de documentos; **clean draft,** saque limpo; **clean surplus,** lucros *mpl* em suspenso distribuíveis.

clear¹, *a.* **1.** (*a*) **clear profit,** lucro líquido; **clear loss,** perda líquida; (*b*) **clear majority,** maioria absoluta (de votos); (*c*) **three clear days,** três dias inteiros e consecutivos. **2. clear accounts,** contas *fpl* em ordem.

clear², *v.tr.* **1.** (*in retail trade*) **to clear old stock,** liquidar, queimar, estoque velho. **2.** *Nau: Cust:* **to clear a ship,** desembaraçar um navio; **to clear goods through (the) customs,** liberar mercadorias na alfândega; **to clear a consignment,** desembaraçar uma partida (de mercadorias). **3. to clear a thousand dollars on a sale,** auferir um lucro líquido de mil dólares de uma venda. **4. to clear a debt,** liquidar, saldar, uma dívida. **5.** *Fin:* **to clear a cheque,** compensar um cheque; **cleared cheques,** cheques compensados.

clearance, *n.* **1.** clearance (sale), liquidação *f*, queima *f*. **2.** *Nau: Cust:* **customs clearance,** desembaraço alfandegário; **clearance papers,** licença *f* para desembarcar ou deixar o porto; **clearance inwards,** desembaraço de um desembarque; **clearance outwards,** desembaraço de um embarque; **3.** *Fin: Bank:* compensação *f*, liberação *f*; *Bank:* **clearance loan,** empréstimo concedido por um dia.

clearing, *n.* *Fin: Bank:* compensação *f*, liberação *f*; **clearing house,** câmara *f* de compensação; **clearing agreement,** acordo *m* de compensação; **clearing arrangements,** acordos para compensação; **clearing dollar,** dólar convênio *m*; **clearing account,** conta *f* de convênio; *UK:* **clearing bank,** banco *m* que participa do sistema de compensação.

clerical, *a.* **clerical work,** trabalho *m* de escritório; **clerical worker,** funcionário *m* de escritório, auxiliar *mf* de escritório; **clerical staff,** pessoal *m* de escritório;

clerical officer, oficial administrativo; *Book-k:* **clerical error,** erro *m* de escrituração.

clerk, *n.* **1.** auxiliar *mf* de escritório, funcionário *m* de escritório, (*of solicitor, etc.*) escrevente *mf*; **bank clerk,** bancário *m*; **chief clerk, managing clerk,** chefe *mf* de escritório; **filing clerk,** *Am:* **file clerk,** arquivista *mf*, fichador *m*; **invoice clerk,** auxiliar de faturamento; **junior clerk,** auxiliar júnior, praticante *mf*, (em um banco); **ledger clerk,** escriturário *m*; **shipping clerk,** despachante *mf*; **wages clerk,** auxiliar de folha de pagamento. **2.** *N.Am:* balconista *mf*, caixeiro *m*; **(hotel) clerk,** recepcionista *mf*; **booking clerk,** (i) despachante *mf* (que vende passagens), (ii) encarregado *m* de reservas.

client, *n.* cliente *mf*.

clientele, *n.* clientela *f*.

climbing, *a.* **climbing prices,** preços *mpl* em elevação; **climbing unemployment,** desemprego *m* ascendente.

clock off, *v.i. Ind:* assinar o ponto na saída.

clock on, *v.i. Ind:* assinar o ponto na entrada.

close¹, *v.* **1.** *v.tr.* (*a*) *Book-k:* **to close the books,** encerrar os livros; (*b*) encerrar (uma conta), liquidar (uma operação); (*c*) encerrar, terminar, (uma reunião); (*d*) **to close a deal,** fechar um negócio. **2.** *v.i.* **the shares closed at $4,** as ações fecharam a $4; **the meeting closed at 3 o'clock,** a reunião se encerrou, terminou, às três horas; **the shops close earlier on Wednesdays,** o comércio fecha mais cedo às quartas-feiras.

close², *a. UK:* **close company,** companhia fechada; companhia com cinco (ou menos) sócios; *Am:* **close corporation,** companhia controlada por poucos acionistas; sociedade fechada.

closed, *a.* fechado, encerrado; **closed account,** conta encerrada; **closed mortgage,** hipoteca *f* que tem um limite fixo de valor; **closed-end investment company,** sociedade *f* de investimento com capital fixo; **closed-end trust,** sociedade fiduciária para administração de capital fixo; *Ind:* **closed shop,**

estabelecimento *m* que só admite empregados sindicalizados.

close down, *v.* **1.** *v.tr.* **to close down a factory,** fechar uma fábrica; **to close down a business,** extinguir, dissolver, um negócio. **2.** *v.i.* fechar, parar; **the shop closed down owing to a lack of customers,** a loja fechou por falta de freguesia; **production closed down,** a produção parou.

close out, *v. N.Am:* **1.** *v.tr.* (*a*) liquidar, queimar, (estoque, mercadorias); (*b*) encerrar (uma conta). **2.** *v.i.* fechar (fábrica, loja, etc.).

close-out, *n. N.Am:* liquidação *f*, queima *f*.

closing, **1.** *a.* último, final; **closing bid,** lance *m* final; **closing date,** data *f* de encerramento, data-limite *f*; **closing rate (of exchange),** taxa *f* (de câmbio) de fechamento; *St.Exch:* **closing prices,** preços *mpl*, cotações *fpl*, de fechamento; *Book-k:* **closing entry,** lançamento *m* de encerramento; **closing trial balance,** balancete *m* final. **2.** *n.* fechamento *m* (de loja, fábrica, etc.); **closing time,** hora *f* de fechamento; **early closing day,** dia *m* em que o comércio fecha mais cedo; **Sunday closing,** repouso *m* dominical.

closing down, *n.* **1.** extinção *f*, dissolução *f*, (de um negócio), encerramento *m* (de uma conta). **2.** fechamento *m* (de loja, fábrica); **closing down sale,** liquidação *f* (por motivo de fechamento).

clothing, *n.* vestuário *m*, roupa *f*; **clothing industry, trade,** indústria *f* de vestuário; **clothing factory,** fábrica *f* de roupas; **articles of clothing,** peças *fpl* de vestuário; **clothing manufacturer,** fabricante *m* de roupas; **clothing store,** loja *f* de roupas; **children's clothing,** vestuário *m* infantil.

coal, *n.* carvão *m*, hulha *f*; **coal industry,** indústria carvoeira; **coal miner,** mineiro *m* de carvão; **coal merchant,** carvoeiro *m*; **coal strike,** greve *f* dos mineiros de carvão.

coast, *v.i.* cabotar.

coaster, *n.* navio *m* de cabotagem.

coasting, *n.* cabotagem *f*; **coasting vessel,**

navio *m* de cabotagem; **to be in the coasting trade,** cabotar.

cocoa, *n.* cacau *m*; **cocoa cultivation,** cacauicultura *f.*

co-creditor, *n.* co-credor *m.*

code, *n.* código *m*; **post(al) code,** código de endereçamento postal; **cable code,** código telegráfico; *Tel:* **international code,** código internacional; **country code,** código do país; **city (area) code,** código (de área) da cidade.

co-director, *n.* co-diretor *m*, co-administrador *m.*

co-emption, *n. Jur:* coempção *f.*

coffee, *n.* café *m*; **coffee planter,** cafeicultor *m*, plantador *m* de café; **coffee plantation,** cafezal *m*, plantação *f* de café; **coffee exchange,** bolsa *f* de café; **coffee market,** mercado *m* de café; **the world coffee prices,** os preços mundiais do café; **coffee crop,** safra cafeeira, safra do café; **coffee futures,** vendas futuras de café; **the Brazilian Coffee Institute,** o Instituto Brasileiro do Café; **freeze-dried coffee,** café liofilizado; **soluble coffee,** café solúvel.

coffer, *n.* **coffers of State,** cofres *mpl* do Estado, fundos públicos.

coin¹, *n.* 1. moeda (metálica); **gold coin,** moeda de ouro; **small coin,** moeda divisionária; *UK:* **coin of the realm,** moeda corrente. 2. *F:* trocado *m*, dinheiro miúdo, quebrados *mpl*; **coin machine,** (i) vendedora automática, (ii) máquina *f* para trocar dinheiro.

coin², *v.tr.* cunhar, amoedar; **coined gold,** ouro monetizado.

coinage, *n.* 1. cunhagem *f*, amoedação *f*, moedagem *f.* 2. moedas *fpl.*

co-insurance, *n.* co-seguro *m.*

co-insure, *v.tr. & i.* co-segurar.

co-insurer, *n.* co-segurador *m.*

collapse¹, *n.* (*a*) quebra *f* (de empresa, banco, etc.); (*b*) craque *m*, colapso *m*, (do mercado); **the collapse of the pound,** o colapso, a degringolada, da libra esterlina.

collapse², *v.i.* (*a*) quebrar; (*b*) (*of market, currency, etc.*) sofrer um colapso; acusar, apresentar, uma queda brusca; cair bruscamente.

collateral, *a. & n.* collateral (security), (i) garantia subsidiária, (ii) penhor *m*, garantia pignoratícia; **collateral loan,** empréstimo *m* sob garantia, empréstimo pignoratício.

collateralize, *v.tr. N.Am:* garantir por penhor (de títulos, etc.).

collect¹, *v.tr.* cobrar; **to collect a debt,** cobrar uma dívida; **to collect bills of exchange,** cobrar letras de câmbio; (*of bank*) **to collect a cheque,** cobrar, receber, um cheque; **to collect taxes,** arrecadar, cobrar, coletar, recolher, impostos; *N.Am:* **collect on delivery (COD),** pagamento *m* na entrega.

collect², 1. *a. N.Am:* **collect call,** chamada *f* a cobrar, telefonema *m* a cobrar; **to make a collect call,** fazer uma chamada a cobrar; **collect shipment,** embarque *m* a cobrar. 2. *adv. N.Am:* **to call collect,** fazer uma chamada a cobrar; **to send a parcel collect,** enviar um pacote com porte a pagar.

collectable/collectible, *a.* (*of debt, etc.*) cobrável; **collectible bill of exchange,** letra *f* de câmbio cobrável; **collectible tax,** imposto *m* arrecadável, cobrável, coletável; *Book-k:* **collectible account,** conta *f* a receber.

collectables/collectibles, *n.pl. Book-k:* efeitos *mpl* a receber.

collecting, *a.* **collecting clerk,** coletor *m*, cobrador *m*; funcionário recebedor (em repartições, etc.); **collecting agency,** agência *f* de cobranças; **collecting department,** departamento *m* de cobranças.

collection, *n.* cobrança *f*; **debt collection,** cobrança de dívidas; **tax collection,** arrecadação *f*, coleta *f*, de impostos; **collection account,** conta *f* de cobrança; **collection charge,** taxa *f* de cobrança; **collection agency,** agência *f* de cobranças; **to attend to the collection of bills of exchange,** encarregar-se da cobrança de letras de câmbio; *Bank:* (*of cheque*) **to send for collection,** remeter para cobrança.

collective, *a.* coletivo; **collective agreement,** acordo coletivo, convênio

coletivo; **collective bargaining,** negociação coletiva.
collector, *n.* (*a*) cobrador *m*, recebedor *m*, (de um cheque, etc.); (*b*) *Adm:* **collector of taxes, tax collector,** coletor *m*, exator *m*; arrecadador *m*, cobrador *m*, recebedor *m*, de impostos; **tax collector's office,** recebedoria *f*, coletoria *f*.
column, *n. Book-k:* coluna *f*.
combination, *n.* (*of business units, etc.*) combinação *f*, integração *f*.
combine, *n.* truste *m*, associação financeira (de empresas); **horizontal combine,** consórcio *m*.
commerce, *n.* comércio *m*, negócios *mpl*; **Chamber of Commerce,** Câmara *f* de Comércio; *Am:* **Secretary of Commerce,** Ministro *m* da Indústria e do Comércio.
commercial, 1. *a.* comercial, mercantil; **commercial art,** arte *f* de propaganda, arte publicitária; **commercial artist,** artista *mf* de propaganda; **commercial attaché,** adido *m* comercial; **commercial bank,** banco *m* comercial; **commercial banking,** atividade bancária comercial; **commercial bill,** efeito *m* comercial; **commercial college,** escola *f* de comércio; **commercial cost,** custo *m* comercial, custo mercantil; **commercial credit,** crédito *m* comercial, crédito mercantil; **commercial hotel,** hotel *m* para caixeiros-viajantes; **commercial invoice,** fatura *f* comercial; **commercial law,** direito *m* comercial; **commercial paper,** efeitos *mpl* de comércio, títulos *mpl* negociáveis de empresas comerciais, papel *m* comercial; **commercial paper houses,** firmas especializadas no desconto de títulos comerciais; **commercial port,** porto *m* comercial; **commercial traveller,** caixeiro-viajante *m*; **commercial vehicle,** (veículo) utilitário *m*; **this shop is not a commercial proposition,** esta loja não é rentável, não oferece lucros; **sample of no commercial value,** amostra *f* sem valor comercial; *Ind:* (*of machine, etc.*) **commercial efficiency,** rendimento econômico; *Am:* **commercial club,** câmara *f* de comércio. **2.** *n. Radio: TV:* comercial *m*.
commercialese, *n.* jargão *m* comercial, linguajar *m* comercial.

commercialism, *n.* mercantilismo *m*.
commercialization, *n.* comercialização *f*.
commercialize, *v.tr.* comercializar (novos, produtos, mercadorias, etc.).
commercially, *adv.* comercialmente.
commission[1], *n.* **1.** comissão *f*; **a ten per cent commission,** uma comissão de dez porcento; **sale on commission,** venda *f* em comissão, venda por comissão; **to work on commission,** trabalhar em comissão, trabalhar por comissão; **to charge 5% commission on a transaction,** cobrar uma comissão de 5% sobre uma operação; **to appoint s.o. as a buyer on commission,** comissionar um comprador; **commission agent,** comissário *m*; **commission broker,** corretor *m* por comissão; (*as factor*) **commission merchant,** comissário financiador. **2. exchange control commission,** comissão de controle de câmbio.
commission[2], *v.tr.* **to commission a market research study from a consultant,** encomendar uma pesquisa de mercado a um consultor.
commitment, *n.* compromisso *m*, obrigação *f* (contratual); *Bank:* **commitment fee,** comissão *f* de compromisso, comissão por imobilização de fundos; **to meet one's financial commitments,** cumprir (com) as suas obrigações financeiras.
committee, *n.* comitê *m*, comissão *f*; **to sit on a committee,** ser membro de um comitê; **management committee,** comitê de direção; *Ind:* **joint production committee,** comissão paritária; *St.Exch:* **the Stock Exchange Committee,** = a Comissão Nacional de Bolsas de Valores.
commodity, *n.* (*a*) mercadoria *f*, bem *m*, artigo *m*, produto *m*; *Trans:* **commodity rates,** tarifas *fpl* de transporte cobradas com base na natureza da mercadoria; (*b*) *pl.* **commodities,** produtos básicos, produtos primários, commodities *mpl*; **international commodities market,** mercado *m* internacional de commodities; **commodities such as meat, sugar and cocoa,** produtos básicos como a carne, o açúcar e o cacau; **commodity agreement,** acordo *m* sobre produtos

básicos; **commodity broker,** corretor *m* de mercadorias; **commodity exchange,** bolsa *f* de mercadorias; **commodity goods,** artigos *mpl* de primeira necessidade; **commodity-money,** moeda-mercadoria *f*; **commodity paper,** saques *mpl* (ou promissórias *fpl*) garantidos por conhecimentos de depósito de mercadorias; **commodity standard,** padrão *m* de mercadoria.

common, *a.* comum; **common carrier,** transportador comum, transportador público; **common cost,** custo comum, custo conjunto; *Ins:* **common average,** avaria *f* comum, avaria grossa; *N.Am:* **common stock, common equity,** ação ordinária; **common stockholder,** possuidor *m* de ação ordinária; *Am:* **common law corporation,** sociedade anônima de fato.

community, *n.* 1. comunidade *f*; **the business community,** a classe dos comerciantes (de uma cidade); **the European Economic Community,** a Comunidade Econômica Européia. 2. **community of interests,** comunhão *f*, comunidade, de interesses.

company, *n.* companhia *f*, sociedade *f*, empresa *f*; **affiliated company,** companhia filiada, companhia coligada; **associated company,** companhia associada; **assurance, insurance, company,** companhia de seguros, seguradora *f*; **bogus company,** sociedade fantasma, sociedade fictícia; **holding company,** sociedade holding, empresa holding, holding *f*; **investment company,** sociedade de investimento; **limited company, joint stock company,** sociedade por ações, sociedade anônima; **mixed company,** sociedade de economia mista; **off-shore company,** companhia constituída no exterior para conseguir vantagens fiscais; **parent company,** sociedade controladora, sociedade de comando; **private company** = sociedade por quotas; **property, real estate, company,** sociedade imobiliária; **public company,** sociedade de capital aberto; **public limited company** = sociedade anônima de capital aberto; **shipping company,** companhia de navegação;

(wholly owned) subsidiary company, companhia subsidiária (integral); **telephone company,** companhia telefônica; **trading company,** trading (company) *f*, sociedade mercantil; **Companies Act,** lei *f* das sociedades; **the company books,** os livros sociais; **company director,** administrador *m*, diretor *m*, de companhia; **company transaction,** operação *f* social, operação da companhia; **company year,** exercício *m* social; **company in the process of formation,** companhia em organização, em formação, em constituição; **company owned,** de propriedade da companhia; **he's a good company man,** ele é dedicado à companhia; **he drives a company car,** ele utiliza um carro da companhia; **the name of a company,** a razão social, a denominação social, de uma companhia; **the objects of the company,** o objeto social; **to dissolve a company,** dissolver uma companhia; **to form, incorporate, a company,** constituir, organizar, uma companhia; **to wind up a company,** liquidar uma companhia.

comparative, *a.* **comparative costs,** custos comparativos.

compensate, *v.tr.* (*a*) indenizar, compensar, reparar; **to compensate s.o. for sth.,** indenizar alguém por algo; (*b*) remunerar, pagar, (alguém).

compensation, *n.* (*a*) indenização *f*, compensação *f*, reparação *f*; **accident compensation,** indenização por acidente; **to pay s.o. compensation in cash,** indenizar alguém em dinheiro; (*b*) **executive compensation,** remuneração *f* do pessoal executivo.

compensatory, *a. Cust:* **compensatory duty,** imposto aduaneiro compensatório.

compete, *v.i.* **to compete with s.o.,** competir, concorrer, com alguém (por um contrato, etc.).

competence, competency, *n.* competência *f*, capacidade *f*, habilidade *f*; **the project is beyond his competence,** o projeto está além da sua competência; *Jur:* **the competence of the courts of Rio de Janeiro,** a competência do foro do Rio de Janeiro.

competent, *a.* competente, hábil, capaz; *Jur:* **competent court,** tribunal *m* competente.

competition, *n.* competição *f,* concorrência *f;* **free competition,** livre concorrência; **unfair competition,** concorrência desleal; **monopolistic competition,** concorrência monopolística; **cut-throat competition,** concorrência predatória.

competitive, *a.* competitivo; **our prices are extremely competitive,** os nossos preços são muito competitivos; **competitive bidding,** concorrência (pública).

competitiveness, *n.* competitividade *f* (de preços, produtos, etc.).

competitor, *n.* concorrente *m,* competidor *m;* **our competitors,** a (nossa) concorrência.

complaint, *n.* (*a*) queixa *f* (da alta de preços, etc.); (*b*) (*officially made*) reclamação *f;* **complaints office (in a firm),** serviço *m* de reclamações; **to make a complaint against s.o.,** fazer uma reclamação contra alguém; **to lodge a complaint with a body,** registrar uma reclamação junto a um órgão.

completion, *n.* **completion of a contract,** assinatura *f* de um contrato.

composition, *n.* **1.** *Jur:* concordata *f,* compromisso *m;* **to apply for a composition,** pedir concordata; **composition to avoid a declaration of bankruptcy,** concordata preventiva; **composition of fifty cents in the dollar,** concordata mediante o pagamento de cinqüenta por cento (das importâncias devidas); **to make a composition,** fazer uma concordata. **2.** estrutura *f;* **composition of debt,** estrutura *f* da dívida; **composition of deposits,** estrutura *f* dos depósitos; **composition of expenditure,** estrutura do dispêndio; **composition of imports,** estrutura das importações.

compound¹, *a.* composto; **compound discount,** desconto composto; *Fin:* **compound interest,** juro(s) composto(s); *Book-k:* **compound entry,** lançamento composto; *Book-k:* **compound interest**

method (of depreciation), cálculo *m* de depreciação baseado em juros compostos.

compound², *v.* **1.** *v.i.* compor, entrar em composição, (com alguém). **2.** *v.tr.* (*a*) capitalizar (juros); (*b*) agravar (problemas).

comprehensive, *a.* **comprehensive planning,** planejamento *m* global; *Ins:* **comprehensive insurance,** seguro compreensivo.

Comptometer, *n. R.t.m:* máquina *f* de calcular.

compulsory, *a.* **compulsory loan,** empréstimo compulsório; **compulsory deposit,** depósito compulsório; **compulsory overtime,** horas extraordinárias compulsórias; *Am:* **compulsory check-off,** dedução compulsória do salário.

computable, *a.* computável, calculável.

computation, *n.* (*a*) cômputo *m,* cálculo *m,* estimativa *f;* **to make a computation of sth.,** fazer o cômputo de algo, calcular algo; **at the lowest computation, it will cost...,** vai custar, no mínimo...; (*b*) **electronic computation,** cômputo eletrônico.

computational, *a.* **computational error,** erro *m* de cálculo.

compute, *v.tr.* computar, calcular; estimar, orçar, (despesas, preços, etc.); **he computed expenditure at 10 000 dollars,** ele computou as despesas em 10.000 dólares.

computer, *n.* computador *m;* **all-purpose computer,** computador universal; **analog computer,** computador analógico; **digital computer,** computador digital; **electronic computer,** computador eletrônico, cérebro eletrônico; **computer accounting,** contabilidade *f* por computador; **computer analyst,** analista *mf* (de sistemas); **computer control,** controle *m* por computador; **computer department,** serviço *m* de computação, setor *m* de computação; **computer engineer,** técnico *m* de computador; **computer expert,** perito *m* em computação; **computer firm,** empresa *f* de computação; **the computer industry,** a indústria de computação; **computer language,** linguagem *f* de

máquina, linguagem de programação; **computer program,** programa *m*; **computer programmer,** programador *m*, programadora *f*; **computer system,** sistema *m* de computação.
computerese, *n.* linguagem *f* de máquina, linguagem de programação.
computerization, *n.* computadorização *f*.
computerize, *v.tr.* (*a*) **to computerize a factory,** instalar um computador numa fábrica, equipar uma fábrica com computador; (*b*) **to computerize wages,** computadorizar a folha de pagamento.
computerized, *a.* **computerized data,** dados computadorizados.
conceal, *v.tr. Fin: Adm:* **to conceal income,** sonegar, ocultar, renda; **concealed asset,** ativo ocultado; **concealed profits,** lucros ocultados; *Jur:* **to conceal evidence,** ocultar provas.
concealment, *n.* sonegação *f* (de renda, lucros, etc.), ocultação *f* (de informações, provas, rendas); **concealment of assets,** sonegação de haveres.
concern¹, *n.* empresa *f*, firma *f*; **industrial concern,** empresa industrial; **business concern,** empresa comercial, casa *f* comercial; *Book-k: etc:* **going concern,** empresa em funcionamento, em andamento; **shop for sale as going concern,** vende-se loja com fundo de comércio.
concern², *v.tr.* (*in correspondence, etc.*) **to whom it may concern,** a quem possa interessar.
concession, *n.* (*a*) concessão *f*; *Ind:* **mining concession,** concessão de mineração; (*b*) (**price**) **concession,** redução *f* de preço, abatimento *m* no preço; **to give a price concession,** conceder uma redução de preço.
concessionaire, *n.* concessionário *m*; (*company*) concessionária *f*; **regional spares concession,** concessionária regional para sobressalentes.
concessionary, **1.** *a.* concessionário. **2.** *n.* concessionário *m*; (*company*) concessionária *f*.
concessioner, *n. Am:* concessionário *m*; (*company*) concessionária *f*.
condition¹, *n.* **1.** condição *f*; **conditions of**

sale, condições de venda; **to lay down conditions for a deal,** determinar, estipular, estabelecer, impor, condições para uma operação; condicionar uma operação; **the conditions laid down in the agreement,** as condições contratuais; as condições estipuladas, estabelecidas, no contrato; **the conditions agreed upon (by the parties),** as condições aceitas de comum acordo; **the terms and conditions of an issue,** os termos e condições de uma emissão, as cláusulas e condições de uma emissão; **express condition,** condição expressa; **implied condition,** condição tácita; **on condition,** sob condição; **on condition that he pays,** sob condição de que ele pague; *Ins:* **condition of average,** regra *f* proporcional. **2.** condição *f*, estado *m*; **the working conditions in the factory,** as condições de trabalho em uma fábrica; **living conditions,** condições de vida; **the goods are in excellent condition,** as mercadorias estão em ótimas condições; **goods in fair condition,** mercadorias em condições aceitáveis; **economic conditions,** condições econômicas; **the condition of the market,** a conjuntura atual do mercado.
condition², *v.tr.* condicionar.
conditional, *a.* condicional; **conditional sale,** venda *f* sob condição; *Fin:* **conditional acceptance,** aceite *m* condicional.
conduct¹, *n.* **the conduct of affairs,** a gestão, a condução, dos negócios.
conduct², *v.tr.* dirigir (as atividades de uma empresa).
conference, *n.* **1.** conferência *f*, reunião *f*; **he is in conference with the manager,** está em conferência com o gerente. **2.** conferência, convenção *f*, congresso *m*; **conference centre,** centro *m* de conferências, centro de convenções; **conference room,** sala *f* de conferências, sala de reuniões; **sales conference,** conferência, reunião, de vendedores; **press conference,** entrevista coletiva à imprensa. **3.** *Nau:* **freight conference,** conferência de fretes.
confidence, *n.* confiança *f*; **confidence in the currency,** confiança na moeda; (*in job*

advertisements) **all applications will be dealt with in the strictest confidence** = asseguramos sigilo profissional, mantemos absoluto sigilo.
confidential, *a.* confidencial; **confidential file,** arquivo *m* confidencial.
confirm, *v.tr.* confirmar; **confirmed credit,** crédito confirmado; **confirmed letter of credit,** carta de crédito confirmada.
confirmation, *n.* confirmação *f.*
confiscate, *v.tr.* confiscar.
confiscation, *n.* confisco *m.*
conflicting, *a.* **conflicting interests,** interesses *mpl* conflitantes.
connection, *n.* conexão *f*, ligação *f.*
consent, 1. *a. Am: Fin:* **consent dividend,** dividendo consentido. **2.** *n.* **with the consent of the majority of the directors,** com o consentimento da maioria dos diretores; **by mutual consent,** por mútuo consentimento.
consequential, *a.* **consequential damages,** danos *mpl* conseqüentes.
consideration, *n.* (*a*) pagamento *m*, remuneração *f*, preço *m*, (de um serviço, etc.); **agreed consideration,** preço combinado (pela compra de uma casa, etc.); **to pay a solicitor a consideration for his services,** remunerar um advogado por seus serviços; (*b*) *Jur:* **good, valuable, consideration,** contraprestação *f* (em contrato bilateral); **for a valuable consideration,** a título oneroso.
consign, *v.tr.* **to consign goods to an agent,** consignar mercadorias a um agente.
consignee, *n.* consignatário *m.*
consignment, *n.* (*a*) consignação *f*; (*loosely*) remessa *f*, expedição *f*; **consignment goods, stocks,** mercadorias recebidas em consignação; **consignment sale,** venda *f* de mercadorias em consignação; **consignment account,** conta *f* para vendas de mercadorias em consignação; **consignment note,** guia *f*, nota *f*, de remessa; nota de consignação; *Am:* conhecimento aéreo; **the agent receives certain goods on consignment,** o agente recebe certas mercadorias em consignação; (*b*) (*goods sent*) **a consignment of grain,** uma partida de

cereais; **a consignment of meat,** uma partida de carne.
consignor, *n.* consignador *m*, consignante *mf*, (*loosely*) expedidor *m.*
consolidate, *v.tr.* **to consolidate a number of firms,** consolidar várias empresas; **to consolidate a debt,** consolidar uma dívida.
consolidated, *a.* consolidado; **consolidated debt,** dívida consolidada; **consolidated annuities, consolidated government stock,** títulos *mpl* de dívida pública consolidada, consolidados *mpl*; *Book-k:* **consolidated accounts,** contas consolidadas, demonstrações consolidadas; **consolidated balance sheet,** balanço consolidado; **consolidated financial statement,** demonstração financeira consolidada; **consolidated income statement,** demonstração consolidada de lucros e perdas; **consolidated surplus,** lucros consolidados não distribuídos; **consolidated group,** grupo consolidado; **consolidated goodwill,** fundo *m* de comércio resultante de uma consolidação.
consolidation, *n.* **the consolidation of two corporations,** a consolidação de duas empresas; *Fin:* **consolidation of a debt,** consolidação de uma dívida; **consolidation policy,** política *f* de consolidação; **consolidation excess,** fundo *m* de comércio resultante de uma consolidação.
consols, *n.pl. Fin:* consolidados *mpl*, títulos *mpl* de dívida pública consolidada.
consortium, *n.* consórcio *m* (de bancos, etc.).
constant, *a. Book-k:* **constant cost,** custo constante, custo fixo.
constituent, *a.* **constituent company,** companhia *f* que faz parte de um grupo (de companhias coligadas).
construction, *n.* construção *f*; **construction industry,** indústria *f* da construção civil; **construction firm,** (empresa) construtora (*f*); **construction materials,** materiais *mpl* de construção; **construction loan,** empréstimo imobiliário para construção; **construction bond,** caução *f* de execução para construtor;

Am: **construction worker,** trabalhador *m* da (indústria de) construção civil.
constructive, *a. Ins:* **constructive total loss,** perda *f* total construtiva; *Am: Fin:* **constructive receipt (of income),** recebimento construtivo (de renda).
consul, *n.* cônsul *m,* consulesa *f;* **honorary consul,** cônsul honorário; **consul general,** cônsul geral.
consular, *a.* **consular agent,** agente *m* consular; **consular invoice,** fatura *f* consular; **consular document,** documento *m* consular; **consular official,** funcionário *m* de consulado; **consular visa,** visto *m* consular; **consular fees,** emolumentos *mpl* consulares.
consulate, *n.* consulado *m.*
consult, *v.tr.* consultar (advogado, médico, etc.).
consultancy, *n.* consultoria *f;* **consultancy fee,** honorário *m* de consultor; **consultancy firm,** (empresa) consultora (*f*), firma *f* de consultoria; **consultancy agreement,** contrato *m* para serviços de consultoria; **to take up a consultancy with a company,** começar a trabalhar para uma companhia como consultor.
consultant, *n.* consultor *m;* **business consultant,** consultor de empresa; **management consultant,** consultor em administração; **personnel consultant,** consultor de pessoal, consultor em recursos humanos; **financial consultant,** consultor financeiro; **tax consultant,** consultor fiscal.
consulting, *a.* **consulting engineer,** consultor *m* de engenharia, engenheiro-consultor *m;* **consulting services,** serviços *mpl* de consultoria.
consumable, *a.* consumível; **consumable goods,** bens *mpl* consumíveis; *Ind:* materiais *mpl* de consumo.
consumer, *n.* consumidor *m;* **consumer behaviour,** comportamento *m* do consumidor; **consumer choice, preference,** preferência *f* do consumidor; **consumer credit,** crédito *m* ao consumidor; **consumer demand,** procura *f* dos consumidores; **consumer franchise,** privilégio *m* de consumo; **consumer goods,** bens *mpl* de consumo, artigos *mpl*

de consumo, produtos *mpl* de consumo; **consumer interests,** interesses *mpl* do consumidor; **consumer markert,** mercado *m* de consumo, mercado consumidor; **consumer needs,** necessidades *fpl* do consumidor, necessidades de consumo; **consumer price index,** índice *m* de preços ao consumidor; **consumer protection,** proteção *f* ao consumidor; **consumer public,** público *m* consumidor; **consumer research,** pesquisa *f* de consumo; **consumer society,** sociedade *f* de consumo; **consumer spending,** gastos *mpl* de consumo; **consumer taste,** gosto *m* do consumidor; **final, ultimate, consumer,** consumidor final.
consumption, *n.* (*a*) consumo *m;* **consumption trends,** tendências *fpl* do consumo; **mass consumption,** consumo em massa; **consumption tax,** imposto *m* de consumo; **home consumption,** consumo interno; (*b*) (*of food*) **unfit for human consumption,** impróprio para consumo.
contain, *v.tr.* conter.
container, *n. Trans:* container *m,* cofre *m* de carga; **container ship,** navio *m* porta-containers; **container shipping,** transporte *m* marítimo de carga containerizada, transporte marítimo em containers; **container firm,** empresa transportadora de carga containerizada; **container berth,** atracadouro *m* para navios porta-containers; **container plane,** avião *m* para carga containerizada.
containerization, *n. Trans:* containerização *f.*
containerize, *v.tr. Trans:* containerizar.
contango[1], *n. Fin: St.Exch:* reporte *m,* taxa *f* de reporte, taxa devida pela demora na liquidação de um negócio; **payer of contango,** reportado *m;* **contangoes are heavy, low,** as taxas de reporte estão altas, baixas; **contango day,** dia *m* de pagamento de taxas de reporte.
contango[2], *v.tr. & i. St.Exch:* conceder um prazo para a liquidação de um negócio mediante pagamento de uma taxa de reporte.
contents, *n.pl.* conteúdo *m* (de caixa, etc.).
contingency, *n. Fin: Book-k:* **contingency**

fund, fundo *m* para contingências; **contingency reserve,** reserva *f* para contingências; *pl.* **contingencies,** contingências *fpl;* **to provide for contingencies,** fazer provisão para as contingências.
contingent, *a.* (*a*) **contingent asset,** ativo *m* de realização contingente; **contingent charge, cost,** despesa *f,* custo *m,* contingente; **contingent liability,** responsabilidade *f* contingente, passivo *m* contingente; **contingent profit,** lucro *m* contingente; (*b*) condicional.
continuation, *n.* *St.Exch:* **continuation operation,** operação *f* de reporte.
continuing, *a.* *Am: Fin:* **continuing appropriation,** verba *f* contínua.
continuous, *a.* *Book-k:* **continuous audit,** auditoria contínua.
contra, *n.* *Book-k:* **contra account** conta compensada; **contra entry,** contralançamento *m,* contrapartida *f;* **as per contra,** em contrapartida; **to settle a debt per contra,** compensar uma dívida com outra.
contraband[1], *n.* contrabando *m,* muamba *f;* **contraband goods,** mercadorias contrabandeadas, contrabando; **contraband cargo,** carga contrabandeada; **to engage in contraband trade,** contrabandear, fazer contrabando.
contraband[2], *v.tr.* 1. contrabandear, fazer contrabando de, (alguma coisa). 2. proibir.
contrabandist, *n.* contrabandista *mf.*
contract[1], *n.* (*a*) contrato *m;* **breach of contract,** violação *f,* infração *f,* de disposições contratuais; **law of contract,** direito *m* contratual; **performance of a contract,** execução *f* de um contrato; **simple contract,** contrato verbal, contrato consensual; **terms of contract,** termos *mpl* contratuais; **under the terms of the contract,** nos termos contratuais; **to acquire sth. under contract,** adquirir alguma coisa por contrato; **to be under contract to a firm,** estar vinculado a uma empresa por (um) contrato; **to bind oneself by contract,** obrigar-se, comprometer-se, por contrato; **to draw up a contract,** estabelecer, redigir, lavrar,

um contrato; **to execute a contract,** celebrar, lavrar, um contrato; **to rescind a contract,** rescindir um contrato; **to sign a contract,** assinar um contrato; **to void a contract,** anular, invalidar, nulificar, irritar, um contrato; **contract of sale,** contrato de compra e venda; **contract for services,** contrato de prestação de serviços; **contract of service (or employment),** contrato de trabalho; **contract price,** preço *m* contratual, preço contratado; *Trans:* **contract of carriage,** contrato de transporte; **contract for delivery,** contrato de entrega; (*b*) (*in building industry, etc.*) **contract work,** empreitada *f;* **this firm only does contract work,** esta empresa só faz obras de empreitada; **to do a painting job under contract,** fazer uma obra de pintura por empreitada; **this engineer works for the government under contract,** este engenheiro está contratado pelo governo; **contract worker,** operário contratado; **contract labour,** mão-de-obra contratada; **contract rate,** tarifa *f* contratual; (*c*) *St.Exch:* **contract note,** boleta *f.*
contract[2], *v.* 1. *v.tr.* **to contract an engineer for three months,** contratar um engenheiro por três meses; **to contract to do sth.,** obrigar-se por contrato a fazer algo; **to contract a loan,** contratar um empréstimo. 2. *v.i.* **to contract for the supply of meat,** fazer contrato para o fornecimento de carne; **to contract with s.o.,** fazer um contrato com alguém; **to contract out,** (i) desobrigar-se por contrato, (ii) confiar uma tarefa manufatureira (a um empreiteiro).
contract[3], *v.tr. & i.* reduzir, contrair.
contracting, *a.* contratante; *Jur:* **the contracting party,** a parte contratante.
contraction, *n.* (i) contração *f* (de crédito), (ii) contenção *f* (de despesas).
contractor, *n.* contratante *mf,* empresa *f* contratante, empreiteiro *m;* **building contractor,** empreiteiro de obras (de construção); **haulage contractor,** empresa *f* de transportes rodoviários, transportadora *f.*
contractual, *a.* contratual; **contractual obligation,** obrigação *f* contratual;

contractual liability insurance, seguro *m* de responsabilidade contratual.
contributed, *a.* *Fin:* **contributed capital,** capital integralizado, capital realizado.
contribution, *n.* contribuição *f*, cota *f*, quota *f*; **pro-rata contribution,** cota-parte *f*, quota-parte *f*; *Ind:* **employer's contributions,** encargos *mpl* sociais; *Adm:* **social insurance contribution,** contribuição previdenciária, contribuição para a previdência social; *Fin:* **contribution of capital,** contribuição *f* ao capital social; *Ins:* repartição *f* de responsabilidade.
contributor, *n.* contribuinte *mf*; *Fin:* acionista *mf* que integraliza as ações subscritas.
contributory, **1.** *a.* contributário; **contributory pension,** pensão contributária. **2.** *n.* *Fin:* acionista *mf* que integraliza as ações subscritas.
control[1], *n.* controle *m*; (*official*) tabelamento *m*; **accounting control,** controle contábil; **cost control,** controle de custo(s); **exchange control,** controle de câmbio, fiscalização *f* cambial; **import controls,** controles de importação; **price control,** controle de preços, **production control,** controle de produção; **quality control,** controle de qualidade; **control account,** conta *f* de controle; **to have control of a business,** controlar uma empresa.
control[2], *v.tr.* controlar; **to control a group of companies,** controlar um grupo de companhias; **to control inflation,** conter, controlar, a inflação; *Pol.Ec:* **to control the economy,** dirigir a economia.
controllable, *a.* **controllable cost,** custo controlável.
controlled, *a.* controlado; **controlled prices,** preços controlados, preços regulamentados; **controlled economy,** economia dirigida; **controlled currency,** moeda controlada, moeda administrada; **controlled company,** companhia controlada.
controller, *n.* controlador *m*.
controlling, *a.* **controlling account,** conta *f* de controle; **controlling interest (in a company),** controle acionário (de uma

companhia); **controlling shareholder,** acionista controlador; **controlling company,** companhia controladora.
convene, *v.* **1.** *v.tr.* **to convene an extraordinary general meeting of the shareholders,** convocar uma assembléia geral extraordinária dos acionistas. **2.** *v.i.* reunir-se; **the managers convene each week,** os gerentes se reúnem toda semana.
convenience, *n.* **convenience goods,** mercadorias *fpl* de compra fácil.
convention, *n.* *Am:* convenção *f* (de empresários, etc.).
conversion, *n.* (*a*) *Fin:* **conversion of debentures into shares,** conversão *f* de debêntures em ações; **conversion privilege,** direito *m* de conversão; **conversion rate,** taxa *f* de conversão, taxa de câmbio; (*b*) **improper conversion of funds,** malversação *f* de fundos.
convert, *v.tr.* (*a*) **to convert dollars into cruzeiros,** converter dólares em cruzeiros; **to convert debentures into shares,** converter debêntures em ações; (*b*) **to convert funds to one's own use,** malversar fundos.
convertibility, *n.* *Fin:* conversibilidade *f*, convertibilidade *f*, (de moedas, títulos, etc.).
convertible, *a.* *Fin:* conversível, convertível; **convertible currency,** moeda *f* conversível; **convertible debenture,** debênture *f* conversível em ações.
conveyance, *n.* *Jur:* transferência *f* de propriedade de imóveis.
cook, *v.tr.* *F:* **to cook the books,** falsificar os livros contábeis.
cooperative, **1.** *n.* cooperativa *f*; **consumers' cooperative,** cooperativa *f* de consumo. **2.** *a.* **cooperative dairy,** cooperativa do leite; **cooperative society,** sociedade cooperativa; **cooperative bank,** cooperativa bancária; **cooperative marketing,** comercialização cooperativa; **cooperative farming,** agricultura *f* em base cooperativista.
co-owner, *n.* co-proprietário *m*, condômino *m*, comuneiro *m*.
co-ownership, *n.* co-propriedade *f*, condomínio *m*.
copartner, *n.* sócio *m*.

copartnership, n. 1. sociedade ƒ em nome coletivo. 2. *Ind:* (industrial) copartnership, participação acionária dos empregados de uma empresa.

copy, n. 1. (a) cópia ƒ, transcrição ƒ; copy typist, datilógrafa ƒ, datilógrafo m; carbon copy, cópia a carbono; top copy, original m; the original and two copies of a document, un documento em três vias; rough copy, rascunho m; fair copy, cópia passada a limpo; file copy, cópia de arquivo; (b) certified (true) copy, cópia autenticada, *Jur:* pública-forma ƒ. 2. advertising copy, texto publicitário.

copyright, n. copirraite m, direitos mpl autorais; the owner of the copyright, o detentor do copirraite; copyright reserved, todos os direitos reservados; copyright agreement, acordo m sobre os direitos autorais; out of copyright, em domínio público; infringement of copyright, violação ƒ dos direitos autorais.

copywriter, n. escritor m de textos publicitários.

corn, n. milho m, cereais mpl; corn chandler, dealer, cerealista m, negociante m de cereais; corn exchange, bolsa ƒ de cereais; corn futures, vendas ƒpl futuras de cereais, vendas de cereais para entrega futura.

corner¹, n. monopólio m, açambarcamento m; to make a corner in wheat, açambarcar, monopolizar, o trigo.

corner², v.tr. açambarcar, monopolizar, (mercadorias, etc.).

cornering, n. açambarcamento m, açambarcagem ƒ.

corporate, a. corporate body, pessoa jurídica; corporate name, razão ƒ social, denominação ƒ social; corporate cash, recursos mpl da empresa; corporate interests, os interesses da empresa; corporate earnings, income, rendimentos mpl de empresa; corporate stocks, ações ƒpl; corporate planning, planejamento m das operações da companhia (ou do grupo); corporate image, imagem ƒ da empresa; *Am:* corporate secretary, secretário m de uma companhia; corporate member, sócio m votante (de uma sociedade).

corporation, n. (a) *Am:* sociedade anônima, companhia ƒ, sociedade por ações; *Jur:* pessoa jurídica; corporation tax, imposto m sobre a renda de sociedades; (b) corporation stocks, títulos emitidos por uma municipalidade; public corporation, *Am:* government corporation, empresa pública, empresa governamental.

correspond, v.i. 1. (of product) to correspond to sample, corresponder à amostra. 2. corresponder-se; to correspond with s.o., trocar, manter, (uma) correspondência com alguém; corresponder-se com alguém.

correspondence, n. correspondência ƒ; correspondence clerk, correspondente mf; business correspondence, correspondência comercial.

correspondent, n. correspondente mf.

cost¹, n. 1. custo m; cost, insurance and freight (CIF), custo, seguro e frete; the cost of a job, o valor de uma obra; cost of living, custo de vida; increased cost of living, aumento m no custo de vida; actual cost, net cost, custo real; depleted cost, custo exaurido; first cost, prime cost, custo primário; fixed cost, custo fixo; historical cost, custo histórico; operating costs, custos de operação, custos operacionais; replacement cost, custo de substituição; standard cost, custo standard, custo-padrão m; target cost, custo predeterminado; unit cost, custo unitário; variable cost, custo variável; weighted average cost, custo médio ponderado; cost account, conta ƒ de custos; cost accountant, contador m de custos, técnico m de contabilidade de custos; cost accounting, contabilidade ƒ de custos, contabilidade industrial; cost analysis, análise ƒ de custos; cost basis (of accounting), base ƒ de custo; cost–benefit analysis, análise de custos e benefícios; cost centre, centro m de custo, centro de cargas; cost conscious, cônscio dos custos; cost control, controle m dos custos; cost cutting, redução ƒ de custos; cost distribution, distribuição ƒ de custos; cost elements, determinantes mpl de custo; cost function, função ƒ custo; cost ledger, razão *m* de custos; **cost overrun,** custos superiores aos previstos; **cost-plus,** custo mais uma taxa determinada (em construção ou fabricação); **cost-plus pricing,** sistema *m* de preços baseado no acréscimo de uma taxa sobre os custos; **cost price,** preço *m* de custo; **cost rate,** taxa *f* de custo; **cost records,** registros *mpl* de custo; **cost recovery,** recuperação *f* de custos; **cost saving,** economia *f*, poupança *f*, de custos; **cost sheet,** folha *f* de custo, ficha *f* de custo; **cost system,** sistema *m* de apuração de custos; **cost unit,** unidade *f* de custo; **cost value,** valor *m* de custo; **to allocate costs,** apropriar custos; **to pass on costs,** repassar os custos; **to sell below cost,** vender abaixo do custo. **2.** *Jur:* custas *fpl*; **to be ordered to pay costs,** ser condenado ao pagamento das custas.

cost², *v.* **1.** *v.tr. & i.* custar; **how much does it cost?** quanto custa? **it costs five dollars,** custa cinco dólares; **a book costing $5,** um livro de cinco dólares; **the house cost $50 000,** a casa custou, ficou em, $50.000. **2.** *v.tr.* **to cost a product,** apurar, determinar, o custo de um produto.

cost-effective, *a.* economicamente rentável.

costing, *n.* custeio *m*, determinação *f*, apuração *f*, (de custos); **batch costing,** custeio por bateladas; **production costing,** contabilidade *f* industrial; **costing department,** seção *f* de contabilidade de custos.

costly, *a.* dispendioso.

cost-push, *n.* aumento *m* de custos de produção que provoca subida de preços ao consumidor.

cost-pusher, *n.* elemento provocador de elevação de preços.

cotton, *n.* algodão *m*; **cotton industry,** indústria algodoeira; **cotton trade,** comércio *m* de algodão; **cotton broker,** corretor *m* de algodão; **cotton futures,** vendas futuras de algodão, vendas de algodão para entrega futura; **spot cotton,** algodão para entrega imediata; **cotton wool,** algodão em rama; **cotton goods,** fazendas *fpl* de algodão, tecidos *mpl* de

algodão; **cotton farming,** cotonicultura *f*; **cotton grower,** cotonicultor *m*.

count, *v.tr.* contar.

counter, *n.* (*a*) *Bank:* caixa *f*; **counter clerk,** caixa *mf*; **counter cheque,** cheque avulso; (*b*) (*in shop*) balcão *m*; **counter clerk,** balconista *mf*, caixeiro *m*, caixeira *f*; **to sell goods under the counter,** vender mercadorias ilícita ou clandestinamente, *F:* vender mercadorias por baixo do pano; (*c*) *St.Exch:* **sales over the counter,** vendas *fpl* de balcão; **over-the-counter market,** mercado *m* de balcão.

counterclaim, *n.* *Jur:* alegação *f* em contrário.

counterfeit, *n.* dinheiro falsificado.

counterfeiting, *n.* falsificação *f*.

counterfoil, *n.* talão *m* (de cheque, conta, recibo, etc.), canhoto *m* (de talão de cheques); **counterfoil book,** talão, livro talonário; **counterfoil waybill,** canhoto de conhecimento.

counterman, *n.* *Am:* empregado *m* de balcão.

countermand, *v.tr.* contramandar, contra-ordenar.

counterpart, *n.* duplicado *m*, duplicata *f*, (de um documento); **counterpart funds,** fundos *mpl* de contrapartida.

countersign, *v.tr.* contra-assinar.

countersignature, *n.* contra-assinatura *f*, contra-firma *f*, segunda assinatura, (em cheque, etc.).

countervailing, *a.* **countervailing rate,** taxa compensatória.

coupon, *n.* cupão *m*, cupom *m*; **coupon redeemable for cash,** cupão conversível em dinheiro; **coupon holder,** possuidor *m* de cupão; **dividend coupon,** cupão de dividendo; **coupon bond,** obrigação *f* com cupão; **cum coupon,** com cupão; **ex coupon,** ex cupão; **coupon rate of interest,** taxa *f* de emissão (de uma obrigação).

cover¹, *n.* **1.** (*a*) *Ins:* cobertura *f*; **open cover,** cobertura aberta; **to operate without cover,** operar a descoberto; **accident cover,** cobertura contra acidentes; **cover note,** nota *f* de cobertura; (*b*) **to lodge stocks as cover for a loan,** depositar títulos em garantia de um empréstimo; (*c*) *St.Exch:* margem *f*;

cover percentage, percentagem *f* de cobertura. **2. under cover,** em envelope fechado; **to send sth. under separate cover,** enviar alguma coisa separadamente. **3. cover charge,** serviço *m* (em restaurante). **cover²,** *v.tr.* (*a*) cobrir (um risco); *Fin:* **to cover a bill,** providenciar o pagamento de uma letra de câmbio; *Ins:* **to be covered against fire, etc.,** ter seguro contra incêndio, etc.; (*b*) *St.Exch:* **to cover a short account,** cobrir um título a descoberto, uma conta a descoberto; **to cover a position,** cobrir uma posição; (*c*) **to cover (one's) expenses,** cobrir as despesas; **this money does not cover his debts,** este dinheiro não cobre as suas dívidas.

coverage, *n.* cobertura *f* (de riscos).

covering, *a.* (*a*) **covering letter,** carta explanatória (que acompanha documento ou pacote); (*b*) *St.Exch:* **covering purchases,** cobertura *f* de títulos a descoberto; aquisições *fpl* na bolsa.

crash, *n.* craque *m.*

crate, *n.* engradado *m*, caixa *f*, caixote *m.*

create, *v.tr.* **to create jobs,** gerar empregos.

credit¹, *n.* (*a*) crédito *m*; **to give s.o. credit,** conceder crédito a alguém; **to open a credit,** abrir um crédito; **to sell on credit,** vender a crédito, vender fiado; **goods on credit,** mercadorias vendidas a crédito; **letter of credit,** carta *f* de crédito; **line of credit,** linha *f* de crédito; **bank credit,** crédito bancário; **consumer credit,** crédito ao consumidor; **corporation credit,** crédito de corporação, crédito capital; **documentary credit,** crédito documentário; **export credit,** crédito ao exportador; **long credit,** crédito a longo prazo; **revolving credit,** crédito rotativo; **sixty days' credit,** crédito de sessenta dias, crédito concedido por sessenta dias; **trade, mercantile, credit,** crédito mercantil; **credit account,** conta *f* de crédito; **credit agreement,** acordo creditício; **credit analysis,** análise *f* de crédito; **credit arrangement,** acordos *mpl* de crédito; **credit bank,** banco *m* de crédito; **credit card,** cartão *m* de crédito; **credit cash,** crédito para retirada em dinheiro; **credit ceiling,** teto *m* de crédito; **credit company,** sociedade *f* de crédito; **credit department,** departamento *m* de crédito, carteira *f* de crédito; **credit expansion,** expansão *f* de crédito, ampliação *f* de crédito; **credit facilities,** facilidades *fpl* para obtenção de crédito; **credit information department,** serviço *m* de cadastro; **credit instrument,** instrumento *m* de crédito; **credit insurance,** seguro *m* de crédito; **credit limit,** limite *m* de crédito; **credit man,** investigador *m* cadastral; **credit manager,** chefe *mf* do departamento de crédito; **credit market,** mercado financeiro; **credit money,** moeda fiduciária; **credit nation,** nação credora; **credit need,** necessidade *f* de crédito, de financiamento; **credit note,** nota *f* de crédito; **credit operation,** operação *f* de crédito; **credit policy,** política creditícia, política de crédito; **credit rating,** (i) informações *fpl* cadastrais, (ii) avaliação *f* de crédito; **to have a good credit rating,** ter um bom cadastro bancário; **credit rationing,** restrição *f* de crédito; **credit restraint,** contenção *f* de crédito; **credit restriction,** restrição *f* de crédito, restrição ao crédito; **credit sale,** venda *f* a crédito; **credit squeeze,** arrocho *m* ao crédito; **credit use,** utilização *f* de crédito; (*b*) *Bank: Book-k:* **credit and debit,** crédito e débito; **credit balance,** saldo credor, saldo positivo; **the credit side (of an account),** o haver; **credit advice,** aviso *m* de crédito; **credit slip,** formulário *m* de depósito, papeleta *f* de depósito; **to enter a sum, pay a sum, to s.o.'s credit,** creditar uma importância a alguém; levar, lançar, uma importância ao crédito de alguém; **tax credit,** crédito fiscal; **frozen credits,** créditos congelados.

credit², *v.tr.* **to credit s.o. with $5000,** creditar $5.000 a alguém, creditar alguém em $5.000, levar $5.000 ao crédito de alguém; **please credit this amount to our current account,** favor creditar esta importância em nossa conta corrente.

creditor, *n.* credor *m*; **joint creditor,** co-credor *m*; **secured creditor,** (i) (*with mortgage*) credor hipotecário, (ii) (*with* *stocks, etc.*) credor pignoratício; **preferential creditor,** credor preferencial, credor privilegiado; **ordinary, unsecured, simple-contract, creditor,** credor quirografário; **creditors' meeting,** concurso *m* de credores; **creditor account,** conta credora; **creditor country,** país credor.

creditworthiness, *n.* capacidade creditícia.

credit-worthy, *a.* merecedor de crédito.

creeping, *a.* **creeping inflation,** inflação moderada.

crop, *n.* colheita *f*, safra *f*, lavoura *f*; **crop estimate,** estimativa *f* de safra, de colheita; **crop insurance,** seguro *m* de colheita; **crop lien,** penhor *m* agrícola; **crop rotation,** rotação *f* de culturas; **crop year,** ano *m* de colheita; **crop yield,** rendimento *m* das culturas.

cross¹, *a. Book-k:* **cross entry,** estorno *m*; **cross trade,** comércio cruzado; *Fin:* **cross rates,** taxas cruzadas.

cross², *v.tr.* **to cross a cheque,** cruzar um cheque; **crossed cheque,** cheque cruzado.

cross-section, *n. Stat:* seção *f* transversal (de população), faixa representativa.

crude, *a.* **crude materials,** matérias-primas *fpl*, produtos não beneficiados; bens intermédios; **crude rubber,** borracha natural, borracha não beneficiada; **crude steel,** aço bruto; **crude oil, petroleum,** petróleo *m* em bruto.

crunch, *n. Am:* **credit crunch,** arrocho *m* ao crédito.

cum, *prep. St.Exch:* **cum coupon,** com cupão; **cum dividend,** com dividendo.

cumulative, *a.* cumulativo; **cumulative dividend,** dividendo acumulado; **cumulative stock,** ação *f* capitalizável.

curbing, *n.* **curbing of inflation,** contenção *f* da inflação.

currency, *n.* **1.** moeda *f*; **payable in currency,** pagável em moeda corrente; **controlled currency,** moeda controlada; **convertible currency,** moeda conversível, convertível; **foreign currency,** divisas *fpl*, moeda estrangeira; **bill in foreign currency,** cambial *f*; **hard currency,** moeda forte; **legal (tender) currency,**

moeda corrente; **multiple currency bond,** título *m* com opção de câmbio; **paper currency,** papel-moeda *m*; **soft currency,** moeda fraca; **currency dealings,** operações *fpl* de câmbio, operações cambiais; **currency note,** moeda-papel *f*; **currency rates,** taxas *fpl* de câmbio, taxas cambiais; **currency reserves,** reservas *fpl* em divisas. **2. the currency of a bill of exchange,** o prazo de uma letra de câmbio.

current, *a.* corrente, atual; **current account,** conta *f* corrente, (*for international balance of payments*) transações *fpl* correntes, *St.Exch:* liquidação *f* corrente; **money on current account,** depósitos *mpl* à vista; **current asset(s),** ativo *m* corrente, ativo realizável a curto prazo; **current budget,** orçamento *m* corrente; **current cost,** custo *m* corrente, custo atual; **current expenditure,** despesa *f* corrente; **current income,** renda *f* corrente, (*of company*) receita *f* corrente; **current liabilities,** passivo *m* corrente; **current money,** dinheiro *m* corrente; **current month,** mês *m* em curso; **current price,** preço *m* corrente; *Book-k: Fin:* **current ratio,** quociente *m* de liquidez, coeficiente *m* de liquidez; *Ind:* **current standard cost,** custo *m* standard corrente; **current year,** ano *m* em curso.

custom, *n.* **1.** freguesia *f*, clientela *f*, (de um negócio, uma firma, etc.); **we are losing custom,** estamos perdendo freguesia; **a custom-built house,** uma casa construída sob encomenda; **a custom-made hat,** um chapéu feito sob encomenda. **2.** *pl.* **customs,** alfândega *f*, aduana *f*; **land (or airport) customs,** alfândega seca; **seaport customs,** alfândega marítima; **customs broker,** corretor *m* de alfândega, despachante aduaneiro; **customs clearance,** desembaraço alfandegário; **customs declaration,** declaração *f* de alfândega; **customs duties,** impostos alfandegários, direitos aduaneiros; **customs examination,** vistoria alfandegária, inspeção alfandegária; **customs formalities,** formalidades alfandegárias; **customs house,** alfândega, aduana; **customs**

officer, official, aduaneiro *m*, funcionário *m* de alfândega; customs seal, chancela alfandegária; customs tariff, pauta *f*, tarifa aduaneira; customs union, união alfandegária, união aduaneira; customs value, valor aduaneiro; customs visa, visto aduaneiro; to clear goods through customs, liberar mercadorias da alfândega; to pass through customs, passar pela alfândega.

customer, *n.* freguês *m*, freguesa *f*, (de uma loja), cliente *mf* (de uma empresa, banco, etc.); regular customer (of restaurant, etc.), freqüentador *m*, habitué *m*; *Bank:* current account customer, titular *mf* de conta corrente; customer needs, necessidades *fpl* do cliente; customer relations, relações *fpl* entre uma casa comercial e seus fregueses; to serve, attend to, the customers, atender os fregueses.

customhouse, *n. Am:* alfândega *f*.

cut¹, *n.* corte *m*, redução *f*,(de preços, etc.); price cuts, cortes nos preços, reduções de preços; expenditure cuts, cortes nas despesas, reduções de despesas.

cut², *v.tr.* to cut prices, reduzir, diminuir, os preços.

cutback, *n.* redução *f* (dos preços, taxas), corte *m* (nos gastos, nas despesas).

cut-off, *n.* cut-off date, data-limite *f*, *Book-k:* data *f* de interrupção de transações; cut-off point, ponto *m* limite.

cut-price, *a.* cut-price meat, carne vendida a preços reduzidos.

cut-throat, *a.* cut-throat competition, concorrência predatória, competição ruinosa.

cycle, *n.* business, trade, cycle, ciclo econômico.

cyclical, *a.* cyclical sales, vendas cíclicas.

D

dabble, *v.i.* **to dabble on the Stock Exchange,** especular, jogar, na Bolsa de Valores (de maneira intermitente, não como profissional).

dabbler, *n.* **dabbler on the Stock Exchange,** pessoa *f* que investe na Bolsa de Valores de maneira intermitente.

daily, *a.* diário, cotidiano; **the expenses of daily life,** as despesas da vida cotidiana; **to employ s.o. on a daily basis,** empregar alguém como diarista, por salário diário; **daily charge (in hotels, etc.),** diária *f*; **daily wage,** diária *f*, salário diário; **daily returns, takings,** receita diária, féria diária (em casa comercial, etc.); **daily (newspaper),** diário *m*, jornal cotidiano; *St.Exch:* **daily closing prices,** preços *mpl* de fechamento do dia; *Fin:* **daily loan,** financiamento, empréstimo, (concedido) por um dia.

dairy, *n.* 1. leiteria *f*; **co-operative dairy,** cooperativa *f* de leiterias; **dairy industry,** indústria *f* de lacticínios, indústria do leite; **dairy produce,** lacticínios *mpl*; **dairy farming,** criação *f* de gado leiteiro, (*on industrial scale*) lacticultura *f*. 2. **dairy (shop),** leiteria *f*.

dairying, *n.* indústria *f* de lacticínios, indústria do leite.

damage¹, *n.* 1. dano(s) *m(pl)*, prejuízo *m*, deterioração *f*; **damage in transit,** (i) dano em trânsito, (ii) *M.Ins:* (*to ships or their cargo*) avaria *f*; *M.Ins:* **damage survey,** avaliação *f* de avaria, de danos; **to suffer damage,** ser danificado, danificar-se, sofrer dano, deteriorar-se; *Jur:* **consequential damages,** danos conseqüentes. 2. *Jur:* indenização *f* por perdas e danos; **to bring an action for damages against s.o.,** intentar, mover, propor, ação de perdas e danos contra alguém; **to sue s.o. for damages,** mover ação de perdas e danos contra alguém; **to be entitled to claim damages,** ter direito a indenização por perdas e danos; **to pay damages,** pagar indenização por perdas e danos; **to be ordered to pay damages,** ser ordenado ao pagamento de uma indenização por perdas e danos.

damage², *v.tr.* (*a*) danificar, estragar, deteriorar, (mercadorias, equipamento, etc.); **the goods were damaged in transit,** as mercadorias foram danificadas em trânsito; (*b*) *M.Ins:* avariar.

damaged, *a.* danificado, deteriorado; avariado.

damp down, *v.tr.* **to damp down the market,** restringir, conter, o mercado; **to damp down consumption,** diminuir, reduzir, o consumo.

data, *n.pl.* (*occ. with sg. const.*) dados *mpl*; **data processing,** processamento *m* (de dados); **data processing card,** cartão perfurado, cartão; **to process data,** processar dados; **data processing system,** sistema *m* de processamento de dados; **data processing department,** seção *f* de processamento; **data handling,** tratamento *m* de dados; **data validation,** validação *f* de dados; **data storage,** armazenamento *m*, armazenagem *f*, de dados; **data retrieval,** recuperação *f* de dados; **data bank,** banco *m* de dados; **data terminal,** terminal *m* (de sistema de processamento de dados).

date¹, *n.* (*a*) data *f*; **delivery date,** data de entrega; **date stamp,** carimbo datador; (*b*) **up to date,** em dia; **to be up to date with instalments,** estar em dia com as prestações; **to be up to date with work,** andar, estar, em dia com o trabalho; **to bring, keep, the accounts up to date,** pôr, manter, a escrituração em dia; (*c*) **to date,** até esta data, até a presente data;

interest to date, juros vencidos até esta data; (d) out of date, fora de moda, antiquado, superado; (e) Fin: date of a bill of exchange, dias mpl de data, dias de vista, prazo m, de uma letra de câmbio; due date, date of maturity, vencimento m; final date, prazo m final, prazo fatal; to buy at long date, comprar a longo prazo; to buy at short date, comprar a curto prazo; to pay at fixed dates, pagar em vencimentos fixos.

date², v.tr. datar (uma carta); dating and numbering machine, máquina f de datar e numerar; to date back, antedatar; to date forward, pós-datar.

dated, a. (in compounds) Fin: long-dated, a longo prazo; short-dated, a curto prazo.

day, n. dia m; (considered as day's work, earnings, etc.) jornada f; an eight-hour day, um dia, uma jornada, de oito horas; 24 clear days, 24 dias inteiros e consecutivos; pay day, dia de pagamento; business day, working day, dia útil, dia de trabalho; day off, dia de folga; day labour, trabalho pago por jornada; day labourer, day worker, diarista mf; day rate, diária f, taxa diária; day shift, turno m do dia, turno diurno; St.Exch: settlement day, dia de liquidação; Nau: lay days, dias de estadia; days of demurrage, dias de sobreestadia; Fin: days of grace, dias de tolerância; day bill, letra a prazo fixo; day loan, financiamento m por um dia; day-to-day loan, empréstimo m sob chamada; one-day option, opção concedida por um dia.

daybook, n. diário m.

dead, a. (a) (inactive) dead season, baixa temporada; dead period, período de inatividade; dead mine, mina f estéril, improdutiva; dead law, lei extinta; Am: dead-letter office, seção de cartas não reclamadas (no correio); Fin: dead money, dinheiro improdutivo, dinheiro empatado; dead market, mercado inativo, mercado parado; (b) dead loan, empréstimo irrecuperável.

deadline, n. prazo m final, limite m de prazo; to meet a deadline, cumprir um prazo.

deadlock, n. impasse m; the talks reached a deadlock, as negociações chegaram a um impasse.

deadweight, n. Nau: peso bruto; the vessel has a deadweight capacity of X tons, a embarcação tem uma capacidade de deslocamento de X toneladas de porte bruto.

deal¹, n. negócio m, transação f; St.Exch: operação f; it's a deal, o negócio está fechado, está combinado; to close a deal, fechar um negócio, uma transação; to call off a deal, cancelar, desistir de, um negocio; firm deal, negócio firme; cash deal, operação à vista; option deal, operação de opção; package deal, contrato m global; deal on joint account, operação em conta de participação.

deal², v.i. 1. to deal with a piece of business, tratar de um negócio; to deal with a customer, atender um freguês; to deal with an order, atender uma encomenda, despachar um pedido. 2. to deal with s.o., tratar, comerciar, com alguém; to deal in grain, comerciar em, negociar com, cereais; Fin: to deal in options, negociar com opções.

dealer, n. (a) negociante mf, comerciante mf; coffee dealer, negociante de café; wool dealer, negociante de lã; Aut: etc: revendedor m, concessionário m; (b) distribuidor m, intermediário m comerciante, fornecedor m; retail dealer, varejista mf; dealer help, assistência f promocional ao varejista; wholesale dealer, atacadista mf; exchange dealer, agente mf de câmbio; antique dealer, antiquário m, comerciante de antiguidades; book dealer, livreiro m; (c) St.Exch: dealer m; operador m que negocia por conta própria; UK: licensed dealer, agente de títulos no mercado de balcão.

dealing, n. 1. dealing in wool, in platinum, comércio m de lã, de platina; St.Exch: dealings for the account, for the settlement, operações fpl a termo; Fin: forward dealings, operações cambiais a termo; share dealings, negócios mpl, operações, com ações; option dealings, negócios mpl com opções. 2. to have dealings with s.o., tratar de negócios com alguém, comerciar com alguém. **3. fair, square, dealing,** lealdade *f* nos negócios.

dear, *a.* **1.** caro, custoso; (*of food, etc.*) **to get dear, dearer,** subir, encarecer; **food is getting dearer every day,** os gêneros alimentícios sobem, encarecem, dia a dia; **2. Dear Sir,** Prezado Senhor, (*more formal*) Illmo. Senhor.

dearth, *n.* escassez *f*, penúria *f*, falta *f*, carência *f*, míngua *f*; *St.Exch:* **dearth of stock,** escassez de títulos.

death, *n.* **death rate,** mortalidade *f*, índice *m* de mortalidade.

debarkation, *n.* desembarque *m*; (*of ship*) descarga *f*, descarregamento *m*.

debenture, *n.* *Fin:* debênture *f*, obrigação *f*; **first, second, third, debenture,** debênture de primeira, segunda, terceira, ordem; **bearer debenture,** debênture ao portador; **floating debenture,** debênture com garantia flutuante; **fixed debenture,** debênture com garantia real; **mortgage debenture,** debênture hipotecária; **convertible debenture,** debênture conversível em ações; **issue of debentures, debenture issue,** emissão *f* de debêntures; **to issue debentures,** debenturar, emitir debêntures; **debenture holder,** debenturista *mf*, obrigacionista *mf*; **debenture register,** registro *m* de debêntures; **debenture loan,** empréstimo debenturístico; **debenture capital,** capital-obrigações *m*.

debit¹, *n.* débito *m*; *Book-k:* carga *f* de conta; **debit and credit,** débito e crédito; **debit entry,** partida devedora; **every debit has a corresponding credit,** cada partida devedora tem uma contrapartida credora; **the debit side (of an account),** o deve; **to enter a sum on the debit side of an account,** debitar uma conta (em uma determinada quantia), levar uma determinada quantia a débito de uma conta; **debit note,** nota *f* de débito; **debit advice,** aviso *m* de débito; **debit account,** conta devedora; **debit balance,** saldo devedor; **account showing a debit balance,** conta deficitária, conta devedora; **account showing a debit balance of $432,** conta que acusa, apresenta, um saldo devedor

de $432; *Book-k:* **debit column,** deve *m*; *Bank:* **direct debit,** débito direto.

debit², *v.tr.* debitar (uma conta); **to debit s.o. with a sum,** debitar a conta de alguém em uma importância, levar uma importância a débito de alguém; **to debit the expenses to his account,** debitar as despesas na sua conta.

debitable, *a.* **charge debitable to the profit and loss account,** despesa a ser debitada na conta de lucros e perdas.

debt, *n.* dívida *f*; **debt owed by us, by the firm,** dívida passiva; **debt owed to us,** dívida ativa; **acknowledgement of debt,** reconhecimento *m* de dívida; **bad debt,** dívida incobrável; **book debt,** dívida contábil; **claimable debt,** dívida reclamável, dívida quesível; (*on balance sheet*) **doubtful debts,** devedores duvidosos; **floating debt,** dívida flutuante; **funded debt, consolidated debt,** dívida fundada, dívida consolidada; **good debt,** dívida certa; **privileged debt,** dívida privilegiada; **the Public Debt, the National Debt,** a dívida pública; **secured debt,** dívida coberta, dívida garantida; **unsecured debt,** dívida quirografária; **debt collector,** cobrador *m* de dívidas; **debt management,** administração *f* da dívida pública; **debt service,** serviço *m*; **to be in debt,** dever dinheiro, ter dívidas; **to go, run, into debt,** endividar-se, contrair dívidas.

debtor, *n.* devedor *m*; **joint debtor,** co-devedor *m*; **absconding debtor,** devedor omisso; *Book-k:* **debtor side (of account),** deve *m*; **debtor account,** conta devedora.

decile, *n.* *Stat:* decil *m*.

decimal, *a.* **decimal point,** vírgula *f* decimal; **decimal system,** sistema *m* decimal.

decision, *n.* decisão *f*, resolução *f*; **to take a decision,** tomar uma decisão; **decision-making,** tomada *f* de decisões.

deck, *n.* **deck cargo,** carga *f* de convés.

declaration, *n.* (*a*) declaração *f*; **statutory declaration,** atestação *f*, (*actual document*) atestado *m*; **customs declaration,** declaração de alfândega; *Adm:* **declaration of income,** declaração de rendimentos, declaração de renda;

Fin: **declaration of a dividend,** declaração de um dividendo; *Jur:* **declaration of bankruptcy,** declaração de falência, decreto *m* judicial de falência; (*b*) *St.Exch:* **declaration of an option,** notificação *f* da intenção de exercer ou não uma opção.

declare, *v.tr.* declarar; **have you anything to declare?** o senhor tem alguma coisa a declarar? **nothing to declare,** nada a declarar; *Fin:* **to declare a dividend,** declarar um dividendo; *St.Exch:* **to declare an option,** notificar a intenção de exercer ou não uma opção.

declared, *a.* **declared value,** valor declarado; **declared income,** renda declarada.

decline[1], *v.* 1. *v.tr.* **to decline a liability,** declinar uma responsabilidade. 2. *v.i.* declinar, baixar, diminuir.

decline[2], *n.* declínio *m* (na economia, etc.); **the economy is in decline,** a economia está em declínio.

decontrol, *v.tr.* **to decontrol the price of meat,** liberar a carne (de controle determinado pelo Estado).

decrease[1], *n.* diminuição *f*, redução *f*; **decrease in exports,** diminuição de, em, exportações; **decrease in prices,** redução, diminuição, baixa *f*, nos preços; **our imports are on the decrease,** as nossas importações estão diminuindo.

decrease[2], *v.* 1. *v.tr.* **to decrease prices,** reduzir, diminuir, baixar, os preços. 2. *v.i.* diminuir, baixar.

decreasing, *a.* **decreasing cost,** custo *m* decrescente.

decree, *n.* decreto *m*; **decree-law,** decreto-lei *m*.

deduct, *v.tr.* deduzir, abater, (**from,** de); **to deduct a percentage from the price,** deduzir, abater, uma porcentagem do preço; **to be deducted,** a deduzir; **to deduct a discount (before payment),** descontar por antecipação; **to deduct 5% from wages,** descontar, deduzir, 5% do salário; **after deducting expenses, brokerage fees, etc.,** deduzidas as despesas, taxas de corretagem, etc.

deductible, *a.* dedutível.

deduction, *n.* dedução *f*, diminuição *f*,

abatimento *m*, desconto *m*; **deduction of expenses from taxable income,** dedução de despesas da renda tributável; **after deductions his take-home pay is $253,** após descontos, seu salário é $253; **deduction from wages,** desconto salarial, desconto do salário; **deduction at source,** desconto na fonte.

deed, *n.* escritura (pública), instrumento *m*; **deed of bargain and sale,** escritura de compra e venda; **title deed,** título de propriedade; **deed of transfer,** escritura de transferência; **deed of partnership,** escritura de associação; **deed of trust,** escritura de fideicomisso; **deed of assignment,** escritura de cessão; **to draw up a deed,** redigir uma escritura; **to execute a deed,** lavrar uma escritura, escriturar.

default[1], *n.* **default of loan terms,** inadimplemento *m*, inadimplência *f*, de condições de empréstimo; **default in paying,** falta *f* de pagamento; **default interest,** juros *mpl* de mora; **in default of payment,** na falta de pagamento, no caso de não pagamento.

default[2], *v.i.* **to default on instalments,** faltar com o pagamento de prestações, não pagar prestações; **to default on a contract,** inadimplir um contrato.

defaulter, *n.* descumpridor *m*; aquele que é inadimplente; *Jur:* revel *m*.

defaulting, 1. *a.* inadimplente. 2. *n.* (*of debtor, etc.*) inadimplemento *m*, descumprimento *m*.

defect, *n.* defeito *m*, falha *f*, imperfeição *f*; **manufacturing defect,** defeito, falha, de fabricação; **latent defect,** defeito latente; **patent defect,** defeito patente, defeito visível.

defective, *a.* defectivo, defeituoso.

defer, *v.tr.* **to defer a meeting,** adiar uma reunião; **to defer an expense,** diferir uma despesa.

deferment, *n.* adiamento *m*, diferimento *m*, (de pagamento).

deferred, *a.* **deferred asset,** ativo diferido; **deferred charge,** despesa diferida; **deferred credit,** crédito diferido; **deferred debit,** débito diferido; **deferred dividend,** dividendo *m* de pagamento diferido;

deferred expense, despesa diferida, pagamento antecipado; **deferred income,** renda diferida; **deferred liability,** (passivo *m*) exigível a longo prazo; **deferred maintenance,** despesas diferidas de manutenção, de conservação; manutenção diferida; **deferred payment,** (i) pagamento diferido, (ii) pagamento em prestações, pagamento a prazo; **cash or on deferred payments,** pagamento à vista ou a prazo.

deficiency, *n.* (*a*) déficit *m*; **to make up a deficiency,** cobrir um déficit; (*b*) déficit orçamentário; **deficiency bill,** crédito suplementar concedido ao governo pelo Banco da Inglaterra para cobrir um déficit; (*c*) **deficiency payment,** subvenção econômica (paga a produtores de gêneros alimentícios, agricultores, etc.); **deficiency account,** demonstração *f* do prejuízo do falido.

deficit, *n.* déficit *m*; **deficit account,** conta deficitária, conta de déficit; **deficit budget,** orçamento deficitário; **deficit financing,** financiamento deficitário; **deficit spending,** despesa deficitária; **balance of payments deficit,** déficit no balanço de pagamentos; **to make up the deficit,** cobrir o déficit.

deflate, *v.tr.* deflacionar.

deflation, *n.* deflação *f.*

deflationary, *a.* deflacionário; **deflationary policy,** política deflacionária; **deflationary measures,** medidas deflacionárias.

defraud, *v.tr.* defraudar, fraudar; **the employee defrauded the firm of 1 million cruzeiros,** o empregado defraudou a firma em um milhão de cruzeiros.

defray, *v.tr.* custear, correr com as despesas de, arcar com as despesas de, (algo); **to defray the rep's travelling expenses,** correr com as despesas de viagem do representante de vendas.

defrayal, *n.* custeamento *m*, custeio *m.*

defunct, *a.* **defunct company,** companhia extinta.

delay¹, *n.* atraso *m* (de pagamento, etc.).

delay², *v.tr.* atrasar (pagamento, entrega, etc.).

del credere, *n.* del-credere *m*; **del credere agent,** comissário *m* del-credere, agente *m* del-credere; **del credere commission,** del-credere *m*; **del credere contract,** (contrato *m*) del-credere.

deliver, *v.tr.* entregar (mercadorias, títulos, etc.); **'goods delivered free',** 'entregas a domicílio'; **delivered on board,** entregue a bordo; **delivered price,** preço *m* de mercadorias entregues.

deliverable, *a.* que pode ser entregue (imediatamente).

delivery, *n.* entrega *f*, (*from shop to home*) entrega a domicílio; *Jur:* tradição *f*; **delivery of goods,** entrega de mercadorias; **parcels awaiting delivery,** pacotes *mpl* a ser(em) entregues; **for immediate delivery,** para pronta entrega, para entrega imediata; **free delivery,** entrega gratuita; **delivery note,** guia *f*, nota *f*, de entrega; **delivery period,** prazo *m* para, de, entrega; **delivery date,** data *f* de entrega; **delivery within one month,** entrega dentro de um mês; **delivery man, boy,** caixeiro *m*, entregador *m*; **to pay on delivery,** pagar na entrega; **delivery schedule,** programa *m* de entregas; *Post:* **postal, mail, delivery,** distribuição *f* do correio; *Post:* **special delivery,** serviço *m* especial de entrega rápida; *St.Exch:* **delivery of stocks,** entrega de títulos; *St.Exch:* **to sell stocks for delivery,** vender títulos para pronta entrega, para entrega imediata.

demand, *n.* 1. (*of workers, etc.*) reivindicação *f*; **wage demands,** reivindicações salariais. 2. **payable on demand,** pagável à vista, pagável contra apresentação; **promissory note payable on demand,** (nota) promissória resgatável à vista, pagável contra apresentação; **demand bill,** letra *f* à vista; *Bank: Fin:* **demand deposit,** depósito a demanda, depósito à vista. 3. *Econ:* demanda *f*, procura *f*; **supply and demand,** oferta *f* e procura; **to meet demand,** suprir a demanda; **to be in demand,** estar procurado; **demand for a product,** procura de um produto, demanda para um produto; **there is little demand for this line,** esta linha está pouco procurada, há pouca demanda para este produto;

demand for labour, procura de mão-de-obra; **aggregate demand,** procura global; **expanding demand,** procura crescente; **derived demand,** procura derivada.
demonstration, *n.* demonstração *f* (de produto, aparelho, etc.).
demurrage, *n.* **1.** *Nau:* sobreestadia *f*, contra-estadia *f*; **demurrage charge,** taxa *f* de sobreestadia. **2.** *Rail:* (*a*) armazenagem *f*; (*b*) (taxa *f* de) armazenagem.
denationalization, *n.* desnacionalização *f*, desestatização *f.*
denationalize, *v.tr.* **to denationalize the coal industry,** desnacionalizar, desestatizar, a indústria carvoeira.
denomination, *n.* *Fin:* **notes in denominations of £5, £10 and £20,** notas *fpl* de £5, £10 e £20; **money of small denominations,** moeda *f* divisionária; **coins of all denominations,** moedas de todos os valores; **notes of small, large, denominations,** notas de pequeno, grande, valor.
department, *n.* **1.** (*a*) departamento *m*, repartição *f*, seção *f*, serviço *m*; **legal department,** departamento jurídico, contencioso *m*; **personnel department,** seção, departamento, de pessoal; **sales department,** departamento de vendas, departamento comercial; **accounts department,** contabilidade *f*; seção, departamento, de contabilidade; **dispatch department,** serviço de expedição; **packing department,** serviço de embalagem; **supply department,** almoxarifado *m*; **design department,** seção de desenho, departamento de desenho; **head of department,** chefe *mf* de departamento, de seção, de serviço; **to solve a problem between the departments concerned,** resolver um problema interdepartamental; (*b*) (*in shop*) **footwear department,** seção, departamento, de calçados; **department store,** loja *f* de departamentos. **2.** ministério *m*; *Am:* **Department of Commerce,** Ministério do Comércio.
departmental, *a.* **1.** (*a*) departamental; **departmental manager,** chefe *mf* de serviço; (*b*) **departmental store,** loja *f*

de departamentos. **2.** *esp. Am:* **at departmental level,** a nível ministerial.
depletable, *a. Book-k: etc:* exaurível.
depleted, *a. Book-k: etc:* depleted cost, custo exaurido, custo residual.
depletion, *n. Book-k: etc:* exaustão *f.*
deposit¹, *n.* **1.** *Bank:* depósito *m*; **on deposit,** em depósito; **deposit at seven days' notice,** depósito com pré-aviso de sete dias; **bank deposit,** depósito bancário; *Am:* **demand deposit,** depósito a demanda, depósito a ordem; *UK:* **fixed deposit,** *Am:* **time deposit,** depósito a prazo fixo; **safe deposit,** depósito em caixa-forte; **term deposit,** depósito de aviso prévio; **deposit account,** conta de depósito; **deposit banking,** operações bancárias com depósitos; **deposit slip,** formulário *m* de depósito; **to place, put, money on deposit,** depositar dinheiro, colocar dinheiro em depósito. **2.** (*on shop purchase*) sinal *m*; **to give a deposit on an item,** dar um sinal por um artigo; **20% deposit and 10 monthly instalments,** um sinal de 20% e 10 prestações mensais; **the landlord requires one month's rent deposit,** o dono de casa exige um mês de aluguel como caução.
deposit², *v.tr.* (*a*) **to deposit money in the bank,** depositar dinheiro no banco; **to deposit shares with a solicitor,** pôr ações na custódia de um advogado; *Publ:* **to deposit a work at the national library,** depositar uma obra na biblioteca nacional; (*b*) **to deposit $100,** penhorar, caucionar, cem dólares; pagar uma caução de cem dólares.
depositary, *n.* depositário *m.*
depositor, *n.* depositante *mf*, depositador *m.*
depository, *n.* depósito *m*, armazém *m*; **furniture depository,** depósito de móveis, guarda-móveis *m.*
depot, *n.* (*a*) depósito *m*, armazém *m*, entreposto *m*; (*b*) *Am:* (i) estação ferroviária, (ii) estação rodoviária.
depreciate, *v.* **1.** *v.tr.* depreciar, desvalorizar, (bens imóveis, mercadorias, etc.); **to depreciate a currency,** desvalorizar uma moeda. **2.** *v.i.* depreciar-se, desvalorizar-se; **the dollar**

has depreciated over the past two years, o dólar desvalorizou-se nos últimos dois anos.
depreciation, n. (a) depreciação f (de um bem imóvel, de ações, etc.), desvalorização f (de uma moeda); (b) Book-k: depreciação, amortização f; **annual depreciation,** depreciação anual; **depreciation charge,** taxa f de depreciação; **the straight-line method of depreciation,** depreciação pelo método linear, depreciação em linha reta; **the reducing-balance method of depreciation,** depreciação por saldo decrescente; **replacement-cost depreciation,** depreciação baseada no custo de recompletamento; **historic-cost depreciation,** depreciação do valor histórico; **provision for depreciation,** provisão f, previsão f, para depreciação; fundo m de depreciação; **depreciation reserve,** reserva f para depreciação; **depreciation accounting,** contabilidade f de depreciação; **depreciation is charged against the profit and loss account,** a taxa de depreciação é levada a débito da conta de lucros e perdas.
depress, v.tr. deprimir (a economia, o mercado, etc.).
depressed, a. **depressed prices,** preços deprimidos.
depression, n. depressão f.
deputy, n. delegado m, suplente mf, representante mf; **deputy chairman,** vice-presidente mf; **deputy manager,** subgerente mf; **deputy director,** diretor adjunto, subdiretor m; **to act as deputy for s.o.,** substituir, suprir, alguém.
description, n. descrição f; UK: **Trade Descriptions Act,** lei f sobre as descrições de produtos e serviços; Ind: etc: **job description,** descrição de cargos, descrição de tarefas.
design¹, n. (a) desenho m, projeto m; **a bid for the design and construction of a new factory,** uma proposta para o projeto e construção de uma nova fábrica; **architectural design,** desenho arquitetônico; **industrial design,** desenho industrial; **product design,** desenho de produto; **design engineer,** (engenheiro)

projetista mf; **design centre,** centro m de exposição de desenhos; (b) (model) modelo m; **this car is our latest design,** este carro é o nosso último modelo.
design², v.tr. desenhar, projetar, (objetos manufaturados, etc.); **to design a building,** projetar um edifício, fazer o projeto de um edifício.
designate, v.tr. designar, nomear; **the board designated him for a new post,** o conselho de administração designou-o, nomeou-o, para um novo cargo.
designation, n. designação f, denominação f, (de mercadorias, produtos, etc.).
designer, n. desenhista mf, projetista mf.
desk, n. (a) carteira f, escrivaninha f, secretária f; **desk pad,** bloco m (de notas); **desk job, desk work,** trabalho m de escritório; **desk room,** espaço alugado em escritório; Am: **desk man,** chefe m de escritório, supervisor m de escritório; (b) (in bank, store) **cash desk,** caixa f; **please pay at the desk,** favor pagar na caixa; (in hotel) **reception desk,** recepção f.
despatch, n. & v. = dispatch¹,².
determinable, a. Jur: **determinable contract,** contrato rescindível, contrato resilível.
determination, n. 1. determinação f (de preços, prazos, etc.). 2. Jur: rescisão f, resiliação f; **determination clause,** cláusula rescisória.
determine, v.tr. 1. determinar, fixar, definir, precisar, (data, prazo, etc.); **the price is determined by demand,** o preço é determinado pela procura; (in contract, etc.) **conditions to be determined,** condições a ser(em) determinadas, definidas, precisadas. 2. Jur: rescindir, resilir, (um contrato).
devaluation, n. desvalorização f.
devalue, v.tr. desvalorizar.
develop, v. 1. v.tr. (a) **to develop the economy,** desenvolver a economia; (b) (in building industry) **to develop a site,** construir sobre um terreno. 2. v.i. desenvolver-se; **the country developed rapidly after the war,** o país se desenvolveu rapidamente após a guerra.
developed, a. desenvolvido.

developer, *n.* **(property) developer,** empresário *m* de imóveis; incorporador *m* (de edifício de apartamentos, lojas, etc.).

developing, *a.* **developing country,** país *m* em desenvolvimento.

development, *n.* (*a*) desenvolvimento *m*; **economic development,** desenvolvimento econômico; **industrial development,** desenvolvimento industrial; **development agency,** agência *f* de desenvolvimento; **development area, zone,** zona *f* de desenvolvimento; **national development plan,** plano *m* nacional de desenvolvimento; **Brazilian development needs,** necessidades *fpl* do desenvolvimento brasileiro; (*b*) **property development,** empreendimento imobiliário; **property development company,** (empresa) imobiliária *f*; **residential development,** parque *m* residencial, conjunto *m* residencial; **a new housing development,** um novo conjunto habitacional, uma nova vila.

deviation, *n.* (*a*) *M.Ins:* desvio *m* (de navio da derrota); (*b*) *Stat:* **standard deviation,** desvio *m* padrão, afastamento *m* padrão, afastamento unitário.

diary, *n.* *Book-k: etc:* diário *m*, borrador *m*; **bill diary,** registro *m* de datas de vencimento de letras (de câmbio).

Dictaphone, *n.* *R.t.m:* ditafone *m*, máquina *f* de ditar.

dictate, *v.tr.* **to dictate a letter to a shorthand typist,** ditar uma carta para uma estenodatilógrafa.

dictation, *n.* ditado *m*; **to take dictation,** escrever o (texto) ditado; **to take dictation in shorthand,** estenografar, taquigrafar, um texto ditado.

difference, *n.* diferença *f*; **difference between the buying and selling price,** diferença entre o preço de compra e o preço de venda; *St.Exch:* **difference between cash and settlement prices,** reporte *m*.

differential, 1. *a. Cust:* **differential duties,** taxas *fpl* diferenciais; *Book-k:* **differential cost,** custo *m* diferencial, custo marginal. 2. *n.* **price differential,** disparidade *f* de preços, diferença *f* de preços; **wage differentials,** diferenças de

salário; *Ind:* **skill differentials,** adicionais *mpl* por habilitações.

digital, *a.* **digital computer,** computador *m* digital.

dip, *v.i.* (*of prices, etc.*) baixar.

direct¹, *v.tr.* dirigir, administrar, (uma firma, uma fábrica, etc.).

direct², *a.* direto; **direct advertising,** propaganda direta; **direct cost,** custo direto; **direct costing,** custeio direto; **direct expenses,** despesas diretas; **direct labour,** mão-de-obra direta; **direct liability,** passivo direto, exigibilidade direta; **direct mailing,** comercialização direta pelo correio; **direct price,** preço direto, preço de fábrica; **direct selling,** venda direta; **direct tax,** imposto direto; **direct taxation,** tributação direta.

direction, *n.* direção *f*, administração *f*, (de fábrica, etc.).

director, *n.* diretor *m*, diretora *f*, (*specifically board member*) administrador conselheiro *m*; **director general,** diretor geral; **board of directors,** conselho *m* de administração, diretoria *f*; **directors' emoluments,** remuneração *f* total dos diretores, dos administradores; **directors' fees,** honorários *mpl* da diretoria, dos administradores; **directors' report,** relatório *m* da diretoria, do conselho de administração; **managing director,** diretor gerente, diretor superintendente; **marketing director,** diretor de marketing, de comercialização; **director's qualification (shares),** (ações *fpl* de) garantia *f* de gestão de diretor.

directorate, *n.* diretoria *f*.

directorship, *n.* direção *f*, diretoria *f*; **to assume the directorship of a factory,** assumir a direção de uma fábrica.

directory, *n.* 1. **telephone directory,** catálogo telefônico, lista telefônica; **trade directory,** anuário *m* do comércio, anuário comercial. 2. *Am:* conselho *m* de administração, diretoria *f*.

directress, *n.* *N.Am:* diretora *f*, administradora *f*.

disburse, *v.tr.* 1. (*a*) desembolsar, despender, gastar; (*b*) (*defray*) custear; **to disburse travelling expenses,** correr com as despesas de viagem. 2. *N.Am:*

distribuir; **to disburse 100 tons of wheat,** distribuir 100 toneladas de trigo.
disbursement, *n.* (*a*) desembolso *m*, gasto *m*; **the disbursement of a government loan,** o pagamento de um empréstimo do governo; (*b*) **disbursements for research projects,** custeio *m* de projetos de pesquisa, fundos *mpl* para projetos de pesquisa; *Am:* **disbursement office,** pagadoria *f* (em repartição pública, etc.).
discharge¹, *n.* **1. discharge of a ship,** descarga *f*, descarregamento *m*, de um navio; **discharge of a cargo,** descarregamento de uma carga; **discharge of a ton of bananas,** descarregamento de uma tonelada de bananas. **2. discharge in bankruptcy,** reabilitação *f* (de falido); **to apply for discharge,** solicitar reabilitação. **3. discharge of a debt,** pagamento *m*, extinção *f*, de uma dívida; **discharge of a debtor from all liabilities,** quitação *f*, liberação *f*, de um devedor de todas as suas obrigações. **4. discharge of a contract,** execução *f*, adimplemento *m*, cumprimento *m*, de um contrato. **5.** (*dismissal*) demissão *f*, destituição *f*, (de alguém de um cargo ou função).
discharge², *v.tr.* **1.** descarregar (um navio, mercadorias de um navio). **2.** *Jur:* reabilitar (um falido); **discharged bankrupt,** falido reabilitado. **3. to discharge a debt,** saldar, pagar, uma dívida; **to discharge s.o. from a debt,** quitar, liberar, alguém de uma dívida; **to discharge one's liabilities,** cumprir (com) as suas obrigações (financeiras); **to discharge an account,** apurar, liquidar, uma conta. **4. to discharge a contract,** executar, adimplir, cumprir, um contrato. **5. to discharge an employee,** demitir, destituir, despedir, um empregado.
dischargeable, *a.* **1.** (falido *m*) reabilitável. **2.** (dívida *f*) pagável.
disclosure, *n.* divulgação *f* de informações sobre as demonstrações; *St.Exch:* disclosure *m*.
discount¹, *n.* (*a*) desconto *m*, abatimento *m*; **to sell at a discount,** vender com desconto, com abatimento; **to give, allow,**

a 10% discount, conceder um desconto, um abatimento, de 10%; **discount for quantities, quantity discount,** desconto por quantidade, desconto quantitativo; **cash discount,** desconto, abatimento, à vista; **seasonal discount,** desconto da temporada; **promotional discount,** desconto promocional; **to allow a discount of 10% off the retail price,** conceder um desconto de 10% sobre o preço a varejo; **discount shop, store,** loja *f* de abatimentos, loja de descontos; (*b*) *Fin:* desconto *m*; **discount rate,** taxa *f* de desconto; **bank discount,** desconto bancário; **true discount,** desconto real; **the discount market,** o mercado aberto, o open market, o open; **discount house,** instituição financeira que desconta letras de câmbio, letras do Tesouro e outros títulos; (*c*) *St.Exch:* deságio *m*; **to be, stand, at a discount,** estar com deságio.
discount², *v.tr.* **to discount bills of exchange,** descontar letras de câmbio; *Book-k: etc:* **discounted cash flow,** valor *m* presente de fluxo de caixa futuro.
discounter, *n.* **1.** descontador *m*. **2.** *Am:* loja *f* de abatimentos, loja de descontos.
discounting, *n.* desconto *m*; **discounting banker,** banco *m* de desconto.
discrepancy, *n.* discrepância *f*, discordância *f*; **statistical discrepancy,** discrepância estatística; **there are certain discrepancies in the accounts,** a escrituração apresenta certas discrepâncias.
discretion, *n.* *Jur:* **in the discretion of the board of directors,** a critério da diretoria.
discretionary, *a.* discricionário; **discretionary power,** poder discricionário; **discretionary income,** renda *f* pessoal disponível após a dedução de pagamentos obrigatórios; *St.Exch:* **discretionary order,** ordem *f* de compra a valor fixo sem especificação dos títulos a ser(em) comprados.
dishonour¹, *n.* recusa *f* de aceite (de uma letra); recusa de pagamento (de um cheque).
dishonour², *v.tr.* **to dishonour a bill,** recusar o aceite de uma letra; **to dishonour a cheque,** recusar o pagamento

de um cheque; **dishonoured cheque,** cheque devolvido por insuficiência de fundos.
dismiss, *v.tr.* demitir, destituir, despedir, (alguém).
dismissal, *n.* demissão *f*, destituição *f*; **notice of dismissal,** aviso prévio dado pelo empregador; **unfair dismissal,** demissão sem motivo justo; **lawful dismissal,** demissão por justa causa.
dispatch¹, *n.* **1.** expedição *f*, envio *m*, remessa *f*; **the dispatch of an order,** a expedição de uma encomenda; **dispatch note,** guia *f* de remessa, nota *f* de remessa; **dispatch department,** (serviço *m* de) expedição. **2.** (*a*) **the dispatch of current business,** o despacho de negócios correntes; (*b*) *Nau:* **dispatch money,** prêmio pago por redução de estadia.
dispatch², *v.tr.* **1. to dispatch a letter,** enviar, remeter, expedir, uma carta; **to dispatch goods,** expedir, despachar, mercadorias. **2. to dispatch current business,** despachar negócios correntes.
dispatcher, *n.* despachante *mf*, expedidor *m*.
dispatching, *n.* expedição *f*, envio *m*, remessa *f*, (de mercadorias, etc.).
dispenser, *n.* vendedora automática; **cash dispenser,** caixa automática.
display¹, *n.* exposição *f*; **on display,** em exposição; **display window, display cabinet, display case,** vitrina *f*; **display unit,** mostrador *m*, mostruário *m*; **display board,** painel *m* (para comunicação visual); *Cmptr:* **visual display unit (VDU),** terminal *m* vídeo.
display², *v.tr.* expor (mercadorias).
disposable, *a.* (*a*) disponível; **disposable personal income,** renda *f* pessoal disponível; **disposable funds,** disponibilidades *fpl*; **disposable assets,** ativo *m* disponível; (*b*) **disposable packaging,** embalagem *f* descartável.
disposal, *n.* (*a*) disposição *f*; **at the customers' disposal,** à disposição da freguesia; **we shall be at your disposal the whole day,** estaremos à sua disposição o dia inteiro; **he always places the car at my disposal,** ele sempre põe o carro à minha disposição; (*b*) venda *f*, traspasse *m*, (de

um negócio), *Jur:* alienação *f*, cessão *f*; **for disposal by public auction,** a ser vendido em leilão, a ser leiloado.
dispose, *v.i.* (*a*) **to dispose of adequate resources for investment,** dispor de recursos suficientes para investimento; (*b*) **to dispose of a consignment of goods on the open market,** vender, colocar, uma partida de mercadorias no mercado livre; **to dispose of a shop,** transferir uma loja; *Jur:* **to dispose of a property,** alienar um imóvel.
dispute, *n.* questão *f*, divergência *f*, diferença *f*; **to settle disputes arising from this contract,** dirimir, resolver, questões decorrentes deste contrato; **labour dispute,** conflito *m* trabalhista, *Jur:* dissídio coletivo.
distribute, *v.tr.* distribuir; **to distribute goods to local wholesalers,** distribuir mercadorias aos atacadistas locais; **to distribute a dividend,** distribuir um dividendo; **distributed profit,** lucro distribuído.
distribution, *n.* distribuição *f*, repartição *f*; **distribution of tasks,** distribuição, divisão *f*, de tarefas; **distribution channel, channel of distribution,** canal *m* de distribuição; **distribution cost,** custo *m* de distribuição; **distribution network,** rede *f* de distribuição; *M.Ins:* **distribution of average,** repartição de avaria; *Fin:* **distribution of a dividend,** distribuição de um dividendo; *Fin:* **distribution of debts,** repartição de dívidas.
distributor, *n.* distribuidor *m*, intermediário *m* comerciante; *Am:* atacadista *mf*.
district, *n.* distrito *m*; **district manager,** gerente *mf* distrital.
disturbed, *a.* **disturbed market,** mercado agitado.
dividend, *n.* dividendo *m*; **dividends in arrears,** dividendos atrasados; **dividend on registered shares,** dividendo de ações nominativas; **cash dividend,** dividendo em dinheiro; **cum dividend, dividend on,** com dividendo; **ex dividend, dividend off,** ex dividendo; **final, year-end, dividend,** dividendo final; **interim dividend,** dividendo intermediário; **preferred (stock)**

dividend, dividendo de ação preferencial; **scrip dividend, stock dividend,** dividendo em ações; **unclaimed dividends,** dividendos não reclamados; **to claim a dividend,** reclamar um dividendo; **to declare a dividend,** declarar um dividendo; **to draw a dividend,** receber um dividendo; **dividend warrant,** ordem *f* de pagamento de dividendo.

dock, *n.* doca *f*; **to work in the docks,** trabalhar nas docas; **dry dock,** doca seca; **floating dock,** doca flutuante; **(wharf) loading dock,** doca de embarque; **unloading dock,** doca de desembarque.

dockage, *n.* **1.** (*a*) atracagem *f*; (*b*) (*payment*) taxa *f* de atracagem; (*c*) (*facilities*) instalações portuárias. **2.** dedução *f* de salário ou preço (por dano ou defeito, etc.).

docker, *n.* doqueiro *m*, estivador *m*.

docket, *n.* (*a*) guia *f* (de entrega, remessa, etc.); (*b*) (*label*) etiqueta *f*; (*c*) recibo *m* da alfândega.

dockyard, *n.* estaleiro *m*.

document, *n.* documento *m*; (*legal*) instrumento *m*; **notarized document,** instrumento público; **working document,** documento de trabalho; **shipping documents,** documentos de embarque, documentação *f* de embarque; **payment against documents,** pagamento *m* contra apresentação de documentos.

documentary, *a.* documentário; **documentary bill,** letra *f* de câmbio acompanhada de documentos; **documentary credit,** crédito documentário.

dollar, *n.* (i) dólar *m* (do Canadá, Austrália, Baamas, Barbados, etc.), (ii) dólar (americano); **dollar area,** zona *f* do dólar; **a five-dollar bill,** uma nota de cinco dólares; **the dollar crisis,** a crise do dólar; **dollar diplomacy,** diplomacia *f* do dólar; **dollar exchange,** letra *f* de câmbio sacada e pagável em dólares fora dos Estados Unidos; **dollar certificate of deposit,** certificado *m* de depósito em dólares; *Econ:* **dollar balances,** saldos *mpl* em dólares.

domestic, *a.* **domestic market,** mercado interno, mercado nacional; **domestic**

production, output, produção *f* nacional; **domestic products,** produtos *mpl* nacionais, produtos de fabricação nacional; **domestic trade,** comércio *m* interno; *Econ:* **gross domestic product,** produto interno bruto.

domicile[1]**,** *n.* domicílio *m*.

domicile[2]**,** *v.tr.* **to domicile a bill,** determinar o lugar em que uma letra de câmbio deve ser paga; **bill domiciled in the United Kingdom,** letra *f* de câmbio pagável no Reino Unido.

domiciliary, *a.* **domiciliary bill,** letra *f* pagável em determinado lugar.

domiciliation, *n.* determinação *f* do lugar de pagamento de uma letra de câmbio.

doorstep salesman, *n.* vendedor *m* de porta em porta.

door-to-door, *a.* door-to-door **(selling, canvassing, etc.),** (venda *f*, angariação *f*) de porta em porta.

dotted, *a.* **dotted line,** picote *m*, linha picotada; **tear out on the dotted line,** destaque no picote.

double, *a.* **double taxation,** dupla tributação; *Am:* **double liability,** responsabilidade dupla; *Book-k:* **double entry,** partida dobrada; **double-entry book-keeping,** escrituração *f* por partidas dobradas, contabilidade *f* a partidas dobradas.

doubtful, *a. Book-k:* **doubtful debts,** devedores duvidosos.

down, *a.* **down payment,** entrada *f*.

down-market, *a.* **down-market goods,** mercadorias destinadas a consumidores de renda baixa.

downsurge, *n. Fin:* queda repentina.

downtown, *n. Am:* centro *m* comercial (de uma cidade).

downtrend, *n.* tendência *f* para a baixa.

downturn, *n.* diminuição *f*, baixa *f*; **downturn in profits,** uma baixa nos lucros; **business showed a downturn,** o comércio acusou, apresentou, uma baixa.

downward, *a.* **downward trend,** tendência *f* para a baixa.

dozen, *n.* dúzia *f*; **half a dozen,** meia dúzia; **six dozen eggs,** seis dúzias de ovos; **to sell items in dozens, by the dozen,** vender artigos às dúzias.

draft¹, *n.* **1.** rascunho *m*, minuta *f*; **to make a draft of a letter,** rascunhar uma carta, fazer o rascunho de uma carta; **draft contract,** minuta de contrato. **2.** *Fin:* saque *m*, letra *f* de câmbio; **the tenor of a draft,** o prazo de um saque, de uma letra de câmbio; **banker's draft,** saque bancário; **sight draft,** saque à vista; **time draft,** saque a termo; **to make a draft on s.o.,** emitir um saque contra alguém. **3.** *Am: Nau:* **the draft of a ship,** o calado de um navio.

draft², *v.tr.* (*a*) **to draft a letter,** minutar, rascunhar, uma carta; **to draft a new contract,** minutar, fazer a minuta de, um novo contrato; (*b*) (*frame*) **to draft the chairman's report,** redigir o relatório do presidente.

drafter, *n.* redator *m.*

drafting, *n.* redação *f* (de um documento).

drain¹, *n.* **drain on capital,** esgotamento *m* de capital; **drain on the economy of the country,** depauperamento *m* da economia do país.

drain², *v.tr.* esgotar, exaurir, (recursos, capital); depauperar (a economia).

draper, *n.* fanqueiro *m*, negociante *mf* de fazendas.

draught, *n. Nau:* calado *m*; **the draught of a ship,** o calado de um navio.

draw, *v.* **1.** *v.tr.* (*a*) **to draw a salary,** perceber, receber, um salário; **to draw a commission,** receber uma comissão; (*b*) **to draw a cheque on a bank,** emitir, sacar, um cheque contra um banco; **to draw a bill of exchange,** sacar uma letra de câmbio; (*c*) **to draw a bond for redemption,** sortear uma obrigação para resgate. **2.** *v.i.* **to draw on s.o. for $100,** sacar contra alguém uma quantia no valor de $100; **to draw on an account,** sacar sobre uma conta.

drawback, *n. Cust:* drawback *m.*

drawee, *n.* sacado *m.*

drawer, *n.* sacador *m*, emitente *mf* (de cheque, etc.); (*on cheque*) **refer to drawer,** devolvido por insuficiência de fundos.

drawing, *n.* **1.** saque *m*; **drawing account,** conta *f* corrente; *Econ:* **special drawing rights,** direitos *mpl* especiais de saque. **2.**

the drawings of a trader or partner, as retiradas de um negociante ou sócio. **3. drawing of bonds for early redemption,** sorteio *m* de obrigações para resgate antecipado.

dress up, *v.tr. F:* **to dress up the accounts,** falsificar a escrituração.

drive, *n.* campanha *f*; **sales drive,** campanha de vendas; **higher output drive,** campanha para aumento de produção.

drop¹, *n.* queda *f*, baixa *f*, (nos preços, etc.); **a slight drop in profits,** uma ligeira queda nos lucros.

drop², *v.i.* baixar, cair; **receipts dropped last month,** as receitas baixaram, acusaram uma baixa, no mês passado; **gold dropped two dollars yesterday,** o ouro caiu (em) dois dólares ontem; **the shares dropped two points,** as ações baixaram dois pontos.

dry, *a.* **dry goods,** fazendas e artigos de armarinho em geral; *Am:* **dry goods store,** = (*approx.*) armarinho *m*, loja *f* de miudezas.

dud, *a. F:* **dud stock,** estoque *m* invendável; **dud cheque,** cheque *m* sem fundos, *F:* cheque frio, cheque borrachudo; **dud note,** cédula falsa, nota falsa.

due, *a.* **1.** devido, exigível, pagável; **bill due on May 1st,** letra *f* de câmbio com vencimento em 1º de maio, vencida em 1º de maio; **balance due,** saldo *m* a pagar, saldo devedor; **the balance due to us (from customers),** o saldo a receber (de clientes); **debts due to us,** dívidas ativas; **debts due from us, by us,** dívidas passivas; **bond due for repayment on June 5th,** obrigação a ser resgatada em 5 de junho; (*of bill, etc.*) **to fall, become, due,** vencer (-se); **bill falling due on July 6th,** letra *f* a vencer em, com vencimento em, 6 de julho; **due date,** (data *f* de) vencimento; **redemption (of bond) before due date,** resgate antecipado (de obrigação). **2. in due form,** na devida forma, nos devidos termos; **contract drawn up in due form,** contrato redigido nos devidos termos; **in due time,** no momento devido, na hora oportuna.

dues, *n.pl.* direitos *mpl*, taxas *fpl*; **taxes and dues,** impostos *mpl* e taxas; **port dues,**

harbour dues, taxas portuárias, direitos portuários; *Am: Ind:* **union dues,** contribuição ƒ sindical.

dull, *a.* (*of market*) inativo.

dump, *v.tr. & i. Econ:* fazer dumping.

dumping, *n.* dumping *m*; lançamento *m* de produtos no mercado internacional pelo preço de custo ou abaixo do custo.

duplicate, 1. *a.* duplicado; **duplicate receipt,** duplicata ƒ de recibo. **2.** *n.* duplicado *m*, duplicata ƒ; **please send in applications in duplicate,** favor enviar requerimentos em duas vias, em duplicata; **duplicate book,** bloco *m* (de faturas, recibos, etc.) em duas vias.

duplicate², *v.* **1.** *v.tr.* **to duplicate 50 copies of a report,** duplicar, multigrafar, 50 cópias de um relatório. **2.** *v.i. Book-k:* (*of entry*) ser lançado duas vezes.

duplicating, *n.* **1. duplicating machine,** duplicador *m*; **spirit duplicating machine,** hectógrafo *m*, duplicador a álcool; **duplicating paper,** (*for spirit duplicating machine*) papel hectográfico; **stencil duplicating machine,** mimeógrafo *m*. **2.**

Book-k: duplo lançamento de uma partida.

durable, *a.* **durable goods,** bens *mpl* duráveis.

dutiable, *a.* sujeito a impostos, taxável; *Cust:* sujeito a impostos alfandegários.

duty, *n.* imposto *m*, direito *m*, taxa ƒ; **customs duty,** imposto aduaneiro, direito alfandegário, taxa alfandegária, direito de alfândega; **liable to duty,** sujeito a imposto; **countervailing, compensatory, duties,** impostos, direitos, aduaneiros compensatórios; **import, export, duty,** imposto de importação, de exportação; **import duty on cars,** imposto de importação sobre automóveis; **to take the duty off certain goods,** isentar certas mercadorias de direitos de alfândega; **stamp duty,** imposto do selo.

duty-free, *a.* livre de impostos, isento de impostos; **duty-free zone,** zona franca; **duty-free goods,** mercadorias *fpl* livres de impostos; **duty-free shop,** (a loja) duty-free ƒ.

E

each-way, *a. St.Exch:* **each-way transaction,** operação *f* em que o comprador e o vendedor são representados pelo mesmo corretor.

early, *a.* **1.** *UK:* **early closing day,** dia *m* em que o comércio fecha mais cedo. **2. an early reply,** uma reposta rápida, uma pronta resposta; **early settlement,** liquidação rápida, pronto pagamento; **at an early date,** dentro em breve; **at your earliest convenience,** o mais breve possível, com a possível urgência; **negotiations are at an early stage,** as negociações estão em estágio inicial. **3. early redemption,** resgate antecipado; **early repayment,** reembolso antecipado; **early termination of contract,** rescisão antecipada de contrato.

earmark¹, *n.* **1.** *Adm: etc:* sinal distintivo. **2.** *Fin:* **under earmark for s.o.,** destinado para alguém, a alguém.

earmark², *v.tr.* **1. to earmark a document,** marcar um documento (com um sinal, etc.). **2.** *Fin:* **to earmark funds,** destinar, reservar, alocar, fundos **(for, para); to earmark funds for a specific purpose,** alocar verbas para um fim específico; **to earmark funds for the construction of a new factory,** alocar, destinar, fundos para a construção de uma nova fábrica; **funds earmarked for investment,** fundos destinados, reservados, para investimento; **to earmark securities,** reservar valores; **earmarked account,** conta alocada para determinado fim; **earmarked gold,** ouro *m* em custódia; **earmarked revenue,** receita vinculada.

earn, *v.tr.* **1.** ganhar, perceber, (salário, ordenado, etc.); **to earn a living,** ganhar a vida; **earned income,** rendimento *m* do trabalho individual. **2.** (*of securities,*

investments, etc.) render; **these bonds earn 7% a year,** estes títulos rendem 7% ao ano; **earned surplus,** lucros não distribuídos; *Ins:* **earned premium,** parte *f* de prêmio retida pelo segurador quando se cancela uma apólice antes do vencimento.

earner, *n.* **earner of foreign exchange,** produtor *m* de divisas.

earnest, *n.* arras *fpl,* sinal *m,* penhor *m;* **earnest money,** sinal em dinheiro.

earning, 1. *n.* **earning power,** (*of individual*) salário máximo que uma pessoa pode conseguir no mercado de trabalho, capacidade *f* salarial, (*of security*) rentabilidade *f* (de um título). **2.** *a.* **earning assets,** títulos *mpl* de rendimento (de banco).

earnings, *n.pl.* (*a*) salário *m,* ordenado *m,* (*of civil servant, etc.*) vencimento *m;* **my earnings were down this month,** ganhei menos neste mês; **loss of earnings,** perda *f* de salário; *Ins: etc:* **pensionable earnings,** salário de contribuição; (*b*) (*profit*) lucro *m;* **gross earnings,** lucro bruto; **net earnings,** lucro líquido; **earnings per share,** lucro por ação; **earnings statement,** demonstração *f* de lucros e perdas; (*c*) (*income*) receita *f,* renda *f,* rendimentos *mpl* (de empresa, etc.); **invisible earnings (of a country),** rendimentos invisíveis (de um país).

ease, *v.* **1.** *v.tr.* (*a*) atenuar, diminuir, reduzir, abaixar, baixar; **the Bank of England should ease the minimum lending rate,** o Banco da Inglaterra deveria reduzir a taxa mínima de empréstimos; (*b*) **to ease the money supply,** facilitar os meios de pagamento; **to ease terms of credit,** facilitar as condições de crédito. **2.** *v.i.* baixar, atenuar-se, amainar; **the gold**

61

price eased yesterday, o preço do ouro atenuou-se ontem.
easement, n. Jur: servidão f.
ease off, v.i. St.Exch: (of prices, etc.) baixar, diminuir, atenuar-se, amainar.
easiness, n. facilidade f; easiness of money, facilidade de dinheiro.
easing, n. easing of the capital market, abrandamento m, atenuação f, do mercado de capitais.
easy, a. 1. fácil; easy payment, pagamento facilitado, pagamento a prestação, pagamento em prestações; easy payments plan, crediário m, facilitário m; to buy on easy terms, comprar a prestação, comprar a crédito, comprar fiado. 2. easy market, mercado calmo, mercado acessível; the coffee price is getting easier, o preço do café está se tornando mais acessível; cotton became easier, o algodão baixou.
echelon, n. escalão m; the executive echelons of the corporation, os escalões executivos da empresa.
econometrician, n. econometrista mf.
econometrics, n.pl. (usu. with sg. const.) econometria f.
economic, a. (a) econômico; the European Economic Community, a Comunidade Econômica Européia; the present economic situation, a conjuntura econômica atual; economic background, base econômica; economic behaviour, comportamento econômico; economic climate, clima econômico; economic crisis, crise econômica; economic development, desenvolvimento econômico; economic distress, desequilíbrio econômico; economic forecasting, previsão econômica; economic goods, bens mpl econômicos; economic growth, crescimento econômico; economic inducement, incentivo econômico; economic management, gestão econômica; economic mismanagement, má administração econômica; economic policy, política econômica; economic survey, pesquisa econômica; Pol.Ec: economic indicators, indicadores econômicos; (b) to be economic, ser lucrativo, ser rentável, render; the project

was not economic owing to the high costs, o projeto não rendeu devido aos altos custos; (c) Am: economic council, organismo constituído de todos os setores da economia que age em capacidade consultiva ou com poder direto.
economical, a. the most economical means of transport, os meios de transporte mais econômicos.
economics, n.pl. (usu. with sg. const.) 1. economia f, ciências econômicas; administrative economics, economia administrativa; applied economics, economia aplicada; welfare economics, economia social e previdencial, economia do bem-estar social. 2. (a) the economics of the export operation are promising, a operação de exportação promete um bom rendimento; (b) the economics of town planning, os aspectos econômicos do urbanismo.
economist, n. economista mf.
economize, v.i. economizar, fazer economias.
economy, n. 1. economia f; the economy of a country, a economia de um país; controlled, managed, planned, economy, economia dirigida; open economy, economia aberta; closed economy, economia fechada; market economy, economia de mercado; mixed economy, economia mista; political economy, economia política; agricultural economy, economia agrícola. 2. pl. economies, economias, economies of scale, economias de escala; to achieve economies in manufacturing costs, fazer economias nos custos de fabricação. 3. domestic economy, economia doméstica. 4. to travel in economy class, viajar em classe econômica, em classe turística.
effect[1], n. 1. (a) efeito m; the effects of the economic crisis, os efeitos da crise econômica; the effects on exports, os efeitos nas exportações, sobre as exportações; (b) to take effect, (i) (of regulation, etc.) entrar em vigor, (ii) (of contract) surtir, produzir, efeito; to be in effect, estar em vigor, vigorar, viger; with effect from January 1st, a partir de 1º de janeiro; we are making provisions to this

effect, estamos tomando providências neste sentido. 2. **personal effects**, bens *mpl* pessoais, objetos *mpl* de uso pessoal, *Jur:* bens móveis.

effect², *v.tr.* efetuar, efetivar, realizar, executar; **to effect payment of a bill**, fazer, efetuar, o pagamento de uma conta; **to effect an insurance**, fazer um seguro.

effective, *a.* 1. (*a*) efetivo; **effective cost of holding idle cash**, custo efetivo da posse de dinheiro inativo; **effective demand**, demanda efetiva; **effective exchange rate**, taxa *f* de câmbio em vigor; (*b*) **effective date**, data *f* de entrada em vigor; **the effective date of a loan**, a data de entrada em vigor de um empréstimo; **as from the effective date of this law**, a contar da data de entrada em vigor desta lei; **the regulations will be effective on, as from, 10 October**, o regulamento vigorará a partir de 10 de outubro. 2. eficaz, eficiente; **an effective administrator**, um administrador eficaz.

efficiency, *n.* (*a*) eficiência *f*, eficácia *f*; **economic efficiency**, eficiência econômica; **efficiency expert**, técnico *m* em estudos de eficiência; (*b*) rendimento *m* (de máquina, etc.).

efficient, *a.* **efficient manager**, gerente *mf* eficaz, eficiente; **efficient working (of machine)**, bom funcionamento; **efficient machine**, máquina *f* eficiente, de grande rendimento.

efflux, *n. Pol.Ec:* **efflux of capital**, saída *f* de capitais.

ejectment, *n. Jur:* ação *f* de recuperação de bens.

elastic, *a.* **elastic supply, demand**, oferta *f*, procura *f*, elástica.

elasticity, *n. Pol.Ec:* **the elasticity of supply and demand**, a elasticidade da oferta e procura; **income elasticity of demand**, elasticidade-renda *f* de procura.

electronic, *a.* eletrônico; **electronic computer**, computador eletrônico; **electronic data processing**, processamento eletrônico (de dados); **electronic engineer**, engenheiro eletrônico; **electronic technician**, técnico eletrônico.

electronics, *n.pl.* (*usu. with sg. const.*)

eletrônica *f*; **the electronics industry**, a indústria eletrônica.

eligible, *a.* **eligible paper**, títulos *mpl* redescontáveis.

embargo¹, *n.* (*a*) fechamento *m* dos portos; (*b*) restrição *f* legal imposta ao comércio; (*c*) proibição *f*; **to put an embargo on the import of horses**, proibir a importação de cavalos; **to lift an embargo**, levantar, suspender, uma proibição; (*d*) *Nau:* embargo *m*, arresto *m*, (de um navio); **to lay an embargo on a ship**, pôr um embargo a um navio.

embargo², *v.tr.* 1. *Nau:* embargar, arrestar, (um navio, etc.). 2. requisitar (um navio, mercadorias, etc.).

embark, *v.* 1. *v.tr.* (*a*) embarcar (mercadorias ou passageiros); (*b*) **to embark one's money in a venture**, investir, inverter, seu dinheiro num empreendimento. 2. *v.i.* (*of passengers*) embarcar(-se).

embarkation, *n.* embarque *m*; **port of embarkation**, porto *m* de embarque.

embezzle, *v.tr.* malversar, desfalcar; **he embezzled a thousand dollars from the firm**, malversou, desfalcou, mil dólares da firma.

embezzlement, *n.* desfalque *m*, malversação *f*, peculato *m*.

embezzler, *n.* malversador *m*, peculador *m*.

emolument, *n.* remuneração *f*.

employ, *v.tr.* (*a*) empregar, contratar, (alguém); (*b*) *Fin:* investir, empregar, (capitais); (*in financial statements, etc.*) **(net) capital employed**, patrimônio (líquido) empregado.

employee, *n.* empregado *m*; *Adm:* **employee's contribution**, contribuição previdenciária (do empregado); **employee participation**, participação *f* (dos empregados) nos lucros; **employee benefits**, vantagens *fpl* adicionais, benefícios *mpl* extras (para os empregados).

employer, *n.* empregador *m*, patrão *m*; (*as body*) **the employers**, os empregadores, a classe patronal: **employers' association**, sindicato *m* patronal, organização *f* patronal; *Adm:* **employer's contributions**,

encargos *mpl* sociais; **employers' liability insurance,** seguro *m* de responsabilidade patronal, seguro dos empregadores contra acidentes de trabalho.
employment, *n.* **1.** (*use*) emprego *m,* aplicação *f,* (de fundos, recursos, etc.). **2.** (*occupation*) emprego, colocação *f,* trabalho *m;* **to be in employment,** estar empregado, ter emprego; **to be without employment,** estar sem emprego, estar desempregado, não ter emprego; **employment agency,** agência *f* de emprego(s); **contract of employment,** contrato *m* de trabalho; **employment market,** mercado *m* de trabalho; **place of employment,** local *m* de trabalho; **to enjoy security of employment,** ter estabilidade no emprego; **full-time employment,** trabalho de tempo integral; **part-time employment,** trabalho de tempo parcial, trabalho de meio expediente; **temporary employment,** trabalho temporário; *Pol.Ec:* **full employment,** pleno emprego.
emporium, *n.* empório *m.*
empties, *n.pl.* cascos *mpl;* **returned empties,** cascos devolvidos.
emption, *n. Jur:* compra *f;* **right of emption,** direito *m* de compra.
en bloc, *adv.* em conjunto.
encash, *v.tr.* **to encash a cheque,** descontar, receber, um cheque.
encashable, *a.* descontável.
enclose, *v.tr.* incluir, juntar, anexar; **to enclose a cheque with a letter,** anexar um cheque a uma carta; **to enclose a list of members with a report,** anexar uma lista de sócios a um relatório; (*in correspondence*) **enclosed herewith, please find enclosed,** anexa-se à presente, segue anexo, (um relatório, etc.).
enclosure, *n.* (documento) anexo *m.*
end¹, *n.* fim *m,* término *m,* final *m,* (do mês, ano, etc.); **at the end of the month,** no fim do mês; **at the end of the financial year,** ao fim do exercício; **to bring sth. to an end,** pôr fim a, dar fim a, ultimar, algo; **to come to an end,** ter fim, chegar ao fim, terminar(-se), acabar; **end product,** produto *m* final, produto acabado.
end², *v.* **1.** *v.tr.* terminar, acabar, concluir,

encerrar; **to end a meeting,** encerrar, terminar, uma reunião; **to end economic aid,** suspender, acabar com, a ajuda econômica. **2.** *v.i.* terminar(-se), acabar, expirar; **your subscription ends on May 31st,** sua assinatura expira em 31 de maio.
endorsable, *a.* **endorsable share,** ação *f* endossável.
endorse, *v.tr.* endossar (documento, cheque, etc.); **to endorse a document with a signature,** endossar um documento com uma assinatura; **to endorse a cheque over to s.o.,** endossar um cheque a, para, alguém; **to endorse a bill of exchange,** endossar uma letra de câmbio; **endorsed bond,** título endossado.
endorsee, *n.* endossado *m,* endossatário *m.*
endorsement, *n.* (*a*) endosso *m,* endossamento *m;* **blank endorsement, endorsement in blank,** endosso em branco; **full endorsement,** endosso em presto, endosso pleno, endosso completo, endosso nominativo; *Jur:* **endorsement pledging as collateral,** endosso em caução, endosso em garantia, endosso pignoratício, endosso-caução *m;* **endorsement giving power of attorney,** endosso procuratório, endosso mandatício, endosso-mandato *m;* (*b*) *Ins:* cláusula *f* suplementar a uma apólice de seguro.
endorser, *n.* endossante *mf,* endossador *m.*
endow, *v.i.* (*of insurance policy*) vencer(-se).
endowment, *n.* dotação *f;* **endowment insurance,** seguro *m* dotal; **endowment mortgage,** crédito imobiliário ligado com seguro dotal; **endowment policy,** apólice *f* dotal.
engineer, *n.* engenheiro *m;* **civil engineer,** engenheiro civil; **consulting engineer,** engenheiro consultor; **design engineer,** (engenheiro) projetista *mf;* **electrical engineer,** engenheiro eletricista; **electronic engineer,** engenheiro eletrônico; **hydraulic engineer,** (engenheiro) hidráulico *m;* **maintenance engineer,** técnico *m* de manutenção; **marine engineer,** engenheiro naval; **mechanical engineer,** engenheiro

mecânico; **metallurgical engineer,** engenheiro metalúrgico; **mining engineer,** engenheiro de minas; **planning engineer,** engenheiro de planejamento; **product development engineer,** engenheiro de desenvolvimento de produto; **production engineer,** engenheiro de produção; **quality control engineer,** engenheiro de controle de qualidade; **(work) safety engineer,** engenheiro de segurança (do trabalho).

engineering, *n.* engenharia *f*; **chemical engineering,** engenharia química; **civil engineering,** engenharia civil; **electrical engineering,** engenharia elétrica; **electrical engineering works,** fábrica *f* de aparelhagem elétrica; **light engineering,** engenharia leve; **marine engineering,** engenharia naval; **mechanical engineering,** engenharia mecânica; **production engineering,** engenharia de produção; **engineering consultant,** engenheiro consultor; **engineering data,** dados técnicos; **engineering department,** departmento *m* de engenharia; **the engineering industry,** a indústria de maquinaria pesada, (*mechanical*) a indústria mecânica; **engineering works, factory,** fábrica *f* de construção de máquinas, fábrica de maquinaria pesada.

enter, *v.* 1. *v.tr. Cust:* (*a*) **to enter goods,** dar entrada de mercadorias; **to enter inwards,** dar entrada (de mercadorias) para importação; **to enter outwards,** dar entrada (de mercadorias) para exportação; (*b*) **to enter (an item) in the ledger,** lançar, registrar, (uma partida) no livro-razão; **to enter an amount against s.o.,** levar, passar, uma importância a débito de alguém; debitar uma importância à conta de alguém; **to enter a share transfer in the share register,** averbar uma transferência de ações no livro de registro de ações; (*c*) **to enter a mortgage at the land registry,** inscrever uma hipoteca no cadastro imobiliário. 2. *v.i.* **to enter into relations,** estabelecer relações; **to enter into negotiations,** iniciar, entrar em, negociações; **to enter into an agreement,** entrar num acordo, concluir um acordo; *Jur:* **to enter into the**

rights of a creditor, estar subrogado aos direitos de um credor.

entering, *n.* (*a*) inscrição *f*, averbação *f*; (*b*) *Book-k:* escrituração *f*, lançamento *m*; **entering clerk,** escriturário *m*.

enterprise, *n.* **free enterprise (economy),** (economia de) livre-empresa *f*; **private enterprise,** a empresa particular, a empresa privada, o setor privado; **state enterprise,** empresa estatal; **enterprise cost,** custo *m* de aquisição de um bem para o proprietário atual; **small-scale enterprise,** empresa pequena, empresa de pequeno porte.

entrepreneur, *n.* empresário *m*, empreendedor *m*.

entry, *n.* (*a*) *Book-k:* lançamento *m*, partida *f*, registro *m*; **single entry,** lançamento simples, partida simples; **compound entry,** lançamento composto, partida composta; **double entry,** partida dobrada, lançamento dobrado, lançamento duplo, registro duplo; **double-entry book-keeping,** escrituraçao *f* por partidas dobradas, contabilidade *f* a partidas dobradas; **contra entry,** contrapartida *f*, contralançamento *m*; **reversing entry, cross entry,** (lançamento de) estorno *m*; **adjusting entry,** lançamento de retificação; **red ink entry,** lançamento em vermelho, lançamento negativo; **wrong entry,** lançamento incorreto, lançamento errado; **to make, post, an entry,** lançar uma partida; **to make an entry of a transaction,** lançar, escriturar, contabilizar, uma transação; **to make an entry against s.o.,** debitar alguém; levar, passar, uma importância a débito de alguém; (*b*) *Cust:* **to make an entry of goods,** dar entrada de mercadorias; **entry inwards,** entrada *f* para importação; **entry outwards,** entrada para exportação; **bill of entry,** nota *f* de entrada; **entry under bond,** entrada sob caução; (*c*) **entry (in a register),** averbação *f*, inscrição *f*, (num livro de registro).

envelope, *n.* envelope *m*; **to put (sth.) in an envelope,** colocar (algo) num envelope; **window envelope,** envelope de janela; **adhesive envelope,** envelope adesivo;

envelope with metal fastener, envelope com fecho metálico; **envelope file,** pasta *f;* (*of bid, etc.*) **in a sealed envelope,** em envelope lacrado, em envelope selado; **airmail envelope,** envelope aéreo; **stamped addressed envelope,** envelope selado e sobrescritado.

equalization, *n.* (*a*) **equalization of wages,** equiparação *f,* nivelamento *m,* de salários; (*b*) **equalization of dividends,** regularização *f* **equalization account,** conta *f* de regularização; **equalization reserve,** reserva *f* para regularização.

equalize, *v.tr.* (*a*) equiparar, nivelar, (salários, etc.); (*b*) regularizar (dividendos).

equate, *v.tr.* **to equate the expenses with the income,** igualar, equiparar, as despesas e a renda.

equation, *n.* *Book-k:* **accounting equation,** igualdade *f* contábil, equação *f* contábil.

equip, *v.tr.* **to equip a factory with new machinery,** equipar, aparelhar, uma fábrica com nova maquinaria.

equipment, *n.* equipamento *m;* **office equipment,** equipamento *m* de escritório; *Fin: etc:* **capital equipment,** imobilizado técnico, (ativo) imobilizado.

equity, *n.* 1. *Jur:* (*a*) eqüidade *f;* (*b*) **equity of redemption,** direito *m* de resgate. 2. *Fin:* direito *m* sobre o patrimônio (de uma empresa); **equity capital, equities,** ações *fpl* ordinárias; **equity market,** mercado *m* de ações.

equivalence, *n.* equivalência *f,* paridade *f; Fin:* **equivalences of exchange,** paridades *fpl* de câmbio.

equivalent, *a.* equivalente; **to be equivalent to,** equivaler a, ser equivalente a; **sum equivalent to £1000 sterling,** importância *f* equivalente a mil libras esterlinas.

error, *n.* erro *m;* **error of calculation,** erro de cálculo; **accounting, book-keeping, error,** erro de escrituração, de contabilidade; **clerical error,** erro de escriturário; **errors and omissions excepted (E. & O. E.),** salvo erro ou omissão (S. E. O.); **sent by error,** enviado por engano; **printing error,** erro

tipográfico, erro de imprensa; **typing error,** erro de datilografia, erro datilográfico; *Stat:* **standard error,** erropadrão *m;* **tally error,** erro de registro; **grouping error,** erro de agrupamento; **sampling error,** erro de amostragem.

escalate, *v.i.* aumentar, subir, (rapidamente).

escalation, *n.* (*a*) aumento rápido *m,* subida rápida; (*b*) (*in contract for services, etc.*) **escalation clause,** cláusula *f* de reajustamento.

escalator, *n.* (*in collective agreement*) **escalator clause,** cláusula *f* de reajustamento.

escapable, *a.* *Book-k:* **escapable cost,** custo evitável.

escape, *n.* **escape clause,** cláusula *f* que permite a revogação ou retratação de um contrato.

establish, *v.tr.* **to establish a firm,** estabelecer, fundar, criar, uma firma; **to establish a tax on alcohol,** estabelecer, criar, um imposto sobre bebidas alcoólicas; **to establish oneself in business,** estabelecer-se, instalar-se, nos negócios; **to establish oneself in a job,** estabelecer-se num emprego.

establishment, *n.* (*a*) estabelecimento *m* (de uma indústria), abertura *f,* criação *f,* fundação *f,* (de uma casa comercial); (*b*) **business establishment,** estabelecimento (comercial), casa comercial; *Book-k:* **establishment charges,** despesas *fpl* de administração geral, despesas gerais; custos indiretos.

estate, *n.* 1. patrimônio *m,* bens *mpl;* **the estate of the late Mr X,** o espólio, a herança, do finado Sr. X; *UK:* **estate duty,** imposto *m* sobre transmissão de propriedade *causa mortis.* 2. (*a*) herdade *f,* quinta *f;* (*b*) **real estate,** bens *mpl* de raíz, bens imóveis, bens imobiliários; **a piece of real estate,** um pedaço de terra; **estate agent,** agente imobiliário, corretor imobiliário, corretor de imóveis; **estate agency,** agencia imobiliária, corretora imobiliária; (*c*) **residential estate,** parque *m* residencial, conjunto *m* residencial; *UK:* **housing estate,** conjunto de habitações pequenas (geralmente alugadas por órgão público); (*approx.*) vila *f*; **the Churchill Housing Estate,** a Vila Churchill.

estimate[1], *n.* (*a*) estimativa *f*; **an estimate of net income,** uma estimativa de renda líquida; **precise estimate,** estimativa exata; **rough estimate,** aproximação *f*, estimativa aproximada; **these figures are a rough estimate,** estas cifras são aproximativas; **to give an estimate of annual output,** dar uma estimativa da produção anual; (*b*) (*for a job, etc.*) orçamento *m*; **free estimate without obligation,** orçamento grátis sem compromisso; **estimate of cost,** estimativa de custo; **rough estimate,** orçamento aproximado; **preliminary estimate,** orçamento preliminar; **building estimate,** orçamento para uma obra de construção; **estimate of expenditure,** orçamento de despesas.

estimate[2], *v.* 1. *v.tr.* (*a*) estimar, fazer estimativa de, (custo, produção, etc.); **the insurance company estimated the loss at £1500,** a companhia de seguros estimou o prejuízo em 1.500 libras esterlinas; (*b*) orçar, fazer orçamento para, (obra, etc.). 2. *v.i.* **to estimate for a painting job,** orçar, fazer orçamento para, uma obra de pintura.

estimated, *a.* **estimated cost,** custo estimado; **estimated value,** valor estimado.

Euro-bond, *n. Fin:* Euro-obrigação *f*.

euro-currency, *n.* euro-moeda *f*; **eurocurrency deposits,** depósitos *mpl* em euro-moedas.

Euro-dollar, *n.* eurodólar *m*.

Euro-loan, *n. Fin:* Euro-empréstimo *m*.

European, *a.* europeu, *fem.* européia; **the European Economic Community,** a Comunidade Ecônomica Européia; **the European Free Trade Area,** a Area Européia de Livre-Comércio; **European Currency Unit (ECU),** Unidade Monetária Européia.

evaluate, *v.tr.* avaliar (casa, quadros, etc.).

evaluation, *n.* avaliação *f*; **job evaluation,** avaliação *f* de cargos.

evasion, *n.* (tax) evasion, sonegação *f* (de impostos).

even, *a.* **even lot,** lote redondo.

eviction, *n. Jur:* despejo *m*; **eviction order,** mandado *m* de despejo.

ex, *prep.* 1. (*out of*) **ex store,** entregue no armazém do vendedor, no depósito do vendedor; **ex works,** entregue na fábrica do vendedor; **price ex works,** preço *m* na porta da fábrica (do vendedor); **ex wharf, ex quay,** desembarcado no cais, posto no cais. 2. (*without*) **ex dividend,** ex dividendo; **ex rights,** ex direitos; **stock quoted ex rights,** ações cotadas ex direitos; **this stock goes ex coupon on 1st August,** estas ações serão cotadas ex dividendo a partir de 1º de agosto.

exceed, *v.tr.* ultrapassar, exceder; **to exceed the share capital by 50%,** ultrapassar o capital-ações em 50%; **the expenditure exceeds the receipts,** as despesas excedem as receitas.

excess, 1. *n.* excesso *m*, excedente *m*; **in excess,** em excesso; **excess of revenue over expenditure,** excedente de receitas sobre despesas. 2. *a.* **excess luggage,** excesso *m* de bagagem; **excess weight,** excesso de peso; **excess load,** sobrecarga *f*, carga excessiva; *Fin:* **excess reserves,** reservas *fpl* excedentes; **excess profits (tax),** (imposto *m* sobre) lucros extraordinários.

exchange[1], *n.* 1. troca *f*, permuta *f*, câmbio *m*; **exchange and barter,** troca e permuta; (*car sales, etc.*) **part-exchange deal,** troca; **we take your old car in part exchange,** aceitamos seu carro usado como entrada, como parte do pagamento; *Fin:* **share exchange,** permuta de ações. 2. (*a*) **foreign exchange,** divisas *fpl*, câmbio; **foreign exchange broker,** corretor *m* de câmbio; **foreign exchange dealer,** agente *mf* de câmbio; **foreign exchange dealings,** operações *fpl* cambiais, operações de câmbio; **foreign exchange earner,** produtor *m* de divisas; **foreign exchange earnings,** receitas *fpl* em divisas, lucros *mpl* em divisas, rendimentos *mpl* em divisas; **foreign exchange market,** mercado *m* de câmbio, mercado cambial; **foreign exchange rate,** taxa *f* de câmbio, câmbio; **at the current rate of exchange,** à

taxa atual de câmbio; **foreign exchange reserves**, divisas *fpl* (estrangeiras); **forward exchange**, operações *fpl* cambiais a termo; **exchange control**, fiscalização *f* cambial, controle *m* de câmbio; **exchange premium**, ágio *m* para contrato de câmbio; **exchange value**, valor *m* cambial; **floating exchange rate**, câmbio flutuante; **official exchange rate**, câmbio oficial; **unofficial exchange rate**, câmbio negro, câmbio paralelo; (*b*) **bill of exchange**, letra *f* de câmbio, cambial *f*; **first of exchange**, primeira via de uma cambial; **second of exchange**, segunda via de uma cambial; **third of exchange**, terceira via de uma cambial; (*c*) *Am:* (*usu.* **exchanges**) letras *fpl* de câmbio, saques *mpl* e outros efeitos. **3.** bolsa *f*; **commodities exchange**, bolsa de mercadorias; **corn exchange**, bolsa de cereais; **stock exchange**, Bolsa de Valores. **4. telephone exchange**, central telefônica.
exchange², *v.* **1.** *v.tr.* trocar, permutar, cambiar; **no perishables exchanged**, não trocamos mercadorias perecíveis; **to exchange one thing for another**, trocar uma coisa por outra; **to exchange shares**, permutar ações; **non-convertible currencies are only exchanged at head office**, moedas não-conversíveis só podem ser trocadas na sede. **2.** *v.i.* **the pound is exchanging better**, a cotação da libra melhorou.
exchangeable, *a.* trocável, cambiável, permutável.
exchanger, *n.* trocador *m*; *Fin:* cambista *mf.*
exchequer, *n.* **the Exchequer**, (i) o fisco, o erário, a fazenda pública, (ii) tesouro público; *UK:* **Chancellor of the Exchequer**, Ministro da Fazenda; *UK:* **exchequer bill**, letra *f* do tesouro; *UK:* **exchequer bond**, título *m* de dívida pública não fundada.
excise¹, *n.* **1.** imposto *m* indireto; imposto de licença (para determinadas atividades); imposto de consumo; imposto sobre produtos industrializados; **excise duty**, imposto de consumo (sobre determinadas mercadorias). **2.** diretoria *f*

de impostos indiretos; **Customs and Excise**, diretoria da alfândega e de impostos indiretos; **Excise Officer**, (i) fiscal *m* de impostos indiretos, (ii) coletor *m* de impostos indiretos.
excise², *v.tr.* tributar, taxar, (bebidas alcoólicas, artigos de luxo, etc.).
exciseman, *n. UK:* (i) fiscal *m* de impostos indiretos, (ii) coletor *m* de impostos indiretos.
exclusion, *n. Ins:* exclusão *f.*
exclusive, **1.** *a.* **car for his exclusive use**, carro *m* para seu uso exclusivo; **exclusive sales contract**, contrato *m* de venda exclusiva; **exclusive of packaging**, gastos *mpl* de embalagem excluídos. **2.** *n. Am:* direito exclusivo (de venda, distribuição, etc.).
execute, *v.tr.* **to execute a task**, executar uma tarefa; **to execute a contract**, lavrar um contrato.
execution, *n.* execução *f* (de uma obra, etc.); lavratura *f* (de um contrato, uma escritura).
executive, **1.** *a.* **executive board**, conselho executivo; **executive position**, cargo executivo; **executive director**, diretor executivo; **executive secretary**, secretária executiva. **2.** *n.* executivo *m*; **sales executive**, executivo de vendas.
exempt¹, *a.* isento, franco, livre, (de impostos, direitos, etc.); **exempt from import duty**, isento do imposto de importação.
exempt², *v.tr.* isentar, franquear, eximir, (de impostos, etc.).
exemption, *n.* isenção *f*, franquia *f*; **exemption clause**, cláusula *f* de isenção.
exercise¹, *n.* (*a*) exercício *m*, desempenho *m*, (de uma função, etc.); (*b*) *St.Exch:* **exercise of an option**, exercício de uma opção.
exercise², *v.tr.* (*a*) exercer, desempenhar, (função, etc.); (*b*) **to exercise preferential rights**, exercer direitos preferenciais; *St.Exch:* **to exercise an option**, exercer uma opção.
ex gratia, **1.** *a.* **ex gratia payment**, pagamento efetuado a título de favor. **2.** *adv.* a título de favor; **he was not entitled to a pension, but the firm gave him a lump**

sum **ex gratia,** ele não tinha direito a uma pensão, mas a empresa lhe pagou um capital a título de favor.

exhaustion, *n.* exaustão *f*, esgotamento *m*, (de recursos).

exhibit, *v.tr.* **1. to exhibit large profits,** apresentar grandes lucros. **2. to exhibit goods in a shop window,** expor mercadorias em uma vitrina.

exhibition, *n.* exposição *f*; **the Car Exhibition,** o Salão do Automóvel; **exhibition stand,** stand *m* de exposições; **exhibition room,** sala *f* de exposições.

exhibitor, *n.* (*at exhibition*) expositor *m*.

expanding, *a.* **expanding market,** mercado *m* em expansão.

expansion, *n.* expansão *f*; **monetary expansion,** expansão monetária.

expectancy, *n. Ins:* **life expectancy,** probabilidade *f* de vida; **life expectancy table,** tábua *f* de mortalidade.

expenditure, *n.* despesa *f*, dispêndio *m*, gasto *m*; **public expenditure,** despesa(s) pública(s); **capital expenditure,** despesas de capital; *Book-k:* **expenditure rate,** taxa *f* de dispêndio.

expense, *n.* **1.** despesa *f*, gasto *m*, dispêndio *m*; **carriage is at our expense,** o transporte corre por nossa conta; **free of expense,** livre de despesas; **no expense involved,** livre de despesas, gratuito; **with all expenses paid,** com todas as despesas pagas; **advertising expenses,** despesas publicitárias, despesas com publicidade; **general expenses,** despesas gerais; **incidental expenses,** (despesas) eventuais *fpl*; **legal expenses,** despesas jurídicas, despesas legais; **petty expenses,** despesas miúdas; **the preliminary expenses of a company,** as despesas de instalação, as despesas de organização, de uma companhia; **selling expenses,** despesas com vendas; **total expenses incurred,** total *m* das despesas feitas; **travelling expenses,** despesas de viagem; **to incur expenses,** fazer despesas; **expense account,** conta *f* de despesas; **expense budget,** orçamento *m* de despesas (autorizadas); *Book-k:* **expense allocation,** apropriação *f* de despesas; *Book-k:* **expense centre,** centro *m* de cargas, centro de custo, centro de

custeio, (de operações); *Book-k:* **expense grouping,** grupamento *m* de despesas. **2.** (*allowance*) *pl.* **expenses,** ajuda *f* de custo; **to allow s.o. his expenses,** reembolsar as despesas de alguém.

expensive, *a.* caro, dispendioso, custoso.

expensiveness, *n.* **the expensiveness of imported foodstuffs,** o alto custo de produtos alimentícios importados.

experience, *n.* experiência *f*, vivência *f*, (de um cargo, em um cargo, etc.).

expert, 1. *a.* perito, especialista; **to be expert,** ser perito (**at, in,** em); **expert opinion,** parecer *m*. **2.** *n.* perito *m*, especialista *mf*; **the new manager is a marketing expert,** o novo gerente é um perito em marketing; **the experts are investigating the matter,** a perícia está investigando o assunto, os peritos estão investigando o assunto; **expert's report,** laudo *m* pericial; **court expert,** perito judicial.

expertise, *n.* perícia *f* (**in,** em).

expiration, *n.* expiração *f* (de um prazo para inscrição, etc.).

expire, *v.i.* expirar; **the registration period expires on the 31st of December,** o prazo para inscrição expira em 31 de dezembro.

expiry, *n.* expiração *f* (de um contrato de arrendamento, etc.).

export¹, *n.* **1.** (*article exported*) artigo exportado; *pl.* **exports,** exportações *fpl*; **visible, invisible, exports,** exportações visíveis, invisíveis; **the U.K. is increasing her exports to Brazil,** o Reino Unido está aumentando suas exportações para o Brasil. **2.** (*exporting*) exportação *f*; **for export,** para exportação; **export bounty,** bônus *m*, subsídio *m*, de exportação; **export credit,** crédito *m* ao exportador; **export credit insurance,** seguro *m* de crédito sobre exportações; **Export Credits Guarantee Department (ECGD),** departamento *m* para garantia de créditos de exportação; **export crop,** safra *f* exportável; **export firm,** (firma) exportadora *f*, exportador *m*; **export house,** (casa) exportadora *f*; **export incentive,** incentivo *m* à exportação; **export licence,** licença *f* de exportação; **export manager,** gerente *mf* de

exportações; **export market,** mercado *m* de exportação; **export order,** encomenda *f* de exportação; **export packing,** empacotamento *m*, embalagem *f*, para exportação; **export product,** produto *m* de exportação; **export quality,** qualidade *f* exportável; **export rebate,** desconto *m* de exportação; **export sales,** vendas *fpl* de exportação.
export², *v.tr.* exportar (**from,** de; **to,** para).
exportable, *a.* exportável.
exportation, *n.* exportação *f.*
exporter, *n.* exportador *m.*
exporting, **1.** *a.* exportador; **exporting nation,** nação exportadora. **2.** *n.* exportação *f.*
extend, *v.tr.* **1. to extend an invoice,** desdobrar uma fatura; **the credit balance is extended on the statement,** o saldo credor está indicado no extrato de conta; *Book-k:* **to extend a balance,** transportar um saldo. **2. to extend a loan,** conceder um empréstimo. **3. to extend the period for the payment of a tax,** prorrogar o prazo para o pagamento de um imposto. **4.** ampliar, estender; **the group is extending its operations,** o grupo está ampliando suas operações. **5.** *UK: Jur:* **to extend a property,** avaliar um bem imóvel.
extension, *n.* **1.** *Book-k:* transporte *m* (de um saldo). **2. extension of credit,**

concessão *f* de crédito. **3.** (*growth*) extensão *f*, ampliação *f*, (de um negócio). **4. the extension of a period for payment,** a prorrogação de um prazo para pagamento. **5.** (*telephone*) ramal *m.*
external, *a.* externo, exterior; **external debt,** dívida (pública) externa; **external commerce, trade,** comércio *m* exterior; **external loan,** empréstimo obtido no exterior; **external account,** (i) conta *f* no exterior, (ii) conta em moeda estrangeira; **external deficit,** déficit *m* no balanço de pagamentos; *Book-k:* **external audit,** exame *m* por auditores externos.
extra, 1. *a.* **to work an extra four hours,** trabalhar quatro horas extras; **extra charge,** sobretaxa *f*, taxa *f* adicional, taxa suplementar; *Ins:* **extra premium,** prêmio *m* adicional; *Fin:* **extra dividend,** dividendo extraordinário. **2.** *adv.* **packing extra,** gastos *mpl* de embalagem excluídos.
extractive, *a.* **extractive industry,** indústria extrativa.
extraordinary, *a.* extraordinário; **extraordinary general meeting,** assembléia geral extraordinária; **extraordinary loss,** prejuízo extraordinário, perda extraordinária; *Book-k:* **extraordinary depreciation,** depreciação extraordinária.
extrapolation, *n. Stat:* extrapolação *f.*

F

face, *n.* **1. face value,** valor *m* nominal, valor facial, (de uma ação, etc.). **2.** face *f* (de um documento), anverso *m* (de uma moeda).

facility, *n.* **1.** facilidade *f*; **facilities for payment,** pagamento facilitado, facilidades de pagamento; *Bank:* **overdraft facilities,** linha *f* de crédito a descoberto. **2.** *usu.pl.* instalações *fpl*; **storage facilities,** entreposto *m*, armazém *m*; **transport facilities,** meios *mpl* de transporte; **customs facilities,** facilidades alfandegárias; *Nau:* **harbour facilities,** instalações portuárias; *Trans:* **loading and unloading facilities,** instalações de carga e descarga.

facsimile, *n.* fac-símile *m*; **copy in facsimile,** cópia fac-similada, cópia fac-similar, cópia em fac-símile.

factor, *n.* **1.** (*a*) (*in commercial transactions*) comissário *m* financiador; empresa *f* que compra contas a receber; (*b*) corretor *m* de mercadorias. **2. factors of production,** fatores *mpl* de produção; **at factor cost,** ao custo de fatores.

factorage, *n.* (*a*) comissão *f* (cobrada por uma empresa que compra contas a receber); (*b*) (*of intermediary*) corretagem *f*.

factoring, *n.* compra *f* de contas a receber.

factory, *n.* fábrica *f*, usina *f*; **car factory,** fábrica de automóveis; **shoe factory,** fábrica de sapatos; **factory-installed component,** componente *m* original; **factory hand, worker,** operário *m*; **factory inspector,** inspetor *m* de fábricas; **factory inspection,** inspeção *f* de fábricas; **factory cost,** custo *m* de fabricação, custo industrial, custo de produção; **factory overheads,** despesas *fpl* gerais de fabricação, gastos *mpl* gerais de fabricação; **factory price,** preço *m* de

fábrica; **factory system,** sistema *m* fabril; *Book-k:* **factory ledger,** razão *m* de custo industrial.

fail, *v.i.* (*of firm, business*) falir.

failed, *a.* *N.Am:* **failed firm,** empresa falida.

failing[1], *n.* falência *f*.

failing[2], *prep.* na falta de; **failing payment,** na falta de pagamento; **failing advice to the contrary,** salvo aviso contrário, na falta de aviso em contrário.

failure, *n.* **1. failure to pay,** falta *f* de pagamento. **2.** (*a*) fracasso *m*, malogro *m*, mau êxito *m*, (de um empreendimento, etc.); (*b*) falência *f* (de uma companhia).

fair[1], *n.* feira *f*, exposição *f*; **book fair,** feira de livros; **trade fair,** feira industrial.

fair[2], *a.* **fair price,** preço justo, justo preço; **fair market value,** justo valor de mercado; **to charge a fair price,** cobrar um preço justo, vender por um preço justo; **fair trading,** (i) livre-troca *f* em condições de reciprocidade, (ii) práticas comerciais justas; **fair wages,** salário justo; **fair wear and tear,** uso *m* e desgaste *m* normal.

faith, *n.* **good faith,** boa fé; **to act in good faith,** agir de boa fé; **purchaser in good faith,** comprador *m* de boa fé.

faithfully, *adv.* *Corr:* **(we remain) yours faithfully,** atenciosamente subscrevemo-nos, com a maior consideração e estima subscrevemo-nos.

fake[1], **1.** *n.* falsificação *f*, imitação *f* fraudulenta. **2.** *a.* **fake document,** documento falsificado, documento falso; **fake signature,** assinatura falsificada, assinatura falsa.

fake[2], *v.tr.* falsificar, imitar fraudulentamente.

fall[1], *n.* baixa *f*, queda *f*, (dos preços, etc.); **heavy fall,** forte queda, queda acentuada;

71

fall in value, desvalorização *f*; fall of the currency, desvalorização *f* da moeda; *St.Exch:* dealing for a fall, operação *f* baixista; to buy on a fall, comprar na baixa.
fall², *v.i.* (*a*) (*of price*) baixar, cair; (*of money*) desvalorizar-se; (*b*) (*of debt*) vencer(-se); to fall due, vencer(-se).
fall back, *v.i.* (*a*) *St.Exch: Fin:* (*of market*) recuar, retrair-se, (*of prices*) baixar; the shares fell back a point, as ações baixaram um ponto; (*b*) to fall back on one's capital, recorrer ao seu próprio capital.
falling, 1. *a.* falling market, mercado *m* (que está) em baixa; to sell on a rising market and buy on a falling market, vender na alta e comprar na baixa; the falling pound, a libra em baixa. 2. *n.* baixa *f*, queda *f*, (de preços), diminuição *f* de valor; falling off, (*of rate, etc.*) diminuição *f* (de taxa, etc.); declínio *m*, enfraquecimento *m*, (de uma indústria), retração *f* (da procura).
fall off, *v.i.* diminuir, declinar, baixar; the takings are falling off, as receitas estão diminuindo, baixando; trade with Brazil is falling off, o comércio com o Brasil está declinando, em declínio.
fall-off, *n.* diminuição *f*, baixa *f*, (nos preços, etc.), retração *f* (da procura).
false, *a.* falso; false coin, moeda falsa; false document, documento falso, documento falsificado; false balance sheet, balanço falso, balanço falsificado.
falsification, *n.* falsificação *f* (de documentos, etc.).
falsify, *v.tr.* falsificar (um documento, uma assinatura, etc.).
fancy, *a.* (*a*) fancy goods, (i) artigos *mpl* de fantasia, (ii) artigos de luxo; (*b*) *F:* fancy price, preço exagerado, preço muito alto.
fare, *n.* passagem *f*, preço *m* de passagem; air fare, passagem aérea; full fare, passagem inteira; half-fare, meia passagem; single fair, passagem de ida; return fare, passagem de ida e volta; bus fare, passagem de ônibus; train fare, passagem de trem; an increase in rail fares, um aumento na tarifa ferroviária.

farm¹, *n.* fazenda *f*; (*small farm*) granja *f*, sítio *m*; sheep farm, fazenda de criação de ovelhas; dairy farm, fazenda de criação de gado leiteiro; stock farm, fazenda de criação de gado; fish farm, estabelecimento *m* de piscicultura; poultry farm, fazenda de criação de aves domésticas; farm labourer, farm worker, trabalhador *m* agrícola; farm products, produce, produtos *mpl* agrícolas.
farm², *v.tr.* 1. (*a*) cultivar, lavrar, (a terra); (*b*) administrar uma fazenda. 2. *Am:* vender o direito de arrecadar (impostos ou outros encargos) a uma entidade privada.
farmer, *n.* fazendeiro *m*, agricultor *m*, cultivador *m*, granjeiro *m*; poultry farmer, criador *m* de aves domésticas; sheep farmer, ovinocultor *m*, criador de ovelhas; stock, cattle, farmer, criador de gado.
farming, *n.* agricultura *f*, lavoura *f*, cultivo *m*, cultura *f*; (*of cattle, etc.*) criação *f*; mixed farming, policultura *f*; single-crop farming, monocultura *f*; fish farming, piscicultura *f*; poultry farming, avicultura *f*; sheep farming, ovinocultura *f*, criação de ovelhas; cattle, stock, farming, criação de gado; *Jur:* farming lease, aforamento *m*.
farm out, *v.tr.* dar (trabalho) de empreitada.
favourable, *a.* (*of terms, etc.*) favorável, vantajoso; on favourable terms, em condições favoráveis.
feasibility, *n.* praticabilidade *f*, viabilidade *f*; feasibility study, estudo *m* de viabilidade; feasibility report, relatório *m* sobre a viabilidade (de um projeto, etc.).
feature, *n. St.Exch: pl.* features, ações negociadas freqüentemente.
federation, *n.* federação *f*; employers' federation = sindicato *m* patronal.
fee, *n.* 1. (*a*) honorário *m*, provento *m*; directors' fees, honorários da diretoria; a solicitor's fees, honorários, proventos, de um advogado; to draw one's fees, receber seus honorários, perceber seus proventos; (*b*) admission fee, (taxa *f* de) entrada *f*; patent fee, taxa de patente; registration

fee, (i) taxa de registro, (ii) (*at college, etc.*) (taxa de) matrícula *f*; **subscription fee**, assinatura *f* (de revista, etc.); cota *f*, cota-parte *f*, mensalidade *f*, (de membro de uma organização, etc.). **2.** *Jur:* **fee simple**, herança *f* sem limitações a herdeiros específicos.

fetch, *v.tr.* **to fetch a high price, a low price**, ser vendido por um preço alto, um preço baixo.

fiat, *n. Fin:* **fiat money**, papel-moeda *m* (inconversível).

fictitious, *a.* fictício; **fictitious assets**, ativo fictício; **fictitious bill (of exchange)**, letra *f* de câmbio fictícia.

fidelity, *n. Am:* **fidelity bond, insurance**, seguro *m* contra infidelidade (de empregado).

fiduciary, **1.** *a.* fiduciário, fiducial; **fiduciary money**, moeda fiduciária; **fiduciary issue**, emissão *f* de moeda fiduciária, emissão de moeda sem lastro. **2.** *n.* fiduciário *m*.

field, *n.* (*a*) mercado *m* (para um produto); (*b*) campo *m*; **field work**, trabalho *m* de campo; **field research**, pesquisa *f* de mercado (mediante observação ou entrevista); *Am:* **field auditor**, auditor interno viajante.

FIFO, *n. see* **first**.

figure, *n.* cifra *f*, número *m*; **in round figures**, em números redondos; **to write a total in figures**, escrever um total em algarismos; **to work out the figures for a deal**, fazer os cálculos referentes a uma transação; **to find a mistake in the figures**, descobrir um erro de cálculo; **his earnings run into five figures**, ele ganha mais de dez mil; **the sales figures**, os números referentes às vendas, o volume das vendas; **the 1975 figures**, os números referentes a 1975; **the June trade figures**, os números da balança comercial do mês de junho; (*on document, etc.*) **check figure**, número de controle.

file¹, *n.* arquivo *m*; **card-index file**, fichário *m*; **we have placed your report in the file, on (the) file**, arquivamos seu relatório; **file copy**, cópia *f* de arquivo; *Am:* **file cabinet, file case**, arquivo, fichário; *Am:* **file card**,

ficha *f* (de arquivo); *Am:* **file clerk**, arquivista *mf*, *F:* papelista *mf*.

file², *v.tr.* **1.** arquivar (documentos, fichas, etc.). **2. to file a petition in bankruptcy**, abrir, confessar, falência.

filing, *n.* arquivamento *m*; **filing system**, sistema *m* de arquivamento; **filing cabinet, filing case**, arquivo *m*, fichário *m*; **filing clerk**, arquivista *mf*, *F:* papelista *mf*; **filing drawer**, gaveta *f* de arquivo; **vertical filing system**, arquivo *m* vertical.

fill, *v.tr.* **1.** (*a*) **to fill a post**, ocupar um cargo; (*b*) **to fill a vacancy**, preencher uma vaga. **2. to fill an order**, executar, atender, uma encomenda.

fill in, *v.tr.* preencher (um formulário); **to fill in the date**, inserir a data.

fill out, *v.tr.* preencher (um formulário).

fill up, *v.tr.* preencher (um formulário).

final, *a.* final; **final dividend**, dividendo *m* final; **final date (for payment, etc.)**, prazo *m* fatal; **final instalment**, última prestação; **final product**, produto acabado.

finance¹, *n.* finanças *fpl*; **public finance**, finanças públicas; **high finance**, altas finanças; **the world of finance**, o mundo financeiro; **questions of finance**, questões financeiras; **finance company, finance house**, financeira *f*, sociedade *f* de financiamento; **finance development corporation** = (*approx.*) fundo *m* de desenvolvimento econômico; **finance bill**, (i) letra *f* de favor, (ii) projeto *m* de lei das finanças.

finance², *v.tr.* financiar, custear; **to finance a building project**, financiar uma obra de construção.

financial, *a.* financeiro; **financial assistance**, ajuda financeira; **financial expense**, despesa financeira; **financial news**, informações financeiras; **financial position**, posição financeira; **financial ratio**, índice financeiro; **financial statement**, demonstração financeira, balanço financeiro; **financial expert**, financista *mf*, financeiro *m*; **the financial world**, o mundo financeiro; **financial year**, ano *m* fiscal, exercício (financeiro), exercício social, (de uma companhia), (*of*

public body, etc.) exercício orçamentário; **financial instrument**, título *m* de crédito.
financially, *adv.* financeiramente; **financially sound**, seguro financeiramente.
financier, *n.* (i) financeiro *m*, financista *mf*, (ii) (*backer*) financiador *m*.
financing, *n.* financiamento *m*; **self-financing**, autofinanciamento *m*.
find, *v.* 1. *v.tr.* (*a*) **to find the money for a project**, (i) achar, conseguir, o dinheiro para um empreendimento, (ii) fornecer os recursos, o dinheiro, para um empreendimento; (*b*) *UK:* **she receives £50 all found**, ela ganha £50 com quarto e refeições. 2. *v.i.* *Jur:* (*of judge*) pronunciar sentença.
fine¹, *n.* multa *f*, penalidade *f*; **liable to a fine of $100**, passível de uma multa de $100, sujeito a uma multa de $100.
fine², *v.tr.* multar (alguém); **to fine s.o. $50**, impor uma multa de $50 a alguém, multar alguém em $50.
fine³, *a.* (*a*) **fine bills**, títulos *mpl* de primeira ordem; **fine trade paper**, efeitos *mpl* de comércio de primeira ordem, títulos *mpl* comerciais de primeira ordem; (*b*) **fine gold**, ouro fino.
fine⁴, *adv.* **prices are cut very fine**, os preços estão reduzidos ao nível mais baixo possível.
fineness, *n.* *Num:* título *m* (de moeda).
finished, *a.* *Ind: etc:* **finished goods**, produtos acabados.
fire, *v.tr.* *F:* **to fire s.o.**, demitir, despachar, despedir, alguém; mandar alguém embora, *F:* botar alguém na rua, dar o bilhete azul a alguém.
firm¹, *n.* firma *f*, empresa *f*, casa *f* comercial; **name, style, of a firm**, razão *f* social, firma; **a large firm**, uma grande empresa, uma firma de grande porte; **a small firm**, uma pequena empresa, uma firma de pequeno porte.
firm², *a.* (*of market, offer, sale*) firme; **these shares remain firm**, estas ações mantêm-se firmes; **firm contract**, contrato *m* firme; **firm demand**, procura *f* constante, demanda *f* constante.
first, *a. & n.* (*a*) primeiro (*m*); **on the first of May, on May 1st**, em 1º de maio; *Fin:*

first of exchange, primeira via de uma cambial; (*b*) *n.pl.* **firsts**, artigos *mpl* de primeira qualidade; (*c*) *Book-k:* **FIFO, first in first out**, FIFO *m*, custeio *m* das saídas em ordem cronológica das entradas; (*d*) *UK:* **first-line managers**, supervisores *mpl* e gerentes *mpl* de nível médio (que estão em contato com os trabalhadores).
fiscal, *a.* fiscal; **fiscal period**, exercício financeiro; **fiscal year**, ano *m* fiscal, exercício financeiro (anual), *Am:* ano *m* contábil; **fiscal policy**, política *f* fiscal; **fiscal tax incentive**, incentivo *m* fiscal.
fish, *n.* peixe *m*, (*esp. for food*) pescado *m*; **fish market**, mercado *m* de peixe.
fishing, *n.* **fishing industry**, indústria pesqueira; **fishing boat**, barco *m* pesqueiro, barco pescador.
fishmonger, *n.* peixeiro *m*.
five-year, *a.* (*of plan, etc.*) qüinqüenal.
fix, *v.tr.* fixar, estabelecer, determinar, (preços, condições, etc.); **to fix the budget**, fazer, determinar, o orçamento; **to fix an interview for three o'clock**, marcar uma entrevista para as três; **the date is not yet fixed**, a data ainda não está marcada; **on the date fixed**, na data marcada.
fixed, *a.* (*a*) fixo; **fixed budget**, orçamento fixo; **fixed charges**, despesas fixas; **fixed cost**, custo fixo; **fixed price**, preço fixo; **fixed(-term) deposit**, depósito *m* a prazo fixo; **fixed income**, renda fixa; **fixed resale price**, preço fixo de revenda; **fixed salary**, salário fixo; **fixed-interest security**, título *m* de renda fixa, título com juros fixos; *Am: Jur:* **fixed trust**, fideicomisso fixo; (*b*) *Book-k:* **fixed assets**, ativo fixo, ativo permanente, (ativo) imobilizado *m*; **fixed capital**, capital fixo, bens *mpl* de ativo fixo; **fixed liability**, passivo imobilizado, passivo exigível a longo prazo.
fixing, *n.* (*a*) fixação *f*, determinação *f*, (de preços, direitos, etc.); (*b*) (*by cartels, etc.*) **price fixing**, fixação de preços.
flat, *a.* 1. **flat market**, mercado calmo. 2. **flat rate**, tarifa única; **flat price**, preço único, preço fixo. 3. **flat refusal**, recusa categórica.

flexibility, *n.* flexibilidade *f* (de preços, etc.).

flexible, *a.* flexível; **flexible budget,** orçamento *m* flexível; **flexible standard cost,** custo *m* standard flexível; **flexible working time, flexible working hours,** horário *m* de trabalho flexível.

flexitime, *n.* horário *m* (de trabalho) flexível.

flier, *n. Am:* especulação temerária.

flight, *n.* **the flight of capital,** a fuga de capitais, a saída de capitais.

float¹, *n.* (*in shop, etc.*) caixa *f* (para troco).

float², *v.tr.* **1.** (*a*) **to float a company,** fundar, criar, uma companhia; (*b*) **to float shares,** lançar ações ao público; **to float a loan,** lançar um empréstimo; *Fin:* **to float securities,** lançar títulos no mercado. **2. to float the pound,** deixar flutuar a libra esterlina.

floatation, *n.* (*a*) **floatation of a company,** criação *f*, fundação *f*, de uma companhia. (*b*) lançamento *m* (de títulos, debêntures); **the floatation of shares,** o lançamento de ações ao público; **the floatation of a loan,** o lançamento de um empréstimo.

floating, *a.* **floating assets,** ativo *m* circulante, ativo corrente; **floating capital,** capital *m* circulante; **floating liability,** passivo *m* flutuante, passivo corrente; **floating debt,** dívida *f* flutuante, dívida exigível a curto prazo; **floating exchange rate,** câmbio *m* flutuante; **floating pound,** libra *f* flutuante; **floating stock,** títulos adquiridos para fins especulativos; *Ins:* **floating policy,** apólice aberta; *Pol.Ec:* **floating population,** população *f* flutuante, população em trânsito; *Am: Pol.Ec:* **floating labour,** mão-de-obra *f* flutuante; *Am: Ind:* **floating inspector,** inspetor *m* que controla a qualidade de mercadorias em diversas etapas do processo de fabricação.

flood, *v.tr.* **to flood the market,** inundar, abarrotar, o mercado.

floor, *n.* **1.** (*a*) *St.Exch:* **the floor,** o pregão (da bolsa de valores), o recinto da bolsa de valores; (*b*) **the factory floor,** as

oficinas (de uma fábrica ou unidade manufatureira). **2.** (*a*) preço mínimo; (*b*) nível mínimo determinado por fatores econômicos. **3.** *N.Am:* (*in store*) **floor manager,** chefe *mf* de departamento, de seção.

floorwalker, *n. Am:* (*in a store*) supervisor *m* (de seção ou departamento).

florist, *n.* florista *mf*, floreiro *m*; **florist's,** casa *f* de flores.

flotation, *n.* = **floatation.**

flotsam, *n.* destroços *mpl* (flutuantes) de naufrágio; fragmentos *mpl* (flutuantes) de navio naufragado.

flourish, *v.i.* prosperar, florescer.

flourishing, *a.* **flourishing trade,** comércio próspero, comércio florescente.

flow¹, *n.* **flow of capital,** movimento *m* de capital, de capitais; **cash flow,** fluxo *m* de caixa; **discounted cash flow,** valor *m* presente de fluxo de caixa futuro; **flow chart,** fluxograma *m*, diagrama *m* de fluxo.

flow², *v.i.* (*of money*) circular.

flower, *n.* **flower show,** exposição *f* de flores; *Am:* **flower shop,** casa *f* de flores.

flow in, *v.i.* (*of money*) entrar.

flow out, *v.i.* (*of money*) sair.

fluctuate, *v.i.* (*of markets, prices*) oscilar, flutuar; **fluctuating foreign exchange rate,** câmbio *m* flutuante.

fluctuation, *n.* oscilação *f*, flutuação *f*.

fly-by-night, *a.* **fly-by-night firm,** empresa *f* financeiramente irresponsável, que não merece confiança.

fold (up), *v.i.* *F:* (*of business, etc.*) fechar, deixar de funcionar; **the restaurant folded owing to a lack of customers,** o restaurante fechou por falta de freguesia.

folder, *n.* **1.** (*publication*) circular *f*, prospecto *m*. **2.** pasta *f* (para papéis).

folio¹, *n.* *Book-k:* fólio *m*; **posting folio,** fólio *m* para lançamento de registros contábeis; **folio reference,** indicação numérica (em diários, razões, documentos, etc.).

folio², *v.tr.* *Book-k:* paginar, numerar (páginas).

following, *a.* seguinte, subseqüente; *St.Exch:* **following settlement, following**

account, dia *m* de liquidação subseqüente.

follow up, *v.tr.* to follow up a letter, enviar uma carta com referência à anterior; **to follow up an order,** seguir, acompanhar, uma encomenda.

follow-up, *n.* acompanhamento *m*, seguimento *m*, (de encomenda, trabalho, etc.); **follow-up letter,** carta *f* de acompanhamento, carta de seguimento; **follow-up work,** (i) trabalho *m* de acompanhamento, trabalho de seguimento, (ii) (*extra*) trabalho adicional.

food, *n.* comida *f*, alimento *m*, alimentação *f*, produtos alimentícios, gêneros alimentícios, víveres *mpl*, comestíveis *mpl*; **food allowance,** ajuda *f* para alimentação, diária *f*; **food imports, exports,** importações *fpl*, exportações *fpl*, de alimentos; **food industry,** indústria *f* de alimentos; **food manufacturer,** fabricante *m* de produtos alimentícios; **food prices,** preços *mpl* de produtos alimentícios; **food production,** produção *f* de alimentos, fabricação *f* de produtos alimentícios; **food products,** produtos alimentícios, gêneros alimentícios; **food value,** valor nutritivo (de produtos alimentícios); **world food markets,** mercados alimentícios mundiais; **canned, tinned, foods,** conservas *fpl*, produtos alimentícios enlatados; **dietetic food,** alimentação dietética; **frozen food,** alimentos congelados, alimentos supergelados; **health foods,** alimentos naturais, alimentos integrais; **the Food and Agriculture Organization,** a Organização para Alimentação e Agricultura.

foolscap, *n.* papel *m* ofício, papel de formato ofício.

foot, *v.tr.* F: 1. to foot the bill, pagar a conta; to foot the expenses, pagar as despesas, arcar com as despesas. 2. N.Am: to foot up an account, somar uma conta.

force, *n.* 1. to be in force, estar em vigor, vigorar, viger; to come into force, entrar em vigor. 2. sales force, quadro *m* de vendas, equipe *f* de vendas; **labour force,** mão-de-obra *f*, força *f* de trabalho.

forced, *a.* Jur: forced sale, venda forçada, liquidação forçada; forced sale value, valor *m* de liquidação forçada.

force down, *v.tr.* to force down prices, forçar uma baixa nos preços.

force up, *v.tr.* to force up prices, forçar uma subida nos preços.

forecast¹, *n.* previsão *f*, prognóstico *m*; sales forecast, previsão de vendas.

forecast², *v.tr.* prever, prognosticar, (a performance de uma companhia, etc.).

foreclose, *v.tr.* Jur: to foreclose a mortgage, executar uma hipoteca.

foreclosure, *n.* Jur: execução *f* (de uma hipoteca).

foreign, *a.* estrangeiro; **foreign(-held) balances,** saldos mantidos no exterior; **foreign bill (of exchange),** letra *f* (de câmbio) pagável no exterior; **foreign capital,** capital estrangeiro, capitais estrangeiros; **foreign currency,** moeda estrangeira, divisas *fpl*; **foreign exchange,** câmbio *m*, divisas *fpl*; **foreign exchange broker,** corretor *m* de câmbio; **foreign exchange dealings,** operações *fpl* de câmbio, operações cambiais; **foreign (exchange) earnings,** receitas *fpl* em divisas; rendimentos *mpl* em divisas, lucros *mpl* em divisas; **foreign goods,** mercadorias fabricadas no exterior; **foreign investment,** investimento estrangeiro; **foreign investor,** investidor estrangeiro; **foreign markets,** mercados externos; **foreign trade,** Am: foreign commerce, comércio exterior, comércio externo; UK: Foreign Office, Ministério das Relações Exteriores.

foreman, *n.* Ind: etc: chefe *m* de turma, encarregado *m* de turma, contramestre *m*, (on roadworks, etc.) capataz *m*, (on building site) mestre-de-obras *m*.

forfeit¹, *n.* (a) (for non-performance of contract) penalidade *f*; forfeit clause (of a contract), cláusula *f* penal (de um contrato); (b) St.Exch: to relinquish the forfeit, renunciar à opção.

forfeit², *v.tr.* (a) perder (algo) por confisco; (b) perder (o direito de fazer algo).

forfeitable, *a.* sujeito a confiscação, confiscável.

forfeiture, *n.* **1.** (*a*) (*confiscation*) confisco *m*, confiscação *f*; (*b*) perda *f* (de direito, etc.). **2.** bem confiscado.

forge, *v.tr.* falsificar, forjar, (documento, assinatura).

forged, *a.* (documento, dinheiro) falsificado, falso, forjado.

forger, *n.* falsificador *m*, forjador *m*.

forgery, *n.* (*a*) falsificação *f*; (*b*) **the signature was a forgery,** a assinatura era falsa, estava falsificada, foi forjada.

form¹, *n.* **1. receipt in due form,** recibo feito na devida forma, nos devidos termos. **2. (printed) form,** formulário *m*, impresso *m*; **application form,** (i) formulário *m* de pedido, de requerimento, (ii) (*for shares*) boletim *m* de subscrição; **telegram form,** impresso para telegrama; **order form,** impresso para encomendas; **blank form,** formulário em branco; **to fill in a form,** preencher um formulário.

form², *v.tr.* fundar, criar, organizar, formar, (uma companhia, etc.).

formality, *n.* **to complete the formalities,** cumprir com, preencher, as formalidades.

formation, *n.* criação *f*, organização *f*, fundação *f*, formação *f*, (de sociedade, etc.); **formation expenses,** despesas *fpl* de organização, despesas de instalação; *Fin:* **capital formation,** formação de capital.

forward, **1.** *a.* *St.Exch: etc:* **forward delivery,** entrega futura; **forward dealings,** operações *fpl* a termo; **forward sales,** vendas *fpl* a termo; **forward market,** mercado *m* a termo; *Bank:* **forward rates,** taxas *fpl* para operações a termo. **2.** *adv.* (*a*) **to date forward a cheque,** pré-datar um cheque; **a forward-dated cheque,** um cheque pré-datado; **carriage forward,** porte *m* a pagar; (*b*) *Fin:* **to buy forward,** comprar a termo; **to sell forward,** vender a termo; (*c*) *Book-k:* **to carry the balance forward,** transportar o saldo; (**carried**) **forward,** transporte *m*.

forward², *v.tr.* (*a*) expedir, despachar, remeter, (mercadorias); (*b*) **to forward a letter,** reexpedir uma carta (a um destinatário que mudou de endereço); **please forward,** favor reexpedir.

forwarder, *n.* (*a*) despachante *mf*, expedidor *m*; (*b*) = **forwarding agent.**

forwarding, *n.* (*a*) expedição *f*, envio *m*, remessa *f*, (de pacotes, etc.); **forwarding agent,** despachante *mf*; **forwarding instructions,** instruções *fpl* para expedição; (*b*) reexpedição *f* (de correspondência a um destinatário que mudou de endereço); **forwarding address,** novo endereço (para reexpedição de correspondência).

foul, *a.* **foul bill of lading,** conhecimento *m* no qual se constata que certas mercadorias têm defeitos.

founder, *n.* fundador *m*, organizador *m*, (de uma empresa, de uma companhia); **founders' shares,** partes beneficiárias (de fundadores), partes de fundador, ações *fpl* de fundador.

fraction, *n.* fração *f*; *Fin:* **fraction of a share,** fração de uma ação; *St.Exch:* **fraction dealings,** operações *fpl* no mercado fracionário.

fractional, *a.* fracionário; **fractional part,** fração *f*; **fractional coin(s), fractional currency,** moeda fracionária, moeda divisionária; *N.Am:* **fractional note,** cédula *f* de pequeno valor.

franc, *n.* franco *m*.

franchise, *n.* **1.** concessão *f* (de direito de exploração ou venda). **2.** *Ins:* franquia *f*.

franchisee, *n.* concessionário *m* (de um direito de exploração ou venda).

franchiser, *n.* **1.** = **franchisee. 2.** = **franchisor.**

franchising, *n.* concessão *f* (de direito de exploração ou venda).

franchisor, *n.* concedente *mf* (de um direito de exploração ou venda).

fraud, *n.* fraude *f*; **to obtain sth. by fraud,** conseguir algo por meio de fraude, por meios fraudulentos.

fraudulent, *a.* fraudulento, fraudatório; **fraudulent balance sheet,** balanço fraudulento; **fraudulent contract,** contrato fraudulento; **fraudulent transaction,** operação, transação, fraudulenta; **fraudulent bankruptcy,** falência fraudulenta, bancarrota *f*; **fraudulent bankrupt,** bancarroteiro *m*.

fraudulently, *adv.* fraudulentamente, por meio de fraude.

free¹, *a.* **1.** *Fin:* **to set funds free,** mobilizar fundos, mobilizar recursos; **the setting free of money,** a mobilização de dinheiro. **2.** livre, franco, isento, **(of,** de); **free currency,** moeda *f* de curso livre; **free market,** mercado *m* livre; **free port,** porto franco, porto aberto, porto livre; **free trade,** livre-comércio *m,* livre-câmbio *m,* livre-troca *f;* **free-trade area,** (i) área *f* de comércio livre, (ii) zona franca; **free-trade policy,** política *f* livre-cambista; **free trader,** (i) livre-cambista *mf,* (ii) *N.Am:* comerciante *mf* independente (dos consórcios); **free of tax,** livre, isento, de impostos; **a tax-free income,** uma renda isenta de impostos; **an interest-free loan,** um empréstimo isento de juros, um empréstimo sem juros; *M.Ins:* **free of all average,** livre de toda avaria; *Cust:* **free of duty, duty-free,** isento de impostos alfandegários, de direitos aduaneiros; *Cust:* **free list,** lista *f* de mercadorias isentas de impostos alfandegários. **3.** **free (of charge),** grátis, gratuito; **free estimate without obligation,** orçamento *m* grátis sem compromisso; **free sample,** amostra gratuita, amostra grátis; **free ticket,** bilhete gratuito; **free admission,** entrada gratuita; **free delivery,** entrega gratuita; *Trans:* **free at quay, on wharf,** posto no cais; **free alongside ship (FAS),** franqueado no costado do navio; **free on board (FOB),** franqueado a bordo, (posto) livre a bordo; *Post:* **post free,** porte pago; *Fin:* **free surplus (of a company),** lucros acumulados à disposição dos acionistas.

free², *adv.* de graça, gratuitamente, grátis.

free³, *v.tr.* (*a*) mobilizar (fundos); (*b*) liberar (mercadorias).

freehold, *a.* **freehold property,** propriedade *f* alodial, bens *mpl* alodiais.

freeze¹, *n.* **1.** **prices and wages freeze,** congelamento *m* de preços e salários, congelamento dos preços e dos salários. **2.** **deep freeze,** congelador *m,* frigorífico *m,* unidade frigorífica.

freeze², *v.tr.* **1.** congelar; **to freeze prices,** congelar os preços; **to freeze an account,**

congelar uma conta. **2.** congelar, frigorificar, (peixe, carne, etc.).

freezer, *n.* congelador *m,* frigorífico *m,* unidade frigorífica.

freezing, *n.* congelamento *m* (dos preços, salários, contas, etc.).

freight¹, *n.* (*cargo, transportation and charge*) frete *m;* (*cargo*) carga *f;* (*transportation*) transporte *m* de carga; **by freight,** a frete, como carga; **freight in,** frete de entrada; **freight out,** frete de saída; **freight out and home, freight out and in,** frete de ida e volta, frete por viagem redonda; **air freight,** (i) frete aéreo, (ii) transporte de carga aérea; **sent by air freight,** expedido por avião, expedido como carga aérea; **dead freight,** (i) frete falso, (ii) penalidade *f* por falta de carregamento; **home freight, outward freight,** frete de volta; **freight charge,** frete *m;* **freight charges paid,** porte pago; **freight conference,** conferência *f* de fretes; **freight market,** mercado *m* de transporte de cargas; **freight rates, freight tariff,** tarifa *f* de fretes; **to pay the freight,** pagar o frete; **to take in freight,** aceitar carga, carregar; *N.Am:* **freight agent,** agente *mf* de carga, despachante *mf;* **freight car,** vagão *m* de carga; **freight elevator,** elevador *m* de carga; **freight train,** trem *m* de carga; *Av:* **freight plane,** avião *m* de carga; *Rail:* **freight depot,** estação *f* de carga.

freight², *v.tr.* **1.** *N.Am:* **to freight a ship with wheat,** carregar um navio com trigo. **2.** **to freight a ship (to s.o.),** fretar um navio (a alguém). **3.** (i) transportar (mercadorias), (ii) despachar, expedir, (como carga).

freightage, *n.* **1.** fretagem *f,* fretamento *m.* **2.** (*cargo*) frete *m,* carga *f.* **3.** *N.Am:* (*charge*) frete.

freighter, *n.* **1.** afretador *m* (de navio). **2.** (i) transportador *m,* (ii) empresa *f* de transportes. **3.** expedidor *m.* **4.** (*a*) *Av:* avião *m* de carga; (*b*) *Nau:* (navio) cargueiro *m.*

friendly, *a.* **friendly society,** sociedade *f* mutuante, mútua *f.*

fringe, *n.* (*in employment*) **fringe benefits,** vantagens *fpl* adicionais, benefícios *mpl* extras; **fringe market,** mercado *m* marginal.

front, *n.* **front (man),** representante *m* (de uma sociedade, da qual geralmente não é acionista); chefe *m* nominal (de uma empresa), porta-voz *m* (de uma organização).

frozen, *a.* (*a*) *Fin:* congelado; **frozen assets,** fundos congelados; **frozen account,** conta congelada; (*b*) **frozen food,** alimentos congelados, alimentos supergelados.

full, 1. *a.* **full payment,** pagamento *m* integral; **full price,** preço *m* integral; (*on bus, etc.*) **full fare,** tarifa plena, tarifa integral; **full weight,** peso máximo; **full liability,** responsabilidade plena, responsabilidade irrestrita; *Trans: etc:* **full load,** carga completa; *Fin:* **full discharge,** quitação *f*; *Ins:* **full cover,** cobertura *f* total; *Pol.Ec:* **full employment,** pleno emprego; *Jur:* **full powers,** plenos poderes. 2. *n.* **capital paid in full,** capital integralizado, capital realizado; **money is refunded in full,** todo o dinheiro pago será reembolsado (em determinadas circunstâncias); **acceptance in full of the conditions,** plena aceitação das condições.

full(-)time, 1. *adv.* **to work full time,** trabalhar em tempo integral. 2. *a.* **full-time employment,** emprego *m* de tempo integral; **full-time employee,** empregado *m* de tempo integral.

fully, *adv.* plenamente, completamente, integralmente; **capital fully paid up,** capital integralizado, capital realizado; **fully paid shares,** ações integralizadas.

functional, *a.* funcional; *Book-k:* **functional accounting,** contabilidade *f* funcional, contabilidade por funções; *Book-k:* **functional statement,** demonstração *f* de custos subdivida por funções.

fund¹, *n.* (*a*) fundo *m*; **International Monetary Fund (IMF),** Fundo Monetário Internacional (FMI); **pension fund, retirement fund,** fundo *m* de pensão, caixa *f* de aposentadoria, fundo de aposentadoria; **revolving fund,** fundo rotativo; **fund account,** conta *f* que

registra as operações de um fundo; **fund asset,** bem (ou ativo) vinculado a um determinado fundo; **fund liability,** passivo *m* de um fundo; **fund obligation,** empenho *m* de um determinado fundo; **fund surplus,** superávit *m* de um fundo; *Fin:* **sinking fund,** fundo de amortização; (*b*) *pl.* **funds,** fundos *mpl*, disponibilidades *fpl*; **funds of a company,** fundos sociais; **to earmark, allocate, funds for sth.,** alocar, destinar, fundos para algo; (*of company*) **to make a call for funds,** fazer uma chamada de capital; *Bank:* **no funds,** sem fundos; *Bank:* **insufficient funds,** insuficiência *f* de fundos; (*c*) *pl.* **funds,** fundos públicos, títulos *mpl* da dívida pública; **fund holder,** possuidor *m* de títulos da dívida pública ou outros valores.

fund², *v.tr.* 1. *Fin:* fundar, consolidar, (uma dívida pública). 2. *UK:* **to fund money,** aplicar dinheiro em fundos públicos. 3. **to fund a pension plan,** criar um fundo para custear um plano de aposentadoria; **to fund a new business,** financiar, dar fundos para, uma nova empresa.

fundable, *a.* (dívida *f*) consolidável.

funded, *a.* 1. **funded debt,** dívida fundada, dívida consolidada. 2. *UK:* **funded capital,** capitais investidos em fundos públicos.

funding, *n.* 1. consolidação *f* (de uma dívida); **funding bonds,** obrigações *fpl* de consolidação. 2. financiamento *m* (de um empreendimento, uma empresa, etc.).

further, *a.* **further orders,** novas encomendas, encomendas adicionais; **for further information,** para maiores informações, para informações complementares, para mais informações; **further to your letter of 15th instant,** com referência à sua carta de 15 do corrente, em resposta à sua carta de 15 do corrente; **further to our telephone conversation,** em complemento ao nosso contato telefônico.

future, 1. *a.* futuro; **future delivery,** entrega futura; **to sell for future delivery,** vender a termo, vender para entrega futura; **future sale,** venda futura, venda para entrega futura; *Fin:* **exchange for future delivery,** operações *fpl* de câmbio a termo, operações cambiais a termo; **future price,** (i) preço futuro, cotação futura, (ii) preço *m* de venda a termo, preço de compra a termo. **2.** *n.pl.* **futures,** vendas futuras; **futures contract,** contrato *m* de venda futura; **futures market,** mercado futuro, mercado a termo.

G

gain¹, *n*. **1.** (*profit*) ganho *m*, lucro *m*; **capital gain**, ganho de capital; **capital gains (tax)**, (imposto *m* sobre) os ganhos de capital. **2.** (*increase*) aumento *m*; **a gain in sales**, um aumento nas vendas; *St.Exch:* **a gain of three points in the morning's trading**, um aumento de três pontos no pregão da manhã.

gain², *v*. **1.** *v.tr.* ganhar, aumentar; **wheat gained two cents just before closing**, o trigo aumentou em dois cêntimos um pouco antes do fechamento; **these stocks are gaining ground**, estes títulos estão subindo. **2.** *v.i.* **to gain from a slump in the market**, lucrar com uma baixa no mercado.

gainful, *a*. *Adm: etc:* **gainful occupation**, trabalho produtor de rendimento.

gallon, *n*. *Meas: UK:* galão *m* imperial (= 4,546 litros); *N.Am:* galão (= 3,85 litros).

galloping, *a*. **galloping inflation**, inflação *f* galopante.

gamble¹, *n*. transação arriscada; empresa arriscada; **pure gamble**, pura especulação.

gamble², *v.i.* **to gamble on the stock exchange**, jogar, especular, na bolsa de valores; **to gamble in wheat futures**, especular em vendas futuras do trigo.

gambler, *n*. *F:* (*on stock exchange, etc.*) especulador *m*.

gambling, *n*. **gambling on the stock exchange**, especulação *f* (na bolsa de valores).

gap, *n*. **deflationary gap**, hiato deflacionário; **trade gap**, déficit *m* no balanço comercial; **(hard) currency gap**, escassez *f* de divisas.

gas, *n*. **1.** gás *m*; **the gas industry**, a indústria do gás. **2.** *Am: F:* gasolina *f*; **gas station**, posto *m* de gasolina.

gazette¹, *n*. **the Official Gazette**, o Diário Oficial.

gazette², *v.tr.* anunciar, publicar, no Diário Oficial.

gazump, *v.tr.* *Brit:* *F:* (*in property transactions*) **to gazump s.o.**, aumentar o preço de venda combinado antes da assinatura do contrato.

gear, *v.tr.* **to gear wages to the cost of living**, reajustar os salários (ao custo de vida); **a company geared for expansion**, uma empresa orientada para a expansão.

gearing, *n*. *Fin:* alavancagem *f*; emprego *m* de capital-obrigações (por uma companhia).

general, *a*. geral; **general meeting**, assembléia *f* geral; **general manager**, diretor *m* geral; (*on agenda of meeting*) **general matters**, assuntos diversos; **general post office**, correio *m* geral; **general store**, loja *f* geral; *Book-k: etc:* **general audit**, exame *m* geral de auditoria; **general cash**, caixa *f* geral, caixa principal; **general accountant**, contador *m* geral, contabilista *mf*; **general journal**, diário *m* geral; **general ledger**, razão *m* geral; **general balance sheet**, balanço *m* geral (completo); **general (operating) expenses**, despesas *fpl* gerais (de operação); *M.Ins:* **general average**, avaria grossa, avaria comum; *Nau:* **general cargo**, carga mista; **General Agreement on Tariffs and Trade (GATT)**, Acordo *m* Geral sobre Tarifas e Comércio; *Jur:* **general partnership**, sociedade *f* em nome coletivo; *Jur:* **general partner**, sócio solidário.

gentleman, *n*. **a gentleman's agreement**, um acordo de cavalheiros.

genuine, *a*. (*a*) **a genuine muscatel**, um moscatel genuíno; **a genuine signature**, uma assinatura autêntica; (*b*) **a genuine buyer,** um comprador sério.

genuineness, *n.* **the bank questioned the genuineness of his references,** o banco pôs em dúvida a autenticidade das suas referências.

get, *v.tr.* **1.** (*a*) (i) conseguir, obter, alcançar; **he got a new job quickly,** conseguiu um novo emprego rápidamente; **the firm got a loan from the development agency,** a firma conseguiu um empréstimo da agência de desenvolvimento; (ii) **I got this car cheap,** comprei este carro barato; (*b*) ganhar, perceber, vencer, receber, auferir, tirar; **the sales manager gets $17 000 a year,** o gerente de vendas ganha $17.000 anuais; **the agent gets 10% commission on the deal,** o agente recebe uma comissão de 10% sobre o valor da transação. **2.** receber; **to get a letter,** receber uma carta; **the strikers got dismissal notices,** os grevistas receberam o aviso prévio.

get out, *v.tr.* (*a*) **to get out a balance sheet,** levantar, preparar, um balanço; (*b*) **to get out an advertising brochure,** publicar uma brochura publicitária.

getup, get-up, *n.* apresentação *f,* disposição *f,* (de mercadorias no supermercado, etc.).

giant, *a. Advert: etc:* **giant packet,** pacote *m* gigante.

gift, *n.* (*a*) *Jur:* doação *f*; **as a gift, by way of gift,** a título gratuito, a título de doação; **deed of gift,** (escritura *f* de) doação; **gift tax,** imposto *m* sobre doações; (*b*) **gift shop,** *Am:* **gift store,** loja *f* de presentes; (*c*) (*on presentation of coupons, etc.*) brinde *m*; **gift voucher,** *Am:* **gift certificate,** cupão *m,* cupom *m,* (dando direito à escolha de mercadoria de determinado valor).

gift-wrap, *v.tr.* embrulhar para presente.

gilt-edge(d), *a. Fin:* **gilt-edge(d) stock(s),** *n.pl.* **gilts,** fundos públicos, títulos *mpl* de toda confiança; **gilt-edge(d) securities,** títulos, valores *mpl,* de toda confiança; **gilt-edge(d) investment,** investimento *m* (em títulos, valores) de toda confiança.

giro, *n. UK:* (*a*) *Post:* **the Giro,** sistema *m* de transferência (de dinheiro); **giro**

cheque, cheque *m* de transferência; (*b*) *Bank:* sistema de transferências bancárias.

give, *v.tr.* **1.** (*a*) dar; **to give sth. in exchange for sth.,** dar algo em troca de outra coisa, trocar algo por outra coisa; **I gave £10 for this radio,** eu dei dez libras esterlinas por este rádio; **what did you give for your car?** quanto deu por seu carro? quanto pagou por seu carro? (i) **to give notice,** avisar, dar aviso, (ii) (*of employer*) **to give s.o. his/her notice,** dar aviso prévio, (*of employee*) **to give in one's notice,** dar aviso prévio; (*b*) *St.Exch:* **to give for the call,** exercer opção de compra a determinado preço; **to give for the put,** exercer opção de venda a determinado preço; **to give an order (to a broker),** dar uma ordem (a um corretor). **2.** (*in a shop, etc.*) **to give an order,** fazer uma encomenda; **to give a receipt,** passar um recibo; **to give a loan (to s.o.),** conceder um empréstimo (a alguém); **to give a service,** prestar um serviço. **3.** *Fin:* **this investment gives 12%,** esta aplicação rende 12%.

give-and-take, *n.* concessões mútuas.

giveaway, *n.* (*a*) brinde *m* (promocional); (*b*) *F:* **these shoes are a giveaway,** estes sapatos são vendidos a preço de banana.

give on, *v.tr. St.Exch:* (*of bull*) pagar a taxa de reporte.

giver, *n. St.Exch:* **giver of option money,** comprador *m* de opções; **giver of stock,** reportado *m.*

glass, *n.* vidro *m*; **glass industry,** indústria *f* do vidro, indústria vidreira; **glass factory,** fábrica *f* de vidro, vidraria *f,* vidraçaria *f*; **glass making, glass manufacture,** fabricação *f* de vidros; **glass manufacturer,** fabricante *m* de vidros, vidraceiro *m*; **glass trade,** comércio *m* de vidros, vidraria *f,* vidraçaria *f*; **crystal glass,** cristal *m.*

glassware, *n.* vidros *mpl,* cristais *mpl,* artigos *mpl* de vidro, vidraria *f.*

glassworks, *n.* vidraria *f,* vidraçaria *f,* fábrica *f* de vidro.

glossary, *n.* **glossary of technical terms,** glossário *m* de termos técnicos.

glut¹, *n.* fartura *f,* pletora *f,* saturação *f*;

there's a glut in the coffee market, há
fartura no mercado do café, o café está
superabundando.
glut², *v.tr.* to glut the market, causar
saturação de mercado; the market is
glutted with cheap imports, o mercado
está saturado de importações baratas.
glutting, *n.* the glutting of the market, a
saturação do mercado.
goal, *n.* meta *f*, objetivo *m*, propósito *m*.
go down, *v.i.* (*of prices, value*) descer,
baixar, cair, diminuir; profits went down
considerably, os lucros cairam, baixaram,
sensivelmente.
going, *a.* (*a*) going concern, (empresa *f*)
em funcionamento, em andamento; 'shop
for sale as going concern', 'vende-se loja
com fundo de comércio'; *Book-k:* going
concern value, valor *m* de funcionamento
(de loja, empresa, etc.); (*b*) the going
black-market rate, a taxa corrente no
mercado negro.
going-to-press, *a. Fin:* going-to-press
prices, os ultimos preços, as últimas
cotações.
gold, *n.* (*a*) ouro *m*; green gold, ouro verde;
ingot gold, ouro em lingotes; pure, fine,
gold, ouro fino; solid gold, ouro maciço;
standard gold, coin cold, ouro de lei; white
gold, ouro branco; gold alloy, liga *f* de
ouro; gold bullion, ouro em barra; gold
content, teor *m* de ouro; gold dust, ouro
em pó; gold foil, ouro em lâmina; gold
leaf, ouro em folha; (*b*) *Fin:* free gold
market, mercado *m* livre de ouro; gold
bond, obrigação *f* resgatável em ouro;
gold-bullion standard, estalão *m* lingote-
ouro; gold currency, gold money, moeda-
ouro *f*, moeda *f* de ouro; gold-exchange
standard, estalão de câmbio ouro-divisas;
gold point, gold point *m*; situação *f* de
equilíbrio cambial nos países de moeda-
ouro; gold reserve, reserva *f* de ouro,
lastro *m*; gold shares, *n.pl.* golds, ações
fpl de empresas de mineração de ouro,
ações de ouro; gold standard, padrão-ouro
m, estalão-ouro *m*; to peg a currency to
gold, cotar uma moeda em relação ao
ouro; gold can be coined freely, a
cunhagem de ouro é livre.
good, *a.* (*a*) a good cheque, um cheque

quente; is the cheque good? o cheque é
bom? good receipt, recibo válido; a good
debt, uma dívida cobrável; he, his credit,
is good for £5000, ele tem crédito até
cinco mil libras esterlinas; (*b*) a good
investment, um bom investimento; to earn
good money, ganhar um bom dinheiro; a
good piece of business, um bom negócio.
goods, *n.pl.* (*a*) *Jur:* bens *mpl*; goods and
chattels, bens móveis; (*b*) mercadorias
fpl, mercancia *f*, bens, produtos *mpl*,
artigos *mpl*; goods and services, bens e
serviços *mpl*, mercadorias e serviços;
goods in transit, mercadorias em trânsito;
goods (sold) on approval, artigos vendidos
a contento; goods on consignment,
mercadorias em consignação; bonded
goods, mercadorias retidas no entreposto
aduaneiro; branded goods, mercadorias
marcadas; canned, tinned, goods,
conservas *fpl*, produtos enlatados, lataria
f; capital goods, bens de capital;
competitive goods, bens concorrentes;
complementary goods, bens
complementares; consumer goods, bens
de consumo, artigos de consumo;
damaged goods, mercadorias danificadas,
estragadas; dry goods, tecidos *mpl*,
fazendas *fpl* e artigos de armarinho em
geral; durable goods, bens duráveis;
economic goods, bens econômicos; knitted
goods, malharia *f*, artigos de malha;
leather goods, artigos de couro;
manufactured goods, (produtos)
manufaturados *mpl*; perishable goods,
bens perecíveis; producer's goods, bens de
produção; representative goods, bens
representativos; saleable, unsaleable,
goods, mercadorias vendáveis,
invendáveis; stolen goods, mercadorias
roubadas; travel goods, artigos de viagem;
wage goods, bens de salário; wasting
goods, bens esgotáveis; wet goods,
molhados *mpl*, mercadorias líquidas; *Ind:*
Book-k: goods in process, produção *f* em
curso, produção em andamento; (*c*) *Rail:*
goods train, trem *m* de carga, trem de
mercadorias; to send sth. by goods train,
by goods service, expedir alguma coisa
por trem de carga; goods station, depot,
estação *f* de mercadorias; goods yard,

pátio *m* de carga; **goods shed,** armazém *m*, galpão *m*, de mercadorias.
goodwill, *n.* aviamento *m*, fundo *m* de comércio; **'for sale with goodwill',** 'vende-se com fundo de comércio'.
go-slow, *n. UK:* greve tartaruga, operação tartaruga, greve passiva.
go up, *v.i.* (*of prices, value, etc.*) subir, (*of product*) encarecer; **bread went up yesterday,** o pão subiu ontem; **food goes up each week,** os gêneros alimentícios encaracem toda semana; **the price of petrol went up by four pence,** o preço da gasolina subiu em quatro penies; **bidding went up to £200,** os lances antingiram, montaram em, importaram em, duzentas libras esterlinas.
government, *n.* governo *m*; **government policy,** a política do governo; **government stock, securities,** títulos *mpl* do governo, fundos públicos; **government bonds,** obrigações *fpl* do governo; **government spending,** despesas públicas; **government loan,** empréstimo público; **government employee,** funcionário público; **government corporation,** empresa pública.
grace, *n.* **period of grace,** prazo *m* de tolerância; **days of grace,** dias *mpl* de tolerância; **to give seven days' grace,** conceder um prazo de tolerância de sete dias; **last day of grace,** prazo fatal, prazo final.
grade¹, *n.* categoria *f*, qualidade *f*, classe *f*; **high-grade farm produce,** produtos *mpl* agrícolas de alta qualidade; **top-grade beef,** carne *f* de boi de primeira qualidade; **low-grade vegetables,** legumes *mpl* de baixa qualidade; **standard-grade coal,** carvão *m* de qualidade-padrão; **grade labelling,** rotulagem *f* baseada na qualidade.
grade², *v.tr.* **1. to grade tomatoes for export,** classificar tomates para exportação; **to grade skilled workers,** categorizar operários especializados; **graded personnel,** pessoal categorizado; **graded hotels,** hotéis classificados. **2. graded tax,** imposto progressivo.
grading, *n.* classificação *f*.
graduated, *a.* **graduated taxation,** tributação progressiva; **graduated income**

tax, imposto de renda progressivo; *UK:* **graduated pension scheme,** sistema *m* de contribuições previdenciais (obrigatórias); *Ins:* **graduated life table,** tábua *f* de mortalidade graduada.
graft, *n. F:* concussão *f*, suborno *m*.
grain, *n.* cereais *mpl*; **the grain market,** o mercado de cereais; **the grain exchange,** a bolsa de cereais.
gram, gramme, *n. Meas:* grama *m*.
grand, *a.* **grand total,** total *m* geral.
grant¹, *n.* subvenção *f*, subsídio *m*; **grant-aided,** subvencionado, pelo Estado.
grant², *v.tr.* conceder, *Jur:* outorgar; **to grant a patent, an exploration licence,** conceder uma patente, um alvará de exploração; **to grant a loan,** conceder um empréstimo; **to grant a request,** atender (a) um pedido; *Jur:* **to grant bail,** conceder liberdade sob caução.
grantee, *n. Jur:* concessionário *m*, cessionário *m*, outorgado *m*.
grantor, *n. Jur:* cedente *mf*, outorgante *mf*.
graph, *n.* gráfico *m*; **graph paper,** papel quadriculado, papel milimetrado.
gratis, 1. *a.* de graça, gratuito. **2.** *adv.* grátis, de graça.
grey, *a.* **grey market,** mercado cinzento.
grievance, *n. Ind: etc:* dissídio *m*; **to set up grievance machinery, a grievance procedure,** instituir um processo de dissídios.
grocer, *n.* merceeiro *m*, comerciante *mf* de secos e molhados; **the grocer's,** a mercearia, a loja de secos e molhados, o armazém, o empório, a venda.
grocery, *n. pl.* **groceries,** secos e molhados *mpl*; *N.Am:* **grocery store,** loja *f* de secos e molhados, mercearia *f*, armazém *m*, empório *m*, venda *f*.
gross¹, *n.* grosa *f*, doze dúzias *fpl*.
gross², *a.* (*a*) bruto; **gross amount,** montante bruto, valor bruto, (de fatura, etc.); **gross book value,** valor escritural bruto; **gross cost,** custo bruto; **gross earning,** renda bruta; **gross income,** renda bruta; **gross loss,** perda bruta, déficit bruto; **gross margin,** margem bruta, lucro bruto; **gross proceeds from the sale of vehicles,** produto bruto da venda de

veículos; **gross profit,** lucro bruto; **gross profit analysis,** análise *f* do lucro bruto; **gross receipt(s),** receita bruta; **gross revenue,** receita bruta; **gross sales,** vendas brutas; **gross weight,** peso bruto; *Econ:* **gross national product (GNP),** produto nacional bruto (PNB); **gross domestic product (GDP),** produto interno bruto (PIB); **gross national income,** renda nacional bruta; **gross national expenditure,** despesa nacional bruta; *Book-k:* **gross profit method of inventory,** método de cálculo do valor do inventário com base no lucro bruto; (*b*) *Nau:* **gross tonnage,** tonelagem bruta; (*c*) *M.Ins:* **gross average,** avaria grossa, avaria comum.

gross³, *v.tr.* dar uma renda, uma receita, bruta de (tantos dólares, cruzeiros, etc.); **the shop is grossing $1700 a week,** a loja está dando, está produzindo, uma receita semanal bruta de $1.700; a receita semanal bruta da loja é de $1.700.

ground, *n.* *Jur:* **grounds of a plaint,** fundamentos *mpl* de uma reclamação.

group, *n.* (*a*) *Ind: etc:* grupo *m*, grupo de sociedades; **this company belongs to the X group,** esta companhia pertence ao grupo X; **group accounts,** demonstrações financeiras (consolidadas) de grupo; (*b*) *Ins:* **group (life) insurance,** seguro *m* (de vida) em grupo; (*c*) **age group,** faixa etária.

growing, *a.* crescente; **a growing industry,** uma indústria em crescimento, em expansão; **a growing demand for fixed-interest loans,** uma demanda crescente para empréstimos com juros fixos.

growth, *n.* crescimento *m*; **economic growth,** crescimento econômico; **rate of growth,** índice *m*, taxa *f*, de crescimento; **growth industry,** indústria *f* em rápido crescimento; *Fin:* **growth stock,** ações *fpl* de uma companhia em rápido crescimento.

guarantee¹, *n.* **1.** (*person*) (*a*) (*guarantor*) fiador *m*, abonador *m*, garante *mf*, garantidor *m*; (*of bill*) avalista *mf*; (*b*) credor garantido. **2.** (*guaranty*) garantia *f* (**against,** contra); **a five-year guarantee,** uma garantia de cinco anos; **this television is under guarantee,** esta televisão está na garantia, está sob garantia; **complete guarantee,** garantia total, garantia absoluta; **guarantee of a bill of exchange,** aval *m* (de uma letra de câmbio); **guarantee fund,** fundo *m* de garantia; **guarantee company,** sociedade *f* de responsabilidade limitada (de acordo com a garantia dada pelos sócios); **guarantee commission,** del-credere *m*. **3.** (*security*) garantia *f*, caução *f*; **to leave sth. as a guarantee,** dar algo em garantia, em caução; caucionar algo.

guarantee², *v.tr.* (*a*) garantir, afiançar, abonar; **to guarantee a debt,** garantir, avalizar, afiançar, uma dívida; **he is guaranteed by his father,** ele é afiançado, abonado, pelo seu pai; **the watch is guaranteed for two years,** o relógio está garantido por dois anos, a garantia do relógio é de dois anos; (*b*) **to guarantee a bill of exchange,** avalizar uma letra de câmbio.

guaranteed, *a.* garantido, afiançado; **guaranteed bond,** obrigação garantida, obrigação afiançada; **guaranteed stock,** títulos garantidos; **guaranteed dividend,** dividendo garantido; **guaranteed minimum wage,** salário mínimo.

guaranteeing, *n.* abonação *f*, abonamento *m*.

guarantor, *n.* fiador *m*, afiançador *m*, abonador *m*, garante *mf*, garantidor *m*; (*of bill of exchange*) avalista *mf*; **to stand (as) guarantor for s.o.,** afiançar, abonar, alguém; ser fiador de alguém.

guaranty, *n.* = **guarantee¹,** 2. and 3.

guild, *n.* (*a*) corporação *f*; (*b*) *Hist:* guilda *f*.

H

habilitate, v.tr. N.Am: emprestar fundos para a operação (de uma fábrica).
habilitator, n. N.Am: financiador m (de operações industriais).
haggle, v.i. regatear, pechinchar.
half, 1. n. metade f; the first half of the year, o primeiro semestre do ano; the Brazilian product costs half the imported one, o produto brasileiro custa a metade do importado; (of goods, etc.) reduced by half, reduzido à metade. 2. a. meio; half a kilo, meio quilo; it cost half a dollar, custou meio dólar; half a dozen, meia dúzia; (in shops, etc.) (it's) on sale at half price, à venda pela metade do preço; half fare, meia passagem; half pay, meio salário; (official) half day, half holiday, meio-feriado m; (of working) half time, meio período, meio expediente; half-time worker, trabalhador m de meio expediente, de meio período.
half-monthly, a. bimensal, semimensal.
halfpenny, n. moeda f de meio pêni.
half-year, n. semestre m.
half-yearly, 1. a. semestral; half-yearly payment, semestralidade f, semestre m, pagamento m semestral; he's paying for his car in half-yearly instalments, ele está pagando seu carro em prestações semestrais. 2. adv. semestralmente.
hallmark[1], n. marca f de contraste (em artefatos de ouro ou prata).
hallmark[2], v.tr. estampar (artefatos de ouro ou prata) com a marca de contraste.
hammer[1], n. (of auctioneer) martelo m; by the hammer, ao correr do martelo; to come under the hammer, ser leiloado, ser vendido ao correr do martelo, em leilão.
hammer[2], v.tr. (a) UK: St.Exch: to hammer a defaulter, declarar a insolvência de um corretor de valores; (b) Fin: to hammer prices, fazer baixar os

preços (mediante vendas a descoberto); (c) to hammer out a contract, negociar um contrato.
hand, n. 1. mão f; it's in the hands of the manager, está nas mãos do gerente; receipt made out in his own hand, recibo feito por seu próprio punho, por sua própria mão; to send a letter by hand, enviar uma carta em mão(s); goods left on one's hands, encalhe m, mercadorias encalhadas; (of business, etc.) to change hands, passer às mãos de um novo dono. 2. (a) in hand, disponível, à disposição; to have some money in hand, ter algum dinheiro disponível, à (sua) disposição; Book-k: cash in hand, dinheiro em caixa, encaixe m, numerário m disponível, bens numerários; stock in hand, mercadorias fpl em estoque; work in hand, trabalho m em curso, em andamento; (b) we have a wide range of goods on hand, (nós) temos um grande sortimento de mercadorias; (c) (of letter, etc.) to come to hand, chegar (ao destino). 3. assinatura f, firma f; to set one's hand to a deed, assinar, firmar, uma escritura; under the hand and seal of X, assinado e selado por X; note of hand, (nota) promissória f. 4. a hand of bananas, uma penca de bananas. 5. Am: braceiro m, (general) operário m; 'hands wanted', 'vagas para braceiros', 'precisa-se de braceiros'; to take on hands, admitir braceiros.
handbook, n. manual m.
handicraft, n. artesanato m.
hand in, v.tr. entregar (requerimento, formulário, etc.); all bids must be handed in by 15 July, todas as propostas deverão ser entregues até o dia 15 de julho; to hand in one's resignation, pedir demissão (por escrito).
handle, v.tr. (a) to handle a lot of business,

tratar de muitos negócios, ter muitos negócios; **to handle large órders,** despachar, atender, grandes encomendas; **to handle a lot of money,** lidar com, trabalhar com, muito dinheiro; **we do not handle these goods,** não comerciamos nestas mercadorias, não negociamos com estas mercadorias; (b) Ind: movimentar; **the port handles X tons of steel a month,** o porto movimenta X toneladas de aço por mês.

handling, n. Ind: movimentação f, manuseio m; **handling charge,** taxa f de manuseio; **handling cost,** custo m de manuseio; **handling facilities,** instalações fpl de manuseio; **cargo handling facilities,** facilidades fpl de manuseio de cargas; **materials handling,** manuseio de materiais, movimentação de materiais.

hand-made, a. feito à mão.

handout, n. circular publicitária.

hand over, v.tr. **to hand over shares as security for a loan,** dar, entregar, ações em caução de um empréstimo; **to hand over a draft for collection,** dar, entregar, um saque para cobrança; **the property will be handed over on 1 June,** a propriedade será transferida em 1° de junho.

handshake, n. **golden handshake,** indenização f por afastamento de cargo (ou emprego).

handwork, n. trabalho m manual; trabalho feito com as mãos (e não com máquina).

handworker, n. trabalhador manual.

harbour, n. porto m; **commercial harbour,** porto comercial; **harbour authorities,** autoridades portuárias; **harbour dues,** direitos portuários; **harbour facilities,** instalações portuárias; **harbour master,** capitão m do porto; **harbour pilot,** prático m (de porto); **to leave harbour,** sair do porto, deixar o porto.

hard, a. 1. (a) Fin: (of price, rate, etc.) firme; elevado e estável; **stocks are harder,** as ações subiram de cotação; (b) Fin: (of currency) forte; **the yen and the Deutschmark are hard currencies,** o iene e o marco alemão são moedas fortes; (c) (of money) **hard money and not**

banknotes, moeda metálica e não cédulas bancárias; **hard cash,** dinheiro vivo, moeda f sonante. **2. this article is hard to sell,** este artigo é de difícil saída. **3. the hard sell,** a venda por métodos agressivos.

harden, v.i. (of prices, etc.) subir, elevar-se, aumentar.

hardening, n. (of prices, etc.) subida f, aumento m, elevação f.

hardware, n. **1.** ferragens fpl; **hardware store,** loja f de ferragens. **2.** Cmptr: hardware m; componentes físicos de um equipamento de computação.

hat, n. Nau: **hat money,** chapéu m (de capitão).

haul¹, n. (a) (act of transporting) transporte m, transportação f; (b) **short-haul operations,** operações fpl de transporte a curta distância; **long-haul operations,** operações de transporte a longa distância; **long-haul jet,** jato m de longo curso.

haul², v.tr. transportar (por caminhão).

haulage, n. transporte m; **road haulage,** transporte rodoviário de carga; **haulage contractor, haulage firm,** (empresa) transportadora f, empresa de transportes rodoviários; **haulage charge,** frete rodoviário.

haulaway, n. Trans: jamanta f, carreta f.

haulier, n. (empresa) transportadora f, empresa de transportes rodoviários.

haven, n. **tax haven,** refúgio m fiscal.

hawk, v.tr. & i. mascatear.

hawker, n. mascate m, vendedor m ambulante.

hawking, n. **share hawking,** venda f de títulos de porta em porta.

head¹, n. **1.** (heading) cabeçalho m. **2. the head of sales,** o chefe de vendas; **the head of the organization,** o diretor, o chefe, da organização; **head of department, departmental head,** chefe de serviço, (in store) chefe de departamento; **head clerk,** chefe de escritório; **head agent,** agente mf principal; **head office,** sede f, (casa) matriz f (de firma, etc.). **3. to pay so much per head,** pagar tanto por cabeça.

head², v.tr. **to head an organization,** chefiar uma organização.

headed, *a.* **headed notepaper,** papel timbrado.

heading, *n.* timbre *m,* cabeçalho *m,* (em papel de carta), cabeça *f* (de página, fatura, etc.); *Book-k:* rubrica *f.*

headquarters, *n.pl.* (*often with sg. const.*) sede *f*; **this organization has its headquarters in New York,** esta organização está sediada em Nova Iorque.

health, *n.* saúde *f*; **health insurance,** seguro-saúde *m,* seguro *m* contra doença; **health service,** serviço *m* de saúde.

hearing, *n.* *Jur:* **bankruptcy hearing,** audiência *f* falencial.

heavily, *adv.* **to be heavily in debt,** estar cheio de dívidas.

heavy, *a.* **1.** pesado; **heavy goods vehicle,** caminhão *m* de carga pesada. **2.** *Fin:* **the market is heavy,** o mercado está em baixa; **a heavy fall in share prices,** uma forte queda nos preços de ações; **heavy expenditure,** despesas elevadas; **heavy losses,** prejuízos *mpl,* perdas *fpl,* importantes; **heavy sales,** vendas maciças. **3. heavy tax,** imposto oneroso, imposto pesado. **4. heavy industry,** indústria pesada.

hedge¹, *n.* *Fin:* cobertura *f* contra um risco; (*commodities market*) operação a termo compensatória; **to buy works of art as a hedge against inflation,** comprar obras de arte para cobrir-se, proteger-se, contra a inflação; *Jur:* **hedge clause,** cláusula *f* de ressalva; **to buy for the account as a hedge,** cobrir-se mediante hedging.

hedge², *v.tr. & i.* cobrir-se mediante hedging; **to hedge by a sale for the account,** cobrir-se mediante uma venda a termo.

hedging, *n.* hedging *m*; operação que consiste na tomada de uma posição no mercado futuro aproximadamente igual — mas em sentido contrário àquela que se detém no mercado à vista.

hereafter, *adv.* daqui em diante.

hereby, *adv.* **we hereby declare that . . .,** declaramos pelo presente que . . . .

herewith, *adv.* em anexo; **our price list is enclosed herewith,** anexamos, anexa-se, a nossa lista de preços.

hidden, *a.* *Fin:* **hidden tax,** imposto disfarçado; **hidden reserve,** reserva oculta.

high, 1. *a.* (*a*) alto, elevado; **to be in a high position in a firm,** exercer um alto cargo, desempenhar uma alta função, numa empresa; **the higher positions are filled by foreigners,** os cargos superiores são ocupados por estrangeiros; (*b*) **high prices,** preços altos, preços elevados; **he wants the highest price possible,** ele quer o melhor preço possível; **to make a higher bid,** oferecer um lance maior; **the high rate of interest,** a taxa elevada de juros, a alta taxa de juros. **2.** *adv.* (*of prices*) **to run high,** estar elevado, estar alto; **costs are running higher than anticipated,** os custos estão acima do nível previsto. **3.** *n.* *Fin:* nível máximo de preços, preço máximo; **the shares have reached a new high,** as ações atingiram um novo recorde; *St.Exch:* **highs and lows,** altas *fpl* e baixas *fpl.*

high-class, *a.* **high-class goods,** mercadorias *fpl* de alta qualidade.

high-grade, *a.* de alta qualidade, de alta categoria.

high-level, *a.* **high-level staff,** pessoal *m* de alto nível.

high-priced, *a.* de alto custo, caro, custoso.

high-proof, *a.* de alto teor alcoólico.

high-quality, *a.* de alta qualidade.

high-ranking, *a.* **high-ranking official,** alto funcionário, funcionário de alto nível.

high-speed, *a.* de alta velocidade.

hike, *v.tr.* *N.Am:* aumentar (preços, etc.).

hire¹, *n.* **1.** (*a*) *N.Am:* admissão *f,* contrato *m,* contratação *f,* (de pessoal, etc.); (*b*) locação *f* (de automóveis); **self-drive cars for hire,** alugam-se carros sem chofer; **car-hire firm,** empresa locadora de automóveis; **hire car,** carro *m* de aluguel; **car-hire charges,** tarifa *f* para locação de automóveis; **the car is on hire,** o carro está sendo alugado; (*c*) **hire purchase,** compra *f* a prestação, compra *f* a prazo; **to buy a television on hire purchase,** comprar uma televisão a prazo, comprar

uma televisão pelo crediário, pelo facilitário. **2.** *esp. N.Am:* (i) salário *m*, paga *f*, (ii) aluguel *m*.
hire², *v.tr.* **1.** *esp. N.Am:* admitir, contratar, (operário, empregado). **2.** (*a*) alugar (carro, etc.); (*b*) *esp. N.Am:* **to hire sth. out**, alugar, locar, (alguma coisa para um freguês, um cliente). **3.** *N.Am:* (*esp. of self-employed*) ser contratado (para trabalhos avulsos).
hired, *a.* **hired car**, carro alugado, carro de aluguel.
hirer, *n.* **1.** alugador *m*, locatário, (de quarto, carro, etc.). **2.** *N.Am:* **hirer (out)**, locador *m*, (empresa) locadora *f*.
historical, *a. Book-k:* **historical cost**, custo histórico, valor histórico; **historical cost accounting**, contabilidade *f* de custos baseada no valor histórico.
hive off, *v.tr.* **to hive off a profitable operation**, vender um setor lucrativo de uma empresa (geralmente para compensar os prejuízos num outro setor).
hoard, *v.* **1.** *v.tr.* açambarcar (mercadorias), entesourar (dinheiro); **hoarded money**, dinheiro *m* de botija. **2.** *v.i.* açambarcar.
hoarder, *n.* açambarcador *m* (de mercadorias), entesourador *m* (de dinheiro).
hoarding, *n.* **1.** açambarcamento *m*, açambarcagem *f*, (de mercadorias), entesouramento *m* (de capitais, etc.). **2.** painel *m* para cartazes.
hold, *v.* **1.** *v.tr.* (*a*) **to hold shares in three companies**, possuir ações de três companhias; **to hold stocks as security for a loan**, deter títulos em garantia de um empréstimo; **to hold stocks for a rise**, reter determinados títulos com vistas a uma alta; **the farmers are holding their wheat to force up the price**, os fazendeiros estão guardando, retendo, o trigo para provocar uma subida no preço; (*b*) **this product is still holding its own after ten years**, este produto ainda vende bem após dez anos de lançamento; (*c*) **to hold a meeting**, realizar uma reunião; **to hold a position**, ocupar, exercer, um cargo; ocupar uma posição; (*d*) **to hold s.o. responsible for the loss, the damage**,

responsabilizar alguém pela perda, pela avaria. **2.** *v.i.* **the prices will hold for 90 days**, os preços terão validade por 90 dias.
hold back, *v.i.* **the buyers are holding back**, os compradores estão se abstendo.
holder, *n.* proprietário *m*, possuidor *m*, dono *m*, titular *mf*, (*bearer*) portador *m*; **the holder of a lease**, o arrendatário; **the holder of a manufacturing licence**, o titular de uma licença de fabricação; **holders of debt claims**, credores *mpl*; **holder of a bank account**, titular de uma conta bancária; **holder of a bill of exchange**, tomador *m*, possuidor *m*, de uma letra de câmbio; *Jur:* **holder on trust of s.o.'s securities**, depositário *m* dos títulos de alguém.
holding, *n.* **1.** *Agr:* arrendamento *m*. **2.** *Fin: etc:* haveres *mpl*, posses *fpl*; carteira *f* (de títulos comerciais ou valores móveis); **to have a holding in a company**, participar de uma companhia, ter uma participação (acionária) em uma companhia, ter um investimento em uma companhia; **holding company**, (empresa) holding *f*, sociedade *f* holding, holding company *f*.
hold on, *v.i.* **to hold on to certain shares**, reter determinadas ações.
hold over, *v.tr.* **to hold over a payment**, adiar um pagamento.
hold up, *v.* **1.** *v.tr.* (*a*) reter; **goods held up at the customs**, mercadorias retidas na alfândega; (*b*) **to hold up payment until the completion of a job**, reter, atrasar, o pagamento até o acabamento de uma obra; **deliveries have been held up owing to a strike**, as entregas atrasaram por causa de greve. **2.** *v.i.* (*a*) (*of prices, shares, etc.*) manter-se (firme, estável, etc.); **prices held up well until closing**, os preços se mantiveram firmes até o fechamento; (*b*) *esp. N.Am:* **to hold up on the money**, reter o dinheiro, atrasar o pagamento do dinheiro.
holiday, *n.* (*a*) feriado *m*; **public, national, official, legal, holiday**, feriado público, dia feriado; **bank holiday**, feriado bancário; (*b*) (*day off*) dia *m* de folga; (*c*) (*vacation*) **a month's holiday**, um mês de férias; **to take three weeks' holiday**,

tirar três semanas de férias; **paid holidays, holidays with pay,** férias remuneradas; **holiday pay,** pagamento *m,* salário *m,* de férias; **to be on holiday,** estar de férias, estar em férias; (*d*) **tax holiday,** período *m* de isenção fiscal (para empresas).

hollow ware, *n. Dom.Ec:* vasilhas *fpl* (de louça, metal, etc., para servir comida ou bebida).

holograph, *n. Jur:* documento hológrafo.

holograph(ic), *a. Jur:* hológrafo; **holograph(ic) will,** testamento hológrafo.

home, *n.* **1.** casa *f* de família, domicílio *m,* residência *f* (familiar); *Jur:* bem *m* de família; **home delivery service,** serviço *m* de entregas a domicílio; **home owner,** dono *m* de casa própria; **home loan,** crédito imobiliário, financiamento *m* habitacional; **home ownership scheme,** sistema *m* para aquisição de casa própria; *Ins:* **home owner's policy,** apólice *f* de seguro de chefe de família, apólice de seguro do lar. **2.** (*a*) *N.Am:* **home economics,** economia doméstica; (*b*) **the Home Counties,** os condados nos arredores de Londres; (*c*) *N.Am: Ind: etc:* **home office,** sede *f,* (casa) matriz *f,* (de uma companhia). **3. home journey,** viagem *f* de volta; **home freight,** carga transportada na viagem de volta; **home port,** porto *m* de origem, de procedência. **4.** (*of the nation*) **home trade,** comércio interno; **home market,** mercado interno, mercado nacional; **home products,** produtos *mpl* nacionais; *UK:* **the Home Office,** o Ministério dos Negócios Interiores.

homecraft, *n.* artes domésticas.

homegrown, *a.* (*a*) caseiro; **homegrown vegetables,** hortaliças caseiras; (*b*) (*of the country*) **homegrown coffee,** café *m* nacional.

home-made, *a.* (*a*) caseiro, feito em casa; (*b*) nacional, de fabricação nacional; **home-made cars,** carros *mpl* nacionais, de fabricação nacional.

homespun, *Tex:* **1.** *a.* (tecido) caseiro, tecido em casa; **homespun linen,** linho caseiro, linho fiado em casa. **2.** *n.* tecido caseiro.

homestead, *n. Am: Jur:* bem *m* de família.

homeward, *a.* **homeward voyage,** viagem *f* de volta.

homewards, *adv.* **loading homewards,** recebendo carga para a viagem de volta.

homework, *n.* trabalho feito em casa.

homeworker, *n.* tarefeiro *m* que trabalha em casa.

honorary, *a.* honorário; **honorary chairman,** presidente honorário; **honorary duties,** funções honorárias.

honour¹, *n.* **acceptance (of protested bill) for honour,** aceite *m* de honra, aceite sob protesto; **the acceptor for honour,** aquele que aceita uma letra de câmbio sob protesto.

honour², *v.tr.* (*a*) **to honour a cheque,** pagar um cheque; **to honour a bill,** (i) aceitar uma letra de câmbio; (ii) pagar uma letra de câmbio; **honoured bill,** (i) letra aceita, (ii) letra paga; (*b*) **to honour one's obligations,** cumprir (com) as suas obrigações; **to honour a contract,** cumprir, adimplir, completar, um contrato.

horizontal, *a.* horizontal; *Am:* global (isto é, para todos os artigos ou pessoas da mesma categoria); **a horizontal increase of 10%,** um aumento global de 10%; *Am: Ind:* **horizontal union,** sindicato *m* para operários da mesma categoria.

horsepower, *n.* horse-power *m,* cavalo-vapor *m;* **horsepower hour,** cavalo-hora *m.*

hosier, *n.* (i) negociante *mf* de meias, (ii) negociante de artigos de malha, de malharia.

hosiery, *n.* comércio *m* de (i) meias, (ii) malharia *f,* artigos de malha; **hosiery counter,** balcão *m* de (i) meias, (ii) malharia, artigos de malha.

hostess, *n.* **air hostess,** aeromoça *f,* comissária *f* de bordo.

hot, *a. Fin:* **hot money,** dinheiro (depositado ou investido) que pode ser retirado com pouco aviso prévio (causando assim pânico no mercado financeiro).

hotel, *n.* hotel *m;* **the hotel industry,** a indústria hoteleira; **the hotel trade,** o comércio hoteleiro; **private, residential, hotel,** pensão *f* (familiar); **hotel accommodation,** acomodação *f* (de hotel); **hotel manager,** gerente *mf* de hotel.

hour, *n.* hora *f*; **to pay s.o. by the hour,** pagar alguém por hora; **to be paid $5 an hour,** ganhar cinco dólares por hora, receber um salário de cinco dólares por hora; **eight-hour day,** jornada *f* de oito horas, dia *m* de oito horas; **office, business, hours,** expediente *m*, horário *m* comercial; **I do this work after hours,** faço este trabalho fora do horário, após o expediente; **rush hour,** hora do rush; *Advert:* **peak viewing hours,** horário *m* nobre.

hourly, *a.* horário; **hourly flights,** vôos horários; **hourly-paid worker,** horista *mf*; **hourly wage, rate, pay,** salário-hora *m*.

house, *n.* **1.** casa *f*, vivenda *f*, habitação *f*, residência *f*; **house telephone,** telefone interno; **house painter,** pintor *m* de paredes; **house coal,** carvão *m* para uso doméstico; **house property,** imóvel *m* residencial, bem *m* residencial; **house duty, tax,** imposto *m* predial; **house agent,** agente imobiliário; *Ins:* **house insurance,** seguro *m* do lar, seguro habitacional. **2.** (*a*) **banking house,** casa bancária; **publishing house,** (casa) editora *f*; **export house,** (casa) exportadora *f*; *Fin:* **clearing house,** câmara *f* de compensação; **house organ,** órgão *m* de circulação interna; (*b*) *St.Exch:* **the House,** a Bolsa; **the members of the House,** os membros, os sócios, da Bolsa. **3.** *Am: Ind: etc:* **packing house,** (i) frigorífico *m*, (ii) fábrica *f* de conservas.

housecraft, *n.* artes domésticas.

household, *n.* família *f*, *Adm:* instituição *f*

familiar; **head of the household,** chefe *m* de família, *Adm:* chefe-de-casal *m*; **household articles,** artigos domésticos; **household appliances,** eletrodomésticos *mpl*; **household expenses,** despesas domésticas; *Ind: etc:* (*of brand, product, etc.*) **household name,** marca *f* de aceitação nacional, produto *m* de grande aceitação.

householder, *n.* (i) dono *m* da casa, (ii) chefe *m* de família.

house-to-house, *a.* **house-to-house selling,** venda *f* de casa em casa.

housewares, *n.pl.* *Am:* aparelhos domésticos, artigos *mpl* de uso doméstico.

housewife, *n.* dona *f* de casa; *Adm:* (*on passport, etc.*) prendas domésticas.

housework, *n.* serviço doméstico.

housing, *n.* alojamento *m* (de pessoas); (*as issue*) habitação *f*; **the housing crisis,** a crise habitacional; *Ind: etc:* **housing allowance,** ajuda *f* para alojamento.

hovercraft, *n.* aerobarco *m*.

hoverport, *n.* estação *f* de aerobarco.

huckster[1]**,** *n.* **1.** mascate *m*, vendedor *m* ambulante. **2.** *Am:* publicitário *m*.

huckster[2]**,** *v.tr.* (*a*) (i) comerciar (em), (ii) retalhar, (determinadas mercadorias); (*b*) regatear.

hypermarket, *n.* hipermercado *m*.

hypothecate, *v.tr.* *Jur:* **to hypothecate land and buildings,** hipotecar terras e prédios; **to hypothecate a ship, a plane,** hipotecar um navio, um avião.

hypothecation, *n.* *Jur:* hipoteca *f*; **hypothecation certificate, letter of hypothecation,** cédula hipotecária, letra hipotecária.

I

ideal, *a. Ind: Book-k: etc:* **ideal standard cost,** custo *m* standard ideal.

idle, *a.* (*a*) ocioso; **idle capacity,** capacidade ociosa, capacidade não utilizada; **idle cost,** custo *m* de capacidade não utilizada; **idle time,** tempo perdido, tempo ocioso; (*b*) **idle money,** dinheiro inativo, dinheiro morto; **capital lying idle,** capital improdutivo, capital não investido; **to let one's money lie idle,** não investir os capitais.

illegal, *a.* ilegal.

illegality, *n.* ilegalidade *f.*

illegally, *adv.* ilegalmente.

illicit, *a.* ilícito.

image, *n.* imagem *f*; **brand image,** imagem de marca; **corporate image,** imagem de companhia.

immovable, *Jur:* 1. *a.* **immovable property,** bens *mpl* imóveis, bens de raíz; **seizure of immovable property,** seqüestro *m* de bens imóveis. 2. *n.pl.* **immovables,** (bens) imóveis *mpl.*

immunity, *n.* isenção *f*, imunidade *f*, (**from,** de); **to request immunity from certain taxes,** pedir isenção de certos impostos.

impact, *n.* impacto *m*; **to have an impact on (prices, etc.),** causar, produzir, impacto sobre (os preços, etc.); **the impact of a publicity campaign,** o impacto de uma campanha publicitária.

impersonal, *a. Book-k: etc:* **impersonal account,** conta *f* impessoal.

implement, *v.tr.* implementar, executar, (um projeto); fazer cumprir, aplicar, (uma lei).

implementation, *n.* execução *f*, implementação *f.*

implied, *a.* **implied contract,** contrato implícito, tácito; **implied terms (of contract),** condições (de contrato)

implícitas; **implied trust,** fideicomisso implícito, fideicomisso tácito.

import[1], *n. usu. pl.* **imports,** importações *fpl*; **postal imports,** importações via postal; **visible and invisible imports** importações visíveis e invisíveis; **import ban,** proibição *f* de importações; **import controls,** controles *mpl* de importação **import credit,** crédito *m* ao importador crédito de importação; **import duty** imposto *m* de importação, taxa de importação; **import financing** financiamento *m* de importações; **import firm,** (empresa, firma) importadora *f* **import licence,** licença *f* de importação **import list,** pauta *f* de importações **import permit,** guia *f* de importação **import policy,** política *f* de importação **import quotas,** contingentes *mpl*, quota *fpl*, cotas *fpl*, de importação; **import restrictions,** restrições *fpl* às importações **import trade,** comércio *m* de importações **import and export trade,** comércio de importações e exportações.

import[2], *v.tr.* importar (mercadorias) **imported goods,** mercadorias importadas **imported from Brazil,** importado de Brasil.

importable, *a.* importável.

importation, *n.* 1. importação *f* (de mercadorias); **for temporary importation** em regime de admissão temporária. 2 *N.Am:* artigo importado.

importer, *n.* importador *m*; (firma importadora *f.*

importing, *a.* importador; **the importing countries,** os países importadores.

impose, *v.tr.* impor; **to impose a tax on sugar,** impor uma taxa sobre o açúcar tributar o açúcar.

imposition, *n.* (*a*) imposição *f* (de taxa etc.); (*b*) imposto *m*, taxa *f.*

impound, *v.tr. Jur:* confiscar, arrestar, (bens de devedor, etc.).

impounding, *n. Jur:* confisco *m*, apreensão *f*, (de bens, documentos, etc.).

impresario, *n.* empresário *m* (de teatro, espetáculos, etc.).

imprest, *n. Adm: Book-k:* **imprest system,** sistema *m* de fundo fixo; **imprest cash, fund,** fundo fixo de caixa.

imprint, *n.* **publisher's imprint,** nome *m* de (casa) editora.

imprinter, *n.* **(credit card) imprinter,** máquina *f* de imprimir (cartões de crédito).

improve, *v.* **1.** *v.tr.* **to improve sales,** melhorar as vendas; **to improve profitability,** melhorar a rentabilidade; **to improve on s.o.'s offer,** oferecer mais que alguém. **2.** *v.i.* melhorar(-se); (*of prices, etc.*) subir, elevar-se; **business is improving,** os negócios estão melhorando; **the market is improving,** o mercado está melhorando.

improved, *a.* (*a*) (*of method, product, etc.*) melhorado, aperfeiçoado; (*b*) **improved offer,** oferta *f* superior.

improvement, *n.* melhoramento *m*, melhoria *f*, benfeitoria *f*; **the tenant made various improvements in the house,** o inquilino fez vários melhoramentos na casa; **job improvement,** melhoramento de cargo.

impulse, *n.* **impulse buying,** compra *f* emocional, compra impulsiva.

imputed, *a.* **imputed value,** valor presumido.

in, *a.* **in tray, basket,** cesta *f* para correspondência de entrada; *Fin:* **in book,** registro *m* de entradas; *Ind: etc:* **in-house training,** treinamento *m* na própria empresa.

inadmissible, *a. Book-k:* **inadmissible assets,** bens *mpl* inadmissíveis.

incentive, *n.* incentivo *m*; **incentive plan, scheme,** plano *m* de incentivos; **production incentives,** incentivos à produção; **incentive pay,** salário-prêmio *m.*

incidence, *n. Fin:* **incidence of taxation,** incidência *f* de impostos.

incidental, *a.* **incidental expenses,** despesas *fpl* adicionais; *Book-k:* **incidental costs,** custos *mpl* adicionais.

include, *v.tr.* incluir, abranger; **price including carriage,** preço *m* incluindo porte; **up to and including December 31st,** até 31 de dezembro inclusive; **to include a new clause in the contract,** incluir uma nova cláusula no contrato.

inclusive, *a.* **inclusive sum,** soma *f* global; **all-inclusive price,** preço *m* global, preço total; **from 4th to 12th February inclusive,** de 4 até 12 de fevereiro inclusive; **inclusive of all taxes,** incluindo todas as taxas, todos os impostos.

income, *n.* renda *f*, rendimento *m*, receita *f*, rédito *m*; **source of income,** fonte *f* de renda; **what are your sources of income?** quais são suas fontes de renda? **annual income,** renda anual, rendimento anual; **disposable income,** renda disponível; **earned income,** rendimentos do trabalho individual; **gross income,** renda bruta; **net income,** renda líquida; **operating income,** renda operacional; **personal income,** renda individual, renda pessoal; **taxable income,** renda tributável, rendimentos tributáveis; **unearned income,** rendimentos não ganhos com o trabalho individual; **income bond,** obrigação *f* de renda variável (pagável somente se houver lucros); **income bracket,** faixa *f* de renda, faixa de salário; **lower-income group,** grupo *m* de renda baixa; **middle-income group,** grupo de renda média; **higher-income group,** grupo de renda alta; **income statement,** balanço *m* de resultados (de empresa), demonstração *f* de lucros e perdas; **(personal) income tax,** imposto *m* de renda (de pessoa física); **income tax return,** declaração *f* de rendimentos; **to live from a private income,** viver de rendas (tais como juros, dividendos, etc.); *Pol.Ec:* **incomes policy,** política *f* de salários; *Pol.Ec:* **gross national income,** renda nacional bruta.

incomings, *n.pl.* receitas *fpl*; **incomings and outgoings,** receitas e despesas *fpl.*

inconvertible, *a.* inconversível, inconvertível.

incorporate, *v.* **1.** *v.tr.* **to incorporate a company,** constituir, organizar, uma

companhia. **2.** *v.i.* organizar-se em sociedade.
incorporated, *a.* *N.Am:* (firma) organizada em sociedade autorizada.
incorporation, *n.* constituição *f,* organização *f,* (de companhia); *Am:* constituição de uma sociedade mercantil; **incorporation expenses,** despesas *fpl* de organização, de instalação.
incorporator, *n.* *N.Am:* fundador *m,* organizador *m,* (de uma sociedade mercantil).
increase¹, *n.* aumento *m,* majoração *f,* acréscimo *m;* **increase of capital,** aumento de capital; **price increase, increase in price(s),** aumento de preço(s), aumento no(s) preço(s); **increase in the cost of living,** aumento do custo de vida; **increase in wages, pay increase,** aumento de salário, aumento salarial; **an increase of 30% on last year,** um aumento de 30% sobre o ano passado; **to be on the increase,** estar aumentando; **increase in value (of property, etc.),** valorização *f* (de bens imóveis, etc.).
increase², *v.* **1.** *v.tr.* aumentar, majorar, elevar, (preços, salários, etc.); **to increase expenditure,** aumentar as despesas; **the increased cost of living,** o aumento do custo de vida. **2.** *v.i.* aumentar, subir, elevar-se; **to increase in size,** aumentar de tamanho; **to increase in price,** aumentar de preço, subir de preço, encarecer.
increasing, *a.* **the increasing cost of petrol,** o custo crescente da gasolina.
increment, *n.* incremento *m,* aumento *m.*
incremental, *a.* **incremental cost,** custo *m* marginal, custo incremental.
incur, *v.tr.* *(a)* **to incur a loss,** acusar um prejuízo, sofrer uma perda; **to incur expenses,** realizar despesas; **to incur debts,** contrair dívidas, endividar-se; *(b)* **to incur a risk,** expor-se a um risco.
indebted, *a.* endividado; **to be heavily indebted towards s.o.,** dever muito dinheiro a alguém, estar muito endividado com alguém.
indebtedness, *n.* endividamento *m.*
indefeasible, *a.* *Jur:* irrevogável.
indemnification, *n.* indenização *f* (of s.o., de alguém); **to pay a sum of money by**

way of indemnification, pagar uma quantia a título de indenização.
indemnify, *v.tr.* indenizar (alguém de, por, alguma coisa).
indemnity, *n.* **1.** garantia *f,* seguro *m,* (contra uma perda, etc.); **indemnity bond, letter of indemnity,** carta *f* de fiança, caução *f.* **2.** indenização *f;* **to pay full indemnity to s.o.,** indenizar alguém totalmente.
indent¹, *n.* encomenda *f* de mercadorias.
indent², *v.i.* **to indent on s.o. for sth.,** encomendar algo a alguém.
indenter, *n.* cliente *mf* que encomenda mercadorias procedentes do exterior.
indenture¹, *n.* *Jur:* *(a)* contrato sinalagmático, contrato bilateral; *(b)* *usu. pl.* **indentures,** contrato de aprendizagem; *(c)* *Am:* contrato para emissão de debêntures.
indenture², *v.tr.* *(a)* contratar; **indentured labour,** mão-de-obra contratada; *(b)* contratar (alguém) como aprendiz.
index, *n.* **1.** (*pl.* **indexes**) índice *m,* índex *m;* **index card,** ficha *f* (de arquivo); **card index,** fichário *m.* **2.** (*pl.* **indices**) **index number,** número *m* índice; **retail price index,** índice dos preços a varejo; **cost of living index,** índice do custo de vida; **overall index,** índice geral; **consumer price index,** índice dos preços ao consumidor; **wholesale price index,** índice dos preços por atacado; **index-linked,** baseado no índice do custo de vida (ou outro índice); **the Financial Times Ordinary Industrial Share Index,** o Índice de Ações Industriais Ordinárias do *Financial Times;* **economic growth index,** índice de crescimento econômico.
indexing, *n.* indexação *f.*
indicator, *n.* **retail-price indicator,** índice *m* dos preços a varejo; **all-items indicator,** índice geral dos preços; *Pol.Ec:* **economic indicators,** indicadores econômicos.
indirect, *a.* indireto; **indirect charges, expenses,** despesas indiretas; **indirect costs,** custos indiretos; **indirect labour,** mão-de-obra indireta; **indirect labour cost,** custo de mão-de-obra indireta; *Ind:* **indirect materials cost,** custo de materiais

indiretos; **indirect selling**, venda indireta; **indirect taxes**, impostos indiretos.

ndorse, *v.tr.* = **endorse**.

ndorsement, *n.* = **endorsement**.

ndorser, *n.* = **endorser**.

nduction, *n.* **induction procedure**, *Am:* **induction program**, procedimento *m* de admissão (de novo empregado).

ndulge, *v.tr.* conceder um prazo de tolerância (a alguém).

ndulgence, *n.* prazo *m* de tolerância (para o pagamento de uma dívida, etc.).

ndustrial, *a.* (*a*) **industrial centre**, centro *m* industrial; **industrial estate, complex,** *Am:* **industrial park**, parque *m* industrial; **industrial exhibition**, exposição *f*, feira *f*, industrial; **industrial training**, treinamento *m* industrial; **industrial worker**, operário *m* (industrial), industriário *m*; **industrial dispute**, conflito *m* trabalhista, *Jur:* dissídio coletivo; **industrial unrest**, agitação operária; **industrial troubles**, distúrbios *mpl* trabalhistas; **industrial relations**, relações *fpl* industriais, relações entre patrão e empregados; **industrial action**, medidas tomadas por operários para acelerar a obtenção das reivindicações; **industrial psychology**, psicologia *f* industrial; (*b*) *Fin:* **industrial bank**, banco *m* industrial; **industrial shares**, ações *fpl* industriais; **industrial property**, propriedade *f* industrial; **industrial goods**, bens *mpl* de produção.

ndustrialism, *n.* industrialismo *m*.

ndustrialist, *n.* industrial *mf*, industrialista *mf*.

ndustrialization, *n.* industrialização *f*.

ndustrialize, *v.* 1. *v.tr.* industrializar. 2. *v.i.* industrializar-se.

ndustry, *n.* indústria *f*; **aircraft industry**, indústria aeronáutica; **basic industry**, indústria básica; **building industry**, indústria de construção civil; **car, motor, industry**, indústria automobilística; **chemical industry**, indústria química; **cottage industry**, indústria caseira; **engineering industry**, indústria mecânica; **fishing industry**, indústria pesqueira; **it's a growing industry**, é uma indústria em expansão, uma indústria em crescimento;

growth industry, indústria em crescimento; **heavy industry**, indústria pesada; **hotel industry**, indústria hoteleira; **iron and steel industry**, indústria siderúrgica; **light industry**, indústria leve; **manufacturing industry**, indústria manufatureira; **mining industry**, indústria de mineração; **oil industry**, indústria petroleira; **service industry**, indústria de serviço; **the service industries**, o setor de serviços, o setor terciário; **shoe industry**, indústria do calçado; **textile industry**, indústria têxtil.

inefficiency, *n.* ineficiência *f*, incompetência *f* (de alguém).

inefficient, *a.* ineficiente, incompetente, ineficaz.

inelastic, *a.* inelástico.

inexecution, *n.* inadimplemento *m*, não execução *f* (de um contrato, etc.).

inexpensive, *a.* barato, de baixo custo.

inexpensively, *adv.* barato, a um preço baixo, por um preço módico; **to live inexpensively**, viver com pouco dinheiro.

inferior, *a.* inferior; **inferior goods**, mercadorias *fpl* inferiores; **of an inferior quality**, de qualidade inferior.

in-firm, *a.* **in-firm training**, treinamento *m* no local de trabalho.

inflate, *v.tr.* (*a*) **to inflate an invoice**, enfestar uma fatura, aumentar o valor de uma fatura; (*b*) *Pol.Ec:* **to inflate (the currency)**, inflacionar (o meio circulante).

inflated, *a.* (preço, etc.) inflacionado; *Pol.Ec:* **inflated currency**, meio circulante inflacionado.

inflation, *n.* *Pol.Ec:* inflação *f*; **rate of inflation**, taxa *f* de inflação, índice *m* de inflação; **galloping inflation**, inflação galopante; **open inflation**, inflação declarada; **runaway inflation**, inflação desenfreada; **suppressed inflation**, inflação contida; **to combat inflation**, combater a inflação; **measures to combat inflation**, medidas anti-inflacionárias; **the fight against inflation**, a luta contra a inflação; **monetary inflation**, inflação monetária; **cost-push inflation**, inflação provocada pelos custos; **demand-pull inflation**, inflação provocada pela procura.

inflationary, *a.* inflacionário, inflacionista; **inflationary gap,** hiato inflacionário; **inflationary policy,** política *f* inflacionista; **inflationary spiral,** espiral inflacionária; **inflationary tendency,** tendência *f* inflacionista.

inflationism, *n. Pol.Ec:* inflacionismo *m.*

inflationist, *n. Pol.Ec:* inflacionista *mf, F:* papelista *mf.*

inflow, *n.* **the inflow of foreign capital,** o influxo, a entrada, de capital estrangeiro.

influx, *n.* **the influx of gold,** a entrada de ouro.

inform, *v.tr. Corr:* **we are pleased to inform you that . . .,** temos o prazer de informar (a) V. S.ª (de) que . . .; **I regret to have to inform you that . . .,** lamento informar (a) V. S.ª (de) que . . .; **we are writing to inform you of the dispatch of . . .,** pela presente informamos (a) V. S.ª da remessa de . . .; **we are informed that . . .,** fomos informados (de) que . . ..

informal, *a.* informal; **informal negotiations,** negociações *fpl* informais; *Book-k:* **informal record,** registro *m* extra-contábil.

information, *n.* informação *f*; **all the necessary information,** todas as informações necessárias; **for your information,** para seu conhecimento; **(strictly) confidential information,** informações confidenciais; **information bulletin,** boletim *m* de informações (de bolsa de valores, etc.); **request for information,** pedido *m* de informações; **for further information apply to the management,** para maiores informações, para mais informações, para informações complementares, favor dirigir-se à gerência; **information bureau,** centro *m* de informações; **information technology,** informática *f.*

informed, *a.* **he's informed on the tax legislation,** ele é bem informado sobre a legislação tributária.

infrastructure, *n.* infra-estrutura *f.*

infringe, *v.tr.* violar, infringir, transgredir.

infringement, *n.* violação *f*, infração *f*, (de um regulamento).

ingot, *n.* lingote *m*; **ingot gold,** ouro *m* em lingote(s).

initial¹, *a.* **initial capital,** capital *m* inicial; *Book-k:* **initial (capital) expenditure,** despesas *fpl* de instalação (de uma companhia); *Ind: etc:* **initial cost,** custo *m* inicial; (*of product*) **initial value,** valor *m* de custo, valor inicial.

initial², *v.tr.* **to initial a draft contract,** rubricar uma minuta de contrato.

inject, *v.tr.* **to inject capital into a firm,** injetar capitais numa empresa.

injection, *n.* **injection of capital into a business,** injeção *f* de capitais num negócio.

injured, *a. Jur:* **injured party,** parte lesada.

inland, *a.* **inland trade,** comércio interno; **inland postage rates,** tarifa *f* para correspondência destinada a um lugar no país; **inland bill,** *UK:* letra *f* pagável no mesmo país, *Am:* letra pagável no mesmo estado; **inland revenue,** rendas internas; *UK:* **the Inland Revenue (Department),** o Fisco; diretoria *f* das rendas internas; **inland revenue stamp,** selo *m* fiscal.

input¹, *n.* **1.** *Econ:* insumo *m*, input *m.* **2.** *Cmptr:* input *m*, entrada *f*; **input device,** unidade *f* de entrada, dispositivo *m* de entrada.

input², *v.tr. Cmptr:* introduzir (dados num computador).

inquiry, *n.* (*a*) **inquiry office,** centro *m* de informações, setor *m* de informações; (*b*) *Ind: etc:* tomada *f* de preços; (*c*) **(public) inquiry,** sindicância (pública), inquérito (público); **judicial inquiry,** inquérito *m* judicial; **administrative inquiry,** inquérito *m* administrativo.

inscribed, *a. Fin:* **inscribed stock,** títulos inscritos (em um livro-registro mantido num banco).

inside, *a. Am:* **inside director,** diretor executivo.

insider, *n. St.Exch:* insider *m*; investidor que tem acesso a uma determinada empresa, recebendo informações ainda não conhecidas pelo mercado; **insider dealing,** operações *fpl* de insiders.

insolvency, *n.* insolvência *f*; **to be in a state of insolvency,** estar insolvente, em estado de insolvência.

insolvent, *a.* insolvente; **to become insolvent,** tornar-se insolvente.

inspect, *v.tr.* inspecionar (uma obra, uma fábrica, etc.); examinar, fiscalizar, (uma contabilidade); verificar (documentos).
inspecting, 1. *a.* **inspecting officer,** inspetor *m*, fiscal *m*, examinador *m*. **2.** *n.* inspeção *f*, fiscalização *f*, exame *m*; **inspecting order,** ordem *f* de inspeção.
inspection, *n.* exame *m*, inspeção *f*, fiscalização *f*, verificação *f*, (de uma contabilidade, documentos, etc.); **by inspection,** por (simples) inspeção.
inspector, *n.* inspetor *m*, fiscal *m*; **inspector of taxes,** fiscal de imposto de renda; *UK:* **factory inspector,** inspetor de fábricas; **customs inspector,** inspetor da alfândega; **inspector of weights and measures,** inspetor de pesos e medidas.
inspectorate, *n.* inspetoria *f*; *UK:* **the Factory Inspectorate,** a inspetoria das fábricas.
instability, *n.* instabilidade *f* (da economia, do mercado, etc.).
instalment, *n.* prestação *f*, parcela *f*; **monthly instalment,** mensalidade *f*, pagamento *m* mensal, prestação mensal; **weekly instalment,** prestação, pagamento, semanal; **annual instalment,** anuidade *f*; **to pay by instalments,** pagar em prestações, em parcelas; **payment in instalments,** pagamento em prestações, pagamento em parcelas, pagamento parcelado; **to buy by instalments, on instalments,** comprar a prazo, comprar a prestação; **instalment plan, scheme,** crediário *m*, facilitário *m*, plano *m* de pagamento; **instalment selling,** venda *f* a crédito (de artigos de consumo); *Fin:* **instalment bond,** obrigação *f* resgatável em parcelas; *Fin:* **instalment loan,** empréstimo *m* reembolsável em prestações, em parcelas.
instant, *a.* **1.** *abbr:* **inst.** *Corr:* corrente (*abbr:* cor.te); **with reference to my letter of the 5th inst.,** com referência à minha carta de 5 do corrente. **2. instant coffee,** café *m* solúvel.
institute, *v.tr. Jur:* **to institute proceedings against s.o.,** processar, acionar, alguém; instaurar processo contra alguém; intentar, mover, ação judicial contra alguém.

institution, *n.* instituição *f*; **financial institution,** instituição financeira; **credit institution,** sociedade *f* de crédito; **investment institution,** sociedade de investimento.
institutional, *a. N.Am:* **institutional advertising,** propaganda *f* institucional; propaganda que ajuda a criar atitudes públicas favoráveis a um determinado serviço ou organização; *Fin:* **institutional investors,** investidores *mpl* institucionais.
in-store, *a.* **in-store promotion,** promoção *f* de vendas em loja.
instruct, *v.tr. Jur:* **to instruct a solicitor,** constituir um advogado.
instruction, *n.* (*a*) *Corr: etc:* **we await your instructions,** aguardamos suas instruções, suas ordens; (*b*) **instruction manual,** manual *m* de instruções.
instrument, *n. Jur:* instrumento *m*; *Fin:* **negotiable instrument,** título *m* de crédito, título negociável.
insurable, *a.* segurável *m*; **insurable interest,** interesse *m* segurável; **insurable risk,** risco *m* segurável.
insurance, *n.* (*a*) seguro *m*; **to take out an insurance against a risk,** contratar um seguro, fazer (um) seguro, contra um risco; **to pay the insurance on a car,** pagar o (prêmio de) seguro de um carro; **(personal) accident insurance,** seguro contra acidentes (pessoais); **all-risks insurance,** seguro total, seguro contra todos os riscos; **burglary, theft, insurance,** seguro contra roubo; **comprehensive insurance,** seguro compreensivo; **credit insurance,** seguro de crédito; **fire insurance,** seguro de incêndio, seguro contra fogo; **group insurance,** seguro em grupo, seguro coletivo; **group life insurance,** seguro de vida em grupo; **health insurance,** seguro-doença *m*, seguro contra doença; **invalidity, disability, insurance,** seguro contra invalidez, seguro-invalidez *m*; **life insurance,** seguro de vida, seguro-vida *m*; **marine insurance,** seguro marítimo; **motor car insurance,** seguro de automóveis; **personal, public, liability insurance,** seguro de responsabilidade civil; **third-party insurance,** seguro contra terceiros;

workmen's compensation insurance, employer's liability insurance, seguro contra acidentes de trabalho; *M.Ins:* hull insurance, seguro de casco; (*b*) insurance agent, agente *mf* de seguros; insurance broker, corretor *m* de seguros; insurance charges, (i) taxas *fpl* de seguro, (ii) despesas *fpl* com seguro; insurance company, seguradora *f*, companhia *f* de seguros; insurance contract, contrato *m* de seguro; (international) insurance market, mercado *m* segurador (internacional), mercado de seguros (internacional); insurance money, indenização paga por uma seguradora; insurance policy, apólice *f* de seguro; insurance premium, prêmio *m* de seguro; (*c*) *Adm:* national, social, insurance, previdência *f* social, seguro social; national insurance contribution, contribuição *f* de previdência social; national, social, insurance benefits, benefícios *mpl* da previdência social, benefícios sócio-securitários.

insure, *v.tr.* segurar, fazer seguro de, (mercadorias, casa, mobiliário, etc.); to insure one's life, segurar-se, fazer um seguro de vida; to insure against theft, segurar contra roubo, contra furto.

insured, *a. & n.* segurado (*m*); the house was insured, a casa estava segurada; insured value, valor segurado.

insurer, *n.* segurador *m.*

intangible, *a. Book-k:* intangible assets, ativo *m* intangível, ativo imaterial; intangible value, valor *m* intangível.

interbank, *a.* interbancário; interbank loans, empréstimos interbancários.

intercompany, *a.* entre companhias (associadas ou coligadas); intercompany profit, lucro *m* sobre transações entre companhias (associadas ou coligadas).

interdepartmental, *a.* interdepartamental; interdepartmental profit, lucro *m* sobre transações entre departamentos da mesma empresa.

interest, *n.* (*a*) juro(s) *m*(*pl*); interest due, payable, juros vencidos, juros pagáveis; interest on a loan, juros sobre um empréstimo; interest on $100, juros sobre $100; accrued interest, juros acumulados;

compound interest, juro composto; fixed interest, juro fixo; simple interest, juro simples; 11% a year interest, 11% de juros anuais, juros de 11% anuais, juros de 11% ao ano; money earning no interest, dinheiro improdutivo, dinheiro inativo; interest-bearing securities, títulos *mpl* que rendem juros; interest-free loan, empréstimo livre de juros, empréstimo gratuito; interest income, rendimento *m* de juros; interest rate, rate of interest, taxa *f* de juro(s); high interest rate, taxa elevada de juros; true rate of interest, taxa de juros efetiva; the interest rate dropped 2%, a taxa de juros caiu (em) 2%; to allow interest to accumulate, deixar acumular os juros; to bring down interest, baixar a taxa de juros; to charge interest, cobrar juros; to lend money at interest, emprestar dinheiro a juros; to pay interest, pagar juros; to yield, bear, interest, render, vencer, juros; (*b*) participação *f*, interesse *m*; what's his interest in the business? qual é seu interesse no negócio? majority interest, participação majoritária; minority interest, participação minoritária; to have an interest in the profits, participar nos lucros; ter parte, participaçao, nos lucros; his interest in the company is $10 000, ele tem $10.000 investidas na companhia; (*c*) to act in the interest of the company, agir no interesse da companhia; conflict of interests, conflito *m* de interesses; conflicting interests, interesses conflitantes; (*d*) *Jur:* interesse *m.*

interested, *a.* the interested parties, os interessados; *Jur:* the interested party, a parte interessada.

interim, *a.* interino, provisório; interim appointment, nomeação provisória; interim report, relatório *m* preliminar; interim audit, exame *m* preliminar; interim dividend, dividendo intermediário, dividendo preliminar.

interlocking, *a.* interlocking boards, diretorias *fpl* de companhias das quais participam, ao menos em parte, as mesmas pessoas.

intermediary, *a. & n.* intermediário (*m*).

intermediate, *a.* intermediário;

intermediate credit, crédito *m* a médio prazo; *Econ:* **intermediate goods,** bens intermédios, bens de produção.
internal, *a.* **internal trade,** comércio interno; *Adm:* **internal revenue,** rendas internas; *Am:* **the Internal Revenue,** a Diretoria das Rendas Internas; *Book-k:* **internal audit,** auditoria interna; *Book-k:* **internal accounting control,** controle contábil interno; *Fin:* **internal rate of return,** taxa interna de retorno.
international, *a.* internacional; **international trade,** comércio *m* internacional; **international law,** direito *m* internacional; **the International Monetary Fund (IMF),** o Fundo Monetário Internacional (FMI); **the international situation,** a conjuntura internacional, a situação internacional; *Fin:* **international settlements,** pagamentos *mpl* internacionais.
intertrade, *n.* relações *fpl* comerciais recíprocas.
interview¹, *n.* entrevista *f;* **job interview,** entrevista para um emprego; **to arrange, fix, an interview with s.o.,** marcar uma entrevista com alguém.
interview², *v.tr.* entrevistar (alguém).
interviewee, *n.* entrevistado *m.*
interviewer, *n.* entrevistador *m.*
inter vivos, *a. Jur:* **inter vivos trust,** fideicomisso *m inter vivos.*
intrinsic, *a.* **intrinsic value,** valor intrínseco.
introduce, *v.tr.* **to introduce a new manager to the board,** apresentar um novo gerente à diretoria; **to introduce a new product onto the market,** lançar um novo produto no mercado.
invalid, *a.* inválido, nulo, írrito; **this passport is invalid,** este passaporte não tem mais validade.
invalidate, *v.tr.* invalidar, anular.
invalidity, *n.* **1.** invalidade *f,* nulidade *f,* (de um ato, uma escritura, etc.). **2.** **invalidity insurance,** seguro-invalidez *m,* seguro contra invalidez; **invalidity pension,** pensão *f* de invalidez.
inventory¹, *n.* **1.** inventário *m;* **to take, draw up, an inventory (of the stocks),** inventariar (os estoques), fazer um

inventário (dos estoques); **inventory book,** livro *m* de inventário; **book inventory,** inventário contábil, inventário segundo os livros; **ingoing inventory,** inventário de entrada (num prédio); **outgoing inventory,** inventário de saída (de um prédio); *Jur:* **benefit of inventory,** benefício *m* de inventário. **2.** *N.Am:* (*a*) estoque(s) *m(pl);* **inventory turnover,** rotação *f,* rotatividade *f,* de estoques; **inventory valuation,** avaliação *f* dos estoques; (*b*) (*act*) inventário *m.*
inventory², *v.tr.* inventariar, fazer o inventário de, (bens e valores de uma sociedade, estoques, etc.).
invest, *v.* **1.** *v.tr. Fin:* investir, aplicar, inverter, colocar, empregar, (capitais em uma companhia, etc.); **to invest money in a business,** investir, aplicar, colocar, dinheiro num negócio; **capital invested,** capital investido, capitais investidos. **2.** *v.i.* **to invest in property,** investir, aplicar, em bens imóveis; **to invest on the stock market,** investir, aplicar, no mercado de valores.
investment, *n. Fin:* investimento *m,* aplicação *f;* **to make investments,** investir recursos; aplicar, empregar, capitais; **investments in securities,** investimentos em títulos mobiliários; **business investments,** investimentos comerciais, aplicações comerciais; **good investment,** bom investimento; **long-term investment,** investimento a longo prazo; **portfolio investment,** investimento em títulos não relacionados à atividade da companhia investidora; **portfolio of investments,** carteira *f* de títulos; **property investment, investment in real estate,** investimento imobiliário; **safe investment,** investimento seguro; **short-term investment,** investimento a curto prazo; **trade investment,** investimento relacionado à atividade da companhia investidora; **investment adviser,** consultor *m,* assessor *m,* de investimentos; **investment bank,** banco *m* de investimento; **investment company,** sociedade *f* de investimento; **investment credit,** crédito *m* para investimento, crédito concedido para a compra de ativo fixo; **investment fund,**

fundo *m* de investimento; **investment goods,** bens *mpl* de investimento; **investment market,** mercado *m* de capitais; **investment policy,** política *f* de investimento; **investment rate,** taxa interna de retorno; **investment ratings,** classificação *f* de títulos conforme sua rentabilidade e segurança, etc.; **investment ratio,** índice *m* de investimento; *UK: Fin: Adm:* **investment income,** rendimento *m* de investimentos.

investor, *n.* investidor *m*; **small investor,** pequeno investidor, pequeno poupador; **institutional investors,** investidores institucionais.

invisible, *Pol.Ec:* 1. *a.* **invisible exports,** exportações *fpl* invisíveis; **invisible imports,** importações *fpl* invisíveis; **invisible earnings,** rendas *fpl* invisíveis; **invisible items of trade,** bens *mpl* invisíveis componentes do balanço de pagamentos. 2. *n.pl.* **invisibles,** invisíveis *mpl.*

invitation, *n.* carta-convite *f*; *Fin:* **invitation to the public to subscribe to a loan,** solicitação *f* de empréstimos públicos; *Ind:* **invitation to tender,** (abertura *f* de) concorrência pública.

invite, *v.tr.* *Fin:* **to invite shareholders to subscribe the capital,** fazer uma chamada de capital.

invoice¹, *n.* fatura *f*; **as per invoice,** conforme fatura; **invoice of origin, original invoice,** fatura original; **consular invoice,** fatura consular; **proforma, pro forma, invoice,** fatura simulada, fatura pro forma; **shipping invoice,** fatura de expedição; **to make out an invoice,** fazer, tirar, uma fatura **(for,** de); **faturar; to settle an invoice,** pagar, liquidar, uma fatura; **the amount is included in the invoice,** o montante está incluído na fatura; **the goods are on a separate invoice,** as mercadorias estão faturadas à parte, as mercadorias estão incluídas numa fatura separada; **invoice book,** livro *m* de faturas, livro-registro *m* de compras; **invoice clerk,** faturista *mf*; **invoice price,** preço *m* de fatura; **invoice value,** valor *m* de fatura; **invoice work,** trabalho *m* de faturamento.

invoice², *v.tr.* 1. faturar (mercadorias); **please invoice me for the goods,** favor faturar as mercadorias em meu nome. 2. *Am:* expedir (mercadorias); **the wheat was invoiced to the Soviet Union,** o trigo foi expedido para a União Soviética.

invoicing, *n.* faturamento *m*; **invoicing machine,** máquina *f* de faturar.

inward, *a.* **inward charges (for a vessel),** despesas *fpl* de entrada (de uma embarcação); **inward bill of lading,** conhecimento *m* de entrada; **inward manifest,** manifesto *m* de entrada; *Book-k:* **inward payment,** pagamento recebido.

inwards, *adv.* **goods inwards,** mercadorias *fpl* a ser(em) importadas.

IOU, *n.* (= **I owe you**) vale *m.*

irrecoverable, *a.* (dívida *f*) incobrável.

irredeemable, *a.* irresgatável; **irredeemable bonds,** obrigações *fpl* sem data fixa para o resgate; **irredeemable paper,** papéis *mpl* não conversíveis.

irregulars, *n.pl.* *N.Am:* artigos *mpl* de qualidade inferior.

irrevocable, *a.* *Jur:* irrevogável.

issuance, *n.* *N.Am:* emissão *f*; **the issuance of new bonds,** a emissão de novas obrigações.

issue¹, *n.* (*a*) *Adm: Fin:* emissão *f* (de ações, bilhetes, selos, etc.); **bonus issue, capitalization issue, scrip issue,** bonificação *f* de ações, bonificação em ações; **rights issue,** emissão de bônus (*mpl*) de subscrição; *Bank:* **issue department,** departamento *m* (que trata da emissão) de títulos e valores; (*b*) *Adm:* **issue card,** cartão *m* para a saída de mercadorias (do almoxarifado, etc.); (*c*) **the latest issue of a magazine,** o último número de uma revista.

issue², *v.tr.* emitir (ações, carteira de identidade, etc.); **to issue a letter of credit,** emitir uma carta de crédito; **to issue a draft on s.o.,** emitir um saque contra alguém.

issued, *a.* **issued capital,** parcela *f* do capital de uma companhia que corresponde a ações já emitidas.

issuing, 1. *a.* *Fin:* **issuing company,** sociedade *f* emitente; **issuing house** = banco *m* de investimento que compra ações emitidas para revendê-las com lucro. **2.** *n.* emissão *f*; **issuing procedures,** procedimentos *mpl* de emissão. **item, 1.** *adv.* (*in accounts, etc.*) item. **2.** *n.* (*a*) artigo *m*; **the items displayed in the shop window,** os artigos expostos na vitrine; **please send the following items,** favor remeter os seguintes artigos; (*b*) *Book-k:* lançamento *m*, partida *f*; **credit item,** lançamento credor; **debit item,** lançamento devedor, lançamento no deve; **balance-sheet items,** componentes *mpl* do balanço; **this item does not appear in our books,** esta partida não está lançada em nossos livros; (*c*) item *m* (de um contrato, etc.); **the items on the agenda,** os assuntos na ordem do dia.

itemize, *v.tr.* discriminar (uma fatura, etc.); **itemized account,** conta discriminada.

J

jacket, *n.* **book jacket,** jaqueta *f*, sobrecapa *f*.

jam, *n.* geléia *f*; **jam manufacturer,** fabricante *m* de geléias; **jam factory,** fábrica *f* de geléias.

jar, *n.* (*general*) vasilha *f*; (*wide-mouthed, short-necked*) pote *m*; (*large, earthenware*) jarro *m*, jarra *f*.

jargon, *n.* **economic jargon,** jargão econômico.

Jason clause, *n. M.Ins:* cláusula *f* que estipula, em contrato de seguro marítimo, que o armador terá cobertura contra quaisquer sinistros ocasionados por defeitos inerentes à embarcação ou às mercadorias transportadas.

jersey, *n. Tex: etc:* jérsei *m*.

jet, *n.* **jet (plane),** avião *m* a jato, jato *m*; **jet cargo aircraft,** avião de carga a jato.

jetsam, *n.* carga alijada ao mar.

jettison¹, *n.* (*a*) *Nau:* alijamento *m*; **jettison of cargo,** alijamento de carga; (*b*) *Av:* alijamento, lançamento *m*, (de carga).

jettison², *v.tr.* (*a*) *Nau:* alijar; lançar a carga ao mar; **to jettison the deck cargo,** alijar a carga de convés; **goods jettisoned,** mercadorias alijadas; (*b*) *Av:* alijar, deslastrar, (mercadorias, carga).

jettisoning, *n. Nau: Av:* alijamento *m*, alijação *f*; *Av:* lançamento *m*.

jeweller, *Am:* **jeweler,** *n.* joalheiro *m*; **the jeweller's,** a joalharia, a joalheria.

jewellery, *Am:* **jewelry,** *n.* (*a*) (*trade*) comércio *m* de jóias; (*b*) (*jewels*) jóias *fpl*, adereços *mpl*.

jingle, *n. Advert:* jingle *m*.

job¹, *n.* **1.** (*a*) (*task*) trabalho *m*, tarefa *f*, obra *f*, serviço *m*; **a building job,** uma obra de construção; **contract job,** obra de empreitada, empreitada *f*; **odd job,** biscate *m*, bico *m*, gancho *m*, galho *m*,

viração *f*; **odd-job man,** biscateiro *m*, biscateador *m*; **a printing job,** um trabalho tipográfico; **to work by the job, to do job work,** fazer obras de empreitada; trabalhar por empreitada, por tarefa; **the painter disappeared without finishing the job,** o pintor (de paredes) sumiu sem ter acabado o trabalho, o serviço; (*b*) *Ind:* **job card,** ficha *f* de custo (da tarefa); **job costing,** cálculo *m* do(s) custo(s) da obra, da tarefa; **job order, ticket,** ordem *f* de serviço, de produção; **job recorder,** relógio registrador da mão-de-obra; **job scheduling,** programação *f* do trabalho; **job site,** canteiro *m* de obras; **to be on the job,** estar no serviço; **on-the-job training,** treinamento *m* no local de trabalho; **off-the-job training,** treinamento fora do local de trabalho; **on-the-job testing,** testes *mpl* na obra. **2.** (*employment*) trabalho *m*, emprego *m*, cargo *m*, serviço *m*, colocação *f*, ocupação *f*, função *f*, ofício *m*; **to look for a job,** procurar (um) emprego, procurar trabalho; **to lose one's job,** perder o emprego; **to resign, throw up, one's job,** demitir-se, pedir demissão do emprego, deixar o emprego; **to be out of a job,** estar sem trabalho, estar desempregado; **my job starts at eight o'clock,** meu trabalho começa às oito; **he has an interesting job,** ele tem um emprego interessante; **job analysis,** análise *f* de cargos, de trabalho; **job centre,** agência *f* de emprego (organizada por órgão do governo); **job description,** descrição *f* de cargo; **job evaluation,** avaliação *f* de cargo(s), de tarefa(s); **job specification,** especificação *f* de cargo; **job security,** estabilidade *f* no emprego. **3.** **job lot,** lote *m* de mercadorias variadas (às vezes de qualidade inferior); **job-lot**

102

quantities, quantidades fabricadas fora de série; **job printing,** impressão *f* de obras de bico, de obras de acidência; **job printer,** impressor *m* de bicos; **job compositor,** compositor *m* de bicos, compositor de fantasia, chapista *m*, obrista *m*, remendeiro *m*.
job², *v.* **1.** *v.i.* (*a*) *N.Am:* (*of craftsman*) trabalhar por empreitada, por tarefa; fazer obras de empreitada; (*b*) biscatear, fazer biscates, fazer bicos; (*c*) (*of wholesaler*) comerciar por atacado; (*d*) *St.Exch:* (*of jobber*) negociar com títulos. **2.** *v.tr.* **to job small building works,** empreitar pequenas obras de construção; *St.Exch:* **to job shares,** (i) negociar com ações, (ii) especular sobre ações.
jobber, *n.* **1.** (*a*) intermediário *m* atacadista, intermediário comerciante; (*b*) *UK: St.Exch:* operador intermediário (que não trata com o cliente). **2.** empreiteiro *m*, tarefeiro *m*.
jobbing, 1. *a.* **jobbing workman,** tarefeiro *m*; **jobbing tailor,** alfaiate tarefeiro; **jobbing gardener,** jardineiro pago por tarefa; **jobbing printer,** impressor *m* de bicos; **jobbing work,** bico *m*, obra-de-bico *f*, obra de acidência, remendo *m*. **2.** *n.* (*a*) empreito *m*; (*b*) comércio *m* de intermediário; (*c*) *St.Exch:* (*of jobber*) compra *f* e venda *f* de títulos; *Pej:* **stock jobbing,** agiotagem *f*; (*d*) *Typ:* impressão *f* de obras-de-bico, de obras-de-acidência.
jobless, *a.* desempregado, sem emprego.
join, *v.tr.* **1. the documents joined to the report,** os documentos anexos ao relatório. **2. to join an organization,** ingressar numa organização, entrar para uma organização, tornar-se membro de uma organização; **to join a company,** começar a trabalhar numa companhia.
joint, *a.* conjunto, comum; **joint action,** ação conjunta; **joint beneficiaries,** beneficiários conjuntos; **joint commission,** comissão conjunta, comissão mista; **joint debt,** dívida conjunta; **joint debtor,** co-devedor *m*; **joint director,** co-diretor *m*; **joint facilities income,** receita *f* de instalações conjuntas; **joint obligation,** obrigação conjunta, obrigação comum;

joint owner, co-proprietário *m*, condômino *m*, comuneiro *m*; **joint ownership,** condomínio *m*, co-propriedade *f*; **joint producer,** co-produtor *m*; **joint production,** co-produção *f*; **joint purchase,** coempção *f*, compra *f* em comum; **joint purchasers,** compradores conjuntos; **joint report,** relatório conjunto; **joint sellers,** vendedores conjuntos; **joint services,** serviços conjuntos; **joint stock,** capital-ações *m*, capital *m* social; **joint-stock company,** sociedade anônima por ações; **joint venture,** sociedade *f* em conta de participação; *Bank:* **joint account,** conta conjunta, conta em comum, conta de participação; *Jur:* **joint and several liability,** responsabilidade conjunta e solidária; *Book-k: Ind: etc:* **joint cost,** custo conjunto; *Econ:* **joint demand, supply,** procura, oferta, conjunta; *Jur:* **joint heir,** co-herdeiro *m*; *Fin:* **joint shares,** ações indivisas, ações possuídas em condomínio; *Adm:* **joint tax return,** declaração *f* (de rendimentos) em conjunto.
jointly, *adv.* juntamente, conjuntamente; **to produce sth. jointly with a foreign manufacturer,** produzir algo juntamente com um fabricante estrangeiro; **to own sth. jointly,** possuir algo em comum; *Jur:* **the contracting parties are jointly and severally liable for the full performance of their obligations,** as partes contratantes são conjunta e solidariamente responsáveis pelo integral cumprimento das suas obrigações.
joker, *n. Am: F:* cláusula disfarçada; artifício *m* contratual.
journal, *n. Book-k:* diário *m*; **journal entry,** lançamento *m* de diário; **journal voucher,** comprovante *m* de lançamento, ficha *f* de lançamento, guia *f* de lançamento; **to make an entry in the journal,** lançar um registro no diário; fazer um lançamento de diário, no diário; **cash journal,** diário de caixa, diário-caixa *m*; **general journal,** diário geral; **ledger journal,** diário-razão *m*; **sales journal,** diário auxiliar de vendas; **simple journal,** diário simples.
journalism, *n.* jornalismo *m*; **television journalism,** telejornalismo *m*.

journalist, *n.* jornalista *mf*.
journalistic, *a.* jornalístico.
journalize, *v.tr.* lançar, registrar, no diário.
journalizer, *n. Book-k:* funcionário encarregado do diário.
journeyman, *n.* oficial *m* (diarista); **journeyman carpenter**, oficial de carpintaria.
journeywork, *n.* trabalho *m* de oficial (diarista).
judge, *n.* juiz *m*.
judgement, *n. Jur:* julgamento *m*, sentença *f*, decisão *f*, juízo *m*; **to give, pronounce, judgement,** dar, pronunciar, sentença, sentenciar, julgar; **judgement debtor,** devedor *m* condenado em juízo a pagar a sua dívida; **judgement note,** documento *m* judicial de dívida.
judicial, *a.* judicial, judiciário; **judicial bond,** caução *f* judicial; **judicial inquiry,** sindicância *f*, inquérito *m*, judicial; **judicial sale,** venda *f* judicial.
jump¹, *n.* **jump in prices,** subida repentina, elevação rápida, de preços.
jump², *v.i.* galgar, subir repentinamente, dar um salto; **prices jumped 10%,** os preços galgaram (em) 10%, deram um salto de 10%.
jumper, *n. Am:* **1.** servente *mf* de entregador. **2.** *Ind:* faz-tudo *m* em fábrica.
jumpiness, *n. F:* **jumpiness of the market,** instabilidade *f* do mercado.
jumpy, *a.* (*of market, etc.*) instável.
jungles, *n.pl. St.Exch: F:* títulos *mpl* de companhias instaladas na África Ocidental.
junior, *a. & n.* (*a*) júnior (*m*), subalterno (*m*), auxiliar (*mf*); **junior position,** cargo *m* para júnior; **junior secretary,** secretária

f júnior; **junior office clerk,** auxiliar *mf* de escritório (júnior); (*in bank*) **junior clerk,** praticante *mf*; **junior accountant,** contador *m* júnior, contador subalterno, contador auxiliar; **junior partner,** (i) sócio minoritário, (ii) sócio mais recente; **junior board,** conselho constituído por pessoal de nível médio; (*b*) **junior creditor,** credor minoritário; **junior mortgage,** hipoteca *f* de segunda ordem; *Fin:* **junior security,** título mobiliário, subordinado em categoria a um outro título mobiliário.
junk, *n.* trastes *mpl*; (*scrap metal*) sucata *f*, ferro velho; (*old clothing*) trapos *mpl*; **junk dealer,** bricabraquista *mf*, adeleiro *m*, ferro-velho *m*, trapeiro *m*, roupavelheiro *m*; **junk shop,** loja *f* de bricabraque, adelo *m*; **junk yard,** depósito *m* de ferro velho, ferro-velho *m*, sucata *f*; **junk food,** comida industrializada de baixa qualidade.
juridical, *a.* jurídico, legal; **juridical person,** pessoa jurídica.
jurisdiction, *n.* jurisdição *f*; (*power, authority*) alçada *f*, competência *f*, foro *m*; (*territory*) vara *f*; **the courts of the city of Rio de Janeiro have the jurisdiction to settle any disputes arising from the contract,** é da competência do foro da cidade do Rio de Janeiro dirimir quaisquer questões decorrentes do contrato.
jurisdictional, *a.* jurisdicional; *Am: Ind:* **jurisdictional strike,** greve *f* para determinar qual sindicato tem jurisdição em determinada área ou indústria.
jurist, *n.* jurisconsulto *m*, jurisperito *m*, jurista *mf*.
juristic, *a.* (*a*) relativo a jurista; (*b*) jurídico; **juristic person,** pessoa jurídica.
jute, *n.* juta *f*.

K

kaffirs, *n.pl. St.Exch:* títulos *mpl* de companhias sul-africanas negociados na bolsa de Londres.

kangaroos, *n.pl. St.Exch:* títulos *mpl* de companhias australianas (de mineração e produtoras de tabaco).

keelage, *n. Nau:* ancoragem *f.*

keen, *a.* (*a*) (*of person*) **a keen businessman,** um perspicaz homem de negócios; **they are keen competitors,** são fortes concorrentes; (*b*) forte, acirrado, intenso; **keen competition,** concorrência acirrada; **there is a keen demand for these stocks,** estes títulos estão sendo intensamente procurados; *UK:* **keen prices,** preços baixos, preços competitivos.

keep, *v.tr.* 1. (*of packed goods, etc.*) 'keep flat', 'não dobrar'; **'keep upright',** 'manter em posição vertical'; **'keep dry',** 'conservar em lugar seco'. 2. **to keep an appointment,** não faltar a um encontro marcado. 3. **to keep the books,** fazer a escrituração dos livros mercantis. 4. **to keep goods in stock,** ter um estoque de mercadorias, ter mercadorias em estoque. 5. **to keep prices down,** conter os preços; **to keep prices up,** apoiar, sustentar, os preços. 6. **to keep sth. back from s.o.'s wages,** deduzir, reter, uma quantia do salário de alguém.

kerb, *n. St.Exch: F:* **business done on the kerb,** operações realizadas após o fechamento da bolsa de valores; **the kerb market,** o mercado livre de títulos não listados na bolsa de valores.

key, *n.* (*a*) **key money,** luvas *fpl*; (*b*) **key post,** função *f* chave, cargo *m* chave; **key industry,** indústria básica, indústria chave; **key personnel,** pessoal *m* chave.

keyboard, *n.* teclado *m.*

keyman, *n. Ins:* **keyman insurance,** seguro *m* de vida de pessoal de alto nível (sendo a empresa beneficiária).

keypunch, *n.* perfuradora acionada por teclado.

kilo, kilogram(me), *n. Meas:* quilo(grama) *m.*

kilometre, *Am:* **kilometer,** *n. Meas:* quilômetro *m*; **distance in kilometres,** distância quilométrica.

kind, *n.* **payment in kind,** pagamento *m* em espécie.

king-size(d), *a. Advert: etc:* de tamanho gigante.

kiosk, *n.* quiosque *m*; **kiosk proprietor,** dono *m* de quiosque, quiosqueiro *m.*

kitchen, *n.* cozinha *f*; **kitchen unit,** móvel *m* de cozinha (comumente embutido); **kitchen utensils,** utensílios *mpl* de cozinha, bateria *f* de cozinha.

kitchenette, *n.* kitchenette *f.*

kitchenware, *n.* utensílios *mpl* de cozinha; **set of kitchenware,** bateria *f* (de cozinha).

kite¹, *n. Fin: F:* (*a*) papagaio *m*, letra *f* de favor; **kite flying,** emissão *f* de letra de favor para obter dinheiro; **kite flyer,** aquele que obtem dinheiro mediante emissão de letras de favor; (*b*) cheque *m* sem fundos.

kite², *v. Fin: F:* 1. *v.i.* (*a*) obter dinheiro mediante letras de favor ou cheques sem fundos; (*b*) (*of prices*) elevar-se, subir, rapidamente; galgar; **tin prices kited in world markets,** os preços do estanho galgaram nos mercados mundiais. 2. *v.tr.* (*a*) provocar (uma subida de preços); (*b*) **to kite a draft,** obter dinheiro mediante um saque sem valor.

kiting, *n. Fin: F: etc:* tipo *m* de fraude por meio de cheques não registrados na escrita.

knitted, *a.* **knitted goods,** malharia *f*, artigos *mpl* de malha.

knitwear, *n.* malharia *f*, artigos *mpl* de malha; **knitwear industry,** indústria *f* de malha, malharia.

knock, *n. Aut.Ins:* **knock-for-knock agreement,** acordo *m* entre seguradoras para cada uma indenizar seu segurado em caso de acidente, sem atribuição de responsabilidades.

knock down, *v.tr.* **1.** (*at auction*) **to knock down a cupboard for $900,** arrematar um armário por $900. **2. to knock down the price of an item,** reduzir o preço de um artigo.

knockdown, 1. *a.* (*a*) **knockdown price,** preço mínimo; (*at auction*) **knockdown bid,** lance mínimo; (*b*) (*in shops, etc.*)

knockdown prices, preços reduzidos; (*c*) **knockdown furniture,** móveis *mpl* desmontáveis. **2.** *n.* (*a*) redução *f* (de preços); (*b*) móvel desmontável.

knock off, *v.tr.* **to knock 5% off the retail price,** abater, descontar, 5% do preço a varejo.

knock-on, *n.* **the knock-on effects of wage increases,** os efeitos cumulativos de aumentos salariais.

knot, *n. Nau:* nó *m*.

know-how, *n.* **to buy foreign know-how,** comprar know-how *m* do exterior; a **know-how agreement,** um acordo sobre a transferência de know-how.

kurtosis, *n. Stat:* curtose *f*, achatamento *m*.

L

label¹, *n.* rótulo *m*, etiqueta *f*; **gummed label**, rótulo gomado, etiqueta gomada; **adhesive, sticky, stick-on, label**, rótulo adesivo, etiqueta adesiva; **self-adhesive label**, etiqueta auto-adesiva; **guarantee label**, rótulo, etiqueta, de garantia; **quality label**, rótulo, etiqueta, de qualidade.

label², *v.tr.* rotular, etiquetar; **consumers require well labelled products**, os consumidores exigem produtos bem rotulados.

labeller, *n.* encarregado *m* de rotulagem.

labelling, *n.* rotulagem *f*, etiquetagem *f*; **product labelling regulations**, regulamento *m* sobre a rotulagem de produtos.

labour, *Am:* **labor**, *n.* **1.** trabalho *m*, labor *m*; **manual labour**, trabalho braçal; **the division of labour**, a divisão do trabalho; **the Ministry of Labour**, o Ministério do Trabalho; **Labour Day**, o Dia do Trabalho; **the International Labour Organization**, a Organização Internacional do Trabalho. **2.** (*a*) *Econ: Ind: etc:* mão-de-obra *f*; **direct, indirect, labour cost**, custo *m* de mão-de-obra direta, indireta; **skilled labour**, mão-de-obra especializada; **semi-skilled labour**, mão-de-obra semi-especializada, semiqualificada; **unskilled labour**, mão-de-obra não especializada, não qualificada; **labour force**, mão-de-obra, força *f* de trabalho; **local labour**, mão-de-obra local; **cheap labour**, mão-de-obra barata; **shortage of labour**, escassez *f* de mão-de-obra; **employer of labour**, empregador *m*, patrão *m*; (*b*) **capital and labour**, o capital e o trabalho; **labour agreement**, convênio coletivo; **labour dispute**, conflito *m* trabalhista, dissídio coletivo; **labour market**, mercado *m* de trabalho; **labour turnover**, rotatividade *f* da mão-de-obra; **labour relations**, relações *fpl* trabalhistas, relações entre empregador(es) e empregados, relações de trabalho; **labour legislation, laws**, legislação *f* trabalhista, leis *fpl* trabalhistas; **labour movement**, movimento *m* trabalhista, movimento operário; **labour troubles**, distúrbios *mpl* trabalhistas; **labour unrest**, agitação operária; *Am:* **labor union**, sindicato *m*; *Am:* **labor court**, tribunal *m* do trabalho; (*c*) *Pol:* **the Labour Party**, o Partido Trabalhista; **Labour won the elections**, os Trabalhistas ganharam as eleições.

labourer, *n.* trabalhador *m*, operário *m*; braçal *m*, braceiro *m*; **unskilled labourer**, operário não qualificado, não especializado; **agricultural labourer, farm labourer**, trabalhador *m* agrícola, trabalhador rural, peão *m*.

labour-intensive, *a.* de alta intensidade de mão-de-obra; **labour-intensive industry**, indústria intensiva de mão-de-obra.

labour-saving, *a.* que poupa o trabalho, que economiza o trabalho; **labour-saving devices**, aparelhos *mpl*, dispositivos *mpl*, que poupam o trabalho (tais como eletrodomésticos).

lack¹, *n.* falta *f*, penúria *f*, míngua *f*, escassez *f*, carência *f*; **lack of resources**, escassez de recursos; **lack of information**, falta, escassez, de informações; **for lack of sufficient data**, por falta de dados suficientes.

lack², *v.tr.* carecer de, não ter; **he lacks the necessary experience**, ele não tem a experiência necessária, falta-lhe a experiência necessária; **they lack the resources for the project**, eles não têm (os) recursos para o projeto.

lade, *v.tr. Nau:* (*a*) carregar (uma embarcação) (**with,** com, de); (*b*) embarcar (mercadorias).

laden, *a.* carregado; **fully laden vessel,** embarcação completamente carregada; **laden in bulk,** carregado a granel; **laden draught,** calado *m* de embarcação carregada.

lading, *n.* (*a*) carregamento *m* (de navio); (*b*) embarque *m* (de mercadorias); **bill of lading,** conhecimento *m* de carga, de embarque, de transporte.

laissez-faire, *n. Pol.Ec:* laissez-faire *m.*

lame, *a.* **lame duck,** *F:* (i) empresa *f* industrial com fraca situação econômico-financeira, (ii) *St.Exch:* especulador *m* que não pode cumprir com seus compromissos.

land¹, *n.* terra *f*, terreno *m*, bens *mpl* de raíz; **arable land,** terra arável; **exhausted land,** terra esgotada, terra cansada; **fallow land,** alqueive *m*, terreno alqueivado, (terreno) pousio *m*; **idle land,** terras não cultivadas; **to buy land,** comprar terra(s), um terreno; *Book-k:* (*on balance sheet, etc.*) **land and buildings,** imóveis *mpl*, edifícios *mpl* e terras *fpl*; **land agency,** (i) administração *f* de terras, (ii) agência imobiliária; **land agent,** (i) administrador *m* de terras, (ii) corretor *m* de terras; **land grant,** doação *f*, concessão *f*, de terras; **land measure,** (i) medida agrária, (ii) sistema *m* de mensuração agrária; **land register,** cadastro *m*, registro público de imóveis; **land registration,** inscrição *f* de imóvel no cadastro; **land registry (office),** cartório *m* do registro geral de imóveis, cadastro *m* de imóveis, cadastro imobiliário, (escritório *m* do) cadastro público; **land tax,** imposto *m* sobre as terras, imposto territorial; **land tenure,** (i) posse *f* da terra, (ii) (*system*) regime fundiário; **land warrant,** certificado *m* de concessão de terras; *Am:* **land bank,** banco *m* de crédito real, de crédito imobiliário; *UK:* **land certificate,** certificado *m* de inscrição no registro geral de imóveis; *Pol.Ec:* **land reform,** reforma agrária.

land², *v.tr.* desembarcar (mercadorias).

landed, *a. Nau: etc:* **landed cost, price,**

preço *m* de mercadorias desembarcadas no cais; **landed terms,** condições *fpl* de venda de mercadorias desembarcadas no cais.

landholder, *n.* possuidor *m* de terras, proprietário *m* de terras.

landing, *n. Nau: etc:* desembarque *m*; **landing certificate,** certificado *m* de desembarque, de descarga; **landing charges,** despesas *fpl* de desembarque; **landing permit,** autorização *f* para desembarque; **landing number,** número *m* de desembarque; **landing weight,** peso *m* de mercadorias desembarcadas.

landlord, *n.* senhorio *m*, dono *m*, proprietário *m*.

language, *n.* língua *f*, idioma *m*; **language school,** escola *f* de línguas; **foreign language,** língua estrangeira; **business language,** linguagem *f* comercial; *Cmptr:* **computer, machine, language,** linguagem de computador, de máquina; *Cmptr:* **source language,** linguagem-fonte *f.*

lapse¹, *n.* **1. after a lapse of three months,** após um prazo de três meses, após um lapso de três meses. **2.** *Jur: Ins:* caducidade *f.*

lapse², *v.i. Jur: Ins: etc:* caducar, cair em desuso; (*of contract*) tornar-se nulo.

lapsed, *a. Jur: Ins: etc:* caduco.

large, *a.* **a large sum,** uma quantia vultosa, uma importância considerável; **a large industry,** uma grande indústria, uma indústria de grande porte; **to trade on a large scale,** comerciar, negociar, em grande escala; **to give a large order,** fazer uma grande encomenda; **to incur large losses,** sofrer grandes prejuízos.

largeness, *n.* grandeza *f.*

large-scale, *a.* **a large-scale operation,** uma operação em grande escala.

large-size(d), *a.* de grande tamanho, vultoso; **a large-size(d) packet,** um pacote grande.

last, *a. Book-k:* **last in first out (LIFO),** custeio *m* de saídas em ordem cronológica inversa das entradas, LIFO *m.*

last-minute, *a.* **a last-minute decision,** uma decisão de última hora.

late, *a.* **1.** (*a*) atrasado, tardio; **late delivery,**

entrega atrasada; (*b*) **there is late
shopping on Fridays,** o comércio fecha
mais tarde nas sextas-feiras; *Post:* **late
collection,** última coleta. **2.** (*of business*)
Martin, late Thomas, Casa Martin,
antiga Casa Thomas, ex-Casa Thomas. **3.
latest date (for delivery, payment, etc.),**
prazo *m* fatal, prazo final, (para entrega,
pagamento, etc.). **4. the latest model,** o
último modelo.
Latin American, *a.* **Latin American Free
Trade Association,** Associação Latino-
Americana de Livre-Comércio.
launch, *v.tr.* **to launch a new product on the
market,** lançar um novo produto no
mercado.
law, *n.* **1.** (*a*) lei *f*; **in accordance with the
law,** na forma da lei, de acordo com a lei;
permitted by law, permitido em lei; **to
enforce a law,** fazer cumprir, aplicar,
uma lei; **law enforcement,** aplicação *f*,
execução *f*, da lei; **for the purpose of this
law,** para os efeitos da presente lei; (*b*)
Pol.Ec: **law of supply and demand,** lei da
oferta e da procura; **law of diminishing
returns,** lei dos rendimentos decrescentes;
Gresham's law, lei de Gresham; **law of
large numbers,** lei dos grandes números;
law of (marginal) substitution, lei das
substituições; **law of free competition,** lei
da livre concorrência. **2.** direito *m*;
administrative law, direito administrativo;
air law, direito aéreo; **bankruptcy law,**
direito falimentar, direito falencial; **civil
law,** direito civil, direito comum;
commercial law, law merchant, direito
comercial; **common law,** direito
consuetudinário, direito costumeiro;
criminal law, direito criminal, direito
penal; **industrial law,** direito industrial;
international law, law of nations, direito
internacional (público); **maritime law,**
direito marítimo; **positive law,** direito
positivo, direito normativo; **tax law,**
direito fiscal, direito tributário. **3.**
(*justice*) **court of law,** tribunal *m* de
justiça; **to go to law,** ir à justiça; **action at
law,** ação *f* judicial; **law department (of a
firm),** departamento jurídico, contencioso
m; **law costs,** custas *fpl* (judiciais); **law
office,** escritório *m* de advocacia.

law-abiding, *a.* cumpridor das leis.
lawbreaker, *n.* violador *m*, infrator *m*, das
leis.
lawful, *a.* **1.** legal; **lawful day,** dia *m* legal,
dia judicial; **lawful age,** maioridade *f*. **2.**
(*permitted*) lícito. **3. lawful contract,**
contrato válido; **lawful currency,** moeda *f*
de curso legal.
lawfully, *adv.* legalmente, licitamente,
legitimamente.
lawfulness, *n.* legalidade *f*, licitude *f*.
lawsuit, *n.* ação *f* judicial, processo *m*,
pleito *m* (judicial), litígio *m*; **to bring a
lawsuit against s.o.,** processar, acionar,
alguém; abrir, instaurar, (um) processo
contra alguém; proceder contra alguém;
intentar, mover, ação judicial contra
alguém.
lawyer, *n.* advogado *m*.
lay, *n. Nau:* **lay days,** dias *mpl* de estadia.
laying off, *n.* **1.** *Ind:* demissão temporária
de trabalhadores. **2.** *Ins:* resseguro *m*,
contra-seguro *m*.
lay off, *v.tr.* **1.** *Ind:* demitir trabalhadores
temporariamente; **the factory is laying off
500 workers until new orders come in,** a
fábrica está demitindo 500 operários
temporariamente até receber novas
encomendas. **2.** *Ins:* **to lay off a risk,**
contratar um resseguro, um contra-
seguro, contra um risco.
lay-off, *n. Ind:* (período de) demissão
temporária de trabalhadores.
lay out, *v.tr. Advert:* leiautar.
layout, *n. Advert:* leiaute *m*.
lead, *n.* **lead time,** prazo *m* entre a data e
entrega de uma encomenda.
leader, *n.* **loss leader,** chamariz *m*, líder *m*
de preço; **market leader,** líder de
mercado.
leading, *a.* **leading shares,** títulos *mpl* de
primeira linha; **a leading shareholder,** um
dos acionistas principais; **available from
leading jewellers',** à venda nas grandes
joalherias; **one of the leading firms in the
country,** uma das maiores empresas do
país; *Advert:* **leading article,** artigo *m* de
ponta (como a oferta da semana).
lease¹, *n.* (contrato de) arrendamento *m*,
contrato *m* de aluguel, de locação; **long
lease, ninety-nine-year lease,** (contrato

de) aforamento *m*, emprazamento *m*, enfiteuse *f*, contrato enfitêutico; **to take on lease,** arrendar, tomar em arrendamento; **to take on long lease,** aforar, tomar por aforamento, por enfiteuse; **to renew a lease,** renovar um contrato de arrendamento; **expiry of a lease,** expiração *f* de um contrato de arrendamento.
lease², *v.tr.* (*a*) **to lease a house to s.o.,** arrendar, alugar, locar, uma casa a alguém; dar uma casa em arrendamento, de arrendamento, a alguém; **to lease land (on a long-term basis),** aforar, emprazar, um terreno; (*b*) **to lease a flat from a property company,** arrendar, alugar, um apartamento de uma imobiliária.
leasehold, 1. *n.* (*a*) arrendamento *m*, (*of long lease*) aforamento *m*; **leasehold insurance,** seguro *m* contra rescisão de contrato de arrendamento; **leasehold mortgage,** hipoteca *f* de direito enfitêutico; (*b*) imóvel tomado em arrendamento. **2.** *a.* (*a*) tomado em arrendamento; (*b*) para ser arrendado.
leaseholder, *n.* arrendatário *m*, locatário *m*; (*holder of a long lease*) enfiteuta *mf*, aforador *m*.
leasing, *n.* arrendamento *m*, locação *f*; *Ind: etc:* (*of vehicles, machinery, etc.*) leasing *m*.
leather, *n.* couro *m*; **leather goods,** artigos *mpl* de couro; **the leather industry,** a indústria de couro; **morocco leather,** marroquim *m*; **patent leather,** verniz *m*.
leave, *n.* licença *f*, licenciamento *m*; (to be) **on leave,** (estar) de licença; **to take leave,** licenciar-se, entrar de licença, tirar licença; **annual leave,** férias *fpl* anuais; **to take one's annual leave in May,** tirar as férias anuais no mês de maio; **unpaid leave,** licença nao remunerada; **sick leave,** licença por motivo de saúde.
ledger, *n.* *Book-k:* livro-razão *m*, razão *m*; **sales ledger,** registro *m* de vendas do razão; **bought ledger,** registro de compras do razão; **ledger clerk,** encarregado *m* do livro-razão.
ledgerless, *a.* *Book-k:* **ledgerless accounting,** contabilidade *f* mediante faturas originais.

leftover, 1. *a.* **leftover stock,** resto *m* de estoque, fim *m* de estoque. **2.** *n.pl.* **leftovers,** sobras *fpl*, restos *mpl*.
legacy, *n.* legado *m*; **to leave s.o. a legacy of £50,** legar a alguém a soma de cinqüenta libras esterlinas; **legacy tax,** imposto *m* sobre legados.
legal, *a.* **1.** (*permitted by law*) legal, lícito, legítimo; **legal commerce,** comércio lícito. **2.** (*a*) (*according to the law, founded upon the law*) legal, jurídico; **legal age,** maioridade *f*; **legal capability,** capacidade *f* legal; **legal costs,** (i) (*in an action*) custas *fpl*, (ii) (*in a transaction*) despesas jurídicas; **legal charges,** despesas jurídicas, honorários *mpl* legais; **legal entity,** pessoa jurídica, pessoa moral; **legal liability,** responsabilidade *f* legal; **legal tender,** moeda *f* de curso legal, moeda corrente; **to take legal action against s.o.,** processar, acionar, alguém; intentar, mover, ação judicial contra alguém; proceder contra alguém; abrir, instaurar, (um) processo contra alguém; (*b*) (*of bank, etc.*) **legal department,** contencioso *m*, departamento jurídico; **legal expert,** jurisconsulto *m*, jurista *mf*, jurisprudente *mf*; **legal adviser,** assessor jurídico, consultor jurídico; **to take legal advice,** consultar um advogado; pedir conselho a um jurisconsulto, a um advogado.
legalization, *n.* legalização *f*, legitimação *f*, autenticação *f*, (de documentos, etc.).
legalize, *v.tr.* legalizar, legitimar, autenticar, (um documento).
legally, *adv.* (i) legalmente, licitamente, (ii) judicialmente, (iii) juridicamente; **legally responsible,** legalmente responsável.
legislation, *n.* legislação *f*; **tax legislation,** legislação tributária; **labour legislation,** leis *fpl* trabalhistas, legislação trabalhista.
lend, *v.tr.* emprestar; dar por empréstimo, em empréstimo, (**sth. to s.o.,** alguma coisa a alguém); **to lend money at interest,** emprestar dinheiro a juros; **to lend against security,** emprestar sobre penhor, mediante penhor.

lendable, *a.* **lendable funds,** fundos *mpl* (disponíveis) para empréstimos.

lender, *n.* emprestador *m*, mutuante *mf*, financiador *m*.

lending, *n.* empréstimo *m*; **lending bank,** banco *m* de crédito; **lending policy,** política *f* de empréstimos; **inter-bank lending,** empréstimos interbancários; **minimum lending rate (MLR),** taxa mínima de empréstimos.

less, 1. *a.* **of less value,** de menos valor; **sums less than $50,** importâncias *fpl* inferiores a $50; **he earns less money than you,** ele ganha menos dinheiro que você. **2.** *prep.* **income less expenses,** renda *f* menos despesas, renda deduzidas as despesas. **3.** *n.* **to sell sth. at less than cost price,** vender alguma coisa abaixo do custo. **4.** *adv.* **this product costs 15% less than any similar product,** este produto custa 15% menos que qualquer produto semelhante; **the box contains three items less than the number ordered,** a caixa contém três artigos a menos do número encomendado; **the imports are no less important than the exports,** as importações são tão importantes quanto as exportações.

lessee, *n.* arrendatário *m*, locatário *m*.

lessor, *n.* arrendador *m*, locador *m*, senhorio *m*.

let, *v.tr.* **1.** alugar, arrendar, locar; 'to be let furnished', 'aluga-se mobiliado'. **2.** *Am:* **to let a contract,** adjudicar um contrato.

letter, *n.* (*a*) carta *f*; **air letter,** aerograma *m*; **airmail letter,** carta aérea; **business letter,** carta comercial; **circular letter,** (carta) circular *f*; **express letter,** carta expressa; **follow-up letter,** carta de seguimento, circular *f*; **registered letter,** carta registrada; **set-form letter,** carta impressa; **letter box,** caixa *f* de correio; **letter paper,** papel *m* de carta; **air-letter paper,** papel aéreo; **letter rates,** tarifa *f* para correspondência postal; **letter scale,** pesa-cartas *m*; (*b*) **letter of acknowledgement (of receipt),** carta de acusação (de recebimento); **letter of advice,** carta de aviso; **letter of application,** carta de requerimento; **letter of appointment,** carta de nomeação; **letter**

of complaint, carta de reclamação, de queixa; **letter of credit,** carta de crédito; **letter of guaranty,** carta de fiança; **letter of introduction,** carta de apresentação; **letter of reference,** carta de recomendação; **letter of resignation,** carta de demissão; *St.Exch: etc:* **letter of allotment,** aviso *m* de atribuição de ações; (*c*) *Jur:* **letter of attorney,** procuração *f*; **letter of hypothecation,** cédula hipotecária, letra hipotecária; **letters patent,** carta patente.

letterhead, *n.* cabeçalho *m*, timbre *m*.

level¹, *n.* nível *m*; **to keep prices at the lowest possible level,** manter os preços no nível mais baixo possível.

level², *v.tr.* nivelar, equiparar, (salários, etc.).

levelling, *n.* nivelamento *m*, equiparação *f*, (de rendas, etc.).

level out, *v.i.* (*of prices*) equilibrar-se.

leverage, *n.* *Fin:* alavancagem *f*; emprego *m* de capital-obrigações (por companhia).

leviable, *a.* **1.** (imposto *m*) arrecadável, coletável. **2.** **leviable goods,** mercadorias *fpl* tributáveis.

levy¹, *n.* **1.** arrecadação *f*, coleta *f*, colheita *f*, (de imposto). **2.** imposto *m*, tributo *m*; **capital levy,** imposto sobre capitais, imposto sobre patrimônio, imposto patrimonial.

levy², *v.tr.* (*a*) arrecadar, cobrar, (impostos, tributos); **to levy a duty on goods,** tributar, taxar, mercadorias; (*b*) **members are levied $x a year for the pension fund,** a contribuição anual de $x é deduzida dos salários dos participantes do fundo de pensão.

levying, *n.* arrecadação *f*, coleta *f*, colheita *f*, (de impostos, tributos, etc.).

liability, *n.* **1.** *Jur:* responsabilidade *f*; **joint and several liability,** responsabilidade conjunta e solidária; **employer's liability,** responsabilidade patronal; **public liability insurance,** seguro *m* de responsabilidade civil; **liability bond,** caução *f* de responsabilidade civil; **contractual liability,** responsabilidade contratual, obrigação contratual. **2.** *Fin:* (*a*) *pl.* **liabilities,** passivo *m*, exigibilidades *fpl*;

assets and liabilities, ativo *m* e passivo; **current liabilities,** (passivo) exigível a curto prazo; **long-term liabilities,** (passivo) exigível a longo prazo; (*b*) **to meet one's liabilities,** cumprir com suas obrigações (financeiras); **this company's liabilities are very large,** esta companhia apresenta elevadas exigibilidades.

liable, *a.* **1.** *Jur:* responsável (**for,** por); **to be liable for,** responder, ser responsável, por; **to be liable for the damage,** ser responsável pelos danos. **2.** (*a*) sujeito (**to,** a); **liable to a fine,** passível de uma multa, sujeito a uma multa; **to render s.o. liable to certain penalties,** sujeitar alguém a determinadas penalidades; **infringements of the provisions of this law render directors liable to . . .,** as infrações aos dispositivos desta lei sujeitam os administradores a . . .; **to be liable for damages,** estar sujeito ao pagamento de uma indenização por perdas e danos; (*b*) **liable to stamp duty,** sujeito ao imposto de selo; **dividends liable to income tax,** dividendos sujeitos ao imposto de renda; **to make liable to a tax,** sujeitar, tornar sujeito, a um imposto. **3. a cargo liable to rot,** uma carga suscetível de apodrecimento.

liberate, *v.tr. Fin:* **to liberate capital,** mobilizar capitais.

liberation, *n. Fin:* **liberation of capital,** mobilização *f* de capitais.

licence, *Am:* **license,** *n.* licença *f,* guia *f,* alvará *m,* autorização *f,* permissão *f;* **driving licence,** carteira *f* de motorista, carteira de habilitação; **export licence,** guia, licença, de exportação; **heavy goods (vehicle) (HGV) licence,** carteira de habilitação para caminhão de carga pesada; **import licence,** guia, licença, de importação; **made, manufactured, under licence,** fabricado sob licença; **manufacturing licence,** licença de fabricação; **operating licence,** autorização para funcionar; **trading licence,** licença de comerciante; *Am:* **liquor license,** autorização para vender bebidas alcoólicas; **licence holder,** licenciado *m;* titular *mf* de licença, de autorização; **to grant a licence,** licenciar, autorizar;

conceder uma licença, uma autorização; **to take out a licence,** tirar uma licença.

license¹, *v.tr.* licenciar, conceder uma licença, outorgar uma autorização; **to license an establishment to sell drink,** conceder a um estabelecimento autorização para a venda de bebidas alcoólicas.

license², *n. Am:* = **licence.**

licensed, *a.* autorizado, licenciado; *UK:* **licensed premises,** estabelecimento autorizado a vender bebidas alcoólicas; **licensed victualler** = (*approx.*) dono *m* de restaurante ou bar.

licensee, *n.* licenciado *m;* titular *mf* de licença, de autorização; (*of restaurant, etc.*) proprietário *m,* dono *m.*

licenser, *n.* licenciador *m,* órgão *m* disciplinador, autorizador *m.*

licensing, *n.* licenciamento *m;* **licensing requirements,** condições *fpl* de licenciamento, condições de concessão de licenças; *UK:* **licensing acts, laws,** leis *fpl* sobre a autorização para a venda de bebidas alcoólicas.

lien, *n.* penhor *m,* direito *m* de retenção; *Jur:* privilégio *m;* **general lien,** privilégio geral; **vendor's lien,** privilégio do vendedor; **lien on goods,** direito de retenção sobre mercadorias; **lien on chattels,** penhor *m* sobre bens imóveis; **lien on income from property,** anticrese *f,* consignação *f* de rendimento.

lienholder, *n.* titular *mf* de privilégio, de direito de retenção.

life, *n.* (*a*) vida *f;* **life of a car,** vida de um automóvel; **working life,** tempo *m* de serviço; **life annuity,** renda vitalícia; **life pension,** pensão vitalícia; **life tenure (of office or position),** vitaliciedade *f;* **life appointment,** cargo vitalício; *Jur:* **life interest,** usufruto *m;* (*b*) *Ins:* **life assurance, life insurance,** seguro *m* de vida, seguro-vida *m;* **expectation of life, life expectancy,** probabilidade *f* de vida; **life (expectancy) table, life table,** tábua *f* de mortalidade; **to be a good life,** ser bom risco (de seguro-vida); (*c*) *Fin:* **life of a loan,** prazo *m* de um empréstimo.

LIFO, *n. see* **last.**

lift, v.tr. **to lift import restrictions,** levantar, suspender, as restrições à importação.

limit¹, n. limite m; **age limit,** limite de idade; **time limit,** prazo m; **size limit,** limite de tamanho; **weight limit,** limite de peso; **limit of free delivery area,** perímetro m de entregas gratuitas a domicílio; Fin: etc: **credit limit, limit of credit,** limite m de crédito, teto m de crédito; **to fix the limit for a budget,** fixar, estabelecer, o teto para um orçamento.

limit², v.tr. limitar, restringir.

limitation, n. **1.** limitação f; **time limitation,** limitação de tempo; **price limitation,** limitação de preços; **limitation of liability,** limitação da responsabilidade. **2.** Jur: prescrição f (extintiva ou liberatória); (in suit) **term of limitation, time limitation,** prazo m de prescrição; **statutes of limitation,** conjunto m de leis que regulam a prescrição; **invalidated by limitation,** prescrito.

limitative, a. limitativo; Jur: **limitative clause,** cláusula restritiva.

limited, a. limitado, restrito; **for a limited period,** por um prazo limitado; **limited liability,** responsabilidade limitada; **limited (liability) company** = sociedade anônima, sociedade de responsabilidade limitada; **limited partnership,** comandita f, sociedade em comandita; **limited expenditure,** despesas limitadas.

line, n. **1.** (a) linha f; **air line,** linha aérea; **bus line,** linha de ônibus; **shipping line,** linha de navegação, companhia f de navegação; (b) Tel: **there's no line,** o telefone não está dando linha; **the line's engaged,** a linha está ocupada; (c) Fin: linha de crédito; (d) Ind: **assembly line,** linha de montagem. **2.** (a) **line of business, of activity,** ramo m de negócios, de atividade; **what's his line?** qual é o ramo dele? **he's in the building line,** ele trabalha na construção civil; (b) linha (de artigos); **the leading lines are household appliances and furniture,** as linhas principais abrangem (aparelhos) eletrodomésticos e móveis.

linen, n. linho m; (as class of goods) roupa branca (de cama, de mesa); **linen draper,**

merchant, linheiro m, fanqueiro m, comerciante mf em linho; **linen drapery,** comércio m de fazendas; **linen industry,** indústria f do linho; **linen manufacturer,** fabricante m de linho.

liner, n. navio m de linha regular; **transatlantic liner,** transatlântico m de serviço regular; **cargo liner,** (navio) cargueiro m de serviço regular; **liner freighting,** transporte m em cargueiro de serviço regular; **liner service,** serviço m de transporte marítimo regular.

liquid, 1. a. Fin: disponível, realizável, real; **liquid assets,** ativo m disponível, disponibilidades fpl, ativo real, ativo realizável; **liquid debt,** dívida líquida. **2.** n. **liquid measure,** medida f de líquidos.

liquidate, v.tr. (a) liquidar (uma sociedade, uma dívida); amortizar (uma dívida); (b) **to liquidate securities,** resgatar títulos.

liquidation, n. liquidação f (de uma sociedade, de uma dívida); amortização f (de uma dívida); resgate m (de títulos); (of company) **to go into liquidation,** entrar em liquidação; **in liquidation,** em liquidação; **voluntary liquidation,** liquidação requerida pela empresa; **compulsory liquidation,** liquidação forçada, liquidação compulsória; **liquidation subject to supervision of court,** liquidação judicial.

liquidator, n. liquidante mf.

liquidity, n. Fin: liquidez f; **liquidity position,** posição f de liquidez; **liquidity preference,** preferência f pela liquidez; **liquidity ratio,** índice m de liquidez; coeficiente m de liquidez; **liquidity shortage,** insuficiência f de liquidez; **liquidity squeeze,** crise f de liquidez.

list¹, n. (a) lista f, relação f; Fin: **list of applicants (for shares, etc.),** lista f de subscritores (de ações, etc.); St.Exch: **list of quotations,** boletim m de cotações; **official list,** boletim oficial; Cust: **free list,** lista de importações franqueadas, de importações isentas; Bank: etc: **list of investments,** carteira f de aplicações; **to make out, draw up, a list,** fazer uma lista, uma relação; **to make out a list of one's assets,** inventariar o patrimônio; (b) **price**

list, catálogo *m*, tabela *f*, lista *f*, de preços; **list price,** preço *m* de tabela, preço de catálogo; **to sell above list price,** vender acima do preço de catálogo; **mailing list,** lista de endereços para remessas postais.

list², *v.tr.* listar, relatar, relacionar, inventariar, (mercadorias, etc.); *Fin:* **listed securities,** títulos listados na bolsa; **listed company** = (*approx.*) sociedade *f* de capital aberto.

listing, *n.* listagem *f.*

literature, *n.* prospectos *mpl* (publicitários, etc.).

litre, *Am:* **liter,** *n. Meas:* litro *m.*

live, *A.* *Fin:* **live claims,** créditos *mpl* admissíveis.

livelihood, *n.* vida *f*, subsistência *f*, meios *mpl* de vida, meios de subsistência; ganha-pão *m*; **to earn a livelihood,** ganhar a vida.

liveliness, *n. Fin:* animação *f* (do mercado).

lively, *a. Fin:* (*of market*) animado.

livery, *n.* **livery company,** corporação *f* da cidade de Londres que antigamente usava uniforme distintivo.

livestock, *n.* gado *m*, criação *f.*

liveware, *n. Cmptr:* pessoal *m* de computação.

living, *n.* 1. (*a*) vida *f*; **standard of living,** nível *m* de vida, padrão *m* de vida; **cost of living,** custo *m* de vida; (*b*) **living in,** alojamento *m* no local de trabalho; **living-in maid,** doméstica *f* residente; **living out,** alojamento fora do local de trabalho; **living out allowance,** ajuda *f* de alojamento. 2. (*a*) (*livelihood*) **to earn one's living,** ganhar a vida; **to work for one's living,** trabalhar para ganhar a vida; **what does he do for a living?** qual é o seu trabalho, a sua profissão? **living wage,** salário *m* de subsistência; (*b*) **living conditions,** condições *fpl* de vida.

load¹, *n. Ind: etc:* carga *f*, carregamento *m*, (de caminhão, navio, etc.); **dead load,** peso morto; **design load,** carga prevista; **dummy load,** carga simulada; **full load,** carga completa, plena carga; **gross load,** peso bruto; **lorry, truck, load,** carga de um caminhão; **ship load,** carga de um

navio; **train load,** carga de um trem completo; **useful load,** carga útil; **wagon load,** carga de um vagão; **working load,** carga normal, carga de funcionamento; **work load,** volume *m* de trabalho; **load(-carrying) capacity,** capacidade *f* de carga; *Nau:* **deck load,** carga de convés; **load displacement,** deslocamento *m* de navio completamente carregado.

load², *v.* 1. *v.tr.* (*a*) carregar (um caminhão, um navio, etc.); **to load a cargo onto a ship,** carregar um navio; **to load a ship with a cargo of wheat,** carregar um navio com uma carga de trigo; (*b*) **to load prices,** carregar os preços; *Ins:* **to load a premium,** carregar um prêmio. 2. *v.i.* (*of ship, etc.*) carregar, receber carga; **ship loading for São Paulo,** navio carregando para São Paulo.

loaded, *a.* 1. (*of ship, lorry, etc.*) carregado. 2. *Ins:* **loaded premium,** prêmio carregado, prêmio comercial.

loader, *n.* carregador *m.*

loading, *n.* carga *f*, carregamento *m*; **the loading and unloading of lorries,** a carga e a descarga de caminhões; **bulk loading,** carregamento *m* a granel; **end-on loading,** carregamento pela ponta traseira; **side loading,** carregamento pelo lado; **loading bay,** vão *m* de carregamento; **loading bridge,** ponte *f* de embarque; **loading chute,** calha *f* de carga; **loading dock,** doca *f* de embarque, embarcadouro *m*, cais *m*; **loading hopper,** tremonha *f* de carga; **loading platform, ramp,** plataforma *f* de carga; **loading skip,** carregador mecânico; **loading yard,** pátio *m* de carga e descarga; *Nau:* **loading port, berth,** porto *m*, atracadouro *m*, de carregamento.

loan¹, *n.* empréstimo *m*; **on loan,** por empréstimo, de empréstimo; **loan at interest,** empréstimo a juros; **loan at notice,** empréstimo a prazo; **loan by the week,** empréstimo a juros semanais; **loan repayable on demand,** empréstimo resgatável quando solicitado; **balance-of-payment loans,** empréstimos no balanço de pagamentos; **call loan, loan at call,** empréstimo sob chamada; **collateral loan, loan on collateral,** empréstimo pignoratício, empréstimo sob garantia; **day loan,** financiamento por um dia; **debenture loan,** empréstimo debenturístico; **foreign loan,** empréstimo externo; **government loan,** empréstimo estatal, empréstimo concedido pelo governo; **interbank loan,** empréstimo interbancário; **internal loan,** empréstimo interno; **long-dated loan, long-term loan,** empréstimo a longo prazo; **mortgage loan, loan on mortgage,** empréstimo hipotecário; **municipal loan,** empréstimo municipal; **overnight loan,** financiamento *m* overnight; **secured loan,** empréstimo caucionado com garantia; **short(-term) loan,** empréstimo a curto prazo; **tied loan,** empréstimo para fins específicos; **time loan,** empréstimo a prazo fixo; **unsecured loan, loan on overdraft,** empréstimo a descoberto; *M.Ins:* **loan on respondentia,** empréstimo a risco; **loan application,** requerimento *m*, pedido *m*, pedido *m*, de empréstimo; **loan capital,** capital-obrigações *m*; **loan market,** mercado *m* de empréstimos; *F:* **loan shark,** usurário *m*, agiota *mf*; **to apply for a loan,** requerer, solicitar, pedir, um empréstimo; **to float a loan,** lançar um empréstimo; **to grant a loan,** conceder um empréstimo; **to issue a loan,** emitir um empréstimo; **to raise a loan,** levantar um empréstimo; **to redeem, repay, a loan,** resgatar, reembolsar, um empréstimo; **to take out, contract, a loan (with s.o.),** contratar um empréstimo (junto a alguém).

loan², v.tr. 1. emprestar (dinheiro a alguém). **2.** *Am:* tomar emprestado, tomar por empréstimo.

loanable, *a.* **loanable funds,** fundos (disponíveis) *mpl* para empréstimos.

loanee, *n.* tomador *m* de empréstimo.

loaner, *n.* emprestador *m*, financiador *m*.

local, *a.* local; **local authorities** = (*approx.*) autoridades *fpl* municipais; **local government** = (*approx.*) administração *f* municipal; **local bank,** (i) banco local, (ii) banco regional; **local agent,** agente *mf*, representante *mf*, local; pracista *mf*; **local trade,** praça *f*, comércio *m* local; **local purchases,** compras feitas na praça.

locking up, *n.* **locking up of capital,** imobilização *f* de capitais.

lock out, *v.tr. Ind:* efetuar um lockout.

lockout, *n. Ind:* lockout *m*.

lock up, *v.tr. Fin:* **to lock up capital,** imobilizar capitais.

lodge, *v.tr.* **to lodge stocks with a bank,** depositar títulos num banco, confiar títulos à guarda, à custódia, de um banco; **securities lodged as collateral,** títulos penhorados, títulos depositados em penhor.

lodging, *n.* **1.** depósito *m* (de dinheiro, títulos, etc.). **2.** *pl.* **lodgings,** alojamento *m*; **lodging house,** hospedaria *f*, pensão *f*.

logbook, *n. Nau: Trans:* livro *m* de bordo, diário *m* de bordo, registro *m* de bordo.

London, *Pr.n.* (*a*) *Geog:* Londres *f*; **Greater London,** a grande Londres; (*b*) londrino, de Londres; **a firm with a London office,** uma firma com escritório em Londres.

long-dated, *a. Fin:* a longo prazo; **long-dated bills,** efeitos *mpl*, letras *fpl*, a longo prazo.

long-distance, *a.* de longa distância; **a long-distance (telephone) call,** (telefonema) interurbano *m*.

longshoreman, *n.* estivador *m*.

longstanding, *a.* antigo; **he's a longstanding customer,** é um freguês antigo; **it's a longstanding debt,** é uma dívida antiga.

long-term, *a.* a longo prazo; **long-term credit, loan,** crédito *m*, empréstimo *m*, a longo prazo; **long-term policy,** política *f* a longo prazo.

loose, *a.* **loose cash, change,** dinheiro miúdo, trocado *m*; **loose goods,** mercadorias *fpl* a granel.

loose-leaf, *a.* de, em, folhas soltas; **loose-leaf ledger,** livro-razão *m* em folhas soltas.

lorry, *n.* caminhão *m*; **heavy lorry,** caminhão pesado; **heavy goods lorry,** caminhão de carga pesada, caminhão para transportes pesados; **five-ton lorry,** caminhão de cinco toneladas; **articulated lorry,** caminhão articulado; **breakdown lorry,** (caminhão de) socorro *m*, guincho *m*, carro-guincho *m*; **lorry driver,** camioneiro *m*, motorista *m* de caminhão.

lose, *v.* **1.** *v.tr.* (*a*) perder, sumir, extraviar, desencaminhar; **the cheque was lost in the post,** o cheque foi extraviado no correio; **he lost his wallet,** ele perdeu sua carteira; (*b*) perder (um direito, dinheiro, etc.); **the company lost ten thousand pounds on the deal,** a empresa perdeu dez mil libras esterlinas na transação; **to lose a lawsuit,** perder uma ação judicial; **to lose a customer,** perder um freguês. **2.** *v.i.* **to lose in value,** perder (o valor), desvalorizar-se; **the shares lost in value,** as ações perderam.

loss, *n.* **1.** (*a*) perda *f*, extravio *m*, sumiço *m*, (de um documento, etc.); *Trans:* **loss in transit,** perda em trânsito; (*b*) **loss of an opportunity,** perda de uma oportunidade; **loss in weight,** perda de peso; **loss of custom,** perda de freguesia. **2.** (*a*) **to sustain, suffer, losses,** sofrer prejuízos, perdas; perder; **to make up one's losses,** compensar as perdas; **to sell at a loss,** vender com prejuízo; **to cut one's losses,** não levar em conta os prejuízos (na ocasião de vender um negócio, etc.); (*b*) *Ins:* sinistro *m*, prejuízo *m*, perda *f*; **to estimate the loss,** avaliar o sinistro, o prejuízo; *M.Ins:* **actual total loss,** perda total efetiva, perda total real; **constructive total loss,** perda total construtiva.

loss-making, *a.* **loss-making services,** serviços deficitários.

lot, *n.* **1.** *Fin:* **the debentures are redeemed by lot,** as debêntures se resgatam por sorteio *m*. **2.** (*a*) (*at auction*) lote *m*; (*b*) lote *m*; **a lot of goods,** um lote de mercadorias; **to sell in lots,** vender por lotes; **to sell in one lot,** vender em bloco, em conjunto; (*for building, etc.*) lote, loteamento *m*, (de terreno para construção, etc.); **to divide a piece of land into lots,** lotar, lotear, um terreno; dividir um terreno em lotes; *Fin:* **a lot of shares,** um lote de ações; *St.Exch:* **odd lot**

trading, negociação *f* de lotes fracionários.

lottery, *n.* loteria *f*; **lottery ticket,** bilhete *m* de loteria; *Fin:* **lottery bond,** obrigação *f* resgatável por sorteio.

low, **1.** *a.* baixo; **low price,** preço baixo, preço competitivo; **at a low price,** a preço baixo; **to keep prices low,** manter os preços baixos, manter os preços em nível baixo; **the rate of exchange is low,** a taxa de câmbio está baixa; **it will cost £100 at the very lowest,** custará cem libras esterlinas no mínimo; **the Dow Jones industrial index is at its lowest in the last 15 months, for 15 months,** o índice industrial Dow Jones registra o nível mais baixo dos últimos 15 meses; **low wages,** salários baixos. **2.** *n.* nível baixo (de ações, etc.); **the Dow Jones index reached an all-time low,** o índice Dow Jones caiu para o seu nível mais baixo.

low-budget, *a.* barato; econômico.

low-cost, *a.* barato; de baixo custo.

lower, *v.tr.* baixar, reduzir; **to lower rents,** baixar os aluguéis; **to lower management charges,** reduzir as taxas de administração.

lowering, *n.* **lowering of prices,** redução *f* dos preços.

low-income, *a.* **low-income consumers,** consumidores *mpl* de renda baixa.

luggage, *n.* bagagem *f*; **hand luggage, cabin luggage,** bagagem de mão; **luggage allowance,** franquia *f* de bagagem; **luggage locker,** guarda-volumes *m* individual.

lump, *n.* **to sell sth. in the lump,** vender alguma coisa a granel; **lump sum,** quantia *f* global; **lump-sum payment,** pagamento *m* de quantia global; **lump-sum contract,** contrato *m* de preço global; *Ins:* **lump-sum benefit,** capital único, pecúlio *m*; *UK:* **the lump,** o conjunto de trabalhadores autônomos na indústria da construção.

luxury, *n.* luxo *m*; **luxury article,** artigo *m* de luxo; **luxury tax,** imposto *m* sobre artigos de luxo; **the luxury trade,** o comércio de artigos de luxo.

M

M, (*abbr.* = **money supply**) *Fin:* **M1** = papel-moeda *m* em poder do público mais os depósitos à vista no Banco do Brasil e bancos comerciais; **M2** = M1 mais depósitos à vista nas Caixas e as LTNs (Letras do Tesouro Nacional) fora do sistema monetário; **M3** = M2 mais 50% dos depósitos a prazo, de poupança, letras de câmbio e letras imobiliárias.

machine, *n.* (*a*) máquina *f*; **adding machine,** máquina de somar, somadora *f*; **business machine,** máquina de escritório; **copying machine,** máquina reprográfica, (máquina) copiadora *f*; **dictating machine,** máquina de ditar; **franking machine,** (máquina) franqueadora *f*; **stamping machine,** máquina de selar; **machine hour rate,** taxa *f* de hora-máquina; **machine output,** produção *f* de máquina; **machine product,** produto mecânico; **machine production,** produção em série, produção em massa, produção mecanizada; **machine shop,** oficina mecânica; *Cmptr:* **machine language,** linguagem *f* de máquina, linguagem de programação; *Ind:* **machine tool,** máquina operatriz, máquina-ferramenta *f*; (*b*) **the machine age,** a era da máquina; (*c*) **the industrial machine,** a máquina industrial.

machine-finished, *a.* acabado à máquina.

machine-made, *a.* feito à máquina.

machinery, *n.* 1. maquinaria *f* (*in speech:* maquinária), mecanismo *m.* 2. **the machinery of commercial life,** a máquina das transações comerciais; **the administrative machinery,** a máquina administrativa, o mecanismo administrativo; *Fin: etc:* **compensation machinery,** procedimento *m* de indenização.

macroeconomic, 1. *a.* macroeconômico. 2. *n.pl.* **macroeconomics,** (*usu. with sg. const.*) macroeconomia *f*.

made, *a.* feito, fabricado, manufaturado, (*of clothing*) confeccionado; **made in Brazil,** fabricado no Brasil, feito no Brasil; **made to measure,** feito sob medida; **made to order,** feito sob encomenda; *Adm: Pol.Ec:* **made work,** trabalho organizado pelo governo para criar empregos.

made-up, *a.* acabado, (*of machine*) montado; **made-up articles,** artigos acabados.

magazine, *n.* revista *f*; **fashion magazine,** revista *f* de moda, figurino *m*; **illustrated magazine,** revista ilustrada.

magnate, *n.* magnata *m*, magnate *m*; **magnate of industry, industrial magnate,** magnata da indústria.

magnetic, *a. Cmptr: etc:* **magnetic cards,** cartões magnéticos; **magnetic disk,** disco magnético; **magnetic tape,** fita magnética.

mail¹, *n.* correio *m*, correspondência *f*; **incoming mail,** correspondência de entrada, correio de entrada; **inward mail,** correspondência (vinda) do exterior; **outgoing mail,** correspondência de saída, correio de saída; **outward mail,** correspondência para o exterior; **mail delivery,** distribuição *f* do correio; **mail order,** encomenda *f* postal, pedido *m* por correspondência; **mail order catalogue,** catálogo *m* para vendas pelo correio; **mail order house, firm,** firma *f* de vendas pelo correio, casa *f* de vendas por correspondência; **mail rates,** tarifa *f* de correspondência; **mail service,** serviço *m* postal; **direct mail advertising,** publicidade direta (pelo correio); **to**

deal with one's mail, tratar da correspondência.

mail², *v.tr.* enviar pelo correio, postar.

mailable, *a. esp. Am:* que pode ser enviado pelo correio.

mailbag, *n.* mala *f* postal.

mailboat, *n.* barco *m* correio.

mailbox, *n. Am:* caixa *f* de correio.

mailing, *n.* postagem *f*, envio *m*, remessa *f*, pelo correio; **mailing machine,** máquina *f* de selar e fechar correspondência; **direct mailing,** mala direta; **mailing piece, sheet,** folheto enviado por mala direta; **mailing list,** lista *f* de endereços para remessas postais; **mailing wrapper,** cinta *f*.

mailman, *n. Am:* carteiro *m*, correio *m*.

main, *a.* principal; **main office,** matriz *f*, casa *f* matriz, sede *f*, administração *f* central, escritório *m* central; **the main building,** o edifício central; **main product,** produto *m* principal; **main plant,** fábrica *f* principal.

mainstay, *n.* ponto *m* de apoio, principal sustentáculo *m*, (da economia).

maintain, *v.tr.* (*a*) manter (relações, uma correspondência, etc.); (*b*) **the improvement in the economy is being maintained,** o melhoramento na economia está sendo mantido; **to maintain the exchange above the gold point,** manter o câmbio acima do gold point; (*c*) manter, conservar, (prédios, máquinas, etc.).

maintenance, *n.* **1.** (*a*) manutenção *f* (de alguém no seu cargo, etc.); **resale price maintenance,** manutenção de preços de revenda; *Fin:* **maintenance of a fund,** manutenção de um fundo; *Am: Ind:* **maintenance of membership,** cláusula pela qual os afiliados a um sindicato se comprometem a pagar as mensalidades durante a vigência de um contrato de trabalho sob pena de perderem o emprego; (*b*) *Jur:* pensão (paga pelo homem divorciado para o sustento da sua ex-mulher e seus filhos). **2.** manutenção, conservação *f*, (de prédios, máquinas, etc.); **preventive maintenance,** manutenção preventiva; **routine maintenance,** manutenção de rotina; **maintenance charges, expenses,** despesas *fpl*, de, com, manutenção, conservação;

maintenance contract, contrato *m* de manutenção; **maintenance cost,** custo *m* de manutenção; **maintenance engineer,** técnico *m* de manutenção; **maintenance imports,** importações *fpl* para manutenção; **maintenance personnel, crew,** pessoal *m*, equipe *f*, turma *f*, de manutenção, de conservação; **maintenance programme,** programa *m* de manutenção; **maintenance requirements,** requisitos *mpl* para manutenção; **maintenance resources,** meios *mpl* de manutenção; **maintenance service,** serviço *m* de manutenção; *Am: Rail:* **maintenance of way,** conservação da via permanente.

maize, *n.* milho (indiano); **maize flour,** farinha *f* de milho.

major, *a.* principal; de grande vulto; **major investment,** investimento vultoso; **major repairs,** consertos *mpl* de grande monta.

majority, *n.* (*a*) maioria *f* (dos votos, etc.); **two-thirds majority,** maioria de dois-terços; **majority decision,** decisão aprovada por uma maioria dos votos; **absolute majority,** maioria absoluta; **relative majority,** maioria relativa; **majority holding, interest, stake,** participação controladora, participação majoritária; **majority shareholder,** acionista majoritário, acionista controlador; (*b*) *Jur:* (*full age*) maioridade *f*.

make¹, *n.* marca *f* (de produto, etc.); **a well-known Brazilian make,** uma marca brasileira de grande aceitação; **cars of all makes,** carros *mpl* de todas as marcas; **a good make of car,** uma boa marca de carro.

make², *v.tr.* **1.** (*a*) fazer, construir; (*b*) fabricar, manufaturar, produzir; **the factory is making 120 machines a week,** a fábrica está produzindo cento e vinte máquinas por semana. **2. to make a bid,** fazer uma proposta; **to make an agreement,** fazer um acordo; **to make a bill of exchange,** emitir uma letra de câmbio; **to make a loan,** fazer um empréstimo; **to make a payment,** efetuar, fazer, um pagamento; **to make a deal,** fazer uma transação; **to make an entry,**

efetuar um lançamento (nos livros contábeis); **to make an impact,** produzir um impacto; **to make a speech,** fazer, pronunciar, um discurso. **3.** (*of person*) **to make $350 a week,** ganhar, perceber, $350 semanais; (*of business*) **the shop is making 250 000 cruzeiros a week,** a loja está rendendo 250.000 cruzeiros por semana; **to make $2000 on the deal,** auferir um lucro de $2.000 com a transação; **to make a profit from sth.,** auferir um lucro de algo; **to make a net profit of $100,** auferir um lucro líquido de $100; **to make a fortune,** ganhar uma fortuna; **to make a good deal by selling cosmetics,** auferir um grande lucro com a venda de cosméticos.

make out, *v.tr.* **to make out a list,** fazer uma lista; **to make out a report,** fazer, redigir, um relatório; **to make out a form,** preencher um formulário; **to make out an invoice,** fazer uma fatura; **to make out a cheque for $100 to s.o.,** emitir, passar, fazer, um cheque de $100 a favor de alguém; **to make out a document in duplicate,** redigir um documento em duas vias.

make over, *v.tr.* transferir, ceder; **he made his share of the inheritance over to his mother,** ele cedeu à mãe sua parte na herança.

maker, *n.* **1.** fabricante *mf,* produtor *m,* construtor *m;* **maker's price,** preço *m* de fábrica. **2. maker of a promissory note,** emitente *mf* de uma promissória.

make up, *v.* **1.** *v.tr.* (*a*) completar, perfazer, inteirar; **the payments make up a considerable total,** os pagamentos perfazem um total considerável; (*b*) **to make up the difference (in an account),** cobrir o déficit, suprir o déficit; (*c*) **to make up back payments,** liquidar pagamentos atrasados; (*d*) (*in shop, etc.*) **to make up an order,** confeccionar um pedido, atender um pedido (juntando vários artigos a serem comprados); **to make up manufactured goods,** embalar, empacotar, manufaturados; (*e*) **to make up the accounts,** ajustar, acertar, as contas; **to make up a balance sheet,**

levantar um balanço. **2.** *v.i.* **to make up for one's losses,** compensar os prejuízos.

making, *n.* **1.** feitura *f,* fabricação *f,* fabrico *m,* produção *f,* (de ferramentas, etc.); confecção *f* (de roupas); construção *f* (de navios); criação *f* (de um cargo); **decision-making,** tomada *f* de decisão, de decisões; **the making of a profit,** a obtenção de um lucro, o auferimento de um lucro. **2.** *Ind: pl.* **makings,** matéria-prima *f.*

making up, *n.* (*a*) compensação *f* (de prejuízos); (*b*) levantamento *m* (de um balanço); ajuste *m,* ajustamento *m,* (de contas); *St.Exch:* **making-up price,** taxa *f* de compensação.

maladjustment, *n. Pol.Ec:* **maladjustment in the balance of trade,** desequilíbrio *m* na balança comercial.

maladministration, *n.* má administração *f.*

mala fide, 1. *adv.* de má fé. **2.** *a.* **mala fide holder,** detentor *m* de má fé; **mala fide purchaser,** adquirente *mf* de má fé.

malinvestment, *n.* investimento mal orientado.

mammoth, *a.* imenso, gigantesco; **mammoth reduction,** redução gigantesca.

man¹, *n.* **1.** homem *m;* **a salaried man,** um assalariado, um salariado; **a non-union man,** um operário não-sindicalizado; *Ind:* **man-hour,** homem-hora *m.* **2.** (*a*) **men's wear,** vestuário masculino; **men's clothing,** confecções masculinas; **men's department,** departamento *m* de vestuário masculino; (*b*) **employers and men,** os patrões e os operários.

man², *v.tr.* prover (uma organização) de pessoal; **to man the production line,** trabalhar na linha de produção; **to man a machine,** manobrar, operar, uma máquina; **to man the night shift,** trabalhar no turno da noite; **the service is manned 24 hours a day,** o serviço funciona 24 horas por dia; **the factory is satisfactorily manned,** a fábrica está provida de pessoal suficiente; **the machine was not manned when the accident occurred,** a máquina não estava sendo operada por um trabalhador competente quando o acidente aconteceu.

manage, *v.tr.* dirigir, gerir, gerenciar, administrar; **to manage a business,** dirigir, administrar, gerenciar, uma empresa; **to manage a factory,** dirigir, gerir, uma fábrica; **to manage a property,** administrar um imóvel; **to manage s.o.'s affairs,** administrar os negócios de alguém; *Pol.Ec:* **managed economy,** economia dirigida.

management, *n.* **1.** (*act of managing*) direção *f*, administração *f*, gerenciamento *m*, gestão *f*, gerência *f*; **management by objectives,** administração por objetivos; **automated production management,** gestão automatizada de produção; **bad management,** má administração, má gestão; **business management,** administração de empresas; **divisional management,** administração departamental; **factory management,** direção, administração, de fábricas; **joint management,** direção conjunta; **personnel management,** direção, administração, de pessoal; **sales management,** direção de vendas; **management ability,** capacidade administrativa; **management accounting,** contabilidade administrativa, contabilidade gerencial; **management board,** conselho diretivo; **management charge,** taxa *f* de administração; **management chart,** organograma *m*; **management company,** sociedade *f* de administração; **management consultant,** consultor *m* em administração; **management fee,** honorário *m* de administração; **management team,** equipe *f* de direção; **management techniques,** técnicas *fpl* de administração; **management theory,** teoria *f* da administração de empresas. **2.** (*persons*) **the management,** a direção, a diretoria, a administração; (*in shop, etc.*) a gerência; **general management,** direção *f* geral; **middle management,** gerentes *mfpl* de nível médio; **top management,** top management *m*, alta direção, os gerentes de alto nível; **negotiations between management and the unions,** negociações *fpl* entre a direção e os sindicatos; (*of shop, restaurant, etc.*) **under new management,** sob nova gerência, sob nova

direção; *Fin:* **management shares,** partes beneficiárias (da direção).

manager, *n.* **1.** gerente *mf* (de loja, departamento, fábrica, etc.), chefe *mf* (de loja, de departamento), diretor *m* (de fábrica), superintendente *mf* (de obra, projeto, etc.); administrador *m* (de bens); **advertising manager,** gerente de publicidade; **assistant manager,** subgerente *mf*; **bank manager,** gerente de banco; **branch manager,** gerente de sucursal; **business manager,** (i) administrador *m* de empresas, (ii) diretor comercial, (iii) empresário *m* (de um cantor, etc.); **contracts manager,** administrador de contratos; (*in store*) **department manager,** chefe de departamento; **departmental manager,** chefe de serviço, chefe de setor; **deputy manager,** subgerente *mf*; **district manager,** gerente distrital; **engineering manager (of a firm),** diretor técnico (de uma empresa); **general manager,** diretor gerente; **hotel manager,** gerente de hotel; **marketing manager,** diretor de marketing, diretor comercial, gerente comercial; **office manager,** chefe de escritório; **personnel manager,** diretor de pessoal, chefe de pessoal; **production manager,** gerente de produção; **purchasing manager,** chefe (do setor) de compras; **sales manager,** gerente de vendas, diretor de vendas, chefe de vendas, diretor comercial; **works manager,** chefe de fábrica. **2.** *Jur:* **receiver and manager,** síndico *m* de massa falida, curador *m* de massas falidas. **3.** *Fin:* **manager trust,** fundo *m* de investimento com grande liberdade quanto à sua política de aplicação.

manageress, *n.* diretora *f*, gerente *f*.

managerial, *a.* gerencial, administrativo; **the managerial class,** a classe gerencial; **managerial structure,** estrutura *f* de administração; **managerial position,** cargo administrativo, cargo de gerência, cargo de chefia; **managerial ability,** capacidade administrativa; **managerial decision,** decisão *f* de caráter administrativo.

managership, *n.* direção *f*, gerência *f*, superintendência *f*, (de empresa, etc.).

managing, *a.* diretor; gerente; **managing director,** diretor gerente, diretor geral, diretor-superintendente *m*; **chairman and managing director,** presidente *mf* (do conselho de administração) e diretor gerente; **managing committee,** comitê *m* de direção, comitê gerencial; **managing partner,** sócio *m* gerente; **managing clerk,** chefe *mf* de escritório; *Nau:* **managing owner,** armador-gerente *m*.

mandate, *n. Bank:* **mandate form,** formulário *m* que contém as assinaturas autorizadas.

mandatory, 1. *n. Jur:* mandatário *m*. **2.** *a.* obrigatório; **mandatory retirement,** aposentadoria compulsória.

man-hour, *pl.* **man-hours,** *n.* homem-hora *m*; **one hundred and twenty man-hours,** cento e vinte homens-hora.

manifest¹, *n. Nau: Av:* manifesto *m* (da alfândega); **inward, outward, manifest,** manifesto de entrada, de saída.

manifest², *v.tr.* declarar (carga) na alfândega, listar (carga) no manifesto.

manipulate, *v.tr.* manipular; **to manipulate accounts,** manipular contas; **to manipulate the market,** manipular o mercado, trabalhar o mercado.

manipulator, *n. F:* especulador *m* que manipula o mercado.

man-made, *a.* sintético, artificial; **man-made fibres,** fibras sintéticas.

manner, *n.* **manner of payment,** modalidade *f* de pagamento.

manning, *n.* (*a*) provisão *f* de pessoal (para organização, serviço, etc.); (*b*) pessoal provido (para organização, fábrica, etc.); **to reduce manning levels,** reduzir o número de operários.

manpower, *n.* recursos humanos, potencial humano, força *f* de trabalho, força humana, mão-de-obra *f*; **manpower control,** controle *m* dos recursos humanos, do potencial humano; **manpower forecasting,** previsão *f* de recursos humanos; **manpower planning,** planejamento *m* de recursos humanos, planejamento da mão-de-obra; **manpower management,** administração *f* de recursos humanos; **manpower shortage,** escassez *f* de mão-de-obra, carência *f* de recursos

humanos; **manpower turnover,** rotatividade *f* da mão-de-obra.

manual, 1. *a.* (*a*) (i) manual, (ii) braçal; **manual work,** trabalho *m* manual; **manual labour,** trabalho braçal; **manual labourer,** trabalhador *m* braçal, braceiro *m*; (*b*) *Ind:* **manual operation,** operação *f* manual; **manual control,** controle *m* manual; **manual feed,** alimentação *f* manual. **2.** *n.* (*a*) manual *m* (de instruções, etc.); (*b*) *Ins:* **manual rate,** taxa *f* oficial de prêmio de seguro.

manually, *adv.* manualmente, à mão.

manufacture¹, *n.* **1.** manufatura *f*, fabricação *f*, (de produtos industriais); confecção *f* (de roupas); **articles of foreign manufacture,** artigos fabricados no exterior, artigos de fabricação estrangeira. **2.** produto industrializado, manufaturado *m*, fabricação *f*, manufatura *f*.

manufacture², *v.tr.* fabricar, manufaturar; confeccionar (roupas, etc.); **manufactured exports,** exportações *fpl* de produtos manufaturados; **manufactured foodstuffs,** alimentos beneficiados; **manufactured goods,** manufaturas *fpl* de consumo, (produtos) manufaturados *mpl*; **manufactured goods tax,** imposto *m* sobre produtos industrializados.

manufacturer, *n.* fabricante *mf*, industrial *mf*; **a leading car manufacturer,** um dos principais fabricantes de automóveis; **manufacturer's agent,** agente *mf* do fabricante; **manufacturer's brand,** marca *f* do fabricante; **manufacturer's recommended price,** preço *m* a varejo recomendado pelo fabricante.

manufacturing, 1. *a.* manufatureiro, fabril, industrial; **manufacturing activity,** atividade manufatureira, atividade fabril; **manufacturing area,** zona *f* industrial, (*of a country*) região *f* industrial; **manufacturing industry,** indústria manufatureira; **manufacturing operation,** atividade manufatureira, operação *f* fabril; **manufacturing process,** processo manufatureiro, processo de fabricação; **manufacturing town,** cidade *f* industrial. **2.** *n.* fabricação *f*, manufatura *f*, confecçao *f* (de roupas); **manufacturing**

control, controle *m* de produção; **manufacturing cost,** custo *m* de fabricação, custo industrial; **manufacturing equipment,** equipamento *m* para fabricação; **manufacturing expenses,** despesas *fpl* de fabricação, despesas industriais; **manufacturing overheads,** gastos *mpl* gerais de fabricação, despesas gerais de fabricação, custos indiretos de fabricação; **manufacturing production, output,** produção manufatureira; **manufacturing statement,** demonstração *f* do custo de fabricação; **economic quantity manufacturing,** quantidade econômica de fabricação, de produção.

margin¹, *n.* 1. (*a*) **the margin between the rates of interest,** a diferença entre as taxas de juros; **the margin of profit, profit margin,** margem *f* de lucro; **gross margin,** margem de lucro bruto; **net margin,** margem de lucro líquido; **margin of error,** margem de erro; **safety margin,** margem, limite *m*, de segurança; **a margin of $100 for unforeseen expenses,** provisão *f* de cem dólares para despesas imprevistas; (*b*) *St.Exch:* margem. 2. (*of page*) margem; **top margin,** margem superior; **bottom margin,** margem inferior; **to write in the margin,** escrever na margem; **to leave a margin,** deixar uma margem.

margin², *v.i. esp. N.Am: St.Exch:* **to margin (up),** pagar a margem.

marginal, *a.* (*a*) marginal; **marginal balance,** saldo *m* marginal; **marginal buying,** compra marginal, compra ao preço do custo da produção; **marginal cost,** custo *m* marginal; **marginal costing,** contabilidade *f* de custos marginais; **marginal costing system,** sistema *m* de custeio marginal; **marginal efficiency of capital,** eficiência *f* marginal do capital; **marginal income,** receita *f* marginal (em indústria, etc.); **marginal producer,** produtor *m* marginal; **marginal productivity,** produtividade *f* marginal; **marginal profit,** lucro *m* marginal; **marginal revenue,** receita *f* marginal; **marginal supply,** suprimento *m* marginal; **marginal utility,** utilidade *f* marginal; (*b*)

marginal note, nota *f* marginal, nota de margem.

marginalism, *n. Pol.Ec:* marginalismo *m*.

marginalist, *n. Pol.Ec:* partidário *m* do marginalismo.

marginally, *adv.* marginalmente; **the shares were marginally lower,** as ações acusaram uma ligeira baixa.

marine, 1. *a.* (*a*) **marine engineering,** engenharia *f* naval; **marine hardware,** ferragens *fpl* de navio; (*b*) **marine insurance,** seguro marítimo; **marine policy,** apólice *f* de seguro marítimo; **marine accident insurance,** seguro contra acidentes marítimos; **marine risk, peril,** fortuna *f* do mar, risco marítimo. 2. *n.* **merchant marine,** marinha *f* mercante.

maritime, *a.* marítimo; **maritime law,** direito marítimo; **maritime trade,** comércio marítimo; **maritime loan,** préstimo *m* a risco; *Ins:* **maritime risk,** risco marítimo, fortuna *f* do mar.

mark¹, *n.* (*a*) marca *f*, sinal *m*; **assay mark,** marca *f* de contraste; **certification mark,** marca de garantia; (*b*) *St.Exch:* cotação *f* (de um título); **to lodge an objection to the mark,** fazer objeção a uma cotação.

mark², *v.tr.* 1. marcar, assinalar; **the packing cases were marked 'breakable',** os caixotes estavam marcados 'frágil'. 2. **to mark (the price of) an article,** marcar o preço em um artigo. 3. *St.Exch:* **to mark stock,** cotar valores.

mark³, *n. Num:* marco *m*.

mark down, *v.tr.* **to mark down,** rebaixar, remarcar (para baixo); **the overcoats have been marked down 20%,** os casacos foram remarcados em 20%; *St.Exch:* **to mark down prices,** baixar as cotações (de determinados títulos).

markdown, *n.* remarcação *f* (para baixo).

market¹, *n.* 1. mercado *m*; **cattle market,** feira *f* de gado; **covered market,** mercado em lugar coberto; **fish market,** mercado de peixe, (*wholesale*) lota *f*; **fruit and vegetable market** = feira livre; **open-air market,** feira (livre); **market day,** dia *m* de feira; **market garden,** horta *f*, chácara *f*; **market gardener,** hortelão *m*; **market place,** praça *f* (em cidade, etc.); **market stall,** barraca *f*. 2. (*a*) **The Common**

Market, o Mercado Comum Europeu; **foreign market,** mercado externo; **world market,** mercado mundial; **free, open, market,** mercado livre; **home market,** mercado interno; **international money market,** mercado monetário internacional; **overseas market,** mercado ultramarino, mercado externo; (*b*) **capital market,** mercado de capitais; **commodity market,** mercado de commodities; **cotton market,** mercado de algodão; **foreign exchange market,** mercado de câmbio; **forward exchange market,** mercado de câmbio a termo; **labour market,** mercado de trabalho; **option market,** mercado de opções; **the property market,** o mercado imobiliário; **retail market,** mercado varejista; **settlement market,** mercado (de valores) a termo; **stock market,** mercado acionário, bolsa *f* de valores; **wholesale market,** mercado atacadista; *St.Exch:* **market order,** ordem *f* ao mercado; (*c*) **black market,** mercado negro, mercado paralelo; **buyer's market,** mercado de comprador; **fringe market,** mercado marginal; **grey market,** mercado cinzento; **jumpy market,** mercado instável; **official market,** mercado oficial; **quiet market,** mercado calmo; **seller's market,** mercado de vendedor; **steady market,** mercado firme, mercado estável; **unofficial market,** *N.Am:* **over-the-counter market,** mercado de balcão; (*d*) **market analysis,** análise *f* de mercado; **market appraisal,** avaliação *f* de mercado; **market demand,** procura *f* de mercado; **market financing,** financiamento *m* de mercados; **market forces,** forças *fpl* do mercado; **market forecast,** previsão *f* de mercado; **market intelligence,** informações *fpl* de mercado; **market interest,** interesse *m* de mercado; **market opportunity,** oportunidade *f* de mercado; **market penetration,** penetração *f* do mercado; **market pressure,** pressão *f* de mercado; **market price,** preço *m* de mercado; **market prospects,** perspectivas *fpl* de mercado; **market research,** pesquisa *f* de mercado; **market segmentation,** segmentação *f* do mercado; **market study,** estudo *m* de mercado;

market survey, levantamento *m* de mercado; **market trend,** tendência *f* do mercado; **market value,** valor *m* de mercado; **down market,** (no) mercado de consumidores de menor renda; **up market,** (no) mercado de consumidores de maior renda; **to be in the market for sth.,** procurar algo (no mercado); **to be on the market, to come onto the market,** estar à venda; **to corner the market in cotton,** monopolizar o mercado de algodão; **to dry up the market,** enxugar, esgotar, o mercado; **to flood the market,** inundar, abarrotar, o mercado; **to play the market,** especular; **to price oneself out of the market,** perder freguesia por causa dos preços excessivos; **to put an article on the market,** colocar, lançar, um artigo no mercado; **to rig the market,** trabalhar, manipular, o mercado; **to upset the market,** desequilibrar o mercado; **there is a ready market for these products,** existe mercado para estes produtos; **the bottom fell out of the market,** o mercado sofreu um colapso

market², *v.tr.* vender, comercializar, mercadejar, (produtos, artigos); negociar (títulos), lançar (um novo produto); **marketed bonds and shares,** títulos negociados.

marketability, *n.* vendabilidade *f* (de um produto), negociabilidade *f* (de títulos, etc.).

marketable, *a.* (*a*) (*of goods*) vendável, comerciável; **marketable product,** produto *m* vendável; **marketable securities,** títulos *mpl* de bolsa, títulos negociáveis na bolsa; (*b*) **marketable value,** valor *m* venal.

marketeer, *n.* (*a*) negociante *mf*, comerciante *mf*; **black merketeer,** traficante *mf*; (*b*) **Common Marketeer,** partidário *m* do Mercado Comum Europeu.

marketing, *n.* 1. marketing *m*, comercialização *f*, mercadologia *f*, mercadização *f*, mercadotecnia *f*, mercadotécnica *f*; **marketing agreement,** acordo *m* de comercialização; **marketing asset,** fator *m* favorável à comercialização; **marketing board,** junta *f* de comercialização; **marketing channels,**

canais *mpl* de distribuição; **marketing cooperative,** cooperativa *f* de comercialização; **marketing costs,** custos *mpl* de marketing, de comercialização; **marketing department,** departamento *m* de marketing, **marketing experience,** experiência mercadológica; **marketing management,** administração mercadológica; **marketing manager,** gerente *mf* de marketing; **marketing method,** método *m* de comercialização; **marketing mix,** composto mercadológico; **marketing money,** verba *f* para comercialização (de um produto); **marketing network,** rede *f* de distribuição; **marketing operation,** operação *f* de marketing; **marketing plan,** plano *m* de comercialização; **marketing policy,** política *f* de comercialização; **marketing productivity,** produtividade *f* em termos de marketing; **marketing research,** pesquisa *f* de marketing, pesquisa de comercialização, pesquisa mercadológica; **marketing study,** estudo mercadológico. **2.** *Am:* gêneros alimentícios colocados à venda.

marketplace, *n.* local *m* do mercado.

marking, *n.* **1.** marcação *f* de preços (numa loja, etc.). **2.** *St.Exch:* cotação *f* (de valores).

mark-on, *n.* margem *f* de lucro.

mark up, *v.tr.* aumentar, majorar, (o preço de mercadorias); aumentar o valor (de uma fatura); *St.Exch:* **prices have been marked up,** os preços subiram.

markup, *n.* **1.** aumento *m* (de preço), remarcação *f* (para cima), majoração *f*. **2.** margem *f* de lucro bruto (de revendedor); (taxa *f* de) markup *m*; **markup pricing,** fixação *f* de preço com base no custo médio acrescido da margem de lucro; **we operate a 2.5 times markup,** nossa taxa de markup é de 2,5.

mart, *n.* **1.** mercado *m*, empório *m*; **money mart,** mercado monetário, mercado financeiro. **2.** **(auction) mart,** casa *f* de leilões; **car mart,** comércio *m* de carros usados.

mass, *a.* (*a*) **mass production,** produção *f* em massa, produção em série, fabricação *f* em série; **mass-production car,** carro

fabricado em série; (*b*) **mass unemployment,** desemprego *m* em massa; **mass communication,** comunicação *f* de massa; **mass media,** mídia *mpl*, meios *mpl* de comunicação de massa; **mass consumption,** consumo *m* de massa; **mass market,** mercado *m* de consumo em massa; **mass purchasing power,** poder aquisitivo total.

mass-produce, *v.tr.* produzir em massa, fabricar em série.

match, *v.tr.* (*a*) igualar, servir de contrapartida a; (*b*) **to match the prices of foreign competitors,** oferecer os mesmos preços que a concorrência estrangeira.

matched, *a.* *St.Exch:* *Am:* **matched orders,** ordens combinadas de compra e de venda (dadas pelo mesmo cliente).

matching, *a.* **matching payment,** pagamento *m* de contrapartida.

material, *n.* **1.** material *m*; matéria *f*; **materials cost,** custo *m* de materiais; **materials management,** administração *f* de materiais; **materials requisition,** requisição *f* de materiais; **materials handling,** manuseio *m* de materiais; **materials testing,** testes *mpl* de materiais; *Econ: Ind:* **raw materials,** materias-primas *fpl*; **unprocessed, unrefined, material,** matéria bruta; **synthetic material,** material sintético; **building materials,** materiais *mpl* de construção; **flooring material,** material para pisos (ou soalhos); **roofing material,** material para telhados. **2.** *Tex:* tecido *m*, fazenda *f*.

matter, *n.* **1.** *Post:* **postal matter,** correio *m*; **printed matter,** impresso *m*. **2.** assunto *m*, questão *f*; **he will deal with the matter tomorrow,** ele tratará do assunto amanhã; **business matters,** negócios *mpl*; **money matters,** assuntos financeiros; **matter of dispute,** assunto contencioso; **that will cost you a matter of £50,** isto custa umas cinqüenta libras esterlinas. *Jur:* **in the matter of . . .,** relativamente a . . . .

mature¹, *a.* (*a*) *Ec:* **mature economy,** economia *f* em estagnação; (*b*) *Fin:* vencido; **a mature bill of exchange,** uma letra de câmbio vencida.

mature², *v.i. Fin:* (*of bill*) vencer-se; **bills**

to mature on Dec. 31st, letras *fpl* a vencer(em) em 31 de dezembro.

matured, *a. Fin:* vencido; matured liability, responsabilidade vencida; matured bonds, obrigações vencidas.

maturity, *n.* (*a*) *Fin:* vencimento *m* (de uma letra, etc.); payable at maturity, pagável no vencimento; date of maturity, (data de) vencimento; *Book-k:* maturity basis, base *f* de vencimento; (*b*) *N.Am:* current maturities, passivo *m* exigível a curto prazo.

maximization, *n.* maximização *f*; maximization of profits, maximização de lucros.

maximize, *v.tr.* maximizar, elevar ao máximo; to maximize total profit, maximizar o lucro total.

maximum, 1. *n.* máximo *m*; to the maximum, ao máximo; up to a maximum of $20, até o valor máximo de $20; to raise production to a maximum, aumentar a produção ao (nível) máximo. 2. *a.* maximum economy, economia máxima; maximum efficiency, rendimento máximo (das instalações fabris); maximum load, carga máxima; maximum price, preço máximo, preço-teto *m*; maximum productivity, produtividade máxima; *Cust:* maximum and minimum tariff system, sistema *m* de tarifas máxima e mínima.

mean, *a.* médio; mean cost, custo médio; mean due date, vencimento médio (para varias obrigações); mean price, preço médio; mean quantity, quantidade média; mean value, valor médio.

means, *n.pl.* (*often with sg. const.*) (*a*) meios *mpl*, posses *fpl*, haveres *mpl*, recursos *mpl*; to live within one's means, viver dentro de suas posses; to live beyond one's means, gastar além de suas posses; *UK: Adm:* means test, investigação da situação financeira de uma pessoa que está solicitando assistência pública; (*b*) means of transport, meios de transporte; means of payment, meios de pagamento; Committee on Ways and Means, Comissão *f* de Meios; Law of Ways and Means, Lei *f* de Meios; *Pol.Ec:* means of production, meios de produção.

measure[1], *n.* 1. (*a*) medida *f*; linear measure, medida de comprimento; square measure, medida de superfície, medida de área; liquid measure, medida de capacidade para líquidos; dry measure, medida de capacidade para secos; standard measure, medida-padrão *f*; metric measure, medida métrica; cubic measure, medida cúbica, medida de volume; weights and measures, pesos *mpl* e medidas; (*b*) *Tail:* made to measure, feito sob medida; (*c*) *Nau:* arqueação *f*. 2. (*instrument for measuring*) medidor *m*; two measures of milk, duas medidas de leite; tape measure, fita métrica, trena *f*. 3. medida, providência *f*; anti-inflation measures, medidas anti-inflacionárias; security, safety, measures, medidas de segurança; measures of conciliation, medidas de conciliação; as an economy measure, como medida de economia; emergency measures, medidas de emergência; preventive measures, medidas preventivas; to take measures, tomar medidas, tomar providências.

measure[2], *v.* 1. *v.tr.* (*a*) medir, tomar as medidas de, (um terreno, etc.); to measure s.o., tomar as medidas de alguém, medir alguém; (*b*) to measure the tonnage of a ship, medir a tonelagem de um navio. 2. *v.i.* the cloth measures two metres, o pano mede dois metros.

measurement, *n.* 1. medição *f*, medida *f*; productivity measurement, medição da produtividade. 2. *Nau:* arqueação *f* (de um navio). 3. *Tail:* to take a customer's measurements, tomar as medidas de um freguês, medir um freguês.

measuring, *n.* measuring apparatus, aparelho *m* de medição; measuring instrument, instrumento *m* de medição; measuring tape, fita métrica, trena *f*.

meat, *n.* meat industry, indústria *f* de carne; meat packaging plant, frigorífico *m* industrial (para carne).

mechanic, *n.* mecânico *m*.

mechanical, *a.* mecânico; mechanical efficiency, rendimento mecânico; mechanical engineering, engenharia mecânica; mechanical industry, indústria mecânica; **mechanical drawing**, desenho técnico, desenho mecânico.

mechanism, *n.* mecanismo *m*, maquinismo *m*; **banking mechanism**, mecanismo bancário; **discount mechanism**, mecanismo de desconto; **price mechanism**, mecanismo dos preços.

mechanization, *n.* mecanização *f*.

mechanize, *v.tr.* mecanizar (agricultura).

media, *n.pl. see* **medium, 2.** (*a*).

mediate, *v.i.* **to mediate between the employers and the strikers**, mediar, atuar como mediador, entre os patrões e os grevistas.

mediation, *n.* mediação *f*; **through the mediation of . . .**, por mediação de . . .; **to resolve a labour dispute through mediation**, resolver um dissídio por mediação; **Mediation Board** = Junta *f* de Conciliação e Julgamento.

mediator, *n.* mediador *m*.

mediatory, *a.* mediador, mediatário.

medical, *a.* **medical insurance**, seguro *m* médico-hospitalar; **medical certificate**, atestado médico; **medical officer**, médico *m* de empresa.

medium, *n.* **1.** intermédio *m*; **through the medium of the press**, por intermédio da imprensa, através da imprensa. **2.** (*a*) meio *m*, órgão *m*, (de divulgação); veículo *m* (de comunicação, etc.); **advertising medium**, veículo publicitário, meio de propaganda; **the media, mass media**, mídia *mpl*, meios de comunicação de massa; **media planning**, planejamento *m* de veículos publicitários; (*b*) **medium of exchange**, meio de troca; *Pol.Ec:* **circulating medium, medium of circulation**, meio circulante. **3.** *Fin: pl.* **mediums**, fundos públicos a médio prazo.

medium-priced, *a.* **medium-priced goods**, mercadorias *fpl* de preço médio.

medium-run, *a.* a médio prazo; **a budget is a medium-run estimate**, um orçamento é uma estimativa a médio prazo.

medium-sized, *a.* de tamanho médio.

medium-term, *a.* **medium-term finance**, financiamento *m* a médio prazo; **medium-term capital flow**, movimento *m* de capitais a médio prazo.

meet, *v.* **1.** *v.tr.* (*a*) encontrar (alguém); **to**

arrange to meet s.o., marcar um encontro com alguém; **the Chairman would like to meet the office staff**, o Presidente gostaria de conhecer o pessoal do escritório; (*b*) **to meet an obligation**, cumprir (com) uma obrigação; **to meet one's expenses**, arcar com as despesas; **to meet a debt**, liquidar, saldar, satisfazer, uma dívida; **to meet a request**, atender (a) uma solicitação; **to meet an order**, atender (a) um pedido; **to meet a bill of exchange**, honrar uma letra de câmbio; **to meet the monthly payments**, cumprir com os pagamentos mensais; **to meet demand**, satisfazer à demanda; **to meet a deadline**, cumprir com um prazo (para a entrega de um trabalho, etc.); *Jur:* **to meet a charge**, responder (em juízo) a uma acusação. **2.** *v.i.* (*a*) encontrar-se, reunir-se; (*of society, assembly, etc.*) **the shareholders will meet at the registered office**, os acionistas se reunirão na sede social; (*b*) **to meet with a loss**, sofrer um prejuízo; **to meet with a refusal**, receber uma recusa.

meeting, *n.* encontro *m*; reunião *f* (de sócios, etc.), assembléia *f* (dos acionistas, etc.); **meeting of creditors**, concurso *m* de credores; **annual meeting, ordinary general meeting**, assembléia geral ordinária; **board meeting**, reunião do conselho de administração; **the extraordinary general meeting of the shareholders**, a assembléia geral extraordinária dos acionistas; **notice of meeting**, convocação *f* de uma reunião, convocação a uma reunião, anúncio *m* de convocação; **the notice of meeting shall state the date, place and time of the meeting**, o anúncio de convocação designará o dia, o local e a hora da assembléia; **place of meeting**, local *m* de reunião; **to address a meeting**, fazer uso da palavra numa reunião, tomar a palavra numa reunião; **to attend a meeting**, assistir a uma reunião, comparecer a uma reunião; **to call a meeting of the shareholders**, convocar uma assembléia dos acionistas; **to close a meeting**, encerrar uma reunião; **to open a meeting**, abrir uma reunião; **to put a**

resolution to a meeting, submeter uma proposta à votação, colocar uma proposta em votação; the meeting will take place tomorrow, a reunião se realizará amanhã; he's at, in, a meeting, ele está em conferência; the manager's going to a business meeting, o gerente está indo a uma reunião de negócios.

member, n. membro m, sócio m, societário m, associado m, afiliado m; board member, membro do conselho (de administração); member of a company, sócio m, acionista mf, de uma companhia; honorary member, sócio honorário; trade-union member, operário sindicalizado, membro de um sindicato, sindicatário m; club member, sócio de clube, clubista mf; member bank, banco associado (de um consórcio, sindicato, etc.); member country, país-membro m (das Nações Unidas, etc.); to become a member of an organization, ingressar numa organização, tornar-se membro de uma organização.

membership, n. 1. qualidade f de membro, societariado m; membership card, carteira f de sócio; membership fee, cota f, contribuição f, de sócio; conditions of membership, condições fpl de admissão como membro; to renew membership, renovar a subscrição de sócio, o título de sócio. 2. (a) (i) grupo m de membros, societariado m, (ii) a totalidade dos membros; (b) Ind: the membership does not accept the employer's offer, os membros do sindicato não aceitam a oferta do patrão.

memo, n. memorando m; memo pad, bloco m de memorando; memo book, agenda f.

memorandum, n. 1. memorando m; memorandum book, agenda f; to make a memorandum of a matter, emitir um memorando sobre um assunto. 2. (a) (in international relations) protocolo m, memorando; the governments signed a memorandum of understanding on their future trading relations, os governos assinaram um memorando de acordo a respeito das suas futuras relações comerciais; (b) Jur: sumário m dos artigos de um contrato; memorandum and

articles of association, contrato m social, estatuto m social, estatutos sociais. 3. Book-k: memorandum account, conta f de compensação.

menswear, n. vestuário masculino.

mention, v.tr. mencionar.

mercantile, a. (a) mercantil, comercial; mercantile affairs, assuntos mpl comerciais; mercantile agency, agência f comercial; mercantile broker, agente mf de câmbio; mercantile credit, crédito m mercantil; mercantile law, direito m comercial; mercantile marine, marinha f mercante; mercantile nation, nação f mercantil; mercantile operations, transações fpl mercantis; mercantile paper, efeitos mpl de comércio; (b) Pol.Ec: the mercantile system, o sistema mercantilista, o mercantilismo.

mercantilism, n. Pol.Ec: mercantilismo m.

mercantilist, a. & n. mercantilista (mf).

merchandise¹, n. mercadoria(s) f (pl).

merchandise², v.tr. 1. comerciar (em algo), negociar (com algo). 2. Mkt: fazer o ajustamento (de um produto), comercializar.

merchandising, n. merchandising m, comercialização f, (in technical use) ajustamento m; leader merchandising, comercialização através de chamariz.

merchant, 1. n. (a) comerciante mf, negociante mf; wine merchant, negociante de vinhos; wholesale merchant, atacadista mf; merchant middleman, intermediário m comerciante; merchant's brand, marca f do comerciante; merchant's mark, marca f de comércio; (b) Scot: & N.Am: comerciante (como dono de loja). 2. a. (a) mercante; merchant bank, banco m mercantil, banco comercial; merchant marine, merchant navy, marinha f mercante; merchant seaman, marinheiro m da marinha mercante; merchant ship, vessel, navio m mercante; merchant shipping, navegação f mercante; merchant tailor, alfaiate m que fornece o tecido para suas confecções; (b) the law merchant, o direito comercial; merchant shipping law, direito marítimo.

merchantable, a. merchantable goods, (i) mercadorias em condições de serem vendidas, mercadorias comerciáveis, (ii) mercadorias vendáveis, que têm boa venda.

merchantman, n. navio m mercante.

merge, v. 1. v.tr. fundir (empresas); he merged the small firms into one large company, ele fundiu as pequenas empresas em uma grande companhia; Jur: rights that are merged in one person, direitos confusos em uma pessoa. 2. v.i. (of banks, etc.) fundir-se.

merger, n. (a) fusão f; industrial merger, consolidação f, fusão, de empresas industriais; merger company, companhia formada pela fusão de duas ou mais empresas; (b) Am: incorporação f, absorção f.

merit¹, n. mérito m, merecimento m; on his merits, por seus méritos; to discuss the merits of a proposal, discutir os méritos de uma proposta; Ind: etc: merit increase, aumento m por merecimento; merit bonus, prêmio m de produção; merit rating, avaliação f da performance dos empregados.

merit², v.tr. merecer; the plan scarcely merits our consideration, o plano mal merece a nossa atenção.

message, n. mensagem f, recado m; advertising message, mensagem publicitária; to leave a message for s.o., deixar um recado para alguém; can I take a message? quer deixar um recado?

messenger, n. mensageiro m; by messenger, por mensageiro; office messenger, contínuo m, bói m; messenger service, serviço m de mensageiro.

Messrs, n.pl. Senhores, abbr. Srs.; Messrs J. Martin & Co., Srs. J. Martin & Cia.

method, n. (a) (research, science) método m; (b) método, maneira f, (de fazer alguma coisa); method of payment, modalidade f de pagamento; method of exporting, método de exportação; Ind: production method, método, processo m, técnica f, de produção; Stat: sampling method, processo de amostragem; Ind: methods engineer, engenheiro m de

métodos; methods study, estudo m de métodos.

methodical, a. metódico, sistemático.

metre, Am: meter, n. Meas: metro m; square metre, metro quadrado; cubic metre, metro cúbico; standard metre, metro-padrão m; running metre, metro corrente.

metric, a. métrico; metric unit, unidade métrica; metric system, sistema métrico; metric ton, tonelada métrica; (of country) to go metric, adotar o sistema métrico.

metrically, adv. metricamente.

metricate, v.i. adotar o sistema métrico.

metrication, n. adoção f do sistema métrico.

microchip, n. Cmptr: condutor m em circuito impresso.

microeconomic, 1. a. microeconômico. 2. n.pl. microeconomics, (usu. with sg. const.) microeconomia f.

microfiche, n. microficha f; on microfiche, em microficha.

microfilm, n. microfilme m; on microfilm, em microfilme.

mid, a. meio; from mid June to mid August, dos meados de junho até os meados de agosto, meados de junho até meados de agosto; St.Exch: mid month, liquidação f quinzenal.

middle, n. meio m, centro m; middle management, gerentes mfpl de nível médio.

middleman, n. intermediário m.

mile, n. milha f; speed limit of 50 miles an hour (50 m.p.h.), velocidade máxima de 50 milhas horárias; statute mile, milha inglesa; nautical, geographical, mile, milha marítima; car mile, milha-vagão f; Av: etc: passenger mile, passageiro-milha m.

mileage, n. Trans: milhagem f (= quilometragem f); mileage (rate), taxa f por milha rodada (para carros alugados, etc.); mileage allowance, ajuda de custo com base nas milhas rodadas (paga aos representantes, etc.).

mill, n. Ind: usina f, fábrica f; steel mill, usina siderúrgica, aciaria f, usina de aço; cotton mill, algodoaria f, cotonaria f.

milliard, n. Brit: bilhão m, bilião m (mil milhões) (N.Am. word: billion).
milligram, milligramme, n. miligrama m.
millilitre, Am: milliliter, n. mililitro m.
millimetre, Am: millimeter, n. Meas: milímetro m.
milliner, n. chapeleiro m.
millinery, n. chapelaria f.
million, n. milhão m; one thousand million, um bilhão, um bilião; two million men, dois milhões de homens; a two-million-pound machine, uma máquina de dois milhões de libras esterlinas.
millionaire, n. milionário m.
mine¹, n. mina f, jazida f; coal mine, mina f de carvão; copper mine, mina de cobre.
mine², v.tr. minerar.
miner, n. mineiro m.
minimal, a. mínimo.
minimization, n. minimização f.
minimize, v.tr. minimizar, reduzir ao mínimo.
minimum, 1. n. mínimo m; to reduce expenses to a minimum, reduzir as despesas ao mínimo. 2. a. minimum quantity, quantidade mínima; minimum price, preço mínimo; minimum guaranteed wage, salário mínimo; minimum weight, peso mínimo; Fin: minimum lending rate (MLR), taxa mínima de empréstimos.
mining, n. mineração f, exploração f de minas; mining company, empresa f de mineração; mining hazards, riscos mpl de mineração; mining industry, indústria f de mineração; mining engineer, engenheiro m de minas; Fin: mining shares, títulos mpl de empresas de mineração.
minor, 1. n. Jur: menor mf. 2. a. menor; it's of minor importance, é de pouca importância; minor expenses, pequenas despesas, despesas miúdas; minor repairs, pequenos consertos; Fin: minor currency, moeda f de menor valor.
minority, n. menoridade f, minoria f; minority holding, interest, stake, participação minoritária; minority shareholder, acionista minoritário.
mint¹, n. the Mint, a Casa da Moeda; Fin: mint par, paridade monetária; mint charges, despesas fpl com cunhagem.

mint², v.tr. cunhar, amoedar, monetizar; minted money, moeda metálica.
mintage, n. 1. cunhagem f. 2. moedas cunhadas. 3. custo m de cunhagem.
minute, n. (a) minutes of a meeting, ata f de uma reunião; to confirm the minutes of the last meeting, aprovar a ata da última reunião; to read the minutes, ler a ata (de uma reunião, convenção, etc.); to take down the minutes, lavrar, fazer, a ata; minute book, livro m de atas; (b) Treasury minute, comunicado m do Ministério da Fazenda; (c) to draft the minute of a letter, redigir a minuta de uma carta.
misapplication, n. (i) malversação f, (ii) mau emprego m (de fundos, bens, etc.).
misapply, v.tr. (i) malversar (fundos, recursos), (ii) empregar mal (fundos, bens, etc.).
misappropriate, v.tr. malversar, desviar, (fundos, etc.).
misappropriation, n. malversação f, apropriação indébita, (de fundos, bens, etc.).
miscalculate, v.tr. & i. calcular mal, fazer um erro de cálculo.
miscalculation, n. cálculo errado, erro m de cálculo.
miscellaneous, a. diverso; miscellaneous assets, bens diversos; miscellaneous expenses, despesas diversas; miscellaneous receipts, receitas diversas, rendas diversas; miscellaneous shares, títulos, valores, diversos (que fazem parte de uma carteira).
miscount¹, n. erro m de cálculo, contagem errada.
miscount², v. 1. v.tr. calcular mal, contar mal. 2. v.i. fazer um erro de cálculo, de contagem.
misdate, v.tr. datar erradamente, colocar data errada em, (carta, cheque, etc.).
misdeliver, v.tr. to misdeliver a letter, entregar uma carta em endereço errado.
misdemeanour, n. Jur: contravenção f penal.
misdirect, v.tr. endereçar mal (uma carta), informar mal (uma pessoa).
misenter, v.tr. fazer um lançamento errado.

misentry, *n.* lançamento errado.
misinvestment, *n.* investimento inapropriado.
mismanage, *v.tr.* administrar mal, gerir mal.
mismanagement, *n.* má administração *f,* má gerência *f.*
misprint, *n.* erro *m* de impressão.
misrepresent, *v.tr.* representar incorretamente.
misrepresentation, *n.* representação incorreta, representação falsa.
misroute, *v.tr.* dirigir mal, encaminhar mal.
misrouting, *n.* encaminhamento errado.
Miss, *n.* senhorita *f;* **Miss Jones,** Senhorita (Sr.^ta) Jones.
mission, *n.* **trade mission,** missão *f* comercial.
mistake, *n.* erro *m,* falta *f;* **mistake in labelling,** erro de rotulagem; **typing mistake,** erro de datilografia, erro datilográfico; **to make a mistake,** (i) cometer um erro, fazer um erro, (ii) enganar-se.
misuse, *n.* abuso *m,* mau uso, uso indevido, uso errado; **misuse of authority,** abuso de autoridade; *Jur:* **fraudulent misuse of funds,** malversação *f* de fundos.
mixed, *a.* misto; **mixed economy,** economia mista; **mixed corporation,** sociedade *f* de economia mista; **mixed rates,** taxas mistas (de câmbio); **mixed reserve,** reserva mista; **mixed surplus,** conta mista de passivo inexigível; *Book-k:* **mixed account,** conta mista (de conta patrimonial e conta de exercício); *Agr:* **mixed farming,** policultura *f,* agricultura mista; *Nau:* **mixed cargo,** (i) carga mista, (ii) navio misto.
mobility, *n.* mobilidade *f* (de mão-de-obra, etc.).
mobilizable, *a.* mobilizável.
mobilization, *n.* mobilização *f.*
mobilize, *v.tr.* mobilizar (capitais, etc.).
mock-up, *n.* maquete *f,* maqueta *f,* (de um edifício, de um navio, etc.).
mode, *n.* **modes of production,** modos *mpl,* formas *fpl,* de produção.
model, *n.* (*a*) modelo (reduzido); **the model of a new factory,** o modelo de uma nova fábrica; (*b*) (*type or design*) modelo; **our latest model,** o nosso último modelo; (*c*) (**fashion**) **model,** manequim *mf,* modelo *mf;* (*d*) **economic model,** modelo econômico.
moderate, *a.* moderado; **moderate income,** renda modesta; **moderate price,** preço módico, preço razoável; **moderate size,** (de) tamanho médio.
modern, *a.* moderno.
modernization, *n.* modernização *f.*
modernize, *v.tr.* modernizar (fábrica, máquinas, etc.).
modest, *a.* modesto.
modular, *a. Const: etc:* modular, modulado; **modular construction,** construção *f* modular; **modular furniture,** móveis modulados.
monetarism, *n. Pol.Ec:* monetarismo *m.*
monetarist, *n. Pol.Ec:* monetarista *mf.*
monetary, *a.* monetário; **monetary agreement, convention,** acordo, convênio, monetário; **monetary area,** zona monetária; **monetary authority,** autoridade monetária; **monetary control,** controle monetário; **monetary correction of fixed assets,** correção monetária do ativo fixo; **monetary counterpart,** contrapartida monetária; **monetary deflation,** deflação monetária; **monetary devaluation,** desvalorização monetária; **monetary equilibrium,** equilibrio monetário; **monetary exchange,** intercâmbio monetário; **monetary expansion,** expansão monetária; **monetary flow,** fluxo monetário; **monetary gold stock,** estoques *mpl* de ouro monetário; **monetary habits,** hábitos monetários; **monetary inflation,** inflação monetária; **monetary management,** controle monetário; **monetary organization,** sistema monetário; **monetary policy,** política monetária; **monetary price,** custo *m* em dinheiro; **monetary reform,** reforma monetária; **monetary standard,** padrão monetário, estalão monetário; **monetary stock,** estoque monetário, massa monetária; **monetary stringency,** austeridade monetária; **monetary survey,** panorama monetário; **monetary unit,** unidade monetária; **monetary value,**

valor monetário; **European Monetary System,** Sistema Monetário Europeu; **International Monetary Fund,** Fundo Monetário Internacional.
monetization, *n.* amoedação *f.*
monetize, *v.tr.* monetizar, amoedar.
money, *n.* **1.** dinheiro *m*, numerário *m*, espécie *f*, moeda *f*; **money and banking,** moeda e crédito; **money as a medium of exchange,** dinheiro como meio de troca; **money as a standard of value,** dinheiro como padrão de valor; **money as a store of value,** dinheiro como guarda de valores; **money of account,** moeda de cálculo, moeda contábil; **price of money,** custo *m*, preço *m*, do dinheiro; **bank money,** moeda escritural; **call money, money at call,** dinheiro reembolsável sob chamada; **cheap money,** dinheiro barato; **commodity money,** moeda-mercadoria *f*; **current money,** moeda corrente, espécie, numerário; **divisional, fractional, money,** moeda divisionária; **fiduciary money,** moeda fiduciária; *(coins)* **gold, silver, money,** moeda(s) de ouro, de prata; **hot money,** dinheiro (depositado ou investido) que pode ser retirado com pouco aviso (causando assim pânico no mercado financeiro); **paper money,** papel-moeda *m*, dinheiro-papel *m*; **ready money,** (i) dinheiro vivo, (ii) dinheiro disponível; **to pay in ready money,** pagar à vista, pagar em dinheiro; **token money,** moeda fiduciária; **the money equivalent of sth.,** o valor (de algo) em dinheiro; **money market,** mercado monetário, mercado financeiro; **money order,** ordem *f* de pagamento, vale *m* postal; **international money order,** vale postal internacional; **money rate,** taxa *f* de juros, taxa de empréstimos; *UK:* **money shop,** agência bancária que fornece serviços para clientes individuais e não para empresas; **money stock, money supply,** meios *mpl* de pagamento, suprimento monetário, oferta monetária; **to be short of money,** ter pouco dinheiro, *F:* estar quebrado, estar limpo; **to be worth a lot of money,** (i) *(of thing)* valer muito dinheiro, (ii) *(of person)* ser rico, *F:* estar cheio de dinheiro; **to coin, mint, money,** cunhar

moeda; **to get one's money back,** recuperar seu dinheiro; **to have money in property,** ter dinheiro em imóveis; **to put one's money in a venture,** investir, colocar, dinheiro num empreendimento. **2.** *Jur: pl.* **moneys, monies,** fundos *mpl* dinheiros, bens pecuniários; **moneys paid out,** desembolsos *mpl*; **moneys paid in,** receitas *fpl*; **public moneys** = *(approx.)* bens pecuniários da União; **sundry moneys owing to s.o.,** diversas importâncias devidas a alguém; **moneys owing to us,** nossos créditos, nossas contas a receber.
moneybag, *n.* saco *m* para dinheiro, sacola *f* para transporte de dinheiro.
money-belt, *n.* cinto *m* para portar dinheiro.
moneychanger, *n.* cambista *mf.*
moneylender, *n.* prestamista *mf*, agiota *mf.*
money-maker, *n.* *(a)* pessoa *f* que faz muito dinheiro; *(b)* negócio rendoso.
money-making, *a.* rendoso, lucrativo.
money-spinner, *n.* produto *m* (ou negócio *m*) muito rendoso, muito lucrativo.
monopolist, *n.* monopolista *mf.*
monopolistic, *a.* monopolístico, monopolista, monopólico.
monopolization, *n.* monopolização *f.*
monopolize, *v.tr.* monopolizar.
monopoly, *n.* monopólio *m*; **to have a monopoly of,** *Am:* **on, sth.,** ter monopólio de alguma coisa; **State monopoly,** monopólio estatal; **buyer's monopoly,** monopólio de compra; **monopoly control,** controle monopolístico, controle monopólico.
month, *n.* mês *m*; **in the month of August,** no mês de agosto; **on 15th July,** em 15 de julho; **at the end of the month,** no fim do mês; **one month's rent,** um mês de aluguel; **once a month,** uma vez por mês; *Fin:* **bill at three months,** letra *f* à vista pagável em três meses.
monthly, **1.** *a.* mensal; **monthly payment,** pagamento *m* mensal, mensalidade *f*; **monthly instalment,** prestação *f*, parcela *f*, mensal; **monthly rent,** aluguel *m* mensal; **monthly loan,** empréstimo *m*

(concedido) por um mês; **monthly contract**, contrato *m* mensal; **the contract will be extended on a monthly basis**, o contrato será prorrogado a base mensal. **2.** *adv.* mensalmente, uma vez por mês, todo mês, todos os meses.

moonlight, *v.i. F:* ter segundo emprego.

moonlighter, *n. F:* pessoa *f* que tem um segundo emprego.

moonlighting, *n. F:* segundo emprego *m*.

mop up, *v.tr. F:* **the losses mopped up all the profits**, as perdas anularam todos os lucros; **to mop up purchasing power**, absorver o poder de compra.

moratorium, *n.* moratória *f*; *Fin: Bank:* carência *f*.

moratory, *a.* moratório.

mortgage¹, *n.* hipoteca *f*; **blanket mortgage, general mortgage**, hipoteca geral; **chattel mortgage**, penhor *m* de bens móveis; **endowment mortgage**, crédito imobiliário ligado com seguro dotal; **first mortgage**, hipoteca de primeira ordem, de primeira classe; **second mortgage**, hipoteca de segunda ordem, de segunda classe; **burdened, encumbered, with a mortgage**, onerado, gravado, com uma hipoteca; **discharge of a mortgage**, baixa *f* de uma hipoteca; **mortgage bank**, banco hipotecário; **mortgage bond, mortgage debenture**, obrigação, debênture, hipotecária; **mortgage certificate**, cédula hipotecária; **mortgage creditor**, credor hipotecário; **mortgage debtor**, devedor hipotecário; **mortgage deed**, escritura hipotecária; **mortgage registrar**, escrivão encarregado da inscrição de hipotecas; **mortgage registration**, inscrição *f* de hipotecas; **mortgage registry**, registro *m* de hipotecas; **to borrow on mortgage**, tomar (dinheiro) emprestado sobre hipoteca, mediante hipoteca; **to create a mortgage**, constituir, fazer, uma hipoteca; **to foreclose a mortgage**, executar uma hipoteca; **to get a mortgage**, conseguir um crédito imobiliário, um empréstimo hipotecário; **to pay off, redeem, a mortgage**, resgatar uma hipoteca; **to raise a mortgage**, levantar um empréstimo hipotecário; **to register a mortgage on a**

house, inscrever uma hipoteca sobre uma casa; **to secure a debt by mortgage**, garantir uma dívida mediante hipoteca.

mortgage², *v.tr.* hipotecar (terra, casa, etc.), (*loosely*) penhorar (títulos e outros bens móveis); **mortgaged estate**, propriedade hipotecada; **he mortgaged the house to a bank**, ele hipotecou a casa a um banco.

mortgageable, *a.* hipotecável.

mortgagee, *n.* credor hipotecário.

mortgager, mortgagor, *n.* devedor hipotecário.

most-favoured, *a. Pol.Ec:* **most-favoured-nation clause**, cláusula *f* da nação mais favorecida.

motion, *n.* **1.** movimento *m*; *Ind:* **time and motion study**, cronometragem *f* de atividades industriais. **2.** (*a*) moção *f*, proposta *f*; **to carry a motion**, fazer aprovar uma moção, uma proposta; **to put forward the motion**, submeter uma proposta à votação; **to speak for the motion**, pronunciar-se a favor da proposta, defender a proposta; **to speak against the motion**, pronunciar-se contra a proposta; (*b*) *Jur:* requerimento *m*.

motivated, *a.* (pessoal, etc.) motivado.

motivation, *n.* motivação *f*; **self motivation**, automotivação *f*.

motivational, *a.* **motivational studies, research**, estudos *mpl* sobre a motivação, pesquisa *f* de motivação.

motivator, *n.* motivador *m*.

motive, *n.* **profit motive**, motivação *f* de lucro.

mount, *v.i.* subir, elevar-se, aumentar.

mounting, *a.* **mounting costs**, custos *mpl* crescentes, custos em alta.

mount up, *v.i.* crescer, subir; acumular-se.

move, *v.* **1.** *v.tr.* (*at meeting, etc.*) propor; **to move that the chairman be re-elected**, propor que o presidente seja reeleito. **2.** *v.i.* vender bem, ter saída.

moveable, *Jur:* **1.** *a.* móvel; **moveable property**, bens *mpl* móveis. **2.** *n.pl.* **moveables**, bens *mpl* móveis.

movement, *n.* (*a*) movimento *m*, circulação *f*, (de capitais, etc.); **upward, downward, movement (of prices, etc.)**, movimento de alta, de baixa, (dos preços, etc.); **the free movement of labour,** o livre movimento da mão-de-obra; **freedom of movement,** liberdade ƒ de movimentos; **movement of freight,** movimento de mercadorias; **movement of money,** movimento de capitais; (*b*) **the trade union movement,** o movimento sindical, o sindicalismo; **he's in the trade union movement,** ele é sindicalista.

move up, *v.i. St.Exch: (of shares)* subir (de novo).

Mr, (*form of address, not used without name*) **Mr Thomas,** (o) Senhor (Sr.) Thomas.

Mrs, (*form of address, not used without name*) **Mrs Thomas,** (a) Senhora (Sr.ª) Thomas.

Ms, M/s, (*form of address, not used without name*) **Ms, M/s, Thomas,** (a) Senhorita (Sr.ᵗᵃ) Thomas.

multilateral, *a.* (acordo, etc.) multilateral.

multimillionaire, *n.* multimilionário *m.*

multinational, *a. & n.* multinacional (*mf*); **multinational bank, corporation,** banco *m*, empresa ƒ, multinacional.

multiple, *a.* múltiplo; **multiple branding,** comercialização ƒ de diversas marcas do mesmo produto (tais como detergentes); **multiple exchange rates,** taxas múltiplas de câmbio; **multiple collection clause,** opção ƒ de praça; **multiple currency**

bonds, títulos *mpl* com opção de câmbio; **multiple activity chart,** gráfico *m* de atividades múltiplas; **multiple management** = participação ƒ dos empregados na direção da empresa; **multiple ownership,** condomínio *m* (de conjunto residencial, etc.).

multiplication, *n.* multiplicação ƒ.

multiplier, *n.* multiplicador *m.*

multiply, *v.* 1. *v.tr.* **to multiply eight by five,** multiplicar oito por cinco. 2. *v.i.* multiplicar, efetuar uma multiplicação.

mutual, *a.* mútuo, recíproco; **to conclude a deal to our mutual advantage,** fechar um negócio em nosso mútuo benefício; **by mutual agreement,** por acordo mútuo; **by mutual consent,** por mútuo consentimento; **mutual concessions,** concessões recíprocas, concessões mútuas; **mutual assurance, insurance,** seguro mútuo; **mutual insurance company,** companhia ƒ de seguros mútuos, sociedade ƒ de seguros mútuos; **mutual benefit society,** mútua ƒ, sociedade mutuante; **member of a mutual benefit society,** mutualista *mf*; **mutual fund,** fundo mútuo, fundo de participação, fundo de aplicação; **mutual stockholding,** recíproco investimento em ações entre duas companhias.

N

naked, *a.* *Jur:* sem garantia, não garantido; **naked bond,** obrigação quirografária.

name[1], *n.* 1. nome *m,* denominação *f,* (de uma companhia ou organização); (*on application form, etc.*) **full name,** nome por extenso, nome completo; **name of a firm, of a company,** razão *f* social, denominação social, (de uma empresa, de uma companhia); (*in articles of association, etc.*) **the company will trade under the name of...**, a companhia girará sob a denominação social de...; **name of an account,** titular *mf* (ou título *m*) de uma conta; **registered (trade) name,** marca registrada; **brand name,** marca *f* de produto; **to set, put, one's name to a document,** assinar, firmar, um documento; **to act in the name of s.o.,** agir em nome de alguém; *UK: St.Exch:* **name day,** segundo dia de liquidação. 2. (*reputation*) nome *m,* reputação *f,* conceito *m*; **a firm with a good name,** uma firma que goza de bom conceito, de boa reputação; uma firma de renome; **a big name in the business world,** um grande nome no mundo comercial.

name[2], *v.tr.* **to name a new chairman,** nomear um novo presidente; **to name s.o. as the new manager,** nomear alguém como o novo gerente, designar alguém para o cargo de gerente; **to name the date for a meeting,** marcar, designar, fixar, a data de uma reunião.

named, *a.* nomeado; **on the named day,** no dia marcado, no dia fixado; *Ins:* **named policy, policy to a named person,** apólice nominativa.

national, *a.* nacional; **national debt,** dívida pública; **national income,** renda *f* nacional; **gross national product (GNP),** produto *m* nacional bruto (PNB); **net**

national product, produto nacional líquido; **national expenditure,** despesas públicas; *Nau:* **national flag,** bandeira *f* nacional; *Adm:* **national insurance,** previdência *f* social, seguro *m* social; **national insurance contribution,** contribuição previdenciária; **national insurance benefits,** benefícios *mpl* da previdência social, benefícios sócio-securitários.

nationality, *n.* nacionalidade *f.*

nationalization, *n.* nacionalização *f,* estatização *f,* (de uma indústria, de uma empresa).

nationalize, *v.tr.* nacionalizar, estatizar.

natural, *a.* natural; **natural gas,** gás *m* natural; **natural fuels,** combustíveis *mpl* naturais; **natural resources,** recursos *mpl* naturais; *Jur:* **natural person,** pessoa física; *Book-k:* **natural grouping,** agrupamento *m* de despesas segundo a natureza; *Ind:* **natural wastage,** redução *f* da mão-de-obra mediante aposentadoria, falecimento, ou afastamento voluntário.

navigation, *n.* navegação *f*; **navigation company,** companhia *f* de transportes marítimos, companhia de navegação; **navigation dues,** direitos *mpl* de navegação.

near, *a.* *Book-k: etc:* **near cash,** disponibilidade(s) *f(pl),* ativo *m* de realização imediata; **near money,** ativo *m* realizável a curto prazo.

necessary, *a.* **necessary condition,** condição necessária; **necessary measures,** medidas necessárias.

necessity, *n.* necessidade *f*; *Book-k:* **necessity certificate,** certificado *m* de necessidade.

need, *n.* necessidade *f.*

negative, *a.* negativo; *Book-k:* **negative goodwill,** fundo *m* de comércio negativo;

Pol.Ec: **negative income tax** = auxílio pago a empregados cujos salários não atingem um determinado nível.

neglected, *a. St.Exch:* **neglected stocks,** títulos não procurados.

negligence, *n.* negligência *f*, descuido *m*; **through negligence,** por negligência; *Jur:* **gross negligence,** negligência grave; *Ins:* **negligence clause,** cláusula *f* (em apólice de seguro) referente à negligência.

negligent, *a.* negligente; **to be negligent (in),** negligenciar, ser negligente (com).

negotiability, *n.* negociabilidade *f* (de um título de crédito).

negotiable, *a. Fin: etc:* (título *m*, efeito *m*) negociável; **stocks negotiable on the Stock Exchange,** títulos de bolsa, títulos negociáveis na bolsa; **negotiable paper,** papéis *mpl*, efeitos, negociáveis; **negotiable instrument,** título negociável, título de crédito; **negotiable warehouse receipt,** warrant *m*, cédula pignoratícia; **not negotiable,** não negociável.

negotiate, *v.* 1. *v.tr.* negociar; **to negotiate a loan,** negociar um empréstimo; **to negotiate a property deal,** negociar uma transação imobiliária; **stocks difficult to negotiate,** títulos *mpl* de pouca negociabilidade; *Fin:* **to negotiate a bill of exchange,** negociar, descontar, uma letra de câmbio. 2. *v.i.* **to negotiate with s.o. for sth.,** negociar algo com alguém; **they refuse to negotiate,** eles recusam negociar, eles se recusam a negociar.

negotiating, *a.* **negotiating bank,** banco negociador.

negotiation, *n.* negociação *f* (de um empréstimo, de um acordo); *Fin:* negociação, desconto *m*, (de uma letra de câmbio); **under negotiation,** em negociação; **by negotiation,** através de negociação, mediante negociação; **negotiation commission,** comissão *f* de negociação; **to enter into, upon, negotiations with s.o.,** entrar em negociações com alguém; **negotiations are proceeding,** as negociações estão em curso; **to break off negotiations with s.o.,** interromper, suspender, negociações com alguém; **to resume negotiations,** retomar as negociações.

negotiator, *n.* negociador *m.*

neon, *n.* **neon sign,** anúncio luminoso a neônio.

nervous, *a.* (*of market*) nervoso, instável, agitado.

net¹, 1. *a.* (*of price, weight, etc.*) líquido; **net avail,** produto líquido do desconto de uma letra; **net book value,** valor líquido segundo os livros; **net current asset,** ativo corrente líquido; **net earnings (on an investment),** renda líquida (de um investimento); **net equity,** patrimônio líquido; **net income,** renda líquida, rendimento líquido, resultado líquido; **net loss,** prejuízo líquido, perda líquida; **net operating profit,** lucro operacional líquido; **net operating revenue,** receita operacional líquida; **net present value,** valor presente líquido (de fluxo de caixa futuro); **net proceeds (of a sale, etc.),** produto líquido (de uma venda, etc.); **net profit,** lucro líquido; **net receipts,** receitas líquidas; **net sales,** vendas líquidas, valor líquido das vendas; **net weight,** peso líquido; **net working capital,** capital de giro; **net worth,** patrimônio líquido, situação líquida, patrimônio próprio; **net worth and reserves,** passivo *m* não exigível. 2. *n.* o (peso, preço. etc.) líquido.

net², *v.tr.* 1. (*of person*) auferir um lucro líquido (de uma certa quantia); **I netted $2000 this month,** auferí, tirei, um lucro líquido de $2.000 este mês. 2. (*of venture, etc.*) render um lucro líquido (de uma certa quantia); **the dry cleaning business nets him $800 a week,** a tinturaria lhe rende um lucro líquido de $800 por semana.

nett, *a.* = net¹ 1.

network, *n.* rede *f*; **distribution network,** rede de distribuição; **television network,** rede de televisão.

never-never, *n. F:* **to buy sth. on the never-never,** comprar algo fiado, comprar algo a crédito, comprar algo pelo crediário.

new, *a.* novo; **new markets,** mercados novos, novos mercados; **a new issue of shares,** uma nova emissão de ações; (*of restaurant, etc.*) **under new management,**

sob nova gerência; **to open up new channels for trade,** abrir novos escoamentos para o comércio; *Ins:* **as new, in a new condition,** como novo, em estado (de) novo; *Ins:* **new for old,** novo por velho.

news, *n.pl.* (*usu. with sg. const.*) (*a*) notícias *fpl*; **news agency,** agência *f* de notícias, agência noticiosa; (*as media programme*) **the news,** o noticiário, o jornal; **the television news,** o telejornal; **the radio news,** o radiojornal; (*b*) **financial news,** informações financeiras, notícias financeiras.

newsagent, *n.* jornaleiro *m.*

newscaster, *n.* noticiarista *mf.*

newsletter, *n.* boletim *m* (de informações), (boletim) informativo *m*; circular *f.*

newspaper, *n.* jornal *m*; **daily newspaper,** diário *m*; **weekly newspaper,** jornal semanal, jornal hebdomadário.

newsprint, *n.* papel *m* de imprensa, papel de jornal.

night, *n.* noite *f*; **night work,** trabalho noturno, serão *m*; **night shift,** turno *m* da noite; **to be on night duty,** estar de serão, de plantão; **night watchman,** guarda-noturno *m*; **night service,** serviço noturno; *Bank:* **night safe,** cofre noturno.

nil, *n.* nulo; **the balance is nil,** o saldo é nulo; **nil return,** demonstração *f* com saldo nulo.

nomenclature, *n.* nomenclatura *f.*

nominal, *a.* nominal; **nominal account,** conta *f* nominal; **nominal amount,** quantia *f* nominal; **nominal value,** valor *m* nominal; **nominal wage,** salário *m* nominal, salário simbólico; *Fin:* **nominal share capital,** capital autorizado.

nominate, *v.tr.* (*a*) nomear, designar, (alguém para um cargo); (*b*) nomear (um candidato); indicar, apresentar, (alguém como candidato); (*c*) *Nau:* **to nominate tankers,** nomear navios-tanques.

nomination, *n.* **1.** (*a*) nomeação *f*, designação *f*, (de alguém para um cargo); (*b*) direito *m* de nomear (alguém para um cargo). **2.** nomeação *f*, indicação *f*, escolha *f*, (de alguém) como (um) candidato.

nominee, *n.* **1.** (*for an annuity, etc.*) beneficiário *m.* **2.** (*for a post*) (*a*) pessoa nomeada, pessoa designada; (*b*) candidato nomeado, candidato indicado; (*c*) *Fin:* **nominee shareholder,** pessoa ou entidade que possui ações em nome de outro (que é o verdadeiro proprietário).

non-acceptance, *n.* *Fin:* falta *f* de aceite (de letra de câmbio); **draft returned under protest for non-acceptance,** saque protestado por falta de aceite.

non-admitted, *a.* *Book-k:* **non-admitted assets,** bens não admitidos (para fins de remuneração de capital, etc.).

non-assessable, *a.* *Adm:* (renda, etc.) não tributável; *Fin:* **non-assessable capital stock,** ações não sujeitas a chamadas.

non-availability, *n.* indisponibilidade *f.*

non-available, *a.* indisponível.

non-breakable, *a.* inquebrável.

non-commercial, *a.* não-comercial.

non-completion, *n.* inadimplemento *m*, falta *f* de cuprimento, descumprimento *m*, (de um contrato, etc.).

non-contributory, *a.* *Adm:* (*of pension scheme*) não-contributário.

non-controllable, *a.* *Book-k:* etc: **non-controllable cost,** custo *m* não-controlável.

non-cumulative, *a.* *Fin:* **non-cumulative dividend,** dividendo não cumulativo.

non-current, *a.* *Fin:* *Book-k:* **non-current assets,** ativo *m* realizável a longo prazo.

non-delivery, *n.* falta *f* de entrega.

none, *pron.* *Adm:* (*in schedules, etc.*) nada.

non-execution, *n.* inexecução *f*, inadimplemento *m*, (de um contrato).

non-executive, *a.* **non-executive director** = diretor *m* que não é empregado da companhia; administrador *m*, conselheiro *m.*

non-fulfilment, *n.* inexecução *f*, inadimplemento *m*, (de um contrato, etc.).

non-interest-bearing, *a.* que não rende juros.

non-member, *n.* **open to non-members,** aberto ao público.

non-negotiable, *a.* (*shares, terms, etc.*) não negociável, inegociável.

non-participating, *a.* (*of insurance*) sem participação nos lucros.

non-payment, *n.* falta *f* de pagamento.

non-productive, *a.* **non-productive labour**, mão-de-obra improdutiva.

non-profit, *a.* *N.Am:* **non-profit organization**, organização *f* sem fins lucrativos.

non-profit-making, *a.* (*a*) deficitário; (*b*) **non-profit-making organization**, organização *f* sem fins lucrativos.

non-recurring, *a.* *Book-k:* **non-recurring expenses**, despesas extraordinárias, despesas eventuais.

non-resident, *a.* não-residente.

non-returnable, *a.* (*of packaging, containers*) descartável; **non-returnable packaging**, embalagem *f* descartável; (*in shop*) 'empties are non-returnable', 'não aceitamos cascos'.

non-scheduled, *a.* **non-scheduled airline**, companhia *f* de aviação comercial sem datas e horários de partidas e chegadas.

non-stock, *a.* *Am:* **non-stock corporation**, empresa *f* que não emite ações.

non-taxable, *a.* *Adm:* (renda, etc.) não-tributável.

non-union, *a.* (operário) não-sindicalizado; **non-union labour**, mão-de-obra não-sindicalizada.

non-voting, *a.* **non-voting equity, non-voting stock**, ações *fpl* sem direito de voto.

no-par, *a.* **no-par share**, ação *f* sem valor nominal.

normal, *a.* normal; **normal price**, preço *m* normal; **normal profit**, lucro *m* normal; **normal return**, renda *f* normal, retorno *m* normal; **normal standard cost**, custo *m* standard normal.

nostro, *a.* *Bank:* **nostro account**, conta que um banco tem com outro banco.

notarial, *a.* *Jur:* notarial.

notarize, *v.tr.* (*of notary*) reconhecer ou autenticar (um documento).

notary, *n.* **notary (public)**, tabelião *m*, escrivão público, notário (público); **notary's office**, cartório *m*, tabelionato *m*, escritório *m* de notário público.

note[1], *n.* 1. nota *f*; **he received a note from the manager**, ele recebeu uma nota do

gerente. 2. (*a*) *Fin:* etc: **note of hand**, promissory note, (nota) promissória *f*; **credit note**, nota de crédito; **debit note**, nota de débito; **discount note**, aviso *m* de desconto; (*b*) **advice note**, aviso; **delivery note**, guia *f*, nota, de entrega; **dispatch note**, guia, nota, de remessa; (*c*) *St.Exch:* **contract note**, boleta *f*. 3. (*banknote*) nota, cédula *f*, bilhete *m* (de banco); **a five hundred cruzeiro note**, uma nota, uma cédula, de quinhentos cruzeiros.

note[2], *v.tr.* notar, anotar, tomar nota; **we note that your account has not been settled**, anotamos que sua conta ainda não foi saldada; **we have noted your order**, tomamos nota da sua encomenda; *Fin:* **to note a bill of exchange**, notar uma letra de câmbio.

notebook, *n.* caderno *m*, agenda *f*, (*small*) caderneta *f*, bloco *m* de notas; *Fin:* etc: livro-registro *m* de promissórias.

notehead, *n.* *esp.* *Am:* cabeçalho *m*, timbre *m*; **notehead paper**, papel timbrado.

notepad, *n.* bloco *m* de notas.

notice, *n.* (*a*) aviso *m*, comunicação *f*, notificação *f*; **notice of delivery**, aviso de entrega; *Nau:* **notice to shipping**, aviso aos navegantes; (*b*) aviso prévio, pré-aviso *m*; **until further notice**, até novo aviso, até a próxima comunicação, até a segunda ordem; salvo aviso (em) contrário; to give notice (to tenant, etc.), dar o aviso prévio (a inquilino, etc.); (*c*) (*in employment*) aviso prévio; **to give notice**, dar o aviso prévio; **period, term, of notice**, prazo *m* de aviso prévio; **to work out one's notice**, trabalhar durante o prazo de aviso prévio; **dismissal without notice**, demissão *f* sem aviso prévio; **subject to three months' notice**, sujeito a três meses de aviso prévio; *Ind:* **strike notice**, aviso de greve; (*d*) **notice of meeting (of shareholders)**, anúncio *m* de convocação de assembléia (de acionistas); (*e*) **at short notice**, sem aviso prévio; **the goods can be delivered at three days' notice**, as mercadorias podem ser entregues dentro (de um prazo) de três dias; *Fin:* **realizable at short notice**, realizável a curto prazo; *Bank:* **deposit at**

7 days' notice, depósito *m* com aviso prévio de sete dias; **notice of withdrawal, withdrawal notice,** aviso prévio para retirada de depósito; (*f*) *Jur:* **notice to quit,** aviso para desocupar um imóvel.

notification, *n.* notificação *f*, aviso *m*; **letter of notification,** carta *f* de aviso.

notify, *v.tr.* **to notify s.o. of sth.,** notificar, cientificar, inteirar, alguém de algo; **to be notified of sth.,** ser notificado de alguma coisa.

notions, *n.pl.* (*in store*) **notions department,** departamento *m*, seção *f*, de aviamentos.

novation, *n. Jur:* novação *f*.

novelty, *n.* (*a*) novidade *f*; (*b*) quinquilharia *f*, bugiganga *f*.

null, *a. Jur: etc:* (*of decree, etc.*) **null and void,** írrito e nulo; **to render a contract null,** anular, invalidar, nulificar, um contrato.

nullification, *n.* anulação *f*, invalidação *f*, nulificação *f*.

nullify, *v.tr.* anular, invalidar, nulificar.

number¹, *n.* **1.** número *m*; **the number of letters received,** o número de cartas recebidas. **2.** (*a*) **reference number,** número de referência; **order number,** número de encomenda; **lot number,** número de lote; **telephone number,** número de telefone; *Ind:* **serial number,** número de série (de fabricação); *Bank:* **cheque number,** número de cheque; (*b*) *Pol.Ec:* **index number,** número-índice *m*. **3.** **the latest number** (**of a magazine**), o último número (de uma revista).

number², *v.tr.* (*consecutively*) numerar.

numerical, *a.* numérico; **numerical analysis,** análise numérica; **numerical data,** dados numéricos.

O

O. & M., *n*. O. & M. *f*, organização (*f*) e métodos (*mpl*).

object¹, *n*. (*a*) objeto *m*, objetivo *m*, propósito *m*; (*in articles of association, etc.*) **the object of the company is . . .**, o objeto social consiste em . . ., a companhia tem por objeto . . .; *Corr:* **the object of this letter is to advise you that . . .**, tem esta por fim comunicar a V. S.ª que . . .; (*b*) *F:* (*in applying for post, etc.*) **salary no object,** não há objeção quanto a salário; **distance no object,** não há objeção quanto a distância.

object², *v.i.* **to object to sth.**, objetar, fazer objeção, opor-se, a alguma coisa; **to object to s.o.**, fazer objeção a alguém.

objection, *n*. **1.** objeção *f*, oposição *f*; **to have no objection to,** não fazer objeção a; **to raise an objection,** levantar uma objeção, objetar; **I have no objection to that proposal,** não faço nenhuma objeção àquela proposta; *St.Exch:* **objection to mark,** objeção à cotação. **2.** obstáculo *m*, inconveniente *m*, incômodo *m*; **the only objection to your project is the cost,** o único inconveniente do seu projeto é o custo.

objective, *n*. objetivo *m*, objeto *m*, finalidade *f*, propósito *m*; **long-term objective,** objetivo a longo prazo; **short-term objective,** objetivo a curto prazo.

obligant, *n*. *Jur: Scot:* obrigado *m*, devedor *m* de obrigação.

obligate, *v.tr.* **to obligate s.o. to do sth.**, obrigar alguém a fazer alguma coisa.

obligation, *n*. obrigação *f*, compromisso *m*, dever *m*, encargo *m*; **to be under an obligation to so sth.**, estar obrigado, ficar obrigado, a fazer alguma coisa; **without any obligation,** sem compromisso; (*in shop, etc.*) **'no obligation to buy',** 'entrada gratuita sem compromisso'; **joint and several obligation,** solidariedade *f*, obrigação solidária; **to meet, fulfil, one's obligations,** cumprir (com) as obrigações; **to fail to meet one's obligations,** inadimplir, não cumprir (com), as obrigações; falhar no cumprimento das obrigações.

oblige, *v.tr.* **1.** (*compel*) (*a*) *Jur:* **to oblige s.o. to pay his debts,** obrigar alguém a pagar suas dívidas; (*b*) **to be obliged to do sth,** estar obrigado a fazer alguma coisa. **2.** (*do s.o. a favour*) fazer um favor a, para, (alguém); **will you oblige me by taking a cheque?** você me faz o favor de aceitar um cheque? **an answer by return of post will oblige,** pede-se a V. S.ª o favor de responder na volta do correio.

obligee, *n*. *Jur:* credor *m* de obrigação.

obligor, *n*. *Jur:* devedor *m* de obrigação.

observance, *n*. cumprimento *m* (de condições de contrato, etc.).

observation, *n*. **marginal observations,** observações *fpl* marginais.

observe, *v.tr.* **1.** cumprir, observar, (as cláusulas de um contrato). **2.** notar, observar, reparar em, (um fato, etc.); **you will observe that there is a mistake in the book-keeping,** você notará que houve um erro na escrituração.

obsolescence, *n*. obsoletismo *m*, obsolescência *f*; *Book-k:* **reserve for obsolescence,** fundo *m* de recompletamento.

obsolescent, *a*. que está se tornando obsoleto.

obsolete, *a*. obsoleto, antiquado, em desuso.

obstacle, *n*. obstáculo *m*; **to put an obstacle in somebody's way,** criar obstáculo ao (progresso, trabalho, etc.) de alguém; **it could have been an obstacle**

to his promotion, podia ter dificultado a sua promoção, ascensão.

obtain, v. **1.** v.tr. obter, conseguir, alcançar, adquirir; **to obtain information that . . .,** informar-se, inteirar-se, de que . . .; **to obtain a loan,** conseguir um empréstimo; **to obtain s.o.'s appointment,** conseguir a nomeação de alguém; **to obtain an appointment through hard work,** conseguir um posto à custa de muito trabalho; **to obtain a week's leave,** tirar, conseguir, uma semana de férias; **the rates obtained at today's market,** as taxas realizadas, os cursos realizados, no mercado de hoje. **2.** v.i. estar em vigor, vigorar, viger; **the system now obtaining,** o sistema vigente; **the practice obtaining in industry,** a prática vigente na indústria.

obtainable, a. obtenível, alcançável; **where is that obtainable?** onde pode-se conseguir isso? onde é que se pode conseguir, obter, isso? **these securities are not obtainable in small lots,** estes títulos não podem ser obtidos em lotes pequenos.

occasional, a. ocasional, eventual.

occupancy, n. **1.** Jur: ocupação f, posse f. **2.** (a) ocupação (de terreno), habitação f (de casa, apartamento, etc.); Am: **industrial occupancy,** uso m (de prédio, terreno) para fins industriais; **residential occupancy,** uso (de imóvel) para fins residenciais; **occupancy expense,** despesa f de ocupação; **'store for rent, immediate occupancy',** 'aluga-se loja com posse imediata'; (b) Am: prédio ocupado, apartamento ocupado; (c) Am: (in restaurant, store, etc.) **'occupancy by more than 160 persons is dangerous',** 'a presença de mais de 160 pessoas é perigosa'. **3.** ocupação, posse, (de cargo).

occupant, n. **1.** (a) morador m, residente mf; **the occupants of the block of flats,** os moradores do edifício de apartamentos; **occupant of a house,** morador; (b) Jur: posseiro m. **2.** titular mf (de cargo).

occupation, n. **1.** ocupação f, profissão f, emprego m, ofício m, serviço m; **what is his occupation?** qual é a sua profissão? qual é o seu trabalho? **without occupation,** desempregado, sem emprego. **2.** Jur: tomada f de posse; **to be in**

occupation of a house, ter a posse de uma casa, (loosely) morar numa casa.

occupational, a. ocupacional, profissional; **occupational disease,** doença profissional (ligada a determinada profissão); **occupational hazard,** risco profissional (ligado a determinada profissão).

occupier, n. morador m, residente mf; Brit: **owner-occupier,** proprietário m residente, dono m de casa própria.

occupy, v.tr. **1.** (a) habitar, morar em, (casa, apartamento, etc.); (b) ocupar; **to occupy a piece of land,** ocupar um terreno. **2.** ocupar, exercer, ficar na posse de, (cargo, etc.); **to occupy an important post,** ocupar um cargo de alto nível.

ocean, n. oceano m; **the Atlantic Ocean,** o Oceano Atlântico; **ocean-carrying trade,** transporte marítimo de longo curso; **ocean bill of lading,** conhecimento m de transporte marítimo; **ocean liner** m; transatlântico m.

ocean-going, a. **ocean-going ship, vessel,** navio m, embarcação f, de longo curso; **ocean-going shipping,** navegação f de longo curso; **ocean-going marine insurance,** seguro marítimo para viagem de longo curso.

odd, a. **1.** (a) (número) ímpar; (b) (i) (usu. = a slightly higher amount) **a hundred-odd packing cases,** cento e tantas caixas para embalagem; (ii) **a few odd grammes over,** alguns gramas mpl adicionais, extras; **keep the odd change,** fique com o troco. **2.** (a) (one of a set or pair) avulso; (b) **odd lot,** lote avulso, lote incompleto; St.Exch: **odd lot trading,** negociação f de lotes fracionários; (c) **odd job,** bico m, biscate m, gancho m, galho m, viração f. **3.** (of clothing) **odd size,** tamanho m especial.

oddments, n.pl. sobras fpl, fim m de estoque; artigos mpl (com defeitos ou fora de moda) geralmente vendidos a preço reduzido.

off, **1.** adv. (a) **our agreement is off,** nosso acordo está desfeito; (b) **my figures were off,** meus cálculos estavam errados; (c) **to allow ten per cent off,** dar, conceder, um abatimento de dez por cento; (d) **sales**

fell off last week, acusou-se uma queda nas vendas na semana passada. 2. *prep.* (*a*) ten per cent off all items, abatimento de dez por cento sobre, em, todos os artigos; to borrow money off s.o., tomar dinheiro emprestado a alguém; (*b*) to have a day off work, tirar um dia de folga; an afternoon off, uma tarde de folga. 3. *a.* off consumption, consumo *m* (de bebidas alcoólicas) fora do local de venda; off licence, (i) licença *f* autorizando a venda de bebidas alcoólicas para consumo fora do local de venda, (ii) estabelecimento *m* onde se vendem bebidas alcoólicas para consumo em outro lugar.

offer¹, *n.* oferta *f*, proposta *f*; (*cut-price goods, etc.*) the best offer in town, a melhor oferta da praça; verbal offer, oferta, proposta, verbal; written offer, proposta, oferta, por escrito; firm offer, oferta, proposta, firme; to make s.o. an offer for sth., apresentar, fazer, uma oferta, uma proposta, a alguém por alguma coisa; to be on offer at $100, estar à venda por cem dólares; *N.Am: Journ:* job offers, ofertas de emprego, 'empregados procurados', 'precisa-se'.

offer², *v.tr.* to offer $2000 for a car, propor, oferecer, dois mil dólares por um carro; to offer oneself for a post, candidatar-se a um cargo; to offer goods for sale, pôr, colocar, mercadorias à venda; 'house offered for sale', 'vende-se casa'; *St.Exch:* the rates offered on government bonds are as follows ..., as taxas oferecidas pelos títulos de dívida pública são as seguintes ....

office, *n.* 1. cargo *m*, função *f*; to perform the office of secretary, desempenhar, exercer, o cargo de secretário; it is my office to examine the books, a minha função é examinar os livros; public office, cargo público; high office, algo cargo. 2. (*a*) escritório *m*, gabinete *m*; branch office, sucursal *f*, filial *f*; business office, escritório comercial; complaints office, serviço *m* de reclamações; government office, repartição pública; head office (of a company), escritório central, matriz *f*, casa *f* matriz, sede *f*; registered office,

sede (social); office block, edifício *m* de escritórios; office boy, bói *m*, contínuo *m*; office clerk, auxiliar *mf* de escritório; office equipment, equipamento *m* de escritório, máquinas *fpl* de escritório; office expenses, despesas *fpl* de escritório; office hours, horário *m* de expediente, expediente *m*; office manager, gerente *mf*, chefe *mf*, de escritório; office management, administração *f* de escritório; office staff, pessoal *m* de escritório; office supplies, material *m* de escritório; office work, serviços *mpl* (gerais) de escritório; (*b*) the manager's office, a gerência; cash office, caixa *f*; box office, bilheteria *f*, guichê *m*.

officer, *n.* funcionário *m*; *Adm:* executive officer, oficial administrador; training officer, chefe *mf* de treinamento; customs officer, funcionário *m* da alfândega, aduaneiro *m*.

official, 1. *a.* (*a*) oficial, oficializado; official document, documento *m* oficial; official practice, prática oficializada; official gold reserves, reservas *fpl* oficiais de ouro; to act in one's official capacity, agir no exercício das suas funções; *Fin:* official quotation, cotação *f* oficial; official market, mercado *m* oficial; *UK:* official receiver, síndico *m* de massa falida; (*b*) official strike, greve autorizada pelo sindicato. 2. *n.* funcionário *m*; government official, funcionário público; *Pej:* burocrata *mf*; minor officials, pequenos funcionários; senior officials, altos funcionários.

officialdom, *n.* burocracia *f*, funcionarismo *m*, funcionalismo *m*, oficialismo *m*.

officialese, *n.* linguagem burocrática, jargão burocrático.

officially, *adv.* oficialmente; stock quoted officially, valores oferecidos com cotações oficiais, títulos registrados (na bolsa).

offload, *v.tr.* descarregar (um excedente de mercadorias, etc.).

off-season, 1. *n.* baixa temporada, baixa estação. 2. *adv.* durante a baixa temporada. 3. *a.* off-season tariff, tarifa *f* de baixa temporada.

offset¹, *n.* compensação *f*; as an offset to

my losses, como compensação pelos meus prejuízos; *Book-k:* compensação.
offset², *v.tr.* (*a*) *Book-k:* compensar; **to offset a debit against a credit,** compensar um débito com um crédito; (*b*) **to offset an error,** estornar, retificar, um erro.
offshore, *a.* **offshore company,** companhia constituída no exterior para conseguir vantagens fiscais.
offtake, *n.* movimento *m* de vendas durante determinado período.
off-the-job, *a.* **off-the-job training,** treinamento *m* fora do local de trabalho.
oil, *n.* (*a*) óleo *m*; (**mineral**) **oil,** óleo mineral, petróleo *m*; **crude oil,** óleo cru, petróleo (em) bruto; **fuel oil,** óleo combustível; **the oil industry,** a indústria petroleira; **oil company,** companhia petroleira; **oil refinery,** refinaria *f* de petróleo; **oil tanker,** (navio) petroleiro *m*, navio-tanque *m*; **oil field,** campo petrolífero; **oil well,** poço *m* de petróleo; **oil truck,** caminhão-tanque *m* para transporte de petróleo; **oil rig,** torre *f* de perfuração (de poços de petróleo); *St.Exch:* **oil shares,** ações *fpl* de companhias petroleiras; (*b*) **vegetable oil,** óleo vegetal; **animal oil,** óleo animal.
oligopolist, *n. Pol.Ec:* oligopolista *mf.*
oligopolistic, *a. Pol.Ec:* oligopolista.
oligopoly, *n. Pol.Ec:* oligopólio *m.*
omnium, *n. UK: St.Exch:* total *m* de títulos (representativos da dívida pública).
on, 1. *prep.* (*a*) *usu.* sobre; **to be on the board of directors,** ser membro da diretoria; **to be on the staff,** fazer parte do quadro de pessoal; (*b*) (*approximation*) **just on $5,** cerca de cinco dólares; (*c*) (*basis*) **on a commercial basis,** em uma base comercial; **to pay a commission on a sale,** pagar uma comissão sobre uma venda; **to work on commission,** trabalhar em comissão, por comissão; **a tax on tobacco,** um imposto sobre o tabaco; **interest on capital,** juros *mpl* sobre o capital; **to borrow money on security,** tomar dinheiro emprestado sobre penhor; **to retire on a pension of $x a year,** aposentar-se com uma pensão de $x ao ano; (*d*) (*in expressions of time*) **on Monday,** na segunda-feira; **on Saturdays**

and Sundays, aos sábados e aos domingos; **on May 5th 1978,** em cinco de maio de 1978; **on and after the 15th,** a partir do dia quinze; **on or about the 12th,** por volta do dia doze; **on application,** mediante solicitação, sob pedido; **payable on sight,** pagável à vista; **on the delivery of the letter,** na entrega da carta; **the commission is paid on presentation of all the necessary documents,** a comissão é paga contra apresentação de todos os documentos necessários; **on commencement of the project,** no início do projeto, quando do início do projeto; (*e*) (*manner*) **on the cheap,** barato; (*f*) (*state*) **on display,** em exposição; **on sale,** à venda; (*g*) (*about, concerning*) **a decision on the pay increase.** uma decisão sobre o aumento de salário; (*h*) (*engaged upon*) **I am here on business,** estou aqui a negócios; **to be on holiday,** estar em férias, de férias; (*i*) **the decision is binding on both parties,** a decisão é obrigatória para ambas as partes; **a cheque on the Banco Português do Ultramar,** um cheque contra o Banco Português do Ultramar; (*j*) **to live on a private income,** viver de rendas. 2. *a.* **on consumption of alcohol,** consumo *m* de bebidas alcoólicas no local de venda; **on licence,** licença *f* autorizando o consumo de bebidas alcoólicas no local de venda.
on call, *a.* (*for repairs, etc.*) **engineer on call,** técnico *m* de plantão.
oncost, *n. Book-k:* custo indireto.
one, 1. *num.a.* um, *f.* uma. 2. *n.* (*a*) um, número um; **one by one,** um por um, um a um; (*b*) **goods that are sold in ones,** mercadorias vendidas por peça; **two for the price of one,** dois pelo preço de um; (*c*) *St.Exch:* unidade *f*; **to issue shares in ones,** emitir ações em unidades.
one-legged, *a. F:* (*contract, etc.*) em condições desiguais.
one-man, *a.* **one-man firm,** firma *f* individual; **one-man market,** mercado fechado, mercado controlado.
one-off, *a.* **one-off offer,** oferta única, oferta exclusiva.
one-price, *a.* de preço único; **one-price counter,** balcão *m* de preço único.

onerous, *a.* (obrigação, imposto, etc.) oneroso; *Jur: esp. Scot:* **onerous contract,** contrato oneroso.

one-sided, *a.* (*of contract*) (i) unilateral, (ii) injusto, parcial.

one-way, *a.* **one-way packing,** embalagem *f* descartável; **one-way ticket,** passagem *f* de ida.

ongoing, *a.* em andamento, corrente.

on-the-job, *a.* **on-the-job training,** treinamento *m* no serviço, no local de trabalho; **on-the-job testing,** testes *mpl* na obra.

open¹, *a.* **1.** (*a*) (*of door, packet, etc.*) aberto; **open packet,** pacote aberto; **the office is open all day,** o escritório está aberto o dia inteiro; (*b*) **open port,** porto aberto, porto livre, porto franco; **open market,** mercado *m* livre; **to sell oil on the open market,** vender petróleo no mercado livre. **2. open contract,** contrato no qual certas disposições não são expostas em termos explícitos; **open ticket,** bilhete *m* em aberto; *Ins:* **open cover,** cobertura ilimitada; **open policy,** apólice aberta. **3.** *Fin:* **open account,** conta aberta; **open credit,** crédito aberto; **open cheque,** cheque aberto, cheque não cruzado; *St.Exch:* **open position,** posição *f* em aberto. **4.** *Pol.Ec:* **open economy,** economia aberta; **open inflation,** inflação declarada. **5. to be open to any reasonable offer,** estar aberto a qualquer proposta razoável, estar disposto a apreciar qualquer proposta razoável.

open², *v.* **1.** *v.tr.* (*a*) abrir (uma carta, etc.); **to open an account,** abrir uma conta; **to open a new shop,** abrir uma nova loja; **to open a branch in Recife,** abrir, criar, fundar, uma filial em Recife; *Fin:* **to open a credit,** abrir um crédito; (*b*) **to open discussions,** abrir, começar, discussões. **2.** *v.i.* (*of shop, etc.*) abrir; **the shops open at 9 o'clock,** as lojas abrem, o comércio abre, às nove horas; *St.Exch:* **coppers opened firm,** as ações das empresas produtoras de cobre abriram firmes.

open-end, *a.* **open-end mortgage,** hipoteca sujeita a condições variáveis; *Fin:* **open-end trust** = (*approx.*) fundo *m* de capitalização ilimitada.

open-ended, *a.* **open-ended contract,** contrato *m* sem limites estabelecidos.

opening, *n.* **1.** (*a*) abertura *f* (de uma conta, um crédito, etc.), criação *f* (de uma filial, etc.); (*b*) abertura, começo *m*, (de discussões, negociações, etc.). **2. the opening up of new markets,** a criação de novos mercados. **3.** vaga *f* (para um cargo), oportunidade *f*; **excellent opening for a young person with a knowledge of English,** vaga excelente para um jovem com conhecimentos de inglês. **4. opening hours,** horário *m* de funcionamento, horário de expediente, horário de serviço; *Book-k:* **opening entry,** partida *f* inicial; *St.Exch:* **opening price,** cotação *f* de abertura, preço *m* de abertura.

open-plan, *a.* **open-plan office,** escritório aberto.

open up, *v.tr.* **to open up new markets in Latin America,** criar novos mercados na América Latina.

operate, *v.* **1.** *v.i.* (*a*) operar, funcionar; *Fin:* **to operate without cover,** operar a descoberto; (*b*) ter vigor, vigorar; **the wage increase will operate from January 1st,** o aumento salarial terá vigor, vigorará, a partir de 1º de janeiro; (*c*) *St.Exch:* operar; **to operate for a rise, a fall,** jogar na alta, na baixa. **2.** *v.tr.* (*a*) (i) (*of person*) **to operate a machine,** operar, fazer funcionar, manobrar, acionar, uma máquina, (ii) (*of part of machine*) **to operate another part,** acionar, fazer funcionar, um outro componente; **operated by hand,** acionado à mão; (*b*) **to operate a business,** dirigir, gerir, uma empresa; **to operate a concession,** explorar uma concessão; **to operate a chain of supermarkets,** dirigir uma cadeia de supermercados.

operating, *a.* (*a*) operacional, de operação; **operating instructions,** instruções *fpl* de funcionamento; **operating standards,** normas *fpl* operacionais; **operating schedule,** programa *m* de operação; **operating personnel,** pessoal operativo; **operating conditions,** condições *fpl* operacionais, condições de funcionamento; (*b*) *Book-k: etc:* **operating cost,** custo *m* operacional;

operating expenses, despesas *fpl* operacionais, gastos *mpl* de funcionamento; operating profit, lucro *m* operacional; operating losses, perdas *fpl* operacionais; operating ratio, índice *m* de operação; operating result, resultado *m* das operações; operating statement, relatório *m* das operações. *Pol.Ec:* operating level of supply, nível *m* operacional de abastecimento.

operation, *n.* (*a*) *Ind:* operação *f*, (*of machine*) funcionamento *m*; exploração *f* (de mina, indústria, etc.); manual operation, operação manual, acionamento *m* manual; (*b*) a firm's operations, as operações, as transações, de uma empresa; machining operations, operações de usinagem; operations management, gestão *f* operacional; operations research, pesquisa *f* operacional; banking operation, operação bancária; *St.Exch:* stock operation, operação de valores, de bolsa; term operation, operação a termo.

operational, *a.* operacional; operational costs, custos *mpl* operacionais; operational efficiency, rendimento *m* de operação, rendimento no funcionamento; operational research, pesquisa *f* operacional; operational planning, planejamento *m* de operações, planejamento operacional; to become operational, tonar-se operacional.

operative, 1. *a.* (*a*) operativo, operante; to become operative, entrar em efeito, em vigor; the rise in wages has been operative since May 1st, o aumento salarial tem vigor, está em vigor, desde 1º de maio; (*b*) operoso, produtivo. 2. *n.* operário *m*.

operator, *n.* operador *m*; operator of a mine, explorador *m* de uma mina; telephone operator, telefonista *mf*; telegraph operator, telegrafista *mf*; machine operator, maquinista *mf*, operador de máquina; *St.Exch:* operador; operator for a fall, a rise, operador que joga na baixa, na alta.

opinion, *n.* (*a*) opinião *f*, parecer *m*, conceito *m*; considered opinion, opinião ponderada; public opinion, opinião pública; opinion poll, sondagem *f* de opinião; in the opinion of the experts, no parecer, na opinião, dos peritos; to express, put forward, an opinion, emitir uma opinião (sobre um assunto); we are of the opinion that . . ., somos de opinião, somos de parecer, que . . .; to express an opinion against a proposal, manifestar uma opinião contrária a uma proposta; to give one's opinion, opinar, dar o seu parecer; to seek s.o.'s opinion, pedir a opinião de alguém; to seek expert opinion, solicitar uma perícia, um parecer pericial; (*b*) *Jur:* counsel's opinion, parecer de jurisconsulto; to take counsel's opinion, consultar um advogado, soliticar um parecer a um jurisconsulto.

opportunity, *n.* oportunidade *f*, ocasião *f*, ensejo *m*; job opportunities, vagas *fpl*, oportunidades de emprego; investment opportunities, oportunidades de, para, investimento; productive opportunities, possibilidades *fpl* de produção; *Econ:* opportunity cost, custo *m* de oportunidade.

opposition, *n.* oposição *f*; to start up (a firm) in opposition to s.o., criar, fundar, (uma firma) em concorrência com alguém.

optimal, *a.* ótimo; optimal resource allocation, distribuição ótima dos recursos.

optim(al)ization, *n.* otimização *f*.

optim(al)ize, *v.tr.* otimizar.

optimum, 1. *n.* ótimo *m.* 2. *a.* optimum conditions, condições ótimas; optimum employment of resources, emprego ótimo de recursos, utilização ótima de recursos.

option, *n.* (*a*) opção *f*; lease renewable at the option of the tenant, contrato *m* de aluguel renovável a critério do arrendatário; bonds redeemable at the option of the Government, obrigações resgatáveis a critério do governo; (*b*) to rent a building with option of purchase, alugar um prédio com opção de compra; (*c*) *St.Exch: etc:* opção *f*; call option, opção de compra; double option, opção dupla; put option, opção do vendedor; option day, dia *m* de vencimento das opções; option deal, operação com opção, negócio com opção; option dealer, corretor *m* de opções; **option dealings,** operações *fpl*, negócios *mpl*, com opções; **option rate,** taxa *f* de opção; **options market,** mercado *m* de opções; **giver of option money,** comprador *m* de opções; **taker of option money,** vendedor *m* de opções; **to buy an option on stock,** adquirir uma opção de compra de títulos; **to declare an option,** notificar a intenção de exercer ou não uma opção; **to give, grant, an option,** conceder uma opção; **to take up an option,** exercer uma opção.

optional, *a.* opcional, facultativo; **optional extras,** acessórios *mpl* opcionais; **optional retirement at sixty,** aposentadoria facultativa aos sessenta anos.

order¹, *n.* **1.** ordem *f*; **workmanship of the highest order,** trabalho *m* de primeira ordem. **2. in alphabetical order,** em ordem alfabética; **in order of dates,** por ordem cronológica. **3.** (*a*) **in order,** em ordem, em forma, nos devidos termos; **this receipt is not in order,** este recibo não está feito nos termos devidos; **is your passport in order?** o seu passaporte está em ordem? **to put the books in order,** pôr os livros em ordem; (*b*) **cargo received in good order,** carga recebida em boas condições; **machine in good (working) order,** máquina *f* em bom estado de funcionamento; **out of order,** fora de funcionamento, enguiçado; **the telephone's out of order,** o telefone não funciona, não está funcionando. **4.** (*a*) ordem, determinação *f*, prescrição *f*; **by order of the management,** por ordem, determinação, da gerência; **I gave orders for the goods to be packed,** mandei embalar as mercadorias; *Jur: Adm:* mandado *m*; **eviction order,** mandado de despejo; (*b*) *Fin:* ordem; **to pay to the order of s.o.,** pagar à ordem de alguém; **pay S. Martin or order,** pagar a S. Martin ou à sua ordem; **cheque to order,** cheque *m* a ordem; **bill to order,** letra *f* a ordem; **order to pay, order for payment,** ordem de pagamento; **order on a bank, banker's order,** ordem bancária; **to pay by banker's order,** pagar por ordem bancária; **postal order, money order,** vale *m* postal; *St.Exch:* **to give a broker an order to sell,**

dar uma ordem de venda a um corretor; **market order,** ordem ao mercado; **stop order,** ordem stop; (*c*) *Trade: Ind: etc:* pedido *m*, encomenda *f*; **order form,** impresso *m* para encomendas; **order book,** livro *m* de encomendas; **to place an order for goods with a manufacturer,** fazer uma encomenda a um fabricante para mercadorias, encomendar mercadorias a um fabricante; **to give effect to an order,** executar, atender, uma encomenda; **to dispatch an order,** expedir, despachar, uma encomenda; **your order will be delivered tomorrow,** a sua encomenda será entregue amanhã; (*in restaurant*) **have you given your order?** o senhor já pediu? **cash with order,** pagamento *m* no ato; **it's on order,** está encomendado, foi encomendado; **we accept telephone orders,** aceitamos encomendas (feitas) pelo telefone; (*of furniture, etc.*) **made to order,** feito sob encomenda; **the order is incomplete,** a encomenda está incompleta; **to give an agent an order to buy,** dar uma ordem de compra a um agente; **purchase order,** ordem de compra; **job order,** ordem de serviço.

order², *v.* **1.** *v.tr.* encomendar, pedir; **to order goods from the firm's Brazilian subsidiary,** encomendar mercadorias à subsidiária brasileira da firma; **to order a taxi,** chamar um táxi. **2.** *v.i.* **to order in a restaurant,** pedir (comida) num restaurante.

ordinary, *a.* (*a*) ordinário, comum, usual; **ordinary general meeting,** assembléia geral ordinária; (*b*) *Fin:* **ordinary share,** ação ordinária; **ordinary shareholder,** titular *mf*, possuidor *m*, de ação ordinária, de ações ordinárias; **ordinary creditor,** credor quirografário.

ore, *n.* minério; **ore docks,** cais *m* de minérios.

organization, *n.* (*a*) organização *f*; **inadequacy of organization,** falta *f* de organização; *Ind: etc:* **organization of work,** organização do trabalho; **organization of labour,** (i) regime *m* de trabalho, (ii) organização dos operários em sindicatos; **organization and methods,**

organização e métodos, O. & M. *f*; **line organization**, organização hierárquica; **organization chart**, organograma *m*; *Am:* (*of corporation*) **organization meeting**, assembléia constitutiva; *Am:* (*of corporation*) **organization expenses**, despesas *fpl* de instalação, de implantação, de organização; **corporations in the process of organization**, sociedades *fpl* em organização; (*b*) (*body*) organização, entidade *f*, organismo *m*; **organization man**, homem *m* de empresa; **the Organization of American States**, a Organização dos Estados Americanos.

organizational, *a.* organizacional; **organizational chart**, organograma *m*.

organize, *v.tr.* & *i.* organizar(-se); **organizing committee**, comitê *m* de organização.

organized, *a.* organizado; **organized labour**, mão-de-obra sindicalizada, operariado organizado em sindicatos.

organizer, *n.* organizador *m*.

orient(at)ed, *a.* orientado; **profit-oriented undertaking**, empresa *f* com fins lucrativos; **export-oriented economy**, economia orientada para exportações.

origin, *n.* origem *f*; **country of origin**, país *m* de origem; **goods of foreign origin**, mercadorias *fpl* de origem estrangeira, mercadorias originárias do exterior; *Cust:* **certificate of origin**, certificado *m* de origem.

original, 1. *a.* original, originário; **original packaging**, embalagem *f* original; **original value**, valor *m* original, valor inicial; **original cost**, custo *m* original; **original document**, documento *m* original; **the original invoice**, o original da fatura; *Fin:* **original capital**, capital *m* inicial; **original subscriber**, subscritor *m* inicial; **original bill**, letra de câmbio vendida antes do endosso. 2. *n.* **the original of a document**, o original de um documento.

ounce, *n. Meas:* (*a*) onça *f*; (*measure of weight*) **avoirdupois ounce** = 28,35 g; **troy ounce** = 31,1035 g; (*b*) (*measure of capacity*) **fluid ounce** = 0,0296 litro.

out, 1. *adv.* (*a*) **the voyage out**, a ida; **voyage out and home**, viagem redonda, viagem de ida e volta; **to insure a ship out and home**, segurar um navio para a viagem de ida e volta; (*b*) **the workmen are out (on strike)**, os operários estão em greve; **money out (on loan)**, dinheiro emprestado, empréstimos *mpl*; (*c*) **to be five dollars out**, estar com cinco dólares a menos; **he's out in his calculations**, seus cálculos estão errados; (*d*) **the lease is out**, o contrato de aluguel expirou; (*e*) **this week's issue is out**, o número desta semana já saiu. 2. *prep.phr.* **out of work**, desempregado; **out of season**, fora da estação; **out of date**, fora de moda, superado, antiquado; **to become out of date**, sair da moda; **my passport is out of date**, meu passaporte não tem mais validade; **out-of-date methods**, métodos antiquados, métodos superados; **out of fashion**, fora de moda; **I'm out of this line**, esta linha de produto está esgotada; **I'm out of stock of pens**, o meu estoque de canetas está esgotado. 3. *a.* **out basket**, **out tray**, cesta *f* (para correspondência) de saída; *Book-k:* **out book**, livro *m* de saídas. 4. *n.pl.* **outs**, *Am: Fin: etc:* débitos *mpl* (especialmente impostos).

outbid, *v.tr.* (*at auction*) sobrepujar (num lance, numa licitação), oferecer um lance maior (que alguém).

outbidder, *n.* licitador *m* vencedor.

outbidding, *n.* oferecimento *m* de sobrelanços.

outbound, *a.* (*a*) **outbound ship**, navio *m* que está de saída, que está de partida, que está partindo; (*b*) (navio, avião *m*) que faz viagem de ida; (*c*) **outbound freight**, carga *f* de saída.

outdoor, *a.* **outdoor staff**, pessoal *m* de serviço externo.

outfitter, *n.* (*a*) fabricante *m* de roupas; (*b*) fornecedor *m* de roupas.

outflow, *n. Fin:* **outflow of gold, exchange**, saída *f* de ouro, de divisas; **inflow and outflow of foreign exchange**, entrada *f* e saída de divisas.

outgo, *n. N.Am:* despesa *f*, gasto *m*.

outgoing, 1. *a.* (*a*) *Ind: etc:* **outgoing shift**, turma *f* que sai do serviço; (*b*) **outgoing mail**, correio *m* de saída, correspondência *f* de saída. 2. *n.pl.* **outgoings**, despesas *fpl*,

gastos *mpl*, dispêndios *mpl*; **the outgoings exceed the incomings**, as despesas excedem às receitas.
outlay, *n.* despesa *f*, gasto *m*, desembolso *m*; *Ind: etc:* **capital outlay**, despesas de capital; **to get back, recover, one's outlay**, reaver, recuperar, as despesas; **without any great outlay**, sem grandes despesas.
outlet, *n.* via *f* de escoamento *m*; **retail outlet**, comércio *m* de varejo, loja *f* de varejo.
outlook, *n.* perspectiva *f*.
outmoded, *a.* antiquado, obsoleto, fora de moda.
out-of-pocket, *a.* **out-of-pocket expenses**, despesas miúdas.
output, *n.* (*a*) produção *f*, output *m*; rendimento *m* (de trabalhador, etc.); **the daily output of a worker**, o rendimento diário de um operário; **the factory's annual output is in excess of 1,000,000 units**, a produção anual da fábrica está superior a 1.000.000 unidades; **unit price of output**, preço unitário da produção; **hourly output**, produção horária; **capacity, maximum, peak, output**, produção máxima; **output bonus**, prêmio *m* de produção; **to reduce, curtail, output**, reduzir, diminuir, a produção; (*b*) *Cmptr:* output.
outright, **1.** *adv.* de uma só vez; **to buy exploration rights outright**, comprar os direitos de exploração em bloco. **2.** *a.* **outright sale**, venda *f* por preço global.
outsell, *v.tr.* **1.** (*of goods*) ser vendido em maior quantidade (que outras mercadorias). **2.** (*of salesman*) vender mais (que outros vendedores).
outside, *a.* (*a*) **outside worker**, trabalhador domiciliário; (*b*) *St.Exch:* **outside market**, mercado *m* livre de títulos não listados na bolsa; **outside broker**, zangão *m*, zângano *m*; **outside transactions**, operações *fpl* no mercado livre de títulos não listados na bolsa.
outsider, *n. St.Exch:* zangão *m*, zângano *m*.
outsize, *n.* (*in retailing, etc.*) tamanho *m* especial; **outsize clothes**, roupas *fpl* de tamanho especial.
outstanding, *a.* (conta *f*, etc.) pendente, a

pagar, a receber; (pagamento) atrasado; **outstanding invoices**, faturas *fpl* pendentes; **outstanding debts (due to us)**, contas a receber; **the outstanding debt**, a dívida a liquidar, a dívida não saldada; **outstanding interest**, juros vencidos; **outstanding notes**, bilhetes *mpl* em circulação; **there is nothing outstanding**, tudo está liquidado.
out-turn, *n.* produção *f*, rendimento *m*.
outvote, *v.tr.* (*usu. in passive*) vencer por votos; **we are outvoted**, estamos minoritários, a maioria dos votos está contra nós.
outward, **1.** *a.* **outward voyage**, viagem *f* de ida; **outward cargo**, carga *f* de ida; **the outward and homeward voyages**, a viagem redonda, a viagem de ida e volta; **outward bill of lading**, conhecimento *m* para carga de ida; **outward freight**, frete *m* de ida. **2.** *adv.* **the ship is outward bound,** (i) o navio está de partida, de saída, (ii) o navio está rumando para o exterior.
over, **1.** *prep.* (*a*) **famous all over the world**, famoso no mundo inteiro; **the news came over the radio**, as notícias chegaram pelo rádio; (*b*) **he is over me in the office**, ele está acima de mim no escritório; **he earns over $500 a week**, ele ganha mais de, acima de, 500 dólares semanais; (*c*) **the parties disagreed over the selling price**, as partes discordaram sobre o preço de venda; (*d*) **to order goods over the phone**, encomendar mercadorias pelo telefone; (*e*) **the figures show an increase of 10% over last year's**, os números acusam um aumento de 10% sobre os do ano passado; **he receives tips over and above his wages**, além do salário recebe gorjetas; (*f*) **over the last, past, three years**, durante os últimos três anos. **2.** *adv.* (*a*) **please turn over**, favor virar a página; (*b*) **difference over or under**, diferença *f* a mais ou a menos; (*c*) **sellers over**, excesso *m* de vendedores; (*d*) **bills held over**, efeitos *mpl* em suspenso. **3.** *n.* **over in the cash**, excedente *m* de caixa; **shorts and overs**, déficits *mpl* e excedentes.
overactive, *a.* (mercado, etc.) superativo.
overage, *n. N.Am:* excedente *m*, excesso *m*.

overall, 1. *a.* total, global; **overall price,** preço *m* global; **overall efficiency,** rendimento *m* global; **overall consumption,** consumo *m* total; **overall plan,** plano *m* geral; **overall company objectives,** os objetivos gerais da companhia. **2.** *n.pl* **overalls,** macacão *m* (de mecânico, etc.).

overassessment, *n.* tributação excessiva.

overbid[1], *n.* (*a*) sobrelanço *m*; (*b*) lanço exagerado.

overbid[2], *v.i.* (*at auction*) (*a*) cobrir o lance anterior; (*b*) oferecer um lance exagerado.

overbidder, *n.* (*a*) aquele que cobre o lance anterior; (*b*) aquele que oferece um lance exagerado.

overbought, *a.* sobrevendido; adquirido por preço excessivo; *St.Exch:* **overbought market,** período *m* de grande atividade na bolsa, quando as cotações estão muito elevadas.

overbuy, *v.tr. & i.* comprar em excesso.

overbuying, *n.* excesso *m* de compras, compras excessivas.

overcapacity, *n. Pol.Ec:* capacidade excessiva.

overcapitalization, *n. Fin:* sobrecapitalização *f.*

overcapitalize, *v.tr.* sobrecapitalizar (uma companhia).

overcertify, *v.tr. N.Am:* **to overcertify a cheque,** visar um cheque por um valor que excede ao saldo do emitente.

overcharge[1], *n.* (*a*) preço excessivo; (*b*) aumento excessivo de preço.

overcharge[2], *v.tr.* (*a*) cobrar em excesso; **he always overcharges foreign customers,** sempre cobra em excesso a clientes estrangeiros; **you are overcharging me by $5,** você está me cobrando $5 a mais (que o preço combinado, etc.); (*b*) **to overcharge (on) an account,** aumentar o valor de uma fatura; **you are overcharging,** você está cobrando demais.

overconsumption, *n.* consumo excessivo.

overdevelop, *v.tr. Pol.Ec:* desenvolver em excesso.

overdevelopment, *n. Pol.Ec:* desenvolvimento excessivo.

overdraft, *n.* descoberto bancário, saque *m* a descoberto, saque sem cobertura; sobregiro *m*; **overdraft facilities,** linha *f* de crédito a descoberto; **to grant a firm overdraft facilities,** conceder a uma empresa uma linha de crédito a descoberto.

overdraw, *v.tr. Bank:* sacar a descoberto; **to overdraw an account,** pôr uma conta a descoberto; **overdrawn account,** conta *f* a descoberto; **to be overdrawn (at the bank),** estar com um saldo (bancário) negativo.

overdue, *a.* (*of payment*) atrasado, (*of bill, etc.*) vencido (e não pago); **interest on overdue payments,** juros *mpl* de mora; **the interest is overdue,** os juros estão atrasados; **overdue payment,** atraso *m*, pagamento atrasado.

overequip, *v.tr.* equipar, aparelhar, em excesso.

overestimate[1], *n.* avaliação excessiva (de preço, etc.), superestima *f.*

overestimate[2], *v.tr.* sobreestimar, superestimar.

overextend, *v.pr.* **to overextend oneself,** comprometer-se além dos recursos disponíveis.

overfreight, *n.* **1.** excesso *m* de peso. **2.** (*price*) frete *m* adicional.

overfull, *a.* **overfull production,** produção *f* excedente.

overhead, 1. *a.* **overhead expenses,** despesas *fpl* gerais, gastos *mpl* gerais. **2.** *n.pl.* **overheads,** despesas gerais, gastos gerais.

overheat, *v.tr. Pol.Ec:* **to overheat the economy,** superaquecer, sobreaquecer, a economia.

overheating, *n. Pol.Ec:* **overheating of the economy,** superaquecimento *m*, sobreaquecimento *m*, da economia.

overindustrialization, *n.* industrialização excessiva.

overinsurance, *n.* seguro excessivo.

overinsure, *v.tr.* segurar em excesso.

overinvest, *v.tr. Fin:* investir em excesso.

overinvestment, *n. Fin:* investimento excessivo, hiperinvestimento *m*, hiperinversão *f.*

overissue[1], *n. Fin:* emissão excessiva (de papel-moeda, etc.).

overissue², *v.tr. Fin:* emitir em excesso (papel-moeda, etc.).

overlapping, *n.* sobreposição *f,* superposição *f.*

overload, *v.tr.* (i) sobrecarregar (um navio, um caminhão, etc.), (ii) saturar (o mercado); **overloaded market,** mercado saturado.

overloading, *n.* (i) sobrecarga *f* (de navio, etc.), (ii) saturação *f* (do mercado).

overmake, *n. Am:* superprodução *f,* produção excessiva.

overman¹, *n. Am:* capataz *m,* chefe *m* de turma.

overman², *v.tr.* colocar pessoal em excesso (em fábrica, rapartição, etc.); **to be overmanned,** estar com excesso de pessoal.

overnight, *a. Fin:* **overnight loans,** financiamentos *mpl* overnight.

overpay, *v.tr.* (*a*) pagar em excesso; **overpaid workmen,** operários remunerados em excesso; (*b*) pagar demais (a alguém).

overpayment, *n.* pagamento excessivo, pagamento em excesso.

overplus, *n. Am:* excedente *m,* excesso *m,* sobra *f.*

overproduce, *v.tr. & i.* produzir em excesso.

overproduction, *n.* superprodução *f,* produção excessiva.

overrate, *v.tr.* (*a*) sobreestimar, superestimar; (*b*) *Fin:* cotar acima do preço (uma ação, etc.); (*c*) *Adm:* tributar em excesso (um contribuinte).

overriding, *a.* principal; *Jur:* **overriding clause,** cláusula derrogatória.

overrun, *v.tr.* **to overrun the estimated costs,** exceder aos custos orçados.

overseas, 1. *a.* externo, exterior, (*strictly*) ultramarino; **overseas market,** mercado externo; **overseas trade,** comércio *m* exterior; **overseas customers,** clientes *mpl* no exterior; **overseas competition,** concorrência estrangeira; **overseas debt,** dívida externa. **2.** *adv.* no estrangeiro, no exterior, (*strictly*) além-mar, ultramar; **to work overseas,** trabalhar no exterior.

overseer, *n.* superintendente *m,* fiscal *m,*

inspetor *m*; *Ind:* contramestre *m,* capataz *m,* chefe *m* de turma.

oversell, *v.tr.* vender em excesso; *St.Exch:* vender a descoberto.

overspend, *v.tr.* gastar além dos recursos.

overstaffed, *a.* (*of firm, etc.*) **to be overstaffed,** estar com excesso de pessoal.

overstock¹, *n.* estoque excessivo.

overstock², *v.tr.* estocar em excesso; **to overstock a shop,** ter estoque excessivo numa loja.

overstocked, *a.* com estoque excessivo.

overstocking, *n.* armazenagem *f* de estoque excessivo.

oversubscribe, *v.tr. Fin:* subscrever (ações) além do limite de emissão.

oversubscription, *n. Fin:* excesso *m* de subscrição.

overtake, *v.tr.* ultrapassar; **demand overtook supply,** a procura ultrapassou a oferta.

overtax, *v.tr.* sobrecarregar (alguém) de impostos, tributar (alguém) em excesso.

overtaxation, *n.* tributação excessiva.

over-the-counter, *a.* **over-the-counter sales,** vendas *fpl* à vista; *N.Am:* **over-the-counter market,** mercado *m* de balcão; **over-the-counter shares,** títulos vendidos no mercado de balcão.

overtime, 1. *n.* horas extraordinárias, (trabalho *m* em) horas extras, trabalho suplementar; **an hour of overtime,** uma hora extra, uma hora de trabalho extraordinário; **all overtime will be paid weekly,** todas as horas extras serão pagas semanalmente; **overtime (payment),** pagamento *m* por horas extraordinárias, por trabalho suplementar. **2.** *adv.* **to work overtime,** fazer horas extras, trabalhar em horas extraordinárias.

overvaluation, *n.* avaliação excessiva.

overvalue¹, *n.* valor excessivo (de moedas).

overvalue², *v.tr.* (*a*) (i) sobreestimar, superestimar, (ii) supervalorizar (uma moeda); (*b*) aumentar o valor (de ativo, etc.).

overweight, 1. *n.* excesso *m* de peso, peso excessivo. **2.** *a.* com excesso de peso; **this package is overweight,** este pacote está

com excesso de peso; **overweight luggage,** excesso de bagagem.
overwork[1], *n.* trabalho excessivo, trabalho extraordinário.
overwork[2], **1.** *v.tr.* sobrecarregar (alguém) de serviço. **2.** *v.i.* trabalhar demais.
owe, *v.tr.* (*a*) dever; **to owe s.o. sth., to owe sth. to s.o.,** dever alguma coisa a alguém; **he owes his brother fifty dollars,** ele deve cinqüenta dólares ao seu irmão; **the sum owed (to) him by the firm,** a importância que lhe deve a firma; **I still owe you for the petrol,** ainda tenho que pagar-lhe a gasolina; (*b*) **I owe you an apology,** tenho que lhe pedir desculpas.
owing, *a.* devido; **all the money owing to me,** todo o dinheiro que me é devido; **the rent owing,** o aluguel atrasado; *Book-k: etc:* **monies owing to the firm,** contas *fpl* a receber.
own, *v.tr.* possuir; ser dono, proprietário, de (alguma coisa); **State-owned company,** empresa pública; **he owns three houses in Portugal,** ele tem três casas em Portugal.

owner, *n.* (*a*) proprietário *m*, possuidor *m*; dono *m*, senhorio *m*, (de prédio, etc.); **owner of thirty shares,** titular *mf*, possuidor, proprietário, de trinta ações; **he's the owner of the boarding house,** ele é o dono da pensão; *Jur:* **rightful owner,** proprietário legítimo; **sole owner,** proprietário único; **bare owner,** titular de propriedade nua; **joint owner,** co-proprietário *m*, condômino *m*, comuneiro *m*; (*b*) *Nau:* **the owners (of a vessel),** os armadores (de uma embarcação); **managing owner,** armador-gerente *m*; **owner charterer,** armador-afretador *m*.

ownership, *n.* propriedade *f*, domínio *m*, posse *f*, senhorio *m* (de chácara, etc.); **bare ownership,** propriedade nua; **joint ownership,** co-propriedade *f*, condomínio *m*; **private ownership,** propriedade particular, propriedade privada; **change of ownership,** mudança *f* de dono, *Jur:* transferência *f* de propriedade; *Jur:* **claim of ownership,** ação petitória; **evidence of ownership,** prova *f* de propriedade.

P

p, *abbr.* = **penny**, *pl.* **pence; one p,** um pêni; **a book costing 50p,** um livro de cinqüenta pênis, penies; **25p each,** vinte e cinco pênis cada um; **10p off the detergent,** um desconto de 10 penies do preço de detergente.

pack¹, *n.* (*a*) pacote *m*, embrulho *m*; **pack of cigarettes,** maço *m* de cigarros; **blister pack,** embalagem *f* contendo o produto em bolha de plástico transparente fixada em base de cartolina; (*b*) (*bale*) fardo *m*, bala *f*, (de algodão, etc.); **pack goods,** mercadorias enfardadas.

pack², *v.tr.* (*a*) embalar, empacotar; **to pack goods in boxes,** encaixotar mercadorias; **to pack the books in brown paper,** embrulhar os livros em papel pardo; (*b*) **to pack meat,** enlatar carne; (*c*) *Nau:* **to pack cargo,** arrumar carga.

package¹, *n.* **1.** embalagem *f*, acondicionamento *m*. **2.** (*a*) fardo *m*, caixote *m*, pacote *m*, embrulho *m*; (*b*) *Am:* **package store,** casa *f* de bebidas (vendidas para consumo fora do local). **3.** **package holiday,** excursão *f*; **a package of economic measures,** um pacote de medidas econômicas; *Fin: etc:* **package deal,** contrato *m*, acordo *m*, global; *Ind:* **package settlement (of claim),** acordo *m* global (sobre uma reivindicação).

package², *v.tr.* (*a*) empacotar, embalar, acondicionar, (mercadorias, etc.); (*b*) enfardar (algodão, lã, etc.).

packaged, *a.* embalado, empacotado.

packager, *n.* embalador *m*, embaladeira *f*, empacotador *m*.

packed, *a.* empacotado, embalado, encaixotado; **packed consignment,** remessa *f* de mercadorias embaladas, de mercadorias encaixotadas.

packer, *n.* **1.** (*person*) (*a*) empacotador *m*, embalador *m*, embaladeira *f*; (*b*) (*of*

meat, etc.) enlatador *m*, fabricante *m* de conservas. **2.** (*device*) empacotadora *f*, empacotadeira *f*, máquina *f* de embalar.

packet, *n.* (*a*) pacote *m*, maço *m*, (de cigarros, etc.); (*b*) **postal packet,** colis *m* postal, encomenda *f* postal.

packing, *n.* **1.** (*a*) (*action of wrapping*) embalagem *f*, empacotamento *m*; **packing charges,** despesas *fpl* com embalagem, gastos *mpl* de embalagem; **packing list,** romaneio *m*; **packing case,** caixote *m* para embalagem; **packing crate,** engradado *m*; **packing cloth, canvas,** tela *f* de embalagem; **packing needle,** agulha *f* para embalagem; **packing paper,** papel *m* de embalagem; **packing room,** embalagem, seção *f* de embalagem; **packing included,** gastos *mpl* de embalagem incluídos; **packing extra,** gastos de embalagem excluídos; **packing agent,** agente empacotador; (*b*) *Nau:* arrumação *f* (da carga); (*c*) enlatamento *m* (de carne, peixe, etc.); **packing house, plant,** frigorífico *m.* **2.** (*material used*) material *m* de embalagem, de acondicionamento; **non-returnable packing,** embalagem descartável.

packthread, *n. Ind: etc:* barbante grosso de enfardar.

pad¹, *n.* bloco *m* (de escrever, etc.); **memo pad, scribbling pad,** bloco de notas.

pad², *v.tr. Am:* aumentar (conta, orçamento, etc.) com ítens falsos; **to pad an account,** enfestar uma conta.

padding, *n. Am:* ítens falsos (de orçamento, conta, etc.).

paid, *a.* **1.** pago, remunerado, assalariado, recompensado; **paid work,** trabalho remunerado; **paid employment,** trabalho assalariado; **paid assistant,** ajudante assalariado; **paid holidays,** férias remuneradas. **2.** (*a*) (*of goods, freight,*

etc.) pago; **paid cash book,** borrador *m* para despesas; (*b*) *Fin:* **paid up,** (*of capital*) realizado, (*of shares*) integralizado; **paid-up shares,** ações integralizadas.
pallet, *n.* paleta *f.*
palletization, *n.* paletização *f* (de mercadorias).
palletize, *v.tr.* paletizar (mercadorias).
pamphlet, *n.* panfleto *m.*
panel, *n.* (*a*) **advertisement panel,** painel *m* para cartazes; (*b*) **consumer panel,** grupo *m* de consumidores que juntam informações sobre determinados produtos.
panic, *n.* pânico *m*; **panic on the Stock Exchange,** pânico na bolsa; **panic measures,** medidas provocadas pelo pânico.
paper, *n.* **1.** (*a*) papel *m*; **airmail paper,** papel aéreo, de avião; **blotting paper,** (papel) mata-borrão *m*; **brown paper,** papel pardo, papel Havana; **carbon paper,** papel-carbono *m*, carbono *m*; **copy paper,** papel de segunda via, papel de cópia; **foolscap paper** = papel ofício; **giftwrap paper,** papel de presente; **glossy paper,** papel acetinado; **graph paper,** papel quadriculado, papel esquadrado; **greaseproof paper,** papel à prova de graxa, papel parafinado; **hand-made paper,** papel de fôrma; **packing paper,** papel de embalagem; **rice paper,** papel de arroz; **ruled paper,** papel pautado; **silver paper,** papel de estanho, papel estanhado, papel prateado, papel de prata, papel argentado; **tissue paper,** papel de seda; **typing paper,** papel para máquina de escrever; **wrapping paper,** papel de embrulho(s); **writing paper,** papel de escrever, de carta; **paper bag,** saco *m* de papel; **paper clip,** clipe *m*, prendedor *m* de papel; **paper parcel,** pacote embrulhado em papel; (*b*) **sheet of paper,** folha *f* de papel; **quire of paper,** mão *f* de papel; **ream of paper,** resma *f* de papel; (*c*) **the paper industry,** a indústria papeleira; **paper manufacturer,** fabricante *m* de papel; (*d*) **to put down on paper,** lançar, pôr, no papel; **the scheme's a good one on paper,** o projeto está bom no papel; **the idea remained on paper,** a idéia ficou no papel; **paper profits,** lucros *mpl* no papel, lucros contábeis. **2.** (*a*) escrito *m*, documento *m*; **the papers of a firm,** os documentos de uma empresa; **ship's papers,** papéis *mpl* de bordo; **clearance papers,** documentos *mpl* de desembaraço (alfandegário); (*b*) *Fin:* *etc:* papéis *mpl*, efeitos *mpl*, valores *mpl*; **commercial, mercantile, trading, paper,** papel comercial; **accommodation paper,** letras *fpl* de favor; **bankable paper,** efeitos bancários, títulos *mpl* negociáveis em banco; **unbankable paper,** títulos não negociáveis em banco; **guaranteed paper,** títulos avalizados; **eligible paper,** títulos redescontáveis; **negotiable paper,** títulos negociáveis; **paper securities,** títulos fiduciários; (*c*) bilhetes (bancários); **paper money,** papel-moeda *m*, dinheiro-papel *m*. **3.** jornal *m*; **daily paper,** diário *m*; **weekly paper,** jornal semanal, hebdomadário (*m*); **Sunday paper,** jornal de domingo; **fashion paper,** figurino *m*, revista *f* de modas; **to write for the papers,** trabalhar em jornalismo.
paperboard, *n.* papelão *m.*
paperboy, *n.* jornaleiro *m*, gazeteiro *m*; vendedor *m*, entregador *m*, de jornais.
paperweight, *n.* pesa-papéis *m.*
paperwork, *n.* trabalho relacionado à preparação ou processamento de documentos, formulários, etc.
par, *n.* par *m*, paridade *f*; valor *m* nominal; **to issue shares at par,** emitir ações ao par; **above par,** acima do par; **below par,** abaixo do par; **par value capital stock,** ações *fpl* com valor nominal; *Fin:* **par of exchange,** paridade monetária, taxa *f* de câmbio ao par; **gold par,** paridade (de) ouro; **par value, value at par,** valor nominal, valor ao par.
parallel, *a.* paralelo (**to, with, sth.,** a algo); **parallel processing,** processamento paralelo.
parcel[1], *n.* **1. parcel of goods,** partida *f*, lote *m*, de mercadorias; *St.Exch:* **parcel of shares,** lote de ações. **2.** pacote *m*, embrulho *m*; **to make, do up, a parcel,** fazer um embrulho; **to do up goods into parcels,** empacotar, embrulhar,

mercadorias; colocar mercadorias em pacotes; **parcel post,** serviço *m* de colis postaux, serviço de encomendas postais; **registered parcel,** encomenda postal registrada; **to send sth. by parcel post,** enviar alguma coisa pelo colis postaux; **insured parcel,** encomenda remetida com seguro; **parcels delivery (service),** serviço de colis postaux; **parcel rates,** tarifa *f* para colis postaux.

parcel², *v.tr.* (*a*) lotar; **to parcel out goods,** lotar mercadorias; (*b*) empacotar, embrulhar; **to parcel up a consignment of books,** embrulhar uma remessa de livros.

parent, *n.* **parent company,** sociedade controladora, sociedade de comando; **parent house, establishment,** casa *f* matriz, matriz *f.*

parity, *n. Fin:* **exchange at parity,** câmbio *m* à paridade, ao par; **fixed parity,** paridade fixa; **exchange parities,** paridades cambiais; **parity ratio,** razão-paridade *f*; **parity table,** tabela *f* de paridades; **parity value,** valor *m* ao par.

part, *n.* (*a*) parte *f*; **part owner,** co-proprietário *m*, condômino *m*, comuneiro *m*; **part ownership,** co-propriedade *f*, condomínio *m*; **part payment,** pagamento *m* parcial; (*car sales, etc.*) **we take your old car in part exchange,** aceitamos o seu carro usado como parte do pagamento; **part of the money was invested,** aplicou-se uma parte do dinheiro; **as part of the advertising campaign,** dentro da campanha de publicidade; **to take part in marketing activities,** tomar parte em atividades de marketing; **to take part in decision-making,** participar na, da, tomada de decisões; **to contribute in part to the expenses,** contribuir parcialmente para as despesas; **to pay in part,** fazer um pagamento parcial; *Nau:* **part shipment,** carga *f* parcial, carga incompleta; **part cargo charter,** afretamento *m* parcial; (*b*) *Ind: etc:* peça *f*, elemento *m*, componente *m*; **spare parts,** peças sobressalentes, peças sobresselentes, peças de reposição, peças de reserva.

partial, *a.* parcial, em parte; **partial damage to goods,** dano *m* parcial a mercadorias; **partial loss,** perda *f* parcial;

partial acceptance of a bill, aceite *m* parcial de uma letra.

participating, *a.* **participating insurance,** seguro *m* com participação nos lucros; **participating policy,** apólice *f* com participação nos lucros; **participating management,** participação *f* dos trabalhadores na administração (da companhia); **participating preferred stock,** ações *fpl* preferenciais de participação.

participation, *n.* participação *f* (**in sth.,** em alguma coisa); **worker participation,** participação nos lucros; **participation loan,** empréstimo concedido por diversas instituições financeiras.

particular, 1. *a.* particular, especial, determinado; *M.Ins:* **particular average,** avaria *f* particular, avaria simples. 2. *n.* pormenor *m*, detalhe *m*, informação *f*, dado *m*; **to give particulars of sth.,** dar informações sobre alguma coisa; **to take s.o.'s particulars,** anotar os pormenores, dados, relativos a alguém; **to ask for further particulars,** requerer informações complementares, maiores informações; **particulars of sale,** descrição *f* de bens imóveis à venda; *Book-k:* **particulars (of an entry),** histórico *m.*

partition, *n. Ins:* **partition of average,** repartição *f* de avaria(s); *Jur:* (*of real estate, etc.*) partilha *f.*

partly, *adv.* em parte, parcialmente; **partly secured creditors,** credores parcialmente garantidos; **partly paid (up) share,** ação não integralizada; **partly paid (up) capital,** capital não realizado.

partner¹, *n.* (*a*) sócio *m*, parceiro *m*; **partner in a firm,** sócio de uma empresa; **senior partner,** sócio principal; **junior partner,** consócio *m*; **managing partner,** sócio-gerente *m*; **active partner,** (sócio) comanditado *m*, sócio em nome coletivo; **special partner, silent partner, secret partner, latent partner, sleeping partner,** (sócio) comanditário *m*; **full partner,** sócio com responsabilidade ilimitada; **working partner,** sócio de indústria; **contracting partner,** contratante *mf*; **to take s.o. on as a partner,** associar alguém, tomar alguém como sócio; (*b*) (*of* *countries*) **trading partners,** parceiros comerciais.

partner², *v.tr.* associar-se a, reunir-se em sociedade com, (alguém).

partnership, *n.* sociedade *f*; **to enter, go, into partnership with s.o.,** constituir uma sociedade com alguém; **the undersigned have gone into partnership,** os abaixo assinados se constituiram, se reuniram, em sociedade; **to take s.o. into partnership,** associar alguém, tomar alguém como sócio; **to take up a partnership in a business,** associar-se a uma empresa; **to dissolve a partnership,** dissolver uma sociedade; **general partnership,** sociedade em nome coletivo; **deed of partnership,** escritura *f* de constituição de sociedade; **articles of partnership,** estatutos *mpl* (de sociedade em nome coletivo, em comandita, etc.); **limited partnership, sleeping partnership,** comandita *f*, sociedade em comandita; **partnership limited by shares,** sociedade em comandita por ações; **industrial partnership,** participação *f* nos lucros.

part(-)time, 1. *a.* **part-time job,** emprego *m* de tempo parcial, de meio-expediente; **part-time secretary,** secretaria *f* de tempo parcial. **2.** *adv.phr.* **to work part time,** trabalhar em tempo parcial, em meio-expediente.

party, *n.* **1.** *Adm: etc:* **working party,** grupo *m* de trabalho. **2.** (*a*) (*to a suit, to a dispute*), parte (interessada), litigante *mf*; **the contracting parties,** as (partes) contratantes; os contratantes; (*b*) **to become party to an agreement,** assinar um contrato, um acordo; **a third party,** um terceiro; **to become a third party to an agreement,** intervir num contrato feito por duas outras partes; **third party insurance,** seguro *m* contra terceiros, seguro de responsabilidade civil; **I'm insured for third party, fire and theft,** tenho seguro contra incêndio, roubo e riscos a terceiros.

pass¹, *n.* passe *m*; **customs, customhouse, pass,** passe *m* alfandegário; **pass book,** caderneta *f* de depósito.

pass², *v.tr.* **1.** *esp. Am:* **to pass a dividend,** deixar de pagar um dividendo; **passed**

dividend, dividendo não declarado. **2. to pass the customs,** ser liberado na alfândega. **3.** aprovar; **to pass an invoice,** aprovar, aceitar, uma fatura; (*of company*) **to pass a dividend of 5%,** aprovar um dividendo de 5%; **to pass a resolution,** aprovar uma proposta, tomar uma deliberação. **4.** (*a*) *Book-k:* **to pass an item to current account,** registrar um lançamento em conta corrente. **5. to pass counterfeit money,** pôr em circulação bilhetes falsos.

passenger, *n.* passageiro *m*; **train passenger,** passageiro de trem; **aircraft passenger,** passageiro de avião; **passenger train,** trem *m* de passageiros; **to send goods by passenger train,** expedir mercadorias em trem de passageiros; **passenger mile,** passageiro-milha *m*.

passing, *n.* (*a*) aprovação *f* (de contas, etc.); (*b*) tomada *f* (de deliberação).

passive, *a.* que não rende juros.

pass on, *v.tr.* **to pass on an increase,** repassar um aumento.

passport, *n.* passaporte *m*.

patent¹, 1. *a.* (*a*) *Jur:* **letters patent,** (carta) patente *f*; (*b*) patenteado; **patent goods,** produtos patenteados. **2.** *n.* patente *f*; **to take out a patent for,** tirar patente de, patentear; **to grant s.o. a patent,** conceder patente a alguém; **to use, exploit, a patent,** explorar uma patente; **patent applied for,** patente já solicitada; **application for a patent,** requerimento *m* de patente; **patent agent,** agente *mf* de patentes; **patent law,** lei *f* de patentes; **patent office,** registro *m* de patentes; **infringement of patent,** violação *f* de patente.

patent², *v.tr.* (i) patentear, tirar patente de (uma invenção), (ii) receber patente (de uma invenção).

patentable, *a.* patenteável.

patented, *a.* patenteado.

patentee, *n.* concessionário *m* de patente.

patenting, *n.* patenteamento *m*.

patentor, *n.* concessor *m* de patentes.

pattern, *n.* **1.** (*a*) padrão *m*, modelo *m*; (*b*) (*as sample*) amostra *f*, espécime *m*; **pattern book,** livro *m* de amostras;

pattern card, cartão *m* de amostras. **2.**
price pattern, estrutura *f* dos preços.
patternmaker, *n.* modelista *mf.*
pawn¹, *n.* penhor *m*, hipoteca *f;* pawn
ticket, cautela *f* de penhor; (*of object*) to
be in pawn, estar em penhor; to put sth. in
pawn, dar alguma coisa em penhor;
penhorar, empenhar, hipotecar, alguma
coisa; to take sth. out of pawn, resgatar
um objeto penhorado, tirar alguma coisa
do penhor.
pawn², *v.tr.* penhorar, empenhar,
hipotecar, (alguma coisa); *St.Exch:*
pawned stock, títulos penhorados.
pawnbroker, *n.* penhorista *mf.*
pawnbroking, *n.* concessão *f* de
empréstimos sobre penhor.
pawnee, *n. Jur:* credor pignoratício.
pawner, *n. Jur:* devedor pignoratício.
pawnshop, *n.* casa *f* de penhores, loja *f* de
penhores, *F:* prego *m.*
pay¹, *n.* **1.** paga *f,* retribuição *f,*
remuneração *f,* (*as wage, etc.*) salário *m*,
vencimento *m*, ordenado *m*; rate of pay,
taxa *f* de remuneração; back pay, salário
atrasado; basic pay, salário-base *m*,
salário básico; equal pay, igualdade *f*
salarial; severance pay, indenização *f* por
afastamento do emprego, por dispensa do
trabalho; sickness pay, salário pago
durante determinado período de doença;
starting pay, salário inicial; take-home
pay, salário líquido; unemployment pay,
auxílio-desemprego *m*; pay cheque,
cheque *m* (de) salário; pay conditions,
condições *fpl* salariais; pay day, dia *m* de
pagamento; pay dispute, conflito *m* sobre
condições salariais; pay packet, pay
envelope, envelope *m* de pagamento; pay
policy, política *f* salarial; pay roll, folha *f*
de pagamento; pay settlement, acordo *m*
salarial; pay slip, contracheque *m*,
holerith *m*; pay talks, negociações *fpl*
salariais; to draw one's pay, receber,
perceber, o salário; *Ind:* call-in pay,
pagamento *m* por presença, pagamento
por comparecimento. **2.** pay desk, caixa *f;*
pay office, caixa *f,* pagadoria *f;* pay
phone, telefone público.
pay², *v.tr. & i.* (*a*) pagar; to pay s.o. $100,
pagar $100 a alguém; I paid him $1000

for the car, lhe paguei $1.000 pelo
automóvel; you have paid too much for it,
você pagou demais por isso; the meat has
been paid for, a carne já foi paga; $2000
to be paid in four instalments, $2.000
pagável em quatro prestações; to pay
cash (down), spot cash, ready money, (i)
pagar em dineiro, (ii) pagar à vista; to
pay in advance, pagar adiantado,
adiantadamente, com antecipação; to pay
in full, fazer, efetuar, pagamento
integral, integralizar um pagamento; pay
as you earn (PAYE), *N.Am:* pay as you
go, tributação *f* na fonte; *N.Am:* to pay as
you go, (i) pagar as faturas prontamente,
(ii) não gastar acima do que se ganha; to
pay sth. (down) on account, (i) dar um
sinal, (ii) fazer um pagamento por conta;
(*b*) to pay at maturity, at due date, pagar
no vencimento; to pay on demand, on
presentation, pagar à vista, contra
apresentação; pay to the order of X,
pagar à ordem de X; (*on cheque*) pay
self, pay cash, pagar em dinheiro; to pay
a cheque into the bank, depositar um
cheque no banco; to pay money into s.o.'s
account, creditar dinheiro na conta de
alguém; (*c*) pagar, remunerar, retribuir,
(os empregados); badly paid job, emprego
mal remunerado; to pay for services,
pagar, remunerar, serviços; (*d*) to pay a
fine, pagar uma multa; to pay (off) a debt,
pagar, liquidar, saldar, uma dívida; to
pay (back) a loan, reembolsar um
empréstimo; to pay (off) a creditor, pagar,
reembolsar, um credor; to pay off
an employee, pagar e despedir um
empregado; to pay off a mortgage,
resgatar uma hipoteca; to pay a bill, (i)
(*also* an account) pagar, saldar, uma
fatura, uma conta, (ii) pagar uma letra;
(*on receipted bill*) paid, pago; carriage to
be paid by sender, porte a ser pago pelo
remetente; to pay s.o.'s expenses, pagar,
arcar com, as despesas de alguém; *Cust:*
to pay duty on sth., pagar os impostos
alfandegários sobre alguma coisa; (*e*)
business that doesn't pay, negócio *m* que
não rende, não dá rendimento, não dá
lucro; it pays to advertise, vale a pena
fazer publicidade.

payable, 1. *a.* pagável, a pagar; **payable at sight, to order, to bearer,** pagável à vista, à ordem, ao portador; **payable on presentation,** pagável contra apresentação; **payable on delivery,** pagável na entrega; **bill payable in one month, two months,** letra *f* (pagável) a um mês, a dois meses; **bill of exchange payable on May 31st,** letra de câmbio com vencimento em 31 de maio; **to make an expense payable out of public funds,** levar uma despesa a débito do Tesouro; **to make a bill payable to s.o.,** sacar uma letra à ordem de alguém; **to make a cheque payable to s.o.,** emitir um cheque em favor de alguém; **cheque payable to bearer,** cheque *m* ao portador; **bonds made payable in dollars,** obrigações *fpl* emitidas em dólares; *Book-k:* **bills payable book,** livro-registro *m* de efeitos a pagar. **2.** *n.pl. N.Am:* **payables,** contas *fpl* a pagar, efeitos *mpl* a pagar.

payback, *n.* recuperação *f* (de capitais investidos), reembolso *m;* **payback period,** prazo *m* de recuperação, de reembolso.

paycheck, *n. Am:* cheque *m* (de) salário.

PAYE, *abbr.* = **pay as you earn,** tributação *f* na fonte.

payee, *n.* beneficiário *m*, tomador *m*, (de cheque, letra, etc.); favorecido *m* (de ordem de pagamento).

payer, *n.* pagador *m*; *St.Exch:* **payer of contango,** reportado *m*.

paying, *a.* (*a*) (*of business, etc.*) lucrativo, rendoso; (*b*) **paying clerk, paying teller,** (caixa) pagador *m*; **paying guest,** inquilino *m* em casa particular.

paying-in, *n.* **paying-in book,** bloco *m* de formulários de depósito; **paying-in slip,** formulário *m* de depósito.

payload, *n.* **1.** totalidade *f* de despesas regulares (de empresa, fábrica, etc.). **2.** carga *f* útil.

paymaster, *n.* pagador *m*; **paymaster's office,** pagadoria *f*.

payment, *n.* (*act or fact of paying*) pagamento *m*, paga *f*; liquidação *f*, satisfação *f*, (de dívida); reembolso *m* (de dinheiro emprestado); realização *f* (de preço); **payment on account,** pagamento por conta; **payment in advance,** pagamento adiantado; **payment of balance,** pagamento *m*, liquidação *f*, do saldo; **payment by cheque,** pagamento *m* em cheque; **payment in full,** (i) pagamento integral, completo, (ii) liquidação *f* (de uma conta), *St.Exch:* integralização *f* (de ações), realização *f* (do capital); **payment in full discharge,** pagamento liberatório (de dívida); **payment by instalments,** pagamento a, em, prestações, pagamento parcelado; **payment of interest,** pagamento de juros; **payment in kind,** pagamento em espécie; **deferment of payment,** diferimento *m* de pagamento; **on payment of $100,** mediante, sobre, contra, pagamento de $100; **subject to payment,** mediante pagamento; **terms of payment,** condições *fpl* de pagamento; **without payment,** de graça, gratuitamente; **cash payment,** pagamento em dinheiro; **cash payments,** pagamentos efetuados pela caixa; **deferred payment,** (i) pagamento diferido, (ii) pagamento a prazo; **down payment,** entrada *f*, sinal *m*, pagamento inicial; **non payment,** falta *f* de pagamento; **to defer payment,** diferir, adiar, o pagamento; **to order, authorize, payment,** autorizar pagamento; **to present a cheque for payment,** apresentar um cheque para pagamento; **to stop payment of a cheque,** suspender o pagamento de um cheque; **to stop payments,** suspender os pagamentos.

pay off, *v.* **1.** *v.tr.* pagar e despedir (empregados). **2.** *v.i.* **the business is paying off,** o negócio é muito lucrativo, é muito rentável.

pay-off, *n. N.Am:* (*a*) pagamento *m*, liquidação *f*; (*b*) lucro *m*; *F:* ajuste *m* de contas.

pay out, *v.tr. & i.* pagar, desembolsar.

payroll, *n.* folha *f* (de pagamento); **to be on the payroll,** fazer parte do quadro de pessoal assalariado (de uma empresa, etc.).

pay up, *v.tr. & i.* pagar (integralmente), saldar, liquidar.

peak, *n.* cume *m*, ápice *m*, máximo *m*; **peak income,** rendimento máximo; **peak year for coal production,** ano *m* de produção recorde de carvão; *Adv:* **peak viewing-time,** horário *m* nobre; *Ind: etc:* **peak output,** produção máxima, produção recorde.

peculate, *v. Jur:* **1.** *v.i.* cometer peculato. **2.** *v.tr.* desfalcar, malversar, (bens públicos, etc.).

peculation, *n. Jur:* peculato *m,* desfalque *m,* malversação *f.*

peculator, *n. Jur:* peculatário *m.*

pecuniary, *a.* pecuniário; **pecuniary difficulties,** dificuldades financeiras; *Jur:* **for pecuniary gain,** com fins lucrativos; **pecuniary offence,** delito *m* de multa.

peer, *n.* **peer group,** grupo *m* de indivíduos da mesma categoria.

peg[1], *n.* **clothes off the peg,** roupa *f* prêt-à-porter.

peg[2], *v.tr.* **to peg prices,** tabelar os preços; **to peg a currency to gold,** cotar uma moeda em relação ao ouro; **to peg the market,** estabilizar o mercado; **to peg meat prices,** fixar os preços da carne (a um nível predeterminado).

pegging, *n.* fixação *f* (a um nível predeterminado), (*by government*) tabelamento *m*; **the pegging of a currency to gold,** a cotação de uma moeda em relação ao ouro.

penalty, *n.* penalidade *f,* multa *f,* pena *f,* sanção *f*; **penalty for nonperformance, contractual penalty,** penalidade contratual, pena convencional; **delay penalty,** multa moratória; (*in contract*) **penalty clause,** cláusula *f* penal; **to set a penalty,** estabelecer o valor de uma penalidade, de uma multa.

pence, *n.pl. see* p, penny.

pending, *a.* (*a*) pendente; **matters pending,** assuntos pendentes; **negotiations pending,** negociações *fpl* em curso; (*b*) (*in office, etc.*) **pending tray,** cesta *f* de documentos ainda não despachados.

penetrate, *v.tr.* penetrar (mercados no exterior, etc.).

penetration, *n.* penetração *f.*

penny, *n.* **1.** (*a*) (*sum of money*) (*abbr. sg. & pl:* p) *pl.* **pence;** pêni *m*; **a ten pence, fifty pence, piece,** uma moeda de dez, cinqüenta, penies, pênis; **I gave 60 pence for the book,** dei 60 penies pelo livro; (*b*)

(*number of coins*) *pl.* **pennies; he gave me the change in pennies,** ele me deu o troco em penies. **2.** *Am:* (*pl.* **pennies**) cêntimo *m.*

pension[1], *n.* pensão *f*; **old-age pension,** (pensão de) aposentadoria *f*; **invalidity pension,** pensão de invalidez; **pension fund,** fundo *m* de pensão, caixa *f* de aposentadoria, fundo de aposentadoria; **contributory pension,** pensão contributária; **to retire on a pension,** aposentar-se; **to commute a pension,** converter uma pensão em um capital.

pension[2], *v.tr.* **to pension (off),** aposentar.

pensionable, *a.* (*a*) (*of person*) quem merece uma pensão; quem tem o direito de receber uma pensão; (*b*) (*of injury, etc.*) que confere o direito a uma pensão; **pensionable age,** idade *f* de aposentadoria; (*c*) (emprego *m*) que dá o direito a uma pensão.

pensionary, 1. *a.* (*a*) pensionário; (*b*) (*of person*) pensionista. **2.** *n.* pensionista *mf.*

pensioner, *n.* pensionista *mf*; **old-age pensioner,** aposentado *m.*

pensioning, *n.* aposentadoria *f.*

per, *prep.* (*a*) por; **sent per carrier,** enviado por transportador; (*b*) **as per invoice,** conforme fatura; **as per sample,** conforme amostra; (*c*) **per cent,** por cento; **ten pence per pound,** dez penies por libra; **100 km per hour,** 100 quilômetros horários; **seven per cent interest,** juros *mpl* de sete por cento; **at what rate per cent was the loan floated?** qual era a taxa de juros para o lançamento do empréstimo? (*d*) **per annum,** por ano, ao ano; **per week,** por semana; **per day, per diem,** por dia; *N.Am:* **the per diem,** a diária; (*e*) **per-share earnings,** lucro líquido por ação; **per capita income,** renda *f* per capita.

percentage, *n.* percentagem *f,* porcentagem *f,* percentual *m,* pecentualidade *f*; **director's percentage,** percentagem (dos lucros) pagável a diretor.

perform, *v.tr.* **to perform a contract,** executar, cumprir, completar, um contrato; **to perform an obligation,** adimplir, executar, cumprir (com), uma obrigação; **to perform a function,**

desempenhar, exercer, uma função; **to perform a service,** prestar um serviço.
performance, *n.* **1.** execução *f*, adimplemento *m*, (de um contrato); cumprimento *m* (de uma obrigação); **performance bond,** garantia *f* de execução, caução *f* de execução. **2.** (*a*) *Ind: etc:* performance *f*, desempenho *m*, rendimento *m*, atuação *f*; **performance appraisal,** avaliação *f* da performance, do desempenho; (*b*) *Ind:* (i) funcionamento *m* (de máquina), (ii) rendimento *m* (de aparelho, etc.); **performance rating,** rendimento nominal. **3.** *Fin:* **profit performance,** rendimento *m*; **earnings performance** (**of shares,** etc.), rentabilidade *f* (de ações, etc.).
peril, *n.* *M.Ins:* **peril of the sea,** risco marítimo, fortuna *f* do mar.
period, *n.* (*a*) período *m*, prazo *m*, termo *m*; (*in contracts, etc.*) **within a period of three months,** dentro (do prazo) de três meses; **delivery period,** prazo de, para, entrega; **completion period** (**of contract,** etc.), prazo de conclusão, de execução; **period of validity,** prazo de validade; *Bank:* **deposit for a fixed period,** depósito *m* a prazo fixo; (*b*) *Fin:* **accounting period,** exercício *m*; **period under review,** exercício em apreço, exercício sob consideração.
periodical, *n.* publicação periódica, revista periódica.
perishable, 1. *a.* perecível; deteriorável; **perishable goods,** mercadorias *fpl* perecíveis; *Nau:* **perishable cargo,** carga *f* perecível. **2.** *n.pl.* **perishables,** bens *mpl*, produtos *mpl*, mercadorias, perecíveis.
perks, *n.pl.* *UK: F:* = **perquisites.**
permanency, *n.* cargo efetivo.
permanent, *a.* (*a*) permanente; **permanent profit flow,** fluxo *m* permanente de lucros; **permanent job,** cargo efetivo; **to be on the permanent staff of a firm,** fazer parte do quadro efetivo de uma empresa; (*b*) *Fin:* (*fixed*) **permanent assets,** ativo *m* permanente, imobilizado *m*.
permanently, *adv.* permanentemente.
permission, *n.* permissão *f*, autorização *f*; **written permission,** autorização por escrito.

permit, *n.* autorização *f*, licença *f*; **building permit,** alvará *m* de construção, autorização para construir; **import permit,** guia *f* de importação; **loading permit,** autorização para carregar; *UK:* **work permit,** permissão *f* de trabalho para estrangeiros.
perquisites, *n.pl.* emolumentos *mpl*; vantagens extras oferecidas pelo emprego.
person, *n.* pessoa *f*, indivíduo *m*; **private person,** particular *m*; **to act through a third person,** agir através de um terceiro; **the persons concerned,** os interessados; **person of independent means,** pessoa que vive de rendas; **policy to a named person,** apólice nominativa; **to deliver to the addressee in person,** entregar somente à própria pessoa; *Jur:* **natural person,** pessoa física, pessoa natural; *Jur:* **juristic, artificial, conventional, person,** pessoa fictícia, pessoa jurídica, pessoa moral, pessoa coletiva.
personal, 1. *a.* (*a*) pessoal; **personal income,** renda *f* pessoal; **personal selling,** venda *f* pessoal; **to make a personal application,** apresentar um requerimento pessoalmente; **personal accident insurance,** seguro *m* contra acidentes pessoais; **personal assistant** (**PA**), secretária *f* particular; *Bank:* **personal account,** conta *f* pessoal, conta particular; *Fin:* **personal share,** ação nominativa; *Cust:* **articles for personal use,** artigos *mpl*, objetos *mpl*, de uso pessoal; **personal effects,** bens *mpl* pessoais; (*b*) (*on letter, etc.*) confidencial; (*c*) *Jur:* **personal estate, personal property,** bens *mpl* móveis. **2.** *n.* *Am: Journ:* anúncio *m* pessoal (classificado).
personalize, *v.tr.* personalizar; **personalized cheque,** cheque personalizado.
personalty, *n.* *Jur:* bens *mpl* móveis.
personnel, *n.* *Ind: etc:* pessoal *m*; **personnel department,** departamento *m* de pessoal; **personnel manager,** gerente *mf*, chefe *mf*, diretor *m*, de pessoal; **personnel management,** administração *f* de pessoal; **personnel rating,** avaliação *f* do pessoal.

petition, *n.* *Jur:* petition in bankruptcy, abertura *f* de falência; to file a petition in bankruptcy, abrir falência, confessar falência.

petrodollar, *n.* petrodólar *m.*

petrol, *n.* gasolina *f;* petrol consumption, consumo *m* de gasolina; petrol station, posto *m* de gasolina.

petroleum, *n.* petróleo *m;* crude petroleum, petróleo (em) bruto; refined petroleum, petróleo refinado; the petroleum industry, a indústria petroleira; barrel of petroleum, barril *m* de petróleo; petroleum products, produtos *mpl* de petróleo; petroleum by-products, petroderivados *mpl,* produtos derivados do petróleo; petroleum coke, coque *m* de petróleo; petroleum gas, gás *m* de petróleo; petroleum jelly, vaselina *f;* petroleum pitch, alcatrão *m* de petróleo.

petty, *a.* petty cash, caixa pequena, fundo *m* para despesas miúdas, fundo de caixa; petty expenses, despesas miúdas, despesas de caixa, gastos *mpl* de pequeno vulto.

phase¹, *n.* fase *f;* to go through a difficult phase, atravessar uma fase difícil.

phase², *v.tr.* (*a*) fazer por fases; (*b*) escalonar (um programa de fabricação, etc.).

phased, *a.* (*a*) por fases, por etapas, progressivo; (*b*) escalonado.

phase in, *v.tr.* introduzir, instalar, progressivamente.

phase out, *v.tr.* eliminar progressivamente, eliminar por fases.

phasing, *n.* execução progressiva; execução por fases, por etapas; escalonamento *m.*

phone¹, *n.* telefone *m,* fone *m;* to be on the phone, (i) estar no telefone, (ii) ter telefone; are you on the phone? (i) você está no telefone? (ii) você tem telefone? who answered the phone? quem atendeu o telefone? phone call, telefonema *m,* chamada (telefônica), ligada *f;* to make a phone call, telefonar, fazer uma chamada (telefônica); to give the news over the phone, dar, passar, a notícia pelo telefone; to speak to s.o. over the phone, falar com alguém pelo telefone; the phone's ringing, o telefone está tocando, está chamando;

phone book, catálogo telefônico, lista telefônica; phone box, *Am:* phone booth, cabina telefônica, cabine telefônica; phone number, número *m* de telefone, telefone.

phone², *v.tr. & i.* to phone s.o., telefonar para alguém, chamar alguém, ligar para alguém; to phone for sth., pedir alguma coisa pelo telefone; to phone for a taxi, chamar um táxi (pelo telefone); to phone through an order, fazer uma encomenda pelo telefone, telefonar uma encomenda.

photocopier, *n.* copiadora *f,* máquina *f* xerox, xerox *m,* xérox *m.*

photocopy¹, *n.* fotocópia *f,* (cópia) fotostática *f,* xerox *m,* xérox *m,* xerocópia *f;* to make a photocopy, tirar uma fotocópia.

photocopy², *v.tr. & i.* fotocopiar, xerocar, xeroxar.

photocopying, *n.* photocopying machine, (máquina) copiadora *f.*

photostat¹, *n.* fotóstato *m.*

photostat², *v.tr. & i.* tirar cópias fotostáticas (de um documento, etc.).

physical, *a.* físico; *Am: Book-k:* physical inventory, inventário físico.

picket¹, *n.* *Ind:* picket (line), piquete *m* (de greve); to put strikers on picket duty, colocar os grevistas de piquete; to cross the picket line, furar o piquete; flying picket, grupo *m* de grevistas que se desloca para reforçar o piquete em outras localidades.

picket², *v.tr.* *Ind:* to picket a factory, (i) colocar piquete em uma fábrica, (ii) fazer piquete em uma fábrica.

picketing, *n.* *Ind:* utilização *f* de piquetes; secondary picketing, utilização de piquetes em empresas indiretamente envolvidas no conflito trabalhista.

pick up, *v.i.* business is picking up, os negócios estão melhorando; prices are picking up, os preços estão subindo de novo.

piece, *n.* pedaço *m,* peça *f;* piece of cloth, pedaço de tecido, de fazenda; piece of clothing, peça de roupa; to sell sth. by the piece, vender algo por peça; a piece of land, um pedaço de terra; *Tex:* piece goods, tecidos *mpl* de tamanho padronizado; *Ind:* **piece wage rates,** salário *m* à base de unidade produzida, salário por peça, por tarefa; **to take piece rates,** ganhar salário por peça, por tarefa.

piecework, *n.* trabalho *m* por peça, por tarefa.

pieceworker, *n.* trabalhador *m* por peça, tarefeiro *m*.

pie chart, *n.* setograma *m*, gráfico *m* de setores.

pier, *n. Nau:* **pier to pier,** cais *m* a cais; **pier to house,** cais a porta.

pig, *n. Ind: etc:* **pig iron,** gusa *f*, ferro-gusa *m*.

pigeonhole¹, *n.* escaninho *m* (de escrivaninha, etc.).

pigeonhole², *v.tr.* arquivar, classificar (solicitações, etc.).

pigeonholing, *n.* classificação *f* (de documentos, etc.).

piker, *n. N.Am: St.Exch:* bolsista *mf*.

pilot, *n.* **1.** *Nau:* prático *m*, piloto *m*; *Av:* piloto; **test pilot,** piloto de prova; **automatic pilot,** piloto automático. **2.** **pilot plant,** instalação *f*, usina *f*, piloto; **pilot sample,** amostra *f* piloto.

pilotage, *n. Nau:* taxa *f* de praticagem, taxa de pilotagem.

pint, *n. Meas:* quartilho *m* (**British pint** = 0,568 litro; **American liquid pint** = 0,473 litro; **American dry pint** = 0,5506 litro).

pioneer, *n.* pioneiro *m*; **pioneer factory,** fábrica pioneira.

pipeline, *n.* oleoduto *m*.

placard¹, *n.* cartaz *m*.

placard², *v.tr.* **1.** afixar cartazes (em parede, etc.). **2.** anunciar em cartazes.

place¹, *n.* (*a*) lugar *m*, local *m*, localidade *f*; **place of residence,** residência *f*, *Jur:* domicílio *m*; **place of work,** local *m* de trabalho; **he got a place in the London office,** ele conseguiu um lugar no escritório de Londres; (*b*) **market place,** praça *f*, mercado *m*, feira *f*; (*c*) *Fin: Bank:* praça *f*; **in the place indicated on the bill of exchange,** na praça indicada na letra de câmbio; **place of payment,** lugar de pagamento; *St.Exch:* (*in quotation*) **place: London, New York,** praça: Londres, Nova Iorque.

place², *v.tr.* (*a*) pôr, colocar; **to place an** amount (of money) to s.o.'s credit, levar uma quantia a crédito de alguém; **to place money in a savings account,** colocar, depositar, dinheiro em uma caderneta de poupança; **to place shares,** colocar, vender, ações; **goods which are difficult to place,** mercadorias *fpl* de difícil colocação, de difícil saída; **to place an order (for goods),** encomendar mercadorias, fazer uma encomenda de mercadorias; **to place a loan,** negociar um empréstimo; **to place $10 000 in bonds,** colocar, aplicar, $10.000 em obrigações; **to place a contract (with someone),** adjudicar um contrato (a alguém); (*b*) **to place s.o. as a sales manager,** colocar alguém no cargo de gerente de vendas; **to place two men on the job,** colocar dois homens na obra.

placement, *n. esp. Am:* colocação *f* (de capitais, etc.).

placing, *n.* colocação *f*, venda *f*, (de títulos, mercadorias); negociação *f* (de empréstimo).

plan¹, *n.* plano *m*, projeto *m*, desenho *m*; *Pol.Ec:* **two-year plan,** plano bienal; **five-year plan,** plano qüinqüenal; **regional development plan,** plano de desenvolvimento regional; *Fin:* **stock option plan,** plano de opções para compra de títulos; *Ins:* **benefit(s) plan,** plano de benefícios; **to draw up, work out, a plan,** estabelecer um plano, um projeto; **to carry out a plan,** executar, implementar, um plano.

plan², *v.tr.* planejar, planificar, projetar; **to plan sales operations,** planejar, planificar, as operações de venda; *Pol.Ec:* **to plan production,** planejar, planificar, programar, a produção.

planned, *a.* planejado, planificado, projetado; **planned economy,** economia dirigida.

planner, *n.* planejador *m*, programador *m*; **town planner,** *N.Am:* **city planner,** urbanista *mf*.

planning, *n.* **1.** *Adm: Const:* planejamento *m*, planificação *f*; **town planning,** *N.Am:* **city planning,** urbanismo *m*; **planning permission** = autorização *f* para construir. **2.** **economic planning,**

planejamento econômico; **production planning,** planejamento, programação *f,* de produção; **sales planning,** planejamento *m* de vendas; **planning department,** serviço *m,* departamento *m,* de planejamento; **company, corporate, planning,** planejamento de operações de empresa; **short-term, long-term, planning,** planejamento a curto prazo, a longo prazo.

plant, *n. Ind:* (*a*) maquinaria *f,* (*in speech:* maquinária), equipamento *m,* aparelhos *mpl;* **plant hire,** locação *f* de equipamentos; **to equip with plant,** aparelhar, equipar, (fábrica, etc.); (*b*) instalação *f* (industrial), usina *f,* fábrica *f;* **plant capacity,** capacidade *f* da usina, da fábrica; **plant manager,** gerente *mf* de usina, de fábrica.

pledge¹, *n.* penhor *m,* arras *fpl,* caução *f,* garantia *f;* **pledge holder,** credor pignoratício; **to set aside as a pledge,** dar em penhor, penhorar, empenhar; **unredeemed pledge,** penhor não resgatado; **valuation of a pledge,** avaliação *f* de um penhor; **value as pledge,** valor *m* de penhor; **to give, put, sth. in pledge,** dar alguma coisa em penhor; **to hold in pledge,** guardar em penhor; **to realize a pledge,** realizar um penhor; **to redeem a pledge,** resgatar um penhor.

pledge², *v.tr.* dar em penhor, penhorar, empenhar; **to pledge property,** penhorar bens, dar bens em penhor; **to pledge securities,** penhorar títulos, dar títulos em penhor, em caução.

pledgee, *n. Jur:* credor pignoratício.

pledger, *n. Jur:* devedor pignoratício, caucionário *m.*

plough back, *v.tr.* **to plough back profits into the business,** reinvestir lucros na empresa.

ploughback, *n.* (*also* **ploughing back**), **ploughback of profits,** reinvestimento *m* de lucros.

plug, *n. Advert:* reclame *m,* reclamo *m,* (indireto, inserido em algum contexto).

plummet, *v.i.* **shares plummeted yesterday,** ontem as ações acusaram uma baixa repentina.

plunge, *v.i. St.Exch:* (*a*) *F:* arriscar

grandes quantias; (*b*) acusar uma baixa repentina.

plunger, *n. St.Exch: F:* especulador *m* que arrisca grandes quantias.

plus, 1. *prep.* mais; **purchase price plus brokerage,** preço *m* de compra mais corretagem. **2.** *a.* (*a*) **the plus side of an account,** os haveres de uma conta, os créditos de uma conta, o haver; (*b*) **plus or minus difference,** diferença *f* a mais ou a menos; **the plus sign,** o sinal mais, o sinal positivo. **3.** *n.* (*a*) sinal *m* mais, sinal positivo; (*b*) vantagem *f* adicional.

pocket¹, *n.* **pocket money,** dinheiro *m* de bolso; **prices to suit every pocket,** preços *mpl* ao alcance de todos; **to be in pocket,** lucrar; **to be \$10 in pocket,** auferir um lucro de \$10; **to be out of pocket (over a transaction),** perder (numa transação); **to be \$10 out of pocket,** perder \$10, sofrer um prejuízo de \$10.

pocket², *v.tr.* (*a*) embolsar (dinheiro); (*b*) *Pej:* malversar (fundos de uma empresa, etc.).

pocketbook, *n.* carteira *f* (para dinheiro ou papéis).

point, *n.* **1.** (*a*) ponto *m;* **point of arrival, of departure,** ponto de chegada, de partida; **point of delivery,** ponto de entrega; **loading point,** ponto de carga; **unloading point,** ponto de descarga; (*b*) **point of sale,** ponto de venda; **point-of-sale advertising,** publicidade *f* de ponto de venda. **2.** (*a*) *Econ:* **point of ultimate use,** ponto de uso final; (*b*) *Book-k: etc:* **break-even point,** ponto morto (de custos), ponto de equilíbrio. **3.** *St.Exch:* (*of prices, securities, etc.*) **to gain, rise, one point,** subir um ponto; **a rise of two points,** uma subida de dois pontos; **to lose one point,** perder, cair, baixar, um ponto; **a fall of one point,** uma queda, uma perda, de um ponto.

policy¹, *n.* política *f,* plano *m* de atuação; **policy of deflation, of inflation,** política deflacionária, inflacionária; **agricultural policy,** política agrícola, política agropecuária; **company policy,** política da empresa; **economic policy,** política econômica; **exchange policy,** política cambial; **financial policy,** política financeira; **fishing policy,** política pesqueira; **government policy,** política do governo; **prices and incomes policy,** política de preços e salários; **sales, selling, policy,** política de vendas; **policy statement,** relatório *m* anual (da diretoria); **to adopt a policy,** adotar uma política; **to follow a policy,** seguir uma política; **to frame a policy,** definir, delinear, uma política.

policy², *n.* (insurance) **policy,** apólice *f* (de seguro); **all-risks policy,** apólice de seguro contra todos os riscos, apólice de seguro total; **(fully) comprehensive policy,** apólice de seguro compreensivo; **fire insurance policy,** apólice de seguro contra incêndio, contra fogo; **floating policy,** apólice aberta; **joint policy,** apólice conjunta; **life insurance policy, life assurance policy,** apólice de seguro de vida; **paid-up policy,** apólice liquidada; **standard policy,** apólice-padrão *f*; **time policy,** apólice (de seguro) a prazo limitado; **with-profits policy,** apólice com participação nos lucros; **policy to bearer,** apólice ao portador; **policy to a named person,** apólice nominativa; **policy for a specific amount,** apólice (de seguro) a quantia fixa; **to draw up, make out, a policy,** estabelecer uma apólice de seguro; **to take out a policy,** fazer um contrato de seguro; *M.Ins:* **marine insurance policy,** apólice de seguro marítimo; **non-marine policy,** apólice de seguro terrestre; **named (ship) policy,** apólice de seguro por navio nomeado; **hull, ship, policy,** apólice de seguro-cascos, apólice de seguro de casco; **round policy,** apólice de seguro por viagem redonda; **voyage policy,** apólice de seguro por viagem.

policyholder, *n.* segurado *m.*

poll, *n.* **poll tax,** imposto *m* de capıtação, imposto per capita.

pollution, *n.* poluição *f*; **environmental pollution,** poluição ambiental; **air pollution,** poluição atmosférica; **noise pollution,** poluição sonora.

pool¹, *n.* 1. grupo *m* (de trabalho); **typing pool,** equipe *f* de datilógrafas (em repartição, escritório, etc.). 2. (*a*) combinação *f* (de recursos); (*b*) sindicato *m* (de negociantes, etc.); *Pol.Ec:* pool *m.*

pool², *v.tr.* (*a*) combinar (recursos, etc.); contribuir (dinheiro) para um fundo comum; (*b*) combinar mediante estabelecimento de sindicato.

pooling, *n.* (*a*) combinação *f* (de fundos, etc.); **pooling arrangements,** acordos *mpl* para a combinação (de recursos, etc.); (*b*) reunião *f* (de interesses empresariais, etc.); organização *f* de um sindicato, de um pool.

poor, *a.* pobre; **poor quality,** qualidade *f* inferior; **poor-quality goods,** mercadorias *fpl* de qualidade inferior.

popular, *a.* popular; **a very popular line,** uma linha de grande aceitação; **this product's still popular in Brazil,** este produto ainda tem boa aceitação no Brasil, tem muita saída no Brasil; **cashmere's popular this year,** a casimira está na moda este ano; **popular prices,** preços *mpl* ao alcance de todos; **popular-priced holiday tours,** excursões econômicas.

popularity, *n.* (i) popularidade *f*, (ii) aceitação *f*, (de um produto, etc.).

population, *n.* população *f*; **population statistics,** estatística *f* populacional, estatística demográfica; **the working population,** a população ativa; **floating population,** população flutuante, população em trânsito.

port, *n.* porto *m*; **port of call,** porto de escala; **port of discharge,** porto de descarga; **port of refuge,** porto de arribada; **port of registration,** porto de matrícula; **in port,** em porto; **commercial port,** porto comercial; **fishing port,** porto pesqueiro; **free port,** porto franco, porto livre; **lake port,** porto lacustre, porto de lago; **ocean port,** porto oceânico; **oil port,** porto petroleiro; **open port,** porto aberto; **river port,** porto fluvial; **sea port,** porto marítimo, porto de mar; **port authority,** autoridade portuária; **port capacity,** capacidade portuária; **port charges, port dues,** taxas portuárias, direitos portuários; **port facilities,** instalações portuárias; **to call at a port,** fazer escala, escalar; **to put into port,** fundear, aportar; **the ship puts into three ports,** o navio faz três escalas.

portable, (*a*) *a.* portátil, transportável; portable plant, instalações portáteis, transportáveis; portable crane, guindaste *m* transportável; portable machine, máquina *f* portátil; (*b*) *a. & n.* portable (typewriter), máquina *f* de escrever portátil.

portage, *n.* (*a*) porte *m*, transporte *m*, frete *m*; (*b*) (*price*) porte *m*, frete *m*, preço *m* de transporte.

porter, *n.* (*at station, airport, etc.*) portador *m*, carregador *m*; (*at hotel*) porteiro *m*; (*in building*) zelador *m*; porter's office, portaria *f* (em hotel, edifício, etc.).

portfolio, *n.* 1. pasta *f* (para documentos, etc.). 2. *Fin: etc:* portfolio of securities, carteira *f* de títulos, de valores; portfolio situation, situação *f* da carteira de títulos; portfolio management, administração *f* de carteira (de títulos); portfolio investment, investimento *m* em títulos; portfolio sales, vendas *fpl* de títulos. 3. pasta *f* ministerial.

portion, *n.* porção *f*, partilha *f*, quinhão *m*; a portion of my money, uma porção do meu dinheiro; *Fin:* portion of shares, lote *m* de ações.

position, *n.* 1. (*a*) posição *f*; competitive position, posição competitiva; (*b*) posição, atitude *f*; to adopt, take up, a position on a question, adotar uma posição sobre um assunto. 2. (*a*) posição, situação *f*, localização *f*; the shop has a good position in the centre of the town, a loja está bem situada no centro da cidade; (*b*) *Post: Bank:* guichê *m.* 3. (*a*) posição, situação, condição *f*; to be in a position to do sth., estar em posição de fazer algo, ter condições para fazer algo; (*b*) financial position, situação financeira; the cash position, a situação da caixa; *Book-k:* net position, situação líquida, patrimônio líquido; position statement, balanço financeiro; (*c*) *St.Exch:* posição; open position, posição em aberto; short position, posição a descoberto; to cover a position, cobrir uma posição. 4. cargo *m*, posição, função *f*; a very responsible position, um cargo, uma posição, de alta responsabilidade; key position, posição-

chave *f*; position description, descrição *f* de cargo; position of trust, cargo *m* de confiança.

possess, *v.tr.* possuir, ter a posse de, fruir a posse de, (um bem); to possess certain rights, ter, gozar de, certos direitos.

possession, *n.* posse *f*; to take possession of a property, tomar posse de um bem imóvel; to have the documents in one's possession, ter os documentos em seu poder; to be in possession of a passport, estar munido de um passaporte; right of possession, direito *m* de posse; vacant possession, posse de imóvel desocupado; 'house for sale with vacant possession', 'vende-se casa desocupada'; *Jur:* actual possession, posse efetiva, posse de fato.

possessor, *n.* possuidor *m.*

post[1], *v.tr.* 1. afixar, colar, (cartazes, avisos, etc.); *PN:* post no bills, proibido colocar cartazes; *St.Exch: etc:* the market rates are posted on the floor, os cursos estão afixados no pregão. 2. inscrever em lista, arrolar. 3. *M.Ins:* to post a ship, anunciar o atraso ou extravio de um navio.

post[2], *n.* (*a*) correio *m*; by return of post, na volta do correio; the first post, a primeira distribuição (do dia); (*b*) correio, posta *f*; the Post Office = o Departamento dos Correios e Telégrafos; to send sth. by post, enviar, mandar, remeter, algo pelo correio; (*c*) post (office), correio; general post office, correio geral; sub post office, branch post office, agência *f* dos Correios e Telégrafos, agência de correio; post office clerk, postalista *mf*, funcionário *m* dos Correios e Telégrafos; post office box, caixa *f* postal; P.O. Box 359, C.P. 359.

post[3], *v.tr.* 1. to post a letter, postar uma carta, pôr uma carta no correio; we posted you a copy of the book, lhe enviamos um exemplar do livro pelo correio. 2. *Book-k:* to post (up) the books, fazer a escrituração; to post an entry, lançar uma partida, um registro, (na escrita contábil); to post an item in the ledger, lançar um registro no razão; to post up the ledger, pôr o razão em dia; my books are posted up, os meus livros de

contabilidade estão em dia. **3. we keep customers posted on any price changes,** informamos os clientes sobre todas as variações de preço.
post⁴, *n.* cargo *m*, emprego *m.*
postage, *n.* porte *m*, taxa *f* postal; **postage rates,** tarifa *f* postal; **postage stamp,** selo *m* postal; (*on insufficiently stamped letter*) **additional postage,** sobretaxa *f*; **postage included,** porte incluído; **postage paid,** porte pago.
postal, *a.* postal; **postal authorities,** administração *f* do correio; **postal charges,** tarifa *f* postal, porte *m*; **postal receipt,** recibo *m* postal; **postal services,** serviços *mpl* postais; **postal order,** vale *m* postal.
postbox, *n.* caixa *f* do correio.
postcard, *n.* cartão *m* postal.
postcode, *n.* código *m* de endereçamento postal (CEP).
postdate, *v.tr.* pós-datar (um documento); pré-datar (um cheque); **to pay with a postdated cheque,** pagar com um cheque pré-datado.
posting, *n.* **1.** (*a*) envio *m* pelo correio, remessa *f* pelo correio; (*b*) postagem *f.* **2.** *Book-k:* (*a*) escrituração *f*; (*b*) (i) lançamento *m* (no razão), (ii) transcrição *f* de registros (do diário para o razão).
postman, *n.* carteiro *m*, correio *m*, distribuidor *m.*
postmark, *n.* carimbo *m* do correio.
postmaster, *n.* agente *m* do correio; *Adm:* **postmaster general,** diretor *m* geral dos correios.
postpaid, *a.* porte pago.
postpone, *v.tr.* **to postpone a meeting,** adiar uma reunião; **to postpone a decision,** pospor uma decisão; **to postpone payment,** diferir pagamento.
postponement, *n.* adiamento *m* (de assembléia, reunião, etc.); diferimento *m* (de pagamento).
potential, 1. *a.* **potential customers,** clientes *mfpl* potenciais. **2.** *n.* potencial *m*; **growth potential,** potencial de crescimento; **industrial potential,** potencial industrial; **monetary potential,** potencial monetário; **sales potential,** potencial de vendas.

pound, *n.* **1.** libra *f* (= 453,6 gramas), libra-peso *f*; **to sell meat by the pound,** vender carne por libra. **2. pound (sterling),** libra (esterlina); **pound note,** nota *f* de uma libra; **five-pound note,** nota de cinco libras; (*of bankrupt*) **to pay 50 pence in the pound,** pagar à razão de cinqüenta penies por libra.
poundage, *n.* taxa *f*, comissão *f*, por libra (peso ou moeda).
power, *n.* **1.** poder *m*; **purchasing power,** poder aquistivo, poder de compra; **bargaining power,** poder de barganha; **earning power,** capacidade *f* salarial. **2.** (*a*) potência *f* (de máquina); (*b*) força *f*, energia elétrica; **power company,** companhia *f* de força e luz, companhia de energia elétrica; **power consumption,** consumo *m* de energia; **power demand,** demanda *f* para energia elétrica; **power cut, power failure,** interrupção *f* da corrente elétrica; **power development,** produção *f* de energia elétrica; **power producer,** produtor *m* de energia; **power system,** rede *f* de energia elétrica; **power station,** usina elétrica. **3.** (*a*) poder, autoridade *f*; **executive power,** poder executivo; **to act with full powers,** agir com plenos poderes; (*b*) **power of attorney,** procuração *f*; **to grant s.o. power of attorney,** passar procuração a alguém.
practical, *a.* prático, útil; **practical suggestions,** sugestões *fpl* úteis; **practical furniture,** móveis práticos, móveis funcionais.
practice¹, *n.* **1.** prática *f*; exercício *m* (de profissão, etc.); **to put one's ideas into practice,** pôr as idéias em prática. **2.** (*a*) prática, uso *m*, praxe *f*, costume *m*, hábito *m*; **local trade practices,** práticas *fpl* comerciais locais, práticas da praça; (*b*) *Ind: etc:* prática, praxe, método *m*; **operating practice,** prática funcional; **standard practice,** prática normal; **management practices,** práticas administrativas, práticas gerenciais. **3.** (*professional business*) **legal practice,** escritório *m* de advocacia.
practice², *v.tr. Am:* = **practise.**
practise, *Am:* **practice,** *v.tr.* **to practise a**

profession, praticar, exercer, exercitar, uma profissão; **to practise as a lawyer,** exercer a profissão de advogado, trabalhar como advogado.
precinct, *n.* **shopping precinct,** área *f* comercial; **pedestrian precinct,** calçadão *m.*
predate, *v.tr.* antedatar.
pre-empt, *v.tr. Jur:* adquirir por preempção.
pre-emption, *n. Jur:* preempção *f*; **to obtain by pre-emption,** obter por preempção.
pre-emptive, *a. Jur:* preemptivo; **pre-emptive right,** direito *m* de preempção.
pre-emptor, *n. Jur:* preemptor *m.*
preference, *n.* preferência *f*; *Pol.Ec: Cust:* sistema *m* de preferências; **imports entitled to preference,** importações *fpl* com direito a regime preferencial; **customs preferences,** preferências alfandegárias; *Fin:* **preference stock, preference shares,** ações *fpl* preferenciais; **preference shareholder,** *Am:* **preference stockholder,** possuidor *m* de ações preferenciais; *Jur:* **preference clause,** cláusula *f* preferencial.
preferential, *a.* (*a*) preferencial; **preferential price,** preço *m* preferencial; *Cust:* **preferential tariff,** tarifa *f* preferencial; *Fin:* **preferential dividend,** dividendo *m* preferencial; (*b*) *Jur:* **preferential right,** preferência *f*, antelação *f*; **preferential claim,** crédito privilegiado; **preferential creditor,** credor privilegiado; **creditor's preferential claim,** direito creditório preferencial, direito de credor privilegiado, de credor preferencial.
preferred, *a. Fin:* **preferred stock,** ações *fpl* preferenciais.
prefinancing, *n.* pré-financiamento *m.*
prejudice[1], *n.* prejuízo *m*, dano *m*; *Jur:* **without prejudice to my rights,** sem prejuízo dos meus direitos, ressalvados os meus direitos; **to the prejudice of s.o.,** em, com, prejuízo de alguém; (*at head of document, letter, etc.*) **without prejudice,** sem prejuízo.
prejudice[2], *v.tr.* (*a*) prejudicar, danificar, causar prejuízo a, (alguém); **without prejudicing my rights,** sem prejuízo dos

meus direitos; (*b*) **the action will not prejudice the decisions to be taken,** a ação não prejudicará às decisões a ser(em) tomadas.
prejudicial, *a.* prejudicial, nocivo, lesivo; **to be prejudicial to s.o.'s interests,** prejudicar os interesses de alguém.
preliminary, 1. *a.* preliminar, prévio; **preliminary meeting,** reunião *f* preliminar; **preliminary data,** dados *mpl* preliminares, antecedentes; **preliminary design,** anteprojeto *m*; **preliminary estimate,** orçamento *m* preliminar; **preliminary work,** trabalho preparatório; **preliminary study,** estudo *m* preliminar; **preliminary survey,** levantamento *m* preliminar; **without preliminary advice,** sem aviso prévio; **to take preliminary steps for sth.,** fazer os preparativos para algo; *Book-k: etc:* **preliminary expenses,** despesas *fpl* de instalação, de organização, de implantação, (de companhia). 2. *n.pl.* **preliminaries,** preparativos *mpl.*
premises, *n.pl.* local *m*, edifício *m*, prédio *m*, recinto *m*; **business premises,** local *m* utilizado para atividades comerciais; **shop premises,** loja *f.*
premium, *n.* 1. prêmio *m*; *Ind:* **to give a premium for increased output,** conceder um prêmio por aumento de produção; *Ind:* **premium bonus (scheme),** (sistema *m* de) salário-prêmio *m*. 2. (*a*) **(insurance) premium,** prêmio *m* (de seguro); **premium charges,** taxas *fpl* de prêmio; **premium increase,** aumento *m* de prêmio; **annual premium,** prêmio anual; **low-premium insurance,** seguro *m* a prêmio reduzido; *Am:* **premium loan,** empréstimo *m* para pagamento de prêmio de seguro; (*b*) (*for flat, etc.*) luvas *fpl*. 3. *Fin:* (*a*) ágio *m*; **2% premium,** ágio de 2%; **at a premium,** com ágio; **exchange premium,** ágio cambial; **premium on gold,** ágio sobre o ouro; **share premium,** ágio sobre a emissão de ações; **to issue shares at a premium,** emitir ações com ágio; (*b*) **premium on redemption,** prêmio de reembolso; *UK:* **premium bonds,** obrigações *fpl* que dão direito a prêmios mediante sorteio; (*c*) **to sell at a premium,** vender com lucro; **antiques are**

at a premium, as antiguidades estão
caríssimas. **4. premium grade petrol,**
gasolina *f* de qualidade superior, *F:*
gasolina azul.
prepack, prepackage, *v.tr.* embalar para
venda ao consumidor.
prepaid, *a.* (*a*) pago antecipadamente,
pago adiantadamente; (*of letter, etc.*)
(com) franquia *f* de porte; **carriage
prepaid,** porte pago, (com) franquia de
porte; *Tg:* **prepaid answer,** resposta paga;
(*b*) *Book-k:* **prepaid income,** receita *f* de
exercícios futuros; **prepaid expenses,**
despesas antecipadas.
preparation, *n.* (*a*) preparação *f*, preparo
m; elaboração *f*; **the samples are in
preparation,** as amostras estão em
preparação; **in course of preparation,** em
preparação, em elaboração; (*b*) *Ind:
etc:* preparação, aprestamento *m*,
aprontamento *m* (de máquina, aparelho,
etc.).
prepare, *v.tr.* (*a*) preparar; **to prepare an
advertising campaign,** preparar uma
campanha de publicidade; **to prepare a
document,** preparar, elaborar, um
documento; **to prepare the way for
negotiations,** preparar o terreno para,
abrir o caminho a, negociações; (*b*)
preparar, aprestar, aprontar, (uma
máquina, etc.); (*c*) **I am prepared to . . .,**
estou disposto, pronto, a . . .; **I am not
prepared to . . .,** não estou disposto a . . .,
recuso-me a . . ..
prepay, *v.tr.* pagar antecipadamente,
adiantar; **to send sth. prepaid,** remeter
algo porte pago.
prepayable, *a.* pagável adiantadamente.
prepayment, *n.* pagamento adiantado.
present¹, *a.* (*a*) (*not absent*) presente; **to
be present at a meeting,** assistir (a) uma
reunião, estar presente a uma reunião;
(*b*) atual, presente; **the present fashion,** a
moda atual, a moda presente; **the present
year,** o ano corrente; **at the present time,**
atualmente, hoje em dia; **present value,**
valor *m* atual; **present capital,** capital
chamado. **2.** *n.* *Jur:* **by these presents,**
pelo presente.
present², *v.tr.* apresentar; **to present a bill
for acceptance,** apresentar uma letra para

aceite; *Jur:* **to present evidence,**
apresentar provas.
presentation, *n.* apresentação *f*; **the
payments will be made on presentation of
invoices,** os pagamentos serão feitos
contra apresentação, quando da
apresentação, das faturas; **presentation of
a bill for acceptance,** apresentação de
uma letra para aceite.
presenter, *n.* apresentador *m* (de letra,
etc.).
presenting, *a.* **presenting bank,** banco
apresentador.
presentment, *n.* **presentment of a bill for
acceptance,** apresentação *f* de uma letra
para aceite.
preservation, *n.* (*of foods, etc.*)
conservação *f*, preservação *f*.
preservative, *n.* conservador *m*.
preserve, *v.tr.* conservar (substâncias
alimentícias, etc.).
preserved, *a.* **preserved food,** gêneros
alimentícios conservados; **preserved meat,**
carne *f* em conserva.
preserving, *n.* conservação *f* (de
substâncias alimentícias).
preside, *v.i.* (*a*) presidir; **to preside at,
over, a meeting,** presidir a uma reunião;
(*b*) **he will preside until the end of the
financial year,** ele presidirá, exercerá as
funções de presidente, até o fim do
exercício.
president, *n.* *esp.* *N.Am:* presidente *mf*
(de uma sociedade por ações).
press, *n.* imprensa *f*; **the TV press,** a
imprensa televisionada; **press agency,**
agência *f* de notícias, agência noticiosa;
press clipping, recorte *m* de jornal; **press
conference,** entrevista coletiva (à
imprensa); **press release,** release *m*,
comunicado *m* (à imprensa).
press-button, *a.* **press-button industry,**
indústria completamente automatizada.
pressure, *n.* pressão *f*; **heavy pressure,**
forte pressão; **pressure group,** grupo *m* de
pressão; **to put pressure on s.o.,**
pressionar, exercer pressão sobre,
alguém; **inflationary pressure,** pressão
inflacionária; **financial pressure,** pressão
financeira; **the pressure of work,** o peso, a
carga, do trabalho.

prestocking, *n.* pré-estocagem *f.*
pre-tax, *a.* **pre-tax profit,** lucro líquido antes do imposto de renda.
pretest[1], *v.tr.* submeter a teste preliminar.
pretest[2], *n.* teste *m* preliminar.
prevailing, *a.* vigente, em vigor.
preventive, *a.* preventivo; **preventive measures,** medidas preventivas; **preventive maintenance,** manutenção, conservação, preventiva.
price[1], *n.* (*a*) preço *m*; **actual price,** preço real; **administered price,** preço administrado; **agreed price,** preço combinado, preço ajustado; **the asking price of this house is too high,** pede-se demais por esta casa; **bargain price,** preço de ocasião, preço de liquidação; **basic price,** preço de base; **cash price,** preço à vista; **catalogue price,** preço de catálogo; **ceiling price,** preço-teto *m*; **competitive price,** preço competitivo, preço de concorrência; **cost price,** preço de custo; **to sell under cost price,** vender abaixo do custo; **current price,** preço corrente; **cut price,** preço reduzido; **direct price,** preço direto, preço de fábrica; **discount price,** preço com desconto; **fair price,** preço justo, justo preço; **firm, steady, price,** preço firme; **fixed price,** preço fixo; **floor price,** preço mínimo (fixo); **full price,** preço integral; *Th: etc:* **half price,** meia-entrada *f*; **it's on sale at half price,** está à venda pela metade do preço; **high price,** preço alto; **at a very high price,** a um preço muito alto; **inclusive price,** preço global; **list price,** preço de tabela, preço de catálogo; **low price,** preço baixo, preço vil; **at the lowest price, at the rock-bottom price,** ao preço mais baixo, *F:* ao preço de banana; **manufacturer's price,** preço de fábrica; **manufacturer's recommended price,** preço recomendado pelo fabricante; **marked price,** preço marcado; **market price,** preço de mercado; **moderate price,** preço módico, preço razoável; **net(t) price,** preço líquido; **purchase price,** preço de compra; **recommended price,** preço recomendado (pelo fabricante); **reduced price,** preço reduzido; **resale price maintenance (RPM),** manutenção *f* de preços de revenda; **reserve price, upset price,** preço mínimo de venda em leilão; **retail price,** preço a varejo, preço de varejo, preço a retalho; **selling price,** preço de venda; **special price,** preço especial; **standard price (of wheat, etc.),** preço de tabela (do trigo, etc.); **support price,** preço de sustentação; **supported price,** preço amparado, preço sustentado; **trade price,** preço de revendedor, preço para revendedores, preço para comerciantes; **unit price,** preço unitário; **wholesale price,** preço por atacado; **price control,** controle *m* dos preços; **price cutting, slashing,** corte *m* de preços, forte redução *f* de preços; (*in industry, etc.*) **price enquiry, inquiry,** tomada *f* de preços, levantamento *m* de preços; **price freeze, price freezing,** congelamento *m* de preços; **price index,** índice *m* dos preços; **price leadership,** liderança *f* de preços; **price level,** nível *m* dos preços; **price line,** linha *f* de preços; **price lining,** alinhamento *m* de preços; **price list,** lista *f* de preços, tabela *f* de preços; **price mechanism,** mecanismo *m* dos preços; **price range,** gama *f* de preços; **price regulation,** regulamentação *f* dos preços; **price tag,** etiqueta *f* de preço; **price war,** guerra *f* de preços; **all at one price,** vende-se tudo por preço único; **what price is that article?** qual é o preço daquele artigo? quanto custa aquele artigo? **to ask a price for an article,** pedir um preço por um artigo; **he charges reasonable prices,** ele cobra preços razoáveis; **what price did you pay for your car?** quanto foi que você pagou por seu carro? **I'll let you have it for a fair price,** lhe vendo por um preço justo; **to fix the price of an article, to set a price on an article,** fixar o preço de um artigo; **to name a price,** fazer um preço; (*of goods*) **to increase in price,** subir de preço, encarecer; acusar, registrar, um aumento, uma subida, de preço; **to force up, push up, prices,** forçar uma subida nos preços; **to force down prices,** forçar uma baixa nos preços; (*b*) *Bank: Fin:* **price of money,** custo *m* do dinheiro, preço do dinheiro; (*c*) *St.Exch: etc:* cotação *f*, curso *m*, preço; **price for the account,** taxa *f* a

termo; **price of allotment,** preço de subscrição; **price of call,** taxa de opção de compra; **price of option,** taxa de opção; **price of put,** taxa de opção do vendedor; **collapse of prices, slump in prices,** queda *f* dos preços, baixa *f* nos preços; **closing price,** preço final, cotação de fechamento; **issue price,** preço de emissão; **market price,** preço de mercado; **marking-up price,** taxa *f* de compensação; **opening price,** cotação de abertura, preço de abertura; **put and call price,** taxa de dupla opção; **spot price,** taxa à vista, (*of commodity*) preço à vista; **price-earnings ratio (PER),** índice *m* preço/lucro (P/L); **to make a price,** fixar uma taxa; **prices are easing off,** os preços estão se atenuando.

price², *v.tr.* **1.** (i) determinar, fixar, o preço de (mercadorias), (ii) marcar o preço (de mercadorias numa loja, etc.); **the book is priced at $4 net,** o livro está à venda ao preço líquido de $4. **2.** informar-se dos preços de (mercadorias, etc.). **3. to price competitors out of the market,** vender a preço baixo para prejudicar a concorrência; **we shall be priced out of the market,** vamos perder freguesia por causa dos nossos preços não-competitivos. **4.** *Pol.Ec:* valorizar.

priced, *a.* **1. high-priced,** de preço elevado, alto; caro; **low-priced,** de baixo preço. **2.** com preços indicados; **everything in the window is priced,** todos os artigos na vitrina estão com os preços marcados.

pricewise, *adv.* em relação aos preços.

pricey, *adv. F:* caro, custoso; **too pricey,** caro demais, caríssimo.

pricing, *n.* fixação *f*, determinação *f*, dos preços; **competitive pricing,** determinação dos preços baseada na concorrência; **pricing policy,** política *f* de preços; **pricing strategy,** estratégia *f* de preços.

primage, *n. Nau:* primagem *f*, chapéu *m*.

primary, *a.* **primary product,** produto básico, produto primário; **primary industries,** setor primário; **primary market,** mercado primário.

prime, *a.* **1.** primeiro, principal; **prime cost,** custo primário, custo direto; *Const: Ind:* **prime contractor,** contratante *m*

principal. **2.** de primeira categoria, de primeira qualidade; **prime meat,** carne *f* de primeira (qualidade); *Fin:* **prime bond,** obrigação *f* de primeira ordem; **prime bills,** efeitos *mpl* de primeira ordem; *esp. N.Am:* **prime (lending) rate,** taxa mínima de empréstimos.

principal, 1. *a.* principal; **principal contract,** contrato *m* principal. **2.** *n.* (*a*) (*person*) diretor *m* (de fábrica, etc.); chefe *mf*, patrão *m*, (de casa comercial); (*in transaction*) mandante *mf*; *St.Exch:* comitente *mf*; *Jur:* **principal and agent,** preponente *m* e preposto *m*; mandante e mandatário *m*; (*b*) principal *m* (de uma dívida); **principal and interest,** principal e juros *mpl*, capital *m* e juros.

principle, *n.* (*a*) princípio *m*; **principle of equal pay,** princípio *m* de igualdade salarial; (*b*) **to reach an agreement in principle,** chegar a um acordo sobre os aspetos fundamentais.

print, *n.* **print shop,** oficina gráfica.

printed, *a. Post:* **printed matter,** impressos *mpl*.

printer, *n.* impressor *m*; **master printer,** mestre-impressor *m*; **printer's ink,** tinta *f* de impressor.

prior, 1. *a.* prévio, anterior, antecedente; **prior contract,** contrato *m* anterior; **without prior notice,** sem aviso prévio; **to have a prior claim,** ter um direito prioritário; *Fin:* **prior claim,** direito creditório preferencial. **2.** *prep.* **prior to negotiations,** antes das negociações.

priority, *n.* (*a*) prioridade *f*, precedência *f*, primazia *f*; **to have priority (over),** ter prioridade (sobre outro direito, etc.); **priority rights,** direitos prioritários; *Jur:* **priority of creditor,** direito *m* de credor privilegiado; (*b*) (*on message*) urgente.

private, *a.* **1.** privado, particular; **private conversation,** conversa *f* particular; **private matter,** assunto *m* particular; **private and confidential,** particular e confidencial; *Jur:* **private contract,** contrato feito por instrumento particular. **2. private trader,** comerciante autônomo; **private bank,** banco privado; **the private sector,** o setor privado; **private enterprise,** empresa privada; **private company** =

sociedade *f* por quotas, companhia controlada por um pequeno grupo de acionistas cujas ações não podem ser negociadas na bolsa; **private limited company** = sociedade por quotas de responsabilidade limitada. **3. private income,** rendimentos *mpl* de capital, rendimentos não ganhos com o trabalho individual; **to live out of, live on, a private income,** viver de rendas; **private property,** (i) propriedade privada, (ii) = entrada proibida.

probation, *n.* (*for job*) estágio *m.*

probationary, *a.* estagiário; **probationary duties,** funções estagiárias.

probationer, *n.* estagiário *m.*

problem, *n.* problema *m*; **problem solving,** resolução *f* de problemas; **problem area,** zona problemática.

procedure, *n.* (*a*) procedimento *m*, processo *m*; *Adm:* **to follow established procedure,** seguir os trâmites normais; **rules of procedure,** regimento interno; (*b*) *Tchn:* **operating, operational, procedure,** procedimento operacional.

proceed, *v.i.* **1.** (*a*) proceder, agir, obrar; **to proceed with caution,** proceder com cautela; **to proceed methodically,** agir metodicamente; (*b*) (*at meeting, etc.*) **the board proceeded to a discussion of the report,** o conselho procedeu a uma discussão sobre o relatório; (*c*) **the inspector's report proceeds thus...,** o relatório do inspetor procede, continua, desta forma...; (*d*) **negotiations are now proceeding,** as negociações estão em andamento, em curso; **to pay as the work proceeds,** pagar conforme o andamento do trabalho. **2.** *Jur:* **to proceed against s.o.,** processar alguém, instaurar processo contra alguém; intentar, mover, uma ação contra alguém.

proceedings, *n.pl.* (*a*) transações *fpl* (de uma assembléia); (*record*) atas *fpl* (de reunião, assembléia, etc.); (*b*) *Jur:* (**legal**) **proceedings, proceedings at law,** processo *m*; ação *f* judicial; **to take, institute, proceedings against s.o.,** processar, acionar, alguém; instaurar processo, intentar ação judicial, contra alguém; **summary proceedings,** processo sumário;

to order proceedings to be taken against s.o., mandar processar alguém.

proceeds, *n.pl.* **the proceeds of a sale,** o produto de uma venda, os proventos de uma venda.

process¹, *n.* **1.** (*a*) processo *m*; *Ind:* **process control,** controle *m* de processos; (*b*) **in process of development,** em via de desenvolvimento; **in process of preparation,** em preparação. **2.** *Jur:* (*a*) ação *f* judicial; (*b*) citação *f*; **process-server,** oficial *m* de justiça, oficial de diligências. **3.** *Ind:* processo, procedimento *m*, método *m*; **manufacturing process,** processo de fabricação.

process², *v.tr.* (*a*) *Ind:* tratar, submeter a processo industrial; beneficiar (produtos agrícolas, etc.); **process(ed) cheese,** queijo industrializado; *Cmptr:* **to process data,** processar dados; (*b*) *Adm: esp. Am:* **to process an application,** processar um requerimento.

processable, *a.* processável; **processable (data),** dados *mpl* processáveis.

processing, *n.* (*a*) *Ind:* tratamento *m* (de matéria-prima, etc.); beneficiamento (de produtos agrícolas); **processing industry,** indústria *f* de beneficiamento, indústria de transformação; **chemical processing,** tratamento químico; (*b*) *Cmptr:* **data processing, information processing,** processamento *m* (de dados); **batch processing,** processamento em bateladas; **serial processing,** processamento em série; (*c*) *Adm: esp. Am:* processamento (de requerimentos, etc.).

processor, *n.* (*a*) *Ind:* técnico *m* de beneficiamento, técnico em tratamento (de matéria-prima, etc.); operário *m* da indústria alimentícia; (*b*) *Cmptr:* (**data**) **processor,** computador *m*; (*c*) *Adm: esp. Am:* funcionário encarregado de processamento (de requerimentos, etc.).

procuration, *n.* (*a*) (i) negociação *f*, (ii) obtenção *f*, (de empréstimo para alguém); (*b*) comissão *f* de abertura (de crédito), comissão para negociação de empréstimo.

procurator, *n. Jur:* procurador *m*, mandatário *m.*

procure, *v.tr.* obter, conseguir, adquirir.
procurement, *n.* (*a*) obtenção *f*, consecução *f*, aquisição *f*; (*b*) *Adm: esp. Am:* (i) abastecimento *m*, suprimento *m*, (ii) serviço *m* de fornecimento; **procurement time,** prazo *m* para fornecimento; *Am:* **procurement clerk,** encarregado *m* de compras; **procurement staff,** compradores *mpl* (de uma empresa).
produce¹, *n.* produtos *mpl* agrícolas; **inland, home, produce,** produtos agrícolas nacionais; **foreign produce,** produtos agrícolas do exterior; **raw produce,** matérias-primas *fpl* (agrícolas); **market garden produce,** produtos hortigranjeiros; **produce broker,** corretor *m* de produtos agrícolas; **produce trade,** comércio *m* de produtos agrícolas.
produce², *v.tr.* 1. apresentar, mostrar, *Jur:* exibir, (documentos, etc.); **he can produce all the necessary documents,** ele pode fornecer todos os documentos necessários; **to produce evidence,** fornecer provas. 2. *Ind:* produzir, fabricar, manufaturar, (carros, máquinas, etc.); **mass-produced goods,** mercadorias produzidas em série, em massa. 3. render, produzir, (lucro, etc.); **the bonds produce a good income,** as obrigações produzem uma boa renda.
producer, *n.* produtor *m*, fabricante *mf*; **coffee producers,** produtores de café; **producer goods,** bens *mpl* de produção.
producing, 1. *a.* (*a*) produtor; **producing centre,** centro produtor; **producing country,** país produtor; **producing industry,** indústria produtora; **oil-producing countries,** países produtores de petróleo; (*b*) **producing capacity,** capacidade produtiva. 2. *n.* = production 1.
product, *n.* (*a*) produto *m*; *Ind:* **basic product,** produto de base; **beauty products,** produtos de beleza; **by-products,** produtos derivados; **end product,** produto final; **finished product,** produto acabado; **raw product,** produto primário; **semi-manufactured product,** produto semi-manifaturado; **waste products,** resíduos *mpl* de operação

fabril; **product advertising,** publicidade *f* de produto; **product analysis,** análise *f* de produtos; **product design,** projeto *m* de produto; (**new**) **product development,** desenvolvimento *m* de (novos) produtos; **product engineer,** engenheiro *m* de produto; **product image,** imagem *f* do produto; **product line,** linha *f* de produtos; **product manager,** gerente *mf* de produto; **product range,** gama *f* de produtos; (*b*) *Pol.Ec:* **gross national product (GNP),** produto nacional bruto (PNB); **net national product,** produto nacional líquido; **gross domestic product (GDP),** produto interno bruto (PIB).
production, *n.* 1. apresentação *f*, *Jur:* exibição *f*, (de documentos, etc.). 2. produção *f*, fabricação *f*, (de bens de consumo, etc.); **production to order,** produção sob encomenda; **drop in production,** queda *f* de produção; **rate of production,** taxa *f* de produção; **batch production,** produção em bateladas; **bulk production,** produção em grandes quantidades; **continuous flow production,** produção contínua; **mass production,** produção, fabricação, em série, fabricação em massa; **planned production,** produção planejada; **quantity production,** produção em quantidade; **production bonus,** prêmio *m* de produção, gratificação *f* por produção; **production car,** automóvel produzido em série; **production chart,** mapa *m*, gráfico *m*, de produção; **production costs,** custos *mpl*, gastos *mpl*, de produção, de fabricação; **production engineering,** engenharia *f* de produção; **production incentives,** incentivos *mpl* à produção; **production line,** linha *f* de produção, linha de montagem; **production machinery,** máquinas *fpl*, maquinismo *m*, maquinário *m*, maquinaria *f*, de produção; **production management,** gerência *f* de produção; **production manager,** gerente *mf*, chefe *mf*, de produção; **production plant,** usina *f*; **production surplus,** excesso *m* de produção; **production unit,** (i) unidade *f* de produção, (ii) equipe *f* de produção.
productive, *a.* (*a*) produtivo, produtor;

(*of capital, etc.*) rendoso; (*b*) *Pol.Ec:* (trabalho, etc.) produtivo.
productiveness, *n.* produtividade *f; Ind:* **productiveness of an enterprise,** rentabilidade *f* de uma empresa.
productivity, *n.* produtividade *f,* produtibilidade *f;* **productivity deal,** acordo *m* sobre produtividade; **raising, stepping up, of productivity,** aumento *m* de produtividade; **productivity bonus,** prêmio *m* de produção; **incentive pay for higher productivity,** incentivos *mpl* à produtividade; **productivity drive,** campanha *f* de produtividade.
profession, *n.* profissão *f;* **liberal profession,** profissão liberal.
professional, **1.** *a.* profissional; **professional practices,** práticas profissionais; **to take professional advice on a matter,** consultar um profissional sobre um assunto; **professional engineer,** profissional *mf* de engenharia; **the professional classes,** as classes profissionais. **2.** *n.* profissional *mf.*
professionalism, *n.* profissionalismo *m.*
professionalize, *v.tr.* & *i.* profissionalizar(-se).
professionally, *adv.* profissionalmente.
proficiency, *n.* competência *f,* habilidade *f,* proficiência *f;* **language proficiency test,** teste *m* de competência lingüística.
proficient, *a.* competente, hábil, proficiente; **candidates should be proficient in Portuguese,** os candidatos devem ter domínio da lingua portuguesa.
profile, *n.* perfil *m;* **company profile,** perfil de empresa; **customer profile,** perfil de freguesia; **market profile,** perfil de mercado.
profit¹, *n.* lucro *m,* benefício *m,* ganho *m;* **profit after taxation,** lucro líquido depois do imposto de renda; **profit before taxation,** lucro líquido antes do imposto de renda; **book profit,** lucro contábil, lucro segundo os livros; **capital profit,** lucro patrimonial; **clear profit,** lucro líquido; **gross profit,** lucro bruto; **net (operating) profit,** lucro (operacional) líquido; **trading profit,** lucro comercial; **profit balance,** saldo positivo; **profit centre,** centro *m* de lucro; **permanent**

profit flow, fluxo *m* permanente de lucros; **profit graph,** gráfico *m* de rentabilidade; **profit and loss,** lucros e perdas *fpl;* **profit and loss account,** conta *f* de lucros e perdas, demonstração *f* de resultados; **profit margin,** margem *f* de lucro; **profit optimization,** otimização *f* de lucro; **profit target,** lucro objetivado, objetivo *m* de lucro; **profits tax,** imposto *m* sobre os lucros; **profit-earning,** rentável; **profit-earning capacity,** rentabilidade *f;* **profit-making,** realização *f* de lucros; **profit-making association,** associação *f* com fins lucrativos; **non-profit-making association,** associação sem fins lucrativos; **profit-taking,** realização *f* de lucros (por especuladores); **profit-volume ratio,** razão *f* lucro/vendas; **to bring in, yield, show, a profit,** dar, apresentar, um lucro; render; **to make a profit on a sale,** lucrar com uma venda; obter, auferir, um lucro com uma venda; (*of company, etc.*) **to move into profit,** tornar-se rentável; **to work a mine at a profit,** explorar uma mina lucrativamente; **profit attributable to proprietors, to members,** saldo deixado à disposição da assembléia; **the profits from the sale of land,** os proventos da venda de terra; **profits on an estate,** rendimentos *mpl* de uma propriedade; *Ind:* **profit sharing (scheme),** (sistema *m* de) participação *f* nos lucros; **profit-sharing bond,** obrigação *f* com participação nos lucros; **profit-sharing employee,** empregado *m* que participa nos lucros; *Ins:* **with-profits policy,** apólice *f* com participação nos lucros; *Pol.Ec:* **profits system,** economia *f* de livre empresa.
profit², *v.* **1.** *v.tr.* beneficiar, favorecer, alguém. **2.** *v.i.* **to profit (from),** lucrar (com); auferir, obter, lucro (com); **to profit from the rise in the price of coffee,** lucrar com o aumento do preço de café.
profitability, *n.* rentabilidade *f,* lucratividade *f;* **profitability index,** índice *m* de lucratividade.
profitable, *a.* lucrativo, rendoso, rentável.
profiteer¹, *n.* explorador *m, F:* tubarão *m.*
profiteer², *v.i.* explorar, *F:* agir como tubarão.

profiteering, *n.* exploração *f.*
profitless, *a.* sem lucro; que não proporciona lucro.
pro forma, *n. & a.phr.* **pro-forma (invoice)**, fatura *f* pro-forma, fatura simulada.
programme[1], *Cmptr. & N.Am:* **program**, *n.* programa *m*; **research programme**, programa de pesquisa; **development programme**, programa de desenvolvimento; **investment programme**, programa de investimento(s); **training programme**, programa de treinamento; **to draw up, arrange, a programme**, estabelecer, elaborar, um programa; *Cmptr:* **source program**, programa-fonte *m*; *Cmptr:* **object program**, programa-objeto *m*.
programme[2], *Cmptr. & N.Am:* **program**, *v.tr.* programar; **programmed management**, administração programada.
programmer, *n. Cmptr:* programador *m*.
programming, *n. Cmptr:* programação *f*; **programming system**, sistema *m* de programação; **programming staff**, pessoal *m* de programação, quadro *m* de programadores; **programming manager**, gerente *mf* de programação.
progress[1], *n.* progresso *m*, andamento *m*, (de obra, campanha publicitária, etc.); **the work is now in progress**, o trabalho agora está em andamento; **the negotiations are making good progress**, as negociações estão progredindo, estão fazendo progresso; **progress report**, relatório *m* sobre o andamento (de uma obra, etc.); *Ind:* **progress chart**, gráfico *m* de andamento.
progress[2], *v.i.* progredir, fazer progresso, evoluir; **industry is progressing**, a indústria está progredindo, está evoluindo.
progression, *n.* progressão *f*; **salary progression curve**, curva *f* de aumento de salários.
progressive, *a.* progressivo; **by progressive stages**, por etapas progressivas; **progressive tax**, imposto progressivo; **progressive increase in taxation**, aumento progressivo de tributação; *Fin:* (*of interest*) **at a progressive rate**, a (uma) taxa progressiva.

prohibit, *v.tr.* proibir, vedar.
prohibition, *n.* proibição *f*, interdição *f*, vedação *f*; **export, import, prohibition**, proibição à exportação, à importação.
prohibitive, *a.* proibitivo; **prohibitive price**, preço proibitivo; *Cust: etc:* **prohibitive import tariffs**, tarifas proibitivas de importação.
project[1], *n.* projeto *m*, esquema *m*, empreendimento *m*, obra *f*; **to carry out a project**, executar um projeto; **project analysis**, análise *f* de projeto; **capital project evaluation**, avaliação *f* de projeto de investimento; **project management**, gerenciamento *m* de projetos, administração *f* de obras.
project[2], *v.tr.* projetar, prever, (resultados, etc.).
projection, *n.* projeção *f*, previsão *f*; **profit projection**, previsão dos lucros.
promise, *n.* promessa *f*; **promise to pay**, promessa de pagamento.
promissory, *a.* **promissary note**, (nota) promissória *f*; **promissory notes payable**, promissórias a pagar; **promissory note made out to bearer**, promissória ao portador; **promissory note made out to order**, promissória à ordem; **the maker and the payee of a promissory note**, o emitente e o beneficiário de uma promissória.
promote, *v.tr.* 1. **to promote the export manager to general manager**, promover o gerente de exportações a diretor geral. 2. (*a*) **to promote the success of a meeting**, promover o bom êxito de uma reunião; (*b*) **to promote sales of a new product**, promover vendas de (um) novo produto; (*c*) fundar, organizar, instalar, (uma sociedade por ações).
promoter, *n.* (*a*) promotor *m*; **sales promoter**, promotor de vendas; (*b*) **company promoter**, fundador *m*, organizador *m*, de sociedade por ações; *Fin:* **promoter's shares**, ações *fpl* de fundador, partes *fpl* de fundador, partes beneficiárias.
promotion, *n.* 1. promoção *f*, ascensão *f*; **promotion prospects**, perspectivas *fpl* de promoção, perspectivas de realização profissional; **promotion by seniority**, promoção por tempo de serviço. 2. (*a*)

promoção (de um novo produto, etc.);
sales promotion, promoção de vendas;
consumer promotion, promoção para
os consumidores; **trade promotion,**
promoção para os revendedores, para os
comerciantes; (*b*) fundação *f*, instalação
f, organização *f*, implantação *f*, (de
sociedade por ações); **promotion money,**
despesas *fpl* de organização, de
instalação, de implantação.
promotional, *a.* promocional; **promotional
campaign, sale,** campanha *f*, venda *f*,
promocional; **promotional material,**
material publicitário.
prompt, 1. *a.* (*a*) pronto, rápido, imediato;
prompt service, serviço rápido; **prompt
action,** medidas imediatas; **prompt
decision,** decisão imediata; **prompt reply,**
resposta imediata, pronta resposta; (*b*)
prompt cotton, prompt sugar, algodão *m*,
açúcar *m*, para entrega imediata, para
pronta entrega. **2.** *n.* prazo *m* (para
pagamento); **prompt note,** nota de venda
(indicando o prazo para pagamento);
prompt day, dia *m* de pagamento (de
títulos, etc.).
promptly, *adv.* prontamente,
imediatamente.
property, *n.* **1.** *Jur:* (**right or title to**)
property, (direito *m* de) propriedade *f*;
intellectual property, bens intelectuais;
literary property, propriedade literária. **2.**
(*a*) propriedade *f*, bens *mpl*, haveres *mpl*;
private property, propriedade privada,
propriedade particular; **public property,**
bens públicos, bens de domínio público;
landed property, propriedade rural; **city
property,** propriedade urbana; **personal
property,** bens móveis; **real property,** bens
imóveis, bens de raíz; **property tax,**
imposto *m* predial e territorial; **damage to
property,** dano *m* a propriedade; (*b*) (i)
imóvel *m*, prédio *m*, (ii) terra *f*; '**property
for sale',** 'vende-se imóvel'; '**property to
let',** 'aluga-se imóvel'; **property developer,**
empresário *m* de imóveis; **property
(development) company,** imobiliária *f*;
property investment, investimento
imobiliário; **property market,** mercado
imobiliário.
proportion¹, *n.* **1.** proporção *f*; **to divide**

expenses in equal proportions, ratear
despesas igualmente, dividir despesas em
partes iguais; **to pay one's proportion of
the expenses,** pagar a sua cota-parte das
despesas. **2.** (*a*) proporção, razão *f*; *Nau:*
**proportion of the net load to the dead
load,** razão entre a carga líquida e o peso
morto; (*b*) **in proportion to sth.,** em
proporção a, com, algo.
proportion², *v.tr.* to **proportion one's
expenditure to one's profits,** proporcionar
as despesas com os lucros.
proportional, *a.* proporcional (**to,** a);
proportional scale, escala *f* proporcional;
Adm: **proportional tax,** imposto *m*
proporcional.
proportionally, *adv.* to **divide expenses
proportionally,** reatear despesas.
proportionment, *n.* rateio *m*, rateamento
m, (de despesas).
proposal, *n.* proposta *f*, oferta *f*; **proposals
for ...,** propostas para ...; **to make a
proposal,** apresentar uma proposta; **he
put forward a proposal for a wage
increase,** ele apresentou uma proposta de
aumento de salário; *Ins:* **proposal of
insurance,** minuta *f* de seguro, proposta
de contrato de seguro.
propose, *v.tr.* (*a*) propor; **the chairman
proposed that the meeting should be
adjourned,** o presidente propôs, sugeriu,
que a reunião fosse suspensa; (*b*) **to
propose a candidate,** propor, apresentar,
um candidato; **to propose a motion,**
apresentar, submeter, uma moção, uma
proposta.
proposer, *n.* proponente *mf*; apresentador
m (de moção).
proposition, *n.* (*a*) proposição *f*, proposta
f; (*b*) *F:* negócio *m*; **it's a big proposition,**
é um negócio, é um negociarrão; **paying
proposition,** negócio rentável.
proprietary, *a.* (*a*) **proprietary product,**
produto patenteado, produto fabricado
pelo detentor do direito exclusivo de
fabricação; **proprietary right,** direito
exclusivo de fabricação; (*b*) **proprietary
company,** companhia fechada;
companhia com cinco (ou menos) sócios.
proprietor, *n.* (*a*) proprietário *m*;
proprietor of a restaurant, dono *m* de

restaurante; **proprietor of a hotel, hotel proprietor,** hoteleiro *m,* dono de hotel; (*b*) **proprietors of a company,** proprietários, acionistas *mpl,* sócios *mpl* de uma companhia, de uma empresa; *Fin:* **proprietors' equity,** patrimônio líquido, patrimônio próprio, situação líquida.

proprietorship, *n.* **1.** (direito *m* de) propriedade *f.* **2.** *Fin:* patrimônio líquido, patrimônio próprio, situação líquida. **3.** (*of business*) firma *f* individual, empresa *f* individual.

pro rata, *adv. & a.phr.* pro rata; **pro rata distribution,** rateio *m,* rateamento *m,* rateação *f.*

prorate, *v.tr. Fin:* ratear (despesas, etc.).

prospect, *n.* perspectiva *f,* expectativa *f;* **market prospects,** perspectivas de mercado, perspectivas comerciais; **career prospects,** perspectivas profissionais; **wage prospects,** perspectivas salariais; *Fin:* (*of shares*) **earning prospects,** perspectivas de rentabilidade.

prospective, *a.* **prospective buyer,** comprador *m* provável.

prospectus, *n.* prospeto *m* (de companhia em organização); *Fin:* **prospectus issue,** oferta pública de ações, emissão *f* de títulos sob regime de subscrição pública.

protect, *v.tr.* **1.** (*a*) proteger, defender; **to protect domestic industries against cheap imports,** proteger as indústrias nacionais contra as importações baratas; **to protect the interests of the company,** proteger, defender, os interesses da companhia; (*b*) *Pol.Ec:* proteger (uma indústria, o comércio de uma nação, etc.). **2.** (*a*) *Fin:* **to protect a bill of exchange,** fornecer fundos para o pagamento de uma letra de câmbio; (*b*) *St.Exch:* **to protect a book,** cobrir uma posição. **3.** *Ins:* **to be protected against fire,** ter seguro contra incêndio.

protection, *n.* (*a*) proteção *f,* defesa *f,* amparo *m,* (**against,** contra); **consumer protection,** proteção ao consumidor, defesa *f* do consumidor; (*b*) *Pol.Ec:* proteção *f;* (*c*) *Ins:* cobertura *f.*

protectionism, *n. Pol.Ec:* protecionismo *m.*

protectionist, *n. & a. Pol.Ec:* protecionista (*mf*).

protective, *a.* protetor; *Pol.Ec:* **protective tariff,** tarifa *f* protecionista.

protest¹, *n.* (*a*) protesto *m,* protestação *f,* reclamação *f;* **to make a protest against,** protestar contra (algo); **to make a written protest,** fazer um protesto por escrito, protestar por escrito; **protest meeting,** reunião *f* de protesto; (*b*) *Fin: etc:* protesto (de letra de câmbio); **acceptance under protest,** aceite *m* sob protesto; **payment under protest,** pagamento *m* sob protesto; **protest for non-acceptance,** protesto por recusa de aceite; **non-payment and protest,** protesto por falta de pagamento; **to note a protest,** notar um protesto; (*c*) *Nau:* **ship's protest,** protesto marítimo.

protest², *v.* **1.** *v.tr.* **to protest a bill,** protestar uma letra, mandar uma letra a protesto. **2.** *v.i.* protestar, reclamar, (**against,** contra).

protestable, *a. Fin:* **protestable bill,** letra *f* protestável.

protested, *a. Fin:* protestado; **protested bill,** letra protestada.

protester, protestor, *n. Fin:* aquele que requer o protesto.

prototype, *n.* protótipo *m.*

prove, *v.* **1.** *v.tr.* (*a*) provar, comprovar, demonstrar, (a verdade de um fato, etc.); (*b*) **to prove claims in bankruptcy,** verificar os créditos (em falência). **2.** *v.i.* **the document proved to be a forgery,** provou-se que o documento era uma falsificação.

provide, *v.* **1.** *v.i.* **to provide against accidents,** prevenir-se, precaver-se, contra acidentes; **to provide for the expenses,** prover às despesas, providenciar às despesas; **this purchase is provided for in the budget,** esta compra está prevista no orçamento; **to provide for a bill,** fornecer os fundos para o pagamento de uma letra; *Ins:* **this risk is not provided for in the policy,** este risco não está coberto na apólice. **2.** *v.tr.* (*a*) estipular (**that,** que + *subj.*)*;* **the contract provides that all payments shall be made in Brazilian currency,** o contrato estipula que todos os pagamentos sejam feitos em moeda brasileira; (*b*) fornecer, prover, suprir, abastecer; **to provide the factory with**

spare parts, fornecer sobressalentes para a fábrica; **to provide all necessary information**, fornecer, proporcionar, todas as informações necessárias; **to provide a service**, prestar um serviço; *Fin:* **to provide a bill with acceptance**, providenciar o aceite de uma letra.
provision, *n.* 1. (*a*) **provision for, against, sth.**, providência *f* para, contra, algo; **we have made provisions to this effect**, tomamos providências neste sentido; (*b*) **provision of capital**, fornecimento *m* de capital. 2. (*a*) *Fin:* **provision for doubtful debts**, provisão *f*, previsão *f*, para devedores duvidosos; **provision for depreciation**, provisão para depreciação, fundo *m* de depreciação; (*b*) *pl.* **provisions**, provisões, provimentos *mpl*, mantimentos *mpl*, víveres *mpl*; **wholesale provisions business**, casa *f* de abastecimentos por atacado, armazém *m* de secos e molhados por atacado. 3. (*in contract*) cláusula *f*, estipulação *f*, condição *f*; **there is no provision to the contrary**, não há cláusula contrária.
provisional, *a.* provisório, interino, provisional; **provisional duties**, funções provisórias, interinas; **provisional agreement**, acordo provisório; **provisional driving licence**, licença provisória para guiar automóvel, *F:* papagaio *m.*
provisionally, *adv.* provisoriamente, provisionalmente; **to sign a contract provisionally**, assinar um contrato provisoriamente.
proviso, *n.* cláusula *f*, estipulação *f*, condição *f*; **with the proviso that**, sob condição de que, contanto que, desde que, + *subj.*
provisory, *a.* provisório, provisional, condicional.
proxy, *n. Jur:* (*a*) procuração *f*; (*b*) (*person*) procurador *m*, mandatário *m.*
psychology, *n.* psicologia *f*; **industrial psychology**, psicologia industrial; **economic psychology**, psicologia econômica.
public, 1. *a.* (*a*) **public authorities**, poder público; **public conveyance**, veículo *m* de transporte coletivo; **public expenditure**, despesas públicas, gastos públicos; **public**

finances, finanças públicas, fazenda *f*; **public holiday**, feriado público, dia feriado; **public image (of product)**, imagem *f* de marca (de produto); **public official**, funcionário público; **public opinion poll**, sondagem *f* de opinião pública; **public relations (PR)**, relações públicas; **public sector**, setor público; **public sector borrowing requirement (PSBR)**, necessidade *f* de empréstimos no setor público; **public transport**, transporte(s) coletivo(s); **public utility company**, **public service company**, empresa *f* de serviços de utilidade pública; *UK:* **public corporation**, empresa pública, empresa governamental; *Am:* **certified public accountant** = perito-contador *m*; *Jur:* **public domain**, domínio público; *Jur:* **public prosecutor**, promotor público; (*b*) **public company**, sociedade anônima de capital aberto, companhia *f* de capital aberto; **public limited company** = sociedade anônima de capital aberto; (*of company*) **to go public**, tornar-se de capital aberto, tornar-se uma companhia de capital aberto; *Fin:* **public offer**, oferta pública de ações. 2. *n.* (*a*) **the (general) public**, o (grande) público; *Fin:* **to issue shares to the public**, emitir ações sob regime de subscrição pública; (*b*) **in public**, em público.
publicity, *n.* publicidade *f*; **publicity campaign**, campanha publicitária, campanha de publicidade; **advance publicity**, publicidade antecipada; **publicity department**, departamento *m* de publicidade; **publicity man**, publicitário *m*; **publicity account**, conta *f* de publicidade; **publicity expenses**, despesas *fpl* com publicidade; **publicity bureau**, **agency**, agência *f* de publicidade.
publicize, *v.tr.* publicar, divulgar, dar publicidade a, (um produto, etc.).
puff¹, *n.* reclame exagerado.
puff², *v.tr.* fazer propaganda exagerada de (um produto).
pull down, *v.tr.* **to pull down prices**, abaixar os preços.
punch, *v.tr. Cmptr: etc:* perfurar; **punched card**, cartão perfurado, ficha *f.*
punt, *v.i. F:* especular na bolsa de valores.

punter, *n. F:* (*a*) bolsista *mf*, especulador *m*; (*b*) freguês *m*.

purchase¹, *n.* compra *f*, aquisição *f*, merca *f*; **cash purchase, purchase for cash,** compra à vista; **credit purchase, purchase on credit,** compra a crédito, compra a prazo; **hire purchase,** compra a prestação, compra a prazo; **hire purchase scheme, hire purchase system,** crediário *m*, facilitário *m*, sistema *m* de compra a prestação; **terms of purchase,** condições *fpl* de compra; **purchase book,** livro *m* de compras, (livro-)registro *m* de compras; **purchase contract, purchase agreement,** contrato *m* de compra e venda; **purchase discount,** desconto *m* sobre compra; **purchase journal,** diário *m* de compras; **purchase money, purchase price,** preço de compra, preço de aquisição; **purchase order,** ordem *f* de compra, pedido *m* de compra; **purchase requistition,** requisição *f* de compra; **purchase tax** = Imposto *m* de Circulação de Mercadorias (ICM); **to buy a television on hire purchase,** comprar uma televisão a prazo, a prestação; comprar uma televisão pelo crediário, pelo facilitário; **to make some purchases,** fazer algumas compras; *Fin:* **forward exchange purchase,** compra *f* de câmbio futura; **spot exchange purchase,** compra de câmbio imediata; *St.Exch:* **bull purchase,** compra a descoberto (por especulador que espera uma alta no mercado); *St.Exch:* **purchase for the settlement,** compra a termo; *Jur:* renda *f* (de terras, etc.).

purchase², *v.tr. & i.* comprar, adquirir, mercar; **to purchase sth. for cash,** comprar alguma coisa à vista; **to purchase sth. on credit,** comprar alguma coisa a crédito, a prazo; comprar alguma coisa fiado.

purchaser, *n.* comprador *m*, adquirente *mf*; (*at auction*) arrematante *mf*, arrematador *m*.

purchasing, 1. *a. Jur:* **purchasing party,** parte compradora; (*at auction*) parte arrematante, parte arrematadora. **2.** *n.* compra *f*, aquisição *f*; **purchasing costs,** gastos *mpl*, custos *mpl*, de aquisição; **purchasing manager,** gerente *mf* de compras; **purchasing department,** departamento *m* de compras; **purchasing agent,** agente *mf* de compras; *Pol.Ec:* **purchasing power,** poder aquisitivo, poder de compra.

pure, *a.* **pure gold,** ouro fino; *Ins:* **pure premium,** prêmio líquido.

pursuance, *n. Jur:* **in pursuance of the terms of the contract,** em conformidade com as condições do contrato.

push, *v.tr.* (*a*) promover a venda (de mercadorias); lançar (uma moda, um produto); (*b*) *St.Exch:* **to push shares,** colocar títulos duvidosos.

push-button, *a. see* **press-button.**

push down, *v.tr.* **to push down prices,** forçar uma baixa nos preços.

push up, *v.tr.* **to push up prices,** forçar um aumento de preços, um aumento nos preços.

put¹, *n. St.Exch:* **put (option),** opção *f* do vendedor; **put and call,** dupla opção.

put², *v.tr.* **1.** pôr, colocar; **to put an article on the market,** colocar um artigo no mercado; **to put a new product on the market,** lançar um novo produto no mercado; **to put an advertisement in the paper,** colocar um anúncio no jornal; **to put one's signature to a contract,** apor a assinatura a um contrato; **to put numbers on packages,** numerar, pôr números em, pacotes; **to put an amount in the receipts, in the expenditure,** lançar uma quantia na conta de receitas, na conta de despesas; **to put a tax on goods,** tributar, taxar, mercadorias. **2. to put a resolution to the meeting,** submeter uma proposta à assembléia; **to put a resolution to the vote,** submeter uma proposta a votação.

put in, *v.tr.* **to put in a bid,** apresentar uma proposta; **to put in a pay claim,** apresentar uma reivindicação salarial.

put up, *v.tr.* **1. to put up the prices,** (i) aumentar, elevar, majorar, os preços, (ii) provocar uma subida de preços, fazer subir os preços. **2. to put up money for a venture,** (i) pôr, colocar, investir, dinheiro num empreendimento, (ii) fornecer os fundos para um empreendimento. **3. put up in tubes,** embalado em tubos.

Q

quadruple¹, *a. & n.* quádruplo (*m*); **profits quadruple those, (the) quadruple of those, of the previous year,** lucros *mpl* quatro vezes maiores que os do ano anterior.
quadruple², *v.* **1.** *v.tr.* quadruplicar, redobrar, reduplicar. **2.** *v.i.* quadruplicar(-se).
quadruplicate¹, **1.** *a.* quádruplo, quadruplicado; **quadruplicate copy,** quarta via. **2.** *n.* **in quadruplicate,** em quatro vias.
quadruplicate², *v.tr.* **1.** quadruplicar. **2.** fazer em quatro vias.
quadrupling, *n.* quadruplicação *f.*
qualification, *n.* **1.** reserva *f*, ressalva *f*, restrição *f*; **to accept without qualification,** aceitar (i) sem reserva, (ii) sem condições. **2.** requisito *m*, habilitação *f*, qualificação *f*; **the qualifications for the job,** as qualificações para o cargo; **to have the necessary qualifications for the job,** ter as qualificações necessárias para o cargo, preencher os requisitos necessários para o cargo; **candidates should bring their qualifications with them,** os candidatos deverão comparecer munidos dos seus diplomas; **professional qualification,** diploma *m* profissional. **3. qualification shares,** ações *fpl* de garantia (de gestão).
qualified, *a.* **1.** (*a*) qualificado, habilitado; **to be qualified for the job,** preencher os requisitos exigidos pelo cargo; **qualified engineer,** engenheiro qualificado; **he's not qualified to drive the lorry,** ele não está habilitado para dirigir o caminhão; **qualified staff,** pessoal qualificado; (*b*) autorizado, competente. **2. qualified approval,** aprovação *f* sob reserva(s), aprovação com ressalvas; **qualified acceptance,** aceitação *f* condicional, (*of bill of exchange*) aceite *m* condicional.

qualify, *v.* **1.** *v.tr.* (*a*) **to qualify s.o. for (doing) sth., to do sth.,** habilitar alguém para, a, fazer algo; *Jur:* autorizar, apacitar, alguém a fazer algo; **to qualify oneself for a job,** conseguir as qualificações necessárias para um emprego; (*b*) fazer reservas, ressalvas, (quanto a uma aprovação, etc.). **2.** *v.i.* conseguir as qualificações necessárias (**for sth.,** para algo).
qualifying, *a.* **1.** (*a*) qualificativo, qualificador; **qualifying exam,** prova *f*, concurso *m*, de habilitação; **qualifying certificate,** certificado *m* de habilitação; (*b*) *Fin:* **qualifying shares,** ações *fpl* de garantia (de gestão). **2.** restritivo; **qualifying statement,** declaração restritiva, declaração modificativa.
quality, *n.* (*a*) qualidade *f*; (*degree of excellence*) **of good, high, quality,** de qualidade superior, de alta categoria, de alto gabarito; **of poor quality,** de qualidade inferior; **of the best quality,** de primeira qualidade, categoria, classe; (*b*) (*excellence*) **quality goods,** mercadorias *fpl* de qualidade, de categoria; **quality newspaper,** jornal *m* de categoria; *Ind:* **quality control,** controle *m* de qualidade.
quantify, *v.tr.* quantificar.
quantity, *n.* (*a*) quantidade *f*, porção *f*; **a small quantity of...,** uma pequena quantidade, porção, de...; **a (large) quantity of...,** uma (grande) quantidade, porção, de...; **marketable quantity of shares,** quantidade negociável de ações; **to buy sth. in large quantities,** comprar algo em grandes quantidades; **quantity discount,** desconto *m* por quantidade, desconto quantitativo; *Cust:* **the quantity permitted,** a quantidade permitida (de cigarros, bebidas alcoólicas, etc.); *Ind:* **quantity production,**

quart

quota

produção *f* em quantidade, produção em série; **economic production quantity,** quantidade econômica de produção; **econ..mic order quantity,** quantidade que torna uma encomenda econômica; *Pol.Ec:* **quantity theory of money,** teoria quantitativa da moeda; **quantity theorist,** partidário *m* da teoria quantitativa da moeda; (*b*) *Const:* **quantity surveyor,** calculista *mf* de obra; **bill of quantities** = planilha *f* (de preços).

quart, *n. Meas:* quarta *f* (**English quart** = 1,136 litro; **American liquid quart** = 0,946 litro; **American dry quart** = 1,101 litro).

quarter, *n.* **1.** quarto *m*, quarta parte; **three-quarters,** três-quartos; **three and a quarter,** três e um quarto; **a quarter (of a pound) of coffee,** um quarto (de uma libra) de café; **it's a quarter cheaper,** é um quarto mais barato. **2.** trimestre *m*; **to be paid by the quarter,** a ser pago por trimestres, em prestações trimestrais, em trimestralidades; **quarter's rent,** aluguel *m* trimestral; **quarter day,** dia *m* em que se faz pagamento trimestral.

quarterly, 1. *a.* trimestral, trimestre, trimensal; **quarterly salary,** salário *m* trimestral; **quarterly subscription,** assinatura *f* trimestral. **2.** *n.* publicação trimestral. **3.** *adv.* trimestralmente.

quasi, *a.* quase; **quasi contract,** quase-contrato *m*; **quasi money (ratio),** (índice *m* de) quase-moeda *f*.

quay, *n.* cais *m*, molhe *m;* **ship moored alongside the quay,** navío atracado ao cais; **quay berth,** atracadouro *m*; (*of goods*) **ex quay,** posto no cais, desembarcado.

quayage, *n.* **1.** direito *m* de cais, taxa *f* de atracagem. **2.** acostagem *f*, acomodação *f*, no cais.

quayside, *n.* terreno situado ao lado do cais; **quayside worker,** estivador *m*; **quayside crane,** guindaste portuário.

query¹, *n.* **if you have any queries, please get in touch,** se tiver alguma pergunta, entre em contato conosco.

query², *v.* **1.** *v.i.* **to query if, whether,...,** perguntar se.... **2.** *v.tr.* **to query a decision,** questionar uma decisão.

question¹, *n.* questão *f*, pergunta *f*; **the matter in question,** o assunto em questão, em apreço, em discussão; **the scheme is out of the question,** a projeto está fora de cogitação; **it is a question of good planning,** é uma questão de bom planejamento; **the question arose whether...,** surgiu a questão de saber se...; **to call into question,** pôr em dúvida, questionar, (um projeto, etc.).

question², *v.tr.* **1. to question the employees,** interrogar, perguntar, os empregados (sobre algo). **2.** questionar (um plano, etc.).

questionnaire, *n.* questionário *m*; **to fill in a questionnaire,** preencher um questionário.

quick, *a.* rápido; **quick sale,** venda rápida; **quick returns,** lucros rápidos; **quick recovery,** recuperação rápida; *Fin:* **quick assets,** valores *mpl* realizáveis imediatamente.

quid, *n. UK: F:* libra (esterlina); **he earns ninety quid a week,** ele ganha noventa libras por semana.

quid pro quo, *n. Pol.Ec:* permuta *f*; compensação *f*.

quiet, *a.* **quiet market,** mercado calmo.

quietus, *n.* quitação *f* (de obrigação, de dívida).

quit, *v.tr.* **1. to quit a job,** deixar um emprego; **to quit a rented flat,** desocupar um apartamento alugado; *Jur:* **notice to quit,** aviso *m* para desocupar um imóvel. **2.** quitar, liberar, alguém (de uma dívida).

quits, *a. F:* **he is quits with his creditors,** ele está quite com seus credores.

quittance, *n.* (*a*) quitação *f*; (*b*) (recibo *m* de) quitação.

quorum, *n.* quorum *m*; **to form, constitute, a quorum,** formar um quorum.

quota, *n.* (*a*) cota *f*, cota-parte *f*, quota *f*, quota-parte *f*; **to contribute one's quota,** pagar, contribuir com, sua cota-parte; (*b*) cota, quota, contingente *m*; **sales quota,** cota de vendas; (*c*) **quota sampling,** amostragem *f* por cotas; (*d*) (taxa *f* de) contingenciamento *m*; **quota system (of distribution),** contingenciamento *m*; **import quotas,** contingentes, cotas, de importação; **to apportion, fix, quotas for imports,** estabelecer cotas de importação.

quotable, *a.* (título *m*) cotizável, quotizável.

quotation, *n.* (*a*) *St.Exch: etc:* cotação *f*, preço *m*, curso *m*; **the latest quotations,** os últimos preços, as últimas cotações; **opening quotations,** cotações *fpl* de abertura; **closing quotations,** cotações de fechamento; **stock admitted to quotation,** ações admitidas à cotação; (*b*) *Ind: etc:* **quotation for the supply of ingots,**

proposta *f* de preço para o fornecimento de lingotes.

quote¹, *n. F:* = **quotation** (*b*).

quote², *v.tr.* **1.** *Adm:* **please quote references,** favor mencionar as referências. **2.** (*a*) propor (preço, etc.); **to quote a price for the supply of screws,** propor um preço para o fornecimento de parafusos; (*b*) *St.Exch:* cotar (ações, etc.); **shares quoted at 90p,** ações cotadas a noventa penies; **stock officially quoted,** valores registrados.

quotient, *n.* quociente *m*, coeficiente *m*.

R

rack, *n.* **1. rack rent,** aluguel *m* exorbitante. **2.** *Am:* **rack jobber,** atacadista especializado no fornecimento de produtos não alimentícios para redes de supermercados.

racket, *n. F:* negociata *f*, mamata *f*, papata *f*.

raid¹, *n. St.Exch:* **raid (on the market),** corrida *f* (na bolsa); venda de ações combinada por especuladores para provocar uma baixa no mercado; *Fin:* **dawn raid,** aquisição repentina de controle de uma companhia.

raid², *v.tr.* **to raid the market,** invadir o mercado (de um concorrente); *St.Exch:* combinar a venda de determinadas ações para provocar uma baixa no mercado.

rail, *n.* estrada *f* de ferro, ferrovia *f*, linha férrea; (*of goods*) **free on rail,** franco sobre vagão; **rail transport,** transporte ferroviário; **to send goods by rail,** expedir mercadorias por via férrea; **rail traffic,** trânsito, tráfego, ferroviário; **rail (freight) charges,** fretes ferroviários.

railage, *n. UK:* (i) transporte ferroviário, (ii) frete ferroviário.

railroad, *n. N.Am:* estrada *f* de ferro, ferrovia *f*, linha férrea.

railway, *n.* estrada *f* de ferro, ferrovia *f*, linha férrea; **railway station,** estação ferroviária; **delivery at railway station,** entrega *f* na estação ferroviária; **railway guide, timetable,** horário *m* dos trens; **railway transport,** transporte ferroviário, transporte por via férrea; **railway traffic,** trânsito, tráfego, ferroviário; **railway parcels service,** serviço ferroviário de encomendas; **works with railway facilities,** usina *f* com instalações ferroviárias; **railway system,** rede ferroviária; *Fin:* **railway shares,** ações *fpl*

das ferrovias; **railway stock,** títulos *mpl* das empresas ferroviárias.

raise¹, *n. F: & N.Am:* aumento *m* (de salário).

raise², *v.tr.* **1. to raise a question,** levantar uma questão. **2.** (*increase*) **to raise the price of coffee,** aumentar, majorar, elevar, o preço do café; **to raise the value of the pound,** valorizar a libra esterlina, aumentar o valor da libra esterlina; **to raise s.o.'s salary,** aumentar o salário de alguém; *N.Am:* **to raise a cheque,** aumentar (fraudulentamente) o valor de um cheque. **3.** (*a*) **to raise money,** levantar dinheiro; **how much can you raise at the bank?** quanto é que você pode levantar no banco? **to raise funds by subscription,** conseguir fundos mediante subscrição; **to raise money on an estate,** levantar dinheiro mediante hipoteca de uma propriedade; (*b*) **to raise taxes,** estabelecer impostos. **4. to raise a ban,** levantar uma proibição. **5. to raise cattle,** criar gado.

raising, *n.* aumento *m*, majoração *f*, elevação *f*, (de preços, tarifas, etc.); **the raising of the minimum lending rate,** o aumento da taxa mínima de empréstimos.

rake in, *v.tr. F:* **to rake in the money,** fazer muito dinheiro, faturar.

rake off, *v.tr. F:* tirar (uma porcentagem, etc.).

rake-off, *n. F:* percentagem *f*, porcentagem *f*, comissão *f*, (ilícita ou não); **to get a rake-off on all business with Brazilian firms,** perceber uma comissão sobre todos os negócios fechados com firmas brasileiras.

rally¹, *n.* revigoramento *m* (de preços, ações).

180

rally², *v.i. St.Exch:* (*of shares, prices, etc.*) revigorar(-se). **rallying**, *n.* revigoramento *m* (de preços, etc.). **random**, **1.** *n.* **to choose sth. at random,** escolher algo no acaso, a esmo. **2.** *a.* (*a*) *Mkt:* **random sample,** amostra aleatória; **random sampling,** amostragem aleatória; *Stat:* **random test,** amostra tirada a esmo; **random error,** erro *m* acidental; (*b*) *Ind: etc:* **random lengths,** comprimentos diversos. **range¹**, *n.* (*a*) **price range,** faixa *f* de preços; **within a range of . . .,** dentro de uma faixa de . . .; **range of products,** gama *f* de produtos; **salary range,** faixa salarial; **the shop has a wide range of goods,** a loja tem um grande sortimento, uma grande variedade de mercadorias; **the supermarket has a wide range,** é um supermercado sortido; (*b*) **the range of an advertising campaign,** o campo, o âmbito, de uma campanha publicitária; **this firm extended the range of its activities,** esta firma ampliou seu campo de ação, seu âmbito de ação. **range²**, *v.i.* **incomes ranging from $10 000 to $12 000,** rendas *fpl* (que estão) na faixa de $10.000 a $12.000. **rank¹**, *n.* **1. the rank and file of the workers,** a massa do operariado. **2.** categoria *f,* classe *f* social; **the higher ranks of the civil service,** os altos funcionários, os funcionários públicos de alto nível. **3.** *Fin: etc:* ordem *f,* classe *f,* (de crédito, hipoteca, etc.). **rank²**, *v.* **1.** *v.tr. Jur:* **to rank creditors (in bankruptcy),** classificar os credores em ordem prioritária. **2.** *v.i.* (*a*) (*of creditor, claimant, etc.*) **to rank after s.o.,** ser classificado após alguém (na ordem de prioridade); **to rank before s.o.,** ter prioridade, preferência, sobre alguém; **to rank equally with s.o.,** ter a mesma classificação que alguém (com relação a outros credores, etc.); (*b*) *Jur:* (*of claim in bankruptcy*) ser admitido na verificação de créditos; **to rank after sth.,** ser classificado após algo (na ordem de prioridade); **to rank before sth.,** ter prioridade, preferência, sobre algo; **to**

rank equally (with sth.), ter a mesma classificação (que algo); **preference shares of all issues shall rank equally,** as ações preferenciais de todas as emissões terão a mesma classificação; **shares that rank first in dividend rights,** ações que dão ao seu possuidor prioridade no recebimento de dividendos. **ranking**, *n.* **1.** classificação *f* (dos credores, etc.) em ordem de prioridade. **2.** hierarquia *f* (em empresa, organização, etc.). **ratable**, *a.* = **rateable.** **rate¹**, *n.* **1.** (*a*) taxa *f,* razão *f; rate of decline, decrease,* taxa de decréscimo, de diminuição; **rate of domestic investment,** taxa de investimento interno; **rate of increase,** taxa de aumento; **rate of turnover,** taxa de rotação, taxa de giro, (de mercadorias, de capitais); **rate per cent,** percentagem *f,* porcentagem *f;* **hourly rate,** salário-hora *m;* **prevailing rate of pay,** nível *m* predominante de salário; **standard wage rate,** salário-base *m;* **starting rate,** salário inicial; **at the rate of ten a minute,** à razão de dez por minuto; **at the rate of £3 an hour,** à razão de três libras horárias, por hora; **at the present rate of growth,** à taxa atual de crescimento; **to pay s.o. at the rate of $200 a week,** pagar alguém à razão de $200 por semana, à base de $200 semanais; (*b*) **things are progressing at an extraordinary rate,** as coisas estão avançando com extraordinária rapidez. **2.** *Fin: Adm: etc:* taxa *f;* **rates for money on loan, money rates,** custo *m,* preço *m,* do dinheiro; **rate of discount,** taxa de desconto; **rate of exchange,** taxa de câmbio; **rate of interest,** taxa de juros; **(expected) rate of return,** taxa (esperada) de retorno; **bank rate,** taxa bancária; **buying rate,** taxa de compra; **inter-bank rate,** taxa inter-bancária; **market discount rate,** taxa de desconto no mercado livre; **minimum lending rate (MLR),** *Am:* **prime (lending) rate,** taxa mínima de empréstimos; **multiple exchange rates,** taxas múltiplas de cambio; **selling rate,** taxa de venda; *Adm:* **rate of income tax,** alíquota *f* de imposto de renda; *St.Exch:*

backwardation rate, taxa de deporte; **contango rate,** taxa de reporte; **demand, sight, rate,** taxa à vista, curso *m* à vista; **forward rate,** taxa a termo, curso a termo. **3.** tarifa *f*, preço *m*, (de transporte, etc.); **rate-fixing,** tarifação *f*, taxação *f*; **commission rates,** taxas de comissão; **fixed rate,** tarifa fixa; **flat rate,** tarifa única; **hotel rates,** preços *mpl* de hotel, preços hoteleiros; **special rate,** tarifa especial; **standard rate,** tarifa global; *Post:* **postage, postal, rates,** tarifa postal; **cable rates,** tarifa para telegramas; **inland rates,** tarifa para correspondência destinada a um lugar no país; **letter rates,** tarifa para correspondência postal; **newspaper rate,** tarifa para remessa de jornais; **overseas rates,** tarifa para remessa de correspondência para o exterior; **parcel rates,** tarifa para remessa de colis postaux; **printed paper rate,** tarifa para remessa de impressos; **telex rates to Brazil,** tarifa de telex para o Brasil, tarifa para transmissão de telex para o Brasil; *Cust:* **preferential rates,** tarifa preferencial; *Trans:* **flat mileage rate,** frete fixo por quilômetro rodado; *Rail:* **(passenger or freight) rates,** tarifa ferroviária; **freight rates,** fretes ferroviários; **to fix the rates to be charged,** tarifar, fixar os preços por tarifa. **4.** *UK: Adm:* **rates** = taxas municipais, baseadas no valor locativo do imóvel taxado; **water rate,** taxa de água; **to put a rate on a building,** taxar um imóvel na base do seu valor locativo.

rate², *v.tr.* **1.** avaliar (algo), fixar o valor (de algo). **2.** taxar, tarifar; **to rate a property at a certain sum,** taxar um imóvel em uma certa quantia baseada no seu valor locativo; *Ins:* **to rate s.o. up,** aumentar o prêmio de alguém.

rateable, *a.* avaliável; *UK: Adm:* taxável; **rateable value of a property,** valor locativo taxável, tributável, de um imóvel.

ratepayer, *n.* contribuinte *mf* de taxas municipais baseadas no valor locativo do imóvel taxado.

ratification, *n. Jur: etc:* ratificação *f*, homologação *f*.
ratify, *v.tr. Jur: etc:* ratificar, homologar; **to ratify a contract,** aprovar um contrato.
rating, *n.* **1.** (*a*) *Ind:* avaliação *f*; **performance rating,** (i) avaliação da performance (de empregado, etc.), (ii) (*of machine*) rendimento *m* nominal; **work-force rating,** avaliação de rendimento da mão-de-obra; (*b*) tarifação *f* (de transportes, mercadorias, etc.); (*c*) (i) taxação *f*, (ii) lançamento *m* de impostos locais; (*d*) classificação *f* (de um veículo, etc.). **2. credit rating,** informações *fpl* cadastrais; **to have a good credit rating,** ter um bom cadastro bancário; **the market rating of a company,** o valor de mercado das ações de uma companhia.
ratio, *n.* **1.** razão *f*, proporção *f*, relação *f*; **in the ratio of one to three,** na proporção, na razão, de um a três; **direct ratio,** razão direta. **2. cover ratio,** taxa *f* de cobertura; **mark-up ratio,** taxa *f* de mark-up. **3.** *Fin: Book-k:* **capital–output ratio,** índice *m* capital-produção; **liquidity ratio,** índice de liquidez; **current ratio,** índice de liquidez corrente; **acid-test ratio,** índice de liquidez estática, índice de liquidez geral; **price–earnings ratio (PER),** índice *m* preço/lucro (P/L); **profit–volume ratio,** razão lucro-vendas, taxa *f* de lucro sobre vendas.
rationale, *n.* análise fundamentada.
rationalization, *n.* racionalização *f* (de indústria, etc.).
rationalize, *v.tr.* racionalizar.
rationing, *n.* racionamento *m*.
raw, *a.* **raw land,** terra não cultivada; **raw material,** matéria-prima *f*; *Cmptr:* **raw data,** dados não processados.
re, *prep.* **re your letter of March 8th,** com referência à sua carta de 8 de março.
react, *v.i.* (*of prices*) reagir.
reaction, *n.* reação *f*; **strong reaction of sterling on the foreign exchange market,** forte reação do esterlino no mercado cambial; **chain reaction,** reação em cadeia.
read, *v.tr.* ler; **he read the report to the shareholders,** ele leu o relatório para os

acionistas; **to take the minutes as read,** aprovar a ata sem leitura; *Adm: etc:* **read and approved,** lido e achado conforme.

readjust, *v.tr.* reajustar (salários, etc.).

readjustment, *n.* reajustamento *m* (de salários, etc.).

ready, *a.* **1. ready cash,** dinheiro vivo; **ready money,** (i) dinheiro vivo, (ii) dinheiro disponível; **to pay in ready money,** pagar em dinheiro; *Fin:* **ready capital,** capital *m* circulante. **2. goods that meet with a ready sale,** mercadorias *fpl* que têm muita saída, que têm boa aceitação.

real, *a.* **1.** real; **real income,** renda *f* real; **real wages,** salário *m* real; **the real value of money,** o valor real do dinheiro. **2. real estate, property,** bens *mpl* de raíz, bens imóveis; **a piece of real estate,** um imóvel; *N.Am:* **real estate agent,** agente imobiliário; **real estate agency,** agência imobiliária.

realizable, *a. Fin:* realizável; **realizable project,** projeto realizável; **realizable assets,** ativo *m* realizável, ativo real.

realization, *n.* (*a*) **realization of a project,** realização *f* de um projeto; (*b*) *Fin:* realização *f* (do ativo, etc.); conversão *f* (dos haveres em dinheiro); (*c*) *Jur:* transformação *f* de bens móveis em bens imóveis.

realize, *v.tr.* (*a*) realizar (projeto, plano, etc.); (*b*) *Fin:* **to realize assets,** realizar o ativo, converter os haveres em dinheiro; **to realize an investment,** realizar um investimento; **to realize a profit on a transaction,** auferir lucro com uma operação; (*c*) *Jur:* transformar (bens móveis em bens imóveis); (*d*) (*of goods*) **to realize a high price,** ser vendido por um preço alto; (*of person*) **he realized a good price on the sale of his house,** ele obteve um bom preço com a venda da sua casa.

realizer, *n.* realizador *m* (de capitais, etc.).

realizing, *n.* = realization.

realtor, *n. N.Am:* corretor *m* de imóveis, agente imobiliário.

realty, *n.* bens *mpl* imóveis, bens de raíz, propriedade imobiliária.

ream, *n.* **a ream contains twenty quires of paper,** uma resma contém vinte mãos de papel.

reapply, *v.i.* solicitar, requerer, de novo.

reappoint, *v.tr.* nomear, designar, de novo; (*of dismissed official, etc.*) reintegrar, readmitir.

reappointment, *n.* (*of dismissed official, etc.*) reintegração *f*, readmissão *f*.

reapportion, *v.tr.* repartir de novo.

reappraisal, *n.* reavaliação *f*.

reappraise, *v.tr.* reavaliar.

reasonable, *a.* razoável; **reasonable prices,** preços *mpl* razoáveis; **reasonable offer,** oferta *f* razoável; **we are open to any reasonable offer,** aceitamos qualquer oferta razoável.

reassess, *v.tr.* **1.** fazer um novo lançamento (de um contribuinte). **2.** reavaliar (danos, prédio, etc.).

reassessment, *n.* **1.** novo lançamento. **2.** reavaliação *f*.

reassurance, *n. Ins:* resseguro *m*.

reassure, *v.tr. Ins:* ressegurar.

rebate¹, *n.* **1.** abatimento *m*, desconto *m*; *N.Am:* (*as from wholesaler to retailer*) bonificação *f*; *Adm:* **tax rebate,** devolução *f* do imposto de renda. **2.** (*refund*) reembolso *m*.

rebate², *v.tr. N.Am:* **1. to rebate retailers,** bonificar os varejistas, conceder uma bonificação aos varejistas. **2.** conceder um abatimento.

reborrow, *v.tr.* tomar emprestado de novo.

rebound¹, *n.* **sharp rebound of the market,** acentuado revigoramento, acentuada reanimação, do mercado.

rebound², *v.i.* (*of market*) revigorar(-se), reanimar-se.

rebuttal, *n. Jur:* réplica *f*.

rebutter, *n. Jur:* réplica *f*.

recalculate, *v.tr.* recalcular.

recalculation, *n.* recálculo *m*.

recapitalization, *n. Fin:* recapitalização *f*.

recapitalize, *v.tr.* recapitalizar.

recede, *v.i.* retroceder, declinar; *St.Exch:* **the shares receded three points,** os títulos declinaram, baixaram, três pontos.

receipt¹, *n.* **1.** receita *f*, féria *f*, renda *f*; **operating receipts,** receitas operacionais; **receipts and expenditure,** receitas e

despesas *fpl*; (*of trader, etc.*) **the day's receipts,** a receita, a féria, do dia. **2.** recepção *f*, recebimento *m*; *Corr:* **I am in receipt of your letter of June 9th,** acabo de receber, recebí, a sua carta, estou de posse da sua carta, de 9 de junho; **to acknowledge receipt of a letter,** acusar a recepção, o recebimento, de uma carta, acusar recebida uma carta; **on receipt of your letter,** após o recebimento da sua carta; **the goods will be sent on receipt of your cheque,** as mercadorias serão enviadas no recebimento do seu cheque; **within five days of receipt of the notification,** dentro de cinco dias após o recebimento da notificação. **3.** recibo *m*, recepisse *m*, quitação *f*; **to make out a receipt in duplicate,** passar um recibo em duas vias; **warehouse receipt,** recibo de depósito, recibo de armazenagem, conhecimento *m* de depósito; **receipt for payment,** recibo de pagamento, quitação; **airmail receipt,** recibo de via aérea; **dock receipt,** recibo de doca; **railway receipt,** recibo ferroviário; *Fin:* **application receipt for shares,** recibo de subscrição de ações.
receipt², *v.tr.* passar recibo (de pagamento, etc.); **to receipt an invoice,** assinar uma fatura.
receivable, 1. *a.* **bills receivable,** efeitos *mpl* a receber; **accounts receivable,** contas *fpl* a receber. **2.** *n.pl.* *N.Am:* **receivables,** efeitos a receber.
receive, *v.tr.* **1.** (*a*) receber (notícia, carta, etc.); **on receiving the invoice,** no recebimento da fatura; **to receive money,** receber dinheiro; **to receive one's salary,** receber o salário; **received the sum of $100 from Mr. X,** recebemos do Sr. X a importância de $100; (*on bill*) **'received with thanks',** 'recebido'; (*b*) **to receive an invitation,** receber um convite; **the proposal was very well received,** a proposta foi muito bem recebida; **the board received the delegation in the library,** o conselho de administração recepcionou a delegação na biblioteca. **2. to receive** (**stolen goods**), receptar (furto).
receiver, *n.* **1.** (*a*) recebedor *m*; destinatário *m* (de carta, etc.); (*b*) *N.Am:* recebedor *m*; **receiver's office,**

recebedoria *f*; (*c*) **receiver in bankruptcy, official receiver,** curador *m* de massas falidas, síndico *m* de massa falida; (*d*) **receiver** (**of stolen goods**), receptador *m*, receptor *m*, encobridor *m*, escondedor *m*; (*e*) *St.Exch:* **receiver of contango,** reportante *mf*, reportador *m*. **2.** (**telephone**) **receiver,** receptor *m* (do telefone), fone *m*.
receivership, *n.* (**official**) **receivership,** curadoria *f*, curatela *f*; **to put a company into receivership,** colocar uma empresa em regime de curadoria, de curatela.
receiving, 1. *a.* **receiving clerk, teller,** caixa *mf*, recebedor *m*, cobrador *m*; **receiving agent,** agente *m* recebedor. **2.** *n.* (*a*) recebimento *m*, recepção *f*; **receiving of goods,** recebimento de mercadorias; **receiving certificate,** certificado *m* de recepção, de recebimento; (*b*) **receiving** (**of stolen goods**), receptação *f* (de furto); (*c*) *Jur:* **receiving order,** mandado *m* de curadoria.
reception, *n.* (*at hotel, etc.*) recepção *f*; *N.Am:* **reception clerk,** recepcionista *mf*, encarregado *m* da recepção; (*b*) **to give a reception for s.o.,** dar uma recepção para alguém.
receptionist, *n.* recepcionista *mf*, encarregado *m* da recepção; **the receptionists of a hotel,** a recepção de um hotel; **head receptionist,** chefe *mf* da recepção.
recession, *n.* *Pol.Ec:* recessão *f*.
recessive, *a.* recessivo.
recipient, *n.* (*a*) destinatário *m* (de carta, etc.), beneficiário *m* (de um cheque); **recipient of a pension,** pensionista *mf*; (*b*) *Jur:* donatário *m*.
reciprocal, *a.* recíproco, mútuo; **reciprocal concessions,** concessões recíprocas; *Jur:* **reciprocal contract,** contrato *m* bilateral, contrato sinalagmático.
recital, *n.* *Jur:* exposição *f* (de fatos, etc.).
reckon, *v.* **1.** *v.tr.* contar, computar; **to reckon sth. among, with, the assets,** contar algo no ativo. **2.** *v.i.* contar, calcular.
reckoner, *n.* **1.** (*person*) calculador *m*,

contador *m*. **2. ready reckoner,** tabela *f* de cálculos.
reckoning, *n*. **1.** conta *f*, contagem *f*, cômputo *m*, cálculo *m*; **to be out in one's reckoning,** errar no cálculo, no cômputo; fazer um erro de cálculo, de cômputo. **2.** (*bill*) nota *f*.
recognition, *n*. **brand recognition,** identificação *f* de marca.
recognized, *a*. **recognized agent,** agente acreditado, agente autorizado; **recognized merchant,** comerciante autorizado.
recommend, *v.tr.* **to recommend the agent to the new manufacturer,** recomendar o agente ao novo fabricante; **to recommend a candidate for a post,** recomendar um candidato para um cargo; **to recommend a hotel,** recomendar um hotel.
recommendation, *n*. **1.** recomendação *f*; *Fin:* **recommendation of dividend,** proposta *f* de dividendo. **2. stockbroker's list of recommendations,** lista *f* de títulos recomendados pelo corretor.
recomputation, *n*. recálculo *m*; reavaliação *f* (de estoque, etc.).
reconcile, *v.tr.* *Book-k:* reconciliar, conciliar.
reconciliation, *n*. *Book-k:* reconciliação *f*, conciliação *f*; **reconciliation of surplus,** demonstração *f* dos lucros não distribuídos.
reconstitute, *v.tr.* reorganizar (uma sociedade, etc.).
reconstitution, *n*. reorganização *f* (de uma sociedade, etc.).
reconstruct, *v.tr.* reconstruir (a economia); reorganizar (uma sociedade).
reconstruction, *n*. reconstrução *f* (da economia, etc.); reorganização *f* (de uma empresa).
record¹, *n*. **1.** nota *f*, registro *m*, inscrição *f*; **sales record,** registro de vendas. **2.** *pl.* **records,** arquivo *m*, registros, *Jur:* auto(s) *m(pl)*; **copy enclosed for your records,** anexa-se copia para o seu arquivo. **3.** antecedentes *mpl*; **work record, service record,** antecedentes profissionais, vida *f* profissional. **4.** recorde *m*; **record profits,** lucros *mpl* recordes; **record output,** produção *f* recorde. **5. the record industry,** a indústria de discos.

record², *v.tr.* registrar, averbar, inscrever.
record-breaking, *a*. **record-breaking profits,** lucros *mpl* recordes.
recoup, *v*. **1.** *v.tr.* (*a*) reaver, recuperar; **to recoup one's losses,** recuperar-se dos prejuízos; (*b*) reembolsar, indenizar, compensar; **to recoup coffee planters their losses,** reembolsar aos cafeicultores as suas perdas. **2.** *v.i.* recuperar-se (dos prejuízos, etc.).
recoupable, *a*. **recoupable losses,** (i) perdas *fpl* reembolsáveis (a alguém), (ii) perdas recuperáveis.
recoupment, *n*. (i) reembolso *m*, (ii) recuperação *f*.
recourse, *n*. recurso *m*, expediente *m*, meio *m*; **to have recourse to a reserve,** recorrer a uma reserva; **to have recourse to fraud,** usar de meios fraudulentos; *Jur:* **recourse against third parties,** recurso contra terceiros.
recover, *v*. **1.** *v.tr.* (*a*) *Ind:* **to recover by-products from coal,** recuperar produtos derivados do carvão; (*b*) **to recover one's investment,** recuperar o investimento; **to recover a debt,** recuperar, cobrar, recobrar, uma dívida; **to recover costs by increased prices,** recuperar os custos mediante aumento de preços; **to recover losses,** recuperar-se das perdas; *Jur:* **to recover damages from s.o.,** fazer-se indenizar por alguém. **2.** *v.i.* **the market is recovering,** o mercado está recuperando-se; **the shares recovered just before closing,** as ações se recuperaram pouco antes do fechamento.
recovery, *n*. **1.** (*a*) *Ind:* **recovery of ore,** recuperação *f* de minério; (*b*) **recovery of expenses,** recuperação de despesas. **2. recovery of the market, prices, etc.,** recuperação, retomada *f*, do mercado, dos preços, etc.; **the recovery began just before closing,** a recuperação começou pouco antes do fechamento; **economic recovery,** recuperação econômica.
recruit, *v.tr.* recrutar.
recruiting, *n*. recrutamento *m*.
rectification, *n*. retificação *f*, correção *f*, (de um erro, etc.); *Book-k:* (*as cross-entry*) estorno *m*.

rectify, *v.tr.* retificar, corregir; *Book-k:* estornar (um lançamento).

recurrent, *a.* **recurrent expenses,** despesas periódicas.

red, 1. *a. Book-k:* **the red side,** o deve; **red-ink entry,** lançamento *m* em vermelho, lançamento negativo; *Am: F: (of account)* **to go into red ink,** apresentar um saldo negativo, um saldo devedor. **2.** *n. F:* **to be in the red,** (i) *(of person)* estar endividado, estar cheio de dívidas, (ii) *(of account)* apresentar um saldo devedor, um saldo negativo; **at last I'm out of the red,** finalmente a minha conta está com saldo credor, saldo positivo.

redeem, *v.tr. (a) Jur:* **to redeem (a property from a charge, etc.),** redimir, remir, (uma propriedade de um ônus, etc.); *(b)* **to redeem a debt,** resgatar uma dívida; **to redeem shares, debentures,** resgatar ações, debêntures; **to redeem a loan,** reembolsar um empréstimo; **to redeem a mortgage,** resgatar uma hipoteca.

redeemability, *n.* resgatabilidade *f.*

redeemable, *a.* resgatável; *Jur:* remível, redimível.

redeemer, *n.* resgatador *m*; *Jur:* redimidor *m.*

redemption, *n. (a) Fin:* resgate *m* (de ações, obrigações, etc.), amortização *f* (de empréstimo); **accelerated redemption, redemption before due date,** resgate antecipado; **redemption date,** data *f* de resgate; **redemption value,** valor *m* de resgate; **redemption fund,** fundo *m* para resgate; **redemption premium,** prêmio *m*, ágio *m*, de resgate; **redemption table,** tabela *f* (dos valores) de amortização; **redemption yield,** rendimento *m*, renda *f*, de resgate; *(b) Jur:* redenção *f* (de uma propriedade); **sale with power, option, of redemption,** retrovenda *f*, retrato *m*, resgate convencional; **to sell with an option of redemption,** retrovender; **covenant of redemption,** contrato *m* de resgate.

redeploy, *v.tr. Adm: Ind:* **to redeploy (the sale staff),** reorganizar (o pessoal de vendas).

redeployment, *n. Adm: Ind:* reorganização *f.*

rediscount¹, *n.* **1.** redesconto *m.* **2.** *F:* papéis redescontados.

rediscount², *v.tr.* redescontar.

rediscountable, *a.* redescontável.

rediscounter, *n.* redescontador *m.*

redistribute, *v.tr.* redistribuir.

redistribution, *n.* redistribuição *f.*

redraft¹, *n.* **1.** nova redação (de um documento, etc.). **2.** *Fin:* ressaque *m*, recâmbio *m.*

redraft², *v.tr.* redigir (um documento) de novo.

redraw, *v.i. Fin:* ressacar.

reduce, *v.tr.* reduzir, diminuir; **to reduce prices, expenses, etc.,** reduzir os preços, as despesas, etc.; **to reduce taxation,** reduzir os impostos; **to reduce the value of the shares,** baixar o valor das ações; **to reduce the working week from 48 to 40 hours,** reduzir a semana de trabalho de 48 para 40 horas; **to reduce metres to centimetres,** reduzir metros em centímetros.

reduced, *a.* reduzido; **reduced price,** preço reduzido; **furniture for sale at reduced prices,** vendem-se móveis a preços reduzidos.

reduction, *n.* redução *f*, diminuição *f*; **reduction of prices, salaries,** redução de preços, salários; **reduction of capital,** redução de capital; **to make a reduction on an article,** conceder uma redução sobre um artigo.

redundancy, *n.* (i) excesso *m* de mão-de-obra, (ii) *(loosely)* *pl.* **redundancies,** demissões *fpl* por excesso de mão-de-obra; **redundancy payment,** indenização paga ao empregado demitido por excesso de mão-de-obra.

redundant, *a.* (empregado) demitido por excesso de mão-de-obra.

re-employ, *v.tr.* reempregar, recolocar, (pessoas); reaplicar (capitais, etc.).

re-employment, *n.* recolocação *f* (de pessoas); reaplicação *f* (de capitais, etc.).

re-engage, *v.tr.* readmitir (um empregado demitido).

re-enter, *v.tr.* **1.** **to re-enter a job,** reingressar num emprego. **2.** *Book-k:* to

re-enter an amount, fazer um novo lançamento de uma quantia.

re-entry, *n.* reingresso *m*; *Book-k:* novo lançamento.

re-equip, *v.tr.* reequipar.

re-equipment, *n.* reequipamento *m*, reequipagem *f.*

re-establish, *v.tr.* restabelecer.

re-establishment, *n.* restabelecimento *m.*

re-exchange, *n.* **1.** (*process*) recâmbio *m.* **2.** (*draft*) ressaque *m*, recâmbio *m.*

re-export¹, *n.* reexportação *f*; **re-export trade,** comércio *m* de reexportações.

re-export², *v.tr.* reexportar.

re-exportation, *n.* reexportação *f.*

re-exporter, *n.* reexportador *m*; **a firm of re-exporters,** uma empresa reexportadora.

refer, *v.* **1.** *v.tr.* (*a*) **to refer a matter to s.o.,** submeter um assunto à apreciação de alguém; **all applications will be referred to the competent authorities,** todas as solicitações serão encaminhadas, dirigidas, às autoridades competentes; (*b*) (*of bank*) **to refer a cheque to drawer,** recusar o pagamento de um cheque sem fundos, devolver um cheque por insuficiência de fundos; **referred to drawer,** devolvido por insuficiência de fundos. **2.** *v.i.* (*a*) (*correspondence*) **I am pleased to refer to your letter of August 8,** tenho o prazer de referir-me à sua carta de 8 de agosto; **referring to your letter,** com referência à sua carta; **he will have to refer to the board of directors,** ele terá de consultar o conselho de administração; (*b*) (*of statement, document, etc.*) **this article refers to extraordinary general meetings,** este artigo se refere, diz respeito, às assembléias gerais extraordinárias.

referee, *n.* **1.** *Jur:* árbitro *m*; **board of referees,** junta *f* arbitral. **2.** referência *f*; **please give the names of two referees,** favor dar os nomes de duas referências.

reference, *n.* **1.** submissão *f* (de uma questão a uma autoridade, etc.). **2. terms of reference,** termos *mpl* de referência; **with reference to my letter of 9th June,** com referência à minha carta de 9 de junho; **the document has reference to ...,** o documento se refere a ...; **to make reference to (a fact, etc.),** fazer referência, referir-se, a (um fato, etc.). **3.** (*at head of letter, etc.*) **my reference FJ,** a minha referência FJ; **Ref. PX,** Ref. PX, Ref.ᵃ PX; **reference number,** número *m* de referência; **when replying quote reference no. ...,** ao responder, queira citar referência número .... **4.** referência(s), fontes *fpl* de referência; **to give s.o. a reference,** dar, fornecer, uma referência sobre alguém; **to have good references,** ter boas referências; **to take up s.o.'s references,** tomar informações sobre alguém; **to give s.o. as a reference,** dar o nome de alguém como referência; **written references are required,** exigem-se referências por escrito; **you may use my name as a reference,** você pode usar meu nome como referência; **letter of reference,** carta *f* de recomendação; **bank reference,** referência bancária; **trade reference,** referência comercial; *Bank:* **reference file (on customers),** cadastro *m* (de clientes).

refinancing, *n.* *Fin:* refinanciamento *m.*

reflate, *v.tr.* *Pol.Ec:* reflacionar.

reflation, *n.* *Pol.Ec:* reflação *f.*

reflect, *v.tr.* refletir; **this increase reflects the rise in oil prices,** este aumento reflete a subida dos preços do petróleo.

refloat, *v.tr.* *Fin:* relançar (empréstimo, etc.).

refloating, *n.* *Fin:* relançamento *m.*

reforestation, *n.* reflorestamento *m*; **reforestation programme,** programa *m* de reflorestamento.

reform¹, *n.* reforma *f*; **tax reform,** reforma tributária.

reform², *v.tr.* reformar (o sistema monetário, etc.).

reforwarding, *n.* **reforwarding by rail,** reexpedição *f* por ferrovia.

refresher, *n.* **refresher course,** curso *m* de reciclagem; **refresher training,** treinamento *m* de reciclagem.

refrigerate, *v.tr.* *Ind:* refrigerar, frigorificar; **refrigerated lorry,** caminhão frigorífico.

refrigeration, *n.* refrigeração *f*, frigorificação *f*; **the refrigeration**

industry, a indústria frigorífica; **refrigeration car,** carro frigorífico; **refrigeration unit,** unidade *f* de refrigeração; **refrigeration plant,** frigorífico *m*.
refund[1], *n.* devolução *f*, reembolso *m*; *Jur:* restituição *f*.
refund[2], *v.tr.* **1.** reembolsar (uma despesa, etc.); devolver (uma quantia paga indevidamente, etc.); *Jur:* restituir (uma quantia, etc.); **to refund postage,** reembolsar o porte; **all taxes paid by the contractor will be refunded by the client,** todos os impostos pagos pelo contratante serão reembolsados pelo cliente. **2. to refund s.o.,** reembolsar alguém.
re-fund, *v.tr. Fin:* (*a*) **to re-fund a debt,** reconsolidar uma dívida; (*b*) refinanciar (uma operação, etc.).
refundable, *a.* reembolsável.
refusable, *a.* **refusable money,** moeda *f* que não tem curso legal.
refusal, *n.* **1.** (*a*) recusa *f*; **refusal to pay,** recusa de pagamento; **flat refusal,** recusa categórica; (*b*) **refusal of goods,** rejeição *f*, não-aceitação *f*, de mercadorias (por serem defeituosas, etc.). **2.** direito *m* de recusar, de rejeitar; direito de preempção; **we have first refusal of, on, the house,** temos preferência para a compra da casa.
refuse, *v.tr.* **1.** (*a*) recusar (uma oferta, etc.); (*b*) **to refuse to do sth.,** recusar fazer algo, recusar-se a fazer algo; **to refuse to pay,** recusar-se a pagar, recusar pagamento. **2.** rejeitar (mercadorias, uma obra); **to refuse delivery,** não aceitar a entrega (de algo); **to refuse s.o. sth.,** recusar algo a alguém; *Adm:* **to refuse the registration of a document, etc.,** negar o arquivamento de um documento, etc.
regain, *v.tr.* recuperar (tráfego, freguesia, etc.).
region, *n.* região *f*.
regional, *a.* regional; **regional development bank,** banco *m* de desenvolvimento regional.
register[1], *n.* (*a*) (livro *m* de) registro *m*, registo *m*; **to enter in a register,** inscrever, averbar, assentar, num registro; **register of shareholders,** livro de registro de ações nominativas; *Adm:* **trade register,**

registro do comércio; **land register,** cadastro *m*; *Nau:* **register tonnage,** tonelagem *f* de registro; (*b*) **cash register,** caixa registradora.
register[2], *v.tr.* registrar; inscrever, assentar, num registro; **to register a company,** registrar uma sociedade; **to register a security,** registrar um título; **foreign investors have to be registered with the Central Bank of Brazil,** os investidores estrangeiros têm de registrar-se no Banco Central do Brasil; **to register a transfer of shares,** arquivar, averbar, uma transferência de ações; *Post:* **to register a letter,** registrar uma carta.
registered, *a.* (*a*) registrado, inscrito; arquivado, averbado; **registered trademark,** marca registrada; (*b*) *Fin:* **registered security,** título nominativo; **registered bond,** obrigação nominativa; **registered share,** ação nominativa; **registered capital,** capital autorizado; (*c*) *Post:* **registered letter,** carta registrada; **registered mail,** correio registrado; (*d*) **registered office,** sede *f* social (de empresa comercial); (*e*) *Am:* **registered accountant,** contador licenciado.
registrar, *n.* escrivão *m*.
registration, *n.* registro *m*, matrícula *f*, inscrição *f*, averbação *f*, assentamento *m*; arquivamento *m* (de documento, etc.); taxa *f* de registro; **land registration,** registro cadastral; **registration of mortgage,** inscrição hipotecária; **registration of trademark,** registro de marca comercial; **registration number,** (i) *Aut:* número *m* de chapa, número de placa, número de matrícula, (ii) *Adm:* número de registro, número de inscrição; *Adm: Post: etc:* **registration fee,** taxa *f* de registro; **registration of a letter,** registro de uma carta; *Nau:* **ship's registration,** registro *m* de navio; *Fin:* **registration and transfer fees,** taxas *fpl* de registro e transferência.
registry, *n.* **1.** (*act*) registro *m*, inscrição *f*, assentamento *m*, averbação *f*. **2.** (*state*) *Nau:* **certificate of registry,** certificado *m* de registro. **3.** (*place*) cartório *m*, arquivo

m; **land registry**, cartório de imóveis. **4.**
(*book*) livro *m* de registro.
regression, *n.* **regression analysis**, análise
f de regressão.
regressive, *a.* **regressive taxation**,
tributação regressiva.
regular, *a.* **1.** regular; **regular service to
New York**, serviço *m* regular para Nova
Iorque; **regular income**, renda *f* regular,
renda constante; **regular salary**, salário
fixo; **regular customer**, freguês *m*, cliente
mf, habitual; **regular staff**, pessoal
efetivo. **2. regular price**, preço *m* usual.
regularity, *n.* regularidade *f*.
regularization, *n.* regularização *f*.
regularize, *v.tr.* regularizar.
regulate, *v.tr.* **to regulate imports**, regular,
regulamentar, as importações; **to regulate
expenditure**, regular, conter, as despesas;
the government regulates price levels, o
governo regula os níveis de preços; **to
regulate money supply**, controlar o
suprimento monetário.
regulation, *n.* **1. regulation of retail sales**,
regulamentação *f* das vendas a varejo;
price regulation, tabelamento *m* de
preços, regulamentação *f* dos preços. **2.**
export regulations, regulamento(s) *m(pl)*
sobre as exportação; **health and fire
regulations**, regulamentos sobre saúde
e incêndio; **customs regulations**,
regulamentos alfandegários.
rehabilitate, *v.tr.* reabilitar (uma pessoa);
reorganizar (as finanças públicas, etc.);
modernizar (uma indústria).
rehabilitation, *n.* reabilitação *f*;
reorganização *f* (das finanças públicas,
etc.); modernização *f* (de uma indústria).
reimbursable, *a.* reembolsável.
reimburse, *v.tr.* **1.** reembolsar (dinheiro
gasto). **2. to reimburse s.o. (for) sth.**,
reembolsar algo a alguém; **to be
reimbursed for one's expenses**, ser
reembolsado das suas despesas.
reimbursement, *n.* reembolso *m*.
reimport[1], *n.* reimportação *f*.
reimport[2], *v.tr.* reimportar.
reimporting, *n.* reimportação *f*.
reinstate, *v.tr.* reintegrar (funcionário
destituido no seu cargo, etc.).
reinstatement, *n.* reintegração *f* (de

alguém no seu cargo).
reinsurance, *n. Ins:* resseguro *m*, contra-
seguro *m*; **reinsurance company**,
(companhia) resseguradora; **reinsurance
policy**, apólice *f* de resseguro.
reinsure, *v.tr. Ins:* ressegurar.
reinsurer, *n. Ins:* ressegurador *m*.
reinvest, *v.tr.* reinvestir, reaplicar,
recolocar.
reinvestment, *n.* reinvestimento *m*,
reaplicação *f*, recolocação *f*.
reissue[1], *n. Fin:* reemissão *f*.
reissue[2], *v.tr. Fin:* reemitir.
reject[1], *n.* (*of goods*) refugo *m*; **reject
shop**, loja *f* de artigos defeituosos.
reject[2], *v.tr.* rejeitar, recusar, (uma oferta,
etc.); rejeitar, refugar, (mercadorias,
produtos).
relate, *v.i.* **to relate to an agreement, a
plan**, relacionar-se a um acordo, um
plano; referir-se, dizer respeito, a um
acordo, um plano; **agreement relating to
the import of tractors**, acordo relativo,
referente, concernente, à importação de
tratores.
related, *a.* relacionado (**to**, a, com);
industries related to shipbuilding,
indústrias relacionadas, ligadas, à
construção naval; **related markets**,
mercados relacionados; **questions related
to a subject**, questões relativas a um
assunto.
relation, *n.* (*a*) relação *f*; **in relation to . . .**,
em relação a . . ., com respeito a . . .; (*b*)
pl. **relations**, relações; **to have business
relations with . . .**, manter relações
comerciais com . . .; **labour relations**,
relações trabalhistas, relações entre
empregador e empregados, relações de
trabalho; **industrial relations**, relações
industriais; **public relations (PR) (officer)**,
(assessor *m* de) relações públicas, *F:*
relações-públicas *mf*; *Pol.Ec:* **relations of
production**, relações de produção.
release[1], *n.* **1.** (*a*) (*act*) quitação *f* (de
uma dívida), liberação *f* (de alguém) de
uma dívida, de uma obrigação; **release
from a mortgage**, baixa *f* de uma
hipoteca; (*b*) *Ind: etc:* **day release**, licença
concedida a um empregado (geralmente
uma vez por semana) para fins de

aperfeiçoamento profissional; (c) *Cust:*
release of goods from bond, liberação de
mercadorias do entreposto aduaneiro. **2.**
(*document*) quitação *f*, recibo *m.*
release², *v.tr.* **1.** (*a*) quitar, liberar,
libertar, (alguém de uma obrigação);
quitar (um devedor); (*b*) *Ind: etc:* lançar
(um novo modelo, produto, etc.). **2.** *Jur:*
(*a*) renunciar (a um direito, etc.); (*b*) **to
release a debt,** remitir uma dívida.
re-lease, *v.tr.* arrendar novamente.
relet, *v.tr.* arrendar, alugar, novamente.
reletting, *n.* renovação *f* de arrendamento.
reliability, *n.* confiabilidade *f* (de um
produto, etc.), fidedignidade *f* (de um
empregado).
reliable, *a.* **reliable employee,** empregado
m de confiança; **reliable product,** produto
m confiável; **reliable firm,** empresa firme,
empresa segura; **reliable guarantee,**
garantia segura, garantia sólida; **reliable
sources,** fontes *fpl* fidedignas.
rely, *v.i.* **1. to rely on imports,** depender de
importações. **2. to rely on the sales staff,**
confiar no pessoal de vendas.
reminder, *n.* (*a*) **(letter of) reminder,** (carta
f de) lembrança *f*; (*b*) **reminder of
account,** aviso *m* de atraso de conta
vencida.
remission, *n.* remissão *f* (de dívida, etc.).
remit, *v.tr.* **1.** remitir (uma dívida). **2. to
remit a sum to s.o.,** remeter, enviar, uma
quantia a alguém.
remittance, *n.* remessa *f*; **remittance of
funds,** remessa de dinheiro; **foreign
remittance,** remessa para o exterior;
remittance slip, guia *f* de remessa.
remittee, *n.* destinatário *m* (de remessa).
remitter, *n.* remetente *mf*.
remitting, *a.* (*of bank, etc.*) remetente.
remnants, *n.pl.* restos *mpl*, sobras *fpl*, (de
tecido, etc.).
remove, *v.tr.* **to remove from circulation,**
retirar da circulação.
remunerate, *v.tr.* **1. to remunerate s.o. for
his services,** remunerar alguém por seus
serviços, retribuir os serviços de alguém.
2. remunerar, retribuir, (um serviço).
remuneration, *n.* remuneração *f* (**for,**
por), retribuição *f* (**for,** por); **his
remuneration for services rendered,** (a)

sua remuneração pelos serviços
prestados.
remunerative, *a.* remunerador,
remunerativo.
render, *v.tr.* **1. to render services,** prestar
serviços; **to render an account,** prestar
uma conta, prestar contas; **as per account
rendered, to account rendered,** conforme
conta entregue. **2. to render possible,**
possibilitar.
rendering, *n.* **rendering of accounts,**
prestação *f* de contas.
renegotiate, *v.tr.* renegociar.
renegotiation, *n.* renegociação *f*.
renew, *v.tr.* renovar, reformar, revalidar;
to renew stocks, renovar os estoques; **to
renew a lease,** renovar um contrato de
arrendamento; **to renew an authorization,**
revalidar uma autorização; **to renew a
subscription,** renovar uma assinatura.
renewal, *n.* renovação *f* (de estoques);
revalidação *f* (de uma autorização, etc.);
reforma *f* (de uma letra de câmbio);
renewal bill, ressaque *m*; *Jur:* **renewal of a
lease,** renovação *f* de um contrato de
aluguel; **renewal by tacit agreement,**
recondução tácita.
rent¹, *n.* (*a*) aluguel *m*; *Jur:* renda *f*; **to owe
three months' rent,** dever três meses de
aluguel; **'for rent',** 'aluga-se'; **quarter's
rent,** aluguel trimestral; **rent control,**
controle *m* de aluguéis; **rent-free
(accommodation),** acomodação gratuita;
(*b*) **ground rent,** foro *m*; aluguel *m* de
terra.
rent², *v.tr.* (*a*) (*let*) alugar, locar; **I rented
him the house for three years,** aluguei-lhe
a casa por três anos; (*b*) (*hire*) alugar; **to
rent a house from the tenant,** subalugar
uma casa do arrendatário.
rental, *n.* aluguel *m*, locação *f*; *Jur:* renda
f; **rental value,** valor locativo (de uma
casa, etc.); **car rental,** locação, aluguel,
de automóveis; **car rental firm,** locadora *f*
de automóveis; **self-drive car rental,**
locação de automóveis sem chofer; (**car**)
rental rates, tarifa *f* de locação; **rental
car,** carro *m* de aluguel.
renter, *n.* *Am:* locatário *m*.
renting, *n.* locação *f*, aluguel *m*.
reopen, *v.* **1.** *v.tr.* reabrir; **the shopkeeper**

reopened the shop after lunch, o
comerciante reabriu a loja depois do
almoço; **to reopen negotiations,** reabrir
negociações. **2.** *v.i.* **the shops reopen on
Monday,** o comércio se reabre na
segunda-feira.
reopening, *n.* reabertura *f.*
reorder[1], *n.* nova encomenda.
reorder[2], *v.tr.* encomendar de novo; fazer
nova encomenda (de, para, mercadorias),
renovar o pedido (de mercadorias).
reorganization, *n.* reorganização *f.*
reorganize, *v.* **1.** *v.tr.* reorganizar. **2.** *v.i.*
(*of company, etc.*) reorganizar-se.
rep, *n. F:* (= **representative**) representante
mf; **local rep,** pracista *mf;* **sales rep,**
representante de vendas.
repack, *v.tr.* reempacotar, reembalar.
repacking, *n.* reempacotamento *m,*
reembalagem *f.*
repair[1], *n.* conserto *m;* **to be under repair,**
estar em conserto; **repair shop,** oficina *f*
de consertos.
repair[2], *v.tr.* consertar, reparar.
repairable, *a.* consertável.
repatriation, *n. Fin:* remessa *f* de lucros.
repay, *v.tr.* **1. to repay a loan,** reembolsar
um empréstimo. **2. to repay s.o.,**
reembolsar alguém.
repayable, *a.* reembolsável.
repayment, *n.* pagamento *m,* reembolso
m; **repayment of a debt,** liquidação *f* de
uma dívida; **loan due for repayment in
August,** empréstimo *m* a vencer no mês
de agosto; **repayment capacity,**
capacidade *f* de pagamento de um
empréstimo.
repeat[1], *n.* **repeat (order),** pedido renovado.
repeat[2], *v.tr.* **to repeat an order,** renovar
um pedido.
replace, *v.tr.* substituir; **the board replaced
the incompetent manager,** a diretoria
substituiu o gerente incapaz.
replaceable, *a.* substituível.
replacement, *n.* substituição *f,* reposição
f; **replacement cost,** custo *m* de reposição,
de substituição; *Book-k:* **replacement
method,** método *m* de depreciação
baseado na substituição; *Ins:* **replacement
value,** valor *m* de reposição; *Ind: etc:*

replacement part, peça *f* de reposição,
sobressalente *m,* sobresselente *m.*
reply[1], *n.* resposta *f;* (*in correspondence*) **in
reply to your letter,** em resposta à sua
carta, respondendo à sua carta; *Post:*
(business) reply card, cartão *m* resposta
(comercial), carta *f* resposta (comercial);
reply envelope, envelope-resposta *m;* (*of
telegram, envelope*) **reply paid,** resposta
paga.
reply[2], *v.i.* **to reply to a letter,** responder a
uma carta.
report[1], *n.* (*a*) relatório *m,* laudo *m,* (**on,**
sobre); **to make, draw up, a report,** fazer,
redigir, um relatório; **to present, render, a
report,** apresentar, submeter, entregar,
um relatório; **joint report,** relatório
conjunto; **annual report (of a company),**
relatório anual; **directors' report,**
relatório da diretoria; **chairman's,
president's, report,** relatório do presidente
do conselho de administração; **auditors'
report (on accounts),** parecer *m* dos
auditores (sobre as peças contábeis); (*b*)
Journ: reportagem *f.*
report[2], *v.* **1.** *v.tr.* (*a*) comunicar, relatar,
(um fato, etc.); **our Paris office reports a
drop in prices,** o nosso escritório em Paris
informa sobre, comunica, uma queda nos
preços; *Ins:* **to report a claim,** comunicar
um sinistro; (*b*) *Cust:* **to report a vessel,**
declarar a carga de uma embarcação. **2.**
v.i. (*a*) **to report on something,** relatar
algo, fazer um relatório de, sobre, algo;
(*b*) **the sales manager reports to the
managing director,** o gerente de vendas se
reporta ao diretor gerente.
repossess, *v.tr.* recuperar, retomar,
devolver ao vendedor; **the car was
repossessed because the buyer could not
keep up with the instalments,** o carro foi
retomado porque o comprador não podia
cumprir com as prestações.
repossession, *n.* recuperação *f,*
retomada *f.*
represent, *v.tr.* representar.
representation, *n.* representação *f;*
worker representation, representação dos
trabalhadores.
representative, 1. *a.* representativo;
representative sample, amostra

representativa. **2.** *n.* representante *mf*;
sales representative, representante de
vendas; **district representative,**
representante distrital; **foreign
representative,** representante no exterior;
sole representative of a firm,
representante exclusivo de uma empresa.
representativeness, *n.*
representatividade *f*.
reprocess, *v.tr.* reprocessar (sucata, etc.).
reprocessing, *n.* reprocessamento *m*.
repudiate, *v.tr.* negar, rejeitar, (uma
dívida); repudiar (um contrato).
repudiation, *n.* negação *f*, rejeição *f*, (de
uma dívida); repúdio *m* (de um contrato).
repurchasable, *a.* recomprável.
repurchase[1], *n.* reaquisição *f*; **sale with
option of repurchase,** retrovenda *f*,
resgate *m* convencional; **repurchase
agreement,** cláusula *f* de retrovenda.
repurchase[2], *v.tr.* recomprar, readquirir;
**sale subject of right of vendor to
repurchase,** retrovenda *f*, resgate *m*
convencional.
repurchaser, *n.* recomprador *m*.
request[1], *n.* pedido *m*, solicitação *f*; **by
request,** a pedido; **on request,** sob pedido;
request for funds, solicitação de dinheiro,
de recursos.
request[2], *v.tr.* pedir, solicitar; **to request
s.o. to do sth.,** pedir a alguém que faça
algo; **customers are requested to retain
their receipts,** pede-se aos fregueses reter
os recibos; **to request sth. from s.o.,** pedir
algo a alguém; **your order was dispatched
as requested,** a sua encomenda foi
expedida conforme pedido.
requirement, *n.* exigência *f*, requisito *m*.
requisition, *n. Ind:* requisição *f*, pedido *m*,
(de materiais, etc.).
resale, *n.* revenda *f*; **resale price,** preço *m*
de revenda; **resale value,** valor *m* de
revenda; **resale price maintenance (RPM),**
manutenção *f* de preços de revenda.
resaleable, *a.* revendível.
rescheduling, *n.* **rescheduling of debt,**
reescalonamento *m* de dívida.
rescind, *v.tr.* rescindir, anular; *Jur:* resilir.
rescindable, *a.* rescindível, anulável; *Jur:*
resilível.
rescinding[1], *a.* (cláusula) rescisória.

rescinding[2], **rescission,** *n.* rescisão *f*.
research[1], *n.* pesquisa *f*; **to do research,**
pesquisar, fazer pesquisas; **advertising
research,** pesquisa de propaganda;
consumer research, pesquisa de consumo;
market research, pesquisa de mercado;
marketing research, pesquisa de
marketing, de comercialização, pesquisa
mercadológica; **sales research,** pesquisa
de vendas; **opinion research,** pesquisa de
opinião; **field research,** pesquisa de
campo; *Ind:* **industrial research,** pesquisa
industrial; **product research,** pesquisa de
produto; **research and development (R. &
D.),** pesquisa e desenvolvimento; **research
centre,** centro *m* de pesquisa(s); **research
organization,** órgão *m* de pesquisa;
research work, trabalho *m* de pesquisa.
research[2], *v.tr. & i.* **to research sth., on
sth., into sth.,** pesquisar algo, fazer
pesquisas sobre algo.
researcher, *n.* pesquisador *m*.
reservation, *n.* **1.** (*in hotel, restaurant,
etc.*) reserva *f*; **to make a reservation,**
fazer uma reserva; **reservations clerk,**
encarregado *m* das reservas. **2.** *Jur:*
ressalva *f*, reserva *f*, restrição *f*; **to enter
reservations in respect of a contract,** fazer
reservas a respeito de um contrato;
without reservations, sem reservas.
reserve[1], *n.* **1.** (*a*) *Fin: Book-k:* **reserve for
bad debts,** reserva *f* para dívidas
incobráveis, fundo *m* de dívidas
incobráveis; **reserve for doubtful accounts,**
reserva, provisão *f*, para devedores
duvidosos; **reserve for maintenance of
working capital,** reserva para
manutenção de capital de giro; **reserve
provided by the articles,** reserva
estatutária; **bank reserves,** reservas
bancárias; **capital reserves,** reservas de
capital, reservas patrimoniais; **cash
reserve,** encaixe *m*, reserva em dinheiro;
contingency reserve, reserva de
contingência, reserva para imprevistos,
fundo *m* de previsão; **depreciation reserve,**
reserva para depreciação, fundo de
depreciação; **foreign-currency reserves,**
reservas cambiais, reservas de divisas;
gold reserve, reserva de ouro, reserva-
ouro *f*; **hidden reserve,** reserva oculta;

legal reserve, reserva legal; **revenue reserves**, reservas de lucros não distribuídos, reservas não exigíveis; **reserve account**, conta *f* de reserva; **reserve asset**, ativo *m* de reserva; **reserve currency**, moeda *f* de reserva, moeda-reserva *f*; **reserve fund**, fundo de reserva; **reserve position**, situação *f* das reservas; *Bank:* **reserve ratio**, coeficiente *m* de reservas; **required reserve**, reserva exigida, encaixe mínimo, reserva legal; (*b*) *Ind: etc:* **oil reserves**, reservas de petróleo; **coal reserves**, reservas de carvão. **2.** (*at auction, etc.*) **reserve price**, preço mínimo de venda.
reserve², *v.tr.* reservar; *Publ:* **all rights reserved**, todos os direitos reservados.
reship, *v.tr.* reembarcar, reexpedir.
reshipment, *n.* reembarque *m*, reexpedição *f*.
residual, *a.* **residual cost**, custo *m* residual; **residual value**, valor *m* residual; *Book-k: Fin:* **residual net profit**, lucro líquido residual.
residuary, *a.* **residuary outlay**, resíduo não amortizado de um dispêndio; *Jur:* **residuary legatee**, legatário *m* residual.
resign, *v.* **1.** *v.tr.* **to resign an office**, resignar, renunciar a, demitir-se de, um cargo; **to resign a job**, pedir demissão de um emprego. **2.** *v.i.* demitir-se, pedir demissão; **to resign from a position**, demitir-se, pedir demissão, de uma posição.
resignation, *n.* demissão *f*, renúncia *f*; **to give (in), hand in, send in, tender, one's resignation**, pedir demissão, demitir-se; **to accept s.o.'s resignation**, aceitar a demissão de alguém.
resistance, *n.* resistência *f*; **consumer resistance**, resistência do consumidor.
resolution, *n.* deliberação *f* (de assembléia geral, etc.), resolução *f*, decisão *f*; (*before being carried*) proposta *f*; **to put a resolution to the meeting**, submeter uma proposta à apreciação da assembléia; **to pass, carry, adopt, a resolution**, aprovar uma proposta, tomar uma deliberação; **at general meetings, resolutions shall be carried by an absolute majority**, as deliberações da assembléia

geral serão tomadas por maioria absoluta de votos; **to reject a resolution**, rejeitar uma proposta.
resource, *n.* (*a*) **resource allocation**, alocação *f* de recursos; **financial resources**, recursos financeiros; **liquid resources**, disponibilidades *fpl*; **limited resources**, recursos limitados; **resources and uses**, recursos e aplicações *fpl*; (*b*) *pl.* **resources**, *N.Am: Fin:* ativo *m* disponível.
respect¹, *n.* (*reference*) respeito *m*; **with respect to...**, com respeito a..., concernente a...; **in respect of...**, a respeito de..., no que diz respeito a...; **in this respect**, neste respeito; *Jur:* **in respect that...**, considerando que.....
respect², *v.tr.* **to respect a clause in a contract**, respeitar uma cláusula contratual.
respite, *n.* prorrogação *f* de um prazo; **to grant a respite for payment**, prorrogar o prazo para um pagamento.
responsibility, *n.* responsabilidade *f*, encargo *m*, obrigação *f*; **his responsibilities include personnel training**, as suas obrigações, funções, abrangem o treinamento de pessoal; *Fin: Ind:* **responsibility costing**, custeio *m* por responsabilidade.
responsible, *a.* **1.** (*a*) **responsible for personnel training**, responsável pelo treinamento de pessoal; **responsible to s.o.**, responsável perante alguém; **to be responsible to s.o. for sth.**, responder, responsabilizar-se, ser responsável, por algo perante alguém; (*b*) **to hold s.o. responsible for sth.**, responsabilizar alguém por algo, considerar alguém responsável por algo. **2.** (*a*) responsável, digno de confiança; **the cashier is a responsible employee**, o encarregado da caixa é um empregado responsável; (*b*) **(very) responsible position**, posição *f*, cargo *m*, de (alta) responsabilidade.
re(-)staff, *v.tr.* admitir novo pessoal para (um hotel, etc.).
restate, *v.tr.* reafirmar, reformular.
restaurant, *n.* restaurante *m*; **self-service restaurant**, restaurante auto-serviço.
restaurateur, *n.* dono *m* de restaurante.
restock, *v.tr.* reabastecer (**with**, de).

restocking, *n.* reabastecimento *m.*

restrain, *v.tr.* restringir (crescimento, expansão).

restraint, *n.* wage restraint, restrição *f* aos salários, restrição de salários; restraint of trade, restrição ao comércio, restrição de comércio, restrição à livre concorrência.

restrict, *v.tr.* restringir, limitar, conter, (despesas, produção, etc.); *Adm:* *etc:* restricted document, documento reservado; restricted market, mercado restrito, mercado limitado; restricted credit, crédito restrito, crédito limitado.

restriction, *n.* restrição *f*; restriction of expenditure, contenção *f* das despesas; credit restrictions, restrições ao crédito; import restrictions (on farm machinery, etc.), restrições à importação (de maquinaria agrícola, etc.).

restrictive, *a.* restritivo; *Ind:* restrictive practices, práticas restritivas; restrictive covenant, acordo restritivo; restrictive endorsement, endosso restritivo; *Pol.Ec:* restrictive policy, política *f* de contenção; *Jur:* restrictive clause, cláusula restritiva.

restructure, *v.tr.* reestruturar.

restructuring, *n.* reestruturação *f.*

result¹, *n.* resultado *m* (of, de); to yield results, produzir resultados; as a result of the rise in prices, em conseqüência da subida dos preços; *Fin:* operating, trading, results, resultados operacionais.

result², *v.i.* the negotiations resulted in a large contract, as negociações resultaram, redundaram, em um contrato importante.

resultant, *a.* resultante.

resupply, *v.tr.* reabastecer (with, de).

resurgence, *n. Pol.Ec:* revigoramento *m.*

retail¹, *n.* varejo *m*, retalho *m*; to sell (goods) (*N.Am:* at) retail, vender (mercadorias) a varejo, a retalho; retail trade, comércio *m* a varejo, comércio varejista; retail dealer, varejista *mf*, retalhista *mf*, retalheiro *m*; retail price, preço *m* a varejo, preço de varejo, preço a retalho; retail price index (RPI), índice *m* dos preços a varejo; retail market, mercado *m* varejista.

retail², *v.* 1. *v.tr.* vender a varejo. 2. *v.i.* (*of* goods) ser vendido no varejo, a varejo, a retalho (at, for, a certain price, a, por, um certo preço); these overcoats retail at $100, estes casacos são vendidos no varejo por $100.

retailer, *n.* varejista *mf*, retalhista *mf*; retailer's brand, marca *f* do varejista.

retain, *v.tr.* to retain s.o.'s services, contratar os serviços de alguém; retaining fee, sinal *m* para a contratação dos serviços de alguém.

retained, *a.* retained earnings, income, profits, lucros não distribuídos.

retainer, *n.* sinal *m* para a contratação dos serviços de alguém.

retention, *n. Ind: etc:* retention money, retenção *f* (contratual), retenções de garantia.

retire, *v.* 1. *v.tr.* (*a*) aposentar (alguém); (*b*) *Fin:* to retire coins, retirar moedas de circulação; to retire bonds, resgatar obrigações; to retire a loan, reembolsar um empréstimo. 2. *v.i.* to retire from the office of chairman, retirar-se do cargo de presidente; to retire from business, retirar-se dos negócios, abandonar os negócios; (*on a pension*) aposentar-se (com uma pensão).

retired, *a.* retired bank employee, bancário aposentado.

retirement, *n.* 1. aposentadoria *f*; optional retirement, aposentadoria facultativa; compulsory retirement, aposentadoria obrigatória; minimum retirement age, idade mínima de aposentadoria; retirement pension, pensão *f* (de aposentadoria); retirement plan, plano *m* de pensões, de aposentadoria; *Ind:* retirement table, tábua *f* de mortalidade. 2. *Fin:* retirement of coins, retirada *f* de moedas de circulação; retirement of bonds, resgate *m* de obrigações; retirement of a loan, reembolso *m* de um empréstimo; retirement of outstanding debt, resgate antecipado de dívida pendente.

retiring, *n.* retiring age, idade *f* de aposentadoria.

retrain, *v.tr.* reciclar.

retraining, *n.* reciclagem *f.*

retrench, *v.* 1. *v.tr.* reduzir, diminuir,

(despesas). **2.** *v.i.* economizar, fazer economias.
retrenchment, *n.* redução *f*, diminuição *f*; **policy of retrenchment**, política *f* de redução de despesas.
retrieval, *n.* recuperação *f* (de perda, etc.).
retrieve, *v.tr.* recuperar.
retrospective, *a.* **retrospective effect**, efeito retroativo; **retrospective increase**, aumento retroativo; **to be retrospective**, retroagir.
return¹, *n.* **1.** volta *f*, retorno *m*, regresso *m*; **by return (of post)**, na volta do correio; **return address**, endereço *m* do remetente; **return journey**, viagem *f* de volta; **return ticket**, passagem *f*, bilhete *m*, de ida e volta; *Nau:* **return freight**, carga *f* de retorno. **2.** (*a*) (*takings*) *pl.* **returns**, receita(s) *f(pl)*, féria *f*; **gross returns**, receitas brutas; (*b*) (*profit*) rendimento *m*, retorno, lucro *m*; **rate of return**, taxa *f* de rendimento, taxa de retorno; **return on capital invested**, retorno sobre capital investido; **return on fixed-yield investments**, rendimento de aplicações de renda fixa; *Pol.Ec:* **law of diminishing returns**, lei *f* dos rendimentos decrescentes. **3.** (*a*) devolução *f*, retorno, (de mercadorias estragadas, ou que não obtiveram venda, etc.); *pl.* **returns**, devoluções *fpl*, mercadorias devolvidas, (*of books, newspapers, etc.*) *F:* encalhe *m*; **(goods) on sale or return**, mercadorias (deixadas) em consignação; *Post:* **return address**, endereço *m* do remetente; (*b*) reembolso *m* (de quantia paga em excesso); *Fin:* **return of a capital sum**, reembolso de um capital; (*c*) **in return for sth.**, em troca de algo. **4.** (*a*) relatório *m* (oficial); *Adm:* recenseamento *m* (da população); **sales return**, relatório de vendas; (*in bank, etc.*) **weekly return**, demonstração *f* semanal; (*b*) **income tax return**, declaração *f* de rendimentos, declaração do imposto de renda. **5.** *Advert:* *pl.* **returns**, respostas *fpl* a propaganda enviada pelo correio.
return², *v.tr.* **1.** devolver, restituir, (um objeto, etc.); reembolsar (uma quantia, um empréstimo); **he returned the capital sum in two years**, ele reembolsou o

capital em dois anos; **to return an amount paid in excess**, reembolsar uma quantia paga em excesso; **he returned the damaged goods to the manufacturer**, ele devolveu as mercadorias estragadas ao fabricante; *Post:* **returned letter**, carta devolvida ao remetente. **2.** *Fin:* render; dar um rendimento, um lucro; **investment that returns high interest**, aplicação *f* que renda altos juros. **3.** **to return one's income at $12 000**, declarar uma renda de $12.000; **the liabilities are returned at $10 000**, o passivo está avaliado em $10.000.
returnable, *a.* (*a*) (*of money, etc.*) restituível; (*b*) **all empties are returnable**, todos os cascos podem ser devolvidos; **damaged goods are returnable**, as mercadorias estragadas podem ser devolvidas.
revalorization, *n. Fin:* revalorização *f* (de uma moeda, etc.).
revalorize, *v.tr. Fin:* revalorizar (uma moeda, etc.).
revaluation, *n.* (*a*) reavaliação *f* (de um imóvel, etc.); **revaluation of assets**, reavaliação do ativo; (*b*) *Fin:* revalorização *f* (de uma moeda, etc.).
revalue, *v.tr.* reavaliar (um imóvel, ativo); *Fin:* revalorizar (uma moeda, etc.).
revenue, *n.* **1.** renda *f*, receita *f*; **gross operating revenue**, receita operacional bruta; **sales revenue**, receita de vendas; **revenue account**, (i) demonstração *f* dos resultados, (ii) conta *f* de receitas; **revenue asset**, capital *m* circulante; **revenue reserve**, reserva *f* de lucros não distribuídos, reserva não exigível. **2. the Public Revenue**, (i) a receita pública, (ii) o fisco, o erário, a fazenda pública; **revenue authorities**, agentes *mpl* do fisco; **revenue collection**, coleta *f* fiscal; **revenue duty**, direito *m* fiscal; **revenue office**, coletoria *f*; **revenue stamp**, selo *m* fiscal.
reversal, *n.* **1.** *Book-k:* estorno *m*; lançamento *m* de uma partida inversa. **2.** *Jur:* anulação *f*, revogação *f*, (de uma decisão).
reverse¹, *a. Book-k:* **reverse entry**,

lançamento inverso, partida inversa; estorno *m*.

reverse², *v.tr. Book-k:* **to reverse an entry,** estornar um lançamento; anular uma partida mediante lançamento de partida inversa.

reversion, *n. Jur:* reversão *f*; **reversion clause**, cláusula *f* de retrovenda.

reversionary, *a. Jur:* reversível; **reversionary right**, direito *m* de reversão; **reversionary annuity**, anuidade *f* reversível.

review¹, *n.* 1. revisão *f*; *Jur:* **review of a decision**, revisão de uma decisão. 2. *Publ:* revista *f*.

review², *v.tr.* **to review salaries**, revisar os salários.

revival, *n.* **economic revival,** recrudescimento *m* das atividades econômicas.

revive, *v.* 1. *v.i.* (*of business, economy, etc.*) revigorar-se, renovar-se, reanimar-se; **the economy is reviving**, a economia está revigorando-se; **the market has revived since the election**, o mercado se reanimou desde a eleição. 2. *v.tr.* **to revive trade**, revigorar, renovar, reanimar, o comércio.

revocable, *a.* revogável; **revocable credit**, crédito *m* revogável; **revocable letter of credit**, carta *f* de crédito revogável; *Jur:* **revocable clause**, cláusula *f* revogável.

revocation, *n. Jur:* revogação *f*, anulação *f*.

revoke, *v.tr. Jur:* revogar; **the articles may be revoked in the following cases . . .**, os estatutos podem ser revogados nos seguintes casos . . . .

revolutionize, *v.tr.* revolucionar (uma indústria).

revolving, *a. Fin:* **revolving credit**, crédito rotativo.

rich, 1. *a.* rico; **the invention made him rich,** a invenção enriqueceu-o, tornou-o rico. 2. *n.* **the rich and the poor**, os ricos e os pobres.

rid, *v.tr.* **to rid oneself of an obligation,** quitar-se, livrar-se, de uma obrigação; **it is hard to get rid of these articles**, estes artigos não têm saída.

rider, *n.* aditamento *m*; (*separate document*) anexo *m*, apêndice *m*; *Ins:* cláusula adicional (pela qual modifica(m)-se determinada(s) cláusula(s) de um contrato de seguro).

rig¹, *n.* **oil rig**, estrutura *f* de produção e perfuração.

rig², *v.tr. Fin: St.Exch:* manipular (o mercado).

rigger, *n. Fin: St.Exch:* especulador *m* que manipula o mercado.

right, *n.* direito *m*; **by right(s)**, de direito; **right of disposal**, direito de alienação; **right to strike**, direito de greve; **to give, grant, a right**, conceder um direito; **rights granted by contract**, direitos contratuais; **operating rights**, direitos de operação; *Fin:* **application rights**, direitos de subscrição; **rights issue**, emissão *f* de bônus (*mpl*) de subscrição; **cum rights**, com direitos.

rightful, *a.* legítimo; **rightful owner**, dono, proprietário, legítimo; **rightful claim**, reivindicação legítima.

rigid, *a.* **rigid wages**, salários rígidos.

rigidity, *n.* **rigidity of wage rates**, rigidez *f* dos salários.

ring, *n.* (*a*) sindicato *m*, cartel *m*; **price ring**, coalizão *f* (de vendedores), grupo *m* de produtores que fixam os preços; (*b*) *St.Exch:* **the Ring**, o pregão.

ring up, *v.tr.* (*a*) **to ring s.o. up**, ligar, dar uma ligada, para alguém; telefonar a, para, alguém; tocar para alguém; (*b*) **to ring up a sale**, marcar uma venda numa caixa registradora.

rise¹, *n.* aumento *m*, subida *f*, alta *f*, elevação *f*, (de preços, etc.); **(pay) rise,** aumento salarial, aumento de salário; **to ask (one's employer) for a rise**, pedir um aumento de salário; **the rise in the cost of living**, o aumento do custo de vida; **the rise in the price of wheat**, o encarecimento do trigo; **food prices are on the rise**, os gêneros alimentícios estão encarecendo, os preços dos gêneros alimentícios estão em alta; *St.Exch:* **to speculate on, operate for, a rise**, jogar na alta.

rise², *v.i.* subir, aumentar, elevar-se, picar; **prices are rising**, os preços estão em alta, estão subindo; **coffee rose three cents**, o café subiu (em) três cêntimos; **production rose 8%**, a produção aumentou 8%; **everything has risen in the last six months**, tudo encareceu nos últimos seis meses.

rising, *a.* (*a*) crescente; **rising prices,** preços *mpl* ascendentes, preços crescentes, preços em alta; **the problem of rising prices,** o problema da subida dos preços; **rising cost,** custo *m* crescente; **rising demand,** demanda *f* crescente; **rising market,** mercado *m* (que está) em alta; **rising unemployment,** desemprego *m* crescente; **to speculate on a rising market,** jogar na alta; (*b*) **rising generation,** nova geração.

risk, *n.* risco *m*, perigo *m*; **to take a risk,** arriscar-se, aventurar-se; **to run the risk of losing a contract,** correr o risco de perder um contrato; **the risks of an undertaking,** os riscos de um empreendimento; **to evaluate the risks in an investment,** avaliar os riscos de um investimento; *Fin:* **risk allowance,** margem *f* de risco; **risk bearing,** aceitação *f* de risco; **risk capital,** capital *m* de risco; *Ins:* **insured risks,** riscos segurados; **uninsured risks,** riscos não cobertos pelo seguro; **theft risk,** risco de roubo; **fire risk,** risco de incêndio; **all risks policy,** apólice *f* de seguro contra todos os riscos; **war risks,** riscos de guerra; **risk unit,** unidade *f* de risco; **risk management,** administração *f* de riscos; **risk margin,** margem *f* de risco; (*of underwriter*) **to underwrite a risk,** aceitar, subscrever, um risco; **to spread a risk,** pulverizar um risco.

risk-free, *a.* **risk-free investment,** investimento *m* livre de riscos.

rival, *a. & n.* rival (*mf*), concorrente (*mf*).

road, *n.* rodovia *f*, estrada *f* (de rodagem), autovia *f*; **road tax,** taxa rodoviária; **road transport,** transporte(s) rodoviário(s); **road haulage,** transporte rodoviário de carga; **road haulage firm,** empresa *f* de transportes rodoviários; *F:* **to be on the road,** trabalhar como caixeiro-viajante.

roasted, *a.* **roasted coffee,** café torrado.

roasting, *n.* torrefação *f*.

rock-bottom, *a.* **rock-bottom price,** preço mais baixo, preço mínimo.

rocket, *v.i.* (*of prices*) subir rapidamente.

role, *n.* **the role of money in the economy,** a função da moeda na economia.

roster, *n.* rol *m*, lista *f*; *Adm:* **promotion roster, advancement roster,** tabela *f* de ascensão profissional.

rostering, *n.* *Ind:* **flexible rostering,** sistema *m* de trabalho a base de horário flexível.

rotation, *n.* rotação *f*, rodízio *m*; **job rotation,** rotação de cargos; **the members of the board will take the chair in rotation,** os conselheiros presidirão por turnos; *Agr:* **crop rotation,** rotação, afolhamento *m*, alternação *f*, de culturas.

rough, *a.* aproximado, aproximativo; **rough average,** média aproximada; **rough estimate,** aproximação *f*, estimativa aproximada; **rough calculation,** cálculo aproximado; **rough draft,** rascunho *m*, minuta *f*; **rough handling (of goods),** manuseio grosseiro (de mercadorias); *Agr:* **rough rice,** arroz *m* em casca; *Ind: etc:* **rough quartz,** quartzo *m* em bruto.

round, *a.* redondo, arrendondado; **round number,** número redondo, número inteiro; **round sum,** montante redondo, montante arredondado; **in round figures,** em números redondos; **round table,** mesa redonda; **round trip,** viagem *f* de ida e volta; **round trip ticket,** passagem *f* de ida e volta; *Am: St.Exch:* **round lot,** lote redondo.

round down, *v.tr.* arredondar para baixo.

rounding, *n.* **rounding off of a sum,** arredondamento *m* de uma soma; **rounding up,** arredondamento para cima; **rounding down,** arredondamento para baixo.

roundsman, *n.* *Am:* entregador *m*.

round up, *v.tr.* arredondar para cima.

route¹, *n.* (*description*) itinerário *m*, roteiro *m*; (*direction*) rota *f*, caminho *m*; **on route for,** a caminho de; **trade route,** rota mercante; **shipping route,** rota de navegação; **sea route,** rota marítima; **air route,** rota aérea.

route², *v.tr.* enviar (por caminho determinado).

routeman, *n. N.Am:* entregador *m.*

routine, *n.* (*a*) rotina *f*, rotineira *f*; office routine, rotina de escritório; routine work, trabalho rotineiro; (*b*) *Cmptr:* rotina.

routing, *n. Ind:* routing sheet, roteiro *m* de produção.

row, *n.* row of figures, (i) (*horizontal*) linha *f*, (ii) (*vertical*) coluna *f*, de algarismos.

royalty, *n.* royalty *m*; (*of author, etc.*) direito *m* de autor; *pl.* royalties, direitos autorais; patent royalties, direitos de patente; oil royalties, royalties petroleiros.

rubber, *n.* borracha *f*; rubber plantation, seringal *m*; rubber tree, seringueira *f*; rubber-processing equipment, máquinas *fpl* para a indústria de borracha.

rule¹, *n.* regra *f*, regulamento *m*; company rules, regulamento interno de uma empresa; operating rules, regras operacionais.

rule², *v.* 1. *v.tr.* governar. 2. *v.i.* the prices are ruling high, os preços estão se mantendo elevados; the prices ruling at the moment, os preços atuais, os preços vigentes, os preços vigorantes.

rule off, *v.tr.* sublinhar (o último lançamento de um diário, etc.).

rule out, *v.tr.* eliminar.

ruling, *a.* ruling prices, preços *mpl* atuais, vigentes, vigorantes.

run¹, *n.* 1. trial run (of a new plant, machine, etc.), funcionamento *m* de ensaio (de nova instalação, máquina, etc.), (*of vehicle*) viagem *f* de ensaio. 2. the run of the market, as tendências do mercado. 3. a run on the banks, uma corrida nos bancos; a run on sterling, uma corrida para o esterlino, uma grande demanda para o esterlino; there was a great run on that line, essa linha teve grande aceitação, muita saída; essa linha estava muito procurada.

run², *v.* 1. *v.i.* (*a*) (i) the bill has fifteen days to run, a letra vence dentro de quinze dias; the rule runs for one year, o regulamento vigora por um ano; (ii) (*of amount, number*) the increase runs to around ten thousand dollars, o aumento atinge, monta a, importa em, cerca de

dez mil dólares; (*b*) prices are running high, os preços estão elevados em geral; (*c*) eggs run at about 70p a dozen, os ovos custam cerca de 70p uma dúzia; (*d*) to run in the red, operar deficitariamente; (*e*) to run ahead, superar, exceder; production is running ahead of consumption, a produção excede o consumo. 2. *v.tr.* (*a*) to run a cheap line, vender uma linha barata; (*b*) to run a business, a factory, etc., dirigir, gerir, um negócio, uma fábrica, etc; (*c*) (*of newspaper, etc.*) to run an advertisement, publicar um anúncio.

runaway, *a.* runaway inflation, inflação desenfreada.

run down, *v.tr.* reduzir, diminuir, (o pessoal); deixar esgotar (o estoque).

run-down, *a.* precário, arruinado, em estado ruinoso.

rundown, *n.* (*a*) (i) (*of items*) levantamento pormenorizado, (ii) (*of event, situation, etc.*) sumário *m*; (*b*) redução *f*, diminuição *f*, (do pessoal de uma empresa, etc.).

run into, *v.tr. & i.* 1. (*a*) to run into debt, endividar-se, contrair dívidas; (*b*) his income runs into thousands of pounds, sua renda se eleva a milhares de libras. 2. that will run me into considerable expense, isto vai sair muito caro para mim.

runner, *n.* (*a*) mensageiro *m*, rápido *m*, próprio *m*; *esp. Am:* bank runner, coletor *m* de banco; (*b*) *Fin:* agente *mf* de banco (que vende títulos, procura novos clientes, etc.); (*c*) artigo *m* de elevado índice de vendas.

running, 1. *a.* (*a*) running account, conta *f* corrente; running expenses, (i) despesas *fpl* correntes, (ii) despesas de funcionamento, despesas operacionais; (*b*) for five days running, durante cinco dias consecutivos. 2. *n.* (*a*) funcionamento *m* (de máquina, etc.); (*of car, etc.*) running costs, custos *mpl* de manutenção; (*b*) direção *f*, gerência *f*, (de empresa, fábrica, etc.).

run up, *v.tr.* (*a*) to run up a debt, an account, deixar acumular uma dívida, uma conta; (*b*) (*at auction*) **to run up the bidding,** forçar os lances para cima.

rural, *a.* rural; **rural agent,** agente *mf* rural; **rural area,** zona *f* rural; **rural bank,** banco *m* rural; **rural credit expansion,** ampliação *f* do crédito rural; **rural economy,** economia *f* rural, economia agrícola; **rural loan,** empréstimo agropecuário; **rural staples,** produtos *mpl* agrícolas.

rush¹, *n.* 1. **the rush hour,** a hora do rush;

the week-end rush, o rush do fim de semana; (*in shops, etc.*) **the closing-time rush,** o rush da hora de fechamento. 2. **rush order,** pedido *m* urgente; **rush job, work,** trabalho *m* urgente.

rush², *v.tr.* *Ind: etc:* **to rush a job,** fazer um trabalho às pressas; **to rush an order,** executar, atender a, um pedido, às pressas, com toda a urgência.

rye, *n.* centeio *m.*

S

sack¹, *n.* **1.** *F:* to give s.o. the sack, demitir, despedir, despachar, alguém; *F:* mandar alguém embora, dar o bilhete azul a alguém, botar alguém na rua; to get the sack, ser despedido, despachado; *F:* ser mandado embora, botado na rua. **2.** *Ind:* etc: saco *m.*

sack², *v.tr. F:* demitir, despedir, despachar, (alguém); *F:* mandar (alguém) embora, dar o bilhete azul (a alguém), botar (alguém) na rua.

sacrifice¹, *n.* sacrifício *m;* (i) venda *f* com prejuízo, (ii) mercadorias vendidas com prejuízo; to sell sth. at a sacrifice, vender algo com prejuízo, vender algo abaixo do custo; **sacrifice prices**, preços sacrificados, preços abaixo do custo.

sacrifice², *v.tr.* vender (mercadorias) com prejuízo, vender (algo) abaixo do custo.

sacrificial, *a.* (venda *f*) com prejuízo; (preço) sacrificado, abaixo do custo.

safe, **1.** *n.* cofre *m,* cofre-forte *m,* caixa-forte *f; Bank:* **night (deposit) safe**, cofre noturno; **safe deposit**, depósito *m* em caixa-forte; **safe-deposit box**, cofre de aluguel (em banco); *Am:* **safe-deposits company**, empresa *f* que aluga caixas-de-segurança para a guarda de valores. **2.** *a.* (*a*) **safe keeping**, custódia *f;* **to place, deposit, securities in safe keeping**, depositar títulos em custódia; (*b*) **safe investment**, investimento seguro; **safe return**, rendimento seguro.

safeguard¹, *n.* garantia *f,* salvaguarda *f.*

safeguard², *v.tr.* to safeguard the interests of the shareholders, proteger, salvaguardar, os interesses dos acionistas.

safety, *n.* segurança *f;* **safety vault**, caixa-forte *f* (de banco, etc.); **safety device**, dispositivo *m* de segurança; **safety equipment**, equipamento *m* de segurança; **safety measures**, medidas *fpl* de segurança; **fire safety regulations**, regulamento *m* sobre a proteção contra incéndios; *Ind:* **industrial safety**, segurança industrial; **this factory has a good work safety record**, esta fábrica tem um bom recorde de segurança do trabalho; **safety factor**, fator *m* de segurança.

sag¹, *n.* baixa *f,* queda *f,* (dos preços, etc.).

sag², *v.i.* (*of prices, etc.*) baixar, cair.

sagging, *a.* **sagging prices**, preços *mpl* em baixa, em declínio; **sagging market**, mercado *m* em baixa.

sail, *v.i.* navegar; **the vessel sails tomorrow**, o navio sai do porto amanhã.

salaried, *a.* (*a*) assalariado, salariado; **salaried staff**, pessoal *m* de nível médio (geralmente mensalista); (*b*) (*of post, etc.*) assalariado, remunerado com salário (mensal).

salary, *n.* salário *m,* ordenado *m,* (calculado a base anual ao contrário do 'wage' que é sempre semanal); **to draw one's salary**, auferir, perceber, receber, o seu salário; **starting salary**, salário inicial.

sale, *n.* **1.** venda *f;* **bill of sale**, (*formal*) escritura *f* de venda, (*informal*) nota *f* de venda; **for sale, on sale**, à venda; **terms, conditions, of sale**, condições *fpl* de venda; **cash sale**, venda à vista; **credit sale**, venda a crédito; **ready sale**, venda imediata, venda fácil; **sale discount**, desconto *m* de venda, desconto comercial; **sale value**, valor *m* venal, valor de venda; **'business for sale'**, 'traspassa-se negócio', 'transfere-se negócio'; **'house for sale'**, 'venda-se casa'; **goods on sale or return**, mercadorias (deixadas) em consignação; **sale with option of repurchase**, retrovenda *f,* resgate *m* convencional, retrato *m;* **to put sth. up for sale**, pôr algo à venda; **these articles are not for sale**, estes artigos não estão à venda; *St.Exch:* **sale for the account,** venda a termo; (*for commodities, etc.*) **forward sale,** venda para entrega futura, venda futura; **sales agent,** agente *mf* de vendas; **sales analysis,** análise *f* das vendas; **sales area,** área *f*, território *m*, de vendas; **sales book,** livro-registro *m* de vendas; **sales budget,** orçamento *m* de vendas; **sales clerk,** caixeiro *m*, balconista *mf*, vendedor *m*; **sales commission,** comissão *f* de, sobre, vendas; **sales contract,** contrato *m* de vendas; **sales department,** departamento *m* de vendas; **sales drive,** campanha *f* de vendas; **sales finance company,** companhia financiadora de vendas; **sales force,** equipe *m* de vendas, quadro *m* de vendas, pessoal *m* de vendas; **sales forecast,** previsão *f* de vendas; **sales literature,** literatura *f* de vendas; **sales management,** direção *f*, administração *f*, de vendas; **sales manager,** gerente *mf* de vendas; **sales planning,** planejamento *m* de vendas; **sales policy,** política *f* de vendas; **sales promotion,** promoção *f* de vendas; **sales revenue,** receita *f* de vendas; **sales tax,** imposto *m* sobre as vendas; Imposto de Circulação de Mercadorias; **sales turnover,** faturamento *m* de vendas, movimento *m* de negócios, volume *m* de negócios. **2.** (*event*) (*a*) **sale by auction, auction sale, sale to the highest bidder,** leilão *m*, leiloamento *m*, almoeda *f*, arrematação *f*, hasta *f*, praça *f*; **to attend a sale,** assistir a uma venda pública; *Jur:* **compulsory, forced, sale,** hasta pública forçada, venda forçada; (*b*) (**clearance**) **sale,** queima *f*, liquidação *f*; (**bargain**) **sale,** feira *f*; **there's a sale of household appliances next week,** tem uma feira de eletrodomésticos na semana que vem; **sale goods,** mercadorias vendidas em liquidação, mercadorias liquidadas, mercadorias queimadas; **sale price,** preço *m* de liquidação.

saleable, *a.* (*of goods, etc.*) vendável, vendível, que tem boa venda; **saleable value,** valor *m* venal, valor de venda.

saleroom, *n.* salão *m* de vendas.

salesgirl, *n.* vendedora *f*, moça *f* de vendas; (*in shop*) caixeira *f*, balconista *f*.

saleslady, *n.* vendedora *f*, senhora *f* de vendas; (*in shop*) caixeira *f*, balconista *f*.

salesman, *n.* vendedor *m*, homem *m* de vendas; (*in shop*) caixeiro *m*, balconista *m*; (*local rep*) pracista *m*; **travelling salesman,** caixeiro-viajante *m*.

salesmanship, *n.* arte *f* de vender, habilidade *f* para vender.

salespeople, *n.pl.* vendedores *mpl*; (*in shop*) caixeiros *mpl*, balconistas *mfpl*; força *f* de vendas, equipe *f* de vendedores.

saleswoman, *n.* vendedora *f*, senhora *f* de vendas; (*in shop*) caixeira *f*, balconista *f*.

salt, *n.* sal *m*; **salt mine,** salina *f*; **salt mining,** mineração *f* do sal.

salvable, *a. Ins:* salvável.

salvage¹, *n.* **1.** (*right*) salvagem *f.* **2.** (*operation*) salvamento *m.* **3.** (*a*) (*property saved*) salvados *mpl*, sucata *f*, material recuperado; (*b*) proventos *mpl* da venda de salvados; (*c*) **salvage value,** (i) (*of wreck, etc.*) valor *m* de salvados, (ii) *Book-k:* (*of fixed asset*) valor de sucata, valor residual.

salvage², *v.tr.* salvar (de incêndio, de naufrágio, etc.); recuperar material perdido (em naufrágio, incêndio, etc.); fazer salvamento (de navio, carga, etc.).

salvageable, *a.* salvável.

salvaged, *a.* salvado; **salvaged goods, property,** salvados *mpl*; material recuperado.

salvaging, *n.* salvamento *m*; recuperação *f* e utilização *f* de material perdido (em naufrágio, etc.).

sample¹, *n.* (*a*) amostra *f* (de trigo, de aço, de papel de parede, etc.); **up to sample,** conforme a amostra; **free sample,** amostra grátis; **sample book,** livro *m* de amostras; **to buy sth. from sample,** comprar algo baseado na amostra; (*on postal packet, etc.*) **sample of no** (**commercial**) **value,** amostra sem valor (comercial); (*b*) **sample survey,** pesquisa *f*, levantamento *m*, por amostragem; *Stat:* **representative sample,** amostra representativa; **master sample,** amostra principal.

sample², *v.tr.* (*a*) tirar amostra de (algo); (*b*) *Stat:* amostrar.

sampling, *n.* amostragem *f*; **household**

sampling, amostragem de domicílios; **bulk sampling,** amostragem de conjunto; **cluster sampling,** amostragem baseada em conglomerados; **random sampling,** amostragem aleatória; **sampling design,** planejamento *m* de amostragem; **sampling error,** erro *m* de amostragem; **non-sampling error,** erro alheio à amostragem; **sampling staff,** coletores *mpl* de dados para amostragem; **sampling tolerance,** tolerância *f* de amostragem.

sanction[1], *n.* sanção *f*, aprovação *f*.

sanction[2], *v.tr.* sancionar, aprovar; **sanctioned by usage,** consagrado pelo uso; **sanctioned failures,** falências decretadas.

sanitary, *a.* **sanitary measure,** medida sanitária; **sanitary survey, inspection,** inspeção sanitária.

satisfaction, *n.* satisfação *f*, liquidação *f*, pagamento *m*; **job satisfaction,** satisfação profissional; **consumer satisfaction,** satisfação do consumidor.

satisfy, *v.tr.* **to satisfy a customer,** satisfazer um freguês; **to satisfy a debt,** satisfazer, saldar, liquidar, uma dívida; **to satisfy an obligation,** cumprir com uma obrigação.

saturate, *v.tr.* saturar (o mercado).

saturation, *n.* saturação *f*; **market saturation,** saturação do mercado; **saturation point,** ponto *m* de saturação; **the market has reached saturation point,** o mercado está saturado.

save, *v.* 1. *v.tr.* (*a*) **to save a company from bankruptcy,** salva uma empresa de falência; (*b*) **to save money,** poupar, economizar, dinheiro; **to save energy,** conservar, economizar, poupar, energia; **to save labour,** economizar mão-de-obra; **to save time,** ganhar tempo. 2. *v.i.* **to save on fuel,** fazer economias no uso de combustível.

saver, *n.* poupador *m*, depositante *mf*.

save up, *v.tr. & i.* economizar (juntando), poupar, aforrar, amealhar; **he saved up his wages for the ticket,** economizou o ordenado para comprar a passagem.

saving[1], *n.* (*a*) economia *f*, poupança *f*; **labour saving,** (i) economia de trabalho, (ii) *Ind: etc:* economia de mão-de-obra; **saving in handling costs,** economia nos

custos de manuseio; **a 10% saving on oil,** uma economia de 10% em petróleo; **to make a saving of 100 tons a day,** fazer uma economia de 100 toneladas diárias; **energy-saving measures,** medidas *fpl* de conservação de energia; (*b*) *pl.* **savings,** poupança(s), economias; **savings-and-loan association,** banco *m* de poupança e empréstimos; **savings bank,** banco *m* de poupança, caixa econômica, caixa de depósito; **savings book,** caderneta *f* de poupança; **savings account,** conta *f* de poupança; **savings bonds,** títulos *mpl* de poupança; **savings scheme,** plano *m* de poupança; **to live on one's savings,** viver das suas economias.

saving[2], *a.* **saving clause,** ressalva *f*, cláusula restritiva.

saw[1], *n.* serra *f*.

saw[2], *v.tr.* serrar; **sawn wood,** madeira serrada.

sawdust, *n.* serradura *f*.

sawmill, *n.* serraria *f*.

scab, *n.* F: fura-greve *mf*.

scale[1], *n.* (*a*) escala *f*; **scale of wages,** escala de salários; **scale of charges,** tarifa *f*, tabela *f* de preços; **scale of output,** escala de produção; **sliding scale,** escala móvel; **economy of scale,** economia *f* de escala; (*b*) escala (de um mapa, de um gráfico estatístico); **scale drawing,** desenho *m* em escala; **scale model,** modelo *m* em escala, modelo reduzido; **on a large, small, scale,** em grande, pequena, escala; **small-scale firm,** empresa *f* de pequeno porte, empresa pequena.

scale[2], *v.tr.* **to scale up, down, (prices, etc.),** aumentar, reduzir, (os preços, etc.) de acordo com uma escala; **to scale down production,** diminuir a produção.

scaling, *n.* graduação *f* (de preços, etc.).

scalp, *v.tr. St.Exch: F: esp. N.Am:* **to scalp stocks,** especular sobre títulos, fazer especulação de pequeno vulto sobre títulos.

scalper, *n. St.Exch: F: esp. N.Am:* especulador *m*.

scalping, *n. St.Exch: F: esp. N.Am:* especulação *f* (de pequeno vulto).

scarce, *a.* escasso, raro; **to become scarce,** escassear, minguar, rarear; **scarce**

currency, moeda escassa, moeda forte; scarce resources, recursos escassos.

scarcity, n. escassez f, míngua f, falta f, (de dinheiro, mão-de-obra, etc.); scarcity of capital, escassez de capital; scarcity value, valor m em razão de escassez existente.

scattergram, n. Stat: diagrama m de dispersão.

schedule¹, n. 1. (a) Jur: anexo m (a um instrumento, etc.); (b) nota explicativa. 2. (a) Ind: etc: relação f, catálogo m, (de máquinas, peças, etc.); (part of bid) schedule of prices, planilha f de preços; schedule of freight charges, tabela f de fretes; (b) Adm: cédula f; income-tax schedules, cédulas declarativas do imposto de renda; (c) Jur: (in bankruptcy) balanço m (do ativo e do passivo); (d) schedule of insurance, lista detalhada de todos os itens cobertos por uma apólice de seguros. 3. (a) roteiro m, plano m, programa m; work, operating, schedule, programa m de trabalho, de operação; (b) (stressing timing) horário m, cronograma m, (de obras, etc.); to be on schedule, estar em dia; to be behind schedule, estar atrasado (na execução de uma obra, etc.); he has a heavy schedule today, a sua agenda de hoje está muito tomada; Ins: schedule bond, seguro m contra a infidelidade de determinados empregados.

schedule², v.tr. 1. Jur: anexar (cláusulas a um contrato, etc.). 2. arrolar, catalogar, inscrever em uma lista; to schedule prices, tarifar os preços; scheduled prices, preços tarifados; Ind: Book-k: scheduled cost, custo programado, custo standard; Adm: scheduled taxes, impostos mpl cedulares. 3. programar (uma operação, a produção).

scheduler, n. Ind: programador m (de operações, obras, etc.).

scheduling, n. Ind: programação f.

scheme, n. 1. (a) Jur: scheme of composition (between debtor and creditors), concordata f; (b) profit-sharing scheme, sistema m de participação nos lucros; bonus scheme, plano m de gratificação; incentive

scheme, esquema m, plano, de incentivo; Ins: benefit scheme, plano de benefícios. 2. esquema, plano, projeto m; preliminary scheme, anteprojeto m, estudo preparatório de projeto.

science, n. ciência f; management science, ciência da administração.

scientific, a. científico; scientific research, pesquisa científica; scientific management, organização científica do trabalho, administração científica, administração racional.

scientist, n. cientista mf.

scope, n. 1. escopo m, extensão f, finalidade f, (das operações de uma firma, etc.). 2. campo m, oportunidade f; there is scope for increasing exports, há campo para aumentar as exportações.

scrap¹, n. sucata f, ferro velho; scrap dealer, merchant, sucateiro m, ferro-velho m; scrap heap, depósito m de ferro velho, montão m de sucata; scrap yard, pátio m de sucata; Book-k: etc: scrap value, valor m de sucata, (of salvage) valor de salvados.

scrap², v.tr. pôr (uma máquina, etc.) fora de serviço; sucatar (instalações, máquinas, etc.); to scrap a project, abandonar um projeto.

screen, v.tr. selecionar (pessoal).

screening, n. seleção f (de pessoal); triagem f.

scrip, n. Fin: 1. (a) cautela provisória (de ação), certificado m de portador de ações; (b) ação f de bonificação; scrip dividend, dividendo m em ações; scrip issue, emissão f de ações de bonificação. 2. Am: papel-moeda m (emitido numa crise).

scrutineer, n. escrutinador m (em eleição).

scrutinize, v.tr. examinar, escrutinar.

sea, n. mar m; at sea, em alto mar; by sea, por mar; to put to sea, fazer-se ao mar; sea damages, avarias fpl do mar; sea transportation, transporte marítimo.

seaborne, a. (of trade) marítimo; (of goods) transportado por via marítima.

sea-going, a. sea-going trade, comércio marítimo.

seal¹, n. selo m, sinete m, (official)

chancela *f*; **lead seal**, selo de chumbo;
wax seal, selo de cera, selo de lacre;
customs seal, selo alfandegário (de cera
ou chumbo).
seal², *v.tr.* **1.** selar (um documento, etc.);
(*with wax*) lacrar, (*with lead*) chumbar,
(caixa de mercadorias, etc.); **sealed bid**,
oferta lacrada; **the bid should be
submitted in a sealed envelope**, a proposta,
a oferta, deve ser apresentada num
envelope lacrado. **2. to seal (up)**, fechar;
to seal a letter, a parcel, fechar uma
carta, um pacote.
sealing, *n.* selagem *f*, (*with lead*)
chumbagem *f*; **sealing wax**, lacre *m*.
seaport, *n.* porto marítimo, porto de mar.
search¹, *n.* **1.** busca *f* (**for**, de);
investigação *f*, pesquisa *f*, (**into**, de); **to
make a search for sth.**, buscar, procurar,
algo; *Jur:* **title search** = (*approx.*)
certidões trintenárias. **2.** *Cust:* revista *f*;
to make a search of somebody's luggage,
passar revista, dar revista, na bagagem de
alguém; **right of search**, direito *m* de
revista; **search warrant**, mandado *m* de
busca.
search², *v.tr.* *Cust:* passar revista (na
bagagem, etc.).
searcher, *n.* *Cust:* funcionário
encarregado de passar revistas.
searching, *n.* *Cust:* revista *f*.
season, *n.* (*a*) estação *f*, temporada *f*,
época *f*; **the seasons of the year**, as
estações do ano; **the busy season**, a alta
temporada, a alta estação; **the slack
season**, a baixa temporada, a baixa
estação; **the holiday season**, a estação de
férias; **out of season**, fora de estação; **end
of season sale**, liquidação *f* de fim de
estação, de fim de temporada; (*b*) **the
cherry season**, a estação das cerejas;
fruits in season, frutas da época, da
estação; **mangoes are in season now**,
agora é época de mangas, agora é tempo
de mangas; (*c*) **season ticket**, bilhete *m* de
transporte para temporada; **to take out a
season ticket**, comprar um bilhete de
transporte para temporada; **season ticket
holder**, titular *mf* de bilhete de transporte
para temporada.
seasonal, *a.* estacional, sazonal; **seasonal

worker**, trabalhador *m* sazonal; **seasonal
unemployment**, desemprego *m* sazonal;
seasonal demand, procura *f* sazonal;
seasonal fluctuations, flutuações *fpl*
sazonais; **seasonal index**, índice *m* de
variação estacional; **seasonal peak**, ponto
máximo estacional; *Stat:* **seasonal
variation**, variação *f* sazonal, estacional.
seasoned, *a.* **seasoned securities**, títulos
confirmados; títulos que gozam de grande
aceitação pública.
seaworthiness, *n.* condições *fpl* de
navegabilidade; **certificate of
seaworthiness**, certificado *m* de
navegabilidade.
seaworthy, *a.* **seaworthy vessel**,
embarcação *f* em condições de
navegabilidade.
second, 1. *a.* segundo; **second half of the
month**, segunda quinzena; **second half
year**, segundo semestre; **second mortgage**,
hipoteca *f* de segunda ordem. **2.** *n.* artigo
m com defeito.
secondary, *a.* segundário; **secondary
industry**, indústria secundária, setor
secundário; **secondary liability**,
responsabilidade secundária; **secondary
reserves**, reservas secundárias; **secondary
securities**, valores *mpl* de segunda ordem.
second-class, 1. *a.* de segunda classe;
second-class mail, correio *m* de segunda
classe. **2.** *adv.* **to travel second-class**,
viajar em segunda classe.
second-grade, *a.* de segunda categoria,
de segunda ordem.
second-hand, 1. *a.* de segunda mão,
usado; **second-hand car**, carro usado;
second-hand car dealer, comerciante *mf*
de carros usados; **second-hand market**,
mercado *m* de artigos de segunda mão. **2.**
adv. **to buy sth. second-hand**, comprar
algo em segunda mão.
second-rate, *a.* (*a*) inferior; de qualidade
inferior; (*b*) **second-rate stocks**, títulos
mpl de segunda ordem.
secrecy, *n.* sigilo *m*.
secret, 1. *a.* **secret reserve**, reserva oculta,
reserva secreta. **2.** *n.* **industrial secret**,
segredo *m* industrial.
secretarial, *a.* **secretarial work**, trabalho
m de secretária; **secretarial services**,

serviços *mpl* de secretariado; **secretarial course,** curso *m* de secretariado.

secretary, *n.* (*a*) secretária *f*, (*male*) secretário *m*; **private secretary,** secretária particular; **senior, executive, secretary,** secretária sênior, executiva; **Secretary-General,** Secretário-Geral; (*b*) **the Secretary for Trade and Industry,** o Ministro da Indústria e Comércio.

section, *n.* (*a*) seção *f*; **the document is divided into three sections,** o documento está dividido em três seções; (*b*) (*in store, etc.*) **menswear section,** seção de roupas masculinas; (*in firm*) **personnel section,** seção de pessoal, setor *m* de pessoal; (*c*) *Stat: etc:* **cross-section of the population,** seção transversal da população; (*d*) *esp. Am:* **the business section of a town,** a zona comercial de uma cidade.

sectional, *a.* **sectional manager,** chefe *mf* de seção.

sector, *n.* setor *m*; **private sector,** setor privado; **public sector,** setor público; **industrial sector,** setor industrial; **sector loan,** empréstimo *m* para determinado setor; *Pol.Ec:* **money-creating sectors,** setores criadores da moeda; *Stat: etc:* **sector chart,** gráfico *m* de setores.

secular, *a.* secular; **secular growth,** crescimento *m* a longo prazo; **secular price,** preço *m* secular; **secular trend of prices,** tendência *f* secular dos preços; **secular upward drift,** tendência secular para o aumento.

secure¹, *a.* **secure investment,** investimento seguro.

secure², *v.tr.* 1. *Nau:* segurar, amarrar, prender, (uma carga no porão, etc.). 2. **to secure a debt,** garantir uma dívida; **to secure a creditor,** dar uma garantia (hipotecária ou pignoratícia) a um credor; **secured creditor,** (i) (*with mortgage or lien*) credor hipotecário, (ii) (*with moveables*) credor pignoratício; **secured loan,** empréstimo caucionado, empréstimo com plena garantia; **to secure a debt by mortgage,** garantir uma dívida mediante hipoteca; **mortgage secured on property,** hipoteca *f* sobre bens. 3. conseguir, obter, (preços, condições especiais, etc.).

security, *n.* 1. (*a*) segurança *f*; **security service (in firm, etc.),** serviço *m* de segurança; (*b*) *Adm:* **social security,** seguro *m* social, seguridade *f* social, previdência *f* social; **social-security regulation,** regulamento sócio-securitário; (*c*) **security of employment, job security,** estabilidade *f* no emprego. 2. (*a*) garantia *f*, caução *f*, fiança *f*; (*object given*) penhor *m*; **collateral security,** garantia subsidiária, garantia pignoratícia; **security for a debt,** garantia de uma dívida; **to give a security,** prestar, dar, uma caução, uma fiança, uma garantia; **to give sth. as (a) security,** dar algo em caução, em garantia; caucionar algo; **to lodge a security,** depositar um penhor; (*b*) (*person*) fiador *m*; **to stand, become, security for s.o.,** afiançar, abonar, alguém; ser fiador de alguém, ser avalista de alguém; 3. *Fin:* (*usu. pl.*) **securities,** títulos *mpl*, valores *mpl* (mobiliários), papéis *mpl*; **government, gilt-edged, public, securities,** fundos públicos; **registered securities,** títulos nominativos; **marketable securities,** títulos de bolsa, títulos negociáveis na bolsa; **to float securities on the market,** colocar, lançar, títulos no mercado; **the securities market,** o mercado de valores, (*the Stock Exchange*) a bolsa de valores; **securities account,** conta *f* de títulos; **securities dealt in for the account,** títulos vendidos em operação a termo; **securities held in pawn,** títulos recebidos em penhor.

sedentary, *a.* sedentário.

seed, *n.* semente *f*; **seed cotton,** algodão *m* em caroço; **seed farm,** campo *m* de multiplicação de sementes; **seed testing laboratory,** laboratório *m* de ensaio de sementes.

segment, *n.* segmento *m* (do mercado, etc.).

seize, *v.tr. Jur:* apreender, confiscar, arrestar, seqüestrar, embargar, (mercadorias, etc.); **seized money,** moeda seqüestrada.

seizure, *n. Jur:* arresto *m*, embargo *m*, confisco *m*, seqüestro *m*.

select, *v.tr.* selecionar, escolher.

selected, *a.* **selected wine,** vinho

selecionado; *Fin:* **selected investments,** investimentos selecionados, aplicações selecionadas.

selective, *a.* seletivo; **selective control,** controle seletivo; **selective demarketing,** descomercialização seletiva; **selective selling,** venda selecionada.

self-adhesive, *a.* auto-adesivo.

self-balancing, *a. Book-k:* **self-balancing ledger,** razão *m* no qual os saldos devedores compensam os saldos credores.

self-employed, *a.* (trabalhador) autônomo; por conta própria.

self-financing, 1. *n.* autofinanciamento *m.* **2.** *a.* **self-financing enterprise,** empreendimento *m* autofinanciável.

self-insurance, *n.* auto-seguro *m.*

self-liquidating, *a.* **self-liquidating loan,** empréstimo *m* auto-amortizável.

self-management, *n.* autogestão *f.*

self-moving, *a. Jur:* semovente.

self-service, *n.* auto-serviço *m.*

self-sufficiency, *n.* auto-suficiência *f;* **economic self-sufficiency,** auto-suficiência econômica; **national self-sufficiency,** autarquia *f,* autarcia *f,* auto-suficiência (nacional).

self-sufficient, *a.* auto-suficiente.

sell, *v.* **1.** *v.tr.* vender; colocar (mercadorias); **to sell sth. back to s.o.,** revender algo a alguém; **difficult to sell,** de venda difícil; **to sell sth. by auction,** arrematar algo, vender algo em leilão; **to sell by weight,** vender a peso; **to sell in bulk,** vender a granel; **to sell sth. for cash,** vender algo à vista; **to sell sth. on credit,** vender algo fiado, a crédito; **to sell on instalments,** vender a prazo; **to sell sth. at a loss,** vender algo com prejuízo; **to sell sth. dear, cheap,** vender algo caro, barato; **he sold me the car for one hundred pounds,** ele me vendeu o carro por cem libras esterlinas; **he's selling the books on commission,** ele está vendendo os livros em commissão; **to sell goods wholesale,** vender mercadorias por atacado; **to sell goods retail,** vender mercadorias a varejo; *St.Exch:* **to sell short, to sell a bear,** vender a descoberto. **2.** *v.i.* **our classified ads sell,** os nossos classificados vendem; **this book sells well in France,** este livro

vende bem na França; **the apartments are selling at $80 000,** os apartamentos estão sendo vendidos por $80.000, os apartamentos estão a, por, $80.000.

seller, *n.* **1.** (*person*) vendedor *m; St.Exch: etc:* **seller's market,** mercado *m* de vendedor; **seller's option,** opção *f* do vendedor; **sellers over,** excesso *m* de vendedores. **2.** (*thing*) **good seller,** artigo *m* que vende bem, que tem boa venda, que tem muita saída; **bad seller,** artigo que encalha, que não tem saída.

selling, *n.* venda *f,* vendagem *f,* colocação *f,* (de mercadorias); **direct selling,** venda direta; **door-to-door selling, house-to-house selling,** venda de porta em porta, de casa em casa; **selling agent,** agente *mf* de vendas; **selling commission,** comissão *f* de sobre, vendas; **selling cost,** custo *m* de venda; **selling expense,** despesa *f* de vendas, despesa com vendas; **selling point,** (i) ponto *m* de venda, (ii) vantagem *f* especial de um produto; **selling practices,** práticas *fpl* de venda, de vendagem; **selling price,** preço *m* de venda; **selling techniques,** técnicas *fpl* de venda; **selling off, out,** liquidação *f* (de estoque).

sell off, *v.tr.* liquidar (mercadorias, saldos).

sell out, *v.* **1.** *v.tr.* liquidar (um negócio). **2.** *v.i.* esgotar-se; **the book sold out in a week,** o livro esgotou-se em uma semana.

sellout, *n.* **the new product was a sellout,** o novo produto teve venda total, saída total; o novo produto se esgotou.

sell up, *v.tr.* vender todos os bens (na liquidação de uma firma, etc.).

semester, *n.* semestre *m.*

semi-annually, *adv.* semestralmente.

semi-automated, *a.* semi-automático.

semi-durables, *n.pl.* semiduráveis *mpl.*

semi-finished, *a.* semi-acabado; **semi-finished steel,** produtos *mpl* de aço semi-acabados.

semi-industrialized, *a.* semi-industrializado.

semi-manufactured, *a.* semimanufaturado.

semi-manufactures, *n.pl.* (produtos) semimanufaturados.

semi-senior, *a.* **semi-senior accountant,** contador *m* semisênior.

semi-skilled, *a.* (trabalhador) semi-especializado, semiqualificado.

semi-variable, *a. Book-k: Ind: etc:* **semi-variable cost,** custo *m* semivariável.

send, *v.* **1.** *v.tr.* (*a*) enviar, mandar, (alguém); (*b*) enviar, remeter, (uma carta, um telegrama, um pacote); expedir (um pacote, um telegrama); passar (um telegrama); **to send goods by train,** enviar, expedir, mercadorias por trem; 'send your order today', 'envie seu pedido ainda hoje'. **2.** *v.i.* **to send for s.o.,** mandar chamar, mandar buscar, alguém.

sender, *n.* remetente *mf* (de carta, etc.); **to return to the sender,** devolver ao remetente.

send forward, *v.tr.* expedir (carga).

send in, *v.tr.* enviar (algo ao seu destino); entregar (uma solicitação, um pedido); **he sent in his bill,** ele entregou sua fatura; **to send in one's resignation,** pedir demissão.

send off, *v.* **1.** *v.tr.* enviar; **to send off a letter,** pôr uma carta no correio; **to send off a telex,** mandar um telex; **to send off goods,** expedir mercadorias; **to send off money,** remeter dinheiro. **2.** *v.i.* **to send off for goods,** encomendar mercadorias pelo correio.

send out, *v.tr.* enviar, expedir, (carta, etc.); **to send out a circular,** distribuir uma circular (pelo correio).

senior, **1.** *a.* sênior; **senior accountant,** contador *m* sênior; **senior secretary,** secretária *f* sênior; **senior official,** alto funcionário, funcionário de categoria superior; **senior clerk** = chefe *mf* de escritório; **senior partner,** sócio *m* principal; *Fin:* **senior debt,** dívida prioritária, dívida principal; **senior shares,** ações *fpl* preferenciais. **2.** *n.* sênior *m.*

seniority, *n.* antiguidade *f*; **to be promoted by seniority,** ser promovido por antiguidade, por tempo de serviço.

sensitive, *a.* **sensitive market,** mercado *m* sensível.

sensitivity, *n.* **sensitivity training,** educação *f* da sensibilidade.

separable, *a. Book-k:* **separable cost,** custo *m* separável, custo identificável.

sequence, *n.* seqüência *f*; **sequence analysis,** análise *f* seqüencial; *Book-k:* **sequence check,** verificação *f* seqüencial.

sequester, sequestrate, *v.tr. Jur:* seqüestrar, apreender, (os bens de um devedor, etc.).

sequestration, *n. Jur:* seqüestração *f*, seqüestro *m*; **writ of sequestration,** mandado *m* de busca e apreensão.

serial, *a.* serial, seriado, seriário, em série; **serial manufacture,** fabricação seriada, em série; **serial number,** número *m* de série, número de ordem, *Ind:* número serial (de fabricação); *Fin:* **serial bonds,** obrigações *fpl* (ou debêntures *fpl*) resgatáveis em série, por série.

serialize, *v.tr. Ind: etc:* fabricar em série.

serially, *adv.* em série, por série.

series, *n.inv.* série *f*; **bonds redeemable in series,** obrigações *fpl* resgatáveis em série, por série.

servant, *n.* **public servant,** empregado público, funcionário *m* (no serviço público), servidor público; **civil servant,** funcionário público; **career civil servant,** funcionário público admitido por concurso; **to become a civil servant,** entrar no serviço público; *Am:* **appointive civil servant,** funcionário público nomeado.

serve, *v.* **1.** *v.tr.* (*a*) **to serve an apprenticeship,** fazer o aprendizado; (*b*) **to serve a customer,** atender um freguês (numa loja), servir um freguês (num restaurante); **to serve s.o. lunch,** servir o almoço a alguém; **this solicitor has served the firm since its foundation,** este advogado serve à firma desde a fundação. **2.** *v.i.* **to serve in a shop,** trabalhar como balconista (numa loja).

service¹, *n.* **1.** (*a*) serviço *m*; **ten years' service,** dez anos de serviço; **promotion according to length of service,** promoção *f*, ascensão *f*, por tempo de serviço, por antiguidade; **service record,** folha *f* de serviço; **contract of service,** contrato *m* de trabalho; (*b*) (*in hotel, etc.*) serviço, atendimento *m*; **service charge,** (taxa *f* de) serviço; **ten per cent service charge,** serviço de dez por cento; **service station,**

posto *m* de serviço; (*c*) *Adm: Ind: etc:* **contract service,** serviço contratual; **contract for services,** contrato *m* de prestação de serviços; **24-hour service,** serviço dia e noite, serviço permanente; (*d*) **to bring, put,** (a machine, a vehicle) **into service,** pôr (uma máquina, um veículo) em funcionamento; **service life** (**of a machine**), vida *f* util (de uma máquina). **2. services rendered,** serviços prestados; *Pol.Ec:* **goods and services,** bens *mpl* e serviços, mercadorias *fpl* e serviços; **service industry,** indústria terciária, setor terciário, indústria de serviços. **3. the civil service,** o serviço público. **4. public services,** serviços públicos; **postal service,** serviço postal; **telecommunications service,** serviço de telecomunicações; **social services,** serviços sociais. **5.** (*maintenance, etc.*) assistência técnica, revisão *f*; **service network,** rede *f* de assistência técnica; **after-sales service,** serviço pós-vendas, serviço de assistência técnica. **6.** *Fin:* (debt) **service,** serviço *m*.

service², *v.tr.* **to service a car,** revisar, fazer a revisão de, um carro; *Fin:* **to service a debt,** efetuar o serviço de uma dívida; efetuar os pagamentos a título de juros e amortização de uma dívida.

servicing, *n.* (*a*) revisão *f* (de carro, etc.); (*b*) *Fin:* (debt) **servicing,** serviço *m*; **servicing cost,** custo *m* de serviço.

session, *n.* sessão *f*; *St.Exch:* sessão (de bolsa); **closing session,** sessão de fechamento.

set¹, *n.* conjunto *m*, jogo *m*, (de ferramentas, etc.); bateria *f* (de cozinha); aparelho *m* (de louça); *Book-k:* **set of accounts,** escrita *f*; conjunto de documentos e registros relativos a uma escrita; **set of invoices,** jogo *m* de faturas.

set², *a.* set price, preço fixo.

set³, *v.tr.* **to set a value on sth.,** avaliar algo; **to set a time for a meeting,** marcar a hora de uma reunião.

setback, *n.* revés *m*; **to suffer a setback,** sofrer um revés.

set off, *v.tr.* **to set off a debt,** compensar uma dívida; **to set off a gain against a loss,** compensar uma perda com um ganho.

set-off, *n.* compensação *f*; *Book-k:* lançamento compensado.

set out, *v.tr.* (*a*) **to set out the terms of a contract,** expor as condições de um contrato; **as set out in article 2,** conforme exposto no artigo 2; (*b*) (*arrange*) dispor (mercadorias num balcão, etc.), (*display*) expor (artigos numa vitrina).

set-out, *n.* exposição *f* (de artigos, etc.).

setting up, *n.* implantação *f*, instalação *f*, estabelecimento *m*, (de indústria, fábrica, etc.); criação *f* (de uma firma); organização *f* (de um comitê).

settle, *v.* **1.** *v.tr.* (*a*) determinar, fixar, combinar, assentar, (dia e hora para um encontro, etc.); **the terms were settled,** as condições foram combinadas; (*b*) resolver (uma questão); fechar (um negócio); (*c*) liquidar, saldar, (uma conta); **to settle one's bills,** saldar, pagar, as contas; (*d*) **to settle an annuity on, upon, s.o.,** doar, legar, uma renda vitalícia a alguém. **2.** *v.i.* **to settle for sth.,** concordar em aceitar algo; **I settled for $100,** concordei em aceitar cem dólares.

settled, *a.* (*a*) (assunto) combinado, decidido; (problema) resolvido; (*b*) (*of bill, etc.*) liquidado, saldado, saldo; **settled accounts,** contas liquidadas.

settle down, *v.i.* (*a*) **to settle down to work,** pôr-se a trabalhar; (*b*) (*of market*) acalmar(-se), amainar.

settlement, *n.* (*a*) resolução *f* (de uma questão), esclarecimento *m* (de uma dúvida), liquidação *f* (de um assunto); **wage settlement, pay settlement,** acordo *m* salarial; (*b*) pagamento *m* (de uma dívida, de uma conta), liquidação, apuração *f*, (de uma conta); **settlement of accounts,** liquidação de contas, apuração de contas; **international settlements,** pagamentos internacionais; *Ins:* **settlement of claims,** liquidação de sinistros; *St.Exch:* liquidação, apuração; **dealings for settlement,** operações *fpl* a termo; **settlement day,** dia *m* de liquidação; **yearly settlement,** liquidação anual; (*c*) **legal settlement** (*between trader and creditors*), concordata *f*; (*d*) **settlement of an annuity on s.o.,** doação *f* de uma renda vitalícia a alguém; (*e*) núcleo *m* de povoamento; **settlement programme**, programa *m* de colonização.

settling, *n.* (*a*) fechamento *m*, conclusão *f*, (de um negócio), resolução *f* (de uma questão); (*b*) **settling (up)**, liquidação *f*, apuração *f*, (de uma conta); **settling of accounts**, ajuste *m* de contas; *St.Exch:* **settling day**, dia *m* de liquidação.

set up, *v.* **1.** *v.tr.* (*a*) criar, organizar, fundar, (uma firma); **to set up a business**, montar, criar, abrir, um negócio; **to set up shop**, abrir, montar, uma loja; (*b*) **to set s.o. up in business**, estabelecer alguém nos negócios. **2.** *v.i.* **to set up in business**, estabelecer-se nos negócios; **to set up as a chemist**, estabelecer-se como farmacêutico.

set-up, *n.* organização *f*; *Ind:* **set-up time**, tempo *m* de preparo de (uma máquina).

severance, *n. Ind: etc:* demissão *f*, dispensa *f*, despedida *f*; **severance pay**, indenização *f* por rescisão do contrato de trabalho, indenização por afastamento do emprego.

shadow, *n.* **shadow price**, preço-sombra *m*, preço *m* de conta.

shake-out, *n. St.Exch: F:* insolvência *f* (de especuladores).

shake-up, *n. F:* reorganização drástica (do pessoal).

shaky, *a.* **shaky business**, negócio fraco; **shaky undertaking**, empreendimento pouco seguro; **shaky currency**, moeda *f* frágil.

sham, *a.* **sham company**, empresa fictícia; **sham dividend**, dividendo fictício.

share¹, *n.* **1.** (*a*) porção *f*, parte *f*; **to divide sth. into equal shares**, dividir algo em partes iguais; **to have a share in ...**, participar, ter parte, em ..., partilhar de ...; **share in the profits**, participação *f* nos lucros; **to go shares with s.o.**, partilhar com alguém; **to win a sizable share of the market**, conseguir uma parcela considerável do mercado; (*b*) **fair share**, quinhão justo, quinhão devido. **2.** cota *f*, cota-parte *f*, quota *f*; **to pay one's share of the running costs**, pagar a sua cota-parte nos custos de funcionamento. **3.** *Fin:* ação *f*, título *m*, papel *m*, valor *m*; (*in partnership*) cota, quota; **bearer**

share, ação ao portador; **bonus share**, ação bonificada, ação de bonificação, filhote *m*; **founder's share, promoter's share**, parte beneficiária, parte de fundador, ação de fundador; **fully paid(-up) share**, ação integralizada, ação liberada; **ordinary share**, ação ordinária; **partly paid(-up) share**, ação não integralizada; **preference, preferred, share**, ação preferencial, ação privilegiada; **qualification share**, ação de garantia (de gestão); **registered, personal, share**, ação nominativa; **share capital**, capital-ações *m*; **share certificate**, certificado *m* de ação (ou de ações); **share exchange**, permuta *f* de ações; **share index**, índice *m* de ações; **share issue**, emissão *f* de ações; **share market**, mercado acionário, mercado de valores, de títulos; **share premium**, ágio *m* sobre a emissão (de ações); **share register**, livro-registro *m* dos acionistas; **share warrant**, cautela *f* de ação (ou ações) ao portador; **to hold shares**, possuir, deter, ações.

share², *v.tr. & i.* **to share (in) the profits**, participar dos lucros, nos lucros; ter parte nos lucros; **to share out the work**, distribuir, repartir, o trabalho; **to share out the profits among the workers**, repartir os lucros entre os trabalhadores, os operários.

sharecropper, *n. Agr:* meeiro *m*.

sharecropping, *n.* plantio *m* a meias.

shareholder, *n. Fin:* acionista *mf*, acionário *m*; **registered shareholder**, possuidor *m* de ações nominativas; **shareholder's equity**, patrimônio líquido (de uma empresa); **shareholder's funds**, capital *m* social e reservas.

shareholding, *n.* **1.** possessão *f* de ações; **employee shareholding**, participação *f* patrimonial dos empregados. **2.** X's **shareholding**, as ações possuídas por X.

share-out, *n.* distribuição *f*, repartição *f*.

sharing, *n.* **1.** repartição *f*, partilha *f*. **2.** participação *f*; **profit sharing**, participação nos lucros.

shark, *n. F:* vigarista *mf*.

sharp, *a.* abrupto, acentuado; **sharp rise in interest rates**, subida acentuada nas taxas de juros; **sharp drop in interest rates**, baixa acentuada nas taxas de juros; **sharp rise in prices,** forte elevação *f,* acentuada elevação, nos preços; **sharp fluctuations,** bruscas oscilações.

shave, *v.tr.* *F:* **to shave advertising expenditure,** reduzir as despesas publicitárias.

sheet, *n.* folha *f;* **sheet of paper,** folha de papel; **sheet of steel,** folha de aço; **sheet of plywood,** folha de madeira compensada; **balance sheet,** (folha de) balanço *m;* **cost sheet,** folha de custo; *Stat:* **spread sheet,** folha de análise; *Ind:* **order sheet,** folha de pedido; **work sheet,** folha de cálculos; **job sheet, time sheet,** folha diária de trabalho, folha de serviço; **attendance sheet,** folha de presença.

shelf, *n.* prateleira *f;* **shelf life,** vida *f* de prateleira; **shelf space,** espaço *m* de prateleira; (*of goods*) **to stay on the shelves,** encalhar, não ter saída.

sheltered, *a.* *Pol.Ec:* **sheltered industry,** indústria protegida contra concorrência estrangeira.

shift, *n.* **1.** *Ind: etc:* (*a*) (*session*) turno *m;* **day shift,** turno diurno, turno do dia; **night shift,** turno noturno, turno da noite; **swing shift, evening shift,** turno vespertino; **rotating shift,** turno em rodízio; **split shift,** turno dividido; **an eight-hour shift,** um turno, uma jornada, de oito horas; **to work eight-hour shifts,** trabalhar em turnos de oito horas; (*b*) (*personnel*) turma *f;* **day shift,** turma do dia; **night shift,** turma da noite. **2.** mudança *f,* deslocamento *m;* **shift of demand,** deslocamento de demanda; **shift between reserve assets,** mudança na composição das reservas.

shiftwork, *n.* *Ind:* trabalho *m* em turnos.

ship¹, *n.* navio *m;* **sea-going ship,** navio de alto bordo; **merchant ship,** navio mercante; **cargo ship,** (navio) cargueiro *m,* navio de carga; **container ship,** (navio) porta-containers *m;* **refrigerator ship,** navio frigorífico; **ship chandler,** fornecedor *m* de provisões para navios; **ship's papers,** papéis *mpl* de bordo; **ship's register,** registro *m* de bordo.

ship², *v.tr.* **1.** (*load*) embarcar (mercadorias, etc.); **shipped bill of lading,**

conhecimento *m* de carga embarcada. **2.** (*dispatch*) expedir, despachar, remeter; **the goods were shipped by rail,** as mercadorias foram expedidas via férrea, por trem.

shipbroker, *n.* corretor marítimo, corretor de navios.

shipbrokerage, *n.* corretagem marítima.

shipbuilder, *n.* engenheiro *m* naval; (*of firm*) construtor *m* de navios.

shipbuilding, *n.* construção *f* naval, construção de navios; **the shipbuilding industry,** a indústria de construção naval.

shipment, *n.* **1.** (*a*) embarque *m,* carregamento *m,* (de mercadorias); **shipment terms,** condições *fpl* de embarque; (*b*) expedição *f,* remessa *f,* despacho *m,* (de mercadorias) (via marítima). **2.** (*goods shipped*) remessa *f;* **gold shipment,** remessa de ouro; **to clear a shipment,** liberar, desembaraçar, um embarque.

shipowner, *n.* armador *m.*

shipper, *n.* expedidor *m.*

shipping, *n.* **1.** (*a*) embarque *m* (de uma carga); **shipping advice,** aviso *m* de embarque; **shipping agent,** agente marítimo; **shipping bill,** conhecimento *m* de embarque; **shipping charges,** despesas *fpl* de embarque; **shipping clerk,** despachante *mf* (de companhia de navegação); **shipping company,** companhia *f* de navegação, empresa *f* de navegação; **shipping dock,** doca *f,* cais *m;* **shipping documents,** documentos *mpl* de embarque; **shipping instructions,** instruções *fpl* para remessa; **shipping line,** linha *f* de navegação; **shipping list,** romaneio *m;* **shipping permit,** guia *f* de embarque; **shipping port,** porto *m* de embarque; **shipping rates,** taxas *fpl* de embarque; **shipping services,** serviços *mpl* de embarque; **shipping space,** espaço *m* disponível para transporte de mercadorias; **shipping ton,** tonelada *f* de embarque; **shipping weight,** peso *m* de embarque; **shipping yard,** pátio *m* de embarque; (*b*) expedição *f,* remessa *f,* (de mercadorias por via marítima). **2. the shipping of a country,** a marinha mercante de um país; **movement of**

shipping, movimento *m* da navegação; coastwise shipping, navegação de cabotagem, navegação costeira; ocean-going shipping, navegação de longo curso; river shipping, navegação fluvial; shipping routes, rotas marítimas.
shoot up, *v.i.* (*of prices, costs*) galgar, elevar-se repentinamente.
shop¹, *n.* 1. loja *f*, casa *f* comercial; baker's shop, padaria *f*; grocer's shop, mercearia *f*, loja de secos e molhados, armazém *m*, venda *f*; shoe shop, sapataria *f*; toy shop, loja de brinquedos; duty-free shop, duty-free *f*; loja que goza de imunidade fiscal; to set up shop, montar uma loja; to keep a shop, ter uma loja; to shut up shop, liquidar um negócio, fechar uma loja, um negócio; shop assistant, caixeiro *m*, caixeira *f*, balconista *mf*, vendedor *m* de loja, vendedora *f* de loja; shop window, vitrina *f*, vitrine *f*. 2. *Ind: etc:* oficina *f*, fábrica *f*; the shop floor, os operários; shop steward, delegado *m* sindical (na empresa), delegado de empresa; assembly shop, oficina de montagem; shop foreman, mestre *m* de oficina; shop number, número *m* de fábrica; shop order, ordem *f* de serviço, de fabricação; shop test, ensaio *m* de oficina, de fábrica; closed shop, estabelecimento que só admite operários sindicalizados. 3. *F:* to talk shop, falar dos próprios negócios, falar de assuntos profissionais. 4. *Advert:* agência *f* de propaganda, de publicidade.
shop², *v.i.* fazer compras; to shop around, ir ou telefonar a diversas lojas a fim de conhecer e comprar pelo melhor preço.
shopgirl, *n.* caixeira *f*, balconista *f*, vendedora *f* (de loja).
shopkeeper, *n.* lojista *mf*, dono *m* de loja, comerciante *mf*.
shopkeeping, *n.* comércio *m* lojista.
shoplifter, *n.* ladrão *m* de loja.
shoplifting, *n.* furto *m* em loja.
shopper, *n.* comprador *m*, freguês *m* de loja.
shopping, *n.* compras *fpl*; to do one's shopping, fazer as compras; shopping bag, sacola *f*; shopping centre, shopping center *m*, centro *m* comercial; shopping district, distrito *m* comercial; shopping hours,

horário *m* de expediente comercial; shopping list, relação *f* de compras; window-shopping, ato *m* de olhar as vitrinas sem entrar na loja para comprar; *Econ: etc:* shopping goods, artigos *mpl* de consumo comparados.
shop-soiled, *a.* usado ou gasto por exposição ou manuseio em loja.
shopwalker, *n.* supervisor *m*, superintendente *mf* de seção (em uma grande loja).
short, 1. *a.* (*a*) *Fin:* short bills, bills at short date, letras *fpl* a curto prazo; deposit, loan, at short notice, depósito *m*, empréstimo *m*, a curto prazo; short rate, taxa *f* a curto prazo; (*b*) (*of weight, measure, etc.*) insuficiente; to give short weight, vender abaixo do peso combinado; short weight, peso *m* a menos, falta *f* de peso; the weight is 50 grams short, faltam 50 gramas no peso; it is 10 cruzeiros short, estão faltando dez cruzeiros; I am twenty pounds short, estão me faltando vinte libras esterlinas; short delivery, entrega *f* insuficiente; short shipment, remessa *f* de mercadorias inferior à constante na fatura comercial; short supply, escassez *f*, estoque escasso, suprimento reduzido; coal is in short supply, o carvão está em falta; *Ind:* to be on short time, trabalhar em regime de semana reduzida; the receipts fall short of expectations by five thousand dollars, as receitas são inferiores em cinco mil dólares à quantia prevista; (*c*) (*of person*) to be short of work, carecer de trabalho, ter trabalho insuficiente; to be short of raw materials, estar com escassez de matérias-primas; to be short of staff, carecer de pessoal; I'm short of money, está me faltando dinheiro, não tenho dinheiro bastante; (*d*) *St.Exch:* short sale, venda *f* a descoberto; short contract, contrato *m* de venda a descoberto; short covering, cobertura *f* de um título (etc.) a descoberto; short account, conta *f* que registra as vendas de títulos a descoberto. 2. *n.* (*a*) short in the cash, déficit *m* na caixa; (*b*) *St.Exch:* (i) venda *f* a descoberto, (ii) (*person*) baixista *mf*. 3. *adv. St.Exch:* (*a*) a descoberto; to sell

short, vender a descoberto, jogar na baixa; (b) a curto prazo.

shortage, n. (a) escassez f, deficiência f, falta f, carência f; Fin: desfalque m; shortage of staff, of labour, escassez f de pessoal, de mão-de-obra; shortage of raw materials, escassez, carência, de matérias-primas; shortage of money, falta de dinheiro; shortage in the cash, déficit m na caixa; to make up, to make good, the shortage, suprir o déficit; (b) M.Ins: etc: pl. shortages, perdas fpl.

short-dated, a. Fin: (letra f) a curto prazo.

shortening, n. Fin: shortening of credit, redução f de crédito.

shortfall, n. deficiência f, insuficiência f; Fin: déficit m.

shorthand, n. estenografia f, taquigrafia f, logografia f; shorthand typing, estenodatilografia f; shorthand typist, estenodatilógrafa f, estenodatilógrafo m; to take sth. down in shorthand, estenografar, taquigrafar, algo.

short-handed, a. com poucos operários, com falta de operários, de empregados; the factory is short-handed owing to the holidays, a fábrica está com poucos operários devido às férias.

short-staffed, a. carente de pessoal; to be short-staffed, estar com falta de pessoal, de mão-de-obra.

short-staple, a. short-staple cotton, algodão m de fibra curta.

short-term, a. Fin: etc: a curto prazo; short-term assets, ativo m a curto prazo; short-term credit, crédito m a curto prazo; short-term liabilities, passivo m a curto prazo, exigível m a curto prazo; short-term loan, empréstimo m a curto prazo; short-term notes, títulos mpl (de vencimento) a curto prazo; short-term paper, efeitos mpl, papéis mpl, a curto prazo; short-term trend, tendência f a curto prazo.

show¹, n. (a) exposição f (de mercadorias, etc.); the Motor Show, o Salão do Automóvel; fashion show, fashion show m, desfile m de moda; show window, vitrina f, vitrine f; television show, show m, espetáculo m, de televisão; (b) show

house, casa (decorada) em exposição; show flat, apartamento (decorado) em exposição; (c) voting by a show of hands, votação f por aclamação, por mãos erguidas.

show², v.tr. (a) mostrar, expor; to show the factory to a client, mostrar a fábrica a um cliente; to show one's products at an industrial fair, mostrar, expor, os seus produtos em uma feira industrial; (b) apresentar, acusar; the balance sheet shows a loss, o balanço apresenta um déficit, o balanço acusa uma perda; the accounts show a net profit of..., as demonstrações financeiras apontam um lucro líquido de...; the market is showing signs of recovery, o mercado está apresentando sinais de recuperação; the reserves shown on the balance sheet, as reservas apresentadas no balanço; to show the surplus as an extraordinary reserve, caracterizar o superávit como uma reserva extraordinária.

showcard, n. Am: (i) cartaz m, (ii) mostruário m.

showcase, n. mostruário m, mostrador m, vitrina f, vitrine f.

showroom, n. sala f de exposição.

shredder, n. máquina fragmentadora de papel.

shrimp, n. camarão m; shrimp boat, barco m para a pesca do camarão.

shrink-wrapping, n. embalagem f a vácuo (que permite a visualização do produto).

shut, v. 1. v.tr. fechar (uma loja, etc.); Book-k: (on transfer books, etc.) shut for dividend, encerrado para lançamento dos dividendos. 2. v.i. the shops shut at 6 p.m., as lojas fecham às 18 horas.

shut down, v. Ind: 1. v.tr. to shut down a factory, fechar uma fábrica; to shut down production, fazer cessar a produção. 2. v.i. (a) fechar; the factory shut down owing to a lack of orders, a fábrica fechou por falta de pedidos; (b) (of production, etc.) parar, cessar; production shut down in the machine shop, a produção parou, cessou, na oficina mecânica.

shut-down, a. fechado; (halted) parado.

shutdown, *n.* *Ind:* (*a*) (*closure*) fechamento *m*; **shutdown point,** ponto *m* de fechamento; (*b*) parada *f* (de fábrica, de produção), cessação *f* de trabalho, paralisação (temporária) (de fábrica, de produção).

shut-out, *n.* *Ind:* lock-out *m*, greve *f* de patrões, greve patronal.

sick, *a.* doente; **sick leave,** licença *f* para tratamento de saúde; **sick pay,** salário pago em período de doença.

sickness, *n.* doença *f*; **sickness benefit,** auxílio-doença *m*; **to draw sickness benefit,** perceber o auxílio-doença.

side, *n.* **1.** *Book-k:* **credit side,** haver *m*; **debit side,** deve *m*. **2.** *St.Exch: etc:* **the other side,** a outra parte (em uma transação). **3. reverse side (of a letter of credit),** verso *m* (de uma carta de crédito). **4. side effect,** efeito *m* colateral.

sidehead, *n.* *Book-k: etc:* título *m* de linha de tabela (em contraste com os cabeçalhos das colunas).

sideline, *n.* **1.** ocupação secundária, *F:* biscate *m*, gancho *m*. **2.** linha *f* suplementar (de artigos, mercadorias, etc.).

sight¹, *n.* (*a*) **at sight,** à vista; **sight assets,** ativo *m* à vista; **sight bill (of exchange), bill at sight,** letra *f* (de câmbio) à vista; (*as invoice*) **sight bill,** duplicata *f* à vista; **sight deposit,** deposito *m* à vista; **sight draft, draft at sight,** saque *m* à vista; **bill payable at 20 days' sight,** letra à vista pagável em 20 dias, letra pagável a 20 dias de vista; **sight liabilities,** obrigações *fpl* à vista; (*b*) *N.Am:* **'on sale sight unseen',** 'à venda sem inspeção prévia', 'vende-se sem inspeção prévia'; *Cust:* **sight entry,** declaração provisória.

sight², *v.tr.* **to sight a bill,** visar uma letra para aceite.

sign, *v.tr.* assinar, firmar; **to sign a cheque,** assinar um cheque; **to sign a contract,** assinar, firmar, um contrato; **sign here,** assine aquí; *Fin:* **to sign a bill of exchange,** aceitar uma letra de câmbio.

signatory, *a. & n.* signatário (*m*); **signatory to a contract,** signatário de um contrato.

signature, *n.* assinatura *f*, firma *f*; **to put one's signature to a letter,** apor a sua assinatura em uma carta; **authenticated, certified, signature,** assinatura reconhecida; **for signature,** para assinatura; **the signature of a firm, corporate signature,** assinatura social.

signer, *n.* signatário *m*.

signing, *n.* assinatura *f* (de contrato, requerimento, etc.); aceite *m* (de letra de câmbio); **signing machines,** máquinas assinadoras.

sign off, *v.i.* (*of workers in factories, etc.*) assinar o ponto (na saída).

sign on, *v.* **1.** *v.tr.* contratar, admitir, (operário, empregado). **2.** *v.i.* (*a*) (*of workers*) ser admitido, ser contratado; *F:* **to sign on for the dole,** requerer o auxílio-desemprego; (*b*) (*of workers in factories, etc.*) assinar o ponto (na entrada).

silent, *a.* **silent partner,** sócio comanditário, comanditário *m*.

silicon chip, *n.* condutor *m* em circuito impresso.

silver, *n.* (*a*) prata *f*; **coin silver,** prata para cunhagem; **commercial silver,** prata comercial; **fine silver,** prata fina; **sterling silver,** prata de lei; **silver bullion,** prata em barras; **silver certificates,** certificados *mpl* de dépositos feitos em prata; **silver foil,** folha *f* de prata; **silver ore,** minério *m* de prata; **silver paper,** papel prateado; **silver plate,** baixela *f* de prata, prataria *f*; **silver standard,** padrão *m* de prata; **silver wire,** fio *m* de prata; (*b*) **a pound in silver,** uma libra em moedas de prata.

simple, *a.* (*a*) simples; **simple average,** média *f* simples, média aritmética; **simple interest,** juro(s) simples; *Book-k:* **simple journal,** diário *m* simples; *Ind:* **simple cost function,** função *f* de custo simples; (*b*) *Jur:* **simple contract,** contrato *m* verbal, contrato consensual; **simple contract creditor,** credor quirografário.

single, *a.* **single collection,** cobrança *f* simples; **single-crop economy,** economia baseada em monocultura; **single decision,** decisão isolada; **single-entry book-keeping,** contabilidade *f* por partidas simples; **single fare,** passagem *f* de ida; **single line,** linha *f* de via única; **single loan,** empréstimo isolado; **single payment,**

pagamento único; **single premium,** prêmio único; **single sum,** importância paga de uma só vez; **single tax,** imposto único.

sink, *v.tr.* **1. to sink money in trade,** aplicar dinheiro no comércio. **2. to sink a loan,** amortizar um empréstimo; **to sink the national debt,** amortizar a dívida pública.

sinking, *n.* **sinking fund,** fundo *m* de amortização.

sir, *n. Corr:* **(Dear) Sir(s),** Ilustríssimo(s) Senhor(es) (*abbr:* Ill.^mo(s) Sr(s).), Amigo(s) e Senhor(es) (*abbr:* Am.^o(s) e Sr(s).); (*less formal*) Prezado(s) Senhor(es).

sister, *n.* **sister company,** companhia coligada.

sit-down, *n.* **sit-down strike,** greve *f* de braços cruzados, greve branca.

site, *n.* (*land*) terreno *m*; **(building) site,** canteiro *m* de obras (de construção); *Book-k:* **site audit,** exame *m* de auditoria no local das atividades (da empresa).

sit-in, *n.* ocupação *f* (de fábrica, etc.).

situation, *n.* **1.** situação *f*; **financial situation,** situação financeira; **overall economic situation,** conjuntura econômica. **2.** emprego *m*, colocação *f*; **to get, obtain, a situation,** colocar-se, conseguir um emprego; **vacant situation,** vaga *f* para emprego; (*in advertisements*) **'situations vacant',** 'precisam-se', 'empregados procurados'; **'situations wanted',** 'oferecem-se', 'empregos procurados'.

size, *n.* **1.** tamanho *m*, dimensão *f*, volume *m*, grandeza *f*, medida *f*; **size of a firm,** tamanho de uma firma; **size of the market,** dimensão do mercado; **size of a loan,** volume, montante *m*, de um empréstimo. **2.** número *m* (de roupa, sapato, etc.).

sizeable, *a.* **sizeable business,** negócio *m* considerável; **sizeable sum,** quantia *f* considerável.

skeleton, *n.* **skeleton staff,** pessoal reduzido, plantão reduzido.

skew, skewed, *a. Stat:* assimétrico.

skewness, *n. Stat:* assimetria *f*, distorção *f*.

skill, *n.* habilidade *f*, destreza *f*,

competência *f*; **skill differentials,** adicionais *mpl* por habilitação.

skilled, *a.* hábil; **skilled work,** trabalho especializado; **skilled worker,** operário especializado, operário qualificado, trabalhador habilitado, oficial *m*; **skilled labour,** mão-de-obra especializada; **skilled manpower,** força de trabalho qualificada; **skilled carpenter,** oficial de carpintaria.

skimmed, *a.* **skimmed (powder) milk,** leite em pó desnatado.

skimming, *a.* **skimming price,** preço muito elevado; **skimming pricing,** fixação *f* de preço muito elevado (para determinado produto).

skyrocketing, *a. Am:* em rápida ascensão.

slack, *a.* frouxo, inativo, pouco animado, de pouca movimentação; **the market is slack,** o mercado apresenta-se frouxo, o mercado está inativo; **the market remained slack,** o mercado manteve-se com reduzida movimentação; **the slack season,** a baixa temporada; **slack business,** marasmo *m*; **slack demand,** demanda fraca; **slack time in business,** relaxamento *m* das atividades comerciais.

slacken, *v.i.* enfraquecer.

slackness, *n.* inatividade *f* (do mercado), reduzida movimentação (dos negócios), enfraquecimento *m* (da demanda).

slate, *v.i. Am:* **to slate for production,** programar para produção.

sleeper, *n.* (sócio) comanditário *m*.

sleeping, *a.* **sleeping partner,** (sócio) comanditário *m*.

slice, *n.* **slice of the market,** fatia *f* do mercado.

slide back, *v.i.* resvalar; retornar (para situação anterior).

sliding, *a.* **sliding scale,** escala *f* móvel (de salário, tarifas, preços, etc.).

slight, *a.* **slight increase,** pequeno aumento.

slip, *n.* **1.** (*a*) **slip of paper,** papeleta *f*, papelzinho *m*; (*b*) (*for special purpose*) ficha *f*, comprovante *m*; *Ind: etc:* **pay (advice) slip,** contracheque *m*, holerith *m*; *Bank:* **deposit slip, paying-in slip,** formulário *m* de depósito; **sales slip,** ficha de vendas; **remittance slip,** guia *f* de

remessa; (*c*) *Ins:* minuta *f* de apólice assinada pelas partes contratantes. **2. book-keeping slip,** erro *m* de escrituração.
slogan, *n.* slogan *m*, moto *m*; palavra *f* (ou frase *f*) de propaganda.
slot-machine, *n.* (máquina *f*) caçaníqueis *m*; máquina distribuidora automática.
slow, 1. *a.* **slow growth,** crescimento lento; **slow increase,** incremento vagaroso, aumento lento; **slow market,** mercado inativo; **slow period,** período *m* de pouca movimentação comercial; **slow rate,** baixa taxa; **business is slow,** os negócios estão lentos, estão pouco animados; **he's a slow payer,** ele é um mau pagador. **2.** *adv.* **to go slow,** fazer uma greve tartaruga, fazer uma greve passiva.
slow-burning, *a.* **slow-burning inflation,** inflação lenta.
slow down, *v.tr.* **to slow down production,** diminuir a produção.
slowdown, *n.* (*a*) diminuição *f*, redução *f*, (da produção, etc.); (*b*) *Am:* greve *f* tartaruga.
slowly, *adv.* lentamente, devagar.
slow-moving, *a.* **slow-moving stock,** estoque *m* de pouca movimentação.
sluggish, *a.* **sluggish growth,** crescimento lento.
slump¹, *n.* baixa repentina (de preços, cotações, etc.); **the slump in the coffee market,** o colapso do mercado de café; **the economic slump,** a crise econômica, a depressão.
slump², *v.i.* (*of prices, etc.*) baixar, cair, subitamente.
slush, *n. F:* **slush fund,** caixa preta.
small, *a.* pequeno; **small change,** trocado *m*, dinheiro miúdo; **small shopkeeper,** pequeno comerciante; **the smaller industries,** as pequenas indústrias; **small investors,** pequenos investidores; **small income,** renda modesta, rendimento modesto; **small loan,** pequeno empréstimo; *Journ: F:* **small ads,** pequenos anúncios.
small-scale, *a.* em pequena escala; **small-scale firm,** empresa *f* de pequeno porte; **small-scale plant,** fábrica *f* de pequenas dimensões.

smash, *n.* falência *f*; ruina financeira; (*of numerous firms, banks, etc.*) craque *m.*
smoking, *n.* **smoking articles,** artigos *mpl* para fumantes.
smooth out, *v.tr.* **to smooth out fluctuations,** suavizar as flutuações.
smoothing, *n. Stat:* aplainamento *m.*
smuggle, *v.* **1.** *v.tr.* contrabandear, fazer contrabando de, (caixas de uísque, etc.); passar; **to smuggle goods into the country,** fazer entrar mercadorias de contrabando; **to smuggle goods out of the country,** fazer sair mercadorias de contrabando. **2.** *v.i.* contrabandear, fazer contrabando.
smuggler, *n.* contrabandista *mf*, muambeiro *m.*
smuggling, *n.* contrabando *m*, muamba *f.*
snake, *n. Pol Ec:* **the (monetary) snake,** a serpente (monetária).
soar, *v.i.* (*of prices*) galgar, subir bruscamente.
soaring, 1. *a.* (*of prices, etc.*) que estão galgando, em rápida elevação. **2.** *n.* elevação repentina (de preços, etc.).
social, *a.* social; **social accounting,** contabilidade *f* social; **social benefit,** benefício *m* social; **social cost,** custo *m* social; **social desirability,** conveniência *f* social; **social development,** desenvolvimento *m* social; **social income flow,** fluxo *m* de renda social; **social insurance,** seguro *m* social, previdência *f* social; **social liability,** ônus *m* para a sociedade; **social mobility,** mobilidade *f* social; **social welfare,** bem-estar *m* social.
society, *n.* (*a*) sociedade *f*; **consumer society,** sociedade de consumo; **affluent society,** sociedade afluente; **industrial society,** sociedade industrial; (*b*) *Ins: etc:* **benefit society,** sociedade mutuante, mútua *f*; *UK:* **building society,** sociedade cooperativa de hipotecas e empréstimos, sociedade de crédito imobiliário; **loan society,** sociedade de crédito, associação *f* de poupança e empréstimo.
soft, *a.* (*a*) **soft currency,** moeda desvalorizada, moeda fraca; **soft money,** moeda inflacionada; (*b*) **soft goods,** (i) bens *mpl* de consumo que devem ser substituídos em pouco tempo; (ii) *UK:* tecidos *mpl*, fazendas *fpl*, artigos *mpl* de

armarinho; (c) St.Exch: (of shares) fraco; (d) **soft market,** mercado calmo; **soft loan,** empréstimo m em condições suaves; (e) **soft sell,** venda f de forma não agressiva; (f) **soft steel,** aço m doce.

software, n. software m; conjunto m de dados e informações com os quais se alimenta um computador.

sole, a. único, exclusivo; **sole proprietor,** proprietário único; **sole proprietorship,** firma f individual; **sole trader,** comerciante mf independente; **sole agent,** agente exclusivo; **sole distributor,** distribuidor exclusivo; **sole rights,** direitos exclusivos; Jur: **sole legatee,** legatário m universal.

solicit, v.tr. **to solicit orders,** solicitar pedidos.

solicitor, n. 1. UK: advogado m (que não pleiteia). 2. Am: angariador m.

solution, n. Jur: **solution of continuity,** solução f de continuidade.

solvability, n. solvência f, solvabilidade f.

solve, v.tr. **to solve a problem,** resolver, solucionar, um problema.

solvency, n. solvência f, solvabilidade f.

solvent, a. solvente, solvável, solvível; **solvent debt,** dívida f exigível e cobrável; **solvent company,** companhia f solvível; **solvent credit,** crédito m de primeira qualidade.

sophisticated, a. **sophisticated form (of product),** forma sofisticada (de produto); **sophisticated product,** produto sofisticado; **sophisiticated management,** administração atualizada e moderna.

sort, v.tr. classificar, separar.

sorter, n. (a) (machine) classificadora f, separadora f; (b) (person) classificador m, separador m.

sound, a. **goods in sound condition,** mercadorias fpl em boas condições, em bom estado; **sound basis,** base segura; **sound currency,** moeda f firme; **sound financial position,** boa situação financeira; **sound value,** valor correto.

soundness, n. 1. bom estado, boas condições, (de mercadorias, etc.). 2. **the soundness of a firm,** a solidez, a estabilidade, a firmeza, de uma empresa;

soundness of a business, excelência f de um negócio.

source, n. (a) fonte f; **source of income,** fonte de renda; **taxed at source,** tributado na fonte; **deducted at source,** deduzido, retido, na fonte; (b) **official source,** fonte oficial, fonte autorizada; **reliable sources,** fontes fidedignas; (c) **source of employment,** fonte de trabalho; **source of supply,** fonte de oferta, de suprimento; (d) **source document,** documento-fonte m, documento m de origem; (e) Book-k: etc: **source-and-disposition statement,** demonstração f da origem e aplicação de fundos, demonstração de recursos obtidos e aplicados.

soya bean, Am: **soybean,** n. feijão-soja m, soja f; **soybean cake,** torta f de soja; **soybean oil,** óleo m de soja.

space out, v.tr. **to space out payments,** escalonar pagamentos.

spare, a. 1. disponível; **spare capital,** capital m disponível, fundos mpl disponíveis. 2. **spare parts,** (peças fpl) sobressalentes mfpl, sobresselentes mfpl; peças de reposição, peças de reserva.

special, a. especial; **special allowance,** concessão f especial; **special assessment,** tributação f especial; **special customs invoice,** fatura alfandegária; **special customs warehouse rules,** regime aduaneiro extraordinário; **special delivery,** entrega rápida, correspondência f para entrega urgente; **special drawing rights,** direitos mpl especiais de saque (contra o Fundo Monetário Internacional); (at meeting, etc.) **special majority,** maioria qualificada; **special offer,** oferta f especial; **special order,** encomenda f especial; **special price,** preço m especial; **special-purpose computer,** computador especializado; **special-purpose financial statement,** balanço elaborado para fins especiais; **special rates (of carriage),** tarifas fpl especiais (de transporte); **special uses,** usos mpl, fins mpl, especiais; Book-k: **special audit,** exame m especial; **special fund,** fundo m especial; **special item,** item extraordinário; **special reserve fund,** fundo m de reservas especiais; Am:

special-revenue fund, fundo *m* resultante de receitas especiais.
specialist, *n.* especialista *mf.*
speciality, *Am:* **specialty,** *n.* especialidade *f.*
specialization, *n.* (*area*) especialidade *f*; (*act*) especialização *f.*
specialize, *v.i.* **to specialize in marketing,** especializar-se em marketing.
specialized, *a.* especializado; **specialized training,** treinamento especializado; **specialized services,** serviços especializados.
specialty, *n.* (*a*) *Jur:* **specialty contract,** contrato *m* formal, contrato solene; (*b*) *Am:* (= **speciality**) **specialty goods,** especialidades *fpl*; **specialty salesman,** vendedor especializado.
specie, *n.* moeda metálica, moeda sonante; **to settle a bill in specie,** pagar uma conta em moeda sonante; *Fin:* **specie clauses,** cláusulas *fpl* de pagamento em moeda específica.
specific, *a.* específico; **specific duty,** imposto específico.
specification, *n.* especificação *f*; **job specification,** (*position*) especificação de cargo, (*project*) especificação de obra; **standard specifications,** normas *fpl*; **the specifications of a contract,** as estipulações de um contrato; *Tchn: Ind:* **platform construction specifications,** especificações para a construção de uma plataforma; *Book-k:* **specification cost,** custo *m* de especificação, custo standard.
specify, *v.tr.* especificar, particularizar; **the report specified all the details,** o relatório especificou todos os pormenores; **as specified in the agreement,** conforme especificado, estipulado, no acordo; **unless otherwise specified,** salvo indicação em contrário.
specimen, *n.* espécimen *m*, espécime *m*, amostra *f*; **specimen contract,** modelo *m* de contrato; **specimen invoice,** modelo de fatura; **specimen signature,** modelo de assinatura.
speculate, *v.i. Fin:* especular; *F:* agiotar; **to speculate on the Stock Exchange,** especular na bolsa de valores; **to speculate for a rise, for a fall,** jogar na alta, na

baixa; **to speculate in coffee,** especular sobre o café, com o café.
speculating, *n. Fin:* especulação *f.*
speculation, *n. Fin: St.Exch:* especulação *f*; **speculation in shares,** especulação sobre títulos; **to buy sth. on speculation,** comprar algo para fins especulativos; **risky speculation,** especulação arriscada.
speculative, *a. Fin:* especulativo; **speculative motive,** motivo *m* de especulação; **speculative purchases,** compras especulativas.
speculatively, *adv.* especulativamente.
speculator, *n. Fin:* especulador *m*; *F:* agiota *mf.*
spend, *v.tr.* gastar, despender; **he spent all his salary in three days,** ele gastou, despendeu, todo o seu ordenado em três dias; **to spend too much,** gastar demais, despender em demasia; **he spent everything on the project,** gastou tudo no projeto.
spender, *n.* gastador *m.*
spending, *n.* despesa *f*; **public spending, government spending,** despesas públicas; **spending cuts,** cortes *mpl*, reduções *fpl*, nas despesas, nos gastos; **spending surge,** rápido incremento dos gastos; *Pol.Ec:* **spending power, spending capacity,** poder aquisitivo, poder de compra.
sphere, *n.* esfera *f*; zona *f* de influência.
spiral¹, *n.* espiral *f*; **the rising spiral of prices,** a espiral ascendente de preços; **inflationary spiral,** espiral inflacionária.
spiral², *v.i.* (*of prices, etc.*) subir com rapidez; **spiralling cost,** custo *m* em rápida elevação.
split, *v.tr. Fin:* **to split shares,** dividir, fracionar, ações; **split share,** ação desdobrada; *Ind: etc:* **split shift,** turno dividido.
split-off, *n. Am:* emissão *f* de ações aos acionistas de uma companhia subsidiária, contra devolução de parte das ações da companhia matriz.
split-up, *n. Am:* emissão *f* de ações de bonificação, transferência *f* de bens de uma companhia, para formação de outra subsidiária.
spoil, *v.* 1. *v.tr.* estragar, deteriorar,

(mercadorias, etc.). **2.** *v.i.* estragar-se, deteriorar-se.

spot, *n.* **1.** local *m* (para instalação de uma fábrica, etc.); **spot check,** controle *m*, verificação *f*, inspeção *f*, de artigos escolhidos ao acaso. **2.** *pl.* **spots,** mercadorias *fpl* para pronta entrega; **spot cash,** dinheiro *m* de contado; **spot contract,** contrato *m* à vista; **spot exchange rate,** taxa *f* de câmbio no ato da transação; **spot price,** preço *m* para entrega imediata; **spot sale,** venda *f* para entrega imediata; **spot market,** (i) mercado *m* à vista; (ii) mercado do disponível; **spot commodities,** mercadorias *fpl* disponíveis, mercadorias para pronta entrega, para entrega imediata; **spot copper,** cobre *m* disponível.

spread¹, *n.* *Fin:* diferença *f* entre o preço de compra e o preço de venda; margem *f* de lucro bruto; diferença entre o preço de fábrica e o preço de venda ao consumidor; *Stat:* **spread sheet,** folha *f* de análise.

spread², *v.tr.* **1. to spread instalments over three years,** distribuir, espaçar, as prestações por três anos; **to spread a risk,** distribuir um risco, *Ins:* pulverizar um risco. **2.** *Book-k:* lançar detalhadamente.

spurt, *v.i.* (*of debt, etc.*) aumentar rapidamente.

squeeze¹, *n.* **credit squeeze,** restrição *f* ao crédito, arrocho *m* ao crédito.

squeeze², *v.tr.* **to squeeze credit,** restringir o crédito; **to squeeze taxpayers,** apertar, arrochar, os contribuintes; **to squeeze profits,** reduzir os lucros; **to squeeze a profit from a deal,** auferir lucro de uma transação mediante medidas de contenção; *St.Exch:* **to squeeze the bears,** apertar os baixistas.

stability, *n.* estabilidade *f*.

stabilization, *n.* estabilização *f* (da moeda, dos preços, etc.); **exchange stabilization fund,** fundo *m* de estabilização cambial.

stabilize, *v.* **1.** *v.tr.* estabilizar (os preços, a moeda, etc.). **2.** *v.i.* **prices finally stabilized,** finalmente os preços se estabilizaram.

stabilizing, *a.* **stabilizing agreements,** acordos *mpl* visando à estabilização; **stabilizing factors of the market,** fatores *mpl* estabilizadores do mercado; **stabilizing mechanisms,** mecanismos *mpl* de estabilização; **to have a stabilizing influence on prices,** exercer uma influência estabilizadora sobre os preços.

stable, *a.* estável; **stable currency,** moeda *f* estável; **stable prices,** preços *mpl* estáveis.

staff¹, *n.* pessoal *m*, quadro *m*, (com exclusão da mão-de-obra); **office staff,** pessoal de escritório; **staff manager,** gerente *mf*, chefe *mf*, do pessoal; **staff auditor,** contador *m* do quadro (de uma firma de contadores públicos, ou de uma empresa); **senior staff,** pessoal *m*·sênior, funcionários *mpl* de alto nível.

staff², *v.tr.* prover (um escritório) de pessoal.

stag, *n.* *St.Exch:* especulador *m* (que subscreve uma nova emissão para revender as ações com lucro).

stage¹, *n.* etapa *f*, fase *f*, estágio *m*; **in stages,** por etapas; **two-stage growth,** crescimento *m* em duas etapas.

stage², *v.tr.* **to stage an exhibition,** organizar uma exposição.

stagflation, *n.* *Pol.Ec:* estagflação *f*.

stagger, *v.tr.* escalonar (pagamentos, etc.).

staggering, *n.* escalonamento *m*.

stagnant, *a.* (*of economy, prices, etc.*) estanque, estagnado, parado, estacionado.

stagnate, *v.i.* (*of trade, etc.*) estagnar-se, estancar, ficar estagnado.

stagnating, *a.* estanque, estagnado, em estagnação.

stagnation, *n.* estagnação *f*, marasmo *m*.

stake¹, *n.* interesse *m*, participação *f*, (numa firma, etc.); **to have a stake in a firm,** ter um interesse numa firma.

stake², *v.tr.* **1.** arriscar (uma importância). **2. to stake an undertaking,** financiar um empreendimento.

stale, *a.* (*a*) *Fin:* **stale market,** mercado pouco movimentado; (*b*) *Jur:* caduco; (*c*) **stale cheque,** cheque não apresentado por muito tempo após emissão; **stale dated**

bill of lading, conhecimento *m* de embarque de data antiga.

stamp¹, *n.* **1.** (*device*) carimbo *m*, timbre *m*, estampilha *f*, selo *m*, sinete *m*; **rubber stamp,** carimbo (de borracha), timbre; **date stamp,** carimbo datador; **stamp pad,** almofada *f* para carimbo. **2.** (*mark*) selo *m*, carimbo, estampilha, sinete; **official stamp,** selo oficial. **3. revenue stamp,** selo fiscal, estampilha; **ad valorem stamp,** selo proporcional; **stamp tax, duty,** imposto de selo; **excise stamp tax,** selo de consumo. **4.** *Post:* **postage stamp,** selo (postal), selo do correio.

stamp², *v.tr.* **to stamp a document,** selar, carimbar, timbrar, um documento; **to stamp a passport,** carimbar um passaporte; **to stamp a letter,** selar uma carta; **to stamp the word 'fragile' on a box,** estampar numa caixa a palavra 'frágil'; **stamped paper,** papel timbrado.

stamping, *n.* carimbagem *f*, selagem *f*, (de documentos); estampagem *f* (de mercadorias); **stamping machine,** (i) máquina *f* de carimbar, de selar, (ii) máquina de estampar.

stand¹, *n.* **1.** stand *m*, pavilhão *m*, (em uma exposição, etc.). **2.** mostruário *m*; banca *f* de venda. **3.** *Agr:* plantação *f*.

stand², *v.i.* (*a*) **the contract stands,** o contrato continua em vigor; (*b*) **to stand (as) security for s.o.,** afiançar alguém, ser fiador de alguém; (*c*) **securities standing in the company's books at . . .,** títulos registrados nos livros sociais no valor de . . .; (*d*) **the balance stands at $70,** o saldo é de $70; **the amount standing to your credit,** o seu saldo credor.

standard, 1. *n.* (*a*) *Fin:* padrão *m*, estalão *m*; **gold standard,** estalão-ouro *m*, padrão-ouro *m*; **gold-bullion standard,** estalão lingote-ouro; **monetary standard,** padrão monetário, moeda-padrão *f*, estalão monetário; (*b*) **standard of living, living standard,** nível *m* de vida, padrão de vida; **high standard of living,** elevado padrão de vida; **rise in living standards,** elevação *f* do nível de vida; **standard of wages,** padrão salarial; *Fin:* **standard of rate,** taxa *f* de juros vigente; (*c*) (*rule*) *Ind: etc:* norma técnica; **standard for the painting of**

offshore production platforms, norma para a pintura de plataformas marítimas de produção. **2.** *a.* standard, padronizado, normal; **standard car,** carro *m* standard; **standard model,** modelo *m* padrão; **standard conditions,** condições *fpl* padrão; **standard practice,** prática *f* normal; **standard size,** tamanho *m* normal, tamanho padrão; **standard grade,** qualidade-padrão *f* (de um produto); **standard weight,** peso-padrão *m*; **standard metre,** metro-padrão *m*; *Book-k: Ind: etc:* **standard cost,** custo *m* standard, custo-padrão *m*, custo padronizado; **standard labour rate,** taxa *f* standard de mão-de-obra; **standard price,** preço *m* padrão, preço standard, preço padronizado; **standard profit,** lucro *m* standard, lucro padronizado; *Adm:* **standard rate of taxation,** alíquota *f* normal de tributação; **to pay tax at the standard rate,** pagar imposto à alíquota normal.

standardization, *n.* padronização *f*, estandardização *f*, (da indústria, dos processos de fabricação, etc.); uniformização *f* (do sistema de medidas); normalização *f* (de processos, métodos, etc.).

standardize, *v.tr.* padronizar, estandardizar, uniformizar, (sistema, etc.); normalizar (processos, métodos).

standardized, *a.* padronizado; **standardized size,** dimensão padronizada; **standardized work,** trabalho padronizado.

standby, *n.* reserva *f*; **standby credit,** crédito *m* de reserva, (*IMF*) abertura *f* de crédito a favor de um país para utilização quando necessário; **standby loan,** empréstimo *m* condicional; **standby underwriting,** contrato *m* de subscrição residual do lançamento de títulos mobiliários; *Ind:* **standby equipment,** equipamento *m* auxiliar (para emergências); **standby pay,** pagamento *m* por comparecimento (efetuado mesmo quando o operário não tem trabalho para fazer).

standing, 1. *a.* **standing price,** preço fixo; **standing cost,** custo fixo; **standing expenses,** despesas fixas; *Bank:* **standing order,** ordem (bancária) permanente. **2.**

n. (*a*) **debt of long standing,** dívida antiga, dívida de longa data; (*b*) **standing of a firm,** importância *f*, prestígio *m*, de uma firma; **financial standing of a business,** situação financeira de uma empresa; **firm of recognized standing,** firma bem conceituada, firma de reconhecida solidez.

stand off, *v.tr.* **to stand off workers,** demitir os operários temporariamente (por falta de trabalho, materiais, etc.).

standpoint, *n.* **from the commercial standpoint,** do ponto de vista comercial.

standstill, *n.* parada *f*, paralisação *f*; **trade is at a standstill,** o comércio está parado, paralisado.

staple, 1. *a.* principal, básico; **staple article,** artigo *m* de consumo geral; **staple industry,** indústria *f* principal; **staple commodities,** produtos básicos; **staple trade,** comércio *m* regular. **2.** *n.* grampo *m.*

stapler, *n.* grampeador *m.*

starting, *n.* **starting price,** preço *m* inicial; **starting date (of a project),** data *f* de início (dum projeto); *Am: Book-k:* **starting load cost,** custo *m* preliminar da operação, custo pre-operacional.

state¹, *n.* **1.** estado *m*; **state-owned bank,** banco *m* estatal; **state-owned company,** empresa *f* estatal, empresa pública; **state-owned economy,** economia estatizada. **2.** estado, situação *f*; **state of affairs,** situação dos negócios; **state of bankruptcy,** estado falimentar.

state², *v.tr.* declarar, expor, especificar; **to state all income,** declarar toda a renda; **to state the reasons for a decision,** expor os motivos de uma decisão; justificar, fundamentar, uma decisão; **to state an account in dollars,** apresentar uma conta em dólares.

stated, *a.* **stated capital,** capital declarado; **stated liability,** passivo declarado; **stated value,** valor declarado, valor facial, valor par; *Book-k: etc:* **account stated,** conta confirmada pelo devedor.

statement, *n.* **1.** exposição *f* (de motivos, razões, etc.), declaração *f*, afirmação *f*; (*report*) relatório *m*; *Jur:* termo *m*; **false statement,** declaração, afirmação, falsa;

Fin: **income statement, statement of income,** declaração de renda. **2.** balanço *m*, demonstração *f*; **statement of account,** extrato *m* de conta, demonstração de conta; **statement of affairs,** balanço geral, demonstração da situação patrimonial; **statement of assets and liabilities,** balanço geral, balanço patrimonial, demonstração da situação patrimonial; **statement of funds,** balanço de competência; **statement of revenue and expenditure,** conta *f* de lucros e perdas, demonstração de receitas e despesas; **statement of net worth,** demonstração do capital social e o correspondente passivo exigível; **bank statement,** extrato bancário, extrato de conta bancária.

stationery, *n.* material *m* de escritório.

statistic, *n.* **1.** dado estatístico. **2.** *pl.* **statistics,** estatística *f*; **external trade statistics,** estatística sobre o comércio exterior.

statistical, *a.* estatístico; **statistical data,** dados estatísticos; **statistical distribution,** distribuição estatística; **statistical sampling,** amostragem estatística; **statistical tool,** instrumento estatístico; **statistical table,** quadro estatístico.

statistician, *n.* estatístico *m.*

status, *n.* (*a*) **social status,** status *m* social; **financial status,** situação financeira; **status inquiry,** levantamento *m* de informações cadastrais (sobre pessoa, empresa, etc.); (*b*) *Jur:* estado *m* civil.

statute, *n.* **1.** *Jur:* **statute of limitations,** prescrição *f*; **debt barred by statute of limitations,** dívida atingida por prescrição. **2.** *pl.* **the statutes,** os estatutos (de uma sociedade, associação, etc.); leis *fpl.*

statutory, *a.* **1.** regulamentar, legal; **statutory audit committee,** conselho *m* fiscal; **statutory declaration,** atestado *m*; **statutory holidays,** férias regulamentares; **statutory reserve,** reserva *f* legal. **2.** (*according to the statutes*) estatutário; **statutory provision,** disposição estatutária.

steadily, *adv.* constantemente.

steadiness, *n.* **steadiness of prices,** estabilidade *f* dos preços; **steadiness of**

the **market**, estabilidade do mercado; **the steadiness of the dollar**, o equilíbrio do dólar.

steady[1], *a.* 1. (*a*) **a steady increase in the price of coffee**, um aumento constante no preço do café; **steady demand**, procura *f* firme; **steady market**, mercado *m* firme, mercado mantido; (*b*) **steady job**, emprego *m* permanente. 2. (*of person*) **steady worker**, trabalhador sério, trabalhador assíduo.

steady[2], *v.i.* (*of prices, etc.*) tornar-se mais estável, mais firme.

steam, *n.* **steam navigation**, navegação *f* a vapor; **steam transportation**, transporte *m* a vapor.

steamship, *n.* **steamship agency**, agência *f* de navegação; **steamship company**, companhia *f* de navegação.

steel, *n.* aço *m*; **steel cartel**, cartel *m* do aço; **the steel industry**, a indústria siderúrgica; **steel works**, aciaria *f*, usina siderúrgica.

steep, *a. F:* **steep price**, preço muito alto, preço exagerado.

sterling, 1. *n.* (*a*) esterlino *m*; **sterling fell on the foreign exchange markets**, o esterlino caiu nos mercados cambiais; (*b*) prata *f* de lei. 2. *a.* (*a*) **pound sterling**, libra esterlina; **the sterling zone**, a zona esterlina; **sterling balances**, saldos *mpl* em esterlino; (*b*) **sterling silver**, prata *f* de lei.

steward, *n. Ind:* **shop steward**, delegado *m* sindical (na empresa), delegado de empresa.

sticker, *n.* etiqueta adesiva.

stiff, *a.* (*a*) **stiff price**, preço muito alto, preço exagerado; (*b*) **stiff market**, mercado *m* altista; (*c*) **stiff competition**, concorrência acirrada.

stiffen, *v.* 1. *v.tr.* provocar subida (nos preços, etc.). 2. *v.i.* (*of prices*) firmar-se, tornar-se firme.

stiffness, *n.* firmeza *f* (do mercado, etc.).

stipulate, *v.tr.* **to stipulate a guarantee**, estipular uma garantia; **to stipulate (in writing) that ...**, estipular (por escrito) que ...; **it is stipulated that all payments shall be made in the national currency**, estipula-se que todos os pagamentos deverão ser feitos na moeda nacional.

stipulated, *a.* estipulado.

stipulation, *n.* estipulação *f*.

stock[1], *n.* 1. estoque *m*, sortimento *m*; **stock in hand, stock in trade**, estoque *m*, estocagem *f*; mercadorias *fpl* à venda, para revenda; **in stock**, em estoque; **depletion, exhaustion, of stocks**, esgotamento *m* de estoques; **stock balance**, saldo *m* de estoque; **stock book**, livro *m* de estoque, livro de entradas e saídas de mercadorias; **stock card**, ficha *f* de estoque; **stock chart**, mapa *m* de estoque; **stock clearance**, liquidação *f* de estoque; **stock control**, controle *m* de estoque, gestão *f* de estoques; **stock-sales ratio**, razão *f* estoque/vendas; **stock turnover**, rotação *f* de estoques; **stock valuation**, avaliação *f* de estoques; (*of goods*) **to be out of stock**, estar em falta, estar esgotado; **to build up a stock**, fazer, formar, um estoque; **to clear, sell off, a stock**, liquidar, queimar, um estoque; **to consume, exhaust, stocks**, esgotar os estoques; **to put goods into stock**, estocar mercadorias, colocar mercadorias no almoxarifado; **to take stock**, fazer o inventário, inventariar (o estoque); **our stocks are running out**, os nossos estoques estão se esgotando; **we are out of stock**, os nossos estoques estão esgotados. 2. *Fin:* *pl.* **stocks**, ações *fpl*, valores *mpl*, títulos *mpl*; **stocks and shares**, títulos e valores mobiliários; **stocks held as security**, títulos recebidos em garantia; **stocks held for a rise**, valores retidos na expectativa de uma alta; **fully paid stocks**, títulos integralizados, títulos liberados; **government stock(s)**, títulos do governo, fundos públicos; **stock exchange**, bolsa *f* de valores; **stock market**, mercado *m* de títulos, de valores; **stock ticker**, máquina impressora das cotações da bolsa de valores; **to take delivery of stocks**, receber títulos; *St.Exch:* **to take in stock, to borrow, carry, stock**, adquirir ações mediante reporte; **stock certificate**, certificado *m* de ação, cautela *f*; **stock dividend**, dividendo *m* em ações; **stock ledger, stock register**, (livro-)registro *m* de ações, de acionistas; *Am:* **stock option,** opção *f* de compra de ações.

stock², *v.tr.* **1.** sortir, abastecer, prover, (uma loja) (**with,** de); **a shop well stocked with . . .,** uma loja bem sortida de . . .. **2.** estocar, ter em estoque; **I don't stock this article,** não tenho, não vendo, este artigo.

stockbroker, *n.* corretor *m* de valores, corretor de bolsa; **stockbroker's fee,** (taxa *f* de) corretagem *f*.

stockbrokerage, *n.* corretagem *f* de valores.

stockbroking, *n.* corretagem *f* de valores.

stockholder, *n.* acionista *mf*; detentor *m*, possuidor *m*, de título(s); **stockholder of record,** acionista constante dos registros de uma companhia em determinada data; **stockholder's equity,** passivo *m* inexigível, capital *m* mais reservas inexigíveis; **preference stockholder,** possuidor *m* de ação preferencial, de ações preferenciais.

stockholding, *n.* investimento *m* em ações.

stocking, *n.* sortimento *m*, abastecimento *m*, provisão *f*, (de uma loja).

stockist, *n.* estoquista *mf*.

stock-keeper, *n.* almoxarife *m*.

stocklist, *n.* **1.** inventário *m*. **2.** *St.Exch:* boletim *m* da bolsa de valores.

stockpile¹, *n.* estocagem *f*, reservas *fpl*, (de matérias-primas, etc.).

stockpile², *v.tr. & i.* estocar, armazenar, (matérias-primas, etc.); acumular reservas.

stockpiling, *n.* estocagem *f*, armazenamento *m*, armazenagem *f*, acumulação *f* de reservas.

stockroom, *n.* almoxarifado *m*, armazém *m*, depósito *m*.

stocktaking, *n.* levantamento *m* do estoque, inventariação *f*; **the yearly stocktaking,** o inventário anual.

stop¹, *n.* **1.** *Fin: St.Exch:* ordem *f* stop; ordem dada ao corretor para vender (ou comprar) título ao ser alcançada determinada cotação; **stop loss,** ordem de venda para evitar possível prejuízo. **2.** *Fin:* (ordem de) suspensão *f* de pagamento (de cheque); **to put a stop on a cheque,** suspender o pagamento de um cheque.

stop², *v.tr.* **1.** *Cust:* **to stop goods,** reter mercadorias (na alfândega); **goods stopped at the customs,** mercadorias retidas na alfândega. **2. to stop (payment of) a cheque,** suspender o pagamento de um cheque; **to stop bankruptcy proceedings,** suspender o processo falencial. **3.** *Jur:* (*of a firm*) **to stop payments,** suspender os pagamentos. **4. to stop an amount from s.o.'s wages,** reter, deduzir, uma quantia do salário de alguém. **5. to stop an order,** cancelar um pedido. **6. to stop inflation,** conter a inflação.

stopgap, *n.* **stopgap measure,** medida provisória.

stoppage, *n.* **1.** suspensão *f*; **stoppage of payments,** suspensão de pagamentos. **2. stoppage of pay,** retenção *f*, dedução *f*, de uma parte do salário. **3.** *Ind:* parada *f*, paralisação *f*, interrupção *f*, (na produção, etc.).

stopping, *n.* suspensão *f* de pagamento (de um cheque).

storage, *n.* **1.** armazenagem *f*, armazenamento *m*, estocagem *f*; **storage charges,** (despesas *fpl* de) armazenagem; **storage capacity,** capacidade *f* de armazenamento; **cold storage,** armazenamento frigorífico; **cold storage building,** frigorífico *m*; **cold storage insurance,** seguro *m* de mercadorias estocadas em frigorífico. **2.** armazéns *mpl*, depósitos *mpl*, (de uma casa comercial), guarda-móveis *m*; **the shop has little storage,** a loja tem pouco espaço para armazenamento; **storage tank,** tanque *m* para armazenamento, de depósito; **storage yard,** pátio *m* de depósito; **to take goods out of storage,** retirar mercadorias do armazém, do depósito. **3.** *Cmptr:* armazenagem *f*, armazenamento *m*, memória *f*; **disk storage,** armazenamento de dados em disco, memória em disco; **magnetic storage,** armazenamento magnético, memória magnética; **main storage,** armazenamento principal, memória principal; **permanent storage,** memória fixa; **program storage,** armazenamento de programa.

store¹, *n.* **1.** (*a*) armazém *m*, depósito *m*; (*in factory, etc.*) **the stores,** o almoxarife; **bond store,** armazém de depósito da alfândega; **cold store,** entreposto frigorífico, depósito frigorífico; *Ind:* **stores requisition,** requisição *f* ao almoxarifado; (*b*) reservas acumuladas (de matérias-primas, etc.), materiais armazenados em depósito. **2.** loja *f*; **grocery store,** armazém *m*, mercearia *f*; **general store,** loja geral; **department store,** loja de departamentos; **chain store,** loja pertencente a uma cadeia; **a chain of stores,** uma cadeia de lojas; **cooperative store,** loja cooperativa; *Am:* **dime store,** loja de artigos variados de preço baixo (como as Lojas Americanas); *Am:* **store credit,** crediário *m* em casa comercial; **store unit,** unidade *f* varejista (pertencente a uma cadeia de lojas).

store², *v.tr.* (*a*) armazenar, colocar em depósito, (mercadorias, etc.); (*b*) receber em depósito; (*c*) *Cmptr:* armazenar (dados).

storehouse, *n.* armazém *m*, depósito *m*, almoxarifado *m*.

storekeeper, *n.* almoxarife *m*.

storeroom, *n.* depósito *m*, almoxarifado *m*, armazém *m*.

storing, *n.* armazenamento *m*, armazenagem *f*.

stow, *v.tr.* *Nau:* estivar (carga em embarcação), arrumar (carga no porão).

stowage, *n.* (*a*) estiva *f*, arrumação *f*; (*b*) taxa *f* de estiva; (*c*) lugar *m* de armazenagem no navio.

straddle, *n.* *Am: Fin:* contrato *m* de dupla opção.

straight, *a.* **1.** (*of flight*) direto; sem escalas. **2.** **straight bill of lading,** conhecimento *m* não negociável; **straight letter of credit,** carta de crédito confirmada e irrevogável; **straight receipt,** recibo *m* normal de entrega de mercadorias.

straight-line, *a.* **straight-line (method of) depreciation,** depreciação *f* em linha reta, depreciação pelo método linear.

strain¹, *n.* sobrecarga *f*.

strain², *v.* **1.** *v.tr.* **to strain resources,** exigir o máximo emprego de recursos. **2.** *v.i.* (*of interest rates*) **to strain upward(s),** subir acentuadamente.

strategic, *a.* estratégico.

strategy, *n.* estratégia *f*.

stratified, *a.* *Stat:* **stratified sampling,** amostragem estratificada.

streamline, *v.tr.* modernizar (a economia, a produção, etc.).

streamlining, *n.* modernização *f* (da economia, da produção, etc.).

street, *n.* **street broker,** corretor *m* de valores que não é sócio de uma bolsa (operando no mercado livre).

strengthen, *v.* **1.** *v.tr.* **to strengthen production,** fortalecer a produção. **2.** *v.i.* (*of demand, etc.*) intensificar-se.

strengthening, *n.* fortalecimento *m* (da moeda, da economia, etc.).

strict, *a.* estrito, rígido; **strict import controls,** estrito controle das importações; **strict cost price,** preço *m* de custo exato.

strike¹, *n.* *Ind:* greve *f*, parede *f*; **go-slow strike,** greve tartaruga; **lightning strike,** greve relâmpago; **official strike,** greve autorizada pelo sindicato; **sit-down strike,** greve de braços cruzados, greve branca; **sympathy strike, sympathetic strike,** greve de solidariedade; **token strike,** greve de advertência; **unofficial, wildcat, strike,** greve sem autorização do sindicato; **strike breaker,** fura-greve *mf*, fura-paredes *mf*; **strike committee,** comitê *m* de greve; **strike leaders,** líderes *mpl* grevistas, líderes paredistas; **strike movement,** movimento *m* grevista, movimento paredista; **strike notice,** aviso *m* de greve; **strike pay,** pagamento feito ao grevista pelo sindicato; **no-strike clause,** cláusula *f* contra-greve; **to be on strike,** fazer greve, estar em greve; **to go on, come out on, strike,** entrar em greve.

strike², *v.* **1.** *v.tr.* (*a*) **to strike a bargain,** fechar um negócio; **to strike a balance,** fazer um balanço; **to strike a dividend,** distribuir um dividendo; (*b*) *Ind:* **to strike oil,** descobrir petróleo. **2.** *v.i. Ind:* (i) entrar em greve, (ii) fazer greve; **the right to strike,** o direito de greve; **to strike in sympathy,** fazer uma greve de solidariedade.

striker, *n.* *Ind:* grevista *mf*, paredista *mf*.

striking, *n. St.Exch:* **striking price**, preço combinado (para a compra ou venda de um título).

stringency, *n. Econ:* escassez *f*.

strong, *a.* forte; **strong currency**, moeda *f* forte; **strong demand**, forte procura *f*; **strong economic position**, forte posição econômica; **strong market**, mercado *m* firme.

structural, *a.* estrutural; *Econ:* **structural inflation**, inflação *f* estrutural; **structural unemployment**, desemprego *m* estrutural.

structure¹, *n.* estrutura *f* (da economia, do comércio varejista, etc.); **wage structure**, estrutura dos salários; **market structure**, estrutura do mercado; **price structure**, estrutura dos preços; *Fin:* **cross-rate structure**, estrutura das taxas cambiais.

structure², *v.tr.* estruturar.

structuring, *n.* estruturação *f*.

stub, *n.* talão *m*, canhoto *m*, (de bloco de cheques, recibos, etc.).

stunt, *v.tr.* impedir (o crescimento de alguma coisa).

style, *n.* **1.** **style of a firm**, razão *f* social, denominação *f* social, razão comercial. **2.** estilo *m*; **advertising style**, estilo publicitário; **style of management**, estilo de administração, de gestão; (*in fashion*) **the twenties style**, o estilo da década de vinte; **the latest style**, a última moda.

sub-account, *n.* subconta *f*.

sub-agency, *n.* subagência *f*.

sub-agent, *n.* subagente *mf*.

sub-charter¹, *n.* subfretamento *m*.

sub-charter², *v.tr.* subfretar (um navio).

sub-charterer, *n.* subfretador *m*.

subcommittee, *n.* subcomitê *m*, subcomissão *f*.

subcontract¹, *n.* subcontrato *m*, sublocação *f*.

subcontract², *v.tr. & i.* subcontratar; **to subcontract s.o. for the job**, subcontratar alguém para a obra; **he is subcontracting the painting to a firm**, ele está subcontratando uma firma para a pintura.

subcontractor, *n.* subempreiteiro *m*; sublocatário *m*; *Jur:* subcontratante *mf*.

subdivision, *n.* subdivisão *f*; *Econ:*

subdivision of labour, subdivisão de mão-de-obra.

subject¹, *a.* sujeito (**to**, a); **subject to stamp duty**, sujeito a imposto de selo; **the decision is subject to confirmation**, a decisão é sujeita a confirmação; **subject to authorization**, sujeito a autorização, mediante autorização; **prices subject to 5% discount**, preços sujeitos a um desconto de 5%.

subject², *v.tr.* **to subject foreign goods to heavy duties**, sujeitar mercadorias estrangeiras a impostos pesados.

sub-lease¹, *n.* (contrato *m* de) sublocação *f*, subarrendamento *m*.

sub-lease², *v.tr.* sublocar, subarrendar, (casa, terras, etc.).

sub-leasing, *n.* sublocação *f*, subarrendamento *m*.

sub-lessee, *n.* **1.** sublocatário *m*, subarrendatário *m*. **2.** *Ind: etc:* subempreiteiro *m*.

sub-lessor, *n.* sublocador *m*.

sub-let¹, *n.* subaluguel *m*, sublocação *f*.

sub-let², *v.tr.* **1.** subalugar, sublocar; **he sub-let a room in his flat**, ele subalugou um quarto do seu apartamento. **2.** subcontratar (alguém para uma obra).

sub-letter, *n.* sublocador *m*.

sub-letting, *n.* **1.** sublocação *f*, subaluguel *m*. **2.** subcontratação *f*.

subliminal, *a.* subliminar, subliminal; **subliminal advertising**, propaganda *f* subliminar.

sub-loan, *n. Fin:* subempréstimo *m*.

sub-manager, *n.* subgerente *m*.

sub-manageress, *n.* subgerente *f*.

submit, *v.tr.* submeter, apresentar, (um relatório, etc.).

sub-office, *n.* sucursal *f*, filial *f*.

subordinate, *a.* **1.** subordinado, secundário, inferior. **2.** subalterno, subordinado; **subordinate official**, funcionário subalterno.

subordinated, *a.* subordinado; **subordinated debt**, dívida subordinada; **subordinated loan**, subempréstimo *m*.

sub-rent¹, *n.* aluguel pago por um sublocatário.

sub-rent², *v.tr.* subalugar.

subscribe, *v.* **1.** *v.tr.* (*a*) **to subscribe**

shares, subscrever ações; **subscribed capital,** capital subscrito; (*b*) *Jur:* **to subscribe a contract,** subscrever um contrato. **2.** *v.i.* (*a*) *Fin:* **to subscribe to an issue,** subscrever uma emissão; (*b*) **to subscribe to a publication,** assinar uma publicação.

subscriber, *n.* (*a*) *Fin:* **subscriber for shares,** subscritor *m* de ações; (*b*) assinante *mf* (de uma publicação, etc.); *Tel:* **subscriber's number,** número *m* de assinante; **subscriber trunk dialling (STD),** discagem direta a distância (DDD).

subscription, *n.* (*a*) *Fin:* subscrição *f*; **subscription for shares,** subscrição de ações; **subscription form,** boletim *m* de subscrição; **subscription list,** lista *f* dos subscritores; **subscription right,** direito *m* de subscrição; **subscription warrant,** bônus *m* de subscrição; **subscription in cash,** subscrição em dinheiro; **subscription in securities,** subscrição em títulos; **subscription receivable,** capital *m* a integralizar; (*b*) **subscription to a newspaper,** assinatura *f* de um jornal.

subsidiary, *a.* subsidiário; **subsidiary coin,** moeda divisionária; *Fin:* **subsidiary company,** (companhia) subsidiária *f*; **subsidiary loan,** empréstimo subsidiário; *Book-k:* **subsidiary account,** subconta *f*, conta subsidiária, conta de segundo grau, de terceiro grau; **subsidiary ledger,** sub-razão *m*, razão subsidiário, razonete *m*.

subsidize, *v.tr.* subvencionar, subsidiar.

subsidy, *n.* subvenção *f*, subsídio *m*; **export subsidy,** subsídio para exportação; **farm subsidies,** subsídios (aos preços dos produtos) agrícolas.

subsistence, *n.* subsistência *f*; **subsistence agriculture,** agricultura *f* de subsistência; **subsistence economy,** economia *f* de subsistência; **subsistence level,** nível *m* de subsistência; **subsistence sector,** setor *m* de subsistência.

substandard, *a.* de qualidade inferior.

substitute¹, *n.* substituto *m*.

substitute², *v.tr.* substituir (**for,** por).

substitution, *n.* substituição *f*; **substitution effect,** efeito substitutivo;

Econ: etc: **intercommodity substitution,** substituição entre mercadorias.

subtenancy, *n.* sublocação *f*, subarrendamento *m*.

subtenant, *n.* sublocatário *m*, subarrendatário *m*.

subventionary, *a.* subvencional.

succeed, *v.i.* **1. to succeed in business,** alcançar êxito nos negócios. **2. to succeed to a business,** suceder (a outrem) na propriedade e/ou direção de uma empresa.

success, *n.* sucesso *m*, êxito *m*; **the new product is a great success,** o novo produto é um grande sucesso.

successful, *a.* bem sucedido.

sue, *v.tr. & i. Jur:* **to sue an absconding debtor,** processar, acionar, demandar, um devedor omisso; **to sue (s.o.) for damages,** mover, intentar, uma ação de perdas e danos (contra alguém).

sugar, *n.* açúcar *m*; **the sugar industry,** a indústria açucareira; **sugar plantation,** canavial *m*, plantação *f* de cana-de-açúcar; **sugar production,** produção açucareira; **sugar refinery,** refinaria *f* de açúcar; **sugar terminal,** terminal açucareiro; **sugar merchant,** açucareiro *m*, negociante *m* de açúcar; **sugar futures,** vendas *fpl* de açúcar para entrega futura, vendas futuras de açúcar; **spot sugar,** açúcar disponível, açucar para entrega imediata; **August sugar,** açúcar para entrega em agosto.

suitable, *a.* adequado, apropriado; **suitable investment climate,** clima *m* favorável ao investimento.

sum¹, *n.* (*a*) soma *f*, total *m*, montante *m*, monta *f*; **sum total,** soma dos totais, total geral, soma total; **to amount to the sum of £250,** somar £250, atingir a soma de £250, elevar-se, montar, à soma de £250; *Book-k:* **sum-of-the years method,** método *m* de depreciação baseado na soma dos anos; (*b*) **sum of money,** quantia *f* em dinheiro, importância *f*; **large sum,** grande importância, vultosa soma.

sum², *v. Am:* **1.** *v.tr.* **to sum the costs,** somar os custos. **2.** *v.i.* **the expenses sum to $3000,** as despesas somam $3.000, importam em $3.000.

summary, 1. *n.* resumo *m*, sumário *m*; summary of loan activity, sumário do movimento de empréstimos. 2. *a. Jur:* summary proceedings, processo sumário.
summons, *n. Jur:* citação *f.*
sundries, *n.pl.* sundries account, conta *f* de diversos.
sundry, *a.* diverso; sundry creditors, credores diversos; sundry expenses, despesas diversas, gastos diversos.
sunk, *a.* sunk cost, (i) custo *m* de aquisição de ativo fixo, (ii) custo empatado.
superannuation, *n.* pensão *f* de aposentadoria.
supercargo, *n. Nau:* 1. encarregado *m* da carga (no navio). 2. agente *mf* de carga marítima (no exterior).
superfine, *a.* superfino.
supermarket, *n.* supermercado *m.*
supertax¹, *n.* sobretaxa *f.*
supertax², *v.tr.* impor sobretaxa (a alguém).
supervise, *v.tr.* supervisar, supervisionar; fiscalizar.
supervision, *n.* supervisão *f*; fiscalização *f.*
supervisor, *n.* supervisor *m*; *Adm:* fiscal *mf.*
supervisory, *a.* supervisory agency, agência fiscalizadora.
supplement, *n. Journ:* caderno *m.*
supplementary, *a.* suplementar; supplementary cost, custo fixo; supplementary finance, financiamento *m* suplementar; supplementary taxation, tributação adicional; supplementary wage, salário *m* adicional, salário suplementar; *UK:* supplementary benefit, benefício *m* social discrecionário.
supplier, *n.* fornecedor *m*, abastecedor *m*, supridor *m*; supplier industry, indústria *f* auxiliar.
supply¹, *n.* 1. suprimento *m*, fornecimento *m*, abastecimento *m*; supply conditions, terms of supply, condições *fpl* de fornecimento. 2. (*a*) supply and demand, oferta *f* e procura *f*, oferta e demanda *f*; the management of supply, a regulamentação da oferta; the supply and demand picture, o quadro da oferta e da procura; the supply of labour, o

suprimento de mão-de-obra; (*b*) *Pol.Ec: Fin:* the money supply, os meios de pagamento, o suprimento monetário, a oferta monetária; supply of capital, suprimento de capital.
supply², *v.tr.* fornecer, abastecer, suprir; to supply raw materials to a factory, fornecer matérias-primas para uma fábrica; to supply share capital, participar no capital social.
support¹, *n.* apoio *m*, sustentação *f*; price support, apoio, amparo *m*, aos preços; sustentação dos preços; support price, preço *m* de sustentação, preço mínimo.
support², *v.tr.* apoiar, sustentar, amparar, (os preços, etc.); supporting document, comprovante *m*; supporting facilities, medidas *fpl* de apoio; *Book-k: etc:* supporting record, registro comprobatório.
surcharge, *n.* (*a*) sobretaxa *f*; import surcharge, sobretaxa de importação; graduated surcharges, sobretaxas graduais, sobretaxas graduadas; (*b*) preço *m* adicional.
surety, *n.* (*a*) garantia *f*, fiança *f*; surety bond, caução *f*; (*b*) (*person*) caucionário *m*, caucionante *mf*, fiador *m*; to stand surety for s.o., afiançar alguém; dar, prestar, caução por alguém; surety for a loan, fiador para um empréstimo.
suretyship, *n.* responsabilidade *f* de fiador.
surge, *n.* rápido incremento.
surplus, 1. *n.* excedente *m*; *Fin:* superávit *m*; exportable surplus, excedente exportável; farm surpluses, excedentes agrícolas; budget surplus, superávit orçamentário; surplus on invisibles, superávit das transações invisíveis; surplus country, país superavitário; surpluses and deficits, excedentes e déficits; *Book-k: etc:* (earned) surplus, lucros acumulados, lucros não distribuídos; free surplus, lucros acumulados (à disposição dos acionistas); available surplus, lucros disponíveis; surplus reserve, reserva *f* de lucros não distribuídos; surplus charge, despesa levada diretamente a débito dos lucros não distribuídos; surplus at date of

acquisition, superávit na data de aquisição, superávit adquirido. **2.** *a.* **surplus stock,** estoque *m* excedente.

surrender, *n. Ins:* **surrender value (of a policy),** valor *m* de resgate (de uma apólice); **cash surrender value,** valor de resgate em dinheiro.

surtax, *n.* sobretaxa *f.*

survey, *n.* levantamento *m*; **market survey,** levantamento de mercado; **postal, mail, survey,** levantamento realizado pelo correio; **sampling survey,** levantamento por amostragem.

suspend, *v.tr.* (*a*) suspender; **to suspend payments,** suspender os pagamentos; **to suspend work for two days,** suspender o trabalho por dois dias; (*b*) **to suspend an official,** suspender um funcionário.

suspense, *n.* (*a*) **bills in suspense,** efeitos *mpl* em suspenso; (*b*) *Book-k:* **suspense account,** conta suspensa, conta provisória, conta transitória, ativo suspenso, ativo transitório.

suspension, *n.* (*a*) suspensão *f*; *Jur:* **suspension of payment(s),** suspensão de pagamentos; (*b*) **suspension of an official,** suspensão de um funcionário.

swap¹, *n.* troca *f*, permuta *f*, permutação *f*; **stock swap,** permuta de títulos; **swap arrangement,** acordo *m* swap, acordo de troca; acordo de crédito recíproco a curto prazo, realizado entre dois bancos centrais; **swap facilities,** facilidades *fpl* de crédito recíproco.

swap², *v.tr.* trocar, permutar; **to swap oil for technology,** trocar o petróleo pela tecnologia.

swell, *v.tr.* **to swell an account,** enfestar, aumentar, uma conta.

swelling, *a.* crescente.

swindle¹, *n.* trapaça *f*, *F:* conto-do-vigário *m.*

swindle², *v.tr.* trapacear, *F:* passar o conto-do-vigário (em alguém).

swindler, *n.* trapaceiro *m*, *F:* vigarista *mf.*

swing¹, *n.* **swing credit,** margem *f* de crédito recíproco; *Am:* **swing shift,** turno vespertino.

swing², *v.tr. F:* **to swing a deal,** fechar um negócio.

symbol, *n.* símbolo *m.*

syndicate¹, *n.* sindicato *m*, consórcio *m*; **member of a syndicate,** sindicatário *m*, membro *m* de um sindicato; **banking syndicate,** sindicato de bancos; **to form a syndicate,** formar um sindicato; **underwriting syndicate,** (i) grupo *m* que subscreve uma emissão de títulos mobiliários, (ii) *Ins:* sindicato de aceitações.

syndicate², *v.* **1.** *v.tr.* **to syndicate a loan,** sindicalizar um empréstimo. **2.** *v.i.* sindicalizar-se, sindicar-se.

synthetic, *a.* **synthetic rubber,** borracha sintética; **synthetic fibre,** fibra sintética.

system, *n.* (*a*) sistema *m*; **decimal system,** sistema decimal; **metric system,** sistema métrico; **accounting system,** sistema contábil; **system of accounts,** sistema de contas, sistema de contabilização; **cost system,** sistema de apuração de custos; **price system,** sistema de preços; **management system,** sistema de administração, de gestão; **computer system,** sistema de computadores; *Book-k:* **voucher system,** sistema de comprovantes; *Cmptr:* **card system,** sistema de cartão; **batch system,** sistema de processamento em bateladas; **systems analysis,** análise *f* de sistemas; **systems analyst,** analista *mf* de sistemas; *Econ:* **international monetary system,** sistema monetário internacional; (*b*) *Econ:* **quota system,** contingenciamento *m.*

systematic, *a.* sistemático; **every organization chart should be systematic,** todo organograma deve ser sistemático.

systematization, *n.* sistematização *f.*

systematize, *v.tr.* sistematizar.

T

table, *n.* **1.** mesa *f.* **2.** tabela *f*, tábua *f*, quadro *m*, mapa *m*; **table of weights and measures,** tabela de pesos e medidas; **interest table,** tabela de juros; *Ins:* **life tables, mortality tables, actuaries' tables,** tábuas de mortalidade; **redemption table,** tabela de amortização.

tabular, *a.* tabular.

tabulate, *v.tr.* **1.** classificar (resultados), catalogar (mercadorias). **2.** (*on typewriter*) tabular.

tabulated, *a.* disposto em forma tabular.

tabulating, *n.* **1.** *Cmptr: etc:* **tabulating card,** cartão perfurado; **tabulating machine,** tabuladora *f.* **2.** = **tabulation 1.**

tabulation, *n.* **1.** disposição *f* em tabela. **2.** (*on typewriter*) tabulação *f.*

tabulator, *n.* tabulador *m*; **tabulator key,** tecla *f* do tabulador.

tacit, *a.* tácito; **tacit agreement,** convenção tácita; *Jur:* **renewal by tacit agreement,** renovação tácita.

tactical, *a.* tático.

tactics, *n.pl.* tática *f.*

tag, *n.* **price tag,** etiqueta *f* de preço.

take¹, *n.* receita *f*, féria *f*; **the day's take,** a féria do dia.

take², *v.tr.* **1. to take home $150 a week,** perceber, receber, ganhar, $150 por semana. **2.** *St. Exch:* (*of dealers, etc.*) to **take one's profits,** realizar os seus lucros. **3. to take an amount out of s.o.'s income,** deduzir uma quantia da renda de alguém. **4. to take delivery of goods, to take the goods (delivered),** receber, aceitar, as mercadorias (entregues). **5. to take a loan,** tomar, fazer, um empréstimo. **6.** (*of secretary, etc.*) to **take (down) a letter,** anotar uma carta ditada. **7. to take a risk,** assumir um risco. **8. to take stock,** fazer o inventário. **9. to take legal advice,** consultar um advogado. **10. to take the**

necessary steps, tomar as providências necessárias.

take back, *v.tr.* receber de volta, receber em devolução; **we do not take back empties,** não aceitamos cascos.

take-home, *a.* **take-home pay,** salário líquido.

take in, *v.tr.* **1.** (*of boat*) **to take in cargo,** aceitar, receber, carga; carregar. **2.** *St. Exch:* to take in stock,** vender títulos com ágio.

take off, *v.tr.* **1. to take sth. off (the price of sth.),** deduzir, abater, uma quantia (do preço de algo). **2. to take a day off,** tirar um dia de folga.

take-off, *n.* **1.** *Econ:* arrancada *f*, demarragem *f.* **2.** elevação brusca (de preços).

take on, *v.tr.* to **take on staff,** admitir, contratar, pessoal.

take out, *v.tr.* to **take out a patent,** tirar uma patente; *Ins:* to **take out an insurance,** contratar um seguro, fazer um seguro.

take over, *v.tr.* to **take over a post,** assumir, tomar posse de, um cargo; **to take over a business,** assumir um negócio; *Fin:* to **take over a company,** adquirir controle de uma companhia; **to take over the liabilities of a firm,** assumir o passivo de uma empresa.

takeover, *n.* *Fin:* aquisição *f* de controle de companhia; **takeover bid,** oferta pública de aquisição de controle.

taker, *n.* **1.** tomador *m.* **2.** *St.Exch:* (*contangoes*) reportante *mf*, reportador *m*; **taker for a put,** operador *m* que exerce opção de compra; **taker for a call,** operador *m* que exerce opção de venda.

take up, *v.tr.* **1. to take up a bill,** aceitar uma letra, pagar uma letra; **to take up shares,** subscrever ações; **to take up an**

228

offer, aceitar uma oferta; *St.Exch: etc:* **to take up an option,** exercer uma opção. **2.** (*of representative*) **to take up a line of goods,** encarregar-se da venda de uma linha de mercadorias.

takings, *n.pl.* receita *f*, féria *f*, apurado *m*, (de casa comercial, etc.); **the day's takings,** a féria do dia; **the takings are good,** a receita é boa.

talk, *n.* **1. pay talks,** negociações *fpl* sobre salários. **2.** *F:* **sales talk,** conversa *f* de vendedor.

tally¹, *n.* **1. the tally trade,** o comércio de vendas a prestações. **2.** (i) contagem *f*, registro *m*, (ii) marcação *f*, rotulagem *f*, rotulação *f*, (de caixas, mercadorias, etc.); **tally clerk,** encarregado *m* da marcação ou contagem de mercadorias; **tally sheet,** (i) folha *f* para registrar contas, (ii) folha de registro (de mercadorias, etc.); *Stat:* **tally error,** erro *m* de registro.

tally², *v.* **1.** *v.tr.* registrar, marcar, (mercadorias); etiquetar, rotular, (caixas, mercadorias, etc.); conferir (caixas, etc.). **2.** *v.i.* (*of plans, etc.*) corresponder; (*of accounts*) concordar, bater; **these accounts do not tally,** estas contas não concordam, não batem.

tallying, *n.* (i) marcação *f*, (ii) registro *m* (de mercadorias, etc.).

tangible, *a.* **tangible asset,** ativo *m* tangível; **tangible property,** bens *mpl* tangíveis, bens físicos; **tangible value,** valor *m* tangível.

tankage, *n. Ind: etc:* (*a*) armazenagem *f* em tanques; (*b*) preço *m* de armazenagem em tanques.

tanker, *n.* (*a*) navio-tanque *m*, navio-cisterna *m*; **oil tanker,** (navio) petroleiro *m*; (*b*) carro-tanque *m*, caminhão-tanque *m*.

tanned, *a.* **tanned hide,** couro curtido.

tanner, *n.* curtidor *m*.

tannery, *n.* curtume *m*.

tanning, *n.* curtimento *m*; **tanning oils,** óleos *mpl* para curtume.

tap, *v.tr.* **1. to tap resources,** aproveitar-se de recursos. **2. to tap oil,** extrair petróleo.

tape, *n.* **1.** fita *f*; **magnetic tape,** fita magnética; **perforated, punched, tape,** fita

perfurada. **2.** *F:* **red tape,** burocracia *f*, papelada *f*, formalidades *fpl*.

tare¹, *n.* tara *f*; **actual tare,** tara real; **average tare,** tara média; **to ascertain the tare,** calcular a tara; **allowance for tare,** desconto *m* pela tara; **to allow for the tare,** conceder um desconto pela tara.

tare², *v.tr.* tarar, tarear.

target, *n.* meta *f*, objetivo *m*; **target cost,** custo predeterminado; **target market,** mercado visado; **target price,** preço visado, preço objetivado; **target setting,** fixação *f* de objetivos; **production target,** objetivo de produção.

tariff¹, *n.* tarifa *f*; **ad valorem tarif,** tarifa ad-valorem; **customs tariff,** tarifa alfandegária; **full tariff,** tarifa plena; **preferential tariff,** tarifa preferencial; **reduced tariff,** tarifa reduzida; **sliding-scale tariff,** tarifa em escala móvel; **specific tariff,** tarifa específica; **tariff agreement,** acordo tarifário; **tariff barriers,** barreiras tarifárias; **tariff laws,** leis tarifárias; **tariff protection,** proteção alfandegária; **tariff system,** sistema tarifário.

tariff², *v.tr.* tarifar.

tariffing, *n.* tarifação *f*.

task, *n.* tarefa *f*; **task force,** força-tarefa *f*; **task report,** relatório *m* de tarefas; *Ind:* **task work,** (i) trabalho *m* por tarefa, (ii) empreitada *f*, empreita *f*.

tax¹, *n.* imposto *m*, taxa *f*, contribuição *f*, tributo *m*; *Adm:* (*amount paid or collected*) coleta *f*; **taxes and dues,** impostos e taxas; **tax on buildings,** imposto predial; **tax on turnover,** imposto de circulação de mercadorias; **assessed tax,** imposto lançado; **capital tax,** imposto sobre capital; **capital gains tax,** imposto sobre ganhos de capital; **capital transfer tax,** imposto sobre transferências de capital, **capitation tax, head tax,** capitação *f*, imposto de capitação; **corporation tax,** imposto sobre a renda das sociedades; **direct taxes,** impostos diretos; **entertainment tax,** imposto sobre diversões públicas; **graduated income tax,** imposto de renda progressivo; **hidden tax,** imposto disfarçado; **income tax,** imposto de renda; **income tax return,** declaração *f* de rendimentos, declaração do imposto de renda; **indirect taxes**, impostos indiretos; **land tax**, imposto territorial; **luxury tax**, imposto sobre artigos de luxo; **manufacturing, excise, tax**, imposto sobre produtos industrializados; **payroll tax**, imposto sobre os salários; **proportional tax**, imposto proporcional; **road tax**, taxa rodoviária, taxa de viação, imposto de viação; **schedule tax**, imposto cedular; **value-added tax (VAT)**, imposto sobre o valor adicionado, sobre o valor agregado; **withholding tax**, imposto retido na fonte; **tax avoidance**, isenção *f* fiscal; **tax base**, base *f* impositiva, base para tributação; **tax benefit**, benefício *m* fiscal; **tax bracket**, faixa *f* de tributação; **tax burden**, carga tributária, ônus *m* fiscal; **tax collection**, arrecadação *f*, coleta *f*, cobrança *f*, recolhimento *m*, de impostos; **tax collection slip, tax payment slip**, guia *f* de recolhimento fiscal; **tax collector**, coletor *m* de impostos, arrecador *m*, cobrador *m* de impostos, recebedor *m* de impostos; **tax (collector's) office**, coletoria *f*, recebedoria *f*, exatoria *f*; **tax consideration**, consideração *f* de ordem fiscal; **tax credit**, crédito *m* fiscal; **tax cut**, redução *f* de impostos; **tax-deductible**, dedutível do rendimento tributável; **tax differential**, diferença *f* de tributação; **tax dodging**, sonegação *f* fiscal, sonegação de impostos; **tax evasion**, sonegação fiscal, sonegação de impostos; **tax exemption**, isenção *f* fiscal, isenção de imposto(s); **tax farming**, venda *f* pelo Estado a entidade particular de direitos de arrecadar impostos; **tax-free**, isento de imposto(s); **tax haven**, refúgio *m* fiscal; **tax holiday**, período *m* de isenção fiscal; **tax incentive**, incentivo *m* fiscal; **tax legislation**, legislação tributária, legislação fazendária; **tax lien**, penhora *f* pelo não-pagamento de impostos; **tax-paying capacity**, capacidade tributária; **tax purposes**, fins *mpl* de tributação; **tax rebate**, devolução *f* do imposto de renda; **tax receipt**, receita *f* fiscal, recebimento *m* de impostos; **tax relief**, desagravo *m* fiscal; **tax return**, declaração *f* de rendimentos, declaração do imposto de

renda; **tax revenue**, receita *f* fiscal, renda tributária; **tax sale**, venda *f* em hasta pública de direitos de arrecadar impostos; **tax subsidy**, subsídio concedido sob a forma de isenção fiscal; **tax system**, sistema tributário; **tax year**, ano *m* fiscal, exercício *m*; **tax yield**, renda tributária, receita *f* fiscal; **to collect a tax**, arrecadar, cobrar, coletar, colher, recolher, imposto; **to levy a tax on sth.**, tributar, taxar, algo.

tax², *v.tr.* taxar, tributar; **to tax foreign investors**, tributar os investidores estrangeiros; **to tax capital gains**, tributar, taxar, os ganhos de capital.

taxable, *a.* tributável, taxável; **taxable article**, artigo *m* tributável, artigo taxável; **taxable income**, renda *f* tributável; **taxable profit**, lucro *m* tributável.

taxation, *n.* tributação *f*, taxação *f*; **the taxation authorities**, o fisco, a fazenda pública; **rate of taxation**, alíquota *f* de tributação; **highest scale of taxation**, nível mais alto da escala tributária; **supplementary taxation**, tributação adicional; **double taxation**, dupla tributação; **taxation at source**, tributação na fonte, desconto *m* na fonte.

taxpayer, *n.* contribuinte *mf*, tributário *m*.

team¹, *n.* equipe *f* (de operários, etc.).

team², *v.i.* *N.Am:* trabalhar como camioneiro.

teamster, *n.* *N.Am:* camioneiro *m*.

technical, *a.* técnico; **technical advice**, orientação técnica; **technical difficulty**, dificuldade *f* de ordem técnica; **technical problem**, problema *m* de natureza técnica; **technical standard**, norma técnica; **technical term**, termo técnico; **technical manager**, gerente, diretor, técnico; **technical adviser**, assessor técnico; **technical expert**, técnico perito; **technical assistance contract**, contrato *m* de assistência técnica.

technicality, *n.* 1. tecnicidade *f*. 2. detalhe técnico; termo técnico.

technician, *n.* técnico *m*.

technique, *n.* técnica *f*; **management techniques**, técnicas de administração; **marketing techniques**, técnicas de

marketing, de comercialização; **sales, selling, techniques,** técnicas de venda.
technocracy, *n.* tecnocracia *f.*
technocrat, *n.* tecnocrata *mf.*
technocratic, *a.* tecnocrático.
technological, *a.* tecnológico; **technological development,** desenvolvimento tecnológico; **technological gap,** diferença *f* de nível tecnológico; **technological forecasting,** previsão tecnológica; **technological level,** nível tecnológico.
technologist, *n.* tecnologista *mf,* tecnólogo *m.*
technology, *n.* tecnologia *f*; **advanced technology,** tecnologia avançada; **information technology,** informática *f.*
Telecom, *n. R.t.m:* **British Telecom,** a empresa de telecomunicações da Grã-Bretanha.
telegram, *n.* telegrama *m*; **telephoned telegram,** telegrama fonado, fonograma *m*; **to send a telegram,** passar um telegrama, mandar um telegrama.
telegraph¹, *n.* telégrafo *m*; **telegraph service,** serviço telegráfico.
telegraph², *v.tr. & i.* telegrafar; **to telegraph news of a deal,** telegrafar a notícia de uma transação.
telegraphic, *a.* telegráfico; **telegraphic address,** endereço telegráfico; *Bank: etc:* **telegraphic transfer,** ordem telegráfica de transferência, transferência telegráfica.
telephone¹, *n.* telefone *m*, fone *m*; **by telephone,** pelo telefone; **dial telephone,** telefone automático; **house telephone, inter-office telephone,** telefone interno; **subscriber's telephone,** telefone de assinante; **telephone answering machine,** respondedor automático de chamadas telefônicas; **telephone box, telephone booth,** cabine, cabina, telefônica; **telephone call,** chamada telefônica, telefonema *m*, telefonada *f*, ligada *f*; **telephone company,** companhia telefônica; **telephone connection,** ligação telefônica; **telephone dial,** disco (telefônico); **telephone directory,** lista telefônica, catálogo telefônico, guia telefônico; **telephone exchange,** central telefônica, estação telefônica; **telephone**

message, recado telefônico; **telephone number,** número *m* de telefone, telefone *m*; **telephone operator,** telefonista *mf*; **telephone selling,** venda *f* pelo telefone; **telephone switchboard,** mesa telefônica; **to speak to s.o. on the telephone,** falar com alguém pelo telefone; **we accept telephone orders,** aceitamos encomendas pelo telefone.
telephone², *v.tr. & i.* telefonar; **to telephone s.o.,** telefonar para alguém; **to telephone s.o. a message,** telefonar um recado para alguém, dar um recado a alguém pelo telefone.
telephonist, *n.* telefonista *mf.*
teleprinter, *n.* teleimpressor *m*, teletipo *m*; **teleprinter operator,** teletipista *mf*, teleimpressor *m.*
teletypewriter, *n. Am:* = **teleprinter.**
teletypist, *n.* teletipista *mf*, teleimpressor *m.*
telewriter, *n.* = **teleprinter.**
telex¹, *n.* telex *m*; **telex subscriber,** assinante *mf* de telex; **telex operator,** operador *m* de telex; **telex network,** rede *f* de telex; **telex rates,** tarifa *f* (para transmissão) de telex; **to send a message by telex,** enviar um recado por telex.
telex², *v.tr. & i.* telexar.
teller, *n.* caixa *mf* (de banco); **paying teller,** caixa pagador; **receiving teller,** caixa recebedor.
temporary, *a.* temporário, provisório, interino, temporâneo; **temporary post,** cargo temporário; **temporary staff,** pessoal temporário; **temporary employment,** trabalho temporário; **temporary measures,** medidas provisórias; **temporary investment,** investimento temporário; *Cust:* **temporary admission,** admissão temporária.
tenancy, *n.* inquilinato *m*; **terms of tenancy,** condições *fpl* de arrendamento, de locação, de aluguel; **period, term, of tenancy,** prazo *m* de locação, de arrendamento; *Jur:* **tenancy at will,** ocupação *f* de propriedade a critério do proprietário.
tenant, *n.* inquilino *m*, locatário *m*, alugador *m*, arrendatário *m*; **business, commercial, tenant,** locatário comercial.

tendency, *n.* tendência *f;* **a growing tendency,** uma tendência crescente; **market tendencies,** tendências do mercado; **strong upward tendency, bullish tendency,** forte tendência para a alta; **strong downward tendency,** forte tendência para a baixa; **deflationary tendency,** tendência deflacionária.

tender[1], *n.* **1.** proposta *f,* oferta *f;* **to invite tenders for the construction of a road,** abrir concorrência para a construção de uma estrada; **to make a tender, put in a tender,** apresentar uma proposta; **sealed tender,** oferta lacrada, proposta apresentada em envelope lacrado; **allocation to lowest tender,** adjudicação *f* a quem oferecer o preço mais baixo; **tender documents,** documentação relacionada com uma proposta. **2.** *Fin:* **tender of securities,** oferta *f* de títulos; **tender rate,** taxa *f* de oferta; *Am:* **tender offer,** oferta pública de aquisição de controle. **3. tender for public loans,** solicitação *f* de empréstimos públicos. **4. legal tender,** moeda *f* de curso legal, moeda legal, moeda corrente; **to be legal tender,** ter curso legal; **tender by word,** oferta *f* verbal de pagamento.

tender[2], *v.* **1.** *v.i.* **to tender for a contract,** apresentar uma proposta em concorrência (pública) para um contrato; **to tender for a supply of goods,** apresentar proposta para fornecimento de mercadorias; **party tendering for work on a contract,** proponente *mf,* concorrente *mf.* **2.** *v.tr.* oferecer (serviços, dinheiro, etc.); **to tender one's resignation,** demitir-se, pedir demissão; **to tender payment,** oferecer pagamento.

tenderable, *a.* **tenderable cotton,** algodão *m* comerciável.

tendering, *n.* apresentação *f* de proposta(s).

tenor, *n.* **the tenor of a draft,** o prazo de um saque.

tenure, *n.* (*a*) (período de) posse *f* (de um imóvel, etc.); (*b*) **security of tenure,** (i) estabilidade *f* no emprego, (ii) = (*approx.*) contrato *m* de aluguel que só pode ser rescindido caso o inquilino não

cumpra com as condições de arrendamento.

term, *n.* **1.** prazo *m,* termo *m;* **the term of a lease,** o prazo de um contrato de arrendamento; **during the term of a contract,** durante o prazo de um contrato, durante a vigência de um contrato; **term of office,** período *m* de cargo; **term of payment,** prazo de pagamento, prazo para pagamento; **term of validity,** prazo de validade; **term of redemption,** prazo para o resgate; **term insurance,** seguro *m* a prazo fixo; *Fin:* **the term of a bill,** o prazo de uma letra; *Am:* **term loan,** empréstimo *m* a prazo fixo; **term bonds,** obrigações *fpl* que têm o mesmo vencimento. **2.** *pl.* **terms,** (*a*) termos, condições *fpl,* cláusulas *fpl,* (de um contrato, etc.); **according to the terms and conditions of the contract,** de acordo com os termos e condições do contrato; **on these terms,** nestes termos, nestas condições; **the terms and conditions laid down in this contract,** os termos e condições previstos, estabelecidos, neste contrato; *Fin: Jur:* **to come to terms with one's creditors,** transigir, chegar a um acordo, com os seus credores; *Econ:* **terms of trade,** relação *f* de intercâmbio, termos de intercâmbio, relações de comércio; (*b*) **terms of payment,** condições *fpl* de pagamento, modalidades *fpl* de pagamento; **easy terms,** pagamento facilitado, pagamento em prestações; **we give easy terms,** facilitamos o pagamento; **to buy sth. on easy terms,** comprar algo a prestação; **terms of sale,** condições de venda. **3. technical terms,** termos técnicos. **4. terms of reference,** termos de referência. **5. to be on good terms with s.o.,** estar em boas relações com alguém.

terminable, *a.* (*of contract, etc.*) rescindível, resilível; (*of annuity*) a prazo fixo, a prazo determinado.

terminal, 1. *a.* terminal; *Ind: etc:* **terminal wage,** salário pago a um empregado demitido; **terminal market,** (i) mercado *m* a termo, (ii) mercado terminal. **2.** *n. Trans:* terminal *m;* **cold storage terminal,** terminal frigorífico; **grain terminal,** terminal de cereais; **air terminal,** terminal aéreo; *Cmptr:* **computer terminal,** terminal de computador.

terminate, *v.tr.* (*a*) terminar; (*b*) **to terminate a contract,** rescindir, anular, dissolver, um contrato.

termination, *n.* **termination of a contract,** rescisão *f*, anulação *f*, de um contrato.

territorial, *a.* territorial; **territorial jurisdiction,** jurisdição *f* territorial; **territorial waters,** aguas *fpl* territoriais.

territory, *n.* território *m* (de agente, representante, etc.); **sales territory,** território de vendas.

test¹, *n.* (*a*) prova *f*, teste *m*; **to undergo a test,** submeter-se a uma prova, a um teste; **vocational test, occupational test, trade test,** teste vocacional; **aptitude test,** teste de aptidão, de habilitação; *Cmptr:* **diagnostic test,** teste-diagnóstico *m*, diagnóstico *m*; *Ind:* **acceptance test,** teste de recepção, prova de homologação; **efficiency test,** prova de rendimento; **field test,** prova na obra, prova no local; **factory test,** teste de fábrica, prova na fábrica; **laboratory test,** teste de laboratório; **test certificate,** resultado *m* de teste; **performance test,** teste de funcionamento; *Book-k:* **acid-test ratio,** índice *m* de liquidez geral, de liquidez estática; (*b*) **test sales,** vendas *fpl* experimentais.

test², *v.tr.* testar, experimentar, (um novo tipo de máquina, etc.); verificar (pesos e medidas, etc.); **to test applicants for a post,** testar os candidatos para um cargo; **to test out a scheme, a plan,** testar um esquema, um plano.

test-check, *v.tr. Book-k:* conferir por amostragem.

testify, *v.tr. & i.* atestar, dar testemunho.

testimonial, *n.* atestado *m*, atestação *f*; (*for an employee, etc.*) carta *f* de recomendação; *Am: Advert:* atestado sobre a qualidade de um produto ou serviço passado por uma pessoa famosa para fins publicitários.

testing, *n.* testagem *f*, ensaio *m*, prova *f*; verificação *f*; *Ind:* **field testing,** testagem na obra, no local; **product testing,** testagem de produtos; **testing equipment,** aparelhos *mpl* de testagem; **testing**

laboratory, laboratório *m* de ensaios; **testing room,** sala *f* de ensaios, de testagem.

textile, **1.** *n.* produto *m* têxtil, tecido *m.* **2.** *a.* **the textile industry,** a indústria têxtil; **textile products,** produtos têxteis.

thank, *v.tr.* agradecer.

thaw, *v.tr.* **to thaw frozen funds,** liberar fundos congelados.

theme, *n.* tema *m.*

theoretical, *a.* teórico, teorético.

theory, *n.* teoria *f*; **economic theory,** teoria econômica; **management theory,** teoria da administração; **communication theory,** teoria da comunicação; **information theory,** teoria da informação; **theory of interest,** teoria de juros; **theory of tariff structure,** teoria das tarifas aduaneiras.

thin, *a.* **thin market,** mercado limitado.

third, **1.** *n.* terço *m*, terça parte; **on the third of January,** no dia três de janeiro, em três de janeiro; **two-thirds of the takings,** dois-terços da receita; **a discount of a third, one third off,** um desconto, um abatimento, de um terço (do preço), no valor de um terço (do preço); **third of exchange,** terceira via de uma cambial. **2.** *a.* terceiro; **third copy,** triplicata *f*, terceira cópia; **the Third World,** o terceiro mundo; **third-class,** de terceira classe; **third currency,** moeda *f* de um terceiro país; **a third party,** um terceiro; **to disclose information to third parties,** divulgar informação a terceiros; **third-party insurance,** seguro *m* contra terceiros, seguro de responsabilidade civil; **third-party risk,** risco *m* contra terceiros; **third-party liability,** responsabilidade civil; *Am:* **third-class mail,** correio *m* de terceira classe.

three, *n. & a.* três (*m*); **three cities,** três cidades; *Ind:* **three-shift system,** sistema *m* de trabalho em três turnos.

threshold, *n. Ind:* **threshold agreement,** acordo *m* entre empregador e empregados para aumento salarial em conformidade com determinada subida no índice do custo de vida; **threshold worker,** empregado novo, empregado recém-contratado.

thriving, *a.* (*of person, industry*) próspero, florescente.

throughput, *n. Ind:* débito *m*; *Cmptr:* capacidade *f* de processamento.

throw-outs, *n.pl.* artigos rejeitados.

thruput, *n. N.Am:* = throughput.

tick¹, *n.* **1.** *F:* crédito *m*; **to buy sth. on tick,** comprar algo a crédito, comprar algo fiado. **2.** (*mark*) tique *m*, tico *m*.

tick², *v.tr.* ticar.

ticker, *n.* **ticker tape,** fita *f* de teleimpressor.

ticket, *n.* (*a*) (*for transport, entertainments, etc.*) bilhete *m*, tiquete *m*; **theatre ticket,** entrada *f*, ingresso *m*, de teatro; **train ticket,** passagem *f* de trem, bilhete de trem; **single ticket,** bilhete de ida; **return ticket,** bilhete de ida e volta; **season ticket,** bilhete de transporte para temporada; (*b*) **price ticket,** etiqueta *f* de preço; (*c*) (*coupon*) cupom *m*, cupão *m*; (*d*) *St.Exch:* ficha *f* (em que se registra uma operação).

tick off, *v.tr.* ticar.

tie¹, *n.* **1.** (*in vote*) empate *m*. **2.** (*link*) elo *m*.

tie², *v.tr.* relacionar, vincular; **tied aid,** ajuda (estrangeira) vinculada; **tied loan,** empréstimo *m* que obriga o tomador em país estrangeiro a adquirir, no país credor, os ítens de que necessita.

tie up, *v.tr.* **to tie up capital,** imobilizar capitais, (*in unprofitable ventures*) empatar capitais.

tie-up, *n.* **1. tie-up of capital,** imobilização *f* de capitais, de recursos. **2.** associação *f* (de casas comerciais, etc.).

tight, *a.* (*a*) **tight money,** moeda escassa, dinheiro escasso; **tight credit conditions,** condições restritas de crédito; (*b*) **tight bargain,** negócio apertado, operação apertada; *Ind:* **tight rate, tight time value,** salário por tarefa muito baixo.

tighten, *v.* **1.** *v.tr.* (*a*) **to tighten economic controls,** reforçar os controles econômicos; (*b*) **to tighten the money supply,** restringir os meios de pagamento, restringir o suprimento monetário; **to tighten credit,** restringir o crédito; **to tighten expenditure,** restringir as

despesas. **2.** *v.i.* (*of money*) tornar-se escasso.

tightening, *n.* aperto *m*; **tightening of credit,** restrição *f* de crédito, contração *f* de crédito; **tightening of money conditions,** aperto nas condições monetárias; **tightening of the money supply,** restrição dos meios de pagamento, restrição do suprimento monetário.

tightness, *n.* aperto *m*; **tightness of money,** escassez *f* do dinheiro; **tightness of credit,** restrição *f* do crédito.

till¹, *n.* gaveta *f* de caixa registradora, *UK:* caixa registradora; **till money,** dinheiro *m* em caixa.

till², *v.tr.* cultivar, lavrar, amanhar.

tillable, *a.* arável, cultivável.

tillage, *n.* cultivo *m*, amanho *m*, do solo.

timber, *n.* madeira *f* de construção; **timber yard,** depósito *m* de madeira.

timberland, *n.* madeiral *m*.

time, *n.* **1.** (*a*) tempo *m*; **idle time,** tempo ocioso, período *m* de inatividade; **lost time,** tempo perdido; **loss of time,** perda *f* de tempo; **to save time,** economizar, poupar, tempo; (*b*) *Ind: etc:* **time and motion study,** estudo *m* de tempos e movimentos, cronometragem *f* de atividades industriais; **time clock,** relógio *m* de ponto; **time card,** cartão *m* de ponto; **time chart,** cronograma *m*; **time sheet,** folha *f* de ponto; *Cmptr:* **time sharing,** compartilhamento *m* do tempo; *Fin: Am:* **time-interest ratio,** índice *m* de tempo/juro; *Stat:* **time series,** série cronológica, série temporal. **2.** hora *f*; **closing time,** hora de fechamento; **in time,** a tempo; **on time,** na hora; **in one's own time,** fora do horário de serviço (sem ser pago); **time zone,** fuso horário; *Ind:* **time work,** trabalho *m* remunerado por hora; **time wage rates,** salário horário, salário pago por horas trabalhadas. **3.** *Fin:* (*of bill of exchange*) **time after sight,** prazo *m* para o pagamento de uma letra à vista; **time for protest,** prazo para o protesto; **time to pay,** prazo de tolerância para pagamento; **latest time,** prazo fatal; **end of the time (allowed),** expiração *f* do prazo (concedido); **within a reasonable (period**

of) **time,** dentro de um prazo razoável; **to obtain an extension of time for payment,** conseguir uma prorrogação do prazo para pagamento; **time bill,** letra *f* a prazo (fixo); **time deposit,** depósito *m* a prazo fixo; **time draft,** saque *m* a prazo fixo; **time insurance,** seguro *m* a prazo fixo; **time money,** empréstimos *mpl* a prazo fixo; *Ins:* **time policy,** apólice *f* de seguro a prazo fixo; *St.Exch:* **dealings for time,** operações *fpl* a termo; **time bargain,** negócio *m* a termo; *Nau:* **time for shipment,** prazo para o carregamento, para embarque. **4. time lag,** desfasagem *f*; intervalo *m* de tempo.
timekeeper, *n. Ind:* apontador *m*; encarregado *m* da folha de ponto.
timesaving, *a.* que economiza tempo.
timetable, *n.* (*of services, etc.*) horário *m*; (*of project or job*) cronograma *m*.
tin, *n.* **1.** estanho *m*; **tin-coated,** estanhado, revestido de estanho; **tin plate,** folha-de-flandres *f*, chapa estanhada, lata *f*; **tin mill,** usina *f* de folha-de-flandres. **2. tin** (**can**), lata *f*.
tinned, *a.* **tinned foods,** gêneros (alimentícios) enlatados.
tip, *n.* **1.** (*gratuity*) gorjeta *f*, gratificação *f*. **2.** *St.Exch:* informação *f* confidencial.
title, *n.* título *m*, direito *m* de propriedade (imobiliária); **title deed,** documento comprobatório de propriedade; escritura *f*.
titleholder, *n.* titular *mf*.
tobacco, *n.* tabaco *m*, fumo *m*; **tobacco crop,** cultura fumageira; **tobacco economy,** economia fumageira; **tobacco industry,** indústria fumageira.
today, *adv.* hoje; **today's price,** o preço de hoje.
token, *n.* (*a*) (*small disc*) ficha *f*; **gift token,** vale *m* para presente; (*b*) **token payment,** pagamento simbólico; **token rise,** aumento simbólico (de salário); (*c*) **token money,** moeda fiduciária; (*d*) **token strike,** greve *f* de advertência.
tolerance, *n. Ind: Cust: etc:* tolerância *f*; **manufacturing tolerance,** tolerância de fabricação; **permissible tolerance,** tolerância admissível, tolerância permitida; **assembly tolerance,** tolerância

de montagem; **standard tolerance,** tolerância normal.
toll, *n.* pedágio *m*; **toll road,** estrada *f* em que se paga pedágio.
ton, *n.* **1.** tonelada *f*; **long ton, gross ton,** (of **2240 lb** = 1016,06 kg) tonelada longa, tonelada inglesa; **short ton, net ton,** (of **2000 lb** = 907,185 kg) tonelada curta, tonelada americana; **metric ton** (of **1000 kg** = 2204,6 lb), tonelada métrica. **2.** *Nau:* (*a*) **register ton,** tonelada de arqueação, tonelada de registro; (*b*) **measurement ton,** tonelada de medição; **freight ton,** tonelada de frete.
tone, *n. Fin:* **the tone of the market,** a tendência do mercado.
tonnage, *n.* **1.** *Nau:* tonelagem *f*; **registered tonnage,** tonelagem de arqueação, tonelagem de registro; **gross tonnage,** tonelagem bruta; **net tonnage,** tonelagem líquida; **bill of tonnage,** certificado *m* de tonelagem; **deadweight tonnage,** tonelagem de porte bruto. **2.** total *m* de embarcações exprimido em termos de tonelagem. **3.** imposto *m* sobre o peso de carga transportada.
tonne, *n.* (= **metric ton**) tonelada métrica.
tontine, *n. Ins:* tontina *f*.
tool, *n.* (*a*) ferramenta *f*; **machine tool,** máquina-ferramenta *f*; **tools of the trade,** instrumental *m* de trabalho (de carpinteiro, etc.); *F:* **to down tools,** (i) parar de trabalhar, (ii) entrar em greve; (*b*) **tool of analysis,** instrumento *m* de análise.
top[1], *a.* superior; **top-quality goods,** mercadorias *fpl* de qualidade superior; **the top price,** o preço mais alto, o melhor preço; **top post,** alto cargo; **top executive,** alto executivo; **top management,** a alta direção, os gerentes de alto nível; **top copy,** original *m*; **top priority,** urgência *f*, prioridade máxima.
top[2], *v.tr.* superar.
top out, *v.i.* (*of prices, etc.*) chegar ao ponto máximo.
tot, *v.* **1.** *v.tr.* **to tot up a column of figures,** somar uma coluna de números; **to tot up expenses,** somar as despesas. **2.** *v.i.* **the expenses tot up to £500,** as despesas

somam £500, importam em, montam a, £500.

total¹, 1. *a.* total, inteiro, completo, integral, global; **total account,** conta *f* total, importe *m*; **total amount,** importância *f* global, soma *f* total; **total amount of created income,** fluxo *m* total de renda criada; **total amount of invoice,** valor *m* total da fatura; **total amount of the product,** totalidade *f* do produto; **total assets,** total *m* do ativo; **total capital formation,** total da formação de capital; **total commitments,** total de compromissos, total de obrigações; **total cost,** custo *m* total; **total demand,** demanda *f* total; **total domestic supply,** oferta interna total; **total expenditure,** gasto *m* total, dispêndio *m* total; **total funds for capital formation,** total dos recursos para formação de capital; **total liabilities,** total do passivo; **total loss,** perda *f* total; **total marketing,** comercialização *f* global; **total output,** produção *f* total; **total overall exports,** total geral exportado; **total quality control,** controle *m* de qualidade em todas as fases de fabricação; **total revenue,** receita *f* total; **total spending,** dispêndio *m* total; **total supply,** oferta *f* total, suprimento *m* global; **total utility,** utilidade *f* total; **total volume,** volume *m* total. **2.** *n.* total *m*, soma *f*; **sum total, grand total,** total geral, soma dos totais; **to calculate the total of the amounts,** totalizar as somas, as importâncias; **the total amounts to $105,** a soma se eleva a $105.

total², v. 1. *v.tr.* somar, adicionar, totalizar, (as despesas, etc.). **2.** *v.i.* **to total (up to),** somar, elevar-se a, montar a, importar em, (uma quantia, um número, etc.).

totalization, *n.* totalização *f.*

totalize, *v.tr.* totalizar.

touch, *v.i.* **to touch at port,** tocar um porto.

tourism, *n.* turismo *m.*

tourist, *n.* turista *mf*; **Spain has a very important tourist trade,** na Espanha, o turismo é muito importante; **the tourist trade,** o turismo; **tourist agency,** agência *f* de turismo; **tourist centre,** centro turístico; **tourist class,** classe *f* turista,

classe de turismo; **tourist guide,** guia turístico; **tourist hotel,** hotel *m* de turismo, hotel turístico; **tourist industry,** indústria turística, setor *m* de turismo; **tourist information,** informação turística, informações turísticas; **tourist revenue,** renda *f* do turismo; **tourist visa,** visto *m* de turista.

trade¹, *n.* **1.** (*occupation*) ofício *m*, ocupação *f*, arte *f*, trabalho *m*; **trade school,** escola *f* profissional, escola de artes e ofícios; **to carry on a trade,** exercer, exercitar, um ofício; **he's a carpenter by trade,** ele é um carpinteiro por ofício. **2.** comércio *m*, intercâmbio *m* comercial, negócios *mpl*, mercância *f*; **export, import, re-export, trade,** comércio de exportação, de importação, de reexportação; **foreign trade,** comércio exterior; **home, domestic, inland, trade,** comércio interno; **international trade,** comércio internacional; **overseas trade,** comércio exterior, comércio ultramarino; **retail trade,** comércio varejista; **wholesale trade,** comércio atacadista; **world trade,** comércio mundial; *Nau:* **coastal trade,** cabotagem *f*; **trade acceptance,** aceite *m* comercial, duplicata *f*; **trade agreement,** acordo *m* (sobre intercâmbio) comercial; **trade area,** área *f* de comércio; **trade balance, balance of trade,** balança *f* comercial; **trade bank,** banco *m* comercial; **trade barrier,** barreira *f* comercial; **trade bill,** efeito *m* de comércio, título *m* mercantil, letra *f* de câmbio; **trade catalogue,** catálogo *m* de revendedor; **trade credit,** crédito *m* mercantil (concedido pelo fornecedor); **trade directory,** guia *f* comercial, anuário *m* comercial; **trade discount,** desconto *m* de revendedor, desconto para revendedor, desconto comercial; **trade fair,** feira *f* industrial; **trade gap, trade deficit,** déficit *m* na balança comercial; **trade name,** (i) denominação *f* comercial, (*of firm*) razão *f* social, (ii) (*registered*) marca registrada; **trade price,** preço *m* para revendedor; **trade sanctions,** sanções *fpl* comerciais; **to be in the coffee trade,** comerciar em café, negociar com café, fazer o comércio cafeeiro; **to be in trade,**

comerciar, negociar, fazer negócios; **to do a good trade,** fazer bons negócios, fazer um bom negócio; **trade is at a standstill,** o comércio está parado, está paralizado. **3.** (*a*) classe *f* (profissional); **trade association,** entidade *f* de classe, associação *f* de classe, associação profissional; **trade journal,** revista *f* profissional, revista de classe; (*b*) **trade union,** sindicato *m*; **trade union movement,** movimento *m* sindical; **trade union member,** membro *m* de um sindicato, sindicatado *m*, sindicatário *m*; **trade unionism,** sindicalismo *m*; **trade unionist,** (i) membro de um sindicato, sindicatado, sindicatário, (ii) sindicalista *mf.*

trade², *v.* **1.** *v.tr.* (*a*) to trade sth. for sth., permutar, trocar, algo por algo; (*b*) *St.Exch:* to trade shares and other securities, negociar ações e outros valores. **2.** *v.i.* comerciar (**in,** em); negociar, mercadejar, (**in,** com); fazer o comércio (**in, de**).

trade in, *v.tr.* dar (carro, etc.) como parte do pagamento de uma nova aquisição.

trademark, *n.* marca *f* de fábrica, marca comercial; **registered trademark,** marca registrada.

trader, *n.* comerciante *mf*, negociante *mf*, mercador *m*, mercante *mf*; *St.Exch:* operador *m*; **retail trader,** varejista *mf*, lojista *mf*; **sole trader,** comerciante independente; **small trader,** pequeno comerciante.

tradesman, *n.* (*a*) comerciante *m*, lojista *m*, fornecedor *m*; **tradesman's entrance,** entrada *f* de serviço; (*b*) artífice *m*, artesão *m*, oficial *m*.

tradespeople, *n.pl.* comerciantes *mfpl*, negociantes *mfpl*, lojistas *mfpl*, gente *f* do comércio, o comércio.

trading, *n.* comércio *m*, intercâmbio *m* comercial, mercancia *f*; *St.Exch:* as operações, os negócios, o pregão; **trading account,** conta *f* de vendas, conta de operações; **trading area,** (i) área *f* de comércio, (ii) território *m* de venda, (iii) *St.Exch:* pregão *m*; **trading capital,** capital *m* de giro; **trading company,** sociedade *f* comercial, empresa *f* comercial; **trading down,** venda *f* de

produtos abaixo do custo; **trading estate,** parque *m* industrial; **trading floor (of exchange),** pregão (de uma bolsa); **trading partners,** parceiros *mpl* comerciais; **trading port,** porto *m* comercial; **trading post,** (i) posto *m* de trocas, (ii) (*on stock exchange*) posto de negociações; **trading practices,** práticas *fpl* comerciais; **trading profit,** lucro *m* comercial, lucro bruto; **trading result(s),** resultado *m* do exercício; **trading stamp,** vale *m* permutável por mercadorias; **trading up,** venda *f* de produtos de alta qualidade com o fim de manter alto padrão de clientela; **trading vessel,** navio *m* mercante; *St.Exch:* **trading began sluggishly,** o pregão abriu vagaroso; **at the start of trading, at the end of trading,** na abertura, no final, do pregão; *Am:* (*on exchanges*) **trading limits,** limites *mpl* de variação de preço.

tradition, *n.* tradição *f.*

traditional, *a.* tradicional; **traditional exports,** exportações *fpl* tradicionais; **traditional practice,** prática *f* tradicional.

traffic¹, *n.* **1.** (street) **traffic,** trânsito *m*, circulação *f*; **air traffic,** tráfego aéreo; **passenger traffic,** tráfego de passageiros; **rail traffic,** tráfego ferroviário; **road traffic,** tráfego rodoviário, trânsito; **waterway traffic,** tráfego hidroviário; **telephone traffic,** tráfego telefônico; **traffic management,** administração *f* de tráfego; **traffic manager,** chefe *m* de tráfego, chefe de expedição; *Am: Ind: etc:* **traffic department,** departamento *m* de expedição. **2.** (*trade*) tráfego *m*, tráfico *m*, comércio *m*, negócio *m*.

traffic², *v.i.* trafegar, traficar.

trailer, *n.* reboque *m.*

train¹, *n.* **1.** trem *m*; **freight trade, goods train,** trem de carga, trem de mercadorias; **passenger train,** trem de passageiros. **2.** seqüência *f* (de acontecimentos, etc.).

train², *v.tr.* treinar, educar, instruir.

trainee, *n.* estagiário *m*; pessoa *f* em treinamento; trainee *mf*; **trainee manager,** gerente *mf* trainee, **gerente** estagiário, estagiário gerente.

training, *n.* treinamento *m*, educação *f*,

preparação *f*, instrução *f*; **vocational training**, formação *f* profissional; **management training**, treinamento de dirigentes, de gerentes; **executive training course**, curso *m* de treinamento de executivos; **industrial training**, treinamento (na área) industrial; **training manual**, manual *m* de treinamento; **training officer**, chefe *mf* de treinamento; **on-the-job training**, treinamento no exercício do cargo, treinamento no local (de trabalho); **practical training**, estágio *m*; **refresher training course, booster training course**, curso de reciclagem; **further training**, aperfeiçoamento *m* (profissional); **training programme**, programa *m* de treinamento.

tramp, *n. Nau:* **tramp service**, serviço *m* de linha irregular; **tramp ship**, cargueiro *m* de linha irregular.

transact, *v.* 1. *v.tr.* **to transact business with s.o.**, fazer negócio(s) com alguém. 2. *v.i.* transacionar, fazer transações, fazer negócio(s).

transaction, *n.* 1. **the transaction of business**, o comércio, os negócios. 2. transação *f*, operação *f*, (comercial); **cash transaction**, transação, operação, à vista; **business transaction, commercial transaction**, transação comercial, operação comercial; **completed, uncompleted, transaction**, transação completada, não completada; **loan transaction, credit transaction**, operação de crédito; **banking transaction**, operação bancária; **exchange transaction**, operação cambial, operação de câmbio; **forward exchange transaction**, operação cambial a termo; *St.Exch:* **Stock Exchange transactions**, operações de bolsa; **transaction for the account**, operação a termo.

transactor, *n.* negociador *m*, transator *m*.

transfer¹, *n.* (*a*) transferência *f*; **the transfer of a manager to another factory**, a transferência, o deslocamento, de um gerente para outra fábrica; **capital transfer**, transferência de capital; *Bank: etc:* **transfer of funds**, transferência de fundos; **telegraphic transfer**, ordem telegráfica de transferência,

transferência telegráfica; **transfer tax**, imposto *m* sobre a transferência; **transfer of ownership**, transferência de propriedade; **property transfer**, transferência de imóveis, (*inheritance*) transmissão *f* de imóveis; *Adm: etc:* **property transfer tax**, imposto sobre a transmissão de propriedade; *Book-k:* **transfer entry**, registro *m* substitutivo de transferência; **the transfer of an item from one account to another**, a transferência de um lançamento de uma conta para outra; *Fin:* **share transfer**, transferência de ação, de ações; **transfer book**, (livro) registro *m* de transferência de ações nominativas; **transfer day**, dia *m* de lançamento das transferências de ações; *Ec: Adm:* **transfer payments**, transferências correntes; **instrument, deed, of transfer**, termo *m*, escritura *f*, de transferência; **transfer form**, formulário *m* para transferência (de título, de propriedade, etc.); (*b*) *Rail: Av:* baldeação *f*, transbordo *m*, (de mercadorias).

transfer², *v.tr.* (*a*) transferir (ações, renda, etc.); ceder (direito), transmitir (propriedade); **to transfer a debt to another account**, transferir uma dívida para outra conta; **to transfer by endorsement**, transferir por endosso; **to transfer an employee**, transferir, deslocar, um empregado (para outra fábrica, escritório, etc.); (*b*) *Rail: Av:* baldear (mercadorias, passageiros, etc., de um avião ou trem, etc., para outro).

transferability, *n.* mobilidade *f*; qualidade ou caráter do que é transferível; *Jur:* transmissibilidade *f*, cessibilidade *f*; *Fin:* negociabilidade *f* (de uma dívida, de valores).

transferable, *a.* transferível; **transferable credit**, crédito *m* transferível; *Jur:* (propriedade, etc.) transmissível, (direito) cessível; (*of debt*) negociável; *Fin:* **transferable securities**, valores mobiliários, títulos *mpl* negociáveis.

transferee, *n.* (*a*) beneficiário *m* de transferência; pessoa que recebe objeto ou título transferido; **transferee of shares**,

novo possuidor de ações transferidas; (*b*)
Jur: cessionário *m* (de um direito, etc.).
transferor, *n.* transferidor *m*, transferente
mf; *Jur:* cedente *mf*; *Fin:* etc: endossador
m, endossante *mf*, (de efeito de
comércio).
tranship, *v.tr.* baldear (mercadorias).
transhipment, *n.* baldeação *f*, transbordo
m; **transhipment is allowed,** transbordo
(é) permitido; **transhipment is forbidden,
prohibited,** transbordo (é) proibido.
transit, *n.* trânsito *m*; **passengers, goods, in
transit,** passageiros *mpl*, mercadorias *fpl*,
em trânsito; **transit visa,** visto *m* de
trânsito; **transit port,** porto *m* de trânsito;
transit agent, despachante *mf*, agente *mf*
de transportes; **transit dues,** direitos *mpl*
de trânsito; **transit insurance,** seguro *m*
contra acidentes de trânsito; **damage in
transit,** dano causado em trânsito; *Fin:*
transit bills, letras *fpl* em trânsito.
transition, *n.* transição *f*.
transitional, *a.* **transitional arrangements,**
disposições transitórias; **transitional
period,** período transitório; **transitional
unemployment,** desemprego passageiro.
translate, *v.tr. & i.* traduzir.
translation, *n.* tradução *f*; **translation
agency,** agencia *f* de traduções.
translator, *n.* tradutor *m*; **sworn
translator,** tradutor juramentado.
transmission, *n.* transmissão *f* (de um
telex, um recado), expedição *f* (de um
pacote, etc.); *Jur:* transmissão.
transport¹, *n.* **1.** (= **transportation**);
transport risks, riscos *mpl* de transporte;
transport capacity, capacidade *f* de
transporte; **transport cost,** custo *m* do
transporte; **transport expenses,** gastos
mpl, despesas *fpl*, com transporte. **2.**
transporte(s) *m(pl)*; **means of transport,**
meios *mpl* de transporte; **Ministry of
Transport,** Ministério *m* dos Transportes;
air transport, transporte aéreo; **freight
transport,** transporte de carga; **marine
transport,** transporte marítimo; **passenger
transport,** transporte de passageiros;
public transport system, sistema *m* de
transportes coletivos; **rail transport,**
transporte ferroviário; **river transport,**
transporte fluvial; **road transport,**

transporte rodoviário; **urban transport,**
transporte(s) urbano(s); **transport
aircraft,** aerotransporte *m*, avião *m* de
carga; **transport company,** empresa *f* de
transportes; **the transport industry,** a
indústria transportadora, a indústria de
transportes.
transport², *v.tr.* transportar (mercadorias,
passageiros); **to transport goods by lorry,**
transportar mercadorias por caminhão;
to transport goods by rail, *Am:* by
railroad, transportar mercadorias por
ferrovia, via férrea, por trem.
transportable, *a.* (*of goods, etc.*)
transportável.
transportation, *n.* transporte *m*,
transportação *f*; **means of transportation,
transportation method,** transporte, meio
m de transporte; **transportation risks,**
riscos *mpl* de transporte; **transportation
capacity,** capacidade *f* de transporte.
transporter, *n.* (*person*) transportador *m*,
(*firm*) (empresa) transportadora *f*; **car
transporter,** jamanta *f*, carreta *f*.
travel¹, *n.* viagem *f*; **travel agency,** agência
f de viagens, agência de turismo; **travel
agent,** agente *mf* de viagens, agente de
turismo; **travel allowance,** ajuda *f* de
viagem, ajuda de custos para viagens;
travel expenses, despesas *fpl* com viagens;
travel goods, artigos *mpl* para viagem; **the
travel industry,** a indústria turística,
indústria de turismo.
travel², *v.i.* **1.** viajar, fazer uma viagem,
fazer viagens. **2. to travel for a firm,**
trabalhar como caixeiro-viajante para
uma firma.
traveller, *n.* **1.** viajante *mf*; **traveller's
cheque,** traveller's cheque *m*, cheque *m*
de viagem. **2.** (**commercial**) **traveller,**
caixeiro-viajante *m*.
travelling, **1.** *n.* viagens *fpl*; **travelling
expenses,** despesas *fpl* de viagem,
despesas com viagens; **travelling
allowance,** ajuda *f* de viagem, ajuda de
custos para viagens. **2.** *a.* viajante;
travelling salesman, caixeiro-viajante *m*;
travelling auditor, auditor *m* viajante;
travelling buyer, comprador *m* itinerante.
treasurer, *n.* tesoureiro *m*; **treasurer's
office,** tesouraria *f*; **treasurer's report,**

relatório financeiro, relatório *m* do tesoureiro.

treasurership, *n.* tesouraria *f.*

treasury, *n.* tesouraria *f;* tesouro (público); **the Treasury,** o Tesouro, o Ministério da Fazenda, o Erário; **treasury bills,** letras *fpl* do Tesouro; **treasury bond,** bônus *m* do Tesouro; **treasury deficit,** déficit *m* do Tesouro; **treasury guarantee,** garantia *f* do Tesouro; **treasury obligations,** obrigações *fpl* do Tesouro; *Am: Fin:* **treasury stock,** ação readquirida pela própria companhia emitente.

treble¹, 1. *a.* triplo, triple, tríplice. **2.** *n.* triplo *m.*

**treble², ** *v.tr. & i.* triplicar(-se).

trend, *n.* tendência *f;* **the trend of prices,** a tendência dos preços; **market trends,** as tendências do mercado; **downward trend,** tendência para a baixa; **upward trend,** tendência para a alta; **underlying trend,** tendência subjacente; **secular trend,** tendência secular; **economic trend,** tendência econômica; **trend analysis,** análise *f* das tendências; **trend value of exports,** valor *m* tendencial das exportações.

trial, *n.* **1.** ensaio *m,* prova *f,* experiência *f;* **on trial,** a título de experiência, em experiência; **to give a new computer a trial,** ensaiar, experimentar, um novo computador; **trial order,** pedido experimental, pedido tentativo; *Book-k:* **trial balance,** balancete *m* (geral); **to draw up, prepare, a trial balance,** levantar, extrair, um balancete. **2.** *Jur:* julgamento *m,* audiência *f;* **to stand trial,** ser submetido a julgamento.

tribunal, *n.* tribunal *m.*

trip, *n.* **business trip,** viagem *f* de negócios.

triple¹, *a.* triplo, triple, tríplice.

triple², *v.tr. & i.* triplicar(-se); tresdobrar(-se).

triplicate¹, 1. *a.* triplicado, tresdobrado. **2.** *n.* triplicata *f;* **in triplicate,** em três vias, em triplicata.

triplicate², *v.tr.* **1.** triplicar. **2.** redigir (um documento) em três vias, em triplicata.

trouble, *n.* distúrbio *m,* conflito *m;* **labour**

troubles, distúrbios trabalhistas, conflitos trabalhistas.

truck¹, *n.* caminhão *m;* **pick-up (truck),** camioneta *f; Ind:* **fork-lift truck,** auto-empilhadeira *f* de garfo.

truck², *v.i. N.Am:* trabalhar como camioneiro.

trucker, *n. N.Am:* camioneiro *m.*

trucking, *n. N.Am:* trabalho *m* de camioneiro.

true, *a.* **true value,** valor *m* real; **true rate of interest,** taxa *f* de juros efetiva.

trust, *n.* **1.** confiança *f* (in, em); **position of trust,** cargo *m* de confiança; **breach of trust,** abuso *m* de confiança. **2.** *Jur:* fideicomisso *m;* **trust deed,** escritura *f* de fideicomisso; **express trust,** fideicomisso expresso; **implicit trust,** fideicomisso tácito; **revocable, irrevocable, trust,** fideicomisso revogável, irrevogável; **trust fund,** fundo *m* de fideicomisso; **trust company,** companhia fiduciária. **3.** truste *m;* **to group into a trust,** organizar em truste; **business trust, common-law trust,** truste comercial. **4.** *Fin:* **investment trust,** fundo mútuo.

trustee, *n. Jur: (a) (of testamentary estate)* fiduciário *m,* gravado *m;* **trustee's certificate,** certificado fiduciário; *(b)* administrador *m;* *(with power of attorney)* mandatário *m;* **trustee in bankruptcy,** síndico *m* de massa falida; *(c)* **trustee savings bank,** caixa *f* de depósitos sem fins lucrativos.

trusteeship, *n. Jur: (a)* cargo *m* de fiduciário, curadoria *f; (b)* **trusteeship in bankruptcy,** sindicância *f,* sindicato *m,* de massa falida.

turn¹, *n. Fin:* **turn of the market, jobber's turn,** diferença *f* entre o preço de compra e o preço de venda de um corretor.

turn², *v.tr.* **1. to turn a limited partnership into a limited company,** transformar, converter, uma sociedade em comandita em uma sociedade anônima. **2. to turn (sth.) to account,** aproveitar-se de (alguma coisa, etc.).

turn down, *v.tr.* **to turn down an applicant,** reprovar, rejeitar, um candidato; **to turn down a post,** recusar um cargo; **to turn down an offer,** recusar uma oferta.

turnkey, *n. Ind: etc:* **turnkey project,** projeto *m* (de) chave em mãos.

turn out, *v.tr.* produzir, fabricar, manufaturar.

turnout, *n. Ind:* (*a*) produção *f*; (*b*) (i) greve *f*, parede *f*, (ii) grevistas *mfpl*, paredistas *mfpl*.

turn over, *v.tr.* faturar (uma quantia), movimentar (capitais, mercadorias).

turnover, *n.* (*a*) (*billing*) faturamento *m*, giro *m*, movimento *m* de negócios, volume *m* de negócios; *Fin: Book-k:* (*ratio*) índice *m* de rotação; **turnover tax,** imposto *m* de circulação de mercadorias; (*b*) rotação *f*, renovação *f*, circulação *f*, rotatividade *m*, (de estoques); *Ind: etc:* **labour turnover,** rotatividade *f* da mão-de-obra, movimento da mão-de-obra.

two-tier, *a.* **two-tier gold system,** duplo mercado de ouro.

tycoon, *n.* magnata *m*.

type¹, *n.* tipo *m*.

type², *v.tr. & i.* datilografar; escrever, bater, à máquina.

typescript, *n.* texto datilografado.

typewriter, *n.* máquina *f* de escrever, datilógrafo *m*; **portable typewriter,** máquina de escrever portátil; **manual typewriter,** máquina de escrever manual, comum; **electric typewriter,** máquina de escrever elétrica; **typewriter ribbon,** fita *f* de máquina de escrever.

typewritten, *a.* (documento, etc.) datilografado, escrito à máquina.

typing, *n.* datilografia *f*; **typing paper,** papel *m* para máquina de escrever; **typing pool,** equipe *f* de datilógrafas; **typing work,** trabalho datilográfico; **to get a typing job,** conseguir um emprego de datilografia; **shorthand typing,** estenodatilografia *f*.

typist, *n.* datilógrafa *f*, datilógrafo *m*; **typist's error,** erro datilográfico, erro de datilógrafa; **shorthand typist,** estenodatilógrafa *f*, estenodatilógrafo *m*.

U

ultimate, *a.* ultimate consumer, consumidor *m* final; ultimate destination, destinação *f* final.

umbrella, *n.* umbrella agreement, acordo *m* que envolve muitos indivíduos ou grupos.

umpire, *n.* (*in arbitration*) desempatador *m*, superárbitro *m*.

unable, *a.* incapaz; unable to meet obligations, inadimplente.

unacceptable, *a.* não aceitável, não digno de aceitação.

unaccepted, *a.* unaccepted bill, letra não aceita.

unaccounted, *a.* sixty dollars unaccounted for in the accounts, sessenta dólares não registrados na contabilidade.

unadvertised, *a.* não anunciado.

unallotted, *a.* Fin: unallotted shares, ações não atribuídas; Book-k: unallotted appropriation, saldo não distribuído de uma verba.

unallowed, *a.* não permitido.

unanimous, *a.* unânime; unanimous opinion, opinião *f* unânime; subject to unanimous approval, mediante aprovação unânime, sujeito a aprovação unânime.

unanimously, *adv.* the minutes were unanimously approved, a ata foi aprovada por unanimidade.

unapplied, *a.* unapplied cash, fundos *mpl* sem destinação específica.

unappropriated, *a.* Fin: (dinheiro, etc.) não destinado para fim específico; unappropriated income, receita não apropriada; unappropriated earned surplus, lucros *mpl* acumulados sem destinação específica; unappropriated budget surplus, superávit orçamentário não apropriado.

unassured, *a.* não segurado.

unauthorized, *a.* não autorizado, sem autorização; unauthorized trading,

comércio ilícito; unauthorized official, (i) (*if authorization is withdrawn*) funcionário desautorizado, (ii) funcionário sem autorização; 'no entry to unauthorized persons', 'entrada proibida a estranhos'.

unavailability, *n.* indisponibilidade *f.*

unavailable, *a.* unavailable funds, fundos não disponíveis.

unavoidable, *a.* Book-k: unavoidable cost, custo *m* inevitável.

unbalanced, *a.* Book-k: (*of account*) não saldado.

unbankable, *a.* (*of security*) não negociável em banco.

unbought, *a.* (artigo) que não teve venda.

unbundling, *n.* separação *f* de tarifas.

unbusinesslike, *a.* **1.** (*of trader, etc.*) sem espírito comercial. **2.** unbusinesslike procedure, procedimento *m* irregular; unbusinesslike system, sistema contrário às práticas comerciais.

uncalled, *a.* Fin: uncalled capital, capital não chamado; capital subscrito e não desembolsado.

uncharged, *a.* (*a*) não sujeito a taxa; (*b*) não cobrado; uncharged for, gratuito.

unchecked, *a.* (*of account, etc.*) não conferido, não controlado, não verificado.

unclaimed, *a.* (*of dividend, etc.*) não reclamado.

uncleared, *a.* (*a*) Cust: uncleared goods, mercadorias não liberadas pela alfândega; (*b*) (*of debt*) não liquidado, não saldado; (*c*) uncleared cheque, cheque não compensado.

uncollected, *a.* não cobrado, não coletado, não recolhido; uncollected bills, contas *fpl* a receber; uncollected taxes, impostos não recolhidos.

uncollectible, **1.** *a.* incobrável, não cobrável, não coletável; uncollectible

242

notes, bills, títulos *mpl,* contas *fpl,* incobráveis. **2.** *n.pl.* **uncollectibles,** títulos *mpl,* contas *fpl,* incobráveis.
uncommercial, *a.* não comercial, estranho às práticas comerciais.
uncompleted, *a.* **uncompleted transaction,** transação não completada.
unconditional, *a.* incondicional, irrestrito; **unconditional acceptance,** aceitação *f* sem reservas, *Fin:* aceite *m* sem reservas; *Fin:* **unconditional liquidity,** liquidez absoluta, liquidez incondicional.
unconfirmed, *a.* não confirmado; **unconfirmed letter of credit,** carta de crédito não confirmada.
unconsolidated, *a. Fin: (of debt)* não consolidado.
uncorrected, *a. Book-k:* não retificado.
uncovered, *a.* (compra *f,* venda *f*) a descoberto; **uncovered advance,** adiantamento *m* a descoberto; **uncovered balance,** saldo *m* a descoberto.
uncrossed, *a.* **uncrossed cheque,** cheque não cruzado.
undated, *a.* sem data; **undated cheque,** cheque não datado; **undated bonds,** obrigações *fpl* sem vencimento fixo.
undelivered, *a.* **undelivered goods,** mercadorias *fpl* não entregues.
under, *prep.* **under consideration,** em consideração; **under seal,** com selo de ofício; **under separate cover,** enviado separadamente; *Cust:* **under bond,** sob retenção alfandegária.
underbid, *v.tr.* oferecer preço menor (que outrem).
undercapitalization, *n. Pol.Ec:* subcapitalização *f.*
undercapitalized, *a. Pol.Ec:* subcapitalizado; **an undercapitalized firm,** uma empresa sem capital e reservas suficientes.
undercharge, *v.tr.* cobrar pouco; cobrar menos que o preço estabelecido.
under(-)consumption, *n. Pol.Ec:* subconsumo *m.*
undercut, *v.tr.* (*a*) fazer uma proposta (ou oferta) mais favorável (que outrem); (*b*) vender por menos (que outrem).
undercutting, *n.* venda *f* a preços inferiores aos da concorrência.

underdemand, *n. Pol.Ec:* subconsumo *m.*
underdeveloped, *a. Pol.Ec:* **underdeveloped countries,** países subdesenvolvidos.
underdevelopment, *n. Pol.Ec:* subdesenvolvimento *m.*
underemployment, *n.* subemprego *m,* subocupação *f.*
underequipment, *n.* subequipamento *m.*
underestimate[1]**,** *n.* subestima *f,* subavaliação *f.*
underestimate[2]**,** *v.tr.* subestimar, subavaliar.
underfreight, *v.tr.* subfretar (um navio, etc.).
undergo, *v.tr.* sofrer, passar por.
under-insurance, *n.* seguro *m* abaixo do valor corrente.
underinsure, *v.tr.* segurar abaixo do valor corrente.
underinvestment, *n.* investimento *m* insuficiente; subinversão *f.*
underinvoice, *v.tr.* subfaturar.
underinvoicing, *n.* subfaturamento *m.*
underlessee, *n.* sublocatário *m.*
underlet, *v.tr.* sublocar, subalugar.
undermanned, *a. (of factory, etc.)* **to be undermanned,** estar com falta de pessoal, de mão-de-obra; não ter pessoal, mão-de-obra, suficiente.
undermentioned, *a.* abaixo mencionado.
underpaid, *a.* mal pago, mal remunerado.
underpay, *v.tr.* pagar insuficientemente; pagar mal, pagar menos que o salário médio (por determinado emprego).
underproduction, *n. Ind:* subprodução *f.*
underquote, *v.tr.* propor, oferecer, preço menor (que outrem).
underrate, *v.tr.* subavaliar, subestimar.
undersell, *v.tr.* 1. vender mais barato que (outrem). 2. vender (mercadorias) abaixo do custo, abaixo do preço a varejo determinado pelo fabricante.
undersign, *v.tr.* subscrever.
undersigned, *a. & n.* **the undersigned,** o abaixo assinado; **we, the undersigned, declare that ...,** nós, (os) abaixo assinados, declaramos que ....
understaffed, *a.* com falta de pessoal, desprovido de pessoal; **to be understaffed,** estar com falta de pessoal, estar

desprovido de pessoal, não ter pessoal suficiente.

understanding, n. 1. (a) compreensão f; (b) entendimento m, acordo m, ajuste m; **according to our understanding,** conforme o nosso entendimento. 2. condição f; **on the understanding that . . .,** sob condição de que, contanto que, desde que, uma vez que + subj.; **on the understanding that compensation is paid,** sob condição de que, desde que, seja paga uma indenização.

undertake, v.tr. (a) **to undertake a market study,** empreender um estudo de mercado; (b) **to undertake an obligation,** assumir uma obrigação; **to undertake a task,** encarregar-se, incumbir-se, de uma tarefa; **to undertake to do sth.,** comprometer-se, obrigar-se, a fazer algo.

undertaking, n. 1. empresa f, empreendimento m; **industrial undertaking,** empresa industrial; **commercial undertaking,** empresa comercial; **joint undertaking,** sociedade f em conta de participação; operação conjunta. 2. compromisso m; **to honour one's undertakings,** cumprir (com) os seus compromissos.

undervaluation, n. subavaliação f, subestima f.

undervalue, v.tr. subavaliar, subestimar; **undervalued currency,** (i) moeda desvalorizada, (ii) moeda cotada abaixo do nível real.

underwrite, v.tr. (a) Fin: subscrever (uma emissão de ações, etc.); (b) Ins: subscrever, aceitar, (o risco de um seguro); **to underwrite a policy,** subscrever uma apólice de seguro.

underwriter, n. (a) Fin: subscritor m (de uma emissão de títulos); (b) Ins: segurador m.

underwriting, n. (a) Fin: subscrição f (de uma emissão de títulos); **underwriting syndicate,** grupo m que subscreve uma emissão de títulos; **underwriting agreement,** contrato m para a subscrição de uma emissão de títulos; **underwriting commitment,** operação f de garantia de emissão; **underwriting commission,** comissão f pela subscrição de uma

emissão de títulos; (b) Ins: aceitação f, subscrição, (do risco de um seguro); **underwriting syndicate,** sindicato m de aceitações.

undischarged, a. (a) Jur: **undischarged bankrupt,** falido não reabilitado; (b) **undischarged debt,** dívida não liquidada, dívida não saldada.

undiscountable, a. **undiscountable bill,** título m, efeito m, não descontável.

undisposed of, a.phr. **stock undisposed of,** mercadorias não vendidas, mercadorias encalhadas, encalhe m.

undistributed, a. não distribuído; **undistributed profits, earnings,** lucros não distribuídos.

undivided, a. não dividido, não repartido; **undivided profits,** lucros não repartidos; Jur: **undivided property,** bens mpl indivisos.

unearned, a. não ganho (pelo trabalho próprio); **unearned income,** rendimento não ganho com o trabalho individual; Jur: **unearned increment (of land),** aumento m de valor (da terra) devido à valorização.

uneconomic, a. 1. não econômico; contrário às leis da economia. 2. (of job, project, etc.) (i) que rende mal, (ii) custoso, dispendioso.

uneconomical, a. antieconômico.

unemployable, a. (a) que não está em condições de ser empregado; (b) que não preenche as exigências de um emprego.

unemployed, 1. a. (a) desempregado, sem emprego; (b) (of capital) não utilizado, não empregado. 2. n.pl. **the unemployed,** os desempregados.

unemployment, n. desemprego m; **unemployment benefit,** auxílio-desemprego m; **unemployment fund,** fundo m de seguro contra o desemprego; **unemployment rate,** índice m de desemprego, taxa f de desemprego.

unendorsed, a. não endossado.

unenforceable, a. Jur: não executório.

unexchangeability, n. Fin: impermutabilidade f (de títulos, etc.)

unexchangeable, a. impermutável.

unexpended, a. Fin: não despendido; **unexpended appropriation,** verba ainda não despendida; **unexpended balance,** saldo ainda não despendido.

unfair, *a.* (*a*) **unfair competition,** concorrência *f* desleal; **unfair trading,** práticas *fpl* comerciais desleais; (*b*) *Ind:* **unfair dismissal,** demissão injusta, demissão infundada.

unfavourable, *a.* desfavorável, adverso, desvantajoso; **unfavourable decision,** decisão *f* desfavorável; **unfavourable balance of trade,** balança *f* comercial desfavorável; *Fin:* **unfavourable exchange,** (taxa *f* de) câmbio *m* desfavorável.

unfunded, *a. Fin:* **unfunded debt,** dívida não consolidada, dívida não fundada.

uniform, *a.* uniforme; **uniform accounting system,** sistema *m* uniforme de contabilidade; **uniform rate of interest,** taxa *f* uniforme de juros.

unilateral, *a.* unilateral; **unilateral contract,** contrato *m* unilateral.

unimpaired, *a.* **unimpaired capital,** capital *m* livre de gravames.

uninsurable, *a.* não segurável; **uninsurable risks,** riscos não seguráveis; **the car is uninsured against theft,** o carro não está segurado contra o robo.

uninsured, *a.* não segurado (**against,** contra).

uninvested, *a.* não investido, não aplicado.

union, *n.* (*a*) união *f*; **customs union,** união alfandegária, união aduaneira; (*b*) (**trade**) **union,** sindicato *m*; **union dues,** contribuição *f* sindical; **union movement,** movimento *m* sindical; **union member,** membro *m* de um sindicato, sindicatado *m*, sindicatário *m*.

unionism, *n.* (*a*) (**trade**) **unionism,** sindicalismo *m*; (*b*) unionismo *m*.

unionist, *n.* (*a*) (**trade**) **unionist,** (i) membro *m* de um sindicato, sindicatado *m*, sindicatário *m*, (ii) sindicalista *mf*; (*b*) unionista *mf*.

unionization, *n.* sindicalização *f*.

unionize, *v.tr.* sindicalizar.

unit, *n.* **1.** unidade *f*; **dwelling unit,** unidade (habitacional); **unit cost,** custo unitário; **unit price,** preço unitário; **unit value index,** índice *m* do valor unitário; **each batch consists of 50 units,** cada batelada

consta de 50 unidades; *Bank:* **unit teller,** caixa-executivo *m.* **2.** unidade (de comprimento, de peso, etc.); **standard unit (of capacity, etc.),** módulo *m*, padrão *m*, (das medidas de capacidade, etc.); **unit of consumption, of production,** unidade de consumo, de produção; **unit of labour, man work unit,** unidade de trabalho humano; **unit of money, monetary unit,** unidade monetária; **unit of value,** unidade de valor; **unit of account,** unidade de conta; **unit of sale,** unidade de venda; **unit of sampling,** unidade de amostragem. **3. unit trust,** fundo mútuo.

unitary, *a.* unitário; **unitary rate,** taxa única (de câmbio); *Pol.Ec:* **unitary elasticity of demand,** elasticidade unitária de procura.

unitization, *n.* unitização *f*.

unitize, *v.tr.* unitizar.

universe, *n. Stat:* universo *m*, população *f*.

unlimited, *a.* ilimitado, irrestrito; **unlimited deposits,** depósitos *mpl* sem limite; **unlimited credit,** crédito *m* em aberto, crédito ilimitado; **unlimited liability,** responsabilidade ilimitada, irrestrita.

unliquidated, *a.* (*of debt, etc.*) não liquidado, não saldado.

unlisted, *a.* (*of securities*) não listado; não cotado na bolsa de valores.

unload, *v.tr.* (*a*) descarregar; **to unload a ship,** descarregar um navio; **to unload sth. from a vessel,** desembarcar algo, descarregar algo de uma embarcação; **to unload goods from a lorry,** descarregar mercadorias de um caminhão; (*b*) *St.Exch:* **to unload stock on the market,** vender títulos em grande quantidade.

unloading, *n.* descarga *f*, descarregamento *m*, (*of goods from vessel*) desembarque *m.*

unmanufactured, *a.* não manufaturado, não fabricado; **unmanufactured materials,** matérias-primas *fpl*.

unmarketable, *a.* não comerciável, invendável, inegociável, não negociável; **unmarketable product,** produto *m* invendável, não negociável; **unmarketable securities,** títulos *mpl* não negociáveis;

Book-k: etc: **unmarketable assets,** ativo *m* não realizável.

unmatured, *a.* **unmatured paper,** títulos não vencidos.

unmerchantable, *a.* invendável.

unmortgaged, *a.* livre de hipoteca(s).

unnecessary, *a.* desnecessário; **unnecessary goods,** bens supérfluos.

unnegotiable, *a.* (*of cheque, etc.*) inegociável, não negociável.

unobtainable, *a.* (*of article, etc.*) não obtenível.

unofficial, *a.* não oficial, extra-oficial; **unofficial strike,** greve não autorizada pelo sindicato, greve sem autorização sindical.

unpaid, *a.* 1. (*of money*) não pago; (*of bill*) não saldado; (*of debt, etc.*) não liquidado, não saldado; **unpaid balance,** saldo *m* a pagar; **unpaid bills,** contas *fpl* a pagar; **unpaid dividend,** dividendo *m* a pagar; **unpaid interest,** juros *mpl* a pagar. 2. (*of post*) não retribuído; (*of person*) não remunerado; **unpaid chairman,** presidente não remunderado; **unpaid services,** serviços não remunerados, serviços prestados gratuitamente.

unpayable, *a.* **unpayable debt,** dívida *f* não liquidável.

unpeg, *v.tr.* **to unpeg the rate,** deixar flutuar a taxa, desvincular a taxa.

unplaced, *a.* (*of shares, etc.*) não colocado.

unpriced, *a.* sem indicação de preço.

unproductive, *a.* improdutivo, não rendoso; **unproductive wages,** salários não produtivos; *Pol.Ec:* **unproductive consumption,** consumo improdutivo.

unproductiveness, *n.* improdutividade *f.*

unprofitable, *a.* não lucrativo, não rendoso; (trabalho, etc.) inútil, estéril.

unprotested, *a.* **unprotested bill,** letra *f* de câmbio não protestada.

unqualified, *a.* 1. (*of personnel, etc.*) não qualificado, não habilitado. 2. (aceitação, etc.) incondicional, irrestrita.

unquoted, *a. St.Exch:* **unquoted securities,** títulos não cotados na bolsa de valores.

unrealizable, *a.* não realizável; **unrealizable property,** bens *mpl* não

realizáveis; **unrealizable capital,** capital *m* não realizável.

unrealized, *a.* (*of assets, etc.*) não realizado; **unrealized revenue,** receita não realizada, receita não ganha; *Fin:* **unrealized exchange gain, loss,** lucro *m*, prejuízo *m*, de câmbio não realizado.

unreceipted, *a.* **unreceipted payment,** pagamento *m* pelo qual não se passou recibo; **unreceipted delivery,** entrega não reconhecida mediante recibo.

unrecovered, *a. Book-k: etc:* **unrecovered cost,** custo *m* a recuperar.

unredeemable, *a.* irredimível, irresgatável.

unregistered, *a.* não registrado, não inscrito.

unremunerative, *a.* pouco rendoso, pouco lucrativo.

unrepaid, *a.* não reembolsado.

unrestricted, *a.* irrestrito; **unrestricted credit,** crédito *m* sem restrições; **unrestricted letter of credit,** carta *f* de crédito negociável em qualquer banco.

unsafe, *a. Fin:* **unsafe investment,** investimento pouco seguro; **unsafe paper,** papéis *mpl*, títulos *mpl*, de valor duvidoso.

unsaleable, *a.* (*of goods*) invendível, invendável.

unsecured, *a.* (*a*) (*of loan, overdraft, etc.*) a descoberto, sem garantia, não garantido; (*b*) quirografário; **unsecured creditor,** credor quirografário; **unsecured debt,** dívida quirografária.

unsettled, *a.* 1. **unsettled market,** mercado instável; **unsettled economic situation,** conjuntura econômica instável. 2. não saldado, não liquidado; **unsettled account,** conta não liquidada, conta a pagar.

unship, *v.tr.* descarregar, desembarcar, (mercadorias).

unshipment, unshipping, *n.* descarregamento *m*, desembarque *m.*

unskilled, *a.* não qualificado, não especializado; **unskilled labour,** mão-de-obra não especializada, mão-de-obra não qualificada; **unskilled worker,** trabalhador, operário, não especializado, não qualificado.

unsold, *a.* não vendido; **unsold goods,**

mercadorias não vendidas, mercadorias que não tiveram venda, que não tiveram saída; (*in shop*) **unsold stocks,** estoques acumulados.

unsound, *a.* (*a*) em mau estado; **the company's financial position is unsound,** a companhia está em má situação financeira; **unsound enterprise,** empreendimento *m* economicamente inviável; (*b*) *Ins:* **unsound risk,** risco *m* de pouco valor.

unspecialized, *a.* não especializado.

unspent, *a.* não despendido.

unsteady, *a.* (*of prices*) variável; (*of market*) instável; **unsteady demand,** procura *f* instável.

unsubscribed, *a.* (capital) não subscrito.

unsuccessful, *a.* malsucedido, malogrado.

untapped, *a.* **untapped resources,** recursos não aproveitados.

untaxed, *a.* (*of person*) não tributado; (*of product, etc.*) isento de impostos.

untransferable, *a.* (*of shares, etc.*) intransferível; *Jur:* (direito) inalienável.

unwarranted, *a.* injustificado.

up, 1. *n.* **the ups and downs of the market,** os altos e os baixos do mercado; (*of shares, etc.*) **to be on the up,** estar em alta. **2.** *adv.* (*a*) (*on packing case, etc.*) **this side up,** este lado para cima; (*b*) **profits are up 25%,** os lucros registram um aumento de 25%; **shares are up at £5,** o valor das ações subiu a £5.

update, *v.tr.* atualizar, pôr em dia.

updating, *n.* atualização *f*.

upgrade, *v.tr.* melhorar (um produto); elevar o nível, elevar a classe, (de um produto); **to upgrade a civil servant,** promover um funcionário público.

upgrading, *n.* **upgrading of consumer tastes,** melhoria *f* das preferências do consumidor.

upkeep, *n.* (despesas *fpl* de) manutenção *f*, conservação *f*.

upset¹, *v.tr.* **to upset the market,** desequilibrar o mercado.

upset², *a.* (*at auctions, etc.*) **upset price** (= **reserve price**), preço mínimo para venda em leilão.

upsurge, *n.* surto *m*, aumento *m*.

upswing, *n.* elevação *f*, alta *f*; fase *f* ascendente.

uptrend, *n.* tendência *f* para a alta, tendência altista.

upturn, *n.* melhoramento *m* (do mercado, preços, etc.); retomada *f* de atividade econômica.

upward, *a.* **upward trend,** tendência *f* para a alta, tendência altista; **upward movement,** movimento *m* para a alta; **prices show an upward tendency,** os preços apresentam uma tendência para a alta; **upward price drift,** movimento *m* ascensional do nível de preços; **upward price pressure,** pressão *f* pela elevação de preços.

urgent, *a.* urgente.

usance, *n.* usança *f*; prazo concedido para pagamento de uma letra de câmbio; *Fin:* **usance draft,** saque *m* a prazo.

use¹, *n.* emprego *m*, uso *m*, utilização *f*; **this product has numerous uses,** este produto tem usos numerosos; **in use,** em uso; **out of use,** fora de uso, em desuso; **joint use,** uso comum, uso coletivo; **to make use of sth.,** empregar, servir-se de, algo; *Cust:* **articles for personal use,** efeitos *mpl* pessoais; **goods for home use,** mercadorias destinadas ao consumo interno.

use², *v.tr.* empregar, usar, servir-se de; utilizar (serviços, dinheiro).

used, *a.* usado; **the used car trade,** o comércio de carros usados.

useful, *a.* útil; **useful life,** vida *f* útil; *Book-k: etc:* **useful expenditure,** despesa *f* útil.

usefulness, *n.* utilidade *f*.

user, *n.* usuário *m*; **telephone users,** usuários do telefone; **post office users,** usuários do serviço dos correios; *Book-k: etc:* **user cost,** custo *m* de utilização.

usual, *a.* usual, habitual, costumeiro; **usual terms,** termos *mpl*, condições *fpl*, usuais; **the usual practice in appointing agents,** a prática usual para a designação de agentes; **usual hours of business,** expediente *m* normal, horário *m* comercial normal; **it is usual to pay a deposit,** é costume pagar-se um sinal.

usufruct, *n.* *Jur:* usufruto *m*.

usufructuary, *n. Jur:* usufrutuário *m*, desfrutador *m*.

usurer, *n.* usurário *m*, agiota *mf*.

utensil, *n.* utensílio *m*; kitchen utensils, utensílios *mpl* de cozinha, bateria *f* (de cozinha).

utility, *n.* 1. utilidade *f*; total utility, utilidade total; *Pol.Ec:* theory of marginal utility, teoria *f* da utilidade marginal. 2. (public) utility company, empresa *f* de serviços de utilidade pública, empresa de utilidade pública; *St.Exch: Fin: pl.* utilities, títulos *mpl* de empresas de utilidade pública.

utilization, *n.* utilização *f* (de serviços, dinheiro, etc.); utilization of a patent, exploração *f* de uma patente; *Ind:* utilization per cent, factor, índice *m* de rendimento (de uma fábrica, etc.).

utilize, *v.tr.* utilizar, servir-se de; explorar, beneficiar-se de, (uma patente, etc.).

V

vacancy, *n.* vaga *f*; **vacancies for typists,** vagas para, de, datilógrafa; **to fill a vacancy,** preencher uma vaga; **to advertise a vacancy in the trade press,** anunciar uma vaga nos órgãos da profissão; **'no vacancies',** 'não há vagas', 'não tem vaga'.

vacant, *a.* vago, vazio; (*only of property, etc.*) desocupado; **vacant lot,** terreno vago, (*uncultivated*) terreno baldío; **vacant apartment,** apartamento vazio, apartamento desocupado; **to become vacant,** ser desocupado, ficar vazio; **the apartment became vacant on Monday,** o apartamento foi desocupado, ficou vazio, na segunda-feira; **the post became vacant,** o cargo vagou, ficou vago; **the post is still vacant,** o cargo continua vago; **vacant possession,** posse *f* de imóvel vazio, de imóvel vago; **'house to let with vacant possession',** 'aluga-se casa vazia'; (*in advertisements*) **'situations vacant',** 'ofertas *fpl* de emprego', 'precisa-se', 'empregados procurados'.

vacate, *v.tr.* 1. vagar, deixar vago, abrir vaga em, (um cargo, uma pasta ministerial, etc.); **to vacate office,** deixar o cargo, vagar o cargo; **to vacate a building,** desocupar um prédio. 2. *Jur:* **to vacate a contract,** anular um contrato.

vacation¹, *n.* férias *fpl*; **to be on vacation,** estar de férias, estar em férias; **to take a vacation,** tirar férias; **vacation pay,** pagamento *m* de férias; **paid vacation,** férias remuneradas; **unpaid vacation,** férias não remuneradas.

vacation², *v.i.* *Am:* estar de férias, estar em férias, gozar as férias, passar as férias, (em determinado lugar).

valid, *a.* válido, legítimo; **to make valid,** tornar válido, validar, legitimar, (documentos, etc.); **valid receipt,** recibo

válido; **air ticket valid for one month,** passagem *f* de avião válida por um mês.

validate, *v.tr.* validar, tornar válido, legitimar, (documentos, etc.).

validation, *n.* validação *f*, legitimação *f*.

validity, *n.* validade *f*, validez *f*; **to extend the validity of a credit,** prorrogar o prazo de um crédito; **validity for shipment and negotiation,** validade para embarque e negociação.

valorization, *n.* *Pol.Ec:* valorização *f*.

valorize, *v.tr.* valorizar.

valuable, 1. *a.* de valor, valioso; **valuable article,** objeto *m*, artigo *m*, de valor; **valuable goods,** objetos de valor; **valuable service,** serviço valioso; *Jur:* **for a valuable consideration,** a título oneroso. 2. *n.pl.* **valuables,** objetos *mpl* de valor.

valuation, *n.* (*a*) avaliação *f*, apreciação *f*; **stock valuation,** avaliação dos estoques, das mercadorias estocadas; **to make a valuation of the goods,** avaliar as mercadorias; **valuation for customs purposes,** avaliação para fins alfandegários; **asset valuation, valuation of assets,** avaliação do ativo; **property valuation,** avaliação de imóveis; **valuation account,** conta *f* de retificação; (*b*) (*value*) avaliação; **I found the valuation too high,** achei a avaliação alta demais; **to put 5% on(to) the valuation of a building,** acrescentar 5% à avaliação do prédio.

valuator, *n.* avaliador *m*.

value¹, *n.* valor *m*, preço *m*; **loss of value,** perda *f* de valor, desvalorização *f*; **of no commercial value,** sem valor comercial; **exchange value,** (i) *Fin:* valor cambial (do dólar, etc.), (ii) *Econ:* valor de troca; **fair value,** valor justo; **invoice value,** valor de fatura; **market value,** valor de mercado; **net value,** valor líquido; **rental value,** valor locativo; **sale value,** valor de venda; **true**

value, valor real; **to be of value,** ser de valor, ter valor; **to get good value for one's money,** comprar por um preço bom; **to lose value,** perder o valor, desvalorizar-se; **to set a low value on the goods,** fixar um valor baixo para as mercadorias; **to set a value upon sth.,** avaliar algo, fixar um valor para algo; **to set too high a value on sth.,** fixar um valor exagerado para algo; **goods to the value of £20,** mercadorias *fpl* no valor de £20; **he gives you good value,** ele vende a preços muito razoáveis; **this book is good value for $3,** por três dólares este livro não é caro; **this book is of great value, of little value,** este livro é de grande valor, de pouco valor; *Fin:* **face value, par value,** valor nominal, valor facial; *Book-k:* **book value,** valor contábil, valor escritural, valor segundo os livros; **value in account,** valor em conta; **value date,** data *f* do lançamento do valor; *Ins:* **insurable value,** valor segurável; **insured value,** valor segurado; **surrender value,** valor de resgate; *Book-k:* **scrap value,** valor de sucata, valor de salvados; *Econ:* **token value,** valor extrínseco; **intrinsic value,** valor intrínseco; **the changing value of money,** o valor variável da moeda, do dinheiro; *Ind: etc:* **value-to-bulk ratio,** razão *f* valor-volume.

value², *v.tr.* avaliar, apreciar, calcular, (o montante de um prejuízo, etc.); **to value the goods,** avaliar as mercadorias; **he valued the car at £300,** avaliou o carro em £300; **to value (sth.) most,** atribuir o máximo valor (a alguma coisa).

value-added, *a.* **value-added tax,** imposto *m* sobre o valor adicionado, imposto sobre o valor agregado.

valueless, *a.* sem valor.

valuer, *n.* avaliador *m*.

valuing, *n* avaliação *f*, apreciação *f*.

variability, *n.* variabilidade *f*.

variable, 1. *a.* variável; **variable costs,** custos *mpl*, gastos *mpl*, variáveis; *Book-k:* **variable cost ratio,** índice *m* dos custos variáveis; **variable expense,** despesa *f* variável; *Ind: etc:* **variable cost accounting,** apuração *f* dos custos variáveis; *Am:* **variable capital**

corporation, sociedade *f* de capital autorizado. **2.** *n. Stat:* variável *f*.

variance, *n.* variação *f*; **cost variance,** variação de custos; **price variance,** variação de preço; **value variance,** variação de valor; **efficiency variance,** variação de eficiência; *Stat:* **random variance,** variação aleatória.

variation, *n.* variação *f*; **annual variation,** variação anual; **seasonal variation,** variação sazonal, variação estacional; **variation of the monetary value of stocks,** variação do valor monetário dos estoques.

variety, *n.* variedade *f*; **variety of goods,** sortimento *m*; **to deal in a variety of goods,** comerciar em várias espécies de mercadorias; *Am:* **variety store,** loja *f* de variedades.

vary, *v.tr.* variar, alterar, mudar, (os termos contratuais, etc.).

vault, *n.* casa-forte *f*, caixa-forte *f*, (em casa bancária, etc.); **vault cash,** dinheiro *m* em caixa-forte.

vegetable, *n. pl.* **vegetables,** legumes *mpl*, hortaliças *fpl*; hortigranjeiros *mpl*; **vegetable extractive industry,** indústria extrativa vegetal.

vehicle, *n.* (*a*) veículo *m*; **freight vehicle,** veículo (para transporte) de carga; **passenger vehicle,** veículo (para transporte) de passageiros; **heavy-duty vehicle,** veículo (para transporte) de carga pesada, veículo de transportes pesados; **(light) commercial vehicle,** veículo comercial (leve); *UK:* **vehicle licensing centre,** serviço *m* responsável pela concessão de licenças autorizando o uso de determinados veículos; (*b*) **advertising vehicle,** veículo (publicitário).

vehicular, *a. Am:* **vehicular capital,** capital investido em veículos; capital aplicado em transporte.

velocity, *n.* velocidade *f*; **velocity of circulation,** velocidade de circulação (de mercadorias); **velocity of money,** velocidade de circulação da moeda.

vend, *v.tr. Jur:* vender.

vendability, *n. Am:* vendabilidade *f*.

vending, *a.* **vending machine,** vendedora automática.

vendor, *n.* (*a*) vendedor *m*; **street vendor,**

vendedor ambulante, camelô *m*; (*with stall*) quitandeiro *m*; (*b*) *Fin:* **vendor's shares,** ações adquiridas por dono de firma convertida em sociedade de capital aberto; (*c*) **sale subject to right of vendor to repurchase,** venda *f* com cláusula de retrovenda; (*d*) *Jur:* **vendor's lien,** privilégio *m* de vendedor.

vendue, *n. Am:* leilão *m*, hasta pública; **vendue crier, master,** leiloeiro *m*.

venture, *n.* empreendimento *m*, especulação *f*; *F:* **it's a new venture,** é um negócio novo; *Fin:* **venture capital,** capital *m* de risco; **joint venture,** sociedade *f* em conta de participação, operação conjunta; associação *f* (com empresa estrangeira, etc.)

verbal, *a.* verbal; **verbal contract, agreement,** contrato *m* verbal; **verbal offer,** oferta *f* verbal.

verification, *n.* verificação *f*, controle *m*.

verifier, *n.* (*machine*) conferidora *f*.

verify, *v.tr.* verificar, conferir, controlar.

vertical, *a.* vertical; **vertical filing system,** arquivo *m* vertical; **vertical integration,** integração *f* vertical; *Fin:* **vertical merger,** fusão *f* vertical; *Ind:* **vertical union,** sindicato *m* cujos membros são todos da mesma indústria.

vessel, *n.* **vessel under Brazilian flag,** navio *m* de bandeira brasileira.

vest, *v.tr.* **to vest the management of a company in the directors,** confiar a administração de uma companhia aos diretores; *Jur:* **to vest s.o. with full powers to do sth.,** conferir plenos poderes a alguém para fazer algo.

vested, *a.* **vested interests,** direitos adquiridos; **to have a vested interest in a concern,** ter um interesse, uma participação, em uma empresa.

viability, *n.* viabilidade *f*.

viable, *a.* (*of plan, etc.*) viável; **commercially viable,** rentável.

vice-chairman, *n.* vice-presidente *mf*.

vice-chairmanship, *n.* vice-presidência *f*.

vice-manager, *n. Am:* subgerente *mf*.

vice-presidency, *n.* vice-presidência *f*.

vice-president, *n.* vice-presidente *mf*.

video, *n.* vídeo *m*; **video cassette,** cassete *m* vídeo; **video demonstration,** demonstração

apresentada por vídeo; **video phone;** videofone *m*; **video player,** reprodutor *m* de vídeo; **video recorder,** gravador *m* de vídeo; **video recording,** gravação *f* de vídeo; **video tape,** video-teipe *m*.

viewpoint, *n.* ponto *m* de vista.

violate, *v.tr.* violar.

visa¹, *n.* visto *m*; **entry, exit, visa,** visto de entrada, de saída; **business visa,** visto para negócios; **customs visa,** visto alfandegário; **transit visa,** visto de trânsito; **tourist visa,** visto de turista.

visa², *v.tr.* visar (um passaporte, etc.); **visaed shipping documents,** documentos de embarque visados.

visible, *a.* visível; **visible imports, exports,** importações *fpl*, exportações *fpl*, visíveis; **visible items of trade,** transações *fpl* visíveis componentes do balanço de pagamentos.

visual, *a.* **visual communication systems,** sistemas *mpl* de comunicação visual.

vital, *a. Stat:* **vital statistics,** estatística demográfica.

vitiate, *v.tr.* anular, invalidar, cancelar, (um contrato, etc.).

vocational, *a.* profissional, vocacional; **vocational training,** formação *f* profissional (a nível médio); **vocational guidance,** orientação *f* profissional; **vocational test,** teste *m* vocacional.

vogue, *n.* moda *f*, voga *f*; **to be in vogue,** estar na moda.

void¹, *a. Jur:* (*of deed, contract, etc.*) nulo, inválido, írrito; **null and void,** írrito e nulo; **to make a clause void,** anular, nulificar, invalidar, uma cláusula.

void², *v.tr. Jur:* anular, nulificar, invalidar, irritar, (um contrato, um documento, etc.).

voidable, *a. Jur:* anulável, nulificável, irritável.

voidance, *n. Jur:* anulação *f*, nulificação *f*, invalidação *f*, (de um contrato, etc.).

volume, *n.* volume *m*; **sales volume,** volume de vendas; **volume discount,** desconto *m* de volume, desconto por quantidade, desconto quantitativo; **volume of orders,** volume de pedidos; **volume of business,** volume de negócios; *Fin:* **profit–volume ratio,** razão *f* lucro-vendas, taxa *f* de lucro sobre vendas; **volume of cheques,** volume de cheques; **volume of transactions,** volume de transações.

voluntary, *a.* voluntário; **voluntary control,** controle voluntário; **voluntary deposit,** depósito voluntário; **voluntary repurchase,** recompra voluntária; *Ret:* **voluntary group,** grupo voluntário; cooperativa *f* de varejistas; *Jur:* **voluntary bankruptcy,** falência solicitada pelo comerciante; **voluntary liquidation, winding-up,** liquidação requerida pela empresa; *Am: Ind:* **voluntary check-off,** dedução *f* de salário autorizada pelo empregado.

vote¹, *n.* **1.** voto *m*, votação *f*; (*right*) direito *m* de voto, direito a voto, direito de votar; **vote of censure,** voto de censura; **vote of confidence,** voto de confiança; **number of votes (cast),** número *m* total de votos; **casting vote,** voto de Minerva, voto de qualidade, (do presidente, etc.); **proxy vote,** voto por procuração; **secret vote,** voto secreto; *coll.* **the trade-union vote,** o sufrágio dos sindicatos; **to cast one's vote,** votar; **to count the votes,** contar os votos; **to put a plan to the vote,** votar um plano, submeter um plano à votação; **to take the vote,** proceder à votação; **the number of votes needed to elect the chairman,** o número de votos necessários para a eleição do presidente; **resoltuion adopted by a majority vote,** deliberação tomada por maioria de votos. **2.** deliberação *f*; **to carry a vote,** votar uma deliberação.

vote², *v.* **1.** *v.i.* votar; **to vote for the candidate,** votar no candidato; **to vote on a proposal,** votar uma proposta, submeter uma proposta à votação; **to vote for a project,** vota um projeto, votar a favor de um projeto; **to vote against a proposal,** votar contra uma proposta; **to vote by a show of hands,** votar por mãos erguidas,

votar por aclamação; **to vote by proxy,** vota por procuração. **2.** *v.tr.* (*a*) **to vote a sum (for a specific purpose, etc.),** votar uma importância (para um fim específico, etc.); (*b*) **to vote s.o. in,** eleger alguém por meio de votos, por votação; **to vote s.o. out,** destituir alguém por votação, por meio de votos.

voter, *n.* votante *mf.*

voting, 1. *a.* votante; **voting member,** sócio *m* com direito de voto, sócio votante. **2.** *n.* votação *f*, voto *m*; **voting stock,** capital *m* votante, capital com direito de voto, ações com direito de voto; **voting power,** direitos *mpl* de voto; **total voting power,** totalidade *f* da votação; **voting paper,** cédula *f* (própria para votação); **to abstain from voting,** abster-se do voto, abster-se de votar; **to declare the result of the voting,** anunciar os resultados da votação.

voucher¹, *n.* (*a*) *Book-k: etc:* comprovante *m*, guia *f* de lançamento; **voucher clerk,** encarregado *m* do sistema de comprovantes; **voucher register,** registro *m* de comprovantes; **voucher system,** sistema *m* de comprovantes; **voucher audit,** exame *m* de comprovantes, exame de guias de lançamento; **voucher payable,** conta *f* a pagar; *Bank: etc:* **voucher cheque,** cheque *m* combinado com comprovante; (*b*) (*acknowledgement of debt*) vale *m*; **voucher for receipt,** recibo *m*; **luncheon voucher,** vale para almoço; **cash voucher,** (i) comprovante de caixa, (ii) cupom *m* que dá direito a desconto sobre determinadas mercadorias; **gift voucher,** vale para presente.

voucher², *v.tr.* comprovar; **to voucher an expense,** comprovar a realização de uma despesa.

W

wage, *n.* salário *m*, paga *f*, ordenado *m* (pago diária ou semanalmente); **current wage rate**, taxa *f* atual de salários; **fair wage**, salário justo; **fixed wage**, salário fixo; **general level of wages**, nível *m* geral de salários; **(guaranteed) minimum wage**, salário mínimo; **hourly wage**, salário-hora *m*; **piece wage**, salário por tarefa; **wage and salary structure**, estrutura *f* de salários e ordenados; **wage and salary survey**, estudo *m* dos rendimentos pagos aos assalariados; **wage and salary workers**, assalariados *mpl*; **wage agreement**, acordo *m* salarial; **wage bill**, custos *mpl* salariais, folha *f* de pagamento; **wage bracket**, faixa *f* salarial; **wage control**, controle *m* salarial; **wage cost**, custo *m* de mão-de-obra, custos *mpl* salariais; **wage cut**, redução *f* salarial; **wage demand**, **wage claim**, reivindicação *f* salarial; **wage determination**, fixação *f* do salário; **wage differentials**, diferenças *fpl* de salário, desníveis salariais; **wage dividend**, abono concedido aos empregados na base dos dividendos distribuídos, participação *f* nos lucros; **wage drift**, tendência *f* dos salários; **wage freeze**, congelamento *m* de salários; **wage goods**, bens *mpl* de salário, bens de consumo pagos como parte do salário; **wage increase**, aumento *m* salarial, aumento de salário; **wage level**, nível *m* salarial; **wage policy**, política *f* salarial; **wage price**, custo *m* salarial; **wage regulation**, regulamentação *f* dos salários; **wage scale**, escala *f* de níveis salariais; **wage settlement**, acordo *m* salarial; **wage structure**, estrutura *f* salarial; **wage system**, sistema *m* salarial; **wage tax**, imposto *m* sobre os salários; **wage-fund theory**, teoria *f* do fundo salarial; **wage-price spiral**, espiral *f* salários-preços; **wages clerk**, auxiliar *mf* de folha de pagamento; **to adjust wages**, reajustar os salários.

wage-earner, *n.* assalariado *m*, salariado *m*.

wage-earning, *a.* assalariado, salariado.

waiting, *n. Ind: etc:* **waiting time**, período *m* de espera.

waive, *v.tr.* **to waive interest**, não cobrar juros; **to waive payment**, sustar pagamento; *Jur:* **to waive a right**, renunciar a um direito, desistir de um direito.

waiver, *n. Jur:* renúncia *f* (de um direito); **waiver clause**, cláusula *f* de renúncia.

waiving, *n.* **waiving of the age limit**, dispensa *f* do limite de idade.

walking, *a. Am: Ind: etc:* **walking delegate**, funcionário designado por um sindicato para vigiar o cumprimento das leis trabalhistas.

walk out, *v.i.* entrar em greve.

walkout, *n.* greve *f*, parede *f*, (não autorizada pelo sindicato e de pouca duração) com abandono do local de trabalho.

wall, *n.* **tariff wall**, barreira tarifária.

wanted, *a.* procurado; **'situations wanted'**, 'empregos procurados', 'precisa-se'; *Fin:* **stocks wanted**, títulos procurados (por corretor, investidor, etc.).

war, *n.* guerra *f*; **price war**, guerra de preços; **tariff war**, guerra tarifária; *Ins:* **war risk**, risco *m* de guerra.

warehouse[1], *n.* armazém *m*, entreposto *m*, depósito *m* (de mercadorias); **furniture warehouse**, depósito de moveis, guarda-móveis *m*; **pier warehouse**, trapiche *m*, **bonded warehouse**, entreposto alfandegário; **warehouse receipt**, recibo *m* de depósito, recibo de armazenagem, conhecimento *m* de depósito; **negotiable**

253

warehouse receipt, warrant *m*, cédula pignoratícia; **warehouse loan,** empréstimo bancário concedido mediante garantia pignoratícia de mercadorias depositadas em armazém; **warehouse company,** companhia *f* de armazéns gerais; *Ins:* **warehouse to warehouse clause,** cláusula *f* de seguro desde o armazém do fornecedor ao armazém do comprador.

warehouse², *v.tr.* depositar em armazém, em entreposto.

warehouseman, *n.* **1.** armazenista *m*, encarregado *m* de armazém, encarregado de depósito. **2.** (*a*) *Am:* companhia *f* de armazéns gerais; (*b*) proprietário *m* de armazém.

warehousing, *n.* armazenagem *f*; **warehousing charge(s),** taxa(s) *f(pl)* de armazenagem, armazenagem.

warning, *n.* aviso *m*, advertência *f*.

warrant¹, *n.* **1.** autorização *f*; *Jur:* **warrant of attorney,** procuração (passada por escrito); *Fin:* **warrant for payment,** ordem *f* de pagamento; **dividend warrant,** ordem de pagamento de dividendo. **2. share warrant,** cautela *f* (de ação ao portador); **subscription warrant,** bônus *m* de subscrição. **3.** (**warehouse**) **warrant,** (**dock**) **warrant,** warrant *m*, cédula pignoratícia; **to issue a warehouse warrant for goods,** warrantar mercadorias; **issuing of a warehouse warrant,** warrantagem *f*; **goods covered by a warehouse warrant,** mercadorias warrantadas. **4.** *Am: Book-k:* (*a*) guia *f* de pagamento; (*b*) guia de lançamento.

warrant², *v.tr.* garantir; **I warrant that the sum shall be paid,** garanto o pagamento da importância.

warranted, *a.* (*a*) garantido; (*b*) autorizado.

warrantee, *n.* beneficiário *m* de uma garantia.

warrantor, *n.* garantidor *m*.

warranty, *n.* **1.** garantia *f* (quanto à qualidade de um produto, etc.). **2.** autorização *f*.

wash, *n. Am:* **wash sale,** venda fictícia; compra *f* e venda *f* quase simultânea de investimentos idênticos; **wash transaction,** operação fictícia (na bolsa, etc.).

wastage, *n. Ind:* perda *f*, desperdício *m*, desgaste *m*.

waste¹, **1.** *a.* excedente, de despejo, de refugo; **waste products,** resíduos *mpl* de operação fabril; **waste paper,** papéis usados; *Ind:* **waste coal,** sobras *fpl* de carvão. **2.** *n. Ind:* resíduos *mpl* (de operação fabril, etc.); *Book-k:* **waste-book,** borrador *m*.

waste², *v.tr.* desperdiçar, esperdiçar, perder, esbanjar, (dinheiro, etc.); **to waste time,** perder tempo; **wasted resources,** recursos desperdiçados.

wasteful, *a.* (*of person*) desperdiçador, desperdiçado, esbanjador, gastador; **wasteful expenditure,** despesas *fpl* inúteis.

wasting, *a.* **wasting assets,** bens fixos consumíveis; *Econ:* **wasting goods,** bens esgotáveis, bens fixos desgastáveis.

water, *n.* água *f*; **water power,** força hidráulica; **water supply,** abastecimento *m* de água.

watered, *a.* **watered capital,** capital aguado, capital diluído; **watered stock,** ações aguadas, ações diluídas; títulos estimados acima do valor real.

waterway, *n.* via *f* fluvial.

wave, *n.* **wave of speculation,** onda especulativa.

waybill, *n.* guia *f*; **air waybill,** conhecimento aéreo.

weak, *a.* (*of market, currency, etc.*) fraco.

weaken, *v.* **1.** *v.tr.* enfraquecer. **2.** *v.i.* (*of market, currency, etc.*) enfraquecer-se, tornar-se fraco; baixar.

wealth, *n.* riqueza *f*, acervo *m*, fortuna *f*; *Pol.Ec:* **wealth using,** utilização *f* da riqueza.

wear, *n.* desgaste *m*, usura *f*; deterioração causada pelo uso; (**fair**) **wear and tear,** uso *m* e desgaste (normal); **wear-and-tear allowance,** provisão *f* para depreciação.

week, *n.* semana *f*; **earnings per week,** salário *m* semanal.

weekday, *n.* dia *m* de trabalho.

weekly, **1.** *a.* semanal, semanário, hebdomadário; **weekly payment,** pagamento *m* semanal; **weekly paper,** jornal hebdomadário, jornal semanário. **2.** *adv.* semanalmente. **3.** *n.* semanário *m*, hebdomadário *m*.

weigh, v.tr. & i. pesar; to weigh twenty kilos of rice, pesar vinte quilos de arroz; to weigh the goods, pesar as mercadorias; this packet weighs one kilo, este pacote pesa um quilo.

weighing, n. pesada f, pesagem f, (de mercadorias, etc.); weighing machine, balança f (de plataforma); weighing car, carro-balança m; weighing tank, balança-tanque f.

weighmaster, n. mestre m de pesadas.

weight¹, n. 1. peso m; dead weight, peso morto; live weight, peso vivo; net weight, peso líquido; gross weight, peso bruto; Fin: legal tender by weight, curso m legal combinado com o peso da moeda; Ind: etc: weight allowance, tolerância f admissível no peso; weight recorder, registrador m de pesos; weight per square metre, peso por metro quadrado; weight list, listagem f de peso. 2. weights and measures, pesos e medidas.

weight², v.tr. Stat: Econ: ponderar; weighted average, média ponderada; weighted index number, número-índice ponderado.

weighting, n. Stat: Econ: ponderação f; weighting system, sistema m de ponderação.

welfare, n. bem-estar m; welfare economics, economia f do bem-estar social, economia social e previdencial; Am: welfare payment, pagamento m de previdência social.

wet, a. wet goods, molhados mpl.

wharf, n. desembarcadouro m, cais m; wharf dues, direitos mpl de cais; price ex wharf, preço m de mercadorias desembarcadas no cais.

wharfage, n. 1. desembarque m, desembarcadouro m, acomodação f no cais. 2. direito m de cais, taxa(s) f(pl) de atracação; taxa portuária.

whereas, conj. Jur: considerando que (+ ind.); whereas the supplier was recommended by the contractor, considerando que o fornecedor foi recomendado pela contratada.

white-collar, a. white-collar worker, white-collar m, colarinho branco m.

wholesale, 1. n. venda f por atacado,

venda em grosso. 2. a. (a) por atacado, em grosso; wholesale price, preço m por atacado; wholesale price index, índice m de preços por atacado; wholesale trade, comércio m atacadista, comércio grossista; wholesale dealer, atacadista mf, grossista mf, negociante mf atacadista; wholesale market, mercado m atacadista; wholesale goods, mercadorias vendidas por atacado; (b) wholesale manufacture, fabricação f em série; (c) Am: wholesale banking, operações bancárias de grande vulto. 3. adv. (a) to sell sth. wholesale, vender algo por atacado; (b) to manufacture sth. wholesale, fabricar, manufaturar, algo em série.

wholesaler, n. (a) atacadista mf, grossista mf, negociante mf atacadista; Am: counter wholesaler, atacadista de balcão; (b) firma f atacadista; wholesaler's brand, marca f do atacadista.

wide, a. amplo; wide market, mercado amplo; wider exchange margins, margens mais amplas (de flutuação cambial); wide-ranging economic effect, efeito econômico de ampla variedade.

widely-accepted, a. widely-accepted currency, moeda f de larga aceitação.

widen, v.tr. alargar, ampliar.

widening, n. widening of capital, ampliação f, aumento m, de capital; widening of production facilities, ampliação de instalações produtivas.

widespread, a. generalizado.

wildcat, a. wildcat strike, greve não autorizada pelo sindicato; F: wildcat bank, banco não merecedor de confiança.

windfall, n. lucro inesperado, lucro imprevisto; windfall losses, perdas sofridas em razão da queda de preços; windfall profit, lucro fortuito.

winding-up, n. liquidação f (de uma companhia); voluntary winding-up, liquidação requerida pela companhia; winding-up under court supervision, liquidação judicial.

window, n. shop window, vitrina f, vitrine f; window envelope, envelope m de janela.

window-dresser, n. vitrinista mf.

window-dressing, n. 1. decoração f de

vitrinas. **2.** *F:* apresentação enganosa (de contabilidade, etc.).

wind up, *v.tr.* **to wind up a meeting,** terminar, encerrar, uma reunião; **to wind up an account,** liquidar, saldar, uma conta; **to wind up a company,** liquidar uma companhia.

wipe off, *v.tr.* **to wipe off a debt,** liquidar, saldar, uma dívida; **thousands of dollars were wiped off share values,** as ações baixaram no valor de milhares de dólares.

wire, *n.* telegrama *m*; **wire transfer,** transferência telegráfica.

with, *prep.* **with average,** com avaria; **with particular average,** cláusula *f* de seguro que cobre perdas parciais ou totais de mercadorias; **with transhipment,** com transbordo.

withdraw, *v.tr.* **1.** retirar (dinheiro do banco, etc.). **2. to withdraw an order,** cancelar, suspender, um pedido.

withdrawal, *n.* (*a*) retirada *f*; **withdrawal of shipping documents,** retirada de documentos de embarque; **withdrawal of capital,** retirada de capital (de uma sociedade, etc.); **withdrawal notice,** aviso prévio para retirada de depósito; (*b*) **withdrawal of foreign capital,** retorno *m* de capital estrangeiro.

withhold, *v.tr.* reter (pagamento, salário, etc.), descontar (parte do salário por dias não trabalhados, etc.); **the firm withheld the payment until the replacement of the broken parts,** a firma reteve o pagamento até a substituição das peças quebradas.

withholding, *n. Am:* retenção *f* (na fonte), desconto *m* (em folha); **withholding tax,** imposto retido na fonte, imposto descontado na folha.

within, *prep.* **within 10 days,** dentro de 10 dias.

witness, *n.* **1.** *Jur:* (*person*) testemunha *f*; **the parties sign this contract in the presence of the undersigned witnesses,** as partes assinam o contrato na presença das testemunhas abaixo assinadas. **2.** *Jur:* **in witness whereof this contract is signed . . .,** em testemunho do qual assina-se este contrato . . ..

word¹, *n.* **word processor,** máquina *f* para o processamento de palavras.

word², *v.tr.* redigir (um documento, telegrama, etc.).

wording, *n.* (*a*) redação *f* (de um documento); (*b*) **(suggested) form of wording (for a cheque, bill of exchange, etc.),** modelo *m*, fórmula *f*, (de cheque, letra de câmbio, etc.).

work¹, *n.* **1.** trabalho *m*; **manual work,** trabalho manual, trabalho braçal, serviço *m* braçal; **office work, clerical work,** trabalho de escritório; **skilled work,** trabalho especializado; **temporary work,** trabalho temporário; **work accident,** acidente *m* de trabalho; **work force,** força *f* de trabalho; **work load,** carga *f* de trabalho; **work period,** período *m* de trabalho; **work schedule,** programa *m* de trabalho, horário *m* de trabalho; **to be at work,** estar no trabalho, estar no serviço; **to get down to work,** começar a trabalhar, pôr mãos à obra; **to go back to work,** voltar ao trabalho; **to stop work,** parar de trabalhar; *Ind:* **work stoppage,** (i) suspensão *f*, cessação *f*, de trabalho, (ii) greve *f*; *Book-k:* **work in progress, work in process,** produção *f* em curso, produção em andamento; produtos *mpl* em andamento, produtos em fabricação, produtos em elaboração, material *m* de produção; *Book-k: Ind:* **works oncost,** despesas *fpl* gerais de produção, de fabricação. **2.** (*task*) trabalho *m*, obra *f*, tarefa *f*, serviço *m*; **to get through a lot of work,** realizar muito trabalho; **the builder left before finishing the work,** o pedreiro saiu antes de terminar o trabalho; **six hours' work,** trabalho de seis horas; **a day's work,** um dia de trabalho, uma jornada; **work sheet,** registro *m* das horas de trabalho; **work ticket,** ordem *f* de serviço, ordem de trabalho. **3.** (*a*) (*employment*) trabalho *m*, emprego *m*; **to be out of work,** estar desempregado, estar sem trabalho, sem emprego; **to be in regular work,** ter um emprego fixo; **an engineer's work is well paid,** o trabalho de um engenheiro é muito bem remunerado; (*b*) (*place of employment*) **he gave me the telephone number of his work,** ele me deu o telefone do trabalho (dele). **4.** *pl.* **works,** usina *f*, instalações *fpl*, fábrica *f*;

chemical works, fábrica de produtos
químicos; iron and steel works, (usina)
siderúrgica *f*; steel works, aceria *f*,
aciaria *f*; car works, fábrica de
automóveis; works committee, comissão
paritária.
work², *v.* 1. *v.tr.* trabalhar; hours worked,
horas trabalhadas; two salesmen work
this region, dois vendedores trabalham
nesta região; to work the land, trabalhar
a terra; to work metals, trabalhar metais.
2. *v.i.* (*a*) trabalhar; he works ten hours a
day, trabalha dez horas por dia; to work
hard, trabalhar muito, *F:* dar duro; to
work to rule, trabalhar estritamente de
acordo com o regulamento como forma
de protesto; (*b*) (*of machine, etc.*)
trabalhar, funcionar; the computer's not
working, o computador não está
funcionando, o computador está
enguiçado, está encrencado.
workability, *n.* (*of plan, etc.*)
practicabilidade *f*, exeqüibilidade *f*,
viabilidade *f*; (*of wood, metal, etc.*)
trabalhabilidade *f*.
workable, *a.* (*of plan, etc.*) practicável,
exeqüível, viável; (*of wood, metal, etc.*)
trabalhável.
worker, *n.* trabalhador *m*, operário *m*;
car worker, operário da indústria
automobilística; steel worker, operário
siderúrgico, metalúrgico *m*; worker
participation, participação *f* dos
empregados na administração da
empresa (com ou sem participação nos
lucros); worker unrest, distúrbios *mpl*
trabalhistas, agitação *f* trabalhista,
conflitos *mpl* trabalhistas.
working, 1. *a.* (i) que trabalha, (ii) que
funciona, em funcionamento; working
group, working party, grupo *m* de
trabalho; working population, população
economicamente ativa; the working class,
a classe operária, o operariado, a classe
trabalhadora. 2. *n.* (*a*) trabalho *m*;
working day, dia *m* de trabalho, dia útil;
working hours, horas *fpl* de trabalho;
(usual) working hours, horário *m* (de
trabalho), expediente *m*; working week,
semana *f* de trabalho; working paper,
documento *m* de trabalho; working

papers, papéis *mpl*, documentos, de
trabalho; working time, duração *f* do
serviço; working conditions, condições *fpl*
de trabalho; working age, idade *f* de
emprego; (*b*) *Fin:* working asset, ativo *m*
circulante, bem *m* de giro; working
balances, saldos *mpl* operacionais;
working capital, capital *m* de giro, capital
de exploração, capital circulante; working
capital fund, fundo *m* de capital
circulante; working capital ratio, índice
m do capital de giro; working expenses,
despesas *fpl* gerais, despesas de
exploração; (*c*) funcionamento *m* (de
sistemas, etc.), execução *f*, aplicação
f, (de lei, convênio, etc.); (*d*)
funcionamento *m* (de uma máquina,
etc.); in good working order, em bom
estado de funcionamento; to be in good
working order, funcionar bem, trabalhar
bem; working load, carga *f* de
funcionamento, carga normal; working
test, prova *f*, teste *m*, de funcionamento;
(*e*) *pl.* workings, mecanismo *m*; the
workings of the modern economy, o
mecanismo da economia moderna.
working off, *n.* the working off of stocks,
a liquidação de estoques.
working out, *n.* (*a*) elaboração *f* (de um
projeto, etc.); (*b*) cálculo *m*, cômputo *m*,
(de juros, etc.).
workman, workingman, *n.* operário *m*,
trabalhador *m*, artífice *m*; workmen's
compensation insurance, seguro *m* contra
acidentes de trabalho; workmen's
compensation laws, leis *fpl* de
indenização por acidentes de trabalho.
workmanlike, *a.* bem acabado, bem
executado, bem feito.
workmanship, *n.* mão-de-obra *f*,
habilidade *f* manual; arte *f* (de operário,
artífice, etc.), acabamento *m*, feitura
f, (de uma obra, etc.); of fine
workmanship, bem acabado, bem
executado; faulty workmanship, execução
defeituosa.
work off, *v.tr.* to work off a debt, (i)
liquidar, saldar, uma dívida pouco a
pouco, (ii) pagar uma dívida mediante
trabalho; to work off a stock of goods,

liquidar um estoque, vender as mercadorias pouco a pouco.
work out, *v.* **1.** *v.tr.* (*a*) **to work out a plan,** elaborar, formular, arquitetar, um plano, um projeto; (*b*) **to work out an account,** calcular, computar, o valor de uma conta; **to work out the cost of a job,** orçar, estimar, o custo de uma obra. **2.** *v.i.* **to work out at (a certain sum),** montar, sair, a (uma determinada quantia); **it works out at fifty dollars,** monta, sai, a cinqüenta dólares.
workpeople, *n.pl.* operários *mpl,* trabalhadores *mpl,* o operariado.
workshop, *n.* oficina *f;* **workshop manager,** chefe *m* de oficina.
world, *n.* mundo *m;* **the financial world,** o mundo financeiro; **world aggregates,** totais *mpl* mundiais; **World Bank,** Banco *m* Mundial; **World Bank Group,** Grupo *m* do Banco Mundial; **world consumption,** consumo *m* mundial; **World Economic Conference,** Conferência Econômica Mundial; **world exports,** exportações *fpl* mundiais; **World Health Organization,** Organização *f* Mundial de Saúde; **world liquidity,** liquidez *f* mundial; **world markets,** mercados *mpl* mundiais, mercados internacionais; **world monetary holdings,** estoque *m* mundial de ouro amoedado; **world money,** moeda *f* universal; **world price,** preço *m* internacional; **world production,** produção *f* mundial; **world recession,** recessão *f* mundial; **world sales,** vendas *fpl* mundiais; **world scarcity, shortage,** escassez *f* mundial; **world trade,** comércio *m* mundial; **trends in world trade,** tendências *fpl* no comércio mundial.
worldwide, *a.* mundial, de âmbito mundial; em todo o mundo; **worldwide economic crisis,** crise econômica mundial; **worldwide letter of credit,** carta *f* de crédito com validade mundial (negociável em todos os países do mundo); **worldwide service,** serviço *m* mundial.
worsen, *v.i.* piorar, agravar-se.
worth, 1. *a.* **to be worth £500,** valer £500; **how much is the cruzeiro worth?** quanto vale o cruzeiro? **the company's worth £3,000,000 on the Stock Exchange,** as

ações da companhia têm um valor total de £3.000.000 na bolsa de valores. **2.** *n.* valor *m;* **of great, little, worth,** de grande, pouco, valor; **a thousand dollars' worth of jewels,** jóias *fpl* no valor de mil dólares; *Fin:* **net worth of a company,** patrimônio líquido, situação líquida, patrimônio próprio, de uma companhia.
worthless, *a.* sem valor; **worthless cheque,** cheque *m* sem fundos, cheque sem valor.
wrap, *v.tr.* **to wrap goods for shipment,** embrulhar mercadorias para embarque.
writ, *n. Jur:* mandado *m,* ordem *f;* **to serve a writ of summons on s.o.,** intimar, notificar, alguém.
write, *v.tr.* escrever (uma carta, etc.); **to write a cheque,** emitir, passar, fazer, escrever, um cheque; **to write a contract,** (i) fazer, estabelecer, um contrato, (ii) redigir um contrato; *Ins:* **to write life insurance,** subscrever apólices de seguro de vida.
write back, *v.tr.* responder por escrito; *Book-k:* transferir um lançamento.
write down, *v.tr.* **1.** tomar nota (de algo) por escrito, apontar (por escrito). **2.** *Book-k:* reduzir o valor contábil (de um bem), reduzir o valor (de um bem) nos livros, amortizar (um bem); **the equipment is written down at 20% a year,** o equipamento se deprecia em 20% ao ano; **written-down value,** valor amortizado (de um bem), valor depreciado (de um bem); **to write down a debt,** abater uma dívida, amortizar uma dívida.
write-down, *n. Am: Book-k:* redução *f* do valor contábil (de um bem), amortização *f* (de um valor do ativo).
write off, *v.tr.* (*a*) *Fin:* **to write off capital,** reduzir o capital; (*b*) *Book-k:* **to write off a bad debt,** cancelar, eliminar, uma dívida incobrável; **to write off £200 for wear and tear,** deduzir £200 por conta de uso e desgaste.
write-off, *n.* cancelamento *m,* eliminação *f,* baixa *f,* (de dívida incobrável).
write out, *v.tr.* escrever por extenso; **to write out a cheque,** emitir, escrever, fazer, passar, um cheque; **to write out an**

invoice, fazer uma fatura; **to write out an order,** fazer uma encomenda por escrito.

write up, *v.tr.* **1.** pôr em dia (contabilidade, livros contábeis, etc.). **2.** *Book-k:* aumentar o valor (de um bem) nos livros.

writing, *n.* **writing paper,** papel *m* de escrever; **writing pad,** bloco *m* de papel (de escrever); **writing desk,** secretária *f*, escrivaninha *f*.

writing back, *n. Book-k:* transferência *f* (de um lançamento).

writing down, *n.* **1.** inscrição *f.* **2.** *Fin:* redução *f* (de capital).

writing off, *n.* **1.** amortização *f* (de capital). **2.** cancelamento *m*, eliminação *f*, baixa *f*, (de dívida incobrável).

written, *a.* **written agreement,** acordo *m* por escrito; **written promise,** promessa *f* por escrito.

wrong, *a.* **wrong decision,** decisão errada.

X

xerographic, *a.* **xerographic techniques,** técnicas xerográficas.

xerography, *n.* xerografia *f.*

Xerox[1], *n. R.t.m:* **Xerox copy,** (fotocópia) xerox *m,* xérox *m;* **Xerox machine,** (máquina) xerox *m,* xérox *m.*

xerox[2], *v.tr.* **to xerox a document,** xerografar, xerocar, xeroxar, um documento.

Y

yam, *n.* inhame *m.*

yard, *n. Meas:* jarda *f* (= 914 mm).

yardstick, *n.* gabarito *m*, medida *f.*

year, *n.* ano *m*; **leap year,** ano bissexto, ano bissêxtil; **calendar year,** ano civil; **he earns £5,000 a year,** ele ganha £5.000 por ano; **current year,** ano em curso, ano corrente; **accounting year, year of account,** exercício *m* contábil; **year under review,** exercício em apreço; **budgetary year,** exercício orçamentário; **commercial year,** ano comercial; **company's financial year,** exercício social; **economic year (of a country),** ano econômico (de um país); **fiscal year, tax year,** ano fiscal; *Book-k:* **audit year,** exercício examinado; *Ind:* **man-year,** homem-ano *m*; **working year,** ano útil; *Stat:* **base-year,** ano-base *m.*

yearbook, *n.* anuário *m*, almanaque *m.*

year-end, *a.* **year-end dividend,** dividendo *m* final de um exercício; dividendo pago no fim do exercício social.

yearling, *n. Fin:* título *m* de crédito a ser resgatado após um ano, no fim do prazo de um ano.

yearly, 1. *a.* anual; **yearly accounts,** contas *fpl* anuais, demonstrações *fpl* anuais; **debt redeemable by yearly payments,** dívida anuitária; **yearly report,** relatório *m* anual. **2.** *adv.* anualmente.

yellow, *a.* **the Yellow Pages,** as Páginas Amarelas; *Am: Ind:* **yellow-dog contract,** contrato *m* que não permite a sindicalização.

yen, *n.* iene *m.*

yield¹, *n.* (*a*) rendimento *m* (de um capital, etc.); (*more specifically*) taxa interna de retorno, taxa interna de rendimento; **the yield on these shares is large,** estas ações rendem muito bem; **net yield,** rendimento líquido; **fixed-yield investment,** investimento *m*, aplicação *f*, a rendimento fixo; **yield rate,** taxa interna de retorno, de rendimento; **tax yield,** renda tributária, receita *f* fiscal; (*b*) **yield of a mine,** rendimento de uma mina; **yield per acre** = produção *f* por hectare; **yield capacity,** rendimento *m*, produtividade *f.*

yield², *v.tr.* (*a*) render, produzir, proporcionar, (lucro, juros); **money that yields interest,** dinheiro *m* que rende juros; **this investment yields a very good return,** este investimento rende muito bem, este investimento dá um rendimento muito bom; **this farm yields a high income,** esta fazenda proporciona um alto rendimento; (*b*) *Ind:* **to yield a variety of by-products,** produzir uma variedade de derivados.

Z

zero, *n.* zero *m*; **to drop to zero,** cair ao zero; **above zero,** acima do zero; **below zero,** abaixo do zero; **zero interest rate,** taxa de juros nula; **zero allowance,** tolerância nula.

zero-rated, *a. UK: (re value-added tax)* **zero-rated,** sujeito ao imposto sobre o valor adicionado à alíquota nula.

zip, *n. Am:* **zip code,** código *m* de endereçamento postal (usado nos Estados Unidos).

zone¹, *n.* zona *f*; **free zone,** zona franca; **sterling zone,** zona esterlina; **wage zone,** zona de salários; **zone pricing,** sistema *m* de preços baseado em zonas geográficas; **industrial development zone,** zona de desenvolvimento industrial; **time zone,** fuso horário.

zone², *v.tr.* zonear, dividir em zonas, (uma área urbana).

zoning, *n.* zoneamento *m*.

zoom, *v.i. (of prices)* **to zoom upward(s),** elevar-se com extrema rapidez.

Common abbreviations
Abreviaturas comuns

a.a.r.	**against all risks,** contra todos os riscos
a/c, A/C	**account,** conta, c/
acc.	**accepted,** aceite
acce.	**acceptance,** aceite
accy.	**accountancy,** contabilidade, Cont.
a.c.v.	**actual cash value,** valor real em dinheiro
ad.	**advertisement,** anúncio
ad val.	**ad valorem,** ad valorem
agcy	**agency,** agência
agt	**agent,** agente
a/o.	**account of,** por conta de, p/c
appro.	**approval, on appro.,** a contento
approx.	**approximately,** aproximadamente
Apr.	**April,** abril, abr.
a/r.	**all risks,** todos os riscos
a/s.	**at sight,** à vista
ass.	**assurance,** seguro
Aug.	**August,** agosto, ag., ag.^{to}
av.	**average,** (i) média, (ii) avaria
avdp.	**avoirdupois,** avoirdupois
back.	**backwardation,** deporte
bal.	**balance,** saldo
b&b	**bed and breakfast**
b/d.	**(balance) brought down,** saldo transportado, transporte
b/e., B/E	**bill of exchange,** letra de câmbio
b/f, B/F	**(balance) brought forward,** saldo transportado, transporte
bkge	**brokerage,** corretagem
B/L	**bill of lading,** conhecimento de carga
BO	**l. branch office,** agência, sucursal **2. buyer's option,** opção de comprador
b.o., B/O	**(balance) brought over,** transporte
b.p., B/P	**bill payable,** efeito a pagar
b.r., B/R	**bill receivable,** efeito a cobrar
b.s., B/S	**1. balance sheet,** balanço **2. bill of sale,** nota de venda
c.	**1. coupon,** cupão, cupom **2. cent,** cêntimo, cênt.
c.a., CA	**1. current account,** conta corrente, c/c **2. current assets,** ativo corrente
C/A, c/a.	**1. capital account,** conta de capital **2. current account,** conta corrente, c/c
c.&f., C&F	**cost and freight,** custo e frete
CB	**cash book,** livro-caixa
c.d.	**cum dividend,** com dividendo, com div.
c.d., C/D	**carried down,** a transportar
cent.	**centime,** cêntimo, cênt.

cert.	**certificate,** certificado
CF	**carriage forward,** porte a pagar
c/f., C/F	**(to be) carried forward,** a transportar
c.i.f., CIF	**cost, insurance and freight,** custo, seguro e frete, cif
cl	**centilitre,** *N.Am*: **centiliter,** centilitro, cl
cm	**centimetre,** *N.Am*: **centimeter,** centímetro, cm
C/N	l. **credit note,** nota de crédito 2. **cover note,** carta de cobertura
Co.	**Company,** companhia, Cia., C.^{ia}
c/o	**care of ...,** ao(s) cuidado(s) de ..., A/C
c.o.d.	**cash on delivery,** *N.Am*: **collect on delivery,** pagamento contra entrega
com(m).	**commission,** comissão
cons.	**consols,** consolidados
convd	**converted,** convertido
corr.	**correspondence,** correspondência
cp.	**coupon,** cupão, cupom
CP	**carriage paid,** porte pago, frete pago
cr., Cr	**credit,** crédito
cum.	**cumulative,** cumulativo
c.w.o.	**cash with order,** pedido acompanhado do respectivo valor
cwt	**hundredweight** = 50kg (aprox.)
DA	**documents against acceptance,** documentos contra aceite
D/A	**deposit account,** conta de depósito
DAP	**documents against payment,** documentos contra pagamento
db.	**debenture,** debênture
d.b.	**day book,** diário
d.d.	**days after date,** dias da vista
DD	**direct debit,** débito direto
Dec.	**December,** dezembro, dez., dez.^{o}
def.	**deferred,** diferido
del.	**delegation,** delegação
dely	**delivery,** entrega
denom.	**denomination,** denominação
dept.	1. **departament,** departamento 2. **deposit,** depósito
dft	**draft,** saque
disc.	**discount,** desconto
div.	**dividend,** dividendo
dol.	**dollar,** dólar
doz.	**dozen,** dúzia(s), dz.
dr., Dr	**debtor,** devedor
E&OE, e.&o.e.	**errors and omissions excepted,** salvo erro ou omissão, S.E.O.
ed.	**edition,** edição, ed.
e.g.	**exempli gratia,** por exemplo, p. ex.
enc., encl.	**enclosure(s), enclosed,** documento anexo
est.	**established,** fundado
ex.	l. **example,** exemplo, ex. 2. **exchange,** câmbio 3. **extra,** extra
Exch.	l. **exchange,** bolsa 2. **Exchequer,** Erário
excl.	1. **excluding,** exclusive 2. **exclusive,** exclusivo
ex cp.	**ex coupon,** ex cupão, ex cupom
ex div.	**ex dividend,** ex dividendo

exec.	1. **executive**, executivo 2. **executor**, testamenteiro, executor
exp.	1. **expense**, despesa 2. **export**, exportação
f.a.a.	**free of all average**, livre de todas as avarias
f.a.s.	**free alongside ship**, franqueado no costado do navio
f/c	**for cash**, à vista
Feb.	**February**, fevereiro, fev., fev.°
fed.	**federation**, federação
f.g.a.	**free of general average**, livre de avaria comum
f.o.b.	**free on board**, franqueado a bordo, posto a bordo, FOB
f.o.c.	**free of charge**, grátis
f.o.r.	**free on rail**, franco sobre vagão
f.p.	**fully paid**, integralizado
f.p.a.	**free of particular average**, livre de avaria particular
Fri.	**Friday**, sexta-feira
F/S	**financial statement**, demonstração financeira
ft	**foot, feet**, pé(s)
g	**gram**, grama, g
g/a.	**general average**, avaria comum
gal	**gallon**, galão
gds	**goods**, mercadorias
GRT	**gross register ton**, tonelada de arqueação bruta
gr. wt	**gross weight**, peso bruto
GT	**gross tonnage**, tonelagem bruta
HO	**head office**, sede, matriz
HP	1. **hire purchase**, compra a prestação 2. **horse power**, cavalo-vapor, c.v.
hr(s)	**hour(s)**, hora(s)
i.e.	**id est (that is)**, isto é, i.e.
imp.	**import**, importação
in(s)	**inch(es)**, polegada(s), pol.
Inc.	**Incorporated**, Incorporada
incl.	1. **included**, incluído 2. **including**, inclusive 3. **inclusive**, inclusivo
info.	**information**, informação
ins.	**insurance**, seguro
inst.	**instant**, corrente, cor.te
int.	**interest**, juros
inv.	**invoice**, fatura
IOU	**I owe you**, vale
J/A	**joint account**, conta conjunta
Jan.	**January**, janeiro, jan. jan.°
jnr, jr	**junior**, júnior
Jul.	**July**, julho, jul.
Jun.	**June**, junho
kg	**kilo(gram)**, quilograma, kg
kl	**kilolitre**, N.Am: **kiloliter**, quilolitro, kl
km	**kilometre**, N.Am: **kilometer**, quilômetro, km

265

km/h	**kilometres per hour,** quilômetros por hora, km/h
kt	**kiloton,** quiloton, kt
l	**litre,** *N.Am:* **liter,** litro, l
lb	**pound(s) (weight),** libra(s), lb.
l/c	**letter of credit,** carta de crédito
led.	**ledger,** livro-razão
Ltd	**Limited,** Limitada, Ltda., Lt.^{da}
m	**1. metre,** *N.Am:* **meter,** metro, m **2. month,** mês, m
m/a	**my account,** minha conta, m/c
Mar.	**March,** março
max.	**maximum,** máximo
memo.	**memorandum,** memorando
min.	**minimum,** mínimo
MO	**1. mail order (business),** venda pelo correio **2. money order,** vale postal
m/o	**my order,** minha ordem, m/o
Mon.	**Monday,** segunda-feira
mortg.	**mortgage,** hipoteca
mpg	**miles per gallon,** milhas por galão
MS	**manuscript,** manuscrito, ms.
M/U	**making-up price,** taxa de compensação
n.	**1. name,** nome, n. **2. nominal,** nominal
NB	**nota bene,** note bem, N.B.
n.c.v.	**no commercial value,** sem valor comercial
NF, N/F	**no funds,** sem fundos
no.	**number,** número, num., n.°, n.
nos	**numbers,** números, n.^{os}
Nov.	**November,** novembro, no., nov.°
NRT	**net register ton,** tonelada de arqueação líquida
n.s.f.	**not sufficient funds,** insuficiência de fundos
Oct.	**October,** outubro, out., out.°
o/d., O/D	**1. on demand,** à vista **2. overdrawn,** a descoberto; **overdraft,** saque a descoberto
o/h	**overheads,** despesas gerais
ono., O.N.O.	**or near(est) offer,** ou melhor oferta
o.p.	**out of print,** esgotado
o.s.	**out of stock,** esgotado
OT	**overtime,** horas extraordinárias
Our ref.	**our reference,** nossa referência, n/referência
oz	**ounce,** onça
p	**1. penny, pence,** pêni, penies, p **2. page,** página, p.
p.a.	**1. per annum,** por ano **2. particular average,** avaria particular
p&p	**postage and packing,** porte e embalagem
pat.	**patent,** patente
pat. pend.	**patent pending,** patente solicitada
pc.	**1. per cent,** por cento **2. petty cash,** caixa pequena **3. price current,** preço corrente
pd	**paid,** pago, pg.
PG	**paying guest,** pensionista

266

pkg.	1. **package,** pacote 2. **packing,** embalagem
pkt	**packet,** pacote, maço
PLC, Plc, plc	**Public Limited Company** = sociedade anônima de capital aberto
PN, P/N	**promissory note,** nota promissória
PO	**postal order,** vale postal
p.p.	1. **per procurationem,** por procuração, p.p. 2. **prepaid,** (porte) pago
pp.	**pages,** páginas, pp.
pr.	**price,** preço
pref.	**preference,** (ação) preferencial
prox.	**proximo,** próximo
PS	**postscript,** pós-escrito, P.S.
pt	1. **payment,** pagamento 2. **pint,** quartilho
p.v.	**par value,** valor ao par
qnty, qty	**quantity,** quantidade
qt	**quart** = 2 quartilhos
qtr	1. **quarter,** quarto 2. **quarterly,** trimestral
rcvd	**received,** recebido, rec.º
RD	**refer(red) to drawer,** (cheque) devolvido por insuficiência de fundos
rd	**road,** rua, R.
re.	**regarding,** com referência a
red.	**redeemable,** resgatável
ref.	**reference,** referência
regd	**registered,** registrado, reg.º
rly	**railway,** estrada de ferro
RSVP	**please reply,** fineza responder
s.a.e.	**stamped addressed envelope,** envelope selado e sobrescritado
Sat.	**Saturday,** sábado
sec.	**secretary,** secretária, secretário, secr.
Sept.	**September,** setembro, set.º
sgd	**signed,** assinado
sh., shr.	**share,** ação
sit.	**situation,** emprego; **sits. vac.,** ofertas de emprego
Snr	**senior,** sênior
s.o.	1. **seller's option,** opção de vendedor 2. **standing order,** ordem bancária permanente
s.o.p.	**standard operating procedure,** procedimento operacional standard
St	**street,** rua, R.
ster.	**sterling,** libra esterlina
stk	**stock,** 1. título, tít., valor 2. estoque
Sun.	**Sunday,** domingo
t.	1. **tare,** tara, T. 2. **ton,** tonelada, t
TA	**telegraphic address,** endereço telegráfico, End. tel.
tel.	**telephone,** telefone, tel.; **tel. no., telephone number,** número de telefone
temp.	**temporary secretary,** secretária temporária
Thurs.	**Thursday,** quinta-feira
tr.	**transfer,** transferência
TT	**telegraphic transfer,** transferência telegráfica
Tues.	**Tuesday,** terça-feira

267

Tx	**Telex**, Telex
ult.	**ultimo**, (mês) passado
u.s.c.	**under separate cover**, (enviado) separadamente
U/W	**underwriter**, segurador
vo.	**verso**, verso, v.$^{\circ}$
WB	**waybill**, guia
w.c.	**without charge**, grátis
Wed.	**Wednesday**, quarta-feira
wt	**weight**, peso
xc.	**ex coupon**, ex cupão, ex cupom
xd.	**ex dividend**, ex dividendo
Your ref.	**your reference**, sua referência, s/referência
yr	**1. year**, ano **2. your**, seu(s), sua(s), s/
&	**ampersand**, nome do símbolo **&**
@	**at**, a
©	**copyright**, direitos reservados
®	**registered trademark**, marca registrada
%	**per cent**, por cento

English abbreviations and acronyms
Abreviaturas e siglas inglesas

AA	Automobile Association
AAA	American Association of Advertising Agencies
AAIA	Associate of the Association of International Accountants
ABAA	Associate of the British Association of Accountants and Auditors
ABIM	Associate of the British Institute of Management
ABTA	Association of British Travel Agents
ACA	Associate of the Institute of Chartered Accountants in England and Wales (or Ireland)
ACAS	Advisory, Conciliation and Arbitration Service
ACCA	Associate of the Association of Certified Accountants
ACGI	Associate of the City and Guilds of London Institute
ACII	Associate of the Chartered Insurance Institute
ACIS	Associate of the Institute of Chartered Secretaries and Administrators
ACMA	Associate of the Institute of Cost and Management Accountants
ACPA	Associate of the Institute of Certified Public Accountants
ACRA	Associate of the Corporation of Registered Accountants
ACTU	Australian Council of Trade Unions
ADB	Asian Development Bank
ADG	Assistant Director-General
ADP	Automatic data processing, processamento automático de dados
AEA	American Economic Association
AFE	Authorization for expenditure
AFL-CIO	American Federation of Labor and Congress of Industrial Organizations
AG	1. Accountant-General, contador chefe 2. Attorney-General 3. Agent-General
AGM	Annual General Meeting, Assembléia Geral Ordinária
AIA	1. American Institute of Accountants 2. Associate of the Institute of Actuaries
AIAA	Associate of the Institute of Accountants and Actuaries
AIB	1. Associate of the Institute of Bankers 2. American Institute of Bankers
AIWM	American Institute of Weights and Measures
ALGOL	*Cmptr*: Algorithmic Language
AMEX	American Express Company
ANPA	American Newspaper Publishers' Association
ANSI	American National Standards Institute = Associação Brasileira de Normas Técnicas, ABNT
AO	1. Accounting officer 2. Administration officer
AOB	Any other business
AP	Associated Press
AR	Annual return, rendimento anual
ARAMCO	Arabian–American Oil Company
ARICS	Associate of the Royal Institute of Chartered Surveyors
ASA	1. Advertising Standards Authority 2. American Standards Association
ASE	American Stock Exchange
ASTMS	Association of Scientific, Technical and Managerial Staffs

ATA	*Am*: 1. Air Transport Association 2. American Trucking Association
BA	British Airways
BB	*Am*: Bureau of the Budget
BCom	Bachelor of Commerce
BEcon	Bachelor of Economics
BHRA	British Hotels and Restaurants Association
BID	Bachelor of Industrial Design
BIF	British Industries Fair
BIM	British Institute of Management
BIS	Bank for International Settlements
BL	British Leyland
B LL	Bachelor of Laws
BNOC	British National Oil Corporation
B of E	Bank of England
BP	British Petroleum
BR	British Rail
BRS	British Road Services
BSBA	Bachelor of Science in Business Administration
BSc	Bachelor of Science
BSC	British Steel Corporation
BSCP	British Standard Code of Practice
BSI	British Standards Institution = Associação Brasileira de Normas Técnicas, ABNT
BSIR	Bachelor of Science in Industrial Relations
BSS	British Standard Specification
BST	1. British Summer Time, hora de verão do Reino Unido 2. British Standard Time, hora legal do Reino Unido
BTA	British Travel Association
BUPA	British United Provident Association
CA	1. Chartered Accountant / *Am*: Certified Accountant, perito-contador 2. Consumers' Association
CAC	*Am*: Consumers' Advisory Council
CAP	1. Common Agricultural Policy, Política Agrícola Comum 2. Code of advertising practice
CARICOM	Caribbean Common Market
CARIFTA	Caribbean Free Trade Area
CBI	Confederation of British Industry
CC	Chamber of Commerce
CCA	Current cost accounting
CCC	Canadian Chamber of Commerce
CED	Committee for Economic Development
CEEC	Council for European Economic Co-operation
CEGB	Central Electricity Generating Board
CEO	Chief Executive Officer
CGI	City and Guilds Institute
CIA	*Am*: Certified Industrial Accountant
CICA	Canadian Institute of Chartered Accountants
CII	Chartered Insurance Institute
CIO	*Am*: Congress of Industrial Organizations
CIS	Institute of Charted Secretaries and Administrators

CITB	Construction Industry Training Board
CM	**Common Market,** Mercado Comum
COBOL	*Cmptr*: **Common Business Oriented Language**
COD	**Cash on delivery** / *N.Am*: **collect on delivery,** pagamento contra entrega
COI	**Central Office of Information**
COMECON	**Council for Mutual Economic Aid,** Conselho de Assistência Mútua
COSIRA	**Council for Small Industries in Rural Areas**
CPA	*N.Am*: **Certified Public Accountant** = perito-contador
CPI	**Consumer Price Index**
CPM	**Critical Path Method,** Método de análise pelo caminho crítico
CPR	**Canadian Pacific Railway**
CS	**Civil Service**
CSC	**Civil Service Commission**
CSE	**Certificate of Secondary Education**
CWS	**Co-operative Wholesale Society**
DA	*Am*: **District Attorney**
DAP	**Documents against payment,** documentos contra entrega
DCF	**Discounted cash flow**
DCom	**Doctor of Commerce**
DComL	**Doctor of Commercial Law**
DDD	*N.Am*: **Direct distance dialing,** discagem direta à distância, DDD
DEcon	**Doctor of Economics**
DHSS	**Department of Health and Social Security**
DIM	**Diploma in Industrial Management**
DipCom	**Diploma of Commerce**
DipEcon	**Diploma of Economics**
DipPA	**Diploma of Public Administration**
DipTech	**Diploma in Technology**
DPP	**Director of Public Prosecutions**
DPR	**Director of Public Relations,** Diretor de Relações Públicas
EAAA	**European Association of Advertising Agencies**
E & OE	**Errors and omissions excepted,** salvo erro ou omissão
ECA	**Economic Commission for Africa**
ECAFE	**Economic Commission for Asia and the Far East**
ECE	**Economic Commission for Europe,** Comissão Econômica para a Europa
ECU	**European currency unit,** Unidade monetária européia, UME
ECWA	**European Commission for Western Asia**
EDP	**Electronic data processing**
EEA	**Exchange Equalization Account**
EEC	**European Economic Community,** Comunidade Econômica Européia, CEE
EEOC	**Equal Employment Opportunities Commission**
EFTA	**European Free Trade Association,** Associação Européia de Livre-Comércio
EGM	**Extraordinary general meeting,** Assembléia Geral Extraordinária
EIB	**European Investment Bank,** Banco Europeu de Investimentos
ELDO	**European Space Vehicle Launcher Development Organization**
EMA	**European Monetary Agreement,** Acordo Monetário Europeu
EMS	**European Monetary System,** Sistema Monetário Europeu
EPU	**European Payments Union,** União Européia de Pagamentos
ERNIE	**Electronic Random Number Indicator Equipment**

ETA	Estimated time of arrival
ETO	European Transport Organization
EURATOM, Euratom	European Atomic Energy Community
EUROCONTROL	European Organization for the Safety of Air Navigation
EXIMBANK	Export and Import Bank (U.S.), Banco de Exportação e Importação dos Estados Unidos
FAO	Food and Agriculture Organization, Organização para Alimentação e Agricultura
FBAA	Fellow of the British Association of Accountants and Auditors
FBCS	Fellow of the British Computer Society
FBIM	Fellow of the British Institute of Management
FCA	Fellow of the Institute of Chartered Accountants in England and Wales (or Ireland)
FCCA	Fellow of the Association of Certified Accountants
FCGI	Fellow of the City and Guilds of London Institute
FCI	Fellow of the Institute of Commerce
FCIA	Fellow of the Corporation of Insurance Agents
FCII	Fellow of the Chartered Insurance Institute
FCIS	Fellow of the Institute of Chartered Secretaries and Administrators
FCMA	Fellow of the Institute of Cost and Management Accountants
FDA	*Am*: Food and Drug Administration
FIA	Fellow of the Institute of Actuaries
FIAC	Fellow of the Institute of Company Accountants
FIB	Fellow of the Institute of Bankers
FIPM	Fellow of the Institute of Personnel Management
FOB	Free on board
FORTRAN	*Cmptr*: Formula Translation
FRICS	Fellow of the Royal Institute of Chartered Surveyors
FSVA	Fellow of the Incorporated Society of Valuers and Auctioneers
FT	Financial Times
FTC	*Am*: Federal Trade Commission, Comissão de Comércio Federal
GAO	General Accounting Officer
GATT	General Agreement on Tariffs and Trade, Acordo Geral sobre Tarifas e Comércio
GCE	General Certificate of Education
GMT	Greenwich Mean Time, tempo universal
GMWU	General and Municipal Workers' Union
GNI	Gross National Income, Renda Nacional Bruta
GNP	Gross National Product, Produto Nacional Bruto (PNB)
HEW	*Am*: Department of Health, Education and Welfare
HGV	Heavy goods vehicle
HMSO	His/Her Majesty's Stationery Office
HNC	Higher National Certificate
HND	Higher National Diploma
HST	High speed train
IAF	International Automobile Federation
IAM	Institute of Administrative Management
IATA	International Air Transport Assocation, Associação Internacional de Transportes Aéreos

272

IBEC	**International Bank for Economic Co-operation,** Banco Internacional para Cooperação Econômica
IBM	**International Business Machines**
IBRD	**International Bank for Reconstruction and Development,** Banco Internacional para Reconstrução e Desenvolvimento, BIRD
ICA	**Institute of Chartered Accountants**
ICAO	**International Civil Aviation Authority Organization**
ICC	**International Chamber of Commerce**
ICI	**Imperial Chemical Industries**
ICMA	**Institute of Cost and Management Accountants**
IDD	**International Direct Dialling,** discagem direta internacional, DDI
IFC	**International Finance Corporation,** Corporação Financeira Internacional
IFTU	**International Federation of Trade Unions**
ILO	**International Labour Organization,** Organização Internacional do Trabalho, OIT
IMF	**International Monetary Fund,** Fundo Monetário Internacional, FMI
IOB	**1. Institute of Bankers 2. Institute of Book-keepers**
IOM	**Institute of Office Management**
IPM	**Institute of Personnel Management**
IPR	**Institute of Public Relations**
IR	**Inland Revenue**
IRS	*N.Am*: **Internal Revenue Service**
ISBN	**International Standard Book Number**
ISC	**International Sugar Council,** Conselho Internacional do Açucar
ISFA	**Institute of Shipping and Forwarding Agents**
ISO	**International Standards Organization**
ITO	**International Trade Organization,** Organização Internacional do Comércio
JAL	**Japan Airlines**
JP	**Justice of the Peace**
KAL	**Korean Airlines**
KLM	**Royal Dutch Airlines**
LAFTA	**Latin American Free Trade Association,** Associação Latino-Americana de Livre-Comércio (ALALC)
LC	**Library of Congress**
LL B	**Bachelor of Laws**
LL D	**Doctor of Laws**
LR	**Lloyd's Register**
LSE	**1. London Stock Exchange 2. London School of Economics**
LV	**Luncheon Voucher**
MBIM	**Member of the British Institute of Management**
MBO	**Management by objectives**
MCom	**Master of Commerce**
MD	**Managing Director**
MEcon	**Master of Economics**
MIS	**Management Information System**
MLR	**Minimum Lending Rate**
MMB	**Milk Marketing Board**
MRP	**Manufacturer's recommended price**
MSc	**Master of Science**

NALGO, Nalgo	National and Local Government Officers' Association
NASA	National Aeronautics and Space Administration
NATO, Nato	North Atlantic Treaty Organization, Organização do Tratado do Atlântico Norte
NC	National Carriers
NEB	National Enterprise Board
NEC	National executive committee
NEDC (also Neddy)	National Economic Development Council
NHS	National Health Service
NI	National Insurance
NPA	Newspaper Publishers' Association
NSB	National Savings Bank = Caixa Econômica
NUPE	National Union of Public Employees
NYSE	New York Stock Exchange
O & M	Organization and Methods
OAP	Old age pensioner
OECD	Organization for Economic Co-operation and Development, Organização para Cooperação e Desenvolvimento Econômico, OCDE
OHMS	On His/Her Majesty's Service
OIT	Office of International Trade
OPEC	Organization of Petroleum Exporting Countries, Organização dos Paises Exportadores de Petróleo, OPEP
OR	Operational research
PA	1. Press Association 2. Publishers Association 3. Personal Assistant 4. Public Address System
PABX	Private automatic branch (telephone) exchange
PAYE	Pay as you earn, imposto deduzido na fonte
PBDS	Publishers and Booksellers Delivery Service
PER	Price–earnings ratio
PERT	Programme, evaluation and review technique
PLA	Port of London Authority
PLR	Public lending right
PMG	1. Postmaster General 2. Paymaster General
PO	Post Office
POB	Post Office Box, Caixa Postal, CP
POP	Post Office Preferred (envelopes)
PPBS	Planning, programming and budgeting system
PPP	Private Patients Plan
PR	Public Relations
PRO	Public Relations Officer
PSBR	Public sector borrowing requirement
PSV	Public Service Vehicle
QANTAS, Qantas	Queensland and Northern Territory Aerial Services
QC	Queen's Counsel
QUANGO, quango	Quasi autonomous non-governmental organization
RE	Royal Exchange
RFD	*Am*: Rural free delivery service
RO	Receiving Office

274

ROI	Return on investment
RPM	Resale/retail price maintenance
RRP	Recommended retail price
RSVP	please reply/answer, fineza responder
SALT	Strategic Arms Limitation Talks
SAS	Scandinavian Airlines System
SAYE	Save as you earn
SDR	Special drawing rights, Direitos Especiais de Saque, DES
SEC	*Am*: Securities and Exchange Commission
SICA	Society of Industrial and Cost Accountants of Canada
STD	Subscriber Trunk Dialling
SWIFT	Society for Worldwide Interbank Financial Telecommunication
TASS	Telegraphic News Agency of the Soviet Union
TGWU	Transport and General Workers' Union
TO	Telegraphic Office
TT	Telegraphic transfer
TU	Trade Union
TUC	Trades Union Congress
TWA	Trans World Airlines
UAW	*Am*: United Automobile Workers
UN	United Nations, Organização das Nações Unidas, ONU
UNCTAD	United Nations Conference on Trade and Development, Conferência das Nações Unidas sobre Comércio e Desenvolvimento
UNDP	United Nations Development Programme, Programa das Nações Unidas para o Desenvolvimento, PNUD
UNIC	United Nations Information Centre, Centro de Informações das Nações Unidas
UNIDO	United Nations Industrial Development Organization, Organização das Nações Unidas para Desenvolvimento Industrial
UNO	United Nations Organization, Organização das Nações Unidas, ONU
UPI	United Press International
UPU	Universal Postal Union, União Postal Universal, UPU
USAID	United States Agency for International Development, Agência dos Estados Unidos para o Desenvolvimento Internacional
USDAW	Union of Shop, Distributive & Allied Workers
USIA	United States Information Agency
USM	1. United States Mint 2. Unlisted Securities Market
USP	Unique selling proposition
USPO	United States Post Office
VAT	Value added tax
VDT	Visual Display Terminal
VDU	Visual Display Unit
VIP	Very important person
WEU	Western European Union
WFP	World Food Program
WFTU	World Federation of Trade Unions
ZIP	*Am*: Zone improvement plan

Countries and currencies
Países e moedas

Country	País	Currency	Moeda
Afghanistan	Afeganistão *m*	Afghani	Afegane *m*
Albania	Albânia *f*	Lek	Lek *m*
Algeria	Argélia *f*	(Algerian) Dinar	Dinar *m* (argelino)
Angola	Angola *f*	(Angolan) Escudo	Escudo *m* (angolano)
Argentina	Argentina *f*	(Argentinian) Peso	Peso *m* (argentino)
Australia	Austrália *f*	(Australian) Dollar	Dólar *m* (australiano)
Austria	Austria *f*	Schilling	Schilling *m*
Bahamas	Bahamas *fpl*	(Bahamian) Dollar	Dólar *m* (bahamense)
Bahrain	Bahrein *m*	Dinar	Dinar *m*
Bangladesh	Bangladesh *m*	Taka	Taka *m*
Barbados	Barbados *mpl*	(Barbados) Dollar	Dólar *m* (barbadiano)
Belgium	Bélgica *f*	(Belgian) Franc	Franco *m* (belga)
Belize	Belize *f*	Dollar	Dólar *m* (da Belize)
Benin	Benim *m*	CFA Franc	Franco *m* (da CFA)
Bermuda	Bermudas *fpl*	Dollar	Dólar *m* (bermudense)
Bolivia	Bolívia *f*	(Bolivian) Peso	Peso *m* (boliviano)
Brazil	Brasil *m*	Cruzeiro	Cruzeiro *m*
Bulgaria	Bulgária *f*	Lev	Lev *m*
Burma	Birmânia *f*	Kyat	Kyat *m*
Burundi	Burundi *m*	(Burundi) Franc	Franco *m* (do Burundi)
Cameroon	Camerum *m*	CFA Franc	Franco *m* (da CFA)
Canada	Canadá *m*	(Canadian) Dollar	Dólar *m* (canadense)
Cape Verde Islands	Cabo Verde *m*	Escudo	Escudo *m*
Cayman Islands	Ilhas Caiman *fpl*	Dollar	Dólar *m*
Central African Republic	República Centro-africana *f*	CFA Franc	Franco *m* (da CFA)
Chad	Chade *m*	CFA Franc	Franco *m* (da CFA)
Chile	Chile *m*	(Chilean) Peso	Peso *m* (chileno)
China	China *f*	Yuan	Yuan *m*
Colombia	Colômbia *f*	(Colombian) Peso	Peso *m* (colombiano)
Congo	Congo *m*	CFA Franc	Franco *m* (da CFA)
Costa Rica	Costa Rica *f*	Colon	Colom *m*
Cuba	Cuba *f*	(Cuban) Peso	Peso *m* (cubano)
Cyprus	Chipre *m*	(Cyprus) Pound	Libra *f* (cipriota)
Czechoslovakia	Tcheco-Eslováquia *f*	Koruna	Coroa *f* (tcheca)
Denmark	Dinamarca *f*	Krone	Coroa *f* (dinamarquesa)
Dominican Republic	República Dominicana *f*	Peso	Peso *m*
Ecuador	Equador *m*	Sucre	Sucre *m*
Egypt	Egito *m*	(Egyptian) Pound	Libra *f* (egípcia)
El Salvador	El Salvador *m*	Colon	Colom *m*
Ethiopia	Etiópia *f*	(Ethiopian) Dollar	Dólar *m* (etiope)

Country	País	Currency	Moeda
Finland	Finlândia f	Markka	Marco m (finlandês)
France	França f	(French) Franc	Franco m (francês)
Gabon	Gabão m	CFA Franc	Franco m (da CFA)
Gambia	Gâmbia f	Dalasi	Dalasi m
Germany (Democratic Republic—GDR)	República Democrática Alemã f	Mark/Ostmark	Marco m oriental
Germany (Federal Republic—GFR)	República Federal da Alemanha f	Mark/Deutschmark	Marco m (alemão)
Ghana	Gana m	Cedi	Cedi m
Gibraltar	Gibraltar m	Pound (sterling)	Libra f (esterlina)
Greece	Grécia f	Drachma	Dracma f
Guatemala	Guatemala f	Quetzal	Quetzal m
Guinea-Bissau	Guiné-Bissau f	Guinean Peso	Peso m (da Guiné-Bissau)
Guinea/Conakry	Guiné-Conacri f	Suli	Suli m
Guyana	Guiana f	(Guyana) Dollar	Dólar m (da Guiana)
Haiti	Haiti m	Gourde	Gourde m
Honduras	Honduras fpl	Lempira	Lempira f
Hong Kong	Hong-Kong m	(Hong Kong) Dollar	Dólar m (de Hong-Kong)
Hungary	Hungria f	Forint	Florim m
Iceland	Islândia f	Krona	Coroa f
India	India f	Rupee	Rupia f
Indonesia	Indonésia f	Rupiah	Rupia f
Iran	Irã m	Rial	Rial m
Iraq	Iraque m	(Iraqi) Dinar	Dinar m (iraquiano)
Ireland	Irlanda f	(Irish) Pound/Punt	Libra f (irlandesa)
Israel	Israel m	(Israeli) Pound	Libra f (israelense)
Italy	Itália f	Lira	Lira f
Ivory Coast	Costa do Marfim f	CFA Franc	Franco m (da CFA)
Jamaica	Jamaica f	(Jamaican) Dollar	Dólar m (jamaicano)
Japan	Japão m	Yen	Iene m
Jordan	Jordânia f	(Jordanian) Dinar	Dinar m (jordaniano)
Kampuchea	Kampuchéia f	Riel	Riel m
Kenya	Quênia m	Shilling	Shilling m (queniano)
Korea (North)	Coréia do Norte f	Won	Won m
Korea (South)	Coréia do Sul f	Won	Won m
Kuwait	Kuwait, Coveite m	(Kuwaiti) Dinar	Dinar m (do Coveite)
Laos	Laos mpl	Kip	Kip m
Lebanon	Líbano m	(Lebanese) Pound	Libra f (libanesa)
Liberia	Libéria f	(Liberian) Dollar	Dólar m (liberiano)
Libya	Líbia f	(Libyan) Dinar	Dinar m (libio)
Liechtenstein	Liechtenstein m	Franc	Franco m (suíço)
Luxembourg	Luxemburgo m	(Luxembourg) Franc	Franco m (do Luxemburgo)
Macao	Macau m	Pataca	Pataca f
Malagasy Republic	República Malgaxe f	(Malagasy) Franc	Franco m (malgaxe)
Malawi	Malaui m	Kwacha	Kuacha m
Malaysia	Malásia f	(Malaysian) Dollar	Dólar m (malasiano)
Mali	Mali m	(Mali) Franc	Franco m (malinês)
Malta	Malta f	(Maltese) Pound	Libra f (de Malta)

Country	País	Currency	Moeda
Mauritania	Mauritânia *f*	CFA Franc	Franco *m* (da CFA)
Mauritius	Maurício *m*	Rupee	Rupia *f*
Mexico	México *m*	Peso	Peso *m* (mexicano)
Mongolia	Mongólia *f*	Tugrik *or* Tughrik	Togrog *m*
Morocco	Marrocos *m*	Dirham	Dirrã *m*
Mozambique	Moçambique *m*	Escudo	Escudo *m* (de Moçambique)
Nepal	Nepal *m*	Rupee	Rupia *f*
The Netherlands	Países Baixos *mpl*	Guilder	Florim *m*
New Zealand	Nova Zelândia *f*	(New Zealand) Dollar	Dólar *m* (neozelandês)
Nicaragua	Nicarágua *f*	Cordoba	Córdoba *f*
Niger	Níger *m*	CFA Franc	Franco *m* (da CFA)
Nigeria	Nigéria *f*	Naira	Naira *m*
Norway	Noruega *f*	Krone	Coroa *f* (norueguesa)
Oman	Omã *m*	Rial (Omani)	Rial *m* (omani)
Pakistan	Paquistão *m*	Rupee	Rupia *f*
Panama	Panamá *m*	Balboa	Balboa *m*
Paraguay	Paraguai *m*	Guarani	Guarani *m*
Peru	Perú *m*	Sol	Sol *m*
Philippines	Filipinas *fpl*	Peso	Peso *m* (filipino)
Poland	Polônia *f*	Zloty	Zloti *m*
Portugal	Portugal *m*	Escudo	Escudo *m*
Qatar	Qatar *m*	Riyal	Rial *m* (de Qatar)
Romania	Romênia *f*	Leu	Leu *m*
Rwanda	Ruanda *f*	(Rwanda) Franc	Franco *m* (ruandês)
Saudi Arabia	Arábia Saudita *f*	Riyal	Rial *m*
Senegal	Senegal *m*	CFA Franc	Franco *m* (da CFA)
Seychelles	Seicheles *fpl*	Rupee	Rúpia *f*
Sierra Leone	Serra-Leoa *f*	Leone	Leone *m*
Singapore	Cingapura *f*	(Singapore) Dollar	Dólar *m* (de Cingapura)
Somalia	Somália *f*	Shilling	Shilling *m* (somálio)
South Africa	Africa do Sul *f*	Rand	Rand *m*
Soviet Union	União Soviética *f*	Rouble	Rublo *m*
Spain	Espanha *f*	Peseta	Peseta *f*
Sri Lanka	Srilanka *m*	(Sinhalese) Rupee	Rupia *f* (cingalesa)
Sudan	Sudão *m*	(Sudanese) Pound	Libra *f* (sudanesa)
Surinam	Surinã *m*	Guilder	Florim *m*
Sweden	Suécia *f*	Krona	Coroa *f*
Switzerland	Suíça *f*	(Swiss) Franc	Franco *m* (suíço)
Syria	Síria *f*	(Syrian) Pound	Libra *f* (síria)
Taiwan	Taiwan *m*	(Tiawan) Dollar	Dólar *m* (do Taiwan)
Tanzania	Tanzânia *f*	Shilling	Shilling *m* (tanzânio)
Thailand	Tailândia *f*	Baht	Baht *m*
Togo	Togo *m*	CFA Franc	Franco *m* (da CFA)
Tunisia	Tunísia *f*	Dinar	Dinar *m* (tunisino)
Turkey	Turquia *f*	(Turkish) Lira	Lira *f* (turca)
Uganda	Uganda *f*	Shilling	Shilling *m* (ugandense)
United Arab Emirates	União dos Emirados Árabes *f*	Dirham	Dirrã *m*

Country	País	Currency	Moeda
United Kingdom / UK	Reino Unido *m*	Pound (sterling)	Libra *f* (esterlina)
United States of America / USA	Estados Unidos *mpl* da América / EUA	(US) Dollar	Dólar *m*
Upper Volta	Alto Volta *m*	CFA Franc	Franco *m* (da CFA)
Uruguay	Uruguai *m*	Peso	Peso *m* (uruguaio)
Venezuela	Venezuela *f*	Bolivar	Bolívar *m*
Vietnam	Vietnam *m*	Dong	Dong *m*
Yemen (North)	Iêmen *m*	(Yemeni) Riyal	Rial *m*
Yemen (South)	Iêmen do Sul *m*	Dinar	Dinar *m* (iemenita)
Yugoslavia	Iugoslávia *f*	Dinar	Dinar *m*
Zaïre	Zaire *m*	Zaïre	Zaire *m*
Zambia	Zâmbia *m*	Kwacha	Kuacha *m*
Zimbabwe	Zimbabue *m*	Zimbabwe Dollar	Dólar *m* (do Zimbabue)

CFA Franc / Franco da CFA = Franco da Comunidade Financeira Africana

279

World time zones
Fusos horários

GMT = 1200 hours/horas

	Hours/ Horas		Hours/ Horas
Adelaide	2130	Luxembourg/Luxemburgo	1300
Algiers/Argel	1300	Madeira	1100
Amsterdam/Amsterdã	1300	Madrid/Madri	1300
Ankara/Ancara	1400	Malta	1300
Athens/Atenas	1400	Mexico City/Cidade do México	0600
Beirut/Beirute	1400	Montevideo/Montevidéo	0830
Belgrade/Belgrado	1400	Montreal	0700
Berlin/Berlim	1300	Moscow/Moscou	1500
Berne/Berna	1300	Nairobi	1500
Bombay/Bombaim	1300	New Orleans/Nova Orleans	0600
Bonn	1730	New York/Nova Iorque	0700
Brasilia/Brasília	0900	Oslo	1300
Brisbane	2200	Ottawa	0700
Brussels/Bruxelas	1300	Panama/Panamá	0700
Bucharest/Bucareste	1400	Paris	1300
Budapest/Budapeste	1300	Peking/Pequim	2000
Buenos Aires	0800	Perth (Austr.)	2000
Cairo	1400	Prague/Praga	1300
Calcutta/Calcutá	1730	Pretoria/Pretória	1400
Cape Town/Cidade do Cabo	1400	Quebec	0700
Caracas	0800	Rangoon	1830
Chicago	0600	Rio de Janeiro	0900
Colombo	1730	Riyadh/Riad	1500
Copenhagen/Copenhague	1100	St Louis (USA)	0600
Delhi	1730	San Francisco/São Francisco	0400
Dubai	1600	Santiago	0800
Dublin/Dublim	1200	Singapore/Singapura	1930
Gibraltar	1300	Stockholm/Estocolmo	1300
Helsinki/Helsinque	1400	Suez	1400
Hobart	2200	Sydney/Sidnei	2200
Hong Kong/Hong-Kong	2000	Tehran/Teerã	1500
Istanbul	1400	Tokyo/Tóquio	2100
Jerusalem/Jerusalém	1400	Toronto	0700
Kuwait City/Kuwait, Coveite	1500	Tunis/Túnis	1300
Lagos	1300	Vancouver	0400
Leningrad/Leningrado	1500	Vienna/Viena	1300
Lima	0700	Warsaw/Varsóvia	1300
Lisbon/Lisboa	1300	Wellington (NZ)	2400
London/Londres	1200		

Weights and measures
Pesos e medidas

Metric measures—
Medidas métricas

Length—Comprimento

1 milímetro (mm)		= 0.0394 in
1 centímetro (cm)	= 10 mm	= 0.3937 in
1 metro (m)	= 100 cm	= 1.0936 yds
1 quilômetro (km)	= 1000 m	= 0.6214 mile

Weight—Peso

1 miligrama (mg)		= 0.0154 grain
1 grama (g)	= 1000 mg	= 0.0353 oz
1 quilograma (kg)	= 1000 g	= 2.2046 lb
1 tonelada (t)	= 1000 kg	= 0.9842 ton

Area—Superfície

1 cm^2	= 100 mm^2	= 0.1550 sq. in
1 m^2	= 10 000 cm^2	= 1.1960 sq. yds
1 are (a)	= 100 m^2	= 119.60 sq. yds
1 hectare (ha)	= 100 ares	= 2.4711 acres
1 km^2	= 100 hectares	= 0.3861 sq.mile

Capacity—Capacidade

1 cm^3		= 0.0610 cu. in
1 dm^3	= 1000 cm^3	= 0.0351 cu. ft
1 m^3	= 1000 dm^3	= 1.3080 cu. yds
1 litro	= 1 dm^3	= 0.2200 gallon
1 hectolitro	= 100 litres	= 2.7497 bushels

Imperial measures—
Medidas inglesas

Length—Comprimento

1 inch (polegada)		= 2,54 cm
1 foot (pé)	= 12 inches	= 0,3048 m
1 yard (jarda)	= 3 feet	= 0,9144 m
1 furlong	= 220 yards	= 201,17 m
1 mile	= 1760 yards	= 1,6093 km
1 nautical mile	= 6080 feet	= 1,8532 km

Weight—Peso

1 ounce (onça)	= 437.5 grains	= 28,350 g
1 pound (libra)	= 16 ounces	= 0,4536 kg
1 stone	= 14 pounds	= 6,3503 kg
1 hundredweight	= 112 pounds	= 50,802 kg
1 ton	= 20 cwt	= 1,0161 toneladas

Area—Superfície

1 sq. in		= 6,4516 cm^2
1 sq. foot	= 144 sq. ins	= 0,0929 m^2
1 sq. yd	= 9 sq. ft	= 0,8361 m^2
1 acre	= 4840 sq. yds	= 4046,9 m^2
1 sq. mile	= 640 acres	= 259,0 hectares

Capacity—Capacidade

1 cu. inch		= 16,387 cm^3
1 cu. foot	= 1728 cu. ins	= 0,0283 m^3
1 cu. yard	= 27 cu. ft	= 0,7646 m^3
1 pint	= 4 gills	= 0,5683 litro
1 quart	= 2 pints	= 1,1365 litros
1 gallon	= 8 pints	= 4,5461 litros
1 bushel	= 8 gallons	= 36,369 litros
1 fluid ounce	= 8 fl. drachms	= 28,413 cm^3
1 pint	= 20 fl. oz	= 568,26 cm^3

US: Dry Measures—
Medidas EUA para secos

1 pint	= 0.9689 UK pt	= 0,5506 litro
1 bushel	= 0.9689 UK bu	= 35,238 litros

US: Liquid Measures—
Medidas EUA para líquidos

1 fluid ounce	= 1.0408 UK fl oz	= 0,0296 litro
1 pint (16 oz)	= 0.8327 UK pt	= 0,4732 litro
1 gallon	= 0.8327 UK gal	= 3,7853 litros

Conversion tables
Tabelas de conversão

Length/Comprimento

Weight/Peso

centímetros	cm or inches	inches (polegadas)	quilogramas	kg or pounds	pounds (libras)
2,54	1	0.39	0,45	1	2.20
5,08	2	0.79	0,91	2	4.41
7,62	3	1.18	1,36	3	6.61
10,16	4	1.58	1,81	4	8.82
12,70	5	1.97	2,27	5	11.02
15,24	6	2.36	2,72	6	13.23
17,78	7	2.76	3,18	7	15.43
20,32	8	3.15	3,63	8	17.64
22,86	9	3.54	4,08	9	19.84
25,40	10	3.94	4,54	10	22.05
50,80	20	7.87	9,07	20	44.09
76,20	30	11.81	13,61	30	66.14
101,60	40	15.75	18,14	40	88.19
127,00	50	19.69	22,68	50	110.23
152,40	60	23.62	27,22	60	132.28
177,80	70	27.56	31,75	70	154.32
203,20	80	31.50	36,29	80	176.37
228,60	90	35.43	40,82	90	198.41
254,00	100	39.37	45,36	100	220.46

quilómetros	km or miles	miles (milhas)	toneladas	toneladas or tons	tons
1,61	1	0.62	1,02	1	0.98
3,22	2	1.24	2,03	2	1.97
4,83	3	1.86	3,05	3	2.95
6,44	4	2.49	4,06	4	3.94
8,05	5	3.11	5,08	5	4.92
9,66	6	3.73	6,10	6	5.91
11,27	7	4.35	7,11	7	6.89
12,88	8	4.97	8,13	8	7.87
14,48	9	5.59	9,14	9	8.86
16,09	10	6.21	10,16	10	9.84
32,19	20	12.43	20,32	20	19.68
48,28	30	18.64	30,48	30	29.53
64,37	40	24.86	40,64	40	39.37
80,47	50	31.07	50,80	50	49.21
96,56	60	37.28	60,96	60	59.05
112,65	70	43.50	71,12	70	68.89
128,75	80	49.71	81,28	80	78.74
144,84	90	55.92	91,44	90	88.58
160,93	100	62.14	101,60	100	98.42

Area/Superfície

hectares	hectares or acres	acres
0,41	1	2.47
0,81	2	4.94
1,21	3	7.41
1,62	4	9.88
2,02	5	12.36
2,43	6	14.83
2,83	7	17.30
3,24	8	19.77
3,64	9	22.24
4,05	10	24.71
8,09	20	49.42
12,14	30	74.13
16,19	40	98.84
20,23	50	123.56
24,28	60	148.27
28,33	70	172.98
32,38	80	197.69
36,42	90	222.40
40,47	100	247.11

Capacity/Volume

litros	litros or gallons	gallons
4,55	1	0.22
9,09	2	0.44
13,64	3	0.66
18,18	4	0.88
22,73	5	1.10
27,28	6	1.32
31,82	7	1.54
36,37	8	1.76
40,91	9	1.98
45,46	10	2.20
90,92	20	4.40
136,38	30	6.60
181,84	40	8.80
227,31	50	11.00
272,77	60	13.20
318,23	70	15.40
363,69	80	17.60
409,15	90	19.80
454,61	100	22,00

Speed—Velocidade

MPH	20	30	40	50	60	70	80	90	100 ($\times 8/5$)
KMPH	32	48	64	80	96	112	128	144	160 ($\times 5/8$)

Temperature—Temperatura

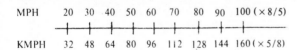

Centigrado
$-18°$ -10 0 10 20 30 40°

0° 10 20 32 40 50 60 70 80 90 100 110°
Fahrenheit

$$C = \frac{5}{9}(F - 32) \qquad F = \frac{9}{5}(C + 32)$$

283

Banco do Brasil

Analysis of Financial Position

Análise das Demonstrações Financeiras

Liabilities

IN 1981, there were only minor changes in the structure of liabilities. Shareholders' equity, as a percentage of total liabilities improved from 8.9% in 1980 to 10.4% in the last fiscal year.

Deposits (demand — Cr$ 671.3 billion, and time — Cr$ 92.1 billion), which represent one of the Bank's major sources of funds, totalled Cr$ 763.4 billion, thus registering a growth of 75.7% in comparison with the previous year.

In 1981, amounts due to correspondent banks and branches grew by 86.5%.

Short and long-term funds borrowed totalled Cr$ 741.7 billion, a growth of 87.1%. They include funds taken locally and abroad.

Sundry Commitments (short and long-term), comprising 58% of total liabilities utilized by the Bank, increased by 108.2%, to Cr$ 3,079.5 billion. They represent the Bank's commitment to the development of priority areas and underline its role as the main financial agent for the Government. The total is mainly composed of a Central Bank special account (Cr$ 1,155.2 billion), other foreign currency payables (Cr$ 889.3 billion), other local currency payables (Cr$ 547.5 billion) and operations for account of the Central Bank (Cr$ 158.5 billion).

LIABILITIES	Cr$ millions	Breakdown (%)
CURRENT AND LONG-TERM	4,761,060	89.7
Deposits	763,407	14.4
Interbank and Interbranch Accounts	142,685	2.7
Funds Borrowed	741,678	14.0
Taxes Collected	33.783	0.6
Other	3,079,507	58.0
Shareholders' Equity	549,720	10.3
Capital Stock	88,128	1.7
Capital Reserves	140,151	2.6
Revaluation Reserves	16,367	0.3
Income Reserves	96,071	1.8
Retained Earnings	209,003	3.9
TOTAL	5,310,780	100.0

At year-end, shareholders' equity (Cr$ 549.7 billion) registered a growth of 134.5%, an expansion significantly greater than the rate of inflation in 1981. Consequently, the equity value of each share of the Bank's capital stock rose to Cr$ 18.71.

The capital stock of Cr$ 88.1 billion is represented by 29,376 million shares, of which 16,470.4 million are ordinary nominal shares and 12,905.6 million are preference bearer shares. It was increased by Cr$ 29,376 million, at the General Shareholders' Meeting held on 28th April 1981, through the incorporation of the monetary correction for 1980. The resolution to incorporate monetary correction for 1981, of Cr$ 85.114 million, will be passed at the General Shareholders' Meeting in 1982.

Revaluation reserves (Cr$ 16.4 billion) increased by 273.5%, as a consequence of monetary correction and the revaluation of the reserves of the Bank's subsidiaries.

Income reserves (Cr$ 96.1 billion) increased by 118.2%, owing to monetary correction and a transfer from retained earnings. Retained earnings reached Cr$ 209 billion, a growth of 186.9%, caused primarily by monetary correction and the retention of a proportion of profits made, in order to strengthen the Bank's capital base with internally generated resources.

Assets

At the close of the year under review the Bank's domestic assets totalled Cr$ 5.3 trillion, a growth of 101.1% over the 1980 figure.

Current and long-term assets accounted for 95.9% of total assets, while permanent assets represented only 4.1% of the total.

The cash balance closed at a figure of Cr$ 77.7 billion, made up of Cr$ 75.4 billion held with the Central Bank and Cr$ 2.3 billion in available cash.

In line with restrictive policies adopted by the Government, credit operations (Cr$ 2,071.4 billion, or 39% of total assets) expanded by only 70.8%.

The account titles of credit operations used in the Bank's balance sheet are in accordance with the norms laid down by the Accounting Plan for Commercial Banks (COBAN), which, as regards loans, differ from the criteria established by the Monetary Budget.

Although considered a liability, provision for bad debts (Cr$ 46.9 billion) is recorded under assets as a deduction from loans. Growth was only 5%, as a consequence of restrictions imposed by Ministry of Finance Directive no. 241.

Loans past due, totalling Cr$ 42.6 billion, represent 2.1% of total credit operations. Although they represent a small percentage of total loans, the Bank is striving to recover such debts.

Passivo

A estrutura do *Passivo* praticamente apresentou mesma regularidade de anos anteriores. Os recursos próprios, registrados no *Patrimônio Líquido*, melhoram sua participação, evoluindo de 8,9% em 1980 para 10,4%.

Os *Depósitos*, uma das mais importantes fontes de recursos para o Banco, somaram Cr$ 763,4 bilhões + 75,7%). Não obstante o expressivo avanço registrado nas contas a prazo — atingiram Cr$ 92,1 bilhões, ultrapassando em 15,2% a meta de captação de Cr$ 80 bilhões —, os depósitos continuam constituídos principalmente da modalidade à vista (87,9%), montante de Cr$ 671,3 bilhões.

O grupamento *Relações Interbancárias e Interdepartamentais*, que reúne as contas de movimento das agências entre si e com correspondentes, cresceu 6,5%.

Englobando aprovisionamentos, repasses, refinanciamentos oficiais, fundos administrados pelo Banco e financiamentos contraídos no exterior, o item *Obrigações por Empréstimos* totalizou Cr$ 741,7 bilhões, incremento de 87,1%.

Grupamento de maior peso (58%) entre os recursos movimentados pelo Banco do Brasil, *Outras Obrigações* apresentou crescimento de 108,2%, atingindo Cr$ 3.079,5 bilhões. Tais rubricas caracterizam as atividades de fomento e de agente financeiro do governo. Destacam-se a Conta de Movimento do Banco Central (Cr$ 1.155,2 bilhões), Obrigações Diversas, em Moedas Estrangeiras (Cr$ 889,3 bilhões), Obrigações Diversas em Moeda Nacional (Cr$ 547,5 bilhões) e recursos para as Operações de Conta do Banco Central (Cr$ 158,5 bilhões).

PASSIVO	Cr$ milhões	Composição (%)
CIRCULANTE E EXIGÍVEL A LONGO PRAZO	4.761.060	89,7
Depósitos	763.407	14,4
Relações interbancárias e Interdepartamentais	142.685	2,7
Obrigações por Empréstimos	741.678	14,0
Obrigações por Recebimentos - Tributos e Encargos Sociais	33.783	0,6
Outras Obrigações	3.079.507	58,0
PATRIMÔNIO LÍQUIDO	549.720	10,3
Capital Social	88.128	1,7
Reservas de Capital	140.151	2,6
Reservas de Reavaliação	16.367	0,3
Reservas e Retenção de Lucros	96.071	1,8
Lucros Acumulados	209.003	3,9
TOTAL	5.310.780	100,0

O *Patrimônio Líquido* (Cr$ 549,7 bilhões) apresentou no final de dezembro de 1981 incremento de 134,5%, bastante superior ao índice de inflação no ano (95,2%). Em decorrência, o valor patrimonial de cada ação do Banco chegou a Cr$ 18,71.

O *Capital Social* de Cr$ 88,1 bilhões está representado por 29.376 milhões de ações, 16.470,4 milhões ordinárias nominativas e 12.905,6 milhões preferenciais ao portador. Foi elevado de Cr$ 29.376 milhões, na Assembléia Geral realizada em 28.4.81, mediante incorporação da correção monetária relativa ao ano de 1980. A correção relativa ao exercício de 1981, no montante de Cr$ 85.114 milhões, será incorporada ao capital na Assembléia Geral Ordinária de 1982.

As *Reservas de Reavaliação* (Cr$ 16,4 bilhões) apresentaram crescimento de 273,5%, em função da correção monetária e de ajustamentos nos saldos de reservas de igual natureza nas sociedades controladas.

As *Reservas e Retenção de Lucros* (Cr$ 96,1 bilhões) elevaram-se em 118,2%, devido à correção do saldo anterior e contabilização de lucros de exercícios anteriores.

O total dos *Lucros Acumulados* chegou a Cr$ 209 bilhões (+ 186,9%), especialmente em razão da correção monetária do saldo inicial e da manutenção de parcelas dos lucros apurados, visando maior capitalização do Banco, com recursos gerados internamente.

Ativo

O *Ativo* do Banco no País alcançou a expressiva cifra de Cr$ 5,3 trilhões, contra Cr$ 2,6 trilhões em 1980.

O grupamento *Circulante e Realizável a Longo Prazo*, que representa a quase totalidade das aplicações, participou com 95,9%, ficando o *Permanente* com apenas 4,1% do total.

As *Disponibilidades* fecharam o exercício com Cr$ 77,7 bilhões: Cr$ 75,4 bilhões de Reservas Bancárias junto ao Banco Central e Cr$ 2,3 bilhões de Caixa.

Com Cr$ 2.071,4 bilhões, ou 39% do *Ativo*, as *Operações de Crédito* tiveram evolução de 70,8% no exercício, coerente com a política contracionista adotada pelo governo.

Os empréstimos e financiamentos constantes do balanço, classificados segundo as normas do Plano Contábil dos Bancos Comerciais — COBAN, diferem dos empréstimos classificados segundo o conceito do Orçamento Monetário, cuja metodologia abrange algumas rubricas inseridas em *Créditos Diversos*.

A Provisão para Créditos de Liquidação Duvidosa (Cr$ 46,9 bilhões), embora de natureza credora, aparece no *Ativo* de forma dedutiva dos empréstimos. Em relação a dezembro de 1980, o incremento foi de apenas 5%, em decorrência da alteração introduzida pela Portaria 241 do Ministério da Fazenda.

Os *Créditos em Liquidação*, no valor de Cr$ 42,6 bilhões, representam 2,1% das Operações de Crédito. Apesar de inexpressivo o percentual desses haveres, o Banco vem empreendendo esforço concentrado para sua recuperação.

ASSETS	Cr$ millions	Breakdown (%)
CURRENT AND		
LONG-TERM	5,091,778	95.9
Cash	77,730	1.5
Credit Operations (*)	2,054,257	38.7
Interbank and Interbranch		
Accounts	351,389	6.6
Sundry Receivables	2,598,853	48.9
Securities and Other		
Assets	9,075	0.2
Prepaid Expenses	474	0.0
PERMANENT	219,002	4.1
Investments	112,867	2.1
Fixed	104,869	2.0
Deferred Charges	1,266	0.0
TOTAL	**5,310,780**	**100.0**

(*) Includes Loans Past Due less Provision for Bad Debts and Unappropriated Income.

Sundry receivables increased by 117.3%, to an amount of Cr$ 2,598.9 billion. This heading includes operations for the account of the National Treasury, particularly concerning payments for wheat and oil, advances on foreign exchange contracts and the application of resources from PASEP, a trust fund for public employees.

Securities form a small part of total assets, although increasing by 83.1%. This comprises the purchase of federal and state securities.

Permanent assets totalled Cr$ 219 billion, an increase of 113.3% over the figure at 1980 year-end. The increase of Cr$ 116 billion was largely due to monetary correction and adjustments made to the value of capital and reserves of the Bank's foreign branches and subsidiaries.

Investments (Cr$ 112.9 billion) include share interests in international financial institutions and Brazilian enterprises as well as the Bank's valuable works of art, museum and historical records.

As a result of monetary correction and the policy of the Bank to develop the acquisition and construction of premises for its operations, fixed assets (Cr$ 104.9 billion) expanded by 129.9% over the figure at 1980 year-end.

Financial Results

Net income for 1981 totalled Cr$ 123.9 billion or 151% more than that recorded in the previous year. Growth, in absolute terms, was Cr$ 74.7 billion. Among the factors that contributed most to this result were earnings from foreign exchange operations and the activities of the Bank's foreign branches and subsidiaries.

Gross revenues (operating and non-operating income), totalled Cr$ 741 billion, registering growth of 145.4% in comparison with the previous year. This result was largely due to income from credit operations, commissions for the rendering of services and foreign exchange earnings. Non-operating income (Cr$ 61. billion) increased by 662%.

Total expenses (Cr$ 392.8 billion) grew by 107%. In 1981, expenses absorbed 53% of revenues as compared with 63% in the previous year, thus showing a marked improvement.

The figure of administrative expenses (Cr$ 244.6 billion) is high principally as a result of expenditure incurred on employees' salaries and social benefits.

The capitalization of retained earnings of Cr$ 30.5 billion is envisaged to strengthen the Bank' capital base with internally generated resources. This in turn, will make it possible to finance growth in operations with less recourse to third party resources.

Shareholders received a total of Cr$ 54.9 billion 133.8% more than that distributed in 1980. Earning per share came to Cr$ 1.87, comprising Cr$ 0.82 in dividends and Cr$ 1.05 in the form of a cash bonus.

Earnings effectively received in 1981 came to Cr$ 1.20 per share (dividends declared in the second half of 1980 and the first half of 1981).

ATIVO	Cr$ milhões	Composição (%)
CIRCULANTE E REALIZÁVEL		
A LONGO PRAZO	5.091.778	95,9
Disponibilidades	77.730	1,5
Operações de Crédito *	2.054.257	38,7
Relações Interbancárias e		
Interdepartamentais	351.389	6,6
Créditos Diversos	2.598.853	48,9
Valores e Bens	9.075	0,2
Despesas de Exercícios		
Futuros	474	0,0
PERMANENTE	219.002	4,1
Investimentos	112.867	2,1
Imobilizado	104.869	2,0
Diferido	1.266	0,0
TOTAL	**5.310.780**	**100,0**

* Inclui *Créditos em Liquidação* e subtrai *Provisão para Créditos de Liquidação Duvidosa* e *Rendas a Apropriar*

O subgrupo *Créditos Diversos,* que registra as operações por ordem e conta do Tesouro Nacional, notadamente os pagamentos de aquisição de trigo e petróleo, adiantamentos sobre contratos de câmbio e os repasses de recursos do Pasep, registrou crescimento de 117,3%, totalizando Cr$ 2.598,9 bilhões.

De pequena representatividade no *Ativo, Valores e Bens* teve seu montante aumentado em 83,1%. Abriga basicamente aplicações financeiras em títulos federais e estaduais.

O grupamento *Permanente* apresentou saldo de Cr$ 219 bilhões, com crescimento de 113,3%, em relação a dezembro de 1980. O aumento de Cr$ 116,3 bilhões decorreu, fundamentalmente, da correção monetária e da contabilização da equivalência patrimonial das agências externas e das empresas controladas no País e no exterior.

O item *Investimentos* (Cr$ 112,9 bilhões) compreende: participações acionárias em organizações financeiras internacionais, que complementam e apóiam as atividades do Banco no exterior; participações em empresas brasileiras, sejam originárias de conversão de créditos ou de interesse governamental; acervo relativo a bens artísticos valiosos, museu e arquivo histórico do Banco.

O *Imobilizado* (Cr$ 104,9 bilhões) apresentou incremento de 129,9% sobre a posição de dezembro de 1980, em decorrência da atualização monetária e dos acréscimos ocorridos, dentro da programação aprovada pelo governo de adquirir ou construir imóveis para as dependências do Banco, buscando oferecer instalações adequadas a clientes e funcionários. O item engloba, entre outros, os imóveis em construção e de uso, móveis e utensílios, sistema de comunicações, segurança e mecanização avançada.

Resultados Financeiros

O lucro líquido apurado no exercício de 1981 atingiu Cr$ 123,9 bilhões, superior em 151,1% ao registrado no exercício anterior. Em termos absolutos o crescimento foi de Cr$ 74,7 bilhões.

Em muito contribuíram para a obtenção desse resultado as operações de câmbio e o resultado líquido das equivalências patrimoniais de agências e subsidiárias integrais no exterior.

As receitas globais atingiram Cr$ 741 bilhões, evoluindo em 145,4% sobre o ano anterior, sobretudo em decorrência do aumento das rendas das operações de crédito, comissões relativas à prestação de serviços e resultado de câmbio. As não-operacionais, ao totalizarem Cr$ 61,8 bilhões, se expandiram em 662%, em virtude preponderantemente de operações de interesse governamental.

O total das despesas (Cr$ 392,8 bilhões) assinalou evolução de 107%, moderado se levado em conta o acréscimo de despesas resultantes da colocação de RDBs. Em 1981, as despesas absorveram 53% das receitas, contra 63% no ano precedente, o que mostra melhoria de desempenho em termos de lucratividade.

Dentre as despesas operacionais, destacaram-se as despesas administrativas, que detêm a maior participação, devido, principalmente, aos custos de pessoal e encargos sociais.

A manutenção da parcela de Cr$ 30,5 bilhões em *Lucros Acumulados* visa propiciar maior capitalização do Banco com recursos gerados internamente, permitindo financiar a expansão das operações com menor aporte de recursos de terceiros.

Aos acionistas foram destinados Cr$ 54,9 bilhões, valor superior em 133,8% à distribuição de 1980 e 315,6% à de 1979. Significou remuneração de Cr$ 1,87 por ação: Cr$ 0,82 de dividendos e Cr$ 1,05 de bonificação em dinheiro. A remuneração efetivamente recebida no ano — relativa ao segundo semestre de 1980 e ao primeiro semestre de 1981 — chegou a Cr$ 1,20.

Income, Expenses and Profit
Percentage Breakdown

	Cr$ billions		Share of total income	
	1981	1981	1980	1979
01. TOTAL INCOME (02 + 08)	740.9	100.0	100.0	100.0
02. Operating Income (03 to 07)	679.1	91.7	97.3	93.7
03. Credit Operations	473.3	63.9	64.9	65.0
04. Exchange Operations	53.2	7.2	8.6	9.2
05. Banking Services	45.6	6.2	8.3	9.6
06. Securities	10.2	1.4	3.3	1.8
07. Other	96.8	13.0	12.2	8.1
08. Non-Operating Income	61.8	8.3	2.7	6.3
09. TOTAL EXPENSES (10 + 16)	392.7	53.0	62.9	64.0
10. Operating Expenses (11 to 15)	392.6	53.0	62.9	63.9
11. Deposits	22.5	3.0	0.2	0.4
12. Funds Borrowed	58.6	7.9	8.5	7.0
13. Administrative	244.6	33.1	37.8	41.8
14. Assets	29.6	4.0	14.1	11.6
15. Other	37.3	5.0	2.3	3.1
16. Non-Operating Expenses	0.1	0.0	0.0	0.1
17. PROFIT (01 − 09)	348.2	47.0	37.1	36.0
18. NET MONETARY CORRECTION	135.3	18.3	13.9	21.5
19. INCOME TAX PROVISION	89.0	12.0	6.9	3.2
20. NET INCOME (17 − 18 − 19)	123.9	16.7	16.3	11.3

Receitas, Despesas e Resultados
Composição Percentual

	Cr$ bilhões	Participação na receita total		
	1981	1981	1980	1979
01. TOTAL DE RECEITAS (02 + 08)	740,9	100,0	100,0	100,0
02. Receitas Operacionais (03 a 07)	679,1	91,7	97,3	93,7
03. Rendas de Operações de Crédito	473,3	63,9	64,9	65,0
04. Resultado de Câmbio	53,2	7,2	8,6	9,2
05. Rendas de Serviços Bancários	45,6	6,2	8,3	9,6
06. Rendas de Valores Mobiliários	10,2	1,4	3,3	1,8
07. Outras Rendas Operacionais	96,8	13,0	12,2	8,1
08. Receitas não Operacionais	61,8	8,3	2,7	6,3
09. TOTAL DE DESPESAS (10 + 16)	392,7	53,0	62,9	64,0
10. Despesas Operacionais (11 a 15)	392,6	53,0	62,9	63,9
11. Despesas de Depósitos	22,5	3,0	0,2	0,4
12. Despesas de Obrigações por Empréstimos	58,6	7,9	8,5	7,0
13. Despesas Administrativas	244,6	33,1	37,8	41,8
14. Despesas patrimoniais	29,6	4,0	14,1	11,6
15. Outras Despesas Operacionais	37,3	5,0	2,3	3,1
16. Despesas não Operacionais	0,1	0,0	0,0	0,1
17. RESULTADO (01 − 09)	348,2	47,0	37,1	36,0
18. RESULTADO DE CORREÇÃO MONETÁRIA	135,3	18,3	13,9	21,5
19. PROVISÃO PARA IMPOSTO DE RENDA	89,0	12,0	6,9	3,2
20. LUCRO LÍQUIDO (17 − 18 − 19)	123,9	16,7	16,3	11,3

BALANCE SHEET

(in thousands of cruzeiros)

ASSETS	31.12.81	31.12.80	31.12.79
CURRENT	**4,113,010,660**	**1,913,857,463**	**1,136,880,109**
Cash	**77,730,714**	**49,717,539**	**3,288,046**
Credit Operations	**1,235,352,138**	**726,871,285**	**448,877,482**
Loans and discounts	498,797,440	309,377,894	235,278,996
Farming loans	752,523,704	430,643,459	221,255,500
(Provision for bad debts)	(3,194,063)	(10,655,089)	(6,366,470)
(Unappropriated income)	(12,774,943)	(2,494,979)	(1,290,544)
Due from Banks and Branches	**351,389,248**	**107,071,736**	**135,210,041**
Receivables and collections outstanding	15,404,975	8,929,805	7,430,098
Correspondents abroad in foreign currencies	244,303,377	91,935,433	63,314,723
Correspondent banks in local currency	123,193	58,267	32,882
Foreign branches in local currency	30,620	89,698	116,913
Interbranch accounts — domestic	91,527,083	6,058,533	64,315,425
Sundry Receivables	**2,441,752,937**	**1,026,320,828**	**547,287,990**
Central Bank collections and deposits	126,827,293	46,872,450	49,792,283
Operations for the account of the Central Bank	2,170,455	3,775,319	6,875,703
Operations for the account of the National Treasury	459,731,568	187,940,415	110,421,078
Advances on exchange contracts	91,839,300	52,920,213	33,213,809
Term bills and documents in foreign currencies	7,254,889	17,824,069	5,635,061
Foreign currency loans	1,185,411	355,640	85,648
Other local currency receivables	705,204,853	266,978,579	146,161,470
Other foreign currency receivables	1,047,772,519	449,798,992	195,220,363
(Unappropriated income)	(233,351)	(144,849)	(117,425)
Securities and Foreign Currency	**6,311,765**	**3,289,800**	**2,215,721**
Fixed income securities	1,673,585	424,254	524,164
Foreign currency	736,878	476,055	341,526
Sundry	3,901,302	2,389,491	1,350,031
Prepaid Expenses	**473,858**	**586,275**	**829**
LONG TERM	**978,768,174**	**623,890,320**	**269,866,645**
Credit Operations	**818,904,964**	**452,557,973**	**253,396,418**
Loans and discounts	518,977,478	276,440,482	119,818,166
Farming loans	301,053,905	196,399,367	136,660,809
Loans past due	42,565,552	13,718,124	9,295,092
(Provision for bad debts)	(43,691,971)	(34,000,000)	(12,377,649)
Sundry Receivables	**157,099,960**	**169,666,524**	**12,781,542**
Central Bank — collections and deposits	—	—	4,583,409
Operations for the account of the Central Bank	281,293	429,876	573,810
Operations for the account of the National Treasury	97,134,589	136,184,033	—
Other local currency receivables	59,684,078	33,052,615	7,624,323
Securities	**2,763,250**	**1,665,823**	**3,688,685**
Fixed income securities	2,281,778	954,833	2,150,248
Sundry	481,472	710,990	1,538,437
PERMANENT	**219,001,337**	**102,674,741**	**54,322,733**
Investments	**112,866,620**	**56,413,214**	**26,988,127**
Foreign branches	46,299,344	23,279,907	7,182,405
Investments in associated companies	50,960,880	26,098,930	15,228,588
Other	15,606,396	7,034,377	4,577,134
Fixed	**104,869,341**	**45,611,807**	**26,962,543**
Bank premises	91,142,940	39,203,707	19,320,387
On-going expansion	23,421,055	10,777,188	9,961,290
Other	23,233,238	10,563,580	6,251,518
(Allowance for depreciation)	(32,927,892)	(14,932,668)	(8,570,652)
Deferred Charges	**1,265,376**	**649,720**	**372,063**
Organization and expansion expenses	2,345,304	1,012,548	510,524
(Allowance for amortization)	(1,079,928)	(362,828)	(138,461)
TOTAL	**5,310,780,171**	**2,640,422,524**	**1,461,069,487**

BALANÇO PATRIMONIAL   (em milhares de cruzeiros)

A T I V O

	31.12.81	31.12.80	31.12.79
CIRCULANTE	**4.113.010.660**	**1.913.857.463**	**1.136.880.109**
Disponibilidades	**77.730.714**	**49.717.539**	**3.288.046**
Operações de Crédito	**1.235.352.138**	**726.871.285**	**448.877.482**
Empréstimos e títulos descontados	498.797.440	309.377.894	235.278.996
Financiamentos rurais	752.523.704	430.643.459	221.255.500
(Provisão para créditos de liquidação duvidosa)	(3.194.063)	(10.655.089)	(6.366.470)
(Rendas a apropriar)	(12.774.943)	(2.494.979)	(1.290.544)
Relações Interbancárias e Interdepartamentais	**351.389.248**	**107.071.736**	**135.210.041**
Pagamentos e recebimentos a liquidar	15.404.975	8.929.805	7.430.098
Correspondentes no exterior em moedas estrangeiras	244.303.377	91.935.433	63.314.723
Correspondentes em moeda nacional	123.193	58.267	32.882
Departamentos e congêneres no exterior em moeda nacional		89.698	116.913
Contas interdepartamentais — País	91.527.083	6.058.533	64.315.425
Créditos Diversos	**2.441.752.937**	**1.026.320.828**	**547.287.990**
Banco Central — recolhimentos e depósitos	126.827.293	46.872.450	49.792.283
Operações de conta do Banco Central	2.170.455	3.775.319	6.875.703
Operações de conta do Tesouro Nacional	459.731.568	187.940.415	110.421.078
Adiantamentos sobre contratos de câmbio	91.839.300	52.920.213	33.213.809
Cambiais e documentos a prazo em moedas estrangeiras	7.254.889	17.824.069	5.635.061
Financiamentos em moedas estrangeiras	1.185.411	355.640	85.648
Outros créditos em moeda nacional	705.204.853	266.978.579	146.161.470
Outros créditos em moedas estrangeiras	1.047.772.519	449.798.992	195.220.363
(Rendas a apropriar)	(233.351)	(144.849)	(117.425)
Valores e Bens	**6.311.765**	**3.289.800**	**2.215.721**
Títulos de renda fixa	1.673.585	424.254	524.164
Valores em moedas estrangeiras	736.878	476.055	341.526
Outros valores e bens	3.901.302	2.389.491	1.350.031
Despesas de Exercícios Futuros	**473.858**	**586.275**	**829**
REALIZÁVEL A LONGO PRAZO	**978.768.174**	**623.890.320**	**269.866.645**
Operações de Crédito	**818.904.964**	**452.557.973**	**253.396.418**
Empréstimos e títulos descontados	518.977.478	276.440.482	119.818.166
Financiamentos rurais	301.053.905	196.399.367	136.660.809
Créditos em liquidação	42.565.552	13.718.124	9.295.092
(Provisão para créditos de liquidação duvidosa)	(43.691.971)	(34.000.000)	(12.377.649)
Créditos Diversos	**157.099.960**	**169.666.524**	**12.781.542**
Banco Central — recolhimentos e depósitos	—	—	4.583.409
Operações de conta do Banco Central	281.293	429.876	573.810
Operações de conta do Tesouro Nacional	97.134.589	136.184.033	—
Outros créditos em moeda nacional	59.684.078	33.052.615	7.624.323
Valores e Bens	**2.763.250**	**1.665.823**	**3.688.685**
Títulos de renda fixa	2.281.778	954.833	2.150.248
Outros valores e bens	481.472	710.990	1.538.437
PERMANENTE	**219.001.337**	**102.674.741**	**54.322.733**
Investimentos	**112.866.620**	**56.413.214**	**26.988.127**
Departamentos no exterior	46.299.344	23.279.907	7.182.405
Investimentos em sociedades ligadas	50.960.880	26.098.930	15.228.588
Outros investimentos	15.606.396	7.034.377	4.577.134
Imobilizado	**104.869.341**	**45.611.807**	**26.962.543**
Imóveis de uso	91.142.940	39.203.707	19.320.387
Imobilizações em curso	23.421.055	10.777.188	9.961.290
Outros bens de uso	23.233.238	10.563.580	6.251.518
(Provisão para depreciação)	(32.927.892)	(14.932.668)	(8.570.652)
Diferido	**1.265.376**	**649.720**	**372.063**
Despesas de organização e expansão	2.345.304	1.012.548	510.524
(Provisão para amortização)	(1.079.928)	(362.828)	(138.461)
TOTAIS	**5.310.780.171**	**2.640.422.524**	**1.461.069.487**

BALANCE SHEET

(in thousands of cruzeiros)

LIABILITIES	31.12.81	31.12.80	31.12.79
CURRENT	**2,752,579,923**	**1,303,719,982**	**731,652,563**
Deposits	**763,407,195**	**434,419,088**	**264,455,831**
Demand	671,268,273	433,505,316	263,114,691
Time	92,138,922	913,772	1,341,140
Due to Banks and Branches	**142,685,422**	**76,522,848**	**36,463,458**
Payments and collections outstanding	3,790,011	2,098,717	1,236,106
Collections in transit	11,389,029	20,160,622	8,005,563
Correspondents abroad in foreign currencies	118,178,281	47,053,390	22,492,218
Correspondent banks in local currency	288,970	250,650	292,571
Payment orders	9,037,910	6,958,952	4,423,063
Foreign branches in local currency	1,221	517	13,937
Funds Borrowed	**331,597,773**	**183,805,489**	**93,546,868**
Central Bank rediscounts	34,812	5,069,906	2,419,454
Funds borrowed locally	126,919,244	64,866,266	27,126,057
Funds borrowed abroad	54,841,692	21,900,604	10,358,950
Foreign currency commitments	149,802,025	91,968,713	53,642,407
Taxes Collected on Behalf of Government Agencies	**33,782,485**	**19,210,519**	**16,719,175**
Sundry Commitments	**1,481,107,048**	**589,762,038**	**320,467,231**
Operations for the account of the Central Bank	42,317,147	23,614,287	30,825,322
Operations for the account of the National Treasury	96,435,581	54,636,082	32,117,615
Provision for payments	177,758,886	51,901,358	39,653,041
Other local currency payables	275,274,154	101,837,094	70,637,733
Other foreign currency payables	889,321,280	357,773,217	147,233,520
LONG TERM	**2,008,480,195**	**1,102,235,077**	**591,012,905**
Funds Borrowed	**410,079,864**	**212,646,000**	**121,505,773**
Funds borrowed locally	211,918,926	132,407,345	84,247,753
Funds borrowed abroad	198,160,938	80,238,655	37,258,020
Sundry Commitments	**1,598,400,331**	**889,589,077**	**469,507,132**
Operations for the account of the Central Bank	116,214,461	61,805,627	27,776,906
Operations for the account of the National Treasury	54,799,639	24,460,374	8,011,427
Provision for payments	−	−	453,025
Central Bank — special account	1,155,179,838	679,109,303	366,048,531
Other local currency payables	272,206,393	124,213,773	67,217,243
SHAREHOLDERS' EQUITY	**549,720,053**	**234,467,465**	**138,404,019**
Capital Stock	88,128,000	58,752,000	39,801,400
Capital Reserves	140,150,979	54,457,508	35,203,832
Revaluation Reserves	16,366,598	4,382,406	2,804,682
Income Reserves	96,071,558	44,025,150	14,995,141
Retained Earnings	209,002,918	72,850,401	45,598,964
TOTAL	**5,310,780,171**	**2,640,422,524**	**1,461,069,487**

BALANÇO PATRIMONIAL (em milhares de cruzeiros)

PASSIVO

	31.12.81	31.12.80	31.12.79
CIRCULANTE	2.752.579.923	1.303.719.982	731.652.563
Depósitos	763.407.195	434.419.088	264.455.831
À vista	671.268.273	433.505.316	263.114.691
A prazo	92.138.922	913.772	1.341.140
Relações Interbancárias e Interdepartamentais	142.685.422	76.522.848	36.463.458
Pagamentos e recebimentos a liquidar	3.790.011	2.098.717	1.236.106
Cobrança efetuada em trânsito	11.389.029	20.160.622	8.005.563
Correspondentes no exterior em moedas estrangeiras	118.178.281	47.053.390	22.492.218
Correspondentes em moeda nacional	288.970	250.650	292.571
Ordens de pagamento	9.037.910	6.958.952	4.423.063
Departamentos e congêneres no exterior em moeda nacional	1.221	517	13.937
Obrigações por Empréstimos	331.597.773	183.805.489	93.546.868
Redescontos e empréstimos do Banco Central	34.812	5.069.906	2.419.454
Obrigações por empréstimos no país	126.919.244	64.866.266	27.126.057
Obrigações por empréstimos externos	54.841.692	21.900.604	10.358.950
Obrigações em moedas estrangeiras	149.802.025	91.968.713	53.642.407
Obrigações por Recebimentos — Tributos e Encargos Sociais...	33.782.485	19.210.519	16.719.175
Outras Obrigações	1.481.107.048	589.762.038	320.467.231
Operações de conta do Banco Central	42.317.147	23.614.287	30.825.322
Operações de conta do Tesouro Nacional	96.435.581	54.636.082	32.117.615
Provisão para pagamentos	177.758.886	51.901.358	39.653.041
Obrigações diversas em moeda nacional	275.274.154	101.837.094	70.637.733
Obrigações diversas em moedas estrangeiras	889.321.280	357.773.217	147.233.520
EXIGÍVEL A LONGO PRAZO	2.008.480.195	1.102.235.077	591.012.905
Obrigações por Empréstimos	410.079.864	212.646.000	121.505.773
Obrigações por empréstimos no país	211.918.926	132.407.345	84.247.753
Obrigações por empréstimos externos	198.160.938	80.238.655	37.258.020
Outras Obrigações	1.598.400.331	889.589.077	469.507.132
Operações de conta do Banco Central	116.214.461	61.805.627	27.776.906
Operações de conta do Tesouro Nacional	54.799.639	24.460.374	8.011.427
Provisão para pagamentos	—	—	453.025
Banco Central, conta de movimento	1.155.179.838	679.109.303	366.048.531
Obrigações diversas em moeda nacional	272.206.393	124.213.773	67.217.243
PATRIMÔNIO LÍQUIDO	549.720.053	234.467.465	138.404.019
Capital Social	88.128.000	58.752.000	39.801.400
Reservas de Capital			
Reservas de Capital	140.150.979	54.457.508	35.203.832
Reservas de Reavaliação	16.366.598	4.382.406	2.804.682
Reservas e Retenção de Lucros	96.071.558	44.025.150	14.995.141
Lucros Acumulados	209.002.918	72.850.401	45.598.964
TOTAIS	5.310.780.171	2.640.422.524	1.461.069.487

INCOME STATEMENT

(in thousands of cruzeiros)

	1981, 1st half	1981, 2nd half	1981	1980	1979
1. OPERATING INCOME	252,353,651	426,792,878	679,146,529	293,802,127	127,210,166
Credit operations	184,795,088	288,521,488	473,316,576	195,971,841	88,283,907
Exchange operations	24,884,611	28,347,421	53,232,032	26,010,671	12,414,927
Banking services	15,903,568	29,678,036	45,581,604	25,054,550	12,981,960
Securities	6,403,234	3,831,651	10,234,885	9,998,877	2,507,497
Other	20,367,150	76,414,282	96,781,432	36,766,188	11,021,875
2. OPERATING EXPENSES	151,594,888	241,044,303	392,639,191	189,778,741	86,840,138
Deposits	1,228,645	21,258,943	22,487,588	526,125	493,764
Funds borrowed	32,654,745	25,976,684	58,631,429	25,575,900	9,477,864
Banking services	2,102	2,545	4,647	3,362	2,098
Administrative	96,402,807	148,175,028	244,577,835	114,217,215	55,949,098
Assets	10,577,985	19,038,534	29,616,519	42,452,187	15,769,466
Other	10,728,604	26,592,569	37,321,173	7,003,952	4,147,848
3. NET OPERATING INCOME	100,758,763	185,748,575	286,507,338	104,023,386	40,370,028
4. NON-OPERATING INCOME	12,131,815	49,697,008	61,828,823	8,114,051	8,553,375
Rent	70,757	100,017	170,774	63,140	37,681
Profit on disposal of assets	286,763	686,696	973,459	231,551	108,176
Profit on disposal of investments	4,182	7,103	11,285	13,468	902
Other	11,770,113	48,903,192	60,673,305	7,805,892	8,406,616
5. NON-OPERATING EXPENSES	53,023	85,329	138,352	67,798	88,701
Losses on disposal of assets	11,400	3,434	14,834	20,978	16,959
Losses on disposal of investments	—	20,438	20,438	2	203
Other	41,623	61,457	103,080	46,818	71,539
6. NET NON-OPERATING INCOME	12,078,792	49,611,679	61,690,471	8,046,253	8,464,674
7. NET MONETARY CORRECTION	(57,490,356)	(77,823,514)	(135,313,870)	(42,102,140)	(29,114,428)
8. INCOME BEFORE TAX	55,347,199	157,536,740	212,883,939	69,967,499	19,720,274
9. INCOME TAX PROVISION	17,231,266	71,726,083	88,957,349	20,704,052	4,377,000
10. NET INCOME	38,115,933	85,810,657	123,926,590	49,263,447	15,343,274
11. EARNINGS PER SHARE	Cr$ 1.30	Cr$ 2.92	Cr$ 4.22	Cr$ 1.68	Cr$ 0.52

DEMONSTRAÇÃO DE RESULTADOS

(em milhares de cruzeiros)

	1º sem/81	2º sem/81	Exercicio/81	Exercicio/80	Exercicio/79
1. RECEITAS OPERACIONAIS	252.353.651	426.792.878	679.146.529	293.802.127	127.210.166
Rendas de operações de crédito	184.795.088	288.521.488	473.316.576	195.971.841	88.283.907
Resultado de câmbio	24.884.611	28.347.421	53.232.032	26.010.671	12.414.927
Rendas de serviços bancários	15.903.568	29.678.036	45.581.604	25.054.550	12.981.960
Rendas de valores mobiliários	6.403.234	3.831.651	10.234.885	9.998.877	2.507.497
Outras rendas operacionais	20.367.150	76.414.282	96.781.432	36.766.188	11.021.875
2. DESPESAS OPERACIONAIS	151.594.888	241.044.303	392.639.191	189.778.741	86.840.138
Despesas de depósitos	1.228.645	21.258.943	22.487.588	526.125	493.764
Despesas de obrigações por empréstimos	32.654.745	25.976.684	58.631.429	25.575.900	9.477.864
Despesas de serviços bancários	2.102	2.545	4.647	3.362	2.098
Despesas administrativas	96.402.807	148.175.028	244.577.835	114.217.215	56.949.098
Despesas patrimoniais	10.577.985	19.038.534	29.616.519	42.452.187	15.769.466
Outras despesas operacionais	10.728.604	26.592.569	37.321.173	7.003.952	4.147.848
3. RESULTADO OPERACIONAL	100.758.763	185.748.575	286.507.338	104.023.386	40.370.028
4. RECEITAS NÃO OPERACIONAIS	12.131.815	49.697.008	61.828.823	8.114.051	8.553.375
Rendas de aluguéis	70.757	100.017	170.774	63.140	37.681
Lucros na alienação de bens	286.763	686.696	973.459	231.551	108.176
Lucros na alienação de investimentos	4.182	7.103	11.285	13.468	902
Outras receitas não operacionais	11.770.113	48.903.192	60.673.305	7.805.892	8.406.616
5. DESPESAS NÃO OPERACIONAIS	53.023	85.329	138.352	67.798	88.701
Perdas na alienação de bens	11.400	3.434	14.834	20.978	16.959
Perdas na alienação de investimentos	—	20.438	20.438	2	203
Outras despesas não operacionais	41.623	61.457	103.080	46.818	71.539
6. RESULTADO NÃO OPERACIONAL	12.078.792	49.611.679	61.690.471	8.046.253	8.464.674
7. RESULTADO DE CORREÇÃO MONETÁRIA	(57.490.356)	(77.823.514)	(135.313.870)	(42.102.140)	(29.114.428)
8. RESULTADO ANTES DO IMPOSTO DE RENDA	55.347.199	157.536.740	212.883.939	69.967.499	19.720.274
9. PROVISÃO PARA IMPOSTO DE RENDA	17.231.266	71.726.083	88.957.349	20.704.052	4.377.000
10. LUCRO LÍQUIDO	38.115.933	85.810.657	123.926.590	49.263.447	15.343.274
11. LUCRO POR AÇÃO	Cr$ 1,30	Cr$ 2,92	Cr$ 4,22	Cr$ 1,68	Cr$ 0,52

STATEMENT OF CHANGES IN SHAREHOLDERS' EQUITY

(in thousands of cruzeiros)

	Capital Stock	Capital Reserves	Revaluation Reserves	Income Reserves	Retained Earnings	Shareholders Equity
BALANCES ON 31.12.79	39,801,400	35,203,832	2,804,682	14,995,141	45,598,964	138,404,019
PRIOR-YEAR ADJUSTMENTS	—	—	—	—	(37,586)	(37,586)
MONETARY CORRECTION	—	18,804,611	702,622	3,750,569	11,405,545	34,663,347
ADJUSTED AND MONETARILY CORRECTED BALANCES	39,801,400	54,008,443	3,507,304	18,745,710	56,966,923	173,029,780
CAPITAL INCREASE	18,950,600	(18,893,335)	—	—	(57,265)	—
CAPITAL ADDITIONS:						
Donations and Grants	—	1,361	—	—	—	1,361
Revaluation of Investments in Subsidiaries	—	—	174,137	—	—	174,137
RESERVE ADJUSTMENTS:						
Reserves Required by By-laws	—	—	—	(23,849)	23,849	-
NET INCOME	—	—	—	—	17,359,791	17,359,791
APPROPRIATIONS FROM INCOME:						
Legal Reserve	—	—	—	867,989	(867,989)	—
Incentive Fund for Technical and Scientific Research	—	—	—	347,196	(347,196)	—
Reserve for Non-Recurring Losses	—	—	—	520,794	(520,794)	—
Cash Dividends (Cr$ 0.20 per share)	—	—	—	—	(5,875,200)	(5,875,200)
Cash Bonus (Cr$ 0.12 per share)	—	—	—	—	(3,525,120)	(3,525,120)
BALANCES ON 30.06.80	58,752,000	35,116,469	3,681,441	20,457,840	63,156,999	181,164,749
PRIOR-YEAR ADJUSTMENTS	—	—	—	1,737,247	(1,806,999)	(69,752)
MONETARY CORRECTION	—	19,310,247	757,291	4,708,711	10,818,577	35,594,826
ADJUSTED AND MONETARILY CORRECTED BALANCES	58,752,000	54,426,716	4,438,732	26,903,798	72,168,577	216,689,823
CAPITAL ADDITIONS:						
Donations and Grants	—	30,792	—	—	—	30,792
RESERVE ADJUSTMENTS:						
Reserves Required by By-laws	—	—	—	(112,695)	112,695	—
Revaluation Reserves	—	—	(56,326)	—	—	(56,326)
Reserve for Unrealized income	—	—	—	(6,750)	6,750	—
NET INCOME	—	—	—	—	31,903,656	31,903,656
APPROPRIATIONS FROM INCOME:						
Legal Reserve	—	—	—	1,595,183	(1,595,183)	—
Incentive Fund for Technical and Scientific Research	—	—	—	638,073	(638,073)	—
Reserve for Non-Recurring Losses	—	—	—	957,110	(957,110)	—
Contingency Reserve	—	—	—	2,039,981	(2,039,981)	—
Reserve for Unrealized Income	—	—	—	12,010,450	(12,010,450)	—
Cash Dividends (Cr$ 0.24 per share)	—	—	—	—	(7,050,240)	(7,050,240)
Cash Bonus (Cr$ 0.24 per share)	—	—	—	—	(7,050,240)	(7,050,240)
BALANCES ON 31.12.80	58,752,000	54,457,508	4,382,406	44,025,150	72,850,401	234,467,465

DEMONSTRAÇÃO DAS MUTAÇÕES DO PATRIMÔNIO LÍQUIDO

(em milhares de cruzeiros)

	Capital Social	Reservas de Capital	Reservas de Reavaliação	Reservas e Retenção de Lucros	Lucros Acumulados	Patrimônio Líquido
SALDOS EM 31.12.79	39.801.400	35.203.832	2.804.682	14.995.141	45.598.964	138.404.019
AJUSTES DE EXERCÍCIOS ANTERIORES . . .	—	—	—	—	(37.586)	(37.586)
CORREÇÃO MONETÁRIA	—	18.804.611	702.622	3.750.569	11.405.545	34.663.347
SALDO AJUSTADO E CORRIGIDO	39.801.400	54.008.443	3.507.304	18.745.710	56.966.923	173.029.780
AUMENTO DE CAPITAL	18.950.600	(18.893.335)	—	—	(57.265)	—
REFORÇOS:						
Doações e Subvenções	—	1.361	—	—	—	1.361
Reavaliação em Controladas	—	—	174.137	—	—	174.137
REVERSÃO DE RESERVAS:						
Reservas Estatutárias	—	—	—	(23.849)	23.849	—
LUCRO LÍQUIDO DO PERÍODO	—	—	—	—	17.359.791	17.359.791
DESTINAÇÕES DO LUCRO:						
Reserva Legal	—	—	—	867.989	(867.989)	—
Fundo de Incentivo à Pesquisa Técnico-Científica .	—	—	—	347.196	(347.196)	—
Fundo para Prejuízos Eventuais . . .	—	—	—	520.794	(520.794)	—
Dividendos (Cr$ 0,20 por ação) . . .	—	—	—	—	(5.875.200)	(5.875.200)
Bonificação em dinheiro (Cr$ 0,12 por ação) .	—	—	—	—	(3.525.120)	(3.525.120)
SALDOS EM 30.06.80	58.752.000	35.116.469	3.681.441	20.457.840	63.156.999	181.164.749
AJUSTES DE EXERCÍCIOS ANTERIORES . . .	—	—	—	1.737.247	(1.806.999)	(69.752)
CORREÇÃO MONETÁRIA	—	19.310.247	757.291	4.708.711	10.818.577	35.594.826
SALDO AJUSTADO E CORRIGIDO	58.752.000	54.426.716	4.438.732	26.903.798	72.168.577	216.689.823
REFORÇOS:						
Doações e Subvenções	—	30.792	—	—	—	30.792
REVERSÃO DE RESERVAS:						
Reservas Estatutárias	—	—	—	(112.695)	112.695	—
Reservas de Reavaliação	—	—	(56.326)	—	—	(56.326)
Reservas de Lucros a Realizar	—	—	—	(6.750)	6.750	—
LUCRO LÍQUIDO DO PERÍODO	—	—	—	—	31.903.656	31.903.656
DESTINAÇÕES DO LUCRO:						
Reserva Legal	—	—	—	1.595.183	(1.595.183)	—
Fundo de Incentivo à Pesquisa Técnico-Científica .	—	—	—	638.073	(638.073)	—
Fundo para Prejuízos Eventuais . . .	—	—	—	957.110	(957.110)	—
Reservas para Contingências	—	—	—	2.039.981	(2.039.981)	—
Reservas de Lucros a Realizar	—	—	—	12.010.450	(12.010.450)	—
Dividendos (Cr$ 0,24 por ação) . . .	—	—	—	—	(7.050.240)	(7.050.240)
Bonificação em dinheiro (Cr$ 0,24 por ação) .	—	—	—	—	(7.050.240)	(7.050.240)
SALDOS EM 31.12.80	58.752.000	54.457.508	4.382.406	44.025.150	72.850.401	234.467.465

STATEMENT OF CHANGES IN SHAREHOLDERS' EQUITY

(in thousands of cruzeiros)

	Capital Stock	Capital Reserves	Revaluation Reserves	Income Reserves	Retained Earnings	Shareholders' Equity
PRIOR-YEAR ADJUSTMENTS	—	—	—	—	3,672,041	3,672,041
MONETARY CORRECTION	—	45,320,761	1,734,235	13,179,547	34,524,343	94,758,886
ADJUSTED AND MONETARILY CORRECTED BALANCES	58,752,000	99,778,269	6,116,641	57,204,697	111,046,785	332,898,392
CAPITAL INCREASE	29,376,000	(29,376,000)	—	—	—	—
CAPITAL ADDITIONS:						
Donations and Grants	—	2,165,904	—	—	—	2,165,904
Revaluation of Investments in Subsidiaries	—	—	4,634,035	—	—	4,634,035
RESERVE ADJUSTMENTS:						
Reserves Required by By-laws	—	—	—	(73,574)	73,574	—
Reserves for Unrealized Income	—	—	—	(10,646,897)	10,646,897	—
NET INCOME	—	—	—	—	38,115,933	38,115,933
APPROPRIATIONS FROM INCOME:						
Legal Reserve	—	—	—	1,905,796	(1,905,796)	—
Incentive Fund for Technical and Scientific Research	—	—	—	762,319	(762,319)	—
Reserve for Non-Recurring Losses	—	—	—	1,143,478	(1,143,478)	—
Fund for Cooperative or Community Rural: Infrastructural Development Programmes	—	—	—	762,319	(762,319)	—
Contingency Reserve	—	—	—	6,660,000	(6,660,000)	—
Cash Dividends (Cr$ 0.34 per share)	—	—	—	—	(9,987,840)	(9,987,840)
Cash Bonus (Cr$ 0.38 per share)	—	—	—	—	(11,162,880)	(11,162,880)
BALANCES ON 30.06.81	88,128,000	72,568,173	10,750,676	57,718,138	127,498,557	356,663,544
PRIOR-YEAR ADJUSTMENTS	—	—	—	—	167,012	167,012
MONETARY CORRECTION	—	64,885,597	4,313,197	18,393,719	49,268,793	136,861,306
ADJUSTED AND MONETARILY CORRECTED BALANCES	88,128,000	137,453,770	15,063,873	76,111,857	176,934,362	493,691,862
CAPITAL ADDITIONS:						
Donations and Grants	—	2,697,209	—	—	—	2,697,209
Revaluation of Investments in Subsidiaries	—	—	1,302,725	—	—	1,302,725
RESERVE ADJUSTMENTS						
Contingency Reserve	—	—	—	(6,660,000)	6,660,000	—
Reserves Required by By-laws	—	—	—	(630,994)	630,994	—
Reserve for Unrealized Income	—	—	—	(6,749)	6,749	—
NET INCOME:	—	—	—	—	85,810,657	85,810,657
APPROPRIATIONS FROM INCOME:						
Legal Reserve	—	—	—	4,290,533	(4,290,533)	—
Incentive Fund for Technical and Scientific Research	—	—	—	1,716,213	(1,716,213)	—
Reserve for Non-Recurring Losses	—	—	—	2,574,320	(2,574,320)	—
Fund for Cooperative or Community Rural: Infrastructural Development Programmes	—	—	—	1,716,213	(1,716,213)	—
Reserve for Unrealized Income	—	—	—	16,960,165	(16,960,165)	—
Cash Dividends (Cr$ 0.48 per share)	—	—	—	—	(14,100,480)	(14,100,480)
Cash Bonus (Cr$ 0.67 per share)	—	—	—	—	(19,681,920)	(19,681,920)
BALANCES ON 31.12.81	88,128,000	140,150,979	16,366,598	96,071,558	209,002,918	549,720,053

DEMONSTRAÇÃO DAS MUTAÇÕES DO PATRIMÔNIO LÍQUIDO

(em milhares de cruzeiros)

	Capital Social	Reservas de Capital	Reservas de Reavaliação	Reservas e Retenção de Lucros	Lucros Acumulados	Patrimônio Líquido
AJUSTES DE EXERCÍCIOS ANTERIORES	—	—	—	—	3.672.041	3.672.041
CORREÇÃO MONETÁRIA	—	45.320.761	—	13.179.547	34.524.343	94.758.886
SALDO AJUSTADO E CORRIGIDO	58.752.000	99.778.269	6.116.641	57.204.697	111.046.785	332.898.392
AUMENTO DE CAPITAL	29.376.000	(29.376.000)	—	—	—	—
REFORÇOS:						
Doações e Subvenções	—	2.165.904	—	—	—	2.165.904
Reavaliação em Controladas	—	—	4.634.035	—	—	4.634.035
REVERSÃO DE RESERVAS:						
Reservas Estatutárias	—	—	—	(73.574)	73.574	—
Reservas de Lucros a Realizar	—	—	—	(10.646.897)	10.646.897	—
LUCRO LÍQUIDO DO PERÍODO	—	—	—	—	38.115.933	38.115.933
DESTINAÇÕES DO LUCRO:						
Reserva Legal	—	—	—	1.905.796	(1.905.796)	—
Fundo de Incentivo à Pesquisa Técnico-Científica	—	—	—	762.319	(762.319)	—
Fundo para Prejuízos Eventuais	—	—	—	1.143.478	(1.143.478)	—
Fundo de Desenvolvimento de Programas Cooperativos ou Comunitários de Infra-estruturas Rurais	—	—	—	762.319	(762.319)	—
Reservas para Contingências	—	—	—	6.660.000	(6.660.000)	—
Dividendos (Cr$ 0,34 por ação)	—	—	—	—	(9.987.840)	(9.987.840)
Bonificação em dinheiro (Cr$ 0,38 por ação)	—	—	—	—	(11.162.880)	(11.162.880)
SALDOS EM 30.06.81	88.128.000	72.568.173	10.750.676	57.718.138	127.498.557	356.663.544
AJUSTES DE EXERCÍCIOS ANTERIORES	—	—	—	—	167.012	167.012
CORREÇÃO MONETÁRIA	—	64.885.597	—	18.393.719	49.268.793	136.861.306
SALDO AJUSTADO E CORRIGIDO	88.128.000	137.453.770	15.063.873	76.111.857	176.934.362	493.691.862
REFORÇOS:						
Doações e Subvenções	—	2.697.209	—	—	—	2.697.209
Reavaliação em Controladas	—	—	1.302.725	—	—	1.302.725
REVERSÃO DE RESERVAS:						
Reservas para Contingências	—	—	—	(6.660.000)	6.660.000	—
Reservas Estatutárias	—	—	—	(630.994)	630.994	—
Reservas de Lucros a Realizar	—	—	—	(6.749)	6.749	—
LUCRO LÍQUIDO DO PERÍODO	—	—	—	—	85.810.657	85.810.657
DESTINAÇÕES DO LUCRO:						
Reserva Legal	—	—	—	4.290.533	(4.290.533)	—
Fundo de Incentivo à Pesquisa Técnico-Científica	—	—	—	1.716.213	(1.716.213)	—
Fundo para Prejuízos Eventuais	—	—	—	2.574.320	(2.574.320)	—
Fundo de Desenvolvimento de Programas Cooperativos ou Comunitários de Infra-estruturas Rurais	—	—	—	1.716.213	(1.716.213)	—
Reservas de Lucros a Realizar	—	—	—	16.960.165	(16.960.165)	—
Dividendos (Cr$ 0,48 por ação)	—	—	—	—	(14.100.480)	(14.100.480)
Bonificação em dinheiro (Cr$ 0,67 por ação)	—	—	—	—	(19.681.920)	(19.681.920)
SALDOS EM 31.12.81	88.128.000	140.150.979	16.366.598	96.071.558	209.002.918	549.720.053

CONDENSED BALANCE SHEET

(in thousands of cruzeiros)

ASSETS

	31.12.81	31.12.80	31.12.79
CURRENT AND LONG TERM	**8,135,303,761**	**3,335,283,700**	**2,034,993,513**
Cash	84,347,135	113,746,353	11,616,763
Credit Operations	3,414,618,657	1,537,361,751	917,895,666
Due from Banks and Branches	1,722,230,475	287,636,742	442,666,710
Sundry Receivables	2,889,387,494	1,381,291,740	653,398,373
Securities and Foreign Currency	11,160,621	7,129,299	8,100,393
Prepaid Expenses	13,559,379	8,117,815	1,315,608
PERMANENT	**181,537,502**	**86,333,166**	**49,590,784**
Investments	66,591,128	33,145,372	20,023,865
Fixed	113,018,929	50,659,646	29,161,961
Deferred Charges	1,927,445	2,528,148	404,958
TOTAL	**8,316,841,263**	**3,421,616,866**	**2,084,584,297**

LIABILITIES

	31.12.81	31.12.80	31.12.79
CURRENT AND LONG TERM	**7,767,121,210**	**3,187,149,401**	**1,946,180,278**
Deposits	3,031,581,077	1,021,561,009	680,451,350
Due to Banks and Branches	297,710,112	110,954,607	119,437,854
Funds Borrowed	1,243,774,732	526,951,223	326,612,777
Taxes Collected on Behalf of Government Agencies	33,782,485	19,210,519	16,719,175
Sundry Commitments	3,160,272,804	1,508,472,043	802,959,122
SHAREHOLDERS' EQUITY	**549,720,053**	**234,467,465**	**138,404,019**
Capital Stock	88,128,000	58,752,000	39,801,400
Capital Reserves	140,150,979	54,457,508	35,203,832
Revaluation Reserves	16,366,598	4,382,406	2,804,682
Income Reserves	96,071,558	44,025,150	14,995,141
Retained Earnings	209,002,918	72,850,401	45,598,964
TOTAL	**8,316,841,263**	**3,421,616,866**	**2,084,584,297**

BALANÇO GERAL CONDENSADO

(em milhares de cruzeiros)

A T I V O	31.12.81	31.12.80	31.12.79
CIRCULANTE E REALIZÁVEL A LONGO PRAZO	**8.135.303.761**	**3.335.283.700**	**2.034.993.513**
Disponibilidades	84.347.135	113.746.353	11.616.763
Operações de crédito	3.414.618.657	1.537.361.751	917.895.666
Relações interbancárias e interdepartamentais	1.722.230.475	287.636.742	442.666.710
Créditos diversos	2.889.387.494	1.381.291.740	653.398.373
Valores e bens	11.160.621	7.129.299	8.100.393
Despesas de exercícios futuros	13.559.379	8.117.815	1.315.608
PERMANENTE	**181.537.502**	**86.333.166**	**49.590.784**
Investimentos	66.591.128	33.145.372	20.023.865
Imobilizado	113.018.929	50.659.646	29.161.961
Diferido	1.927.445	2.528.148	404.958
TOTAIS	**8.316.841.263**	**3.421.616.866**	**2.084.584.297**

P A S S I V O	31.12.81	31.12.80	31.12.79
CIRCULANTE E EXIGÍVEL A LONGO PRAZO	**7.767.121.210**	**3.187.149.401**	**1.946.180.278**
Depósitos	3.031.581.077	1.021.561.009	680.451.350
Relações interbancárias e interdepartamentais	297.710.112	110.954.607	119.437.854
Obrigações por empréstimos	1.243.774.732	526.951.223	326.612.777
Obrigações por recebimentos - tributos e encargos sociais	33.782.485	19.210.519	16.719.175
Outras obrigações	3.160.272.804	1.508.472.043	802.959.122
PATRIMÔNIO LÍQUIDO	**549.720.053**	**234.467.465**	**138.404.019**
Capital	88.128.000	58.752.000	39.801.400
Reservas de capital	140.150.979	54.457.508	35.203.832
Reservas de reavaliação	16.366.598	4.382.406	2.804.682
Reservas e retenção de lucros	96.071.558	44.025.150	14.995.141
Lucros acumulados	209.002.918	72.850.401	45.598.964
TOTAIS	**8.316.841.263**	**3.421.616.866**	**2.084.584.297**

CONDENSED BALANCE SHEET OF THE FOREIGN EXCHANGE DIVISION

(in thousands of cruzeiros)

ASSETS	31.12.81	31.12.80	31.12.79
FOREIGN CURRENCY	**1,301,253,074**	**560,390,189**	**264,597,321**
Correspondents abroad	244,303,377	91,935,433	63,314,723
Term bills and documents in foreign currencies	7,254,889	17,824,069	5,635,061
Sundry accounts	879,504,923	352,374,282	144,184,488
Exporters' contribution quotas receivable	935,942	4,882,747	5,504,204
Loans to local importers	167,331,654	92,541,963	45,531,671
Loans to foreign importers	1,185,411	355,640	85,648
Bank notes and coins	736,878	476,055	341,526
LOCAL CURRENCY	**428,656,534**	**212,173,442**	**109,832,535**
Advances on exchange contracts	91,839,300	52,920,213	33,213,809
Loans and discounts — exchange	150,698,197	91,359,123	40,199,046
Loans to local importers	1,180,803	34,842	550,459
Central Bank — deposits	121,770,076	41,783,106	26,727,232
Correspondents abroad	4,580	537	19,878
Foreign branches — capital account	46,299,344	23,279,907	7,182,405
Foreign branches	30,620	89,698	116,913
Revenue receivable — exchange	785,974	119,696	54,512
Other local-currency receivables	18,546,027	7,282,915	3,541,096
(Unappropriated income)	(579,344)	(182,531)	(109,599)
(Provision for bad debts)	(1,919,043)	(4,514,064)	(1,663,216)
TOTAL	**1,729,909,608**	**772,563,631**	**374,429,856**

BALANCETE SINTÉTICO DA CARTEIRA DE CÂMBIO

(em milhares de cruzeiros)

ATIVO	31.12.81	31.12.80	31.12.79
EM MOEDAS ESTRANGEIRAS	**1.301.253.074**	**560.390.189**	**264.597.321**
Correspondentes no exterior em moedas estrangeiras	244.303.377	91.935.433	63.314.723
Cambiais e documentos a prazo, em moedas estrangeiras	7.254.889	17.824.069	5.635.061
Contas gráficas em moedas estrangeiras	879.504.923	352.374.282	144.184.488
Cotas de contribuição a receber de exportadores	935.942	4.882.747	5.504.204
Créditos registrados em moedas estrangeiras, a receber	167.331.654	92.541.963	45.531.671
Financiamentos em moedas estrangeiras	1.185.411	355.640	85.648
Valores em moedas estrangeiras	736.878	476.055	341.526
EM MOEDA NACIONAL	**428.656.534**	**212.173.442**	**109.832.535**
Adiantamentos sobre contratos de câmbio	91.839.300	52.920.213	33.213.809
Empréstimos e títulos descontados – câmbio	150.698.197	91.359.123	40.199.046
Devedores por créditos liquidados no exterior	1.180.803	34.842	550.459
Banco Central – recolhimentos e depósitos	121.770.076	41.783.106	26.727.232
Correspondentes no exterior em moeda nacional	4.580	537	19.878
Departamentos no exterior – conta capital	46.299.344	23.279.907	7.182.405
Departamentos e congêneres no exterior em moeda nacional	30.620	89.698	116.913
Rendas a receber – câmbio	785.974	119.696	54.512
Outros créditos em moeda nacional	18.546.027	7.282.915	3.541.096
(Rendas a apropriar)	(579.344)	(182.531)	(109.599)
(Provisão para créditos de liquidação duvidosa)	(1.919.043)	(4.514.064)	(1.663.216)
TOTAIS	**1.729.909.608**	**772.563.631**	**374.429.856**

CONDENSED BALANCE SHEET OF THE FOREIGN EXCHANGE DIVISION

(in thousands of cruzeiros)

LIABILITIES	31.12.81	31.12.80	31.12.79
FOREIGN CURRENCY	1,157,301,586	496,795,320	223,368,145
Correspondents abroad	118,178,281	47,053,390	22,492,218
Foreign currency commitments	149,802,025	91,968,713	53,642,407
Sundry accounts	887,994,816	352,890,470	140,269,189
Exporters' contribution quotas payable	1,326,464	4,882,747	6,964,331
LOCAL CURRENCY	312,891,997	157,405,401	82,473,281
Deposits in escrow	14,537,781	32,214,573	17,876,767
Other deposits	51,457	27,123	14,898
Correspondents abroad	25,626	4,717	10,008
Foreign branches	1,221	517	13,937
Funds borrowed abroad	244,540,179	99,043,388	45,987,673
Provision for payments — exchange	44,084,694	17,965,100	14,282,016
Other	9,651,039	8,149,983	4,287,982
INCOME ACCOUNTS	32,606,552	13,761,440	4,957,471
Income from exchange operations — credit balance	28,347,421	14,518,595	7,716,304
Distribution of internal results	—		231
Other revenues	33,131,131	11,953,609	5,464,431
(Other expenses)	(28,872,000)	(12,710,764)	(8,223,495)
NET POSITION	227,109,473	104,601,470	63,630,959
TOTAL	1,729,909,608	772,563,631	374,429,856

BALANCETE SINTÉTICO DA CARTEIRA DE CÂMBIO

(em milhares de cruzeiros)

PASSIVO

EM MOEDAS ESTRANGEIRAS	**1.157.301.586**	**496.795.320**	**223.368.145**
Correspondentes no exterior em moedas estrangeiras	118.178.281	47.053.390	22.492.218
Obrigações em moedas estrangeiras	149.802.025	91.968.713	53.642.407
Contas gráficas em moedas estrangeiras	887.994.816	352.890.470	140.269.189
Cotas de contribuição a entregar	1.326.464	4.882.747	6.964.331
EM MOEDA NACIONAL	**312.891.997**	**157.405.401**	**82.473.281**
Depósitos vinculados	14.537.781	32.214.573	17.876.767
Outros depósitos	51.457	27.123	14.898
Correspondentes no exterior em moeda nacional	25.626	4.717	10.008
Departamentos e congêneres no exterior em moeda nacional	1.221	517	13.937
Obrigações por empréstimos externos	244.540.179	99.043.388	45.987.673
Provisão para pagamentos a efetuar – câmbio	44.084.694	17.965.100	14.282.016
Outras obrigações em moeda nacional	9.651.039	8.149.983	4.287.982
CONTAS DE RESULTADO	**32.606.552**	**13.761.440**	**4.957.471**
Resultados de câmbio – saldo credor	28.347.421	14.518.595	7.716.304
Rateio de resultados internos – câmbio – saldo credor	–	–	231
Outras contas credoras	33.131.131	11.953.609	5.464.431
(Outras contas devedoras)	(28.872.000)	(12.710.764)	(8.223.495)
EXCESSO DOS SALDOS DEVEDORES SOBRE OS CREDORES – VALOR PARA BALANCEAMENTO	**227.109.473**	**104.601.470**	**63.630.959**
TOTAIS	**1.729.909.608**	**772.563.631**	**374.429.856**

STATEMENT OF CHANGES IN FINANCIAL POSITION

(In thousands of cruzeiros)

	1981	1980	1979
1. SOURCES:			
Net income for the year	123,926,590	49,263,447	15,343,274
Depreciation and amortization	4,893,986	1,986,613	890,401
Capital paid-up	29,376,000	18,950,600	10,425,400
Increase in reserves	216,883,118	51,350,199	41,539,396
Resources from third parties originating from an increase in long-term liabilities	906,245,118	511,222,172	280,293,357
TOTAL	1,281,324,812	632,773,031	348,491,828
2. APPLICATIONS:			
Dividends	54,933,120	23,500,800	13,219,200
Increase in:			
Long-term assets	354,877,854	354,023,675	68,819,346
Fixed Assets	63,772,794	20,458,003	11,750,577
Investments	56,453,406	29,425,087	25,593,790
Deferred charges	994,382	455,531	370,620
TOTAL	531,031,556	427,863,096	119,753,533
3. INCREASE IN NET WORKING CAPITAL	750,293,256	204,909,935	228,738,295

CHANGES IN FINANCIAL POSITION:	31.12.81	31.12.80	INCREASE
CURRENT ASSETS	4,113,010,660	1,913,857,463	2,199,153,197
CURRENT LIABILITIES	(2,752,579,923)	(1,303,719,982)	(1,448,859,941)
NET WORKING CAPITAL	1,360,430,737	610,137,481	750,293,256

DEMONSTRAÇÃO DAS ORIGENS E APLICAÇÕES DE RECURSOS

(em milhares de cruzeiros)

	1981	1980	1979
1. ORIGENS DOS RECURSOS:			
Lucro Líquido do Exercício	123.926.590	49.263.447	15.343.274
Depreciação e Amortização	4.893.986	1.986.613	890.401
Realização de Capital Social	29.376.000	18.950.600	10.425.400
Aumento de Reservas	216.883.118	51.350.199	41.539.396
Recursos de Terceiros Originários:			
Do Aumento do Exigível a Longo Prazo	906.245.118	511.222.172	280.293.357
TOTAL DAS ORIGENS	**1.281.324.812**	**632.773.031**	**348.491.828**
2. APLICAÇÕES DOS RECURSOS:			
Dividendos e Bonificação em Dinheiro . . .	54.933.120	23.500.800	13.219.200
Aumento:			
Do Realizável a Longo Prazo	354.877.854	354.023.675	68.819.346
Do Ativo Imobilizado	63.772.794	20.458.003	11.750.577
Dos Investimentos	56.453.406	29.425.087	25.593.790
Do Ativo Diferido	994.382	455.531	370.620
TOTAL DAS APLICAÇÕES	**531.031.556**	**427.863.096**	**119.753.533**
3. AUMENTO DO CAPITAL CIRCULANTE LÍQUIDO 7	**50.293.256**	**204.909.935**	**228.738.295**
MODIFICAÇÕES NA POSIÇÃO FINANCEIRA:	31.12.81	31.12.80	AUMENTO
ATIVO CIRCULANTE	4.113.010.660	1.913.857.463	2.199.153.197
PASSIVO CIRCULANTE	(2.752.579.923)	(1.303.719.982)	(1.448.859.941)
CAPITAL CIRCULANTE LÍQUIDO	1.360.430.737	610.137.481	750.293.256

NOTES TO THE FINANCIAL STATEMENTS

NOTE 1 — THE BANK AND ITS ACTIVITIES

Banco do Brasil S.A., established under charter in 1854 and operating mainly under Brazilian Corporate Law, is a public corporation. Its objectives are to foster domestic production, develop commerce and stimulate foreign trade. The Bank is a monetary authority and is the principal financial agent for the Federal Government, in accordance with the provisions of Law No. 4,595/64.

NOTE 2 — ACCOUNTING PRINCIPLES

The Bank's financial statements have been prepared in accordance with rules laid down by the Central Bank of Brazil and are based on the Companies' Act, to which the Bank is subject. The following accounting principles are adopted by the Bank:

a) All transactions are registered on an accrual basis;

b) Balance sheet items are classified as long or short-term in accordance with articles 179 and 180 of Law No. 6,404/76;

c) Foreign currency-denominated assets and liabilities are stated according to official rates of exchange prevailing on the balance sheet date and assets and liabilities subject to monetary correction are stated according to official indices prevailing on the balance sheet date;

d) The provision for bad debts is based on total outstanding credit operations on the balance sheet date and affords adequate coverage against possible losses;

e) Fixed assets are monetarily corrected according to official indices and — with the exception of land and forests — are depreciated by the straight-line method at the following annual rates: buildings and improvements, 4%; advanced data processing equipment, vehicles, electrical equipment and fixtures, 20%; other items, 10%. The provision for depreciation is also monetarily corrected;

f) Real estate, other than Bank premises, acquired prior to 1st January 1981 is monetarily corrected according to official indices;

g) Vacation pay is treated on a cash basis;

h) Foreign branches are treated as wholly-owned subsidiaries according to the provisions of Law No. 6,404/76, and appear under the main heading "PERMANENT" (subheading "Investments"). This investment is subject to monetary correction and based on the equity method.

NOTE 3 — CHANGES IN ACCOUNTING PRACTICES

The following accounting practices were adopted in the year:

a) The provision for bad debts was based on new limits established by regulations issued by the Ministry of Finance;

b) As required by law, real estate, other than Bank premises, acquired prior to 1st January 1981 was monetarily corrected. Part of this readjustment was registered as income for the year and the remainder attributed to retained earnings, by means of adjustments made to previous years.

NOTE 4 — INVESTMENTS IN SUBSIDIARIES

These are registered under the heading "Investments in Associated Companies" and, based on the equity method, recorded a negative balance of Cr$ 2,255,935 thousand, being a loss on investments of Cr$ 8,192,695 thousand less a revaluation of the reserves of the subsidiaries of Cr$ 5,936,760 thousand.

COMPANIES (In thousands of cruzeiros)	Paid up Capital	Adjusted Shareholders' Equity	Net Income for the fiscal year	Base date	Our share %	Number and kind of shares	Book value at 31.12.81
Banco do Brasil A.G. (Vienna-Austria)	398,645	401,706	6,503	31.12.81	100.00	Wholly-owned subsidiary	401,706
Brasilian American Merchant Bank	63,580	17,932,309	4,844,160	31.12.81	100.00	Wholly-owned subsidiary	17,932,309
Brazilian Finance and Investment Corporation	21,346	36,378	10,315	31.12.81	100.00	Wholly-owned subsidiary	36,378
Companhia Aços Especiais Itabira	12,074,315	19,834,885	(5,425,434)	30.11.81	81.98	6,078,930,717 (1) 105,071,283 (2) 118,443,415 (3)	18,247,802
Banco Brasileiro-Iraquiano S.A.	1,400,000	1,400,000	—	31.12.81	50.00	140,000 (1)	700,000
Riocell Administração S.A.	7,064,721	13,843,995	2,021,048	31.10.81	50.00	1,996,686 (1)	7,761,036
Forjas Acesita S.A.	2,550,825	505,919	(1,548,021)	30.11.81	18.46	272,440,334 (1)	119,595

(1) Ordinary nominal shares   (2) Ordinary bearer shares   (3) Preference shares

NOTAS EXPLICATIVAS

NOTA 1 — O BANCO E SUAS OPERAÇÕES

O Banco do Brasil S.A., fundado em 1854, é uma companhia aberta, de direito privado, regida, sobretudo, pela legislação das sociedades por ações. Tem por objetivo fomentar a produção nacional, promover a circulação dos bens produzidos e incentivar o intercâmbio comercial do País com o exterior. É também autoridade monetária e principal agente financeiro do Governo Federal, nos termos da Lei 4.595/64.

NOTA 2 — DIRETRIZES CONTÁBEIS

Estas demonstrações seguem as normas do Banco Central do Brasil, calcadas na legislação das sociedades anônimas, a que o Banco se sujeita. Em destaque, os princípios e procedimentos contábeis adotados:

a) o regime contábil é o de competência de exercício;

b) a classificação em circulante e longo prazo, do realizável e do exigível, obedece aos arts. 179 e 180 da Lei n.º 6.404/76;

c) os direitos e as obrigações em moedas estrangeiras e os sujeitos à indexação estão ajustados às taxas cambiais ou índices oficiais, na data do encerramento do balanço;

d) a provisão para créditos de liquidação duvidosa tem por base o valor total dos créditos a receber constantes do balanço do final do exercício e proporciona cobertura adequada para eventuais perdas da espécie;

e) o imobilizado está corrigido monetariamente aos índices oficiais, e depreciado — à exceção de terrenos e florestas — pelo método linear às seguintes taxas anuais: edificações e benfeitorias - 4%; sistema de mecanização avançada, veículos, e instalações e equipamentos elétricos - 20%; demais itens - 10%. As depreciações acumuladas também estão corrigidas monetariamente;

f) os imóveis não destinados a uso, adquiridos até o término do exercício anterior, estão corrigidos monetariamente aos índices oficiais;

g) os encargos com férias são reconhecidos por ocasião da sua realização;

h) as agências no exterior recebem o tratamento de subsidiária integral previsto na Lei n.º 6.404/76, estando registradas em "Departamentos no Exterior", no ativo permanente-investimentos, sujeitando-se à correção monetária e avaliação pelo método de equivalência patrimonial.

NOTA 3 — MUDANÇAS DE DIRETRIZES CONTÁBEIS

No presente exercício passaram a ser adotados os seguintes critérios:

a) a provisão para créditos de liquidação duvidosa foi constituída com observância dos novos limites estabelecidos através de portaria do Ministério da Fazenda;

b) em consonância com as disposições de ato normativo específico, os imóveis não destinados a uso, adquiridos até o término do exercício de 1980, foram corrigidos monetariamente. Parte do seu valor foi imputada ao resultado do exercício e o restante levado a lucros acumulados, via ajustes de exercícios anteriores.

NOTA 4 — INVESTIMENTOS EM EMPRESAS CONTROLADAS

Registrados em "Investimentos em Sociedades Ligadas", sua avaliação pelo método de equivalência patrimonial resultou negativa de Cr$ 2.255.935 mil, sendo Cr$ 8.192.695 mil levados a resultado do exercício (despesas), uma vez que Cr$ 5.936.760 mil corresponderam a acréscimo nas reservas de reavaliação dessas empresas.

DISCRIMINAÇÃO (em milhares de cruzeiros)	Capital social realizado	Patrimônio líquido ajustado	Resultado no exercício	Data-base	Nossa participação %	Número e espécie de ações	Valor contábil 31.12.81
Banco do Brasil A.G. (Viena-Áustria)	398.645	401.706	6.503	31.12.81	100,00	Subsidiária integral	401.706
Brazilian American Merchant Bank	63.580	17.932.309	4.844.160	31.12.81	100,00	Subsidiária integral	17.932.309
Brazilian Finance And Investment Corporation	21.346	36.378	10.315	31.12.81	100,00	Subsidiária integral	36.378
Companhia Aços Especiais Itabira	12.074.315	19.834.885	(5.425.434)	30.11.81	81,98	6.078.930.717 ON / 105.071.283 OP / 118.443.415 PP	18.247.802
Banco Brasileiro-Iraquiano S.A.	1.400.000	1.400.000	2.021.048	31.12.81	50,00	140.000 ON	700.000
Riocell Administração S.A.	7.064.721	13.843.995	(1.548.021)	31.10.81	50,00	1.996.686 ON	7.761.036
Forjas Acesita S.A.	2.550.825	505.919		30.11.81	18,46	272.440.334 ON	119.595

NOTE 5 – INVESTMENTS IN ASSOCIATED COMPANIES

Investments in associated companies, registered under the same heading, are stated at monetarily corrected cost. The following is a list of such investments:

COMPANIES	Our share %	Book value at 31.12.81 (in thousands of cruzeiros)
Malibu Palace Hotel	38.05	14,782
European Brazilian Bank Limited	31.89	365,983
Companhia Brasileira de Entrepostos e Comércio	31.16	929,694
Proflora S.A. - Florestamento e Reflorestamento	22.18	56,794
Banque Internationale Pour l'Afrique Occidentale	20.00	1,347,419
Seltom Hotéis S.A.	16.96	14,853
Aços Finos Piratini S.A.	13.56	2,067,379
COBRA - Computadores e Sistemas Brasileiros S.A.	13.01	515,576
Companhia Fábrica de Tecidos Dona Isabel	11.65	91,612
Nutrigel S.A. - Alimentos Supergelados	11.05	9,189
Atlântida Hotéis e Turismo S.A.	11.04	2,956
Nelima Indústria de Relógios S.A.	10.78	69,430
Companhia Brasileira de Participação Agroindustrial	10.47	65,763
Banco Unido de Fomento	10.29	185,999
Kuwait Pacific Finance Company Limited	10.00	24,625

NOTE 6 – INFLATIONARY EFFECTS

Net income for the year was adjusted to reflect inflation in accordance with the rules of monetary correction, pursuant to article 185 of Law No. 6,404/76, broken down as follows:

1981 (in thousands of cruzeiros)

	first half	second half	year
Permanent assets	37,268,530	59,037,792	96,306,322
Investments	18,126,253	29,803,514	47,929,767
Fixed	18,923,658	28,755,597	47,679,255
Deferred charges	218,619	478,681	697,300
Shareholders' Equity	94,758,886	136,861,306	231,620,192
Capital Stock	34,874,595	49,604,081	84,478,676
Capital reserves	10,446,165	15,281,516	25,727,681
Revaluation reserves	1,734,235	4,313,197	6,047,432
Income reserves	13,179,548	18,393,719	31,573,267
Retained earnings	34,524,343	49,268,793	83,793,136
Net (debit balance)	57,490,356	77,823,514	135,313,870

NOTE 7 – CONDENSED BALANCE SHEET OF THE FOREIGN EXCHANGE DIVISION

The condensed balance sheet of the Foreign Exchange Division is required by Circular 409, dated 30th November 1978, of the Central Bank, and aims at an improved presentation of the foreign exchange operations contained in the Bank's balance sheet.

NOTE 8 – PARTICIPATION OF THE FOREIGN EXCHANGE DIVISION IN OPERATING INCOME FROM LOANS UNDER RESOLUTION 63

The total income resulting from such operations of Cr$ 19,369,827,920.16 was registered as income of the Foreign Exchange Division.

NOTE 9 – EXPENSES ON FUNDS BORROWED ABROAD

Such expenses, in the amout of Cr$ 8,462,451,460.03, were incorporated under "Funds borrowed abroad", in the balance sheet.

NOTE 10 – FOREIGN EXCHANGE POSITION

The Bank's foreign exchange position, recorded in memorandum accounts, is as follows:

Forward exchange contracts – purchased	Cr$ 254,877,419,458.33	Dr
Forward exchange contracts – sold.	Cr$ 205,098,607,973.14	Cr
Completed exchange contracts	Cr$ 143,951,487,615.39	Dr
General position of exchange contracts	Cr$ 193,730,299,100.58	Cr
Commitments on credits for import	Cr$ 101,051,755,371.33	Cr

NOTE 11 – CAPITAL STOCK

The Bank's capital stock is fully paid up and comprises 29,376,000,000 non-convertible shares, without par-value, of which 16,470,368,400 (56.07%) are ordinary nominal shares, and 12,905,631,600 (43.93%) are non-voting, preferred bearer shares, the latter taking priority in the distribution of dividends.
Monetary correction of capital stock registered under "Capital Reserves" amounts to Cr$ 85,114,626,954.89, and will be capitalized at the next annual General Shareholders' Meeting.
The Bank is controlled by the National Treasury, which is the major shareholder.

NOTE 12 – ADJUSTMENTS MADE TO PREVIOUS YEARS

The main adjustments that ocurred in the first half year were, primarily, the writing-back of the provision for income tax and rectifications, of little significance made, in the monetary correction of equipment, now calculated by computer.
In the second half year, the main adjustment, as required by law, was the monetary correction of real estate, other than bank premises, acquired prior to 1st January 1981.

NOTE 13 – SHAREHOLDERS' EQUITY

Shareholders' equity amounted to Cr$ 549.7 billion, corresponding to Cr$ 18.71 per share, a growth of 134.5% in the year, while ORTNs (Indexed National Treasury Bonds) increased by 95.57% in the same period. Dividends and a cash bonus distributed in 1981 amounted to Cr$ 1.87 per share, which is a remuneration equivalent to 23.4% of the share value at the beginning of the year.

NOTA 5 — INVESTIMENTOS EM EMPRESAS COLIGADAS

Inscritos em "Investimentos em Sociedades Ligadas" estão avaliados pelo custo de aquisição corrigido monetariamente. São os seguintes:

DISCRIMINAÇÃO	Nossa participação %	Valor contábil Cr$ Mil
Malibu Palace Hotel S.A.	38,05	14.782
European Brazilian Bank Limited	31,89	365.983
Companhia Brasileira de Entrepostos e Comércio	31,16	929.694
Proflora S.A. - Florestamento e Reflorestamento	22,18	56.794
Banque Internationale Pour l'Afrique Occidentale	20,00	1.347.419
Selton Hotéis S.A.	16,96	14.853
Aços Finos Piratini S.A.	13,56	2.067.379
COBRA - Computadores e Sistemas Brasileiros S.A.	13,01	515.576
Companhia Fábrica de Tecidos Dona Isabel	11,65	91.612
Nutrigel S.A. - Alimentos Supergelados	11,05	9.189
Atlântida Hotéis e Turismo S.A.	11,04	2.956
Nelima Indústria de Relógios S.A.	10,78	69.430
Companhia Brasileira de Participação Agroindustrial	10,47	65.763
Banco Unido de Fomento	10,29	185.999
Kuwait Pacific Finance Company Limited	10,00	24.625

NOTA 6 — EFEITOS INFLACIONÁRIOS

Aos resultados foram imputados os reflexos da inflação, com base na sistemática de correção monetária — na forma do art. 185, da Lei 6.404/76 — pelos seguintes valores (Cr$ mil):

	1º sem/81	2º sem/81	Exercício/81
Do Ativo Permanente	37.268.530	59.037.792	96.306.322
Investimentos	18.126.253	29.803.514	47.929.767
Imobilizado	18.923.658	28.755.597	47.679.255
Diferido	218.619	478.681	697.300
Do Patrimônio Líquido	94.758.886	136.861.306	231.620.192
Capital social	34.874.595	49.604.081	84.478.676
Reservas de capital	10.446.165	15.281.516	25.727.681
Reservas de reavaliação	1.734.235	4.313.197	6.047.432
Reservas e retenção de lucros	13.179.548	18.393.719	31.573.267
Lucros acumulados	34.524.343	49.268.793	83.793.136
Resultado (devedor)	57.490.356	77.823.514	135.313.870

NOTA 7 — BALANCETE SINTÉTICO DA CARTEIRA DE CÂMBIO

Elaborado segundo as normas da Circular nº 409, de 30.11.78, do Banco Central do Brasil, tem por objetivo demonstrar, destacadamente, os valores referentes as operações de câmbio, incluídos nos demais demonstrativos financeiros.

NOTA 8 — PARTICIPAÇÃO DA CARTEIRA DE CÂMBIO EM COMISSÕES DE REPASSE DE OPERAÇÕES DA RESOLUÇÃO Nº 63

Foi incorporado como resultado da Carteira de Câmbio o valor de Cr$ 19.369.827.920,16 correspondente a 100% de participação nessas operações.

NOTA 9 — DESPESAS DE OBRIGAÇÕES POR EMPRÉSTIMOS EXTERNOS

Provisionado o valor de Cr$ 8.462.451.460,03 inscrito na rubrica "OBRIGAÇÕES POR EMPRÉSTIMOS EXTERNOS".

NOTA 10 — POSIÇÃO CAMBIAL

É a seguinte, registrada em contas de compensação:

Câmbio Comprado a Liquidar	Cr$ 254.877.419.458,33	D
Câmbio Vendido a Liquidar	Cr$ 205.098.607.973,14	C
Câmbio Liquidado	Cr$ 143.951.487.615,39	D
Movimento de Câmbio	Cr$ 193.730.299.100,58	C
Responsabilidades por Créditos para Importação	Cr$ 101.051.755.371,33	C

NOTA 11 — CAPITAL SOCIAL

Totalmente integralizado, divide-se em 29.376.000.000 ações sem valor nominal, inconversíveis de uma espécie em outra, sendo 16.470.368.400 ações ordinárias nominativas (56,07%) e 12.905.631.600 ações preferenciais ao portador (43,93%), estas sem direito a voto, mas com prioridade na distribuição de dividendos.

A correção monetária do capital, inscrita em "Reservas de Capital" monta a Cr$ 85.114.626.954,89 e será capitalizada na próxima A.G.O.

O Tesouro Nacional é o maior acionista, detendo o controle.

NOTA 12 — AJUSTES DE EXERCÍCIOS ANTERIORES

No 1º semestre decorreram, preponderantemente, da reversão da provisão para pagamento do imposto de renda e de retificações — em montante pouco significativo — da correção monetária das imobilizações em "equipamentos de uso", implantados em sistema computarizado.

No 2º semestre, os principais ajustes originaram-se da correção monetária dos imóveis não destinados a uso, adquiridos até o término do exercício de 1980, em decorrência de ato normativo específico.

NOTA 13 — PATRIMÔNIO LÍQUIDO

O patrimônio líquido de Cr$ 549,7 bilhões, correspondente a um valor patrimonial de Cr$ 18,71 por ação, apresenta uma evolução de 134,5% no ano, período em que as ORTNs tiveram variação de 95,57%. Acrescente-se que em 1981 foram ainda distribuídos Cr$ 1,87 por ação, significando uma remuneração em dinheiro de 23,4% sobre o patrimônio ao início do ano.

NOTE 14 — DIVIDENDS

In accordance with the Bank's by-laws (which require the payment, in each half year, of a minimum dividend of 25% of the Bank's net income) and following the dividend policy adopted in 1979, the amounts listed below were set aside for distribution to shareholders, after several allocations from income required by law and by the by-laws.

A total of Cr$ 33,782.4 million was distributed in dividends in the second half year (Cr$ 54,933.1 million for the whole year). A dividend of Cr$ 0.48 plus a cash bonus of Cr$ 0.67, totalling Cr$ 1.15 per share, was distributed in the second half year (Cr$ 1.87 for 1981 as a whole).

Base period	Dividend	Cash bonus	Total
1979, 1 st half	Cr$ 0.13	Cr$ 0.07	Cr$ 0.20
1979, 2nd half	Cr$ 0.16	Cr$ 0.09	Cr$ 0.25
1980, 1 st half	Cr$ 0.20	Cr$ 0.12	Cr$ 0.32
1980, 2nd half	Cr$ 0.24	Cr$ 0.24	Cr$ 0.48
1981, 1 st half	Cr$ 0.34	Cr$ 0.38	Cr$ 0.72
1981, 2nd half	Cr$ 0.48	Cr$ 0.67	Cr$ 1.15

NOTE 15 — CONDENSED BALANCE SHEET

The condensed balance sheet incorporates all assets and liabilities of the Bank. It includes foreign branches, which are treated as autonomous entities, thus showing higher totals than the standard balance sheet.

NOTE 16 — COMMITMENTS, RESPONSABILITIES AND CONTINGENCIES

The labour contingencies are those of the C.L.T. (Consolidation of Labour Laws) and were considered immaterial.

The Bank is a sponsor of and a contributor to the Banco do Brasil Staff Retirement Fund, which ensures and complements the retirement pay of employees and pensions to their dependents. Guarantees given to third parties (against payment of fees and counterguarantees from the beneficiaries) including bonds, counterguarantees and letters of guarantee, amounted to Cr$ 283.0 million.

The Bank operates the Fund for Sectoral Investments (FISET) and administers the Programme for Formation of Civil Servants Endowment (PASEP), guaranteeing the latter a yield equal to monetary correction plus 3% p.a.

The Bank has credit commitments relating to operations already contracted and is responsible for the administration of custody services, including the custody of the Nation's monetary reserves.

The contingency reserve, in the amount of Cr$ 6,660 million, booked in the first half year was transferred to retained earnings in the second half year, because of a reduction, of a corresponding value, in the shareholders' equity of a subsidiary company, which was based on the equity method in our financial statements.

NOTA 14 — DIVIDENDOS

Em sintonia com os Estatutos, que estipulam dividendo semestral mínimo e obrigatório equivalente a 25% do lucro líquido, e em seguimento à política de dividendos do Banco, adotada a partir de 1979, foram reservadas para distribuição aos acionistas — após realizadas as necessárias destinações legais e estatutárias — Cr$ 33.782,4 milhões no 2º semestre de 1981 (Cr$ 54.933,1 milhões no ano), correspondendo ao dividendo de Cr$ 0,48 e mais uma bonificação em dinheiro de Cr$ 0,67, por ação, no total de Cr$ 1,15 nesse semestre (Cr$ 1,87 no exercício de 1981).

Tivemos assim as seguintes distribuições por ação:.

Período-base	Dividendo	Bonificação em dinheiro	Total
1º sem/79	Cr$ 0,13	Cr$ 0,07	Cr$ 0,20
2º sem/79	Cr$ 0,16	Cr$ 0,09	Cr$ 0,25
1º sem/80	Cr$ 0,20	Cr$ 0,12	Cr$ 0,32
2º sem/80	Cr$ 0,24	Cr$ 0,24	Cr$ 0,48
1º sem/81	Cr$ 0,34	Cr$ 0,38	Cr$ 0,72
2º sem/81	Cr$ 0,48	Cr$ 0,67	Cr$ 1,15

NOTA 15 — BALANÇO GERAL CONDENSADO

Compreende a totalidade dos Ativos e Passivos do Banco, ou seja, engloba as suas dependências no exterior, tratadas como entidades autônomas, apresentando por essa razão total superior ao do Balanço Patrimonial.

NOTA 16 — COMPROMISSOS, RESPONSABILIDADES E CONTINGÊNCIAS

As contingências trabalhistas são as da C.L.T. e foram consideradas não significativas.

O Banco é patrocinador e contribuinte da Caixa de Previdência dos Funcionários do Banco do Brasil, que assegura e complementa a aposentadoria de funcionários e pensão a seus dependentes.

As garantias concedidas a terceiros, mediante encargos financeiros e contragarantias pelos beneficiários — fianças, avais e cartas de garantia — montam a Cr$ 283,0 bilhões.

O Banco é operador do Fundo de Investimentos Setoriais (FISET) e administrador do Programa de Formação do Patrimônio do Servidor Público (PASEP), garantindo a este último uma rentabilidade mínima igual à correção monetária mais juros de 3% a.a.

O Banco tem compromissos de créditos, decorrentes de operações já contratadas, e responsabilidades por administração de serviços de custódia, inclusive da reserva monetária.

A reserva para contingências de Cr$ 6.660 milhões constituída no balanço do primeiro semestre foi revertida, no 2º semestre, para Lucros Acumulados, tendo em vista a baixa do correspondente valor no Patrimônio Líquido de empresa controlada, reconhecida em nossos registros pelo método da equivalência patrimonial.

CONSELHO DE ADMINISTRAÇÃO

Oswaldo Roberto Colin — **Presidente**
Eduardo de Castro Neiva — **Vice-Presidente**
Ângelo Calmon de Sá
Carloman da Silva Oliveira
Carlos Geraldo Langoni
Carlos José Muniz
Cid Heráclito de Queiroz
Luiz de Moraes Barros
Nestor Jost

CONSELHO DIRETOR

Presidente:
Oswaldo Roberto Colin

Vice-Presidentes:
Dinar Goyheneix Gigante
Giampaolo Marcello Falco
Eduardo de Castro Neiva

Diretores:
Alcir Augustinho Calliari
José Luiz Silveira Miranda
Benedicto Fonseca Moreira
Luis Fernando Duarte Siqueira
Amilcar de Souza Martins
Nilson Miranda Motta
Alcio Carvalho Portella
Aléssio Vaz Primo
José Aristophanes Pereira
Antônio Arnaldo Gomes Taveira
Fernando Baptista Martins
Antônio Machado de Macedo
Cesar Dantas Bacellar Sobrinho

CONTADORIA GERAL

Oswaldo dos Santos Pereira
Contador Geral em exercício
Téc. Cont. CRC-DF 4476
CPF 001.717.782-00

OPINION OF THE FISCAL COUNCIL

To the Shareholders:

The Fiscal Council of the Banco do Brasil S.A., exercising its powers pursuant to statutory requirements and the Bank's by-laws, confirms that it has examined the accounting statements for the fiscal period just concluded, which adequately reflect the shareholders' equity situation and financial position of Banco do Brasil S.A. as at 31st December 1981. In the name of its undersigned members, the Council recommends that the accounts and the financial statements submitted to the Shareholders' Meeting be approved by the Shareholders.

Brasília (DF), 21st January, 1982

Odette de Castro Gouveia
João Jabour
Guilherme da Silveira Filho
Maurício Chagas Bicalho
Sergio Andrade de Carvalho

OPINION OF THE INDEPENDENT AUDITORS

To the
Board of Directors and Shareholders of
BANCO DO BRASIL S.A
Brasília - DF

We have examined the financial statements of Banco do Brasil S.A. as at 31st December 1981 and for the year then ended, comprising the balance sheet, the income statement, the statement of changes in financial position and the statement of shareholders' equity, as well as the condensed balance sheets for the foreign exchange division and for the Bank as a whole. Our examination was made in accordance with generally accepted auditing standards, and accordingly included such tests of the accounting records and such other auditing procedures as we considered necessary in the circumstances.
The financial statements of the Bank's foreign branches were examined by other independent auditors whose reports have been made available to us. The financial statements of subsidiaries were examined by other independent auditors.
In our opinion, the aforementioned financial statements, together with the explanatory notes thereto, fairly represent the financial position of Banco do Brasil S.A. as at 31st December 1981 and its income for the year then ended, in accordance with legal and regulatory requirements applicable to banks and with generally accepted accounting principles and, except for the changes referred to in Note 3, with which we concur, were applied on a basis consistent with that of the preceding year.

Brasília (DF), 21st January, 1982

CAMPIGLIA & CIA
S/C AUDITORES INDEPENDENTES
CRC - SP N.º J 756

A.O. Campiglia
Accountant and Auditor

PARECER DO CONSELHO FISCAL

Senhores Acionistas,

O Conselho Fiscal do Banco do Brasil S.A., no uso de suas atribuições legais e estatutárias, declara que examinou as demonstrações financeiras referentes ao exercício recém-findo, que refletem, adequadamente, a situação patrimonial e a posição financeira do Banco do Brasil S.A., em 31.12.81, e, por seus membros abaixo assinados, recomenda que as contas e as referidas demonstrações financeiras submetidas à Assembléia Geral Ordinária sejam aprovadas pelos senhores acionistas.

Brasília (DF), 21 de janeiro de 1982

Odette de Castro Gouveia
João Jabour
Guilherme da Silveira Filho
Maurício Chagas Bicalho
Sergio Andrade de Carvalho

PARECER DOS AUDITORES INDEPENDENTES

Aos Senhores
Diretores e Acionistas do
BANCO DO BRASIL S.A.
Brasília — DF

Examinamos as demonstrações financeiras do BANCO DO BRASIL S.A. em 31 de dezembro de 1981, relativas ao ano findo nessa data, compreendendo o balanço patrimonial, a demonstração do resultado do exercício, a demonstração das origens e aplicações de recursos, a demonstração das mutações do patrimônio líquido, o balancete sintético da carteira de câmbio e o balanço geral condensado. Nosso exame foi efetuado de conformidade com os padrões de auditoria externa geralmente reconhecidos e aceitos, e incluiu as provas e os procedimentos técnicos de auditoria externa na extensão que julgamos necessária segundo as circunstâncias.

As operações e os resultados das agências no exterior, bem como sua situação patrimonial foram auditadas por auditores independentes das respectivas localidades, cujos pronunciamentos examinamos. As demonstrações financeiras das sociedades controladas foram auditadas por outras firmas de auditoria independente.

Em nossa opinião, as demonstrações financeiras antes mencionadas, lidas em conjunto com as Notas Explicativas que as acompanham, representam adequada e fidedignamente a posição financeira e o resultado do BANCO DO BRASIL S.A. em 31 de dezembro de 1981, de conformidade com as normas legais e regulamentares das instituições financeiras e com os princípios de contabilidade geralmente aceitos e, considerando o mencionado na Nota 3, com o que concordamos, aplicados de forma consistente em relação ao ano anterior.

Brasília (DF), 21 de janeiro de 1982.

CAMPIGLIA & CIA
S/C AUDITORES INDEPENDENTES
CRC - SP N.º J 756

A.O. Campiglia
Contador — CRC SP —12179 S/DF —462
Auditor Responsável